Not A Boring Moment
The Chapters of an Artist

Maya B.

Copyright © 2013 Maya B. Krähenmann
All rights reserved.
First edition

No part of this book may be reproduced in any manner whatsoever without written permission except in the case of brief quotations embodied in critical articles and reviews.
In order to maintain their anonymity in some instances, I have changed the names of individuals and places.
I may have changed some identifying characteristics and details such as physical properties, occupations and places of residence.

ISBN 13: 978-1482688764
ISBN-10: 148268876X

DEDICATION

This book is dedicated to my daughters Alexa and Juliette
-
with whom I wish to share my life experiences, and to all my friends who helped me along my way.

CONTENTS

	Preface	i
	Introduction	ii
1	Early Life	1
2	The Married Years	62
3	Free Again	146
4	Sailing with Peter	250
5	Later Years	455
	Retrospectively	618

PREFACE

I lived my life- from adventure to adventure on different parts of the globe, in search of *truth* and freedom and in search of my ideal partner.

Often my friends advised me to write my memoirs. I became good friends with Clemence Dahl, a writer whom I had met in the south of France. We spoke frequently at the Hotel Luxembourg in Lezignan and he took notes of my experiences and wanted to write a book about my life.

He then met a woman from the U.S.A. and the happy pair moved to the United States. Before he left, he told me that I owed it to the world to share my memories, nudging me to write my autobiography. I replied that I would do so when I was older, since I still had some more intensive living ahead of me.

Thanks to Clemence's encouragement, I started to write this book in 2010 and it took me three years to complete it. The following is a true account of the events of my life as I remember them. Others may have a differing viewpoint. I have tried to recreate events, locales and conversations from my memories of them.

I hope that you will enjoy reading my life story as much as I did both living it and writing about it.

INTRODUCTION

My Father's Family. Left to right, back row, My Father (Ruedi),
Uncle Freddy, Aunt Maria, Uncle Fons, Aunt Bethli, Uncle Sepp,
Uncle Beda, Aunt Titi, Uncle Paul, Uncle Benno.

Seated, left to right, Aunt Martheli, Grossmama, Grosspapa,
Aunt Nelli.

My Mother's Family

Alexander Bernhard, Engineer (Neni) and Flavia Bernhard-Dini (Noni) with Uncle Aldo, Pia (who died in childhood) and Aunt Irma.

Maya B.

Neni and Noni

Aunt Irma, Uncle Aldo, Noni, my Mother and Neni

My Mother and Father

My Father and Mother in later years

1 EARLY LIFE

Who I am.

My father Rudolf Wilhelm Josef Krähenmann, born on July 7, 1909, was delivered by my paternal grandfather, Dr. Josef Krähenmann– Hufenus, M.D., at their home in Gossau, St. Gallen, Switzerland. He was the second child of 14 children, in a very close-knit family. My father was handsome and in very strong physical and mental health. His thick, dark-brown curly hair framed his symmetric face with big, warm dark brown eyes. He had a heart-warming smile and was very outspoken, equipped with a great sense of justice. Indeed, a very remarkable man with great intelligence. Not just his great generosity, tolerance, sense of humor, love of life and knowledge, but also his serious intellect made him very loved and admired by family, friends and colleagues alike. My father was the third generation of physicians in our family.

His grandfather, Dr. Josef Krähenmann-Grat, M.D., owned the Castle Risegg, St. Gallen, Switzerland. He bought the most beautiful stud bulls from Europe and opened the first Bircher-Benner Clinic in Switzerland. To this day, he is still known as the strongest man in the history of our family. He was tall, had long hair, a full beard and a moustache. Once, my great-grandfather had a disagreement with the townspeople so he waited until Sunday when they were all inside the church. He then single-handedly put a huge chopping block in front of the church door to lock them all in. It took 2 horses to drag the enormous chopping block away from the church door! Another time, he disagreed with the people in the pub so he emptied the place by grabbing each of the many customers by the collar and seat of their pants and threw them, one by one, out of the first story window onto the lawn. He loved children and was passionate for nature and his stud bulls.

When my father and his brother were young boys, they

smoked a cigarette in one of their grandfather's hay barns. They thought they heard someone approaching the barn and threw away their cigarettes. The barn burned down and the two boys were brought to their grandfather who was inside the castle. He saw immediately how terrified the boys looked. He asked, "Were you scared?' They answered, "Yes, Grandfather." He said to them, "Being scared is punishment enough. I bet you will never do that again." They promised and gave him a hug. It showed what an exceptional, forgiving and unforgettable man he was. My father, his brothers and sisters loved to spend their vacations with their free-spirited grandfather at the castle. This was a welcome change from their religious, authoritarian and conservative upbringing at their home in Gossau.

My parental grandmother, Martha Krähenmann - Hufenus wanted to enter a convent and be a nun. However, her father Paul Hufenus, a well known artist-specialist in lace design who used to own the lace factory Bischofsberger in St. Gallen, would not hear of it. He rewarded her with an Italian masterpiece for agreeing to marry my grandfather. His famous lace collection was the reason the next owner bought his factory.

My parental grandmother was brainwashed into believing that it was her duty to tattletale to her husband when the children played truant from church or played a joke on a child-hating neighbor. As a punishment, they were whipped with the horsewhip and he would say, "We will break your head yet." If they were caught again, he would use the whip on them until they bled.

When my father was twelve years old, he saw his father whip his brother who was lying on the floor with his back bleeding. My father said to their father, "Stop it!" His father shouted, "How do you speak to me?" My father retorted, "THIS is how I speak to you." It woke my grandfather up and he never hit any of his children again. (My Uncle Freddy, my father's brother and the victim, told me about this episode many years later). When I asked my father if it was true that they were treated so cruelly, he said, "Sadly, yes."

"ALL religions cause so much pain and grief in the world."

When men invented gods, they used lies, brainwashing, torture, fear and threats to scare people into submission or death, to fight religious wars to gain power and riches and to brainwash and force men to be soldiers who become murderers and who were often murdered.

Sexuality was seen as sinful and anything other than the missionary position, like cunnilingus, was punishable by law. So was homosexuality and lesbianism. No wonder that caused rape, frustration and perversion. If a soldier (whose mind has been raped) has nothing to do, he will rape women.

In my view, lies are the root of all evil. Brainwashing (lies), cause brain damage. It is high time that the human race started to think, instead of blindly believing and take responsibility for its own actions. Only cowards, bullies or criminals lie. If you have this great gift of life, you are a fool not to live in reality, instead of turning yourself into a brainwashed mentally- ill zombie by lying and cheating, not only to others, but to yourself as well. Can you imagine an honest and peaceful world, that could be a paradise if only everyone were a healthy positive free thinker and not a sick brainwashed negative believer of things like prejudice, racism, sexism, nationalism, hate and fanaticism? It could be Heaven on Earth and balsam for our planet. If the human being is too stupid to understand this, they should be led by intelligent and positive thinking leaders.

It is high time to protect nature, its trees and plant life and to see that animals are our cohabitants and not here to be violated, chained, locked in or exploited. Stop using animals for medical research. Stop vivisection! Stop violence and greed, or it will backfire badly at you. Love and harmony is what both ourselves and our beautiful planet need. To give and to take.

"Vive l' amour!"

My mother was born on November 20, 1912 in Romagnano -

Sesia, Italy. She was named Helena Bernhard. She was a very headstrong woman with a powerful personality, was well-read, cultured and artistic. She was a great beauty with one brown and one blue-grey eye, fine boned and of medium height. She slightly resembled Nefertiti.

    She helped my father in his office and people loved her. Even though she distanced herself from them, she helped everyone that needed her. She was the oldest of 4 children, born to Alexander and Flavia Bernhard – Dini. She grew up in Landquart, Graubuenden, Switzerland, where her father was employed as a machine engineer at the local paper factory.

    He grew up in Wiesen, which lies in the Grison Alps in Switzerland. As a boy, he walked the distance to the University of Chur to study engineering, which entailed a two and- a-half hour walk every day.

    His father, Johannes Bernhard, walked from Wiesen to St. Petersburg, Russia when he was 20 years old. He took on an apprenticeship at a confectionery and coffee shop. He later bought the luxurious coffee shop and married a Russian woman. Fortunately, they were childless since their marriage ended in divorce and after Czar Alexander (a frequent guest in my Great Grandfather's coffee shop) was assassinated, he fled to Switzerland with only what he was wearing. There, he met and married Barbara, a brave young woman from Switzerland who courageously and single-handedly, travelled with a horse and wagon to Russia to recover some of my grandfather's jewels and other treasures. She became the mother of my beloved maternal grandfather who was named Alexander after the Russian Czar, who had been a friend of my maternal great-grandfather.

    My maternal grandmother Flavia Bernhard-Dini, was born in Tivoli, which is near Rome in Italy. She was the first-born of my great grandmother's twenty-one children. After the death of her father, (an engine driver), her mother moved to Rimini and opened a guest house. She married again, but after the birth of her twenty-first child, she had to raise all the surviving children by herself. She lost five children in one year to typhoid fever and some of them died at birth. She was an excellent cook but a very strict and a controlling woman. I remember she tried to force me to eat when my mother and I stayed with her. At home we were allowed to serve ourselves but we always had to eat everything that we put on our plates.

When my daughter Alexa was born in 1961, there were five generations alive on my mother's side.

My great grandmother died at the age of 99 years with all her own teeth still in her mouth and was reading until the very last, without eye-glasses. She had a first class funeral (her last wish) with a glass carriage pulled by four white horses and twenty hired widows who cried, moaned and screamed in so-called grief for a nice package of Italian Lire. Italians like Opera!

My grandmother, Flavia Bernhard-Dini took her first flight from Zurich to Rimini to attend her mother's funeral and she loved being in the airplane. My grandmother died at the age of 96 years.

My great-great-grandmother on my mother's side is remembered as an exceptionally intelligent, sensible and passionate woman of great beauty. She and my great-great-grandfather were so close and in love, that when he passed away at a relatively young age, she too died young, just one hour after his death. She was called 'La Bella Mariella'.

My maternal grandfather, Alexander, was born on July 8, 1884 and he died at the age of 93 in 1997. He would have lived longer if some dilettantish but well meaning people had not advised my grandfather to have a prostate operation against my father's professional advice. After the operation, he was so weak that he died soon after. He could have lived longer with a catheter.

My advice: "Do not take any advice, except from someone professional whom you trust (otherwise it may be hazardous to your health)."

My Great-Great Grandmother

Birth

I was born on July 12, 1940. My mother was seven months' pregnant when she fell down the steps of the Swiss chalet in Flums, St. Gallen, Switzerland and as a result, I was born two months premature. My father, who was a physician, delivered me and built an incubator for me. My mother's milk was pumped off and fed to me from a bottle until I was strong enough to suck on her breasts. I survived by the love and care of my parents and grew to become a very active child, full of energy and fantasy with great love for animals and nature.

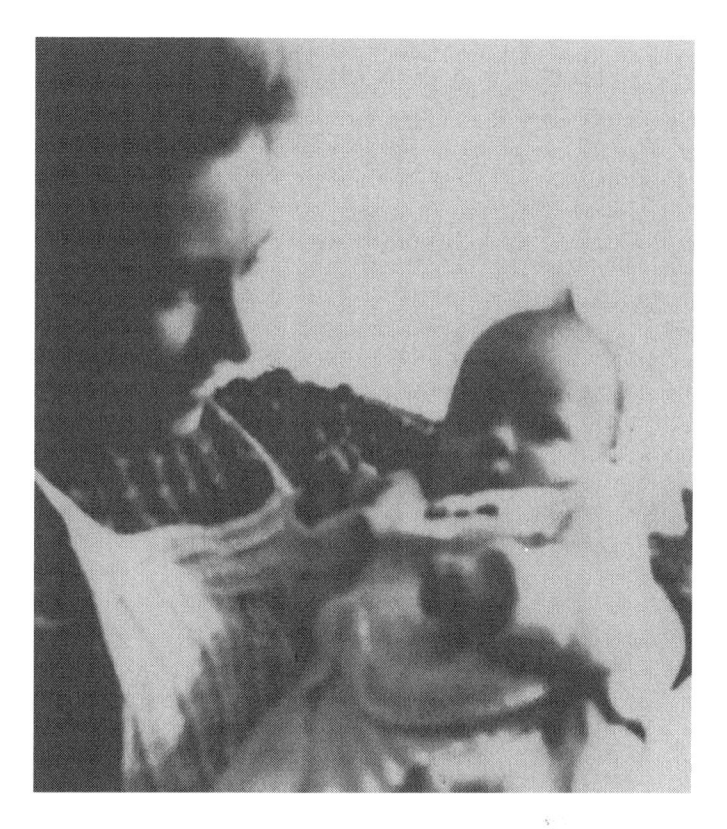

As a baby, with my mother

As a baby, with my Mother

Escape from the Playpen

At the age of 6 months, I escaped from my play pen without anyone ever finding out how I did it. From then on, my parents stopped using the play pen for me.

Waldi and Quakeli

I was walking by the age of 8 months and I can still remember Waldi, our family dog, and our tame King crow Quakeli, whom my father raised by hand feeding him. He was a magnificent blue-black bird, which hated our neighbor, who was a frustrated and bitter old woman. One day she planted seedlings in her garden, while Quakeli watched her from the branch of a tree. When she had finished planting, he flew over and pulled them all out one by one and laid them all on the side. Quakeli must have sensed my father's mixed feelings for that woman who complained bitterly about our beloved bird. Quakeli kept on pulling her plants out and by the third complaint, my father decided to shoot him. With tears in his eyes, he took the gun into the garden and aimed at Quakeli, who flew directly on to the top of the gun. In no way could my father bring himself to pull the trigger. Fortunately, Quakeli soon reached maturity and flew away on his own. He returned with his newly found partner to say good bye. That was the last time my twenty month-older brother Ruedi, my parents and I saw Quakeli but we were all happy for him and his partner to have a family of their own.

With my elder brother, Ruedi

A Work of Art

I woke up in the morning lying in the crib bed that was surrounded by wire mesh, I was there for safety reasons. This inspired me to create my first artwork, using my fingers and the contents of my diaper. My father laughed but my mother had no understanding of my creation and was not at all smiling while cleaning it out of the wire mesh. I was about five months old at the time.

Me as a child

Me as a child

News

My mother told my brother and I that she was expecting a little brother or sister. My parents hired a chubby, jolly cleaning woman who permitted me to ride on her back while she scrubbed the floors. Her name was Frau Bartulet.

The Butter Story

My father had a patient (a farmer's wife) who paid the

medical bill with 1kg of butter. Butter was a rarity in times of the war. I remember the look of horror on my mothers face as she discovered my brother Ruedi shampooing my hair with the whole bar of butter. We both had so much fun that she forgave him with the admonition to never do that again.

My Sister's Birth

When I was 20 months old, my sister Heli was born. I was amazed at how cute she looked. So we were a complete family of five. She was named Helena Marta.

My Sister Heli and I

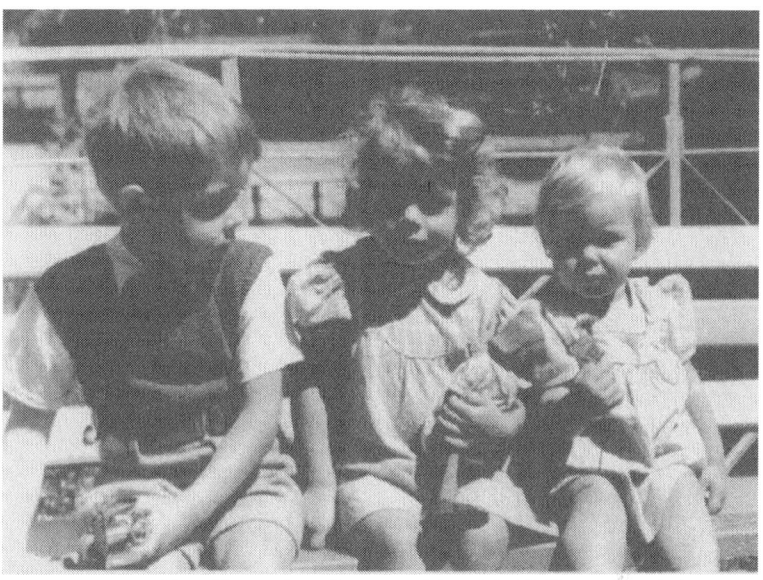

Ruedi, my brother, and I, with Heli on the right

Playing with Drugs

My father's practice also included his own pharmacy. My brother Ruedi and I had the idea to go exploring in it. I was two years old and he was four. We squeezed out tubes of ointment, emptied jars with different colored pills and made sand heaps by opening up packets of worming powder. We had a wonderful time playing in there until my father discovered us. He gave Ruedi and I a good talking to and explained the danger of playing with poisonous remedies to us. I asked of him, "Why do you give poison to patients?" He could not hide his amusement at that question.

A Trip to the Shop

When I was 2 1/2 years old, I took Heli by the hand and we walked home along the path to the village of Flums, across the busy main street, and entered the grocery store to get some fly swatters that I thought it would be fun to have. They asked me to pay, so I told them my mother would do so. To my disappointment rather than giving me the swatters they gave me a bag full of fly papers instead. On the way home we were met by our mother who had been searching for us in panic. She ran up to us, grabbing Heli under one arm while holding my hand to take us home. I found it unjust that I alone was punished, by being locked for 10 minutes in my parent's bedroom, but it was explained to me later that day that my little sister was too young to understand the dangers of going away without telling a parent.

Hernia

My father was visiting a patient, so my mother cooked what she liked. It was some sort of a grain dish I hated, called Griessmus. To make it more palatable she served it with apple sauce. I liked apple sauce and so that I would eat the Griessmus she would mix the two together. When I refused to eat she started to nag me. I thought, "I will do something she will regret!" I pressed my stomach so hard, that it made the hernia on my right side hurt, and then I complained about it. She looked at my groin, then she immediately began to fill the bathtub and she phoned my father at the house that he was visiting. She then put me in to the bath tub and tried to push the hernia back in. I was 2 1/2 years old at the time. My father drove home immediately, then he carried me straight to the car and he drove me to the hospital in Wallenstadt, St. Gallen. They operated on my hernia and I was then strapped to a fenced-in bed, so I could not move enough to endanger the stitches.

There was a very shy and ill boy in another bed in the same room. He was about the same age as I and very quiet. In the morning after the operation when the nurse came in, I was out of my bed wheeling the other bed with the little boy in it all around the room. We were both laughing. This was the first time that they had heard the boy laugh since he entered the hospital. I healed very quickly and once I was back at home my father took the stitches out.

Father's Mountain Practice

My father had a medical practice in the mountains but was getting tired of stitching drunks up every weekend. He also delivered complicated births, putting furs on his skis to get to the mountain farms, sometimes spending all night there and often having to melt snow to wash a newborn baby. After one birth a farmer asked my father to stitch up his goat who had ripped her self on a barbed wire fence. When my father refused and told him to get a vet to do it instead, he begged my father to help his goat since they where so poor. Not only did my father sew up his goat but he also tore up the bill. A few days later when my father visited the mother and baby again, the goat was happily grazing in front of the door. Later he received a huge bag of potatoes from the farmer.

"I hate barbed wire fences and think that those barbaric and cruel things have hurt too many innocent animals and children. They should be declared illegal!"

Often my father would not charge those patients who were poor. Some of them worked at the Flums-rock factory for 35 centimes a day, so how could he charge them the SFr. 3.50 for a consultation, or the SFr. 12.50 for delivering a baby during the war? We were never hungry and people would often pay by bringing us fruit and vegetables from their gardens.

On many occasions my father would have to put seal skins on the bottom of his skis and then walk a long way up to the mountain farms to treat the seriously ill or attend to complicated births. Normal births were helped by a midwife, who would not call the doctor unless it was urgent.

People were only sent to the hospital if the doctors could not handle it. They carried out minor surgery as well and also set most broken bones and put them in casts. The doctors took care of men, women, children and old people. They did pediatrics, internal medicine, dermatology, gynecology, dentistry, urology, cardiology, pulmonology, assisted with births, diagnoses and small operations in most cases and had their own pharmacies with remedies for their patients. Specialists were only consulted in emergencies.

The midwife called my father for a complicated birth. He went as fast as he could and had to use his forceps to deliver the baby. After the baby was born, he waited for the afterbirth to follow and inspected it. The midwife took the afterbirth out of the bowl and whistled. Her dog, a German shepherd, shot out from under the bed, caught and swallowed the placenta in mid air, raising some of the dust from under the bed, which should have been cleaned and inspected by the midwife. Horrified, my father said to her, "What the hell is this dog doing in the room?" She replied, "This is not the only birth my dog has seen and I need him to protect me from frustrated and sex-starved husbands."

I do not remember anything about the war, except that my father was forced to be an officer in the Swiss army and had to go into the medical service, in a mountain valley. If the Nazis had come, there would have been no escape for the Swiss troops. My father sent his pay and cigarette money home to my mother. An uncle took over my fathers practice until he returned home again to my mother.

When my father came home he exchanged his car for a motorbike to save petrol. It was wonderful to have him home again. I was very attached to my father and had a wonderful childhood, loving and understanding parents, a nice environment and grew up in a close-knit family, which continued when we moved to Wil, SG in 1944.

House Calls with my Father

I loved to go out on house calls with my father. He drove a Citroen-Leger, and he always kept mints, jelly snakes or other surprises in the glove compartment of the car for me, so I was never bored while waiting for him when he was visiting the patients. One day, I was playing with the door handle of the car and the door opened while we were travelling at about fifty kilometers per hour. I flew out through the door over a fence and into some grass. It surprised me, that my father worried so much about me. Luckily, he discovered that I had not received so much as scratch. Nothing had hurt me, nor was I suffering from shock. My father immediately got rid of that car, which he loved, but he hated its doors, which opened the wrong way. Not until much later on did he buy another Leger. My sister and brother did not like to go on house calls, they preferred to play or go out with their friends instead.

Visitors

At our home many doctors would meet to discuss medicine. Cases were discussed without mentioning the patient's names. My father came from a family of three generations of physicians and had the experience of running a mountain practice. He was also a connoisseur of fine wines, as were many of the other doctors who often brought him some of their special bottles. Their wives and my mother would also be there. They all sat in the living room.

There was an old tiled oven in the living room that almost reached to the ceiling . Above , there was a small square hole in the ceiling, with a lid that could be opened from my parent's bedroom. My brother, sister and I would listen to the conversations below. I suffered from migraine headaches, to the point where I would fall unconscious, letting everything go. A spied-upon conversation about brain tumors made me imagine that I suffered from a brain tumor every time I had migraine. I sometimes took advantage of this to fake migraines later on during my school years if I did not feel like going to school. Unconsciousness was something that I did not have to fake since not all the migraine attacks were of the same intensity. They ranged from bad headaches to coma. I grew out of migraines at the age of 32 and if I got them again, it was entirely my own fault because they stemmed from a hangover.

Maya B.

Our medieval house in Wil

The front of our house now, the bio (organic) shop, occupies my father's former medical office.

View from my bedroom window

Wil today. My parent's house on the right, behind the bushes.

By the age of four years old, I was fascinated with the four and-a-half story medieval house. At the top, there was a very large two-story attic. On the third floor, there was a balcony overlooking the large terraced garden and the huge pond at the bottom, which was framed all around with hills and woods. Before we moved in, my parents had the balcony fenced in to protect my brother, sister and me from falling. Once when they searched for me, they found me on the balcony sitting on top of the two meter high fence, with my legs pointing toward the garden. I still love heights to this day, to such a degree, that it has often caused me severe problems with uncomprehending people in later life.

Exploring

At the age of 5, I discovered how to open the trap door to get into the attic. While exploring, I found a roof window. Excited, I spotted a stored chair, which I put under the window, enabling me to open it and climb out onto the roof. I never forgot that feeling of joy. The attic became one of my favorite playgrounds. I chose the hours when both parents were in my father's doctor's office, which was located on the ground floor of our home. My mother helped my father in his office, so I was undisturbed in my freedom by the fears of a worrying mother.

Our house was one of many which made up the 400 year old historic city wall. The house next door had a roof terrace. All the houses had different roof levels. Some were more difficult to climb than others. I had years of fun going up and down the old city house roofs, until a woman down in the road lifted her eyes and spotted me. Promptly, she went to tell my parents who immediately ordered me to come back in from the roof and made me promise never to go up there again. So I had to find some other ways to have fun.

Hitch Hike

My brother Ruedi and his best friend Karli, both aged 7, decided to hitch hike. They just went missing and my parents were very upset and frightened. Police were called and searched for the two boys without success. Two days later, they showed up at my grandmother's house with a wolf's hunger and got fed and welcomed. My grandmother even gave them money. She also called my parents and they drove there immediately to pick them up. My brother told us afterwards that they had hidden behind a bank when they spotted a police car coming, and that they had slept in an old shed but they had been cold at night. He also said that they walked the whole way, since no car had stopped for them. This story was passed around the family and friends, as if it had been an act of bravery.

I was 5 years.old at the time and was so impressed with that story, that after one week, I tried to do the same thing. I walked out of town and stopped a truck by standing in front of it with both my arms stretched out to the sides so that the driver had to stop to avoid running me over. He picked me up and with gentle voice, asked me where I was living. He persuaded me to tell him. To my disappointment, he drove me straight back home. He then lifted me out of his truck and took my hand then we entered my home, where he told my parents what had happened. My story did not get treated like an act of heroism and the danger of it was explained to me.

Kindergarten

I was sent to the kindergarten with the option, that if I did not like it, I would not have to go again. It was advent and the kindergarten teacher, a nun, had made a crib where the Baby Jesus was to be laid at Christmas. Each child who talked without being given permission, had to put a stone into Jesus' crib. The others, who were obedient, could put a straw (dry grass) for the comfort of an ugly doll that had the nose chipped from old age. The children with the stones were then supposed to feel guilty for the discomfort they would cause the Baby Jesus doll at Christmas. It all made no sense to me and I did not go back to the kindergarten, which was no fun at all. My mother helped my father at work so I was undisturbed in my freedom by the fears of a worrying mother.

Nun School

I was 6 years old, when many adults said, "Wow! Great! You will be going to school soon." They made it sound like something special. I was really looking forward to it.

On my first day in school, I did not really know what to think. All the girls from my home town had to go to the nun school St. Katharina, while all the boys went to the Allée school house, regardless of their religion.

Even the public swimming pool was segregated. Two hours for men and boys and then two hours for women and girls, while the opposite sex watched over the wooden fence trying to get a glimpse of half-naked bodies, many of them clothed in woolen, hand-knit wet bathing suits, sagging down to their knees when worn by children. The people there were often shivering with blue lips.

Father against Violence

My father told us to never to let a teacher hit us. If one should try it, we were to run home before the teacher could lay a hand on us. After we had learned the alphabet, the teacher was making us write down our first dictation. I made four spelling mistakes. The nun-teacher was about to hit my hand four times with a cane (once for each mistake she said), so I ran home to tell my father who went immediately to the school and told the nun never to hit me or the other children. This nun was tall and skinny, walked with stiff movements, had a green-grey complexion and white dry scaly skin. She stopped hitting us children while in class but told us to remind her to punish us after the class ended. I never reminded her. Those who did, got hit. Some never learned and got hit again and again.

I was a year younger than most, since my birthday was in July and school started in spring and I was a head smaller then the smallest in class. To keep up the respect of the others, I made up for it by having more courage than the rest and an agility almost like a monkey. I could climb trees higher and faster than the others and did not fear to confront the nun-teacher when the class or I had a complaint. I was allowed to invite my friends to our home at any time.

Confession

Since first grade the nuns told us that if we did not go and confess our sins, we would be taken by the devil. The biggest sins were those of a sexual nature. If we did see our brothers, sisters or friends naked, that would be a big sin. So in the third grade, I decided to go and see what confession was all about.

Kaplan Kuster had just gone into the confession booth and having learned the code word, I entered into the dark confession booth too. I said, "Gelobt sei Jesus Christus", as I had learned and Kuster answered as he had learned, "In nomine Patris, Filii et Spiritus Sancti." Next, I had to say, "Amen", and get on my knees and confess my terrible sins to Kaplan Kuster, whom to me represented *The Big Bad One in the Sky*. Kuster sat behind the partition with just a wire mesh covered hole for me to speak through. I told him, that we boys and girls had pulled down our pants to give each other a glimpse of the genitals. (I knew already what my brother looked like but did not want to be a party-pooper). Kuster then asked, "What did you do then? Did you touch each other and did it feel good?" I found his questions more sinful than my glimpse and when Kuster told me, that I had to say twenty Pater Nosters and twenty Hail Mary's, I peed in the confession booth and went home without praying. This was the first and last time I ever went to confession.

"If we recognize our mistakes and take the consequences we gain experience and knowledge. Nature is the best teacher"

Horror

At the bottom of our garden there was the pond, originally built by the city as a reservoir to put out possible fires since the town was burned down on three occasions during medieval times by the warriors of the neighboring village Schwarzenbach, which had been at war with Wil. The warriors of Wil burned Schwarzenbach down a few times as well.

There were all sorts of ducks, several sorts of geese, swans, some black, many species of fish, squirrels, wild birds in abundance and, mice and the odd rat. No wonder it was one of my favorite playgrounds. One day, there was a big, dense, crowd of people blocking the side of the street, along the east side of the pond. It was obviouse to me, that they were looking at something interesting. I wiggled my way through the huge crowd and when I was at front, I could see a drowned woman laying on the ground. She was a resident of the psychiatric clinic in Wil and had committed suicide by drowning herself in the pond. Her cadaver was all blown up and foaming at the mouth and her skin looked a waxy yellowish-white. Her eyes were popping out weirdly and completely red. The poor woman had been missing for a week. I had never seen such a horrible sight before. It caused me many nightmares and sleepless nights. Even so, it did not stop my curiosity. If you have seen the film 'One Flew Over the Cuckoo's Nest', this was the reality of the way psychiatric inmates were treated at that time and until about the 1970s. No wonder some of them looked for a way out.

Kybourg

On Sundays my father drove the whole family to somewhere we had not been before. One Sunday, my parents decided to visit the Kybourg with us. This was a castle with a torture chamber. While my parents explored the castle their way, we children went to find the torture chamber. We were fascinated to explore in there and found all sorts of torture instruments. One was the Iron Bertha. It was a person-like figure with a door on the front and when I opened it I could see the spikes to pierce a person with. I wound myself around the spikes, being agile and skinny enough to succeed, then I asked my brother and sister to close the door and alarm my parents. They ran to tell them to come quickly, "Maya is in the Iron Bertha!" My alarmed parents hurried to the torture chamber and opened the Iron Bertha's door, where I greeted them with laughter.

Fun on Rooftops

I took 5 of my favorite friends (the oldest being 7 years old), home. After we were all given a snack, my mother said to go and play, since she was helping my father. She thought I was taking them to the play room upstairs. Instead, I took them to the attic. Grabbing a washing line, I told them all to take their shoes off so they would not slip on the roof-tiles then we climbed out of the roof window. Once on the roof, I was one hundred percent sure of our safety. I tied the washing line around my waist, attaching all five children to it while I was leading the expedition on the roofs. We kept it a secret and no one found out, until I told my parents much later.

The rooftops!

Adda

One day, my father had a patient whose Fox Terrier had a litter of puppies. This patient asked my dad if he would consider taking a puppy as payment. So my father took us over there to pick out one. We chose a female and named her 'Adda'. What a dog! Adda went everywhere with us. She loved children and let us dress her up and push her in a baby carriage. She sat on the sled with us and all the children knew and loved her. I spent hours with her in the forest where she disappeared a little while to chase deer, rabbits and other animals across my way, which thrilled me to bits.

Unfortunately, Adda died at the young age of four. She suffered so much with distemper, that we begged our father to help her as suggested by him as a last resort, to put her out of her misery. There were no vaccinations against distemper then and 24 dogs died of that epidemic in Wil alone. A child was born to the woman next door and we children believed that baby to be Adda's reincarnation.

Soup

The Nun-teacher told all of us children that the soldiers would hand out free soup under the arches of the town and that we should bring a milk bucket or a container to them, so they could fill it for us to take home. I thought that would be a lovely surprise for my mother so she would not have to cook. The joy was not great, when I came home with the milk bucket full of soup. My mother said that this was meant for the poor people only and added, "What will the people think?" This did not make sense to me, since I had only meant to do her a favor. I had to promise to never bring soup home again.

"It is not important what people think. But it is important what you think of yourself! One has to understand one's own self before one can understand others."

One evening my father returned from a house call with a Chihuahua puppy looking happily out of his waistcoat pocket. It helped to get us over the grief of losing Adda. Fips was his name. He killed rats and brought some home. When he did the same thing with chickens, we started to get complaints along with the bills and (it was always the chicken who laid the most eggs!) my parents gave Fips to a lonely women in the city where there were no chickens.

Jump from 24 meter high bridge

My parents gave me a brand new bicycle for my 10th birthday. Now I really felt free and cycled to the next village, where I went swimming in the river Thur.

There, I met a two year older girl from my home town. Margrit was 12. We decided to jump down from the 24 meter high Schwarzenbach bridge. On the bottom, there was a 4 meter wide hole that had enough depth to jump into. Margrit's bathing suit split from the air pressure. I jumped several times, egged on by an audience clapping and applauding, which I absolutely loved. My parents were told of it before I had a chance to get home and forbade me, to ever jump down from that bridge again. Later, a boy was killed there, when he missed the four-meter diameter hole and the water was not deep enough.

Trapped in a whirlpool

I went swimming alone in the river Thur that same year and I got trapped in a whirlpool. In fetal position, I let myself be pulled by the current to the bottom and quickly pushed off at an angle to the edge of the whirlpool, grabbed the branch of a tree with all my strength and just managed to pull myself out of the water. I suffered a shock and had to rest and recover before cycling back home.

Liberating calves

The butcher across the street had two calves tied up to be slaughtered. They were crying in fear of death so I went over and untied them and they ran for their lives. Unfortunately, they were caught again and my father said, "Maya I can understand you but promise me not to do that again since they will only be caught again and probably have to suffer more from the added frustrations of the butcher. It made sense to me but to this day, I get very upset to see or hear any creature suffer. Other children even went to watch the slaughtering but I stayed away from the slaughter houses and the children who found killing amusing.

My paternal grandfather's death

My grandfather, Dr. MD. Josef Krähenmann, died of his third myocardial infarction, at the age of 70. This was the first time I saw my father with tears in his eyes. He tried to hide them since at this time a man was not supposed to have any feelings. All the children were dressed in white for the funeral and the grown-ups were dressed in black. We first had to say goodbye to my grandfather who was laid out on a bed in the living room of the house. His bed was surrounded with white lilies. A rosary with big cross had been placed in his folded wax-looking hands even though he had not been to church for years. My grandmother stayed religious until she died at the age of 82 many years later. (*Amazing, how brainwashing can cripple a brain for life*). My poor grandmother was put in a nun's-girls finishing school where she was permitted to learn French and piano. She never even learned how to cook. A huge crowd stood in line to do the last honor and say good-bye to my grandfather before they laid him in the coffin. Many people loved and respected him. I watched the coffin being lowered into the hole in the ground and then all the children gently threw a flower on the coffin. I had a bit of a shock when, with a big crash, a shovel of earth was flung over my grandfathers coffin by a rough looking man.

Fräulein Mueller

The children from the old part of the still small town of 6000 inhabitants knew each other well and would see each other frequently. Sometimes we would play hide and seek by hiding in the undertakers' coffins, or many other hiding places. Sometimes they would play ball, which I hated since every time I tried to catch the ball, it would knock me over and caused my nickname to be 'straw'. I refused to play ball and my hated nickname was forgotten. The other thing was that I got quickly bored with games.

One day some of we children met under the arcades of the old town. The news of Fräulein Mueller's death at over 80 was discussed. One of the children asked, "Have you ever seen a dead person?." As the only one, I said, "I saw my grandfather." They all wanted to know what he looked like after he had died, so I suggested to them to pay the last respects to Fraulein Mueller, whose body was still lying in her house. That way they could see a dead person for themselves. So we all agreed to visit her house.

We were greeted by her sister, who said, "Oh it is nice of you children to come and say goodbye to my poor sister." She led us into the dim room, where Fraulein Mueller's body had been laid out, holding a crucifix in her hands, her body covered with a white sheet. Her face was waxen green-white. Her sister lit the candles, which made the dead woman's shadows dance on her face and gave an almost grotesque image. She said to us, "I am busy upstairs. I am sure you children don't mind staying here alone.

When you are finished, call me and I will see you off." As soon as she was out of sight, one of the boys suggested we should see who had the most courage and could hold the dead woman's hand for the longest time. I won. Another boy suggested that we lift her body slightly to find out if it was true that dead bodies have blue spots on the back. It was true. Just as we were looking at the blue spots, a cat meowed and we quickly replaced the white sheet over the sides of the body so that everything looked as it had when we came in. We called the sister, who thanked us for the visit and then we left. I was tortured with nightmares and guilt for many nights after that incident, until I found the courage to tell my parents about it. My father said, "We don't have to worry about the dead. They cannot hurt us any more. It is the living we have to watch out for sometimes."

What a Find!

The whole family was invited over to my maternal grandparents for Easter. The weather was so beautiful that grandparents, uncles, aunts, cousins and all of us had a big feast in the garden. I was exploring in the park and found three baby magpies under a tree. I quickly went to get a box from the cellar and gently placed the young birds in it. I asked the maid for an eye dropper and milk. I soaked some bread in milk and was feeding it to the first bird when my father came up to me. He said, "Maya, put the birds back where you found them- where they fell out of the nest and their mother will take them back." I placed them back under the tree and their mother took back only the two of them that I had not fed.

My father told me I could keep the third one. I raised him by hand, feeding him a mixture of lukewarm milk, ground beef and bread. I named him 'Jacqueli' and back home he learned to fly free in and out of the house. When he wanted to go out, he waited until we opened the window for him. He came shopping with me, sitting on my head or shoulder and picked me up from school, exactly at 4pm. He knew the time. He waited on the house roof opposite the school and when I called him, Jacqueli would fly directly to me. I was the envy of the whole class. Jacqueli slept in our kitchen with the dog and the cat and they all got along very well.

Unfortunately, he was so friendly that he went from window to window to greet the neighbors and when he flew into the open window of a religiously brainwashed and bitter old spinster and landed on her gypsum Holy Mary, she believed my gorgeous Jacqueli to be the devil in disguise and hit him to death with a broom. After that, she was named 'the bird killer' by all the children of Wil who had loved Jacqueli.

My Parent's Friends

The Artist Karl Peterli and his wife Rita, who was a music teacher and amongst my parents best friends, visited us. We children were sent out of the room, which we resented so we sneaked in to our parents bedroom, which was just above the living room. There was a 25 cm hole with a lid on the floor to let the heat rise up from the very large tiled oven, which was built into the living room. We could hear every word being said from there. They were speaking about raising children. The Peterli's said, "The oldest and the youngest of the children usually get more attention than the middle child. One has to be careful to give a middle child the same." I knew that all three of we children got the same love and attention. They also agreed that if one parent said 'Yes', the other parent should also say 'Yes' and the same applied for saying 'No'.

The conversations with the Peterli's inspired my parents and if we wanted something, we always asked our father since he did not suffer from fears and would always say 'Yes'. If he said 'No', he would explain: "I would not do that because of this or that reason." We always listened to him. My mother would generally say 'No' out of over-protection and fear,... *The two things, which can hold back a child's development.*

As the middle child, I enjoyed, getting away with almost everything. The walls in the house were full with artwork, some of them painted by K. Peterli. The Peterli's had a hard time financially. Since there was not enough free wall space to enable my parents to buy more paintings from them. Ruedi, Heli and I were sent to Frau

Peterli for music lessons. Ruedi learned the flute, Heli the violin and I the piano. Often Frau Peterli shared a chocolate with us, before starting the lessons. I loved the music lessons, but not the practicing, forced on us by our well-meaning mother. When Heli played the violin, our dog would sing with her. My mother played piano and my father the violin.

The Gypsy Violin

My father's favorite violin was given to him by his father, who was also a physician and an excellent birth specialist.

One night, a gypsy rang the doorbell and asked my grandfather to help his wife who was in labor and having problems giving birth. My grandfather grabbed his bag and took his horse to follow the worried man into the forest, to where the gypsies were camping. After about an hour's ride on a moonless winter night, my grandfather started to worry. Was he about to get hit over the head and robbed? He continued to follow him. About five minutes later they arrived. My grandfather delivered a healthy baby. It was a difficult breach birth but the mother and baby were well. The gypsy was very happy but said that it was not possible for him to pay and asked if he could bring him the money as soon as he could. My grandfather said that he did not owe him any money but if he could find him a good violin, he would love to buy it from him. Years passed without him hearing anything from the gypsy until one day, when he arrived at my grandfather's house with a violin, which sounded absolutely splendid. He insisted giving this precious violin to my grandfather, who passed it on to my father.

As a boy, my father attended the college in Schwyz where he had an old priest as violin teacher. Many years later, when we already lived in Wil, this teacher visited my father every year, just to play this wonderful violin. He used to come and play it for a couple of hours, eat and drink something and took the train back to Schwyz. Every year, he returned to play the gypsy violin until my very generous father gave it to him as a present. The old priest left with a big grin on his face and he never came back.

The Big Feet

Herr Bollhalder came to our house to give me cello lessons. He played off key and I had to repeat it after him. He then claimed that I played false which was not true and nagged me that my fingernails were too long. He had the biggest feet I have ever seen and had to have his shoes made to measure. Heli and I looked at his feet and cracked up laughing. He used to get angry, which made the whole situation even funnier. I just could not take him seriously and stopped the cello lessons. Heli and I also went to ballet lessons.

A Fight with a Nun

I was 11 years old when I had a fight with a nun-teacher. I had refused to go to church so she told the class to stay away from me because a rotten apple is contagious and it was the fault of my father. No one ever spoke of my father this way. He was loved and respected by all who knew him. I walked out swearing at her and slamming the door as hard as I could, never to return. My parents then agreed that I could go and live with my maternal grandparents who lived in a beautiful and large chalet in Zizers GR.

School at Grandparents

So it came that I went to school in the tiny village of Zizers with only 150 inhabitants. There were two schoolhouses, one for Catholics and the other for Protestants. Boys and girls were together in the classroom. I was in the catholic school and my teacher was Herr Baltasar. All the children at my class ignored me and I found them primitive, narrow minded and ignorant. No-one spoke to me except to yell, "Damned Low-Lander."

I knew then that they behaved this prejudiced way against me for the sole reason that I came from Wil in the low land. Zizers is in the high land. Mind you Zizers and Wil are neighbors in the same canton! I only have two comments, "*Cantonal mentality and brainwashing*" and how small minded can you get? I guess only a few of their brain cells were active.

Elvire Furlemeier

After 6 weeks of being ignored, Elvira had the courage to confront the other children that their behavior was not fair. She became my best friend and suddenly most of the others accepted me but I never trusted them completely. One day, the two most primitive farmers daughters, both fat, plump and red faced, but physically strong like oxen, asked me, "Do you know how your parents made you?" I did not answer and they jumped on top of each other making fornicating movements. I grabbed one of them and slapped her face so they both got up and started to beat me up. I was surprised at their brute force and the only thing I could do was to wiggle out from under them. I avoided most of their blows and ran away. Lucky I could run faster than they could. From then on, I ignored them and when I saw them I made a detour around them.

A Teacher's Failed Attempt to hit me

The male teacher ordered me to take off my jacket during class. My father had bought me the jacket since I liked it so much. My father had given it to me with love and no way was I taking it off, except out of my own free will. He made me come to the front and took a cane that was reinforced with metal. He made me lay my hand open upon his knee. He lifted the cane and before he reached my hand, I pulled back and he hit his upper thigh while I ran to my grandparents to complain. My grandmother went to the school and yelled at the teacher, showing him her Italian temperament. He never tried to hit me again.

Neni and Noni

My grandparents were great. Grandfather 'Neni' was a retired machine engineer and a very happy man who hummed songs while planting the garden. One day, a man walked through the big park belonging to the large, spacious chalet my grandparents lived in. He thought my grandfather was the gardenerand asked him, "What are the owners like?" Grandfather replied, "He drinks too much and she is a tyrant."

My Grandmother 'Noni' loved flowers and was a passionate cook. She was a bit of a house tyrant but did everything for the family. She suffered from more fears than even my mother but less than her mother had. (*The circle of the devil,* which I fortunately managed to break for the sake of my daughters and hopefully also for all future generations!) Noni was afraid to let me go to the cinema in Chur, only one train stop away. Just a week earlier, a woman had committed suicide by flinging herself under the train. I threatened Noni, that I would do the same if she would not let me go. She let me go!

After seeing a film, I walked to Uncle Gusty and Aunt Louise who owned the Hotel White Cross in Chur. They were always very welcoming and treated me to all the ice cream I could eat. I went to see them every time I was in Chur. Sometimes my grandfather accompanied me, which was a special treat. Then we also went to uncle Gusty's sister and her husband, the Defago's. They owned a pub in Chur and Neni loved an occasional cognac he could not enjoy 'in peace' at home. In Zizers, Neni chased to my great disappointment, stags that jumped over the almost two meter-high park wall, out of the vegetable garden. There were also many species of birds, lizards, squirrels, butterflies, bats, etc. It was a wonderful place of discovery for me. There were many trees.

Birch Trees

The birches were my favorite trees. There were 3 big birch trees in the park. The largest was about 15 meters high and my very favorite tree. I climbed it almost every day and even Noni gave up trying to order me down immediately. It was so flexible that I could make it swing about 8 meters from side to side. My passion for this tree was stronger than the orders to stay away. Even the birds knew me and flew freely on and off the tree while I was up it. The birch's silky shimmering white glowing trunk with its elegant leaves fascinated me no end in all the four seasons.

The garden of "Villa Helios" the property where Neni and Noni lived was started by the famous priest, (Pfarrer Kuenzli) who raised herbs for medicine while he as living there. Most of them were still growing in the garden. Pfarrer Kuenzli was a character whose belief was that to give your hand to any one would be very unsanitary. If anyone tried to give him his or her hand he would tell them "You can keep your paw!" There was a beautiful chapel in Villa Helios that the old priest would use for meditation. I loved this room with the gilded wall paper and trim and would have liked it as my personal room.

My grandparents also owned some chickens, a few turkeys and an Entlebucher Mountain Dog called Fido who slept a lot and had a very nice docile character. Fido liked to go walking (slowly) with Neni or me.

Noni was more homebound with her passion for cooking. On the top floor, was an apartment for a single tenant who only came downstairs to have his meals with us. He was a retired hairdresser, dry like a piece of bread and always in a foul mood. Neni said to him, "Isn't my granddaughter beautiful?" and looked at me with grandfatherly pride and love. The pensioner then said to Neni, "M-m- m- yes but her legs are too short." The next pair of shoes I bought had the highest heels I could find. For years to come, I would only wear high heels, even though my legs are the perfect size for my body.

Sunk in Snow and Snow-Blind

The whole class went skiing in Thusis. There were two ski lifts. We were only supposed to go half-way up with the first lift. The second lift to the top, was a no-no. I thought, "Surely no one will miss me if I ski right down from the top." There was deep powdered snow when I came off the top lift and I kept falling. On one fall, my skis came off my bindings and slid down the hill. Trying to recover them, I sunk deeper and deeper into the snow until only my head and shoulders looked out. I started to panic and screamed for help. No one was to be seen until 5 minutes later, when a man on skis found me and helped me out of the deep frozen prison. He then recovered my skis and guided me between his skiis, all the way down to where the rest of the class was and I got yelled at by the teacher, who grounded me for the rest of the day. I was glad to stay in the coffee shop. We then hopped onto the train back to Zizers. The next day, I woke up snow-blind. I was blind for three days and thought about suicide, until my vision came back and restored my joie-de-vivre.

Toothache

My tooth was infected and aching so I called my father who came after the house calls that day, driving for five hours to come to me and to pull my tooth out. It was one of my first molars and I was so glad to have it out. What a father! Unfortunately, he had to go back and attend to his patients.

Episode in Kitchen

Rosa and Noni had a verbal fight in the kitchen. Rosa was a Lilliputian old woman from Tirol who had started to work for my grandparents in 1912, when she was only 16 years old. She had helped to raise my mother, her brother and sister. Everyone loved her including Noni. They just loved fighting over little things and if any one interfered, they both got mad at them. Sometimes, I think that this was their way of having a conversation. The Italian and Tyrolean way! Both of them needed to let off steam from built-up hormones.

1st Fling

There was a boy at school who I admired. He was the most courageous boy. Also, he looked so good. He asked me if I wanted to be his girlfriend. I replied, "Yes." When I found out that he wanted more then a platonic relationship and that he wanted to be a butcher, I suddenly found him unattractive and I told him I did not want to be his girlfriend after all. Soon the year was over and my parents had to make a decision about my future again.

Villa Rhaetzia

My mother suggested that I be enrolled at the Institute "Villa

Rhaetia" in Luzern, since my favorite Aunt Irma and Uncle Freddy with their 3 daughters lived just up the road from that institution and I would be able to spend every week-end with them. My father was against me having to go to that Catholic intern nun school since he had been in such institutions himself. Against his better judgment, my mother insisted. She threatened my father with divorce, if he did not agree with her.

My First Flight

Vacation was not over so 'Papi' (as we called our father) invited all 3 of us to go up in an airplane. He rented a Piper Cub and pilot. I made up my mind while in the air, to earn a pilot's license as soon as I was able to, which I did later on in 1968 but that is another story. Vacation time was over and so 'Mami' as we called our mother and Papi drove me to Lucerne. When we were looking at 'Villa Raetzia', Papi said to Mami, "Poor Maya."

At the Boarding School

All the girls wore black uniforms with white collars. There were nuns ghosting around silently, not one smiled. There was a smell of mildew and holy incense in the dimly lit corridors.

I did not realize how quickly the 2 weeks went before I was brought there again, this time with my packed suitcase. A room with 2 white iron beds was shown to me. There were 2 simple wooden chairs and a plain wooden dresser with 2 rows of drawers, one row for each girl who slept there.

Curious to find out more about the place, I put my clothes and the new horrible black apron dress with the white collar into my side of the dresser and was led with my parents to the office of the mother superior. She greeted us with her clammy, cold and limp hand and a sort of a smile, which looked more like a gas pain, while she said, "Maya will be happy here!"

It was time to say goodbye to my parents, who gave me some pocket money and promised to send me a package that I could share with the other girls if I wanted. When, a few days after the package arrived, I went to pick it up at the Mother Superior's office, she handed it to me opened and the letter in it was also open. I was not used to this, as in my parents' house no one opened any mail with the address of someone else on it. When I bitterly complained, she said with harsh words, "You had better get used to the way it is going to be." She became mother inferior to me. She also said, that if I mentioned one more word about this, I would be punished.

There were two types of nuns. The ones who did the dirty work and prayed, and the ones that prayed and tyrannized the working ones and who did not work. They wore nun's uniforms made of finer cloth than the scratchy ones worn by the other, nicer nuns.

There was one nun we all especially liked. Her name was Sister Ida. She was old and had shoes that hurt her badly since they were too small for her deformed feet. She was hardly able to walk and we told her to get new shoes. She said, that she had asked but new shoes were refused. So all of us girls took up a collection of our pocket money and we asked mother inferior to get a pair of new, comfortable shoes for our favorite nun who was so kind to us all. It was refused but the money was kept. We never found out what our pocket money was used for, except for a so-called 'good cause'. Maybe she bought candles with it?

The girls there were all nice. There were two types of girls, the ones whose parents paid the school fees on time and the ones whose parents did not. The better uniformed nuns made a big difference and treated the poorer girls with more contempt. There was a chapel in this convent school and every morning at 6 o'clock and evening after dinner, we were forced to go and pray in it.

I often fainted while attending morning mass with an empty stomach. The nuns made sure that we did not have any time for ourselves. The food was terrible. The butter was made out of the skin from the top of the hot milk. All vegetables were boiled like mash and nothing was seasoned, except to make it stretch further by pouring a white sauce on it which tasted like flour.

When we wanted to take our weekly bath, we had to show our bathing suits before going in the bathroom. I came out of the bathroom, carrying the bathing suit that I wet in the bath water before getting out of the room and caught a nun looking through the keyhole who claimed she was searching for a needle she had lost on the floor.

I lived for the weekend, when I could spend my time with Aunt Irma and her family, which I enjoyed greatly. My aunt and uncle were so nice and I got along very well with my three cousins, Maya, Verena and Heidi. They were like sisters to me. I could call home from there and speak with my parents, brother and sister in privacy. Time passed quickly when I was there. I always dreaded going back to "Villa Rhaetia."

Walking In the Punishment Hat

We had to go for a walk accompanied by one of the nuns and were forced to walk in a line, in pairs. Every time a boy passed us on the left, we were ordered to turn our heads to the right and when boys were seen on the right we where forced to turn the heads to the left. I did not obey and got punished by having to walk at the end of the two rows of girls, wearing the 'punishment hat'. I wrote a sign and pinned it onto the hat. It said, 'Punished by Institute Villa Rhaetzia'! Everyone who saw my sign on the hat laughed. They did away with the punishment hat after that.

Behavior Class

Twice a week we had to attend two hours of behavior class. The nun said, "Half of all your mothers are murderesses! They use birth control!" Most of us had no idea what the nun was talking about.

I was late for morning mass and was punished by being locked in the bathroom. After about half an hour, I got fed up and opened the window. There was a down spout to the right of the window, which made me decide to go to the public baths for a swim and some sunshine. I could just reach the spout and swung myself onto it, to slide down two stories to freedom. Luckily, I had enough money in my pocket and my bathing suit, which had been drying on the line over the bathtub with me. I enjoyed living in the moment and playing in the water and on the lawn. After that I went to a shop and bought a tube of mayonnaise and sucked it all out in one go. Now I had the necessary strength to go back to that damned institution.

Torture Clinic

Upon my return, I was lectured that it was a sin to go to the public bath since females and males could see each other in sinful costumes. To punish me more, I was forced to go with one nun to their clinic where they stretched the deformed children to try to straighten their backs. Those children had horror and fear written all over their faces and I was forced to watch this torturous ordeal and hear the screams of agony of those poor defenseless children. I suffered from nightmares for a long time.

Ink

My roommate and I put ink into the holy water dish of the dingy chapel. We all went to evening mass. The nuns and the girls (we two included), all crossed ourselves with the ink-mixed holy water. When something like this happened, I was always the one who got questioned first. Of course I pretended innocence but when my roommate who could not lie admitted that she did, it they wanted to throw her out of school. I paid 'Mother Inferior' a visit and told her that it was my idea, that it was my fault and that they should throw me out instead. My roommate got thrown out because her parents were poor and were sometimes late to pay the school fees. So I escaped through the bathroom window down the rainwater pipe and straight to a pay phone and called my parents. They dropped every thing and came to pick me up immediately. I never had to go back to that prison again.

I never learned anything from those nuns anyway. They even killed off my life-long passion for drawing and sketching for the time I was in that sickening institution.

Home Again

I was so happy to be home again and went to the public secondary school. The school was located 2 minutes from our home. The teachers were all male, except for one woman who taught housekeeping and cooking to the girls, while the boys had handicraft. She was a youngish old maid and a terribly boring person, whose cooking was equally tasteless. She was one of those people that were there but not noticed. Her classroom smelled like detergent and moist cleaning rags. She also gave knitting lessons. She wrote a letter of complaint to my parents, which said:

Dear Dr. and Mrs. Krähenmann,
Your daughter Maya has only knitted 4 rows of a wash cloth, if she does not go faster, she will have to repeat the class.

Sincerely Yours,
Miss Hungerbühler

My parents both laughed and found this letter utterly ridiculous.

My First Love, Kurt Benedetti

There was a boy named Kurt Benedetti. We were so in love. He was my first big love and we met each other every day after school. We knew every bench in my hometown and kissed and hugged for hours. We were both not yet in puberty. Our love for each other was pure and platonic.

Tilly, my best friend also had a platonic relationship with a boy. I told my mother that I would be at Tilly's house to do homework and she told her mother that she was doing her homework at my house. This white lie helped us to see our boyfriends in peace and kept our mothers from worrying.

Tilly and I had the same handwriting, so in school she did my arithmetic, which she liked to do, and I did her composition, which I preferred to do. Tilly and I sat next to each other. Herr Sutter, the arithmetic teacher, and Herr Völkli the composition teacher never found out.

About a year passed without any problems about meeting my Love, "Kurt" every day. Then one day, Völkli told my parents, that he had received a complaint. He said, a woman had seen us on the bench near the forest with our clothes off. This was a complete and utter lie, which I suspect was probably made up by Rudi Völkli, (we called him Fudi Rölkli) himself, since he refused to name the so-called woman who made the complaint. Maybe he was jealous.

It was harder and harder to meet Kurt. We missed each other when we were not together until Kurt got into puberty while I was still a child and when he wanted more than kisses and hugs I pushed him out of my life. I was shocked, when I found out in the early 60's that Kurt was killed in a car crash and much later, I met one of his daughters, a very beautiful young lady. We instantly understood each other.

Still Not in Puberty

I was now almost 13 years old and still not in puberty. It started to worry me. Over half the girls had their periods, some since they were 11. Also, I was getting tired of school.

The Secondary School Teachers

My favorite teacher was Herr Winkler, the art teacher. I loved his class and he let me get on with whatever I wanted and gave me all the papers and materials I needed to create whatever I desired.

He also had a terrarium with beautiful vipers in it. The female laid eggs and Herr Winkler took the male out since he did not want to jeopardize the female or her eggs and let the male go free in the place he found it. Only very few of the children and I watched every day with interest if the eggs had hatched. I was the only one that was not afraid of the snakes, knowing that they were not poisonous and I was the only one who could handle the snakes beside Herr Winkler.

One day, the snake man from the Zoo brought a boa constrictor to the class and I was the only one who had it wrapped around my neck, being confident that the man would not have suggested it to me if the snake had been dangerous. I was amazed at the beautiful color of her skin and the warmth of touching her. Before that, I had had the weird idea that snakes would be cold and clammy.

Hässig was our singing teacher. He gave me the creeps. I loved to sing but he yelled with a sharp voice at me, that if I had to sing, I should not sing so loud. He took my joy of singing away from me for years to come. Hässig means, in German, bad-tempered. He lived up to his name and always looked sweaty and greasy. I despised him.

Herr Sutter the arithmetic teacher, walked very stiffly with little careful steps, like the detective Hercule Poirot, but was not so intelligent. He was teased by all of the teenagers. All the teenage girls in the class, decided to stare at his fly and he reddened in the face and went outside. When he came back in we did it again and he dismissed the class. When I think back, I feel that this was a very cruel stunt we played on poor old Herr Sutter. He was old when I was in his class and was still teaching when my daughters went to that same school. Hässig was still there also and caused hardship for my daughters as well.

Professor Brühwiler was a blue-faced old priest. He suffered with bad heart condition high blood pressure and asthma. He came twice weekly to teach us religion. He talked such rubbish that we could not concentrate on it so he screamed with a whistling voice at us. He survived for many years, even though he drank red wine and was known as a gourmet and cigar smoker. There was also a so-called 'maid' who was also his cook living with him. She must have not been a good washerwoman either, since his black clothes were grimy looking.

"Mauchle", was the chemistry, algebra and physics teacher. He was a sadist who hit the boys when passing them by with hectic, nervous and pinched steps, hitting them with the knuckles of his hand on their temples for no reason except for his own sick perversity.

Tilly and I were talking to each other and Mauchle shouted on top of his lungs with a vicious, high pitched voice, "Mmaaaya"! I replied with the same vicious voice but louder "Maaaaauuuchli"! He turned blue in the face and dropped on the floor. Someone called the caretaker who called an ambulance to collect up Mauchle. Mauchle had suffered a heart attack and for one month we had peace from this sadist.

Fortunately, my daughters did not have to experience this sick guy. Mauchle's wife was the girls' swimming teacher. She was also a sadist. We had to go into freezing cold water and stay in it until our faces were blue while she stood fully dressed with a heavy woolen pullover on the outside of the pool.

The Mauchle's had two adopted daughters who were not allowed to have contact with other children and seemed very frightened and shy. I often wondered how they got the right to adopt those girls while loving people had to go to such length to become adoptive parents.

Herr Schawalder the head master and history teacher, called the rest of the teachers for a conference theme, "How to get Maya B. Krähenmann to do her homework." I won. When asked, I replied, "I suffered with a migraine" or "I forgot."

Once out of the school house, I lived in the present and did not let any one steal my precious time. There was hardly enough time to regain my strength before I had to be home for dinner at precisely 6 pm. My mother was very insistent on all of us never being even a minute late. I was school-tired and very relieved and happy when secondary school had finally ended.

The Big Question

My parents asked me to think about what I would like to do with my future. Since I had been away from the "Villa Rhaetia,

Luzern," my love for sketching and color had returned again. I wanted to learn about art so I told them that I wished to study art at the Art Academy in Zurich. My parents agreed, but my mother said, that she had certain conditions for me before she would call the Art Academy to make an appointment for an interview.

Mother's Conditions

My mother's conditions were, first, to wear the ugly dress she had chosen and bought for me. The dress was sugar pink with puffed sleeves and a lace collar. I absolutely hated it and it was not my style I did not care how much she had spent on it. The second condition, was to go to a hairdresser of her choice and have my hair cut and styled. Even though the hairdresser and my mother tried to convince me and said how beautiful I looked, I felt mentally raped and like a phony clown. I preferred my long hair and natural curls. I only won the battle about keeping my finger nails long. From the hairdresser, we went straight to the Art Director. I was so embarrassed by the way I looked, that I felt like hiding under his desk. My mother showed him some drawings that I had done which he liked but then he watched me intently and told my mother, "She is too shy, bring her back in a years time!"

Ecole du Commerce

Meanwhile, my parents decided that I could not pass a year without doing anything and since I did not know which career to choose for myself, I was sent to a career advisor, recommended by friends of my parents. I was 14 years old. He told me that I would die at 24 years old, which I almost did when I had a car accident at 24, but that is another story. He then suggested that I get a commercial education, so I was sent to the Ecole de Commerce in Neuchatel where I could stay with one of my mother's school friends and her family who lived one train station away from school. I did not enjoy staying with that family at all and they treated me as not even a maid should ever be treated. I had to eat in the kitchen with the maid. I preferred to be with the young woman they called 'The maid' and found her to be much nicer than the family.

After 3 long months, I had had a bellyful so I called my parents and told them of the intolerable situation. I quit school and they picked me up. My father said to me, "You can decide what you would like to do but whatever you choose, you have to finish it. Sleep on it and give me the answer as soon as possible." I thought about what I wanted to do and decided to choose an education in ballet.

My Decision

My parents enrolled me at the Ballet Academy "Herta Bammert", in Zurich. I was nearly 15 years old then. I was accepted without a test for, based on my looks and because of already having had ballet lessons.

It was a free school and I could come and go as I pleased but I showed up for almost every class and was in love with all the male teachers.

I admired Harris Plucis who had been with the Sadler's Wells Ballet and taught classical ballet. He was very strict but we learned the most from him. He also had a lot of patience for my lack of concentration and showed me the combination of ballet steps a few more times than he had to do with the others. I suspect that was because I was the most agile in class and he liked me.

Then there was Tonis from India who taught classic, character and expression dance. Tonis was a man with a big heart who was not strict and we all loved him.

Herta Bammert taught classic and tap dancing. When she verbally abused Tonis, we all stuck up for him and threatened her, that if she threw Tonis out, we would all quit her school. Tonis stayed on!

Roy Bosier taught pantomime, which was one of my favorite classes, and Jose Udeta taught flamenco. He was such a fascinating man that I could only concentrate on him and not on the fast steps he tried to teach me.

At 15 1/2 years, I finally got the period. I was so happy not to have to worry anymore if my development was normal. It was as if a big stone had been lifted off me.

My aunt Irma, Uncle Freddy with my three cousins bought a house in Zurich. Aunt Irma was fearless compared to my mother. My mother insisted that I be home by exactly 9 p.m. If I was one minute late, she psycho-tortured me with her fears.

Ballett Academie Herta Bammert, ZH

Jacques Thüring

One day, I played hooky from ballet school to go swimming in Lake Zurich. There I met Jacques Thüring a psychology student. We fell in love. He was the first non-platonic man in my life. He played his favorite classical records to me and asked if I liked them. I had enough classical music in the ballet lessons but did not want to hurt his feelings so I did not tell him of my preference for Elvis Presley, the Platters or Jazz. We made love and he asked me if liked it. Again, I did not want to hurt his feelings and said, "Yes" instead of telling him that it hurt and that I was bitterly disappointed. We made love a few more times and finally I could not stand having to be nice any longer and left him.

To be truthful is better than to be nice - the truth can hurt, but can be dealt with while the pain of even a white lie can linger on and can prevent the pain from healing.

I was also afraid to get pregnant since we only had the hated prophylactics and the birth control pill was not invented until 1964.

I was worried about my sexuality ever since my mother caught me playing with my clitoris. I did not realize that she thought I was doing something bad until I saw the expression of disgust on her face. I had only been 1 1/2 years old and had felt guilty ever since. I tried to stop the addiction without success until I was confronted with real passion in later life.

I also remembered that the career adviser who told me that I would die at the age of 24 and figured since the clitoris felt that good, a real man's penis would be the world's most wonderful feeling. This was what I yearned to experience before I (maybe) would die. I was in some doubt about that. Luckily, another fortuneteller predicted that I would find love and that I would live a long life. I believed him right away.

Cadillac

There was a boy in ballet school who was driven there by a chauffeur in a Cadillac. He was a very nice boy and I told him, that I envied him for being driven by a chauffeur in such a beautiful car. He then said, "You can do that too! My parents are on vacation and they don't need the car so if it suits you, the chauffeur and I will pick you up on Saturday afternoon and we'll go for a ride." I told him that I lived 60 km from Zurich and was delighted to hear him say that the distance was no problem. Thrilled, I accepted and took the train home. Very happy, I told my mother that I was going to be picked up by a boy from class and his chauffeur in a Cadillac.

My mother then became almost hysterical and in a loud voice, she yelled "Under no circumstances will I allow you to go out with them." I asked her, "Why not?" She could not think of an answer - and I should think not, since she did not even know this 15 year old boy. Anyway, it was Friday evening and they would come the next day at 2 p.m. I was glad not to have the boy's address and telephone number, which made it impossible for me to break the date.

When they arrived to pick me up, I squeezed by my mother who was standing in my way and ran out into the Cadillac. The chauffeur asked me where I would like to go so I suggested to him a very nice garden coffee shop with an impressive view. When we arrived there, the chauffeur in his spotless uniform, got out and opened the door for us and we entered the garden of the coffee shop. I felt so proud. No one could take away that feeling. The chauffeur ordered whatever we desired and paid for everything.

After that, I was driven home. When I arrived, (I was not gone more then 1 hour), my mother stood furious in the stairway. When I came toward her, she hit her flat hand so hard in my face, that I fell down the steps. This was the third and last time that she slapped me.

The first time she had slapped me, was when I was five years old and refused to brush my teeth. When she tried to force me, I called her a dumb cow.

The second time her hand slipped, was when I was twelve years of age and came home with a kiss mark on my neck from my first platonic love, Kurt Benedetti.

Now I am not writing this down out of bitterness but to advise all parents, never to slap a child since he or she will never forget an act of hatred. One can speak to a child and explain why one wishes for the child to not do something. Our father always spoke to us and we would always listen to him with the greatest respect. We loved both our parents but I had total admiration for my father who was always just and understanding.

"The one who hits has lost the argument and is therefore the weaker."

My Aunt Irma

My uncle, Prof. Dr. Jur. Alfred Maurer, a handsome and extremely intelligent man who had written famous books about law and his autobiography. He was a judge and adviser to the Swiss Government and had climbed the Matterhorn. Their three beautiful daughters were like sisters to me. Maya, the eldest of my cousins, was a judge in the juvenile court and is now retired. Verena, the middle cousin, is a very feminine and pretty woman who adopted a daughter. Heidi is an author and pianist who is now the grandmother of a beautiful daughter called Ursina, who gave birth to my aunt Irma's first great - grandchild.

Before I was enrolled at the Ballet Academy, the Maurer family moved into a really nice house with big garden in Zurich. Aunt Irma is a beautiful woman both inside and out, with blond hair and blue eyes. She was a kindergarten teacher and was very creative. She had a very gentle nature and had a positive voice and was fearless in contrast to my mother. My mother insisted that I was home by exactly 9 p.m. If I came home just one minute late, she psycho - tortured me with her well-meant fears.

My favorite aunt, Irma, invited me to sleep at their house and gave me the keys. She asked me to call her if I would be back later than 2 a.m. so she would not have to worry. My mother was relieved to see me in good hands and I was happy to finally get my much-needed freedom.

Sometimes I would take some friends from the ballet school to her house and Aunt Irma fed them all. They all envied me for having an aunt like her.

In March 2009, she was 90 years old and I truly hope she will outlive the Queen's mother if she wishes to. She took in an orphaned cat, enjoys the great view and flowers on her balcony and I love her dearly.

My Brother and Sister

I started to think about my life. Even as a small child, I was drawn to the opposite sex. I found it more fun to play with boys than with girls and dolls. I remember watching my brother and his friend at the cemetery competing to see who could pee into the holy-water dish on a grave from the longest distance away. My brother and his friend were then only five years old.

I loved to run, ski, skate, go sledding, draw, sing, climb trees, watch nature, dance and listen to music. When we were teenagers my brother Ruedi measured 1m 80 cm . He had dark brown hair that he combed from his forehead into a big wave and glued with Brylcreem into a "duck's arse" to the back of his head. He shared my passion for dancing. We jitterbugged and rocked and rolled. All the other dancers went to the outside of the dance floor forming a circle around us and applauded for more.

I started to date boys and so did my beautiful sister. Heli had long blond hair, clear blue eyes and a complexion like velvet. She had a very small waist, (hour glass figure) accentuated by wearing wide, flowing skirts and décolleté tops. Almost all of the boys I took home fell in love with Heli, but she only had eyes for a handsome young man from Paris.

She was allowed to invite him and his friend to stay with us providing the two boys stayed at night in the rooms upstairs away from ours. There was no way to sneak unheard up the old creaking staircase. The next morning when I came up stairs to fetch them for breakfast I caught the boys kissing each other on the lips. I felt that I should tell my sister of this incident and when I told her she was so crushed that I wished that I had not told her. I felt so sorry for Heli and was wondering if it would have been better to let her find out by herself. If I had been in her shoes, I would have wanted to know. On the other hand, if she had found out later, she maybe would have been less in love and therefore the truth may have been less painful.

"No one can change the past but one can learn from it."

Werni Hermann

I met Werni Hermann, a dark-haired, blue-eyed man with a strong personality. He had lived in Cuba for a while and was an adventurer. He owned an old Skoda and invited his friend Harry Bietenholz, my sister "Heli" and I to drive it into the woods for its final drive until it would no longer run. Werni drove over tree trunks, branches, lumps and ditches but the Skoda kept on going, so Werni drove the Skoda back home again.

I fell in love with Werni and Heli fell in love with Harry. Harry drove a T- series MG which was a special treat to ride in. We met every weekend because Werni was working and Harry was a student. On weekends, Werni and I or all four of us had a lot of fun together. My parents liked Werni and Harry and when they visited us at home they were always invited for dinner. My mother always stayed in the room with us, to make sure Heli and I did not get pregnant. Little did she know of my great relief every month to be menstruating. Where there is a will, there is a way.

Changed Schools

I had a disagreement with Herta Bammert and quit the Ballet Academy. My parents enrolled me at the Stadt Theatre Ballet School, Zurich, where my teacher was Herr Stebler. He was kind and a gentleman who was blessed with great understanding. I loved to be in his class. I was also taking private acting lessons from Max Amman who taught me at our home once a week. Frau Treichler gave me private lessons in phonetics and singing and gave me back the joy of singing that Hässig had taken away when I was in secondary school. Herr Stebler told me to go to Paris, Studio Wacker, where I could advance. My lack of concentration did not worry him but it worried me. I knew that ballet would be of use to me but for what I did not know until later in life.

Studio Wacker, Paris

At 17 years of age I was enrolled at Studio Wacker, in Paris. My mother and I took a Swissair flight from Zurich airport, then called 'Kloten' to Paris, Orly. Kloten was renamed, because people from Holland laughed at the name *Kloten,* which means *testicles* in their language. I loved the flight and was almost glued to the window, except for the meal, which was served on real dishes with silver plated cutlery, and the free drinks, as many as you wanted were served in real glasses.

In Paris, we found a hotel in the center of town and from there we searched for a room where I could lodge, without success.

In the evening my mother said to me, "Now we will go to the Moulin Rouge, the worst to see in Paris, so I can go back to Switzerland without you having to search for anything else." The Moulin Rouge looked very tame to me and I could not understand why my mother and the older man in the seat next to hers became so upset at a young man wearing silver wings who was only wearing a silver slip and was flying through the air hanging on to a silver rope. I enjoyed the act.

The next day, we looked again for a room for me. No luck again, so my mother said that she would take me back home with her, if we could not find a room the next day. I was getting worried. Happily, and to my relief, we found a room the next day in Danfer-Rocherau. I could relax again.

Danfer-Rocherau was located on the other side of town, almost an hour's ride away from Studio Wacker on the Metro. It was a girl's boarding house and all the girls had to be inside by 9 p.m. Breakfast, lunch or dinner could be eaten there for a reasonable price. The only bed left for me, was in a room with two other girls. One was very shy and quiet but always nice and kind, while the other one was a fire-ball full of fun and temperament. As I found out later, she was in love with a black boy and had had a second key made, so that she could come back in at any time she chose. She also lent me her key so I could have a key made and also enjoy the same freedom as long as we were not caught. We never were!

Before my mother flew home she took me to the Studio Wacker. There, we met one of my teachers, a Mr. Wood from

Russia who gave me an interview. He took one look at me and I did not have to take the test to get into Studio Wacker. Mr. Wood promised my mother to look out for me. As soon as she had gone back to Switzerland, he tried to seduce me but I turned him down. I threatened him, that if he tried again, I would not attend his class any more. He excused himself and respected my wishes.

Violet Verdi, came from London to train at Studio Wacker. Brigitte Bardot studied ballet at Studio Wacker a year before I did. Olega Projenska, 81 years old, looked no more than 60 and came from Russia to teach classical ballet and when I asked her how she managed to look so young. She stood on her head and said, "This is what I do every day" and it makes me feel young. I felt lucky to attend Olega Projenska's class. From then on, I tried to stand on my head as often as possible.

Angeli Davi

My best friend at Studio Wacker was the daughter of rich and famous MD. Angeli was an Indian temple dancer from Switzerland. We went to see the night life in Paris and eat in restaurants. She asked me if I had ever eaten Indian food and I said, "No." So she took me to an Indian restaurant. There was a plate with different sauces on the table and she took a spoon full of the red sauce and said "Open your mouth, this tastes good." I opened my mouth, thinking it was some sort of jam. I felt like my mouth and head was on fire. I perspired and grabbed the glass of water, which I emptied in one go, but it did not help. Then I ate all the rice at great speed and started to get better. I had learned the quick way what concentrated chili sauce was all about. I did not learn to like it until in later life.

Angeli and I went into expensive clubs, accepted a dance with the first man that asked us and then left in a hurry before we had to order an expensive bottle. Since I told Angeli, that I could not afford to consume the way she did, we tried to have fun the inexpensive way.

Sydney Bechet

It was a beautiful spring day in Paris when two classmates and I decided to go exploring. We raced up the stairs to the top of the Eiffel Tower and I won. Then we went to Montparnasse and, walking around, I spotted an underground cafe named LA CHATTE so I suggested to the others to check it out. We went inside and downstairs. It looked empty, except for the waiter behind the bar and a man sitting on a round table. One of my classmates said, "I think that's Sidney Bechet", so I said, "Let's go and ask him." They said, "We can't do that." so I said "Okay, I will go and ask him myself then." and walked over to the round table and asked the man, "Are you Sydney Bechet?" He responded, "Yes." with a warm, velvety voice and a beautiful smile. His eyes had an unforgettable sparkle in them. Pointing at a chair next to him, he asked me to sit down. I told him that I was not alone and pointed to my classmates who were standing on the stairway. Sidney Bechet then said, "Tell them to come and sit with us as well." They accepted with great pleasure and sat down at his table. He then called the waiter and ordered drinks of our choice for all of us. What an unforgettable time with this legend of a man who has enriched our lives so much!

When I found out that he had died in 1959, I got a lump in my throat and could not hold back my tears. His music will live on and I will never, ever forget him.

Werni Herman's and Harry Bietenholz's Visit

They arrived in Paris Studio Wacker in Harry's MG. The MG was red and had a luggage rack on the back. I was happy to see Werni again. Too bad my sister could not come along. Harry said "Let's go and look at a bit of Paris." I said "Can I invite some of my friends?" The boys said "Yes." So I brought five of my friends along. Since the MG only had two seats and there were eight of us, Werni said, "Four of you on the luggage rack and Maya on my knee and one sitting on the top of the door, hanging on, by holding the windshield." This is the way we went through Paris, Champs Elysees, to Sacre Coeur and finally to the castle of Versailles. The

French Police just laughed when they saw us. Of course, Harry drove very slowly.

At Versailles we saw the museum of beautiful horse-drawn carriages. Then we rented two row boats and had a wonderful water fight, splashing each other with the oars. They threw us out, without charging us anything, just so the lake could be peaceful again. We were all soaked to the skin but it was a beautiful, hot day and that did not matter. The next day, Werni and Harry had to leave again.

My Father's Words

Angeli and I had a lot of fun and I thought that my parents were rich. Whenever I needed money, I just called and my parents would send me more. One day, I called home again and my mother called my father to the telephone. He said to me "Maya, we are doing everything to make you happy but if you keep on spending the way you do, I will have to ask you to come home. We have not only you, but your brother and sister to support as well."

My father had never spoken of the financial situation before and since I had the return ticket to Switzerland, I took the first flight home even though Mr. Wood assured me, that if I could stay for rest of the year he would see that I got a job as a soloist at any famous theatre I wanted.

Rigi Blick

Summer, 1958 and at home again, I took courses at the Hotel Rigi Blick in Zurich and visited the classes of Mary Wigwam and Maurice Béjart.

One afternoon, I did not feel like going to classes, so I took the cable car that had been built for the Saffa exhibition across the lake of Zurich. The Saffabahn had seats for two people so I shared with a very handsome Chinese-American man who introduced himself as Howard Fong. We could not understand each other's language but he had a dictionary with him and I understood the word cafe. I accepted his invitation to a cafe.

We found it easy to be together and when he asked me to marry him, just hours after we met, I said, "Yes!" Howard had to leave the next day to fly back and take over his newly bought business, a luxurious beauty salon with his business partner, Wilmar Sick.

I went to my father and asked him for a ticket to the U.S.A., since I wanted to get married. He replied okay, on two conditions. "First you go to cooking school and then you go to England to learn the language. If you still feel this strong about him then, I will agree."

Howard and I wrote frequent love letters to each other and with the help of my dictionary, I learned broken English. We managed to understand each other. I visited a cooking school in St. Gallen, Switzerland.

London

I flew to London where I was going to work as an au-pair girl for a family with a three-month-old baby, where my work consisted of walking with the baby to the park and babysitting. My mother thought it to be a good idea and felt that I would be safe there. She probably wanted me to learn what a responsibility a child would be. I was supposed to have plenty of time to visit a school and learn English.

While visiting the London School of English, I met Peter, a boy from Switzerland, who was going to call me for a rendezvous, to take me out to dinner. The people whom I was supposed to help with their baby, wanted me to make beds, clean, iron, and be a maid. I remembered my father's words, "Maya, whatever you don't want to do, pretend you don't know how to do it." When Peter called on the phone. I was just near it when the woman answered and I heard her say, " No, Maya can't go out with you. She has not done enough work and has to clean tonight."

It was my fifth day there and I grabbed my handbag and ran to the nearest phone booth to call my parents. My father said, "Leave that job and find a room right away and just go to school." I found a room with a bath in a romantic old house with very tolerant family from Australia. In the London School of English, I met a girl who was very depressed and unhappy, working as an au-pair for an older couple.

When she told them that she had met a friend, they invited me to lunch. There was an enormous long table with the woman sitting at one end of the table and the man sitting at the other. We were placed at the sides in the middle facing each other. The place looked dark and dingy and reminded me of a room in an English horror film. No one spoke a word while the lunch was eaten.

After lunch it was the girl's afternoon off and we went out together. My classmate was complaining bitterly about her mental state and so I suggested she leave the job and move in with me. There was an extra sofa in my room she could sleep on until she could find a better job. Little did I know what would face me.

The girl told me that she had grown up in an orphanage and had had nothing but hard times in her life. On top of it all, she was madly in love with a boy who did not feel the same about her. I tried to console her, that we would go out and find her another boy and that she deserved better. I got a bit tired of her whining and with having to put up with all the cut-out film stars she had taped all over the walls of my room.

With her being a pain, I went out on my own and hoped she would do the same. It seemed to be the right thing to do and went so well that we did go out together sometimes. We went to school together but we did not go home together. One day, she was whining again about the boy who did not love her. I went out. When I came back, she was laying unconscious on the bathroom floor.

I found an empty sleeping pill bottle next to her and so I called the ambulance. They pumped out her stomach in the hospital. This happened in 1959 and suicide was a criminal act in England. The police came and sharply questioned me. There was someone from Switzerland coming to pick her up and before taking her back with them, they yelled at me and claimed that it was all my fault. I had only meant to help her. I packed my things and used my return flight ticket to go back to my parents where I took the first job that came my way.

Old City Theatre St. Gallen

I became a dancer at the Old State Theatre S.G. in Switzerland. There was training in the morning, rehearsal in the afternoon, on stage in the evening and then party-time. I loved it. My first dance was in Offenbach's French Can-Can. I was training for my first solo for the coming of the special classical ballet evening. I was really looking forward to this.

Renate Fuchs had to train for my role as well, in case I should fall out. Suddenly she wanted my solo and threatened the director that she would quit the theatre if she was not given the part instead of me. She had been in the theatre much longer than I and had danced parts in other shows that were current, so when she got the part that had been promised to me, I walked out and took the 1/2 hour train ride home.

Unfortunately, the old jewel of a theatre was wrecked to the ground to make room for an ugly parking lot and a square shoe shop.

Heart Block

At home, I did not feel well and it alarmed my father. Then, I was feeling very weak, so he called my mother and carried me upstairs, where he laid me in my bed. My brother and sister, my mother and father stood around the bed and they all thought that I was unconscious. I heard their voices clearly, but faintly, as if very far away and heard my father say poor Maya, she is dying so young. I had no feeling of fear and thought, "No way am I going to die!"

I recovered and my father made an appointment at the practice of his friend, a well known heart specialist who checked my heart and took an electro-cardiogram. He verified the fact that I had suffered a heart block. I was forbidden to dance or do anything strenuous for at least a year. One year later, in the U. S. A., a heart specialist checked my heart and found that it was slightly larger than normal but healthy. He asked to see the previous cardiogram, which I brought to him after it was posted to me from Switzerland. He was amazed that I was telling him the truth, since he could not detect any signs of heart block.

Willi Epper

I fell in love with Willy Epper. His father was as overprotective as my mother. I took the train to St. Gallen every weekday to go to the Hermes, a school for commerce. Willi studied at the E. T. H. (Swiss Federal Institute of Technology Zurich) and planned to later take over the family business of construction. He lived in Gossau. We saw each other every weekend in the company of friends or family. During the week we would write very hot love letters to each other. It was not easy to find private time with each other but we managed. There were two stops on the train from Wil to Gossau and St. Gallen. I called my mother to say that I had missed the train and would take the next one in an hour and a half. She never realized that I was calling from Gossau and not from St. Gallen!

Love is Stronger than Anything

It bothered me that I was, at 19 years of age, still not free to come and go as I liked, as I had in Paris at fifteen and a half or as I had in London just a couple of months before. So, I had to invent a lie for my mother to get the freedom I so desperately needed. I never had to lie to my father. He understood me and I could speak to him about everything. He would lovingly advise me by saying, *"Maya - do what you can."*

Sometimes my father went to see his brother Freddy, who had a very romantic property right on the lake of Zurich. It was an old house with pigsty, and Freddy turned it into a paradise. Those of the family who had thought Freddy was crazy to do so envied him now. Freddy was a lot of fun to be around. He was a garden architect and knew so much about nature. When my father went to see Freddy, he asked, "Maya, would you like to go with me? If not, we could meet in front of the door at 2:00 a.m. That way, if we come home together, your mother would not be worried." My mother did not like to go to Freddy's since he loved to tell raunchy jokes that were not to her liking.

My father was so understanding and generous-thinking that my friends often came to my father for advice because they could not find anyone else to have confidence or understanding.

About six months previously, I had written to Howard that it was too long to have been waiting for him but that a platonic friendship was still possible.

2 THE MARRIED YEARS

Willi and Howard

I asked Willi if he would marry me and he said "No", and that it was senseless to even ask his father, who would not even consider it before he had finished his studies at the E.T.H (Zurich Federal Institute of Technology Zurich) and had more practice in the family business.

Just after he said this, a letter from Howard arrived and he wrote that he was coming to visit me in Switzerland. To my own surprise, I felt my heart surge in my chest. Full of joy, I read the letter to my mother who dictated a letter back to him, stating that I was too young and immature for a relationship. She had me write that I did not yet know what I wanted but that he was welcome to visit us. She made me sign and send the letter and accompanied me to the letterbox.

Howard arrived just two weeks later. He was given a room on the top floor of our house, well away from my room. One night, I tried to sneak upstairs. The old stairway squeaked so loudly, that my parents heard it and I quickly went back to my own room.

The next day, Howard and I went to Zurich and he bought engagement rings. We put the rings on our fingers and called my parents, telling them that we were going to celebrate our engagement. We ate a delicious eight-course feast in a posh restaurant before we went home.

The next morning, Howard asked my father for my hand in marriage. My father looked at Howard and me, and said "Would it not be better to live together for two years before making it legal to see if it would work out?" My mother interrupted him saying, "No daughter of mine is going to live with a man, without getting married first." My father was rather touched that Howard would ask him as this was rarely done during this generation. He took Howard's hand and said, "Please take good care of Maya."

We went to the courthouse to get permission to be married, but had to wait for three weeks. While waiting for the time to get married on October 20, 1960, Howard and I honeymooned in Venice.

We went back to Switzerland for my sister's marriage to Miklos Kiss just five days before our marriage. My parents were not too happy to let my sister Heli get married at only eighteen years of age. I had asked Willi to Heli's marriage and found it to be only polite to dance with him one more time. Howard was upset and I had to explain to him that I would keep a platonic friendship with Willi all my life. Heli's marriage to Miki was wonderful. She looked radiant in her white dress and the ambiance was elegant, classy and fun. The food was excellent and spirits were high. Even Howard cheered up.

Our marriage took place in the office at the Rathaus (City Hall) in Wil. My brother and sister were the witnesses. My parents were there. We did not invite anyone else. We all went out for a fine dinner at the Hotel Derby in Wil where, afterwards, Howard and I spent the night in the honeymoon suite.

My parents were relieved that we only wanted a quiet marriage, since it was unexpectedly soon after Heli's luxurious one. Howard had to be back to attend to his business and flew back to Baltimore, Maryland, U.S.A. the next day, while I had to wait another three months to get the immigrant visa to be with my husband. It was a long wait and I heard afterwards, that mixed marriages were still illegal in the U.S.A. I felt that Howard was a very handsome man, 6 ft tall, well built and energetic. To me, he was the ideal father for my future children and I loved him.

Married to Howard

Finally the time arrived when I got the visa and could join my husband. My parents opened an account for me with SFr. 10'000. I knew this was a sacrifice for them and promised to only use this money in an emergency. When my parents drove me to the airport and the time came to say goodbye, I saw how my father tried to hide his tears. I assured him that we would all see each other again and that I would write and call on the phone, as soon as I arrived in the U.S.A.

The 18-hour flight in the four-engined Sabena plane was great but I looked forward to being in Howard's arms again and was excited that I would soon be in the U.S.A. Howard picked me up at New York airport and we took a taxi to the Hotel Waldorf Astoria where he had a room reserved for us. I felt so happy being in his arms again. Then we went to dinner. For the first time, I ate a real American steak that was so big, that it covered the whole plate. It was so juicy and delicious that I ate it all up, including the baked potato and the salad. Then we went to look at Broadway and it was fascinating to see all the colorful moving neon-light advertisements, some blowing smoke. We had no moving advertisements in Switzerland. Then we went to the top of the Empire State building and other New York landmarks.

The next day, we went shopping and Howard bought me about 10 new dresses, all with matching shoes and handbags and two designer coats, one with real fox fur, and mentioned that it was important for his exquisite business that I looked elegant. I did not mind that in the least.

He took me to meet his sisters MJ and Dolly who lived in Manhattan and we went out together to eat. MJ and her boy friend Joe knew where and which food was best in China town. To me it was as if I were in China. What a colorful and exciting place! We were greeted by the cook and his family who served us the most beautiful and tasty dishes I had ever tasted.

The next day, we left for Baltimore. Howard was living in a very large property and the apartment above his splendid salon was so large, that it did not bother me that we were sharing it with Howard's business partner, Wilmar Sick. Wilmar came from Germany and most of his clients had a crush on him. The older Swiss couple, the Griessers who sold their propriety to Howard and Wilmar and whose business employed 34 people, also left Emma, a black woman, who was an excellent cook with us. They left most of the beautiful furniture as well.

Howard was busy working in his business downstairs so Emma made a special coffee that she and I drank together. Emma disliked children and often said how much the "little brats" irritated her. I wanted to have a baby as soon as possible and get pregnant right away. In the third month after being married, my periods stopped and I found out that I was pregnant. I was deliriously happy and told everyone I knew and met about it. Emma was terribly upset and described a birth to me that sounded like a horror story. She said, "That-there blood was all over them-there walls and on them-there floors."

Howard gave me his second car, an Austin Healey Sprite, which had a number written on both sides and was equipped with a roll bar. He used to race it and all of his trophies, nothing but first and second prizes at the Marlboro racetrack. I found over forty, were hidden in a closet. I loved that little sports car but was stopped by the police the first time I drove the car because it had no muffler. The police let me go and I had a muffler fitted. Often, I just drove around memorizing certain landmarks so that I could find my way back again. That way, I got to know the city of Baltimore and its surroundings very rapidly.

Emma had the day off and I was thinking it would be a nice surprise if I should make lunch with special care and take it downstairs to Howard in the shop's lunchroom. I was sure that he would miss me the way I missed him and would also be happy to see me. The employees were all happy to see me but Howard screamed at me, to never come near his business again unless he asked me to and threw the lunch on the floor. My feelings were badly hurt and I ran upstairs to masturbate in self-pity. My love for him cooled off but I finally managed to forgive him.

Marjorie Lane

Emma had a foul mood as soon as she found out that I was pregnant. I did not want to drink coffee with her any more and so I went swimming. The nearest pool was the Mount Washington pool but when I spotted the big sign with large letters written on it "JEWS, NIGGERS OR DOGS ARE NOT ALLOWED." I could not believe what I had seen and made an immediate 360° turn to head for the zoo instead. I LOVE AND RESPECT ANIMALS MORE THAN MOST PEOPLE!

It was April 1, 1960 when I thought to play a trick. I phoned the shop down stairs and yelled, "The house is on fire!" Then I went to the window and watched the customers, staff and Howard running out of the buildings. I found that the women running out with rollers, plastic or aluminum foil on their heads and wearing aprons looked especially amusing. They looked like scarecrows. I yelled from the window, "April Fools!" Howard did not find this funny at all and gave me a real ear-bashing.

I did not want to have my baby in the house with Emma so we moved into an apartment in a brand-new building in the suburbs. Emma stayed on with Wilmar. One apartment near us was rented by friends and their two little girls. They were from Holland. Their father worked as a hairdresser for Howard. There were six apartments in the house. Another apartment was rented by a young divorced woman from England, who had a little girl. My best friend was Paula Kendros, whose husband was a gynecologist and their little boy, Thomas. They came from Greece. Another apartment was lived in by a young couple from Germany. Yet another apartment was taken by an eccentric old American, a retired schoolteacher who owned a cat, who was so vicious, that the old girl had to wrap a thick, padded blanket around her arm when she carried her cat around so the bites would not hurt her.

Opposite our apartment, lived a middle-aged, very quiet couple from the States. The woman was often alone while her husband went to work. She often invited me to come and drink a cup of coffee with her. I had baked a cake and brought it over to her since she loved sweets. She returned the baking form the next day and it shone brighter than when it was new. So every time the baking form got messy, I baked a cake in it for her and it came back spotless.

This also helped to keep Howard happy, since he was a perfectionist who got bothered by the tiniest little speck of dirt. I could not see dirt, so he hired a cleaning woman for me.

I had just received the news that my father had gotten his pilot's license in a Piper Cub. He had always said that he would wait until we were all grown up before he took flying lessons. I was so proud of my father. When I asked Howard, if I could learn to fly, he said that a woman would not be able to fly. When I told him of the woman who did, he did not want to know and refused to finance flying lessons for me. I found a way to have my dream come true later in life but that is another story.

Meeting my In-laws

Howard had decided to introduce me to his parents and so we drove to Marianna, Arkansas to visit them. I met more family members and some of their friends. I was so happy to be there and they made me feel so welcome.

Father Fong was the best cook and he had a black maid who helped peel the vegetables and who helped with everything else. She had great big eyes and great big lips and a great big belly. She was pregnant, I was pregnant and the cat was also pregnant.

Mother Fong had a big collection of porcelain, all in her favorite color, pink. She loved her beautiful rose garden. I was very impressed by the multitude of varieties and colors, not to speak of the delicious perfumes. What a sight! I loved her roses. I loved her humor also. What a cheerful person!

Howard took me sightseeing and I spotted all the poverty-stricken areas where the ex-cotton pickers lived in ancient wooden shacks, with most of the grown-ups sitting outside on the steps while many children and skinny dogs were playing. Sometimes I saw a few chickens. What surprised me, was that there was a TV antenna on every roof and a washing machine outside.

When the cotton industry replaced men with machines, the plantation industrialists gave the workers, whom they no longer needed, free one-way train tickets to New York. They told them that there was plenty of work for them and their families. Some of the workers left with their whole families on the train. What a nightmare, when they found out that there was no work. Most of them did not know how to read or write and did not have the financial means to survive or turn around to go back. The cruelty and perversity of some of the actions of some of the business people astonishes me.

I am sure there is a way to be wealthy and able to live in your own decent skin with peace of mind.

After many wonderful invitations, meals and interesting times in Arkansas, Howard took me on one of the famous old Mississippi paddle steamers that crossed the Mississippi river. I loved the boat but what turned me off were the four toilets it was equipped with. One was for white men only, one for white women only, one for black men only and one reserved for black women. It was 1960 and Eisenhower was President of the U.S.A. Not until President Kennedy was in office did things get better where racism was concerned. The southern states were known to have a bigger problem with racism.

When Howard was a little boy he was playing with his puppy dog in their fenced-in garden. A policeman saw him and shot his puppy dog. Now, the family is respected by everybody.

Brainwash which stimulates war by using racism, prejudice and nationalism is the cause of inbreeding and illness, (mental and physical) and the less inbreeding there is the more resistant the human race will be to illness and the less chance of being manipulated into war. War is the most polluting of all human activities and should be banned immediately for the urgent improvement of the health of our beautiful planet. The more mixed the human race is the less chances of inbreeding there will be and the less chance of war. There should be a system of defense against the warmongers by all other countries of the world acting together against whoever tries to break the peace in the world. The world is round and should not be squared. Only the restricted believe that world peace is not possible. Thought is more valuable than blind belief.

Howard's mother in her rose garden.

The Birth of Alexa

On August 7, 1961, it was time for my last appointment with gynecologist, Dr. Russel, who was recommended to me by one of Howard's rich clients. He lived on North Charles Street and had the most luxurious waiting room I had ever seen. The floors where covered with the most beautiful oriental rugs and original paintings hung on the walls. The doctor's white Cadillac was prominently parked on the driveway of his posh house, surrounded by the totally manicured garden.

I dreaded those visits to him because every time, he performed an intern examination, by putting his fingers up my vagina. When I asked him why he did that, he said that it was done to every pregnant woman, to feel if everything was alright. This time, he forced his whole hand up and caused me agonizing pain, pulling and pushing my insides. When I demanded to know why he did that, he said that, "The baby was in the wrong position and I had to turn it around." On the way home, I was still in pain.

The next day, blood ran down my legs. I was frightened for my baby and hurried to tell my mother. I also told her of my sudden cramps. She informed me that the water broke and that there was blood in it, which made it look red, since it was the amniotic fluid and that this was nothing to be frightened of. She also told me that the cramps were the labor pains and that all this was normal, except one month early, but it was time to go to the hospital.

I called Howard, who immediately raced all the way home and drove me to the Women's Hospital in Baltimore. Howard sped through all the red lights to get there faster. I was accompanied by my mother. At the desk I was told, "Oh yes, Mrs. Fong, Dr. Russel has already reserved a room for you. Please follow this nurse." My mother and Howard were not allowed to accompany me.

In the room, the nurse, a stocky and butch looking woman with a moustache, ordered me to get undressed and made me lie on the bed. She then put a bracelet with a number around my wrist. When I asked her what this was for, she replied, "In case you die, we know where to put you!" Then she took shaving lotion and sprayed it on my pubic hairs, then shaved them off so close, that she took a layer of skin right off. I ask her why she was doing this and she said, dryly, "For sanitary reasons." I was frightened.

After that, while I was in labor, I was examined by ten medical students in intervals of 5-10 minutes. They all gave me an internal examination and when I asked them why, they all told me that they have to feel how big the opening was where the baby would be coming out. I told each one that I wanted a natural birth and all said, "If that is possible", or something equally unsure. I asked to see Russel but he did not appear. A nurse gave me a spinal injection against my will. They also gave me something that knocked me out.

I woke up briefly to see a pole, which was pressed hard on my stomach and rolled down with great force, held by two medical students on each of my sides, while the other group of students were standing around Russel. Then I passed out again. The next flashback I had, was when Russel held my newborn baby upside down by the feet and slapped its tiny bottom. I heard my baby cry and felt totally helpless. I was shocked and passed out again.

I woke up totally alone in the cold-looking hospital corridor, strapped to a metal bed. I thought I was dying when I could not feel my totally numb legs. Worse, I worried about my baby. I must have laid there for another hour and a half before a nurse came. I asked her, "Where is my baby?" She did not answer and walked away saying that she would go and ask. Then another nurse came and told me that the numbness in my legs would go away soon and that I would be okay. I asked, "Where is my baby? I want to see my baby." She said "That is not possible." "Is my baby okay? Can I see her? Is it a boy or a girl?" "I don't know," she said and added "but the baby is alright." Then, another nurse rolled me into the room and drew the curtain around the hospital bed. She had a stainless steel bowl placed on the floor. She then proceeded to press my stomach until urine flowed out of a tube that had been inserted in my bladder. They had fitted a catheter.

I demanded to see Dr. Russel. Another doctor came and told me that Russel had left on a holiday. It was clear to me, that Russel had induced the birth and reserved a place in that horrible hospital because he had planned to go on vacation. He had not told me a thing about that or warned me at all, that he had planned for his students to learn on me. So, a doctor that I saw for the first time in my life, told me that my baby was a healthy and perfect baby girl. However, she was in an incubator because she was born 1 month premature and only weighed 4 pounds 11 ounces.

Howard and I named our baby

Not A Boring Moment

Alexa Helena Fong

Alexa, after my maternal grandfather Alexander- and Helena after my mother's first name. When I told the new doctor whom I had never seen before, that I wished to breast-feed my baby Alexa, he looked at me in horror and explained that hothouse tomatoes were bigger and sweeter than naturally-grown ones. I told him that a mother's milk was the best I could give to my baby and much better than cow's milk. My breasts were so full with milk that they felt very painful. The doctor wanted me to take pills to dry my breasts off and sign to agree to bottle-feed my baby. I refused to sign and insisted, to at least pump off my breasts and feed the milk to its rightful owner, my baby Alexa. They refused and so in fear that they might let my baby starve, I took the pills and signed. They even threatened, that I could not see my baby until I did what they said. I realized, that I was on the dirty end of the stick and had absolutely no chance of winning the battle, with the people working to the rules of that horrible institution.

In mental anguish, I lit a cigarette and half way down, I pressed it out in the ashtray with the baby powder advertisement on it that was placed on the side table. Howard and my mother were still not allowed to see or visit me until just before I was released the day after having given birth. Just then, on the way out of the hospital, they allowed me to see my gorgeous baby Alexa for the first time.

I could see Alexa through the glass door of the nursery in the arms of a nurse. They had to drag me away heart-broken, since we had to leave our baby there where she spent most of the first 3 weeks of her life in the incubator. They were the longest three weeks in Howard's and my life, even though we visited her every day but were left to stand outside, looking at our beautiful Alexa in the nurse's arms through the glass door. My mother was very sad as well. The nurse was very nice and came out to assure us that she loved our baby, as if it was her own and that she would take very special care of her. I find no words to describe the enormous longing I felt, to hold Alexa in my arms. Howard and my mother were also sharing the suffering. My baby must have suffered even more than I did, firstly through the forced birth, then through the deprivation of mother's milk and absence of the warmth of the mother.

I believe that the baby's pain of being born hurts the baby at least as much as it does the mother!

What happiness, when the time came, to take our beautiful Alexa home with us! Fortunately, my mother could stay and teach me how to change diapers, bathe, feed and take care of Alexa. Alexa suffered from colic for the first 6 months of her life. I believe this to be the fault of the hospital doctors, by inducing the birth and forcing me to take the pills to dry up the milk in my throbbing, painfully full and leaking breasts.

My colleague, artist Marge Mitchell, gave birth in their home where her husband John Blair Mitchell (Professor of Art) cut the cord and their photographer friend immortalized the baby's birth. I received a birth announcement with a row of excellent photographs that documented the B*irth at Home*! I could understand the Mitchells so well for making opposition to the "anything-goes-for-a-Buck" methods of so-called modern medicine and inhumane, sadistic treatments by profiteering doctors and scared hospital staff.

This is my honest opinion. The hospital bill was very high! I was not able to walk properly or sit down, because of the pain, until three weeks after the birth. When I told my father about Dr. Russel and the Women's Hospital in Baltimore, Papi told me that it was not possible to turn a baby who was in the wrong position, after three months of pregnancy and that Russel was a sadist to examine me internally during my pregnancy, which was totally unnecessary. He said, "Promise me, that if you have another child you will come to Switzerland and have it."

I was glad, that Mami could stay two weeks longer before we had to say goodbye until years later. I am so grateful to her. She was such a great help to me even though in the past we had not always seen the world eye to eye. I was just thinking, that thanks to our ancestors, Alexa, and we all, are alive!

If the ancestors had not been where they were at the time they were, and had not made love at the time they did, we would not be here, nor would we be - alive! Thank you, ancestors!

Alexa Helena Fong was born at 3:30 p.m., on August 8, 1961 in Baltimore, MD. She was 1 month premature, but a perfectly formed baby, with dark brown hair, fingernails, beautiful skin and gorgeous big eyes framed with long, shiny eyelashes.

We were such proud parents!

A Proud Mother

Alexa at Home

Howard and I were sleeping late, as poor Alexa suffered from colic and needed to be held by her father, or me . We took turns almost every night until she outgrew the colic at six months of age.

Maya B.

One Sunday morning, Howard and I were woken up by a shot through our bedroom window. Howard called the police who came promptly. They found the bullet stuck in the bedroom wall. From the direction and the way the bullet was stuck, they could investigate where the shot had been fired from. It was a jealous man trying to shoot his woman. Fortunately, he missed her and us!

Our parakeet, Pete not only ate the rim of the lamp shade, but also landed in the middle of the bowl of spaghetti, one of his favorite foods. His cage was always open and he went in at 6:00 pm every evening. If I put my finger in Pete's cage, he would peck me on the cuticle, where it hurts the most. I never disturbed him again. I loved that character of a bird until he got jealous of Alexa and flew onto her cot, trying to peck her. I had to give him away to friends, an older childless couple that fell in love with him the minute they saw him. Pete was very happy. When I visited him, he had the run of the whole house and tried to attack the birds on the bird feeder outside through the window in the living room. I was happy not to have to worry about him.

Alexa was growing nicely. She never crawled as most of the other babies did, but slid really fast on the seat of her pants using her arms and hands to speed along the floor. Then she pulled herself up on a chair or sofa and took her first steps. We were fascinated to watch our daughter's every move. Howard took Alexa's feet in his hands and she laughed with pleasure when he lifted her over his head, balancing her as high as his arms would reach.

Howard and I wanted a better environment for our family. We took a trip to Ruxton in the green suburbs of Baltimore to look at eight acres of woodland on a hill. It was love at first sight. It was Spring. Dogwoods, with their delicate pale pink or silky white blooms laced the greens through the bushes in front of the magnificent trees. Cardinals, Blue Jays and other birds enchanted our ears with music. Raccoons, squirrels, butterflies and chipmunks enjoyed the untamed wilderness. We could easy visualize our dream home on top of the hill.

My Mother with Alexa

Howard bought this beautiful piece of land. He started to design our dream home. He asked my opinion on every new detail of the plans. I could not offer better ideas and approved with pleasure every stage of the planning. He then proceeded to build a model out of plywood. When it was completed, he hired Jim Robertson, a master builder (and pilot). I loved it when he came around to speak of the materials or anything concerning the building of our house. It was my dream to be able to pilot a plane and could ask him anything about flying. He was a handsome man whose eyes sparkled under dark shiny eyebrows that ended in an upward curl of long brow hairs.

Alexa was like sunshine and so beautiful, that wherever I went, she was admired by many people. When Howard was with us and someone came to close to try to kiss Alexa, he was like a cat mother hissing at them, "Go away, we don't need your dirty germs around our baby." This made people feel upset and it embarrassed me. If you keep a child in sterile surroundings, it will not develop enough resistance to illnesses. I kept the house clean but I am not a fanatic or perfectionist where house work is concerned.

Almost every day when Howard was at work, I took Alexa

and we went to see how the building of the house was progressing. In the evening, I reported to Howard about what had been done on our dream house.

Alexa and me at the beach

The Birth of Julie

To give birth, I flew to Switzerland, as I had promised my father. It was so good to stay with my parents. They adored Alexa who was their first grandchild. Howard and I went sightseeing, while my mother watched Alexa. I was 9 months pregnant and feared the birth but was also anxious and longed to give birth to my new baby.

When I was 3 weeks overdue, we went just over the Swiss border to see the German side of the Lake Constance since they planned to induce labor the day after. At night, I got very strong labor pains and woke up my father. He said, "There is no hurry, we will have plenty of time." I said, "No Papi, it's urgent!" He said,"Okay, I'm coming." The suitcase was packed and so Howard, my father and I hurried into the car and my father drove us to the Kantonsspital St. Gallen, while Howard held my hand. I was winding myself in agony. The pains were getting very close together. It took 30 minutes to drive to St. Gallen.

Upon our arrival, they rolled me into the operating room because I had asked them to tie my tubes after the birth. I wanted 2 children and no more and needed permission from an M.D. (my father) and a signature from Howard. It was 2:00 a.m. and the DM who had been called and woken up was not there yet. So, my father scrubbed his hands and put on the rubber gloves, while I felt secure with the presence of my father and contented with Howard holding my hand. As the doctor walked in, he just managed to catch my baby. It took 1 1/2 hrs from the first labor pain to the natural birth of our healthy and beautiful baby *Juliette!*

Juliette Bettina Fong was born on the July 24, 1963, at 10 minutes past 2 a.m. in the presence of her proud father Howard, her proud grandfather DR. med. Rudolf Wilhelm Krähenmann and of course her proud mother Maya B. Fong-Krähenmann.

Julie weighed 3 1/2 kg. Alexa greeted her new sister. My mother, Helena Bernhard greeted her new grandchild and all the family and friends shared our happiness.

Her skin was a bit wrinkled for a couple of days because she was 3 weeks late but she was perfect. She was strong and had no problem to suck milk from my breasts. The cot with Julie in it was rolled next to my bed and she was only taken out for changing and washing. I could hold Julie whenever I wanted. What a pleasant difference to the horrific way I had been treated at the Woman's Hospital in Baltimore!

My mother visited me with Alexa. I never forget the touching, sweet expression of joy on Alexa's face when she first saw her little sister Julie. My mother was very delighted and proud to welcome her new grandchild into the world. I was given many bouquets of flowers and chocolate. My father presented me with a beautiful 18 kt. gold bracelet Certina Watch. I really treasure it.

Alexa and Julie

Alexa and Julie

Julie and Alexa

After Julie's Birth

Just after Julie's birth, the doctor asked, "Are you absolutely sure that you don't want another child? What if you should get divorced and remarried and want another child?" I said, "No, I am absolutely sure. Should I want another child, I would adopt one of those unhappy orphans."

Every animal you adopt, you will get attached to, to a child even more so. By adopting you could help against the population explosion.

So they tied my tubes, something I have never regretted. I could not wish for more precious children. I worship them. 10 days after my having given birth, Howard had to fly back to attend to business. I stayed with my beautiful daughters at my parent's house until Julie was 2 months of age and big enough to travel.

It was not always easy to travel with a 2 year-old and a 2 month-old child. Fortunately, I was a fit 23 year-old and the airhostesses were very nice and helped me. It was hard to carry Alexa, as well as Julie and hold the diaper bag plus my hand luggage. After finding our suitcases in New York, it was time to go through the customs. My mother had given Alexa an apple at the airport in Zurich, which she had not eaten and was then holding in her hand.

At US customs, they wanted to take the apple away from her. I was so proud of the way she defended herself by saying, "This is my apple and my Granny gave it to me." They let her keep it. They then proceeded to take the suitcases apart and when they did not find any thing illegal, they wanted to know what was in the diaper bag. I was tired and so were my children so I snapped at the poor guy who was only doing his job and yelled, "D O P E !" He then reached in to the bag and straight into the shit of a full diaper. I had to laugh. He waved us through to where Howard was waiting for us. What a reunion!

It was a 3 hour drive to Baltimore. Both our children were

sleeping through most of the drive. We arrived all happy, a family of 4, at Sulgrave Avenue. My Old English Sheep Dog greeted us like long-lost friends. Belle was a very good-natured dog who loved children.

My father with Julie and Alexa

My Mother with Alexa and Julie

My grandparents Neni and Noni with Julie and Alexa

With Belle

Bellona Avenue

Finally, the time came when we could move into our beautiful, brand-new house. It looked spectacular! Every one who saw it was enchanted to see our dream house in this beautiful environment. Belle just loved to run in the woods. The house was overlooking beautiful countryside and the whole front façade of the house was made up of two-story high arches in glass. There was a total of ten arches. The glass doors opened onto the huge terrace, which measured the same length as the house and was about eight meters wide. The living room was two stories high. It had glass arches at both sides of the atrium between the kitchen and the living room that permitted us, as in the rest of the house, to watch nature from every angle. The library and master bedroom were overlooking the living room with the beautiful fireplace located in the middle. The bedrooms had en-suite bathrooms. The garages were located on the ground floor under the terrace. Behind was the maid's room, the utility room and a huge playroom. The girls never liked to play in it but preferred to play outside on the terrace or in the living room.

We were given a kitten. Belle and the kitten played all day together and they chased each other through the whole house. Belle then carried the kitten in her mouth. The kitten loved this. The girls loved the animals. The raccoons came to eat the chicken or other food from Belle's dish outside the kitchen. Before they ate it, they dipped it in Belle's water bowl. Belle let them do it. She was friends with all the animals.

I taught Belle how to bring the newspaper to the house. The paper man threw it out of the car window, instead of putting it in the letterbox, as the postman did with letters. The driveway took 4 curves up our land to the house. When I asked Belle, "Do you want to get the paper?" She ran right down to the bottom of the driveway, picked up the paper and brought it straight to me. I then made a big fuss of joy and rewarded her. She was always free and loved to play with the neighbor's German Shepherd, 'Lucky'. She also had the run of the house.

Julie and Alexa with Howard

We could not see the neighbor's houses from our house. We were glad to have the privacy, even though we were on good terms with all of them.

Julie was a sunshine of a baby. She smiled when she woke up and smiled when we kissed her good night. I was so happy to have such adorable little girls, even though it meant a lot of work and sometimes lack of sleep.

Since Howard was a perfectionist, I almost had to become a house slave to please him. He called me on the phone when he was coming home and demanded dinner on the table by the time he entered the house. He changed his shirts 3 times a day and I had to wash, iron, do the shopping, cook, clean, play with the children, feed them, clothe them, feed Belle and the kitten, water the plants, socialize and keep Howard happy.

At least, I hoped he would take me in his arms or that we could have some fun together. We took a baby sitter every weekend. On Friday, he did my hair in his business and then we went to a good restaurant for dinner. Then, we went to a club to have a few drinks before returning back home. Howard knew many people who were very fond of him. On Saturday night, we were either invited to a party or went out for a few drinks and would often meet his acquaintances. At home, we hardly ever had a drink except when we had company.

My wonderful parents had sent their maid over to me. She loved the children and we could trust her with them. She also liked the animals. Trudi, was a robust young farmer's daughter. She wanted to learn how to drive a car. I tried to teach her in my Ford station wagon with automatic gearshift. Trudi insisted on keeping one foot on the brakes and the other on the gas. I tried to hammer it into her head, that the expert where she was going to be tested would not accept that. I also tried to tell her not to slam the brakes down so hard that one could get thrown toward the windshield. She could not take that in either. When she, against my advice, still insisted on going for a driving test, I decided to let her find out for herself. I made a date for her and drove there with her. The expert asked her to drive around the block with him sitting next to her. While I waited, I guessed the results. I saw her driving back slamming the brakes down so hard that the poor guy flew forward and almost hit his head. His face looked green-white then he got out and walked away giving her a real dirty look. I told her that I did not like her to drive my car again since I worried that she would damage the brakes or cause an accident by using both pedals at the same time.

Trudi then got even with me and every time I wanted to go out, she claimed to a have a date with her boyfriend. She would only baby-sit on Friday and Saturday. She soon left to go back to Switzerland. I was glad.

The children were both toilet-trained and I enjoyed them so much. I kept in contact with all my friends and we visited each other. All were in the same position as I. Their husbands were at work until evening and they all had children of about in the same age as Alexa and Julie. We took turns at baby-sitting, so that all the mothers had time for themselves, and their children had a break from their mothers.

The Complete Family

Julie, me, Alexa, Howard

Julie and Alexa grew into the pride of their Father and Mother

My life consisted of being as happy as I could, while waiting for my husband to come home. Then, I would be disappointed at him for growling at every speck of dust around the house, watching football or baseball and being tired while I looked for fun and excitement.

Howard was right, he had had the beautiful house built for me, I had a dishwasher, washer, drier, vacuum cleaner, garbage disposal - all the modern conveniences and a car. Every Sunday morning he asked me, "Do you want it or don't you?" Our sex life was boring.

One day, Howard invited some friends over for dinner the next day. He brought Marge and Bill Courtney home with him. Marge was an artist and Bill was a musician who loved to play the trombone. We saw Marge and Bill almost every day and I especially enjoyed Bill's company. Marge's condition for getting married to Bill, was that he would study law. He was unhappy at not being able to find time to play in the band as well. Law was not his thing.

Howard rented a house on the beach in Ocean City, Maryland for us and our girls and invited Marge and Bill to spend the vacation with us. Howard and Marge always sent Bill and me to get pizzas or something. They made sure that we were often alone together. One day, Bill grabbed me. I fended him off. I had never cheated on Howard and I was not going to but this thing called love was much stronger than me. The more Bill fought for me, the more I desired him. We fell deeply in love.

After the vacation, Bill got an apartment for us to meet once, or if we could, twice a week. I made sure Howard was gone and the children were in good hands before I drove to our meeting place- a parking place at a shopping center, where I sneaked in to Bill's car to go to our love nest. I felt so guilty and yet it was those meetings that kept my marriage going. After many months, it was too much for me to keep this secret and lead a double life. I told Bill that I would not see him any longer since it was a mental strain on me. In retrospect, I knew that my feelings of guilt were brainwash and that Howard was having an affair with Marge, was clear to me. Marge is still my friend.

Nobody owes anyone an explanation.

Marge and Bill had a divorce and both got remarried into a more suitable relationship. I have never seen Bill again. Life went on as usual. I did not understand what it meant to support a family since the material side of my life had been taken care of since my birth. Howard did not understand what it meant to be an every day routine house slave. Things got boring.

Not until one starts to live ones own life and doesn't become bitter does one begin to understand more with each new experience and begin to see that life consists of contrasts.

Shot at on Pony, Birthday Party, Sadistic Teacher

Alexa was in the first class at primary school, while Julie went to the kindergarten of the same Quaker private school, Friends School of Baltimore on Charles Street. It was a school, which had an exceptionally good name and was recommended to us by a few people who had their children there.

I got a phone call from school, explaining that Alexa had been in an accident, that I needed to pick her up from school, but that she was not badly injured. I raced to the school where I found Alexa in a state of shock. A boy had shot her with a BB gun while she was riding a pony. The shot took a piece of skin and hair off the top of her head. I went to the head teacher and gave her hell for allowing BB guns at school and that I would leave my children in their school only if they would ban arms from the school. They banned arms. Fortunately, Alexa's wound healed well but from then on she had a fear of riding ponies and horses.

One of the girls in Alexa's class invited her to her sixth birthday party. I drove her to her friend's home. They invited me to have a drink with them. I accepted gladly and admired their excellent taste and their beautiful house. I found Alexa's friend's parents very interesting, intelligent and kind people. I felt honored to know them. He was a medical doctor and had his own practice. Besides Alexa only one other girl was brought to the party because the family was black. Those low-class, white-trash racists had not even enough decency to excuse themselves.

Every day, I drove my children to the Friends School and Kindergarten, then I picked them up at Noon and drove Alexa back to school at 2:00 p.m. and picked her up again at 4:00 p.m. Julie could stay with me in the afternoons.

One mid day, when I picked the girls up, Alexa seemed nervous and uptight. When I asked her what was wrong, she started to cry and she told me that she was not allowed to tell me. Her teacher had said that otherwise, she would make it much worse for her. I said, "Alexa, I want to know what happened, I promise you that your teacher Mrs. Ball will not be able to hurt you." Alexa then showed me the bruises that were caused by Mrs. Ball and told me that any child who spoke in a way of which she disapproved was made to eat soap! I kept Alexa and Julie at home with a baby sitter and went straight to the school where I entered Mrs. Ball's classroom. Then I yelled at her so loudly, that this sadistic woman became masochistic. I wanted to know why she had hurt my beautiful Alexa and she said, "Because her father is the only father of all the children here, who is not an intellectual." I yelled at the head teacher as well, for employing such a brain-damaged, prejudiced and sadistic person as Mrs. Ball, who was mentally ill and too dangerous to be around innocent children, who could not defend themselves against such mad sadists.

We immediately took both our gorgeous girls out of that damned and so-called 'good' school. What sort of 'Friends' would run such a school? I hope Mrs. Ball was enrolled into a mental hospital or prison.

Sadism is a mental illness and crime, and bullies are cowards who pick on defenseless victims.

Both Alexa and Julie went to the public school in Ruxton, 5 minutes from our house on Bellona Avenue. The children were happy there and learned more than at the previous school.

One afternoon, Julie's teacher called me on the phone. She said, "Mrs. Fong, please come to school right away." I asked why and she told me that it was too terrible to tell me on the phone. I said, "Is anything wrong with my children?" She answered "No." I demanded that she tell me what was wrong, so she said that when she told Julie not to speak in class to the child sitting next to her, Julie said, "You'd better watch what you say to me, because my mother studied Karate." I was relieved that there was nothing wrong with my children and laughed straight out so the teacher started to laugh with me. We both laughed together. There was nothing more said about it.

Laughter is the cure for tension caused by stress originated by lack of time or lack of space. Time should belong to all who can take responsibility for their own actions.

Flying Lessons

As always, Howard left his change on the dresser, which gave me the idea to let the cleaning woman go and do the cleaning myself. That would give me just enough money to have a flying lesson, or sometimes two, every week. I went to Essex Sky Park and made an appointment for my first flying lesson. I then organized for a friend to watch Alexa and Julie, while I took lessons. I did not tell anyone about it and under no circumstances did I want Howard to find out. I feared that he could stop me from making my dream become a reality. I had always wanted to pilot a plane since my father took us up in the Piper Cub when I was 12 years old.

A young pilot named Bob was my flying teacher. He schooled me in a Cessna 150 and a Cessna 175. The moment I was sitting in the plane, I had an instant smile on my face. Bob was a great teacher. Most male students, who shared the flight theory classes with me, looked down on me for being a woman who wanted to fly. When the teacher spoke about the landing gear, I wanted to know what landing gear was. One of the students said, "Go outside and look under the airplane and you will see the 2 black things under there." I went and studied the under side of the airplane but could not see 2 black things. They laughed their stupid heads off, when I did not realize that they meant the wheels.

Bob said to me in private just afterwards, "You are ready to make your first solo flight." I had only had 12 lessons so far and I was happy when he told me this. I believed myself to be ready as well. So I soloed for the first time and became the only student who had soloed after only twelve lessons.

Essex Skypark, Baltimore, and the plane I passed the license in.

The next student took 16 hours before he had the courage. From then on, I was taken seriously by the rest of the flying students. The solo flight was a tremendous experience and I will never forget that feeling as long as I live.

I was so thrilled that I could not keep my secret any longer and told Howard about it. He was really understanding about it (even though our marriage was very unhappy). He told me to hire the cleaning woman again and that he would pay for the rest of the flying lessons and the test. I thought this was really nice of him. I tried to do everything I could to keep him happy as well. But this was not always easy since he was a perfectionist and I felt that I could not be his ideal woman. I did not even hear the nagging any more as long as I could go flying.

Up in the sky, I felt like a goddess and all my worries had gone. I passed the practical test the first time, but flunked the theoretical test. So I bought the Jefferson Airplane test book, a great book to learn theory and studied it for 5 hours every day to be sure to pass the test in theory as well. I passed it and got the private pilot's license in 1968. I had restored my self-confidence and found no one to blame but myself alone, if I was in an unhappy situation.

If you take responsibility for your actions you can find a way to change a situation and improve the quality of your life.

Flying Experiences

After having done blind flying (With hood on so as not to see the instruments on the panel), a blind landing, sky dives, chandelles and lazy eights, the flight expert, who took me for the pilot's license test, told me, "Now you passed the test, you really can learn to fly by making your own experiences."

Whenever I could, weather permitting and there was a Cessna free to go, I went and sometimes I took Alexa and Julie with me. Julie was fascinated with the instruments on the panel of the Cessna and wanted to know what everything was for, also how the radio was used and how you called on the omni. Alexa was fascinated by the landscape from the sky and by the forms of the clouds. Both girls loved to go flying with me.

Howard and I were separating. We made a deal that we would never say a bad word about each other to the children. He wanted to have them every weekend and I agreed.

One weekend, he took Alexa and Julie to Ocean City, MD. He then called me and told me that he would pay for the rental of the plane, if I picked the children up from Ocean City and flew them back to Baltimore. I was delighted. Good thing I picked them up! On the way back, Howard's Pontiac Firebird was hit so hard from behind, that the back of the Firebird was smashed up. Had the children been in the back seats, they could have been killed. I get the shudders just thinking about that. Howard suffered neck injuries. Fortunately, he recovered after a few weeks and looked forward to a new car.

The Cure for Fear of Heights

Howard and I were now legally separated. I met a friend who was deadly afraid of heights. I told him, that if he would pay for the plane rental, I could cure him of his fear, by flying him to Pennsylvania where he had to attend a convention. I convinced him, so he took his briefcase and we drove to Essex sky where we had reserved the plane. The weather was a bit questionable but I did not want to miss this opportunity and so we went up anyway. I dead reckoned (flying by knowing the way without charts). The winds increased and we hit air pockets that nearly tore the steering out of my hand and threw the plane 100 feet downwards. My friend was sitting, crouched in a fetal position, suffering in fear, looking as white as a sheet. I gained some height again and- OOPS here goes another one. This time the plane dropped 60 feet. The clouds got denser and I flew along the river in quite some turbulence. Luckily, I could spot Pennsylvania and called the airport for permission to land. The guy next to me made me very nervous.

They told me which runway was free and I made a very sloppy landing by bouncing off the runway three times, before I stopped the plane. At the airport office, they asked me how the flight was. I told them I flew under the clouds so I could make a forced landing if necessary. They told me, I would have had a lot less turbulence if I had flown over the clouds. I was glad to take their advice on the way back and for the future. My friend did fly back with me after the convention but unfortunately, he was not cured of his fear of heights.

The Cross Country Flight

I remember my father saying to me that

"It takes more guts to stay on the ground than to go up flying in questionable weather."

I never flew in bad weather again. Once, I was flying from Baltimore to Ocean City, MD. Reading the map and looking at the ground, I saw the railroad tracks and the town and found the airport right away. I was late in my flight time but was happy to have found the place. I landed and, being late, I took a short cut across the grass to get to the office quickly. It had been raining the day before and in the middle of the field the Cessna got stuck in the mud. The faster I revved the engine the more the plane dug in and the propeller threw mud over the plane. The guys came out of the office and helped me to get the plane out of the mud. They informed me, that I was in Atlantic City, NJ instead of Ocean City, MD. They were very nice and kind and washed the plane for me and offered me a cup of coffee. They then told me to fly about 20 minutes along the beach to the north and then I would find the Ocean City airport. They promised not to tell a word of this to anyone so I would not get black marks against me. Thanks to the men in Atlantic City, I landed at the Ocean City airport just in time.

On the way back to Baltimore, I took a short cut over a forbidden zone since my airplane was very low on fuel. About 10 miles from Essex sky park I was called on the radio. "Cessna number so and so, what the hell are you doing in this zone?" I answered, "Here is Cessna number so and so I am almost out of fuel and hope not to have to make a forced landing before I get to Essex sky park, over and out." "Woman Pilot! Don't you know that this is a military area and test place for arms? If we catch you once more in any military zone, you will be grounded. Over and out." When I landed and parked the Cessna and entered the office, the airport chief (a very famous pilot and the expert who had tested me for the private pilots license on single engined air planes), already knew about it and gave me a good talking to.

I found out from Bob my flying teacher, that this man had single handedly shot down over 30 German fighter planes and lost an eye during World War II. Bob said, "He has nerves of steel." On a flight back about 1/2 way from Washington to Baltimore, his plane had caught fire. He continued the flight and after landing, he calmly walked away, laid down on the grass and the plane exploded. He was not hurt. He was loved and respected by everyone. His wife was the chief of the office at Essex Sky Park. I wish I could remember their names. Faces I don't forget. That couple I will not forget either. Often, we told each other the newest jokes.

A friend owned a Fokker Triplane. We went out together and had quite a few drinks and then he invited me to go flying that night in his Fokker. I would have loved to have gone up in his plane but thought it to be too much of a risk since we were both not totally sober and I was the mother of 2 children. I said, "No." He started the engine by turning the propeller by hand, climbed into the plane and took off. I watched him doing aerobatics. It looked beautiful when he maneuvered the aircraft with precision through the sky in the magic of the moonlit night. The engine sounded like music. I wished had I trusted him and was sitting in the Fokker with him. He had asked me previously to fly with him but when we got to his plane, birds had made a nest on the propeller and he did not want to move the nest until the young birds had flown. I admired him for it.

The one who respects nature deserves to be respected himself, and the ones who respect life possess real beauty.

Trouble at Home

Howard and I did not get along any more. I felt that he did not understand me and the marriage became a burden. I was an unhappy woman. I created collages and gave all of them away since the people really liked them. I worked in plaster relief and tried to get my mind off my troubles. Every 2 years, except when my parents visited us, we went to see them. Howard figured that if the children and I stayed 3 months for free in Switzerland, it would be cheaper for him to let us go, than to have to provide for us. We made a deal, that while the children and I were overseas, he would move into an apartment. He said that the house was better place for the children to grow up than in the city. I agreed and found this very nice of him. We had a wonderful time with my family and friends in Switzerland.

When we went back to Baltimore, Howard was still in the house. He had not taken it seriously when I told him I wanted a divorce. I insisted that he take an apartment right away and that he sleep in the guest bedroom. When he realized that I meant what I said, he became violent. I found out later in life that almost every man can become violent, when he is losing.

I always made sure that dinner was ready and on the table when Howard came home. I had worked very hard to keep the house clean, the laundry done, the children taken to and picked up from school, the shopping done, the plants watered, and the pets fed. Howard touched a picture frame and showed me his dusty finger. He screamed, "What did you do all day?" When I could not help laughing outright, he hit me in front of the children. I went to the police, who said that they couldn't do anything without witnesses and that my children didn't count as witnesses.

So I went to the Kong Korean Karate teacher who had been awarded the highest of all awards, the red and black belt. I told him, that I was separated and that Howard had hit me and threatened to kill me, rather then give me a divorce. I explained that I had been to the police, who refused to help me and that I was afraid of Howard and wanted to learn how to defend myself and my children.

The teacher said that their training was too hard for a woman and this was why they would not take women in their class. I told them that I had studied ballet and yoga and to please give me a chance.

The whole karate class turned up in their uniforms at the house and threatened Howard, that if he laid a finger on me again, they would make chopped meat out of him.

I was the only woman at that time, who had ever been admitted to Kong Korean Karate and this, only because a karate student volunteered to fight with me. Howard never laid a finger on me again and moved to an apartment near to his business in Village of Cross Keys. Six months later, I graduated to yellow belt and became the first woman that ever had a degree in Kong Korean Karate. Howard and I spoke again. We now were legally separated.

My sister, my brother-in-law "Miki" and their two children moved from Switzerland to San Diego. Howard suggested, that I could drive to California with my Ford Station Wagon and visit my sister and family and that he would take care of the cost. I jumped at this opportunity and one month before summer vacation, Howard moved temporarily back to the house to take care of our sheepdog "Belle." I took Alexa and Julie out of school, packed our things into the car and put a mattress in the back, so the children could sleep when they wanted. I stocked the car with toys plus plenty of drinks and sandwiches. The route was planned and so we started on our

Trip to California

First we went to beautiful green Virginia, over the Appalachian Mountains and slept in a motel with a swimming pool where my girls could recover from the voyage and have a swim. The next day, we continued our trip and watched the spectacular, intensive, pastel sun rise in the Petrified Forest of the Painted Desert in Arizona. Those colors in different shades of gentle to strong colors of blues to different shades, from soft to vivid pinks and melting into lilacs and purples, are lasting memories. Throughout the whole trip, I always drove in the morning and Alexa and Julie were mostly asleep on the mattress in the back of the station wagon. In the afternoon, we went to explore one of the many landmarks and sights and in the evenings we went out.

Everywhere I went, the children went with me. If someone wished to invite me to dinner, we came in a package of 3. I was surprised that they often invited the 3 of us. I always thought that one is not often invited by someone who is happy with just a bit of company. They loved to hear the stories of our adventures during the voyage.

When we got to the town of Marianna, Arkansas, all the men had short beards, which amazed me until I found out that they were in a beard growing contest. The one with the longest beard at the end of 3 months would win the first prize. We headed towards my in-law's house to visit the children's grandparents. I thought that if they did not want to see me, because Howard and I had filed for divorce, I would understand and just go again but they really made us feel welcome. They told me that they understood and that Howard had always been difficult. I told them, that I could not have picked a better father for my children and I know this is the truth. Alexa and Julie love their father truly and he loves them.

Howard's brother Buddy, a very talented architect, was visiting his parents with his BMW motorbike. He asked me if I would like to drive it. I said that I had never driven one and that I didn't want to hurt his bike. Buddy said, "Oh, it's easy to ride." and showed me what to do. He started it for me and I jumped on it. I was happy to be doing well until a red light forced me to stop. I put my foot on the ground and lost my balance and the bike landed on top of me. The car behind me started to honk his horn and I yelled, "Instead of making a lot of noise, you better come and help me get the bike back on the wheels." He did and I drove the BMW straight back to Buddy.

Sissy, the youngest of Howard's sisters was still living at home. She was a very beautiful young lady and we had a really good time. Some more family members and friends came with their favorite dishes and there was one enormous feast after another, always wonderful delicious food. Many gifts were given to Alexa, Julie and I, in Chinese red envelopes containing dollar bills (Chinese lucky money) inside. Father Fong took us to the inside of his grocery shop and insisted on packing my station wagon full of soft drinks, food and toys. It was good to see Edward and Johnny, Howard's two brothers, who worked in their father's business. Every time my mother-in-law found out about an eligible young woman, she made arrangements to match up Edward and Johnny. They then went along and found something wrong with each one of the girls. I was sure they would find a woman of their choice when they were ready. My mother- in-law meant well. The Fong family's generosity is incredible. They are like the Krähenmann family.

Jerry

Then, we drove on to see Howard's youngest brother Jerry,

who was a pilot and at a military airport located in the desert of Arizona. I was amazed at the many hundreds of brand new military jet planes, which were just left to rust in the desert. They never were airborne. More advanced ones were being produced at the same time so they were just abandoned there. Jerry loved to fly the one-man supersonic jet fighter plane he called the "Tweety Bird." He flew the T-37 and the T-38. Jerry flew these souped-up planes to Vietnam which took him 20 hours (He made stops in Hawaii, Guam, Kadena, Okinawa and sometimes at Wake island).

Jerry asked me, "Do you want to race your car with me while I take off in the plane?" "Oh yes", I said and I drove the Ford station wagon on the paved road alongside the Tweety Bird on the runway and floored the gas pedal as soon as Jerry moved. Jerry was lifting off the runway before I could get to the end of the driveway. He won. I was very impressed at Jerry and the Tweety Bird. Jerry later became a pilot for Eastern Airlines.

Continued Adventures in Arizona

We headed west. It was July and the terrible heat was almost unbearable through the desert. The air conditioning was going full blast in our station wagon. There were large advertisements on the side of the road saying things like, "Only 150 miles to the next service station." The asphalt was melted from the heat and bits of rubber from exploded tires were lying at the sides of the road. We had not met one car for at least 1/2 hour so I stepped on the gas pedal.

Then suddenly, the cooler exploded and stopped the air conditioning. I did not know what to do and helplessly inspected what was under the hood. Fortunately, out of the blue, a little sports car drove up behind me and a black man with a big scar across his entire face stepped out. He looked like someone from the underworld. I did not know whether I should be afraid of him or not but the circumstances did not permit me to panic. He was indeed a very nice man and helped me by pulling my car to the next garage which, luckily again, was only 1 1/2 miles away. The garage owner and his wife lived in the middle of the desert, all alone. They took a hose and cooled down the motor and filled the cooler, checked the oil and topped the tank up, while the man who had helped me and I were watching and had a conversation.

Alexa and Julie were happy to run about. The heat did not seem to interfere with their playing. We all had an ice-cold soft drink from the couple's large refrigerator that stood in the garage. We were told not to turn on the air conditioning because it would overheat again. I thanked the nice man, who refused to take anything for his help and paid the couple.

Then we continued our voyage with all the car's windows fully down. The desert was interesting and the moods were beautiful but we longed to see green again. We had seen some vegetation but I did not dare to explore the desert by foot with the children, even though we could have found many species of life there, such as reptiles and beetles, etc. We found a motel with a swimming pool at the end of the desert. What a pleasure to relax in the pool after traversing the desert in the month of July (children's vacation) without air conditioning.

Toward California

We arrived in Santa Fé. There were many Indians selling their handicrafts under the old arches, which sheltered them from the hot summer sun. I bought my children whatever they liked and a pair of Indian hand-made, leather fringed boots, decorated with a multitude of tiny, colorful beads for myself. They were so comfortable that I wore only those boots until they fell apart, except when I had to dress formally and wear high heels.

I spoke to many Indians. Many Indian men were looking unhappy and depressed and weren't sober. Some Indian woman warned me that the intoxicated men could be violent and it was not safe to go near them. They said "Go to Taos Pueblo. That is an interesting place for you to see. So we had something to eat and drink before heading for Taos Pueblo, which is an Indian Reserve in the middle of the desert.

An old Indian woman greeted us and I told her that my children were half Indian and I wanted for them to learn about Indian culture. The woman had a beautiful face, full with wrinkles like a road map and beautiful dark eyes that sparkled full of vitality. I felt very honored to meet her and when she asked us to come to her house, I gladly accepted. She indeed lived in one of the many small, primitive, hard packed, sand-floored but spotlessly clean, single-story terraced houses that the government had built for them on very poor soil. The woman baked a loaf of bread in a handmade oven over a wood fire. She insisted on giving us the loaf of freshly-baked bread as a gift. Then she took us to see their sacred burial ground that hardly any white person is allowed to see.

The Indians danced very wildly just for Alexa, Julie and I. They had their ceremonial clothes on and were made up with different colored paints and feathers. It was fascinating. We said goodbye to the beautiful old Indian woman and all the ones we had had the pleasure of meeting.

There wasn't much to see around the Indian reserve, mainly sand and some semi-precious stones. Not enough to make a living. No one else wanted this land. The government gave the Indians a pension. Since there was not much to do, many of them lost their pride and turned to alcohol. There are plenty of pubs in Santa Fé. The women are more productive than the men and take care of things and produce souvenirs, jewelry, etc. Back in Santa Fé, we went to a pub and I had a cold beer, while the children had a soft drink. We did not stay long because I felt some dark stares from drunken Indian men.

Our next stop was a motel with a swimming pool. We really looked forward to that swim in the pool and to enjoying dinner at a restaurant.

The next day, our journey continued toward Montezuma's Castle. We climbed all over the Indian dwelling inside the cliff. The caves inside were dug out to 3 stories. There were still interesting Indian historic finds there. Beautiful trees surrounded their ancient habitat. Then, we drove on to explore the southern corner of the

Rocky Mountains. Later, we continued toward California.

On the road toward Los Angeles, we spotted an advertisement to visit the set from a cowboy movie, so we turned off and went to see the cowboy film town. When we arrived, they were just staging a bank robbery on horses with stunt men falling out of windows after having pretended to be shot. Alexa and Julie loved it and so did I. The village consisted of only the facades with scaffolding, ladders and lights behind it. There were hardly any tourists.

When we were on the road again, I was stopped by a policeman for speeding on the empty highway. Julie started crying and said to him, "Please don't give my Mommy a fine." The policemen did not have the heart to give me the fine.

The desert was beautiful with very high cacti. We discovered date palms and plantations. We stopped and tasted many different species of dates. There were over 20 different kinds on the plantation. I bought 2 kg of different dates and was told that they are so nourishing, that you could survive by eating 3 of them a day. We finished the whole kg of them while driving, in a few days.

We saw a big dirty cloud of pollution long before we arrived in Los Angeles. We looked at Palm Springs, then pressed on as fast as we could to get out of polluted Los Angeles and took Highway Number 1, all along the Pacific, stopping at romantic little villages next to the sea, where we indulged in ice creams or real Danish pastry while sitting in the cool sea breeze. What a welcome change from having driven through four deserts in the hot summer sun without air conditioning!

Arriving in San Diego

My sister Heli, her husband Miki, their daughter Susie and their son Mathias (my godson), greeted us like long-lost friends. Miki had a job as an atomic engineer and was given the opportunity to work for a Swiss firm in San Diego. They lived in a white house with a garden in the green suburbs. The climate was beautiful, like spring but warmer. The beach, with its wonderful light beige sand invited us to swim. Heli and Miki suggested that they could go to Mexico for three weeks if I took care of all four children. Then, it would be my turn to go on a three-week holiday to wherever I pleased, while they would take care of all our children. This was a great idea and an opportunity for me to fly to Las Vegas. I agreed right away.

After a few days, Heli and Miki left for Mexico, handing me many free tickets for Disneyland. First I took all four children, Alexa (7), Susie (6), Julie (5) and Mathias (4 years old), to the incredible San Diego Zoo. It gave me the impression that we were in the cage, while the animals were free. The next day we went to visit Sea World with the killer whales. I prefer animals, fish or dolphins in the wild. Unfortunately, man's greed has robbed too many species of animals of their natural habitat. Too many have died out, or are endangered.

Problems have solutions! It is not too late, but high time to share the planet with all the other species of life left instead of destroying it for future generations.

Tijuana Mexico

I decided to take all four children to Tijuana. I never locked the station wagon and against everybody's advice, I left it open in Mexico as well. Nothing was ever stolen during the whole voyage. We went to eat tacos, Mexican specialties of crisp corn bread filled with salad, chopped meat, cheese and a spicy hot sauce. All four children loved the tacos and so did I. The owners of the restaurant asked me if all four children were mine, so I said, "Yes." Then they insisted that I only pay half price for everything. The same thing happened when I bought ponchos. I found the people of Tijuana very generous and friendly. They sure like children. The children were a real pleasure to be with. I really felt very proud of all of them.

Back in San Diego, Mathias was looking forward to celebrating his 5th Birthday. I baked a cake, while Alexa, Susie and

Julie decorated it with whatever they thought Mathias would like. They used toy cars, lollipops and toy airplanes. There was just enough room to place the five candles. We did all this while Mathias was asleep and his birthday was the following day. We had a picnic in the garden. I wished I had a camera to capture the beauty of all the children. Alexa, Susie and Julie with pride written all over their faces when they presented their birthday cake to Mathias, surrounded with fresh daisies they had picked from the lawn and the expression of enchantment on the face of Mathias. I saved Disneyland for the last day before Heli and Miki returned.

Disneyland

We drove along the number 1 Highway toward Los Angeles. I loved this route since it went along the seaside and everywhere we stopped there was something interesting to see. The children liked to stop and get ice cream.

Mathias had a tendency to wander off and so I told all of them that if they should be lost, just scream as loud as they could and not to go out of earshot. This worked very well. We arrived in Disneyland. Mathias got lost four times and fortunately, I heard his loud voice and spotted his beautiful red hair in the crowd, so it did not take me long to find him.

Alexa, Julie and Susie all agreed that their favorite attraction, was the singing dolls at 'It's a Small World', representing the children of the world. Matthias liked the little cars electric cars he could sit in and accelerate or use the brakes on. We all sat into a car each and I tripped coming out of mine. My ankle hurt and the guy responsible for the car rides hurried to me and immediately feared that I would sue him, as this is common in the U. S. A. As I had run out of free tickets and had to start watching my finances, I told him that I would not sue him, if he let me and the children have free rides in his cars, until the children became tired of it. He agreed and we rode in the cars for 1 1/2 hours longer.

Then we went to eat and headed back to San Diego. Heli and Miki were back from Mexico. Heli, being blond and blue-eyed looked beautiful anyway, but with the sun tan she looked like a star. Miki looked happy too.

San Francisco

Heli, Miki and I enjoyed the time together with our children. I met some friends of Heli's and Miki's and who invited us to their houses for dinner, coffee or parties. Some of their friends were pilots who flew with the Blue Angels. They were especially interesting to me. Most were single. They all had good stories of flying adventures to tell. Some liked flying so much that on their days off, they would rent an airplane to go up in. I felt that it was time for me to leave Heli and her family to themselves for a while but Heli offered to keep the children while I left for San Francisco.

I had been there before with Howard when he was on a business trip and I loved the place. This time, I chose the route inland through all the vineyards. It felt cold in San Francisco but it was sunny. I loved the cable cars, Chinatown and Fisherman's Wharf where one could eat any kind of seafood. Especially tasty, were the King crab's legs and oysters. Later I found out that the King crabs were imported from Canada. Looking out to sea, you could see sea lions on a tiny island off a cliff. I spent the nights in a motel and ate lonely meals. After a few days, I flew to ' SIN CITY' Las Vegas.

Las Vegas

Looking down toward the ground, I could only see desert and sand. At dusk, when the airplane started to descend for the landing, Las Vegas announced itself with an enormous spectacle of lights. I checked into a room in a big hotel casino. I took a bath, dressed carefully and went gambling. I asked myself, "Do I want a new dress or do I want to gamble?" I reasoned that a new dress would cost $65.00. So I was going to play, pretending to have no more than $65.00 to spend on gambling. First, I went to play blackjack and won. All the drinks were on the house and came frequently. Then I went to have dinner. Tired but happy, I went to sleep. The next day, I swam in the pool and went exploring.

There were many casinos and hotels and there were chapels with green or different-colored neon crosses on top of their towers, which flashed on and off. There were advertisements on billboards outside the chapels, announcing in large blinking neon letters,' WEDDINGS 24 HOURS A DAY.'

I experienced Las Vegas as an over-the-top thrill town that is awake day and night and keeps the adrenalin flowing. It is a fascinating madhouse. I saw an old man with a natural long, white beard and a old tattered sack with his belongings by his side, sitting on the steps of the biggest casino, just shaking his head. I wished I had had a camera.

I was getting a bit lonely and met a friend from Baltimore, while I was playing blackjack. 'Charley' was a professional gambler. He begged me to go to dinner with him, as he was very lonely. He suggested Caesar's Palace, since they were showing 'Hair', the most talked about dinner show in Las Vegas. I accepted, telling him that I could not be more then a friend. I did not want him to be disappointed if he expected more than I wanted to give. I respected Charley, but was not in love with him. He said that my presence would make him happy and so I accepted.

At Caesar's Palace, Charley taught me some tricks for playing blackjack. We gave each other signs about which cards we had and kept on winning. Then we went to eat a delicious multi-course dinner and indulged in champagne, white wine, red wine during the feast and continued with the champagne while watching 'Hair.' Beautiful, well-built people completely naked, sang "Let the sunshine in." while in a circle. They did not look vulgar at all. I enjoyed the show. I don't know what all the fuss was about, calling this show shocking. I guess it was the religious freaks again. At least, those hung- up people cause plenty of free publicity.

I saw Yul Brynner sitting at a table with friends or business men. I went over to him and told him that he was from my homeland. He said, "Are you from Switzerland?" I said, "Yes," and we had a conversation. He was so nice and pleasant but had to get back to the people at his table and I had to go back to Charley.

After the show, Charley asked me to marry him. I told him that I was not even divorced yet, just legally separated. Charley kept on asking and said, "Let's just do it for fun anyway." We were completely drunk as we got married in the chapel. I wore a red mini skirt and a black see-through blouse. He bought an 18 kt. gold ring for me. At 4:00 a.m. Charley ordered the whole big marriage package. We were picked up by a chauffeur in a Cadillac and driven to the chapel where two hired witnesses were waiting to sign the marriage certificate at the court house. Then, as we drank champagne out of a plastic flutes, we returned to the chapel in the Cadillac, where the photographer was waiting to take pictures of us. We were so drunk. We had to hold each other while walking down the aisle so we wouldn't fall. The pastor married us. Back at the hotel, we fell asleep in each other's arms. When I woke up, I spotted a wedding photo standing in a plastic frame on top of the dresser and realized what had happened. I insisted that Charley annul the marriage. Two years in prison for bigamy seemed too high a price to pay for a little fun. We went to the courthouse where Charley bribed the man behind the counter to give him the papers and he destroyed them. We stayed together a day longer before we separated.

I told Charley that I needed time to myself and went off playing roulette until I lost all my gambling money down to a quarter, which I threw into the one-armed-bandit machine and, "bingo!", a lot of money kept coming out. Then an old woman claimed it to be her machine. All the machines are the property of the casino.

I took the money I had won and went back to play and win at blackjack. There, I met Larry from California and fell in love with him. Larry was born on the same date as I. He had to go back to work in California. (Later on, he visited me in Baltimore and I was so afraid of losing him that I lost him.) After having gambled for a solid week, I was tired of being in Las Vegas with Larry gone and flew back to San Diego with $8.00 more in my pocket than before.

Tonsillitis

When I got back to San Diego, I needed a rest. It was good to embrace my girls again and to see everyone. We celebrated Julie's 6th birthday. Julie and all the children and adults had a great time. Suddenly, one child after another, all four children got high fever and complained about pains in the throat. Heli called a pediatrician who came and visited and gave each of the children a very high dose of penicillin. In the 1960s they did not know that too much penicillin would cause problems. When the doctor wanted to remove everybody's tonsils, I called Howard on the phone and asked him to ask our pediatrician in Baltimore for his advice. I trusted Dr. Cordi. He called back and said that our doctor advised against it. All four children recovered well. Alexa and Julie are long grown up and still have their tonsils today in 2013. Two weeks after their recovery, we went on our way to New Orleans.

Toward New Orleans

I was really looking forward to New Orleans. I love Jazz, Blues and Dixieland. We were taking the southern route this time. After days of hard driving, many miles through California, Arizona and New Mexico, we arrived in Texas. We had seen many different landscapes of different deserts, wooded areas, unpopulated and populated areas, agriculture, hills, mountain and tiny villages with names like Paris, Vienna and London.

When we spotted a diner (very large caravan), we stopped to eat the famous Texas breakfast. Our meal included a Texas steak (larger than the diameter of the plate) accompanied by free bacon, eggs (poached, fried or boiled), sausages, hash-brown potatoes, french-fried potatoes, ketchup, mustard, pancakes, muffins, toast, bread, maple syrup, honey, different sorts of jam, butter, orange juice, grapefruit juice, coffee, hot chocolate or milk, fruit and breakfast cereals. You could eat and drink as much as you desired. The most beautiful trucks were parked outside the breakfast trailer. Some were really decorated elaborately, with added lights, painted scenes etc. I was watching a truck driver eating the whole steak, sausages, bacon and the rest of most things that came with it.

What a healthy appetite. I was wondering where he put all that food since he was not fat. Maybe he had a tapeworm. Alexa and Julie ate some of the steak etc. and I asked the waitress for a doggie bag. She placed the left-overs in a big and we ate it with pleasure later on.

Arrival in New Orleans

What a romantic town! It felt like being in France. Most of the balconies of the old town houses were decorated with cast iron railings around them. I found out later, that New Orleans was built by French men. We checked into an old hotel to celebrate Alexa's 8th birthday in the restaurant and rested up to celebrate some more in the evening. We ate something and Alexa and Julie ordered as many sweets and ice cream as they wanted. Then we wanted to go to a jazz concert and the doorman said, "Sorry, no children are allowed." I was angry but pulled myself together since it was Alexa's birthday. I promised the girls that we would find something better somewhere else. We were in the old section of New Orleans and I saw a small sign with handwriting on it saying, '*Jazz Concert, here all night.*' An arrow on it pointed toward a shabby open doorway to steps leading to a basement. We went downstairs to where the wonderful, intense sound of really passionate music could be heard. I told one of the musicians, that it was my daughter's birthday and asked if my children were allowed to come in. He said, "Sure, we'd like you and your children to come in. He asked Alexa, "How old are you?" and she replied, "Eight."

There were two black upright pianos standing in the middle of the cellar with half empty beer glasses standing on them, a drum-set in the corner and the musicians, almost all of them black, played their instruments all over the room. A waitress served us drinks, while the small crowd rotated gently amongst the musicians. The air was smoky but the mood was wonderful. Spiders were guarding their webs on the walls. It reminded me more of a jam session. There seemed to be no tourists but genuine music lovers of all classes, from businessmen to tramps and ladies to whores. It was very colorful and real. Not a boring second. Alexa and Julie loved it.

Suddenly, the musicians played and sang, *"Happy Birthday Alexa."* The bandleader presented her with a poster with all the musician's photographs on it and they all signed it for her. Alexa was thrilled and very proud. We stayed until about 2:00 a.m. and walked to the hotel where we slept until lunchtime the next day. We took it easy until evening, when we went out again.

A man came up to me and asked if I would like to make some money, stripping in his club. I asked, "How much would you pay?" When he mentioned a tempting high price, I said, "Under two conditions. First, I leave the bikini bottom on and second, I want my children sitting in the front row, where I can see them." He said that I could keep my bottom on but that the children were not allowed. So I told him to forget it.

We went to sleep early and left after a visit to the cemetery, where all the dead are buried on top of the ground. Then we continued our voyage to visit my in-laws again in Marianna, Arkansas. The children looked forward to seeing Grandma and Grandpa again.

Visiting Family Again

We drove through Mississippi and continued to Memphis, Tennessee and from there to Marianna, Arkansas. My in-laws were happy to see us again. Friends and family members visited us again, loaded with gifts and delicacies. Alexa and Julie's Uncle Jerry the pilot, was there also. I liked Jerry very much and was happy to see him home safe and in good health after having been at the front in the Vietnam war. In Vietnam, he received 'The Air Medal' and 'The Distinguished Flying Cross' for missions flown. Too many young men came home mentally or physically crippled or in a coffin. Some never got over the feelings of shock of terrifying experiences or guilt, having murdered men of other countries.

War is a perversity which causes the deaths of fathers, husbands, sons, lovers, friends and others. If people could vote for or against war they would surely vote against unless manipulated or because of lack of intelligence. Not only do they pay for the greed of those who enrich themselves from war but also pay again to reconstruct the infrastructure after the damage.

We had a wonderful time with the family in Arkansas. Jerry asked me to take him with us to Baltimore. He insisted on paying for the gasoline. I was thrilled to have his company. Father Fong took us to the grocery store again and filled the car with food, soft drinks, toys and fireworks for Howard. After we said goodbye again, we drove back towards Baltimore.

From Marianna, we drove to Helena and started to cross the Mississippi Bridge, where right in the middle of the bridge we found an abandoned puppy dog. We picked it up and gave it something to eat. He ate so fast, that he couldn't keep the food down. In Memphis, we brought him to a vet, who declared that the dog had the mange and he wanted to put him down. I said a definite no. I planned to bring 'Spotty Rattabrat Fong' (as the girls named him), to my dog Belle's vet. Spotty could hold down small amounts of food and drink water. He seemed tired but okay.

Jerry and I took turns driving. We only slept once in a motel, before getting back home. I only had $5.00 left in my pocket. Howard was happy to see the children again and his youngest brother Jerry, who could only stay with us for one week. I was sad to see him go, but happy that we were able to spend some time with him.

Howard lived in an apartment near his new salon. He and his business partner Wilmar, sold their beauty shop in the city and opened a new, very modern salon in The Village of Cross Keys, towards the Baltimore suburbs, with *no parking problems*, unlike downtown.

Alone with the Children

Howard had taken our bed to his apartment and told me to get a new one, so I ordered a waterbed from California. I had tried one out at a fair in San Diego and was impressed by its comfort. The man who delivered it put it up and also filled it with a ton of water.

He was a flower child and we smoked a joint together. The children were with their father every weekend, so we tried the bed out and had a lot of fun. It cleared my head and I really needed it. I was sad because he had to go back to California.

I soon found new friends and was invited constantly. The children and I went out to eat their favorite Chinese food at 'Me Chung Lo's' restaurant. When I wanted to pay, the owner told me that they did not want me to pay for the time I was separated and that I was welcome with my children at any time.

I was lonely and in search of the ideal man and accepted most invitations. When my friends could not babysit, I had a very dependable sitter. Soon I was known as the wildest woman in Baltimore. I loved to dance on top of bars and was up to constant mischief. People found me fun to be with. I did everything to be happy so that I could remain a happy mother.

Howard came to check up on me and if I had some friends at home he would throw them all out. Things were not easy. He kept me on very little cash. Fortunately my neighbor, Mr. Richter trained chefs for a major hotel chain and brought me whole left-over roasts for my dog Belle, as often as three times a week. Belle shared them with us.

My Friends

I found that my friends were changing from the ones who were together to ones who were single, or miserably married. I was amazed at how many lonely ones were around. Some too bitter to be with, some too corrupt and some who lived lies, some who did nothing but brag, but a few that were intelligent and nice and even fewer who turned me on. I went out every weekend, when Alexa and Julie stayed with their father. He and I had made a deal, that neither one of us would say anything negative to our children about the other. This worked well.

It is perfect when children love both parents even if living together becomes unbearable. Divorce is hard for any child and should not be made more difficult for offspring by their having to take sides.

Different Jobs

Since I was a bit hard up for cash, I took a job as a model. I modeled clothes to swimsuits. I had worked sometimes as a model while I was in ballet school. It was easy and well paid work and did not take me away from the children except for a few hours a week, while they stayed at a friend's house or with a babysitter. I was happy to get out of the house.

I was invited to a party by the people of the fashion world. I accepted. There was a huge buffet of food and a bartender behind a table serving drinks, cocktails, wine etc. There was also a bowl of punch to serve yourself. Around the punch bowl were all sorts of fruit cut, peeled and ready to eat. I took a cup and filled it with punch, putting some of the fruit in with it. I carried it with me to a place in the room and drank it. It tasted delicious but I started to feel weird. I saw people near and then far and the room was moving and distorted. Everything seemed to close in on me. I sat on the floor and held my knees, in a fetal position, terrorized by panic and in fear of going crazy. Some man came over to me and said, "Don' t worry, we only put a little LSD into the punch bowl."

I was very annoyed and would not stay one second more in that crowd. It took all my strength to get up and drive home. In the driveway up to our house, the trees looked so beautiful with fresh, green, young, spring leaves. I parked with all my power and went into our house. The children were staying with their father. I realized, that the snakes moving all over the living room floor were hallucinations, but still tried not to step on them. What was our dream house at one time had turned into a nightmare and prison. There were iron bars all over the windows. I could not stop pacing up and down and my brain was going faster than the speed of light and it took me so much strength to fight and cope with what was happening. I was in panic and survived this trip only by telling myself, that I was stronger than the drugs they had forced on me. The psychological work was harder and more stress, then any physical work I had ever known. I asked myself the question

"What do I want to do?" Instead of *"What does everybody else want me to do?"*

All sorts of questions popped up in my brain. I turned the TV on, which stopped the thought processes for a while and got me off the LSD trip. Wow, I had survived it. I don't regret what happened, but I think people who force drugs on you are criminals. If you decide to try drugs on your own body at your own risk, by all means do so under your own responsibility.

I knew of someone who died of a brain hemorrhage while under the influence of LSD. I believe it can be dangerous. Timothy Leary's belief, forcing LSD on all USA Citizens (or on anyone else) was very IRRESPONSIBLE.

Matchmaking

I answered an "earn while you learn" advertisement in the paper, "A*nyone can do it!"'* I got curious and called. It was a matchmaking business. They taught me how to have lonely people fill in forms with questions. Then, I was supposed to promise that it was almost 100 % sure that they would find a compatible partner if the chemistry was right. That could not be guaranteed. (That way, the business could not be sued). They then sent me off to lonely ones who had called the business to find a partner. The price for the deal was outrageous. If they did not have the means to pay for hope I was supposed to say to them, "I am going out this week end, what will you be doing all alone in your apartment?"

I was sent to a 26-year-old, very shy woman. She filled in the forms but could not afford to spend that high amount of money. Instead of telling her what they had taught me to say, I told her that it was a woman's right to go out where and when she pleased and that she had more chance of finding a partner if she went out. I told her to believe in herself, that she was beautiful and should not take the first man that came along, as there were as many if not lonelier men than women. I told her also, that yoga was good and that she could also take self-defense to help her self-confidence and that the ski slopes were good places to meet people. I walked out of what I considered a dirty business.

Those who enrich themselves on the loneliness of others are low life.

Julie's Accident

I was invited for dinner and went out. I always gave the babysitter Howard's telephone number in case of emergency. Rolfi and Eric, the children from next door were also in our house since their mother could not find a baby sitter. After dinner, I suddenly felt that something was wrong at home. I excused myself and ran to the car heading for home as fast as I could. Howard was at the house and told me that the children had been playing in the swivel chair. Julie had fallen off the chair, hitting her arm on the floor so hard, that her elbow broke and that Julie was in the operation room at Greater Baltimore Mediacal Center. He went straight back to the hospital, while I paid the babysitter. I called my best friend Paula, who took Alexa to their house. Paula's son Thomas, was the same age as Alexa and they got along beautifully.

I raced to the hospital where Julie, her arm in a cast, was laying in the bed in a private room. She was so tired after the operation but she smiled at me and then fell asleep. There were 2 beds in the room so I slept in one. When Julie woke up, she needed pain-killers. I felt so sorry for her. She was only 6 years old. She slept on and off. When she woke up there was the pain again. The next day, the doctor came and found this unusual.

I had to go home and feed Belle's puppies. Howard bred her with a pedigree Old English Sheepdog. It was terrible, since Belle only liked the German Shepherd from next door and they had to force her to mate against my will. It was not surprising that Belle refused to nurse her puppies until I spoke to her and held the three puppies to her teats while complimenting her on what a good mother she was. Belle had the run of the house and the door to the huge terrace was open for her to get in and out. Our cat went in and out and the animals were friends. I left food and water and hurried back to Julie.

This time I stayed with her and slept there for 14 nights. Then they came again to take more x-rays of Julie's elbow and said that I could go home since it would take a while. They told me that I was not permitted to be there with her for at least a couple of hours. So I went to check up on Belle.

When I came back to Julie, she was sound asleep and laying on the bed with her arm in a new cast. Her arm was strapped upwards and attached to a pulley block with a weight pulling downward. Julie could only lay on her back. I asked what had happened and was told that they had to break her elbow again since it was growing together the wrong way. I was very angry that they had not told me anything, before they operated on my little girl again. I am not one of those hysterical women who cannot deal with the truth and felt betrayed.

Howard came to visit Julie after work every day and also visited Alexa each day and on weekends, she stayed with him. I went to see Alexa during weekdays. I missed her but knew that she was in good hands. I fed Julie and washed her, told her stories and wished it were I and not her who had to go through that ordeal.

Poor Julie had to stay on her back for six weeks in total, before she had the cast taken off and could come home. She had to learn to walk again because her leg muscles she had grown so weak during her hospital stay. It was so good to have both my girls and our animals with me at home again. Howard came every day to exercise Julie's arm and hand in warm water while she was squeezing a soft rubber ball in and out. This she had to do for about six months. Fortunately, Julie made a complete recovery. It is time for hospital staff to stop treating people like retards instead of being honest with them.

Belle recovered also and so did the puppies. I find it awful to force a dog or any other living female creature to have sex with a partner of someone else's choice. *This is rape!*

I know what rape means, first hand, but that story will come later in this book. Dogs of so called "pure race" mostly have health defects caused by inbreeding. Belle had frequent visits to the vet, because ear infections in her hanging ears and eye problems until I cut her long hair short over the eyes. She also chased cars since there were no sheep to herd. Many German Shepherds have hip problems and get headaches from their skulls being too tight for their brains. Some turn mad from pain in older age. Most Dachshunds suffer from backache since their spines are too long. St. Bernards suffer in low altitudes and warm climates. Pekinese and other snub nosed dogs suffer from asthma. Scotch Terriers and other dogs with short legs have to be carried up and down steps. Almost all human bred animals have their weaknesses. If you want your bitch to have puppies, let her choose her own partner but be aware that it won't be easy to place the puppies.

If I were to get another dog, I would adopt one. There are too many unhappy dogs in pounds. Dogs rescue people, lead the blind, search for lost ones, cheer up children etc. Dogs are our best friends and totally honest. If a dog bites, it has mostly been mistreated, or neglected or in pain, or has been confined, chained or thought by man to be aggressive. A dog or any animal, like ourselves, needs food, drink, affection, company, freedom, shelter and medical care if required.

If you cannot supply these, you should not acquire a pet. Too many creatures suffer because of ignorance, greed or irresponsibility

Vail, Colorado

Howard said that I deserved a vacation. He knew that I liked to ski. I was very touched when he presented me with a two week skiing holiday package at a really nice hotel in Vail. When I had first come to U.S.A., I was disappointed since I thought that everybody would dress as they do in the cowboy films. I had also expected to find saloons with swinging doors one could kick open with western boots. I took a flight from Baltimore to Denver. In Denver I found that people looked the way I had expected when I first arrived in the country. They wore cowboy hats, boots, fringed leather vests, jeans and western neckties. Only in Denver can you still see that. From there I took a bus over the Loveland pass, where the bus driver let everybody out for a quick move around. We all became slightly dizzy from the sudden high altitude. Then the trip ended in Vail.

Vail looked like a mountain village in Switzerland. Chalets, fondue and other restaurants, ski shops, kiosks with souvenirs and postcards. Even the hotels, restaurants and coffee shops were done in Swiss style. I checked into the hotel. They gave me a very nice room with a bathroom and a window with a view of the village. There was a sauna in the basement and the restaurant was on the ground floor. The ski lift was very near to the hotel. I took a bath, dressed up and went to the restaurant to eat a Fondue Bourgignon and two glasses of succulent red Californian wine. I slept like a baby.

The next day I went skiing. Here in Vail, they measured the snow not in inches but in feet. Well-packed ski slopes on the bottom and a thin layer of new snow on top of the packed snow, where I could leave my fresh traces and push the new snow behind me in a white powder with silver sparkling, misty cloud. The view was spectacular up here. The sun warmed my body without turning the snow to slush and was shining every day for the whole two weeks of my vacation.

After the last run before the closing of the slopes, I went back to the hotel and joined the men in the sauna. The women did not seem to go to the sauna but the men said it was ok for me to use the sauna with them. In Switzerland, it is normal for a group of friends of different sex to use the sauna together. Here it was the same, except for two of the men who believed that I was everybody's. When they tried to touch me up, they got thrown out of the sauna by the other men.

I felt newborn and was totally relaxed. I had dinner and someone invited me for a drink at the bar but I was tired and excused myself and went to bed.

The next day, I skied all day long except for a few breaks at the ski slope restaurant. Just after skiing down the last bit of the bottom slope, I heard that the chair lift was going up for the last time that day. I skied right up to it and tried to get on but one of my skis got trapped between the chair and the ground with my foot on it. It twisted my knee, the lift was stopped and I was taken to the hospital. The doctor said that the ligament of my left knee was torn and had to be put in a cast. I refused a cast since I wanted to go skiing the next day. He said, "You will be glad to get back here tomorrow morning, I will be waiting for you." I woke up with almost unbearable pain and could hardly stand on my leg. I called a taxi to the hotel, which took me straight to the hospital where I very was anxious to have the doctor put a cast on my leg.

While I was in the hospital, I met a man from Texas who asked me to come to his party the next day. He made a date to pick me up the following evening. I was looking forward to his party, he seemed very nice. Afterwards the doctor put the cast on.

Later that day, I tried to ski with the cast on my leg and a friend I had met told me not to ski on it since the risk of falling was too great and could cause the leg to break. He made sense to me and I listened to him but found it hard not to ski. The cast had to stay on my leg for six weeks.

That evening, the Texan sent his chauffeur to pick me up. He brought me to a modern, large chalet that had its own ski lift on the back of the garden behind the chalet. There was quite a crowd there. The host greeted me and introduced some of the guests around him to me. The huge table in the dining room was covered with delicious food from ham, chicken, pork, goose, duck, pheasant and all sorts of fruit to raw vegetables and breads. There were no plates or cutlery. The man who had invited me had found oil in Texas and had the chalet built to his own taste. It was very beautiful. The champagne glasses were constantly filled by a man servant with the best champagne. The people were all dressed up and looked very elegant. Some were wearing beautiful jewelry. The music played wild sounds.

Someone shouted, "Self service by hand at the caveman's table!" I could hardly believe what I saw. I watched people greedily grabbing whole chickens or hams, ripping off some of the meat with their teeth and throwing the rest on the floor or on the wall. I got very upset. When the Texan asked me what was wrong, I told him that I did not understand this behavior. I had seen poverty and people going hungry and did not believe animals should be killed just to waste most of the food. He told me that it would not be wasted, since it would be picked up later and given to someone with many dogs and cats. I stayed a bit longer out of curiosity at what would happen next. After they had eaten and their faces, hands and clothes were covered with grease and gravy, they jumped into the pool. I was still disgusted by the lack of respect for the food. They called me a prude and I gladly left.

Immature non-thinking nouveau-riches, probably also lacking erotic sensitivity. Perhaps even practicing cave-man sex. Maybe foreplay by hitting a champagne bottle over the head before rabbit-like copulation? In no way, was I sticking around to find out!

The hardest thing was to make the best of my remaining 10 days of vacation. I soon met a young man from Mobil, Alabama. We went out together constantly and had a lot of fun. He had tried skiing and did not like it and preferred to be with me. We were both glad not to be alone. He was staying at the same hotel as I was. We really fell in love. My time in Vail was nearly up. We had to make a decision where and how life was going to continue together. I was playing with the idea of living with Alexa and Julie in Mobil but was afraid that it would be hard on the children not to see their father every weekend.

Before deciding, we went out to dinner. We just enjoyed the moment together. While we ate the dessert, a handsome black man was led to the table next to ours and was handed the menu. The man I was with said "Damn niggers, they should ban them from here." I thought I had misheard him. But he repeated, "Damn niggers." I instantly fell out of love with him and saw that I had over-estimated him and told him that I could not love a man who is prejudiced. I walked out while he said, "Dumb broad." With that, he made it easy for me to go on my separate way. Funny, that I had not noticed his prejudice before, and was determined to take a better look at the next guy. The next day, I took a flight back to my children. I longed to take them in my arms again. I also missed Belle and the cat.

Danny

It was great to be back at home with the children but I longed for a life's partner and went out every evening on weekends. We were a big crowd of people who met in several pubs or restaurants in town. I usually returned home still lonely.

One day, someone drove a Cadillac up our driveway and rang the door bell. I opened the door and he introduced himself as "Danny" while presenting me with huge bouquet of flowers. He told me that I was known as the wildest woman in Baltimore and he had heard so much about me that he just had to meet me. My first impression about him was lousy. He was spongy fat and looked vain but very sure of himself and I tried to make him go away. He would not hear of it and insisted on making a date to pick me up for dinner in a high-class restaurant. He refused to go before I agreed to meet him on Saturday evening when Alexa and Julie were staying at their father's place.

I planned to play a trick on Danny and called a musician friend of mine and asked him to come to my house on Saturday before Danny arrived to pick me up and wanted to know if he would be up to some fun. My friend was eager to do so. When he arrived in my house, we lit a big fire in the fireplace of the living room. On the table in front of it stood the big chandelier with all the candles lit. The flowers Danny had given me were standing on the table surrounded by fresh fruit, nuts and all sorts of goodies. Champagne bottles stood also on the beautiful oak, antique coffee table and we had half full flutes placed by the side of the fireplace. My friend looked like a young Greek god with his shiny, dark curly hair and he was perfectly built. I went to open the door, then we both got naked and my friend played romantic music on the silver flute for me. I laid in leisure, enjoying the absolutely beautiful, romantic and sensuous setting, nibbling on a bunch of juicy grapes. The flickering of the candles threw a beautiful vivid light on my friend's perfect skin. I heard Danny coming and called, "Please come in, we are in the living room!" Danny walked in. He stood there for a few seconds, without saying anything and then started to scream in my face, "That's not fair, you have a date with me, go and get dressed!" and he shouted at my friend also to get dressed and to go home. My friend got a little worried and obeyed and so did I.

Danny took me to one of the finest restaurants in town. He was very interested in me and asked me many questions. He ordered cocktails with the before dinner snacks, excellent wine with the main course and cognac with the dessert. This Danny seemed to be a real gourmet. I liked the constant interest he showed in me and started to warm up to him. We went to a piano bar and had a few more drinks. Then he brought me home and I made him wait a whole week before I accepted another date, but was contented enough to open the door when he showed up after a few days.

Alexa and Julie were with me. I made a coffee and he wanted to know everything about my life. I sent him home but he came back almost every day. My loneliness left me and I still did not think he was handsome, but he was tall, wore glasses and listened to every word I said. My daughters liked him.

We ended up in bed together and he was very affectionate. He seemed to do every thing to make me happy. He introduced me to his two best friends. I trusted him. He would make huge sandwiches for all of us. At first I was turned off by the way he spread the bread with butter, then mayonnaise then ketchup and the other half with mustard before filling the sandwich with cheese, tomatoes and whatever meat was around. The children liked it and I learnt to like it also and enjoyed not having to cook. Danny did not stop being interested in me. His questions kept me busy for hours.

Danny invited me to go with him on a business trip to Puerto

Rico. He was selling jewelry to jewelry shop owners and travelled with a big case on wheels full of precious jewels.

He asked for special permission to take the case into the cabin with him and when the hostess asked what the content in the box was, he said "Guns and ammunition for Castro in Cuba." The hostess alarmed the pilot who came and demanded the case to be opened and gave Danny hell for something he had not found funny at all. Danny apologized very humbly and the pilot let him stay in the plane.

We arrived in Puerto Rico and checked into a hotel with a casino. Danny played roulette and when he had lost almost everything he took up credit to keep on gambling. He lost that as well. We went to look at the slums. I was shocked to see that poverty and filth. He did some business for the next few days and we swam in the clear blue water before we flew back home.

Danny lived more at my house than in Pennsylvania where he came from. He demanded my complete trust and faithfulness. I finally gave in and promised. Something happened in my head and our sex life became more pleasurable than I had ever believed it could be. Other men started to admire and fight for me. I loved the state I was in. I was addicted to sex with Danny.

He started to go out with his friends more often. They invited me to come to a party in Pennsylvania. More of his friends and some young women were there. We had smoked cannabis and hashish, as was popular in the 1960s. We all drank wine. Suddenly, I felt fear and paranoia and started to hallucinate and I realized from past experience that the wine was spiked with LSD. Angrily, I told them that I would drive home. Danny told me and one of the young women, "If you go now, you will kill yourself by driving full speed into that wall along side the tunnel." I stayed, knowing from a past experience how hard it was to drive under the influence of LSD, while the young woman left. I found out later, that she must have been hypnotized to crash at full speed into the wall along side that suggested tunnel. I was told that many of her bones were broken and she was forced to spend more than three months in the hospital.

I never forgave Danny and his friends for having forced LSD on me and broke my promise to be faithful to him with myself. This took the magic away from me. I felt as I had before. Men still liked me but they did not admire me the same way any more. After masturbation, bad depressions hit me for the first time in my life. Fortunately, I had my children. Otherwise, I would have probably committed suicide. I never saw Danny or his friends again and was glad of it.

The divorce from Howard was final now, thanks to my best friend Paula Kendros who was the only one of all my friends who was willing to testify that my marriage could not be saved.

The first impression of someone is usually the right one. If someone demands absolute confidence or faithfulness don't give it unless you feel the same. Forcing drugs on someone is a dangerous crime.

Bob

I planned to go and live in Switzerland with my girls and had already started to pack. Every week, I would drive Alexa and Julie to The Village of Cross Keys to spend the weekend with their father.

Between marriages

The neighborhood consisted of town houses and apartments. Howard had moved there out of convenience, since his new business was there. There was a shopping center (called the Square) with a hotel, pharmacy, restaurants, offices, coffee shops and boutiques. For the residents, there was a community house with a billiard room, library and party rental spaces, as well as swimming pools. The whole Rouse Company development had only been built in 1965, in a beautiful wooded Baltimore suburb with plenty of parking spaces. The rich or well-t0-do, felt safe there since the Cross Keys had a gatehouse with a 24–hr guard. All visitors had to sign in and were admitted once the guard verified their invitation with the residents. The guards soon recognized me and would wave me through the gates.

Alexa and Julie were with their father, so I decided to go to the largest village pool. It was a beautiful day and the hot summer sun felt great on my skin. I laid on my back concentrating on the sun and when I opened my eyes, I looked straight in to the eyes of a man. I felt a small orgasm. This was real love. I could feel it. This had never happened to me before.

The man was well built, had longish dark curls and hot sparkling eyes. He introduced himself by a long name and said, but you can call me "Bob." I was instantly hypnotized by this man and would have gone to the end of the world with him. We started a conversation and when he said "Let's do everything together, let no one separate us and if there should be a problem, we won't speak to anyone else about it and solve it together." This was exactly my idea of a relationship as well. It was *real love at first sight.*

Bob was divorced. He invited me to live with him in his townhouse in Cross Keys. There, he introduced me to Leacy. She was a beautiful 60 year-old woman. She was half Cherokee-Indian and half black. She was skinny but full of energy with a beautiful smile. Bob had known Leacy since he was a boy and she had worked for his parents. She loved Bob's gorgeous two sons and all the children. The boys were older than my girls, who were very happy to have 2 instant step-brothers, who felt the same way about having 2 instant step-sisters. Leacy loved all children equally and kept the house immaculate. She also loved animals and spoiled our poodle, Keys.

I was heartbroken when Bob insisted that I give Belle to another family. His house had no land, only a terrace. Belle needed more room. She was used to running free. In the development, dogs were only allowed to walk on leashes.

I went to visit the family where I had placed Belle. The family's children pleaded, "Please don't take Belle away from us!" I was relieved to see that Belle was happy to see me but did not mind staying there when I left. As hard as it was for me to leave her there, I knew that she was in a loving home and would get plenty of attention. Often, I felt homesick for Belle and guilty for not having kept her.

My advice - never give your dog away for anyone.

Jamaican Honeymoon

Bob took me to see the office where he worked. I thought that he worked for his father who he introduced to me. I did not mind what he did as long as he loved me. Bob proposed marriage to me and we waited for the papers to come through. He insisted that I leave behind me all the things that Howard had bought me, like clothes, shoes, jewelry, handbags, gifts etc. and even my 2 fur coats. He then bought me all new clothes. We always wore the same clothes, jeans and tops. He wanted it that way.

We flew to Jamaica for our honeymoon before we could get married. When we arrived, a man called, "Hey, Moan, do you want to buy a joint"? He showed us a huge cone shaped joint about 8 inches long and asked 50 cents for it. We bought it and smoked it in our room at the hotel. It was the best grass we had ever tasted. Real Jamaican.

The Hotel was located at the beach front surrounded by lush trees, bushes and flowers. We swam and enjoyed a cocktail in the sun and then went to town, where we visited a jewelry shop and Bob bought me the most expensive and beautiful gold ring with 3 clear diamonds, handmade by a Jamaican artist. Then we sat in a garden coffee shop and watched the tiniest birds in the world, (the beautifully colored humming birds), eating sugar from the bowls on the tables by hovering in flight over them like little helicopters. Their wings seemed almost transparent from the speed. They probably served as models for the helicopter. Jamaica fascinated us. What a paradise!

Bob seemed to be a hedonist and gourmet. We tasted many delicacies and the finest wines. The costs did not seem to worry

Bob and I did not waste my time by worrying either. I figured that he must have saved up or was well paid for his job. Bob had no shame in bed and we explored every part of our bodies and discovered each other's erogenous zones. I had never felt such pleasure in all my life. We spoke about everything, the past, the present and plans for the future. With Bob I experienced...

With a parakeet in Florida

...My First Passionate Relationship

I wrote to my parents that I was not coming to live in Switzerland, since I was engaged be married to my ideal man- Bob, and we were on honeymoon in Jamaica waiting for my papers to be in order, before we could make the date to be married.

The next day, Bob wanted us to go diving. It was the first time for me, so a diving teacher took me into the swimming pool and showed me how to use the gear properly and taught me the necessary hand signals to communicate with the other divers. After 20 minutes in the pool, he took Bob, me and some others into the sea.

Bob and I stayed close to each other. We saw a lobster defend its territory and we swam in schools of fish. The beauty of sea plants, anemones and other life forms amazed me. A whole new world was opening up for me. We dove down 200 feet. I felt the air go out in my tank and tried to pull the reserve open. It didn't work right away and I gave Bob the signal that I was going up. I panicked and went up as fast as I could. My head ached from the great speed. I learned quickly from my own experience, that one should go up very slowly. They told me after I was out of the water, that it could cause death if one came up too fast.

Bob suggested that we fly from Jamaica to St. Thomas and look at the homosexual beach. I thought this odd and we had our first small argument, standing in the sea, when Bob raised his voice to me and accidentally stood on a sea urchin. I felt sorry for him having to suffer the enormous pain the sea urchin had caused him and made peace while he tried to take out 3 spines. I figured that everyone can have a hang-up and that I would not lose him, if he showed off his body to the homosexuals. Bob had a desire to be admired by everyone and was very vain. He also loved to admire himself in mirrors. I loved him just the same.

We flew to St. Thomas and we walked along the sandy beach where some homosexuals creamed each other with sun tan lotion. Then we spent a wonderful time in beautiful St. Thomas and used the hotel's beach before we flew back to Baltimore.

The children were happy to see us and so were Leacy and Keys, our poodle. Bob had bought his house only a short time ago and it needed decorating. We went shopping for decorations in his new Cadillac. He only bought the finest and best. We went to an antique dealer and found an old damaged stained glass church window, which Bob bought and I repaired. Then we mounted it over the fireplace and lit it from behind. It looked great. Bob ordered special wall paper from Mexico and had smoked glass mirrors installed on the ceiling of the bed room and along a entire wall of the living room. There was a white long-hair shaggy rug on the floor and white leather furniture and glass tables. It resembled an elegant night club.

Leacy kept everything immaculate. She told Alexa and Julie bedtime stories and ironed my jeans. I told her not to iron my jeans and that I did not care if they were wrinkled, but she said, "My lady has to have perfect creases in here jeans."

She refused to eat at the dining room table with us but was happy when one or all of the children ate with her in the kitchen. She also liked a glass of whisky in the evening. We all loved Leacy.

Bob and I were in the delirium of love. When we were invited, we stayed together and hugged and kissed the whole time. People sometimes thought that we behaved antisocially.

Everyone liked it when Fred, Bob's adopted teenage son, played the guitar. He played the lead guitar in a band called "Triggerhappy."

(I recently learned that he also roadied for Jimi Henrix . Today, he is still very active in the music industry. Frederic is an accomplished guitarist and recording artist.)

Alexa and Julie, then 7 and 9 years old, found new friends in the Village. There were 2 adopted neighbor girls, who taught my daughters how to break into houses by putting their arms through the letter slot in the main door and pulling the lever open. They then jumped on the beds or helped themselves to goodies from the fridge. Leacy was no tell-tale, but told me of this, so that I could put a stop to it and prevent them from getting into trouble. I had a good talk with them and asked them how they would like to have others jump on their beds and eat their goodies and told them never to go into someone's house except if they knew the owners and were invited by them. I wanted to know at all times where they were, for their own safety. They listened and never did it again.

Marriage to Bob

We had a small wedding at the Towson Courthouse in Baltimore. All five children attended, along with Bob's brother and his wife as witnesses. It took place in October, 1971. After saying "YES" and signing the marriage certificate, we had an enormous feast at one of the best restaurants in town. I was now the proud Mrs. Tepper.

I had not informed the court that I wanted to keep my Swiss nationality along with my American one because I assumed the bureaucrats already knew this, since I had told them before when I was married to Howard, that I was keeping my Swiss passport. I became a US citizen in 1965. When I went to renew my Swiss passport, the Swiss Embassy informed me that I had lost my Swiss nationality, because I did not advised them before I remarried.

The Swiss embassy informed me that I needed signatures of 12 Swiss citizens, attesting to the fact that I was responsible and trustworthy. This was easy, since my father had 11 living brothers and sisters and my mother had a brother and sister. All the siblings gave their signatures. I got my CH Passport with the name, "Maya Barbara Tepper" on it. The Swiss are allowed to have dual citizenship since Switzerland has had no war for over 650 years and their army is only for defense. I wish all the countries only had a system of defense, so the armies would not need to attack and cause polluting wars.

In our 'threatened nature', it is necessary for men to change their violence for intelligence, for what good is money without food?

Bob ordered a Mercedes 350 SL from Düsseldorf, Germany as my wedding present. There was a waiting list of minimum 2 years, unless someone cancelled their order. I did not mind, since Bob had let me keep the Chevrolet Camaro that Howard had given to me.

Bob's parents invited us to celebrate a Jewish holiday with them, where I tasted my first Jewish specialties at dinner with them. The food was good but very heavy. It was served with a special liqueur, like strong red wine. There, was a variety of food, from vegetables to meats that were spiced differently and unleavened bread. There was a big six-armed candelabra decorated with a Jewish star standing on the formally set table. The mood was formal, but pleasant. No prayers. I was glad for that. After dinner heavy desserts were served. Then we went home and enjoyed a cognac and a joint to help us digest. I preferred Leacy's cuisine.

A few days later, we planned a trip to Switzerland and France. Bob's sons flew to France to visit their mother in St. Tropez. Alexa, Julie, Bob and I flew to Switzerland.

I introduced Bob to my parents and some of my other family members. One was Uncle Freddy, who lived on his romantic property right on the lake of Zurich. Freddy said to my father, "Bob will make Maya terribly unhappy." I overheard it and said "Bullshit."

My daughters chose to stay in Wil with their grandparents. Bob and I went to St. Tropez, in the Alfa Romeo which my father had brought for us from Benno, his youngest brother who owned a garage. Bob bought a Michelin Guide and we went to all the 5-star restaurants along or near our route.

By now, I knew of Bob's work. His father worked for him. He showed me the place he owned. His home improvement business was located in a big warehouse with his large office on the top floor. Bob advertised in the TV magazine every week and I helped to promote his business in TV commercials. He never went to his office, except about once every 3 months to check on this business. I was shocked to discover that he also had some other business investments. He collected the profits annually. He called his worker's his 'whores' and collected his money from them, carrying a gun and threatening them if they didn't pay up.

Bob's parents were Jewish immigrants from Poland and used

to be so poor, that when Bob, as a boy, returned home without money, his father used to beat him. He was never asked how he made the money. Bob had street smarts. He was not daft, but he was without scruples.

By now, we had a few arguments but otherwise had such a good time together. I was addicted to him. I did not want to lose him.

While at the St. Tropez beach bar, I was photographed topless, for *'Time magazine'* and my photo was published in the article of *'The World Topless beach in St. Tropez.'* I was happy not to have to wear a confining bra.

It should not be compulsory to wear clothes into the water only to wear wet unhealthy fashion out of the water.

We also checked out the nudist beach. I saw a man sleeping on his back in the sun and when he woke up, he had a great big erection. He then got up and slowly walked with a smile on his face, calmly into the water. I found this amusing and laughed, which caused a big argument between Bob and me.

I suffered like mad, since I believed that I would not be able to live without him. We usually made up within a few hours, by having a wild erotic session. After that we went and celebrated life some more with champagne and good food and visited a high-class nightclub.

Time magazine, August 28, 1972

We drove to Switzerland and enjoyed a couple of wonderful days with my parents, before we flew back home with my daughters. The boys stayed a little longer with their mother in 'Cogolin' in the house that Bob gave her with their divorce. You could drive to the front of the house and berth your boat at the back of it. It was located in the new built village near St. Tropez. Bob regretted that he had given her the house and I told him that it was the only decent thing for him to do. After all, he had two sons and a past with her.

Back in Baltimore, Bob and I, took all our children frequently to rock concerts. I drove Julie and Alexa to school every day and picked them up later.

In a freak accident, Julie decided to watch a neighborhood baseball game up close and stood behind the batter. As he swung the bat, he didn't realize that she was right behind him and subsequently, struck and broke her nose. We immediately took her to the hospital in the Cadillac, where again, they asked many questions while she was in pain. Bob screamed at them and finally someone took her to the surgeon. We waited in front of the operating room, until Julie came out with a cast on her nose. An hour later, we had to bring her home by taxi because the Cadillac had been stolen. Bob had forgotten to take out the keys from the ignition! Julie's nose healed well. The Cadillac was found where it had run out of gasoline.

After 6 months of constantly being together, mostly in the same room, Bob told me that he was going take guitar lessons. I said "Good idea, when are we starting?" He said, "Not we, but just I." I did not believe him until he really went alone, I could hardly digest it. He had disillusioned me since he had broken our agreement to do everything together. From then on, we had a *tango relationship*.

Bob said, "Let's go to Florida. We drove with the Cadillac all along the East Coast. We stopped in Charleston, a very interesting city. We also fed the seagulls. Then we drove on and stopped at a luxury hotel. When the doormen saw the Cadillac, he ran to open the door for us. His face looked flabbergasted at the sight of us wearing jeans and T-shirts. Bob got a kick out of that.

In Fort Lauderdale, we checked in to the most expensive hotel. Bob was very moody. However, he wanted to go there and I figured he was in a bad mood because of his psoriasis. We went to the Everglades and watched the parrots and the crocodiles. We took a motorboat through the river in the swamps. Then, we went south toward Key West and rented a hobby cat to go day sailing. The wind was very strong and blew the tiny sailing boat over, 3 times. Exhausted after the 3rd time, we went back.

We continued our trip to spend some time in Key West, where homosexual couples were allowed to get married. Then, we drove to Tampa, which had started as a Greek settlement and looks like a Greek village. There are Greek pastries and other specialties offered for sale and we rowed out with Greek sponge fishermen. The water was so deep where the sponges are found, that the divers have to wear bells instead of tanks.

Bob and I had a lot of friction in our relationship. He got very jealous without reason. So did I, it was the first time in my life that I felt this horrible, sick emotion. We drove it away by having an erotic session. We both suffered from folie-a-deux.

Jealousy is an illness that drives your partner away.

Then, we continued along the west coast of Florida and went to enjoy New Orleans. I had been there with my children before and wanted Bob to see this unique place as well. After New Orleans, we managed to get home in one piece and things went well again.

Bob thought it to be good to start a new business together. We decided to buy an old house in town and turn it into a nightclub with a stage for concerts where Fred, Bob's son could play with his band. We had found an old house with plenty of parking place in an up-and-coming area. Now, all we needed was someone who could change it into what we had in mind.

I knew Mr. Robertson who had built the dream house when I was married to Howard. Bob set up a meeting with Mr. Jim Robertson. Jim Robertson asked me, "Can I trust him?" I still wanted to believe in Bob and said, "Yes." So Jim Robertson drew up all the plans to our satisfaction. All of a sudden, and without discussing it with me, Bob sold the old house and refused to pay Jim Robertson for all his intense work. I had no money, (since Howard did not have to pay alimony after Bob married me), so I was unable me to pay the bill. It embarrassed me and caused violent fights between Bob and me. We now had a *love-hate* relationship.

Bob's vanity started to unnerve me. He suffered more than ever from psoriasis and wanted to go to Grenoble for treatments. The phone rang and someone told him that an order for a Mercedes 350 SL had been cancelled and that he could pick it up in Düsseldorf if he did not mind the silver blue exterior and white leather seats. Bob asked me if I liked it and I jumped at it. He told the man, that we would pick it up in 1 week.

We took Alexa and Julie with Keys (our poodle) to Swissair that flew to Zurich. They proudly flew for the first time on their own, with Keys to Zurich. My parents were waiting for them on the other end. The girls told me that, once in flight, Keys was allowed to be free. The flight attendants gave them many toys and gifts and they had a great time in the plane.

Bob and I flew to Düsseldorf, where we were picked up and driven to the Mercedes factory. There, Bob took care of the paperwork and payment and then we continued to Grenoble where we were pampered, massaged and had baths in sulphur-rich water. Bob was injected every day with a syringe of this water.

Then he got very mean to me and started to play cat and mouse with me again, as he had done so often before. He was telling me to go to hell. Often, I used to leave with my children and wondered where to go. When Bob realized that we went to a friend's house, he would come and get me and would make me promise to not ever go away from him again, even if he was difficult. I slowly had my nose full with his mind games. I was not prepared to be psycho-tortured again and said to him, "Okay, I will go for good this time but only if you give me the Mercedes. He gave me some money and I went home to my parents.

On the way home, it was raining like mad. I drove on the then, unrestricted auto route at full speed, about 280 km/hr. It took me only about 4 1/2 hours to drive from Grenoble to Wil, St. Gallen. I had all the confidence in this car, which held so well on the wet road.

My father was impressed with my car. I asked him if he

wanted to drive. He said, "No", but he would like to ride in it. He loved to go to his brother Freddy on the lake, so I suggested that we go there. My mother was happy to have the children to herself and did not want to go with us. My father and I arrived at Freddy's, in 20 minutes, a journey which normally takes 1 hour.

Freddy suggested that he invite us to dinner in a restaurant up on the Zurich Mountain. I drove up to the place at such speed and with such accuracy that all 3 of us were amazed at the performance of the Mercedes. One could not feel the speed in this vehicle the acceleration was tremendous.

We ordered the fish fillets and were enjoying an excellent white wine when the well-fed waitress walked toward us, carrying a platter of food. Freddy said, "Oh, here comes the Cordon Bleu." I said, "But Freddy, we ordered the fish fillets." He said, "I am speaking of the waitress. Two hams with cheese in the middle. We could not help laughing. This egged Freddy on to continue joking. Freddy was known for his sarcasm. Our bellies ached from laughing. That is why my mother did not like Freddy. My father and I dropped Freddy off at his place, had a coffee with him and drove home.

The children, my parents and I were having a good time around the kitchen table, when the phone rang and Bob begged me to come back to him. I tried but could not refuse him. The minute I heard his voice, mad desire overcame me and spoiled any attempt for me to think reasonably. Both my parents advised me to sleep and leave in the morning but the desire left me no option but to leave and join Bob that evening. I drove straight to Geneva, then had a sandwich and coffee and continued straight on.

The Accident

I had full confidence in my new car. I never loved to drive a car as much as the 350 SL, and played 8 track cassettes to keep me company. I was just listening to Jimmy Hendrix, when the steering failed and the car aimed toward a mountain cliff just before Grenoble.

I woke up in a hospital bed in Grenoble with my head stitched up and in a neck brace. The doctor told me that some travelers had heard Jimmy Hendrix and followed the sound. They had found me and called the ambulance, which took me to the hospital, where the doctor stitched my head up without an anesthetic since I was unconscious. He also x-rayed me and showed me that 3 of my neck bones were fractured. I told them to call Bob at the hotel in Grenoble.

Bob stayed the next day to have his treatments and then came to visit me the next evening. I told him that I hadn't seen the doctor since he informed me of what had happened to me. I was grateful for the care but did not want to stay there any longer.

Bob arranged for an ambulance the following day. They put me onto a stretcher and drove very fast with Bob at my side. The ambulance drove straight through the Swiss toll with the sirens turned on. We arrived at my parents' house in Switzerland, where I was carried up to the bedroom. I healed so well, that 3 weeks later, I jumped from the diving board at the hotel pool in St. Tropez.

The accident was investigated. When I had crashed into the cliff, a woman in a Citroen Maserati failed to stop and crashed into the side of my car with such speed, that I flew through the window into the street. The steering rod of the Mercedes 150SL had broken because of a material fault. I heard that this was the cause of a whole series and caused more than 20 accidents, some fatal. Bob informed me later, that the Mercedes people tried to refuse to take the responsibility and had to be taken to court.

Bob, the children, Keys and I flew back to Baltimore. The situation got worse. Bob and I had a fist fight and were rolling on the floor. We were almost at the point of killing each other. Then we made up again. The next day was our first anniversary. Bob gave me a beautiful Omega gold bracelet watch. We then went to see a ballet performance with Rudolf Nureyev. After that, we celebrated with dinner in a luxurious restaurant and enjoyed the nightlife at a piano bar. We then went home and made passionate love.

The next day, I was playing with the children, when Bob came toward me holding a plane ticket to Switzerland. It was a one-way flight ticket for 1 adult and 2 children. We had no argument and I stood there in disbelief and shock. When I did not grab the ticket right away, Bob told Alexa, "Tell your mother that if she does not leave, I will kill her." He would not even speak to me and raised his hand up toward me in a threatening position, as if he was going to hit me. Alexa defended me and told him, "Don't you dare hit my Mom!" and told him what she really thought of him. I admired her bravery. We left the same day with Keys. I could not even say goodbye to the boys or any of my friends. He agreed to pay me, what I would have gotten from Howard, had I not married him.

Back in Switzerland, my parents welcomed us with open arms. What great parents! My father was easy to live with but my mother and I often did not see the world with the same eyes.

Since I wanted us to stay on good terms, I needed to stay independent. I found an apartment in an old farmhouse. It was located in the village of Sirnach, next to Wil. I did not send my children to school since they could do more then read, write and do arithmetic and would learn more by staying with me. We could all sleep as late as we wanted and it would be healthier if they could run free and climb trees. I would not have them robbed of their own time. This was my philosophy and Alexa, Julie and I were okay with that.

The one who was not happy was my mother. She told me that what I was doing, was illegal and it was important to send the children to school. She insisted that they should live with them and go to school in Wil and that I could also live at home with them or visit them whenever I wanted. Alexa and Julie loved their grandparents. After my mother urged me for a month, and since my father also thought it would be better to let my mother have her way, I gave in.

I kept the apartment and was very depressed and lovesick. What saved me, was the consciousness that *Art is my life*. I started to draw, paint and explore all aspects of art. I read about art and artists.

Mr. Schwartz

I spotted a job in the paper. Someone was searching for a poster designer and I went to Zurich to introduce myself and was hired to learn this trade, right away. It was the business of Mr. Schwartz a very nice and intelligent man. He was the first person who placed power tools in my hand and gave me the courage to use them. There were two young men working for him as well and we all went out to decorate shop windows and designed posters. He liked the poster I made for a school, which had the hair of the male pupil woven into a woman. In other words, the pupil will get the woman he dreams of by studying. Mr. Schwartz did not believe it would be a good poster for the school but he said that it was real art. I was searching for the truth and could not make an advertisement for something I did not believe in.

Mr. Schwartz took me to visit many art galleries in Zurich and said, "Look at the style of this artist." He also said, "Go out and start painting outside." We said goodbye and I took his advice to work as a free artist.

I hammered some small nails into the wall to hang some paintings, which caused a big argument with the farmer who I was renting the apartment from. My parents suggested that I come and live with them. They also owned a vacation house in Tessin, the Italian-speaking canton that is in the south of Switzerland. The climate there is sub-tropical and the summers last three months instead of three weeks as in the German-speaking cantons. I loved it in Tessin and my parents let me have the barn that had been converted to an apartment, as an art studio.

I met some artist friends there who helped me to get over my depressions. I felt understood by them and saw parallels in our lives. When my mother was around, I felt a desperate lack of the freedom that I needed to search for a new life partner. My mother told me that a woman can't go out alone and said, "What will people think?" I thought that what I thought of myself, was more important and I did not care what other people were thinking. Most people do not think clearly, anyway. It is I, who has to live in my skin the best way I know how. I found it depressing not to be able to live my life the way I believed to be best.

I had been separated from Bob for three months when a letter arrived from him. He wanted to come and meet me in St. Tropez. I still was in love with him. My father told me to listen to myself and if I was still in love with him, to go and meet him. I found it a bit cowardly of Bob, not to pick me up in Wil, but agreed to meet him at the hotel we had stayed in before. I drove an Opel Olympia, which I had traded with my Uncle Benno for one of my paintings he liked very much.

I arrived in St. Tropez. There was a happy reunion with Bob and we celebrated the usual way, with both of us lying exhausted but happy in each other's arms. We went to the nudist Island "Isle du Levant" and stayed there for a few days when, for no reason I could think of, Bob was getting a foul mood again. I understood that this psychopathic condition would never change and in the three months of separation I had looked at our relationship more critically.

I left Bob for good, before we could kill each other and even abandoned our dream of finding a sailing boat and sailing around the world. I still had the dream but did not know how to realize it.

Bob stopped paying me what he owed me, from the time I refused to let him psycho torture me any longer. I was heart-broken and depressed but stayed firm not to try and run back to him ever again (except when I had to borrow from him to get back to Switzerland, later).

I had overestimated him, in my feverish, hot desire and succeeded in mastering my feelings for him by putting my excess energy into painting, until *love* came to me again. If Bob had ever found the courage to tell me the truth, I could have avoided a lot of pain, suffering and loss of self-confidence.

Lies or silence can make you dwell on a problem for years to come, without finding the right solution while the truth can hurt intensely for a short time; but at least the truth can be dealt with.

I heard many years afterwards, (and not from him) that he went back to his ex-wife Nicole but that did not last. He ended up marrying a third time. I also learned from his family, that he suffered from Bi-Polar disorder but that he never sought treatment for it.

3 FREE AGAIN

Nautilus

After I had left Bob, I went to the beach in St. Tropez, where I had left my car. I laid on my back in the sun and meditated. I consciously relaxed all my tense muscles. When I opened my eyes, a handsome man with long red hair and a beard, was smiling at me and asked, "Do you want an ice cream?" I said, "Yes." He said, "but you have to eat it on that boat." He pointed at an absolutely beautiful wooden sailing boat that was anchored just about 100 meters out from the beach. I had admired that boat previously and had wished to be on it.

He took me to the tender and we motored to *'Nautilus'*. What a ship! He was from Norway and worked on Nautilus as captain. Two crewmembers were working on Nautilus as well. Nautilus looked immaculate. The hull was painted white and the brass work sparkled. The captain, (whose name, to my regret I cannot remember), opened the freezer and I could choose from many different flavors, which one I wanted. He saw my enthusiasm for this boat and told me that he had to pick up the owners in Menton. However, if I liked, I could sail along with them but had to leave the next day, since he was not allowed to invite anyone on board while the owners were on board. I jumped at the chance to be on board.

The captain and I got along as if we had known each other all our lives. We felt instant sympathy. After the sails were set and *Nautilus* was sailing, we retired into the cabin with a bottle of champagne and rolled a joint. The crew members sailed the boat while we made passionate love until they called to tell us that we would arrive in Menton in about 10 minutes. I stayed with him for the night and with tears in our eyes, we embraced each other the next day, both sad to have to go our separate ways. I understood that he did not want to lose his job as captain. He had restored my self-confidence and the belief in my self. I will never forget him.

So, I left Nautilus with the intention of catching a train back to St. Tropez to get my car. I missed the last train that day and decided to hitchhike.

Some cars passed me and then a shady looking character stopped his motorbike and picked me up. I sat on it and believed that if needed, I could fight just one man anytime. He rode the bike very fast and turned into a road to the left of the highway in Nice. I shouted, "Let me off, I want to continue on the highway!" He did not stop and I could not jump off without risking being hurt at this great speed. So I hung on, thinking I could escape as soon as he slowed down.

He rode to a deserted place by a huge wall. He shouted something and two other shady characters showed up so quickly, before I could realize where they were coming from. They grabbed me and pushed me to the ground. Two of them held me down while the third tried to rape me. They all looked Arabian. One had an eye tattooed on the middle of his chest. I was tightening the muscles of my legs so that he did not succeed in ripping off my jeans.

He then got up and tried to push his penis into my mouth, but I looked at him that if he did this, I would bite it off. The whole time while they tried to rape me, I shouted, "How would you like it, if your mother or sister was raped?" When I thought to have lost the battle I screamed, "What the hell do you want, do you want my money?" and threw my bag as far from me as I could. They got up and hurried to pick up my bag. While they searched for my wallet, they also found a small container with marijuana and rolling papers in it. They asked me if I smoked this, so I said, "Of course, but you can have it, but leave me my passport and the rest of the papers." They stole a 1000 Swiss francs note and the rest of the French money from my wallet but left me my papers and disappeared like lightning. I was fortunate to have survived this episode with only a shock.

I then proceeded to find the highway and someone stopped his car to give me a lift to St. Tropez. It was a very nice man, a gardener who was on his way to Cannes. He saw that I trembled and shook and asked me, what was the matter. I told him of my narrow escape from being raped and he insisted on bringing me right to my car in St. Tropez. I got my sketchbook out of the car and drew a portrait of him, which I gave him out of gratitude. He liked it very much and I was pleased that it had turned out so well. It was the first portrait I had ever done.

Then, I was forced to go to Bob and borrow some gasoline money to get back to Switzerland. He was very short with me and I was glad that I did not have to stay longer than a few minutes to tell him I had been robbed before he handed me the cash I needed. Fortune was on my side, when I met a friend in a coffee shop, who offered to pay for my meal, if I would take him along until we got to Geneva. I enjoyed his company.

Reunited With My Daughters

Back with Alexa and Julie at my parent's house, we all went to Tessin. I went out often, which my mother kind of learned to tolerate but never without a little opposition. I met a man from Solothurn. Erich Senn was in the same position I was in. Loneliness drove us together. He asked me to go out with him and we made a date to go to eat in Italy. I called my parents and told them that maybe, I would not be back until the next day. My father said, "If you like, ask him, if he would like to have dinner with us." Erich accepted and I introduced him to my parents and my daughters who all liked him and were happy for me not to be lonely and depressed any longer.

The next day, we planned to go to Italy in Erich's car. While he drove from Ascona toward Brissago he cut a curve, trying to show off his driving skills, which caused a head on collision with an oncoming car. I was wearing high platform shoes and sprained my ankle. No one was seriously hurt. Erich and the other driver wanted to settle the accident between themselves. Erich helped to hide the other driver's car while I was waiting in his wrecked car. When he came back, it was not long before the police arrived from Ascona. He told them that the police from Brissago had been here already and arranged a pickup truck which was surely en-route by now. The police went away and when the police from Brissago arrived, he told them the same story about the Ascona police. He was a quick thinker, to get that easily out of losing his driving license or paying a heavy fine. He then organized someone to pick up his wreck. I threw my high platform shoes over a wall.

He suggested a trip to Spain in my Opel, if he took care of all other costs. My parents said that they wanted to have their grand children with them and that it was okay for me to go to Spain with my new boyfriend. We drove to Barcelona, ate Spanish specialties and soaked up the sun. We drove go-carts and swam in the sea. There were too many buildings and people for my liking and we returned for Solothurn, where he was breeding St. Bernhard dogs in his home.

He had hired a woman to take care of them. There was the father, the mother and five month old puppies. While we were there, he fed them by spearing pieces of meat on a stick and letting them eat from it. He would not permit me to touch them and he did not speak to them or touch them either. I asked him why and he said, that they were all promised and would stay with their parents until they reached six months and would be one-person dogs having affection from them only. This sounded weird and cruel to me.

We went to see some of his friends who had opened a bottle of Absinthe. I had heard of this ancient drink which was declared to be illegal. I was curious to taste it. The glasses were filled almost to the rim and we toasted to each other and said "pro sit." The Absinthe did not seem very strong to me, until I stood up, walked outside and fainted. I promised myself to never touch the stuff again.

Erich started to miss his ex-wife, which again depressed me. I left him to go back to my family. Alexa, Julie and my parents welcomed me but I did not know how to live with my mother's disagreeableness. It caused friction between my parents and gave me more depressions. I felt it was unfair of me to stay at home. When I left, I missed my wonderful daughters and with Bob cutting off my alimony, I did not know where to go.

Just then, a letter from a old admirer arrived. Bijou was one of the two best friends of my brother. He lived in St. Croix U. S. V. I. and asked me to come and visit him. He offered to send me a ticket. My father did not want me to owe anybody anything and insisted on giving me enough money with the promise to put enough into the bank on my arrival, to be able to fly home whenever I wanted. Sad to leave my gorgeous daughters behind but happy that they were in good hands, had many new friends (and contrary to me), did not mind going to school, I started to pack. While I was sad to leave Alexa and Julie, I was also excited to see a new part of the world. We wrote to each other.

U. S. V. I.

I embraced Keys, my parents and Alexa and Julie at the airport and took the flight to Puerto Rico, with a stop in Baltimore. There, I called Bob on the phone and wanted to discuss the divorce. I thought it would be better if we could settle the matter between us, but he refused to speak with me about it. So I told him that I was forced to hire a lawyer.

I went to see Robert C., who had handled my previous divorce. As a former friend of mine, as well as my lawyer, he greeted me with open arms. He was about two meters tall and his friends used to call him purple grape. I once asked him, "Why do they call you purple grape?" He then showed me his penis, which was very small in size and purple in color and said, "This is why."

Now, he proudly introduced his pretty Polish girlfriend to me. In front of her, he pulled his pants down and said, "They can't call me purple grape anymore" and proudly showed me his normal size member. Then he pointed to his girlfriend and said, "THAT is what my angel does for me." She said, "All it needed was exercise!" We all laughed and went out to lunch.

Bob C. tried to talk me into wearing something 'decent', a dress and shoes his girlfriend offered to lend to me. I believed that clothes were not important and insisted on going in my jeans, T-shirt and sandals. I felt comfortable in my clothes and had had enough of fashion musts while married to Howard. I also swore to myself, never to have my hair cut again. Bob C. took me to a more casual restaurant, without a dress code, even though he liked it posh since it would be deducted from his taxes. He took on my case and I told him that I only wanted the alimony that I had had from Howard before marrying Bob. We said goodbye and I took a taxi to the airport and flew to Puerto Rico.

I only carried hand luggage which could be taken with me into the cabin and which was tied with elastic bands to a wheelie cart, which simplified travelling and made it so much easier to get around. Inside my case, I had a second pair of jeans, another T-shirt, a sweater, toothbrush, toothpaste, comb, two pairs of underwear, shampoo, a bikini and a towel. I stacked some canvases between the case and the handle and packed my paints, paintbrushes, turpentine, linseed oil and sketchbook on top of the bag. I also carried a regular handbag containing all my papers and personal things. After looking around Puerto Rico a bit, I took a seaplane to Christianstead, St. Croix.

St. Croix

The owner/pilot of the seaplane greeted me, along with four other passengers and asked all of us to be seated in the six-seat cabin. I could see an empty seat next to the pilot. Once he sat down, I got out of my seat in the cabin and asked him if I could sit beside him, since I had a pilot's license and the flight in his plane would be very interesting to me. He said, "Of course, you're welcome to sit here," and pointed to the seat next to him. It was a beautiful day and the sea was calm. I watched with interest every move he made to start the motor of the sea plane, rolling down the slip way on his landing gear, lowering the floats over the wheels and picking up speed while gliding on the water. The spray of water on each side of the seaplane was a fascinating experience, as was the take off and the whole flight. The pilot and I had a wonderful time in the air. I was fascinated with the view.

When we arrived over St. Croix, he asked me, "Would you like to make an extra round over the Island?" I was thrilled and said, "Yes"! So we flew over the whole island and he showed me what St. Croix looked from the air. What an unforgettable experience! Landing on water was exciting with the spray covering the side windows like a waterfall and the pilot again operated the knob from the cockpit, which pulled the floats up from over the landing wheels to roll the plane up the slipway. Then, he said goodbye to the other four passengers and we had to part as well.

I walked to a pub and called " Bijou ", my brother's friend and told him that I was there. He picked me up and showed me his sailing boat "Flamingo" which was one of the rare original wooden island sailing boats. She was painted red. Bijou loved her and kept her in very good condition. He told me that I could help him sail the boat to Buck Island with some tourists, since he was making his living this way.

After showing me the port, he took me out of the town of Christianstead and up the hill into beautiful lush countryside to his house. It was an old wooden Victorian house with electricity, water and bathroom and had a beautiful view. It was completely private. He then introduced me to his pet. He stuck his whole arm into a big water tank and patted his pet lemon shark with affection. He told me that he had all sorts of fish, seashells and sea creatures in the tank, before he had put the young shark in it, but that the shark had eaten everything. He had to feed him with live fish every day. The shark really liked to be petted and had real affection for Bijou. I studied the shark and saw his slit pupils with eyelids that closed from the bottom upwards. He liked to be petted by me as well and his skin felt like sandpaper. Bijou later felt sorry for his pet, since the tank had become too small for him and freed him, in the place where he had found him.

The day after my arrival, the businesses in town were open and I wanted to deposit the money for the trip back to Switzerland, into a bank. Two of the banks refused to take Swiss francs. Only the

Bank of Nova Scotia accepted them. I kept the rest of the money in my wallet but tried to spend as little as possible, since I liked this island and wanted to stay as long as I could.

Bijou seemed to still be in love with me, like when we were teenagers. I was not in love with him but liked him very much. I was so lonely, that I learned to love him. We went to the boot pier and Bijou would ask bored looking tourists if they wanted to go sailing. Within a short time, he brought no less than four and no more than six people to Flamingo. We sailed with them to Buck Island, a beautiful underwater sanctuary about 1 1/2 hours from St. Croix and 3 hours back. We had sandwiches and drinks on board. There was snorkel gear as well. The people loved it and we never had any one get seasick. I loved to snorkel in this crystal clear blue water and watch the multitude of wild life. Some people were proud to snorkel for their first time. Some sailed with us again and some invited us to dinner or drinks. It was fun and a good and healthy life and we were surrounded by beauty.

All was well until Bijou's ex-girlfriend showed up and when I heard him say to her, "You are so sexy," I packed my things and left. I went to my favorite pub to drown my sorrows with some friends. There, I had a drink with Bob from the sailing sloop 'Mongoose'. I told him that I had left Bijou, so he asked me to sail tourists with him and to stay with him on Mongoose. He was almost 10 years younger. I was 32 and he was 22 but I loved him and agreed to stay with him. I knew that he was a man and I was a woman. Nothing else mattered at the time.

We let the tourists sail the boat while we smoked a joint in the cabin and made hot passionate love. I drew a portrait of him. We had a wonderful, happy time. Too bad it did not last. He believed in free love and so did I, but I wanted my ideal man who would accept me for being Maya and would love me forever. I never played second fiddle and we split up.

Afterwards, I ate at the Holger Danske Hotel, which specialized in twenty different kinds of hamburgers besides other food and ordered a Russian burger with coleslaw, I had been there once before and was impressed with their Hawaiian burger with pineapple and curry sauce. Maybe it would cheer me up.

Then, I headed to my favorite pub, where I could leave my luggage behind the bar any time I wanted. My friends Sonny and Dusty were there. They were best friends and lived in the rain forest, where they had built a tree house in a mahogany tree. They had attached a rope ladder onto their tree house, which they pulled up for safety at night. Sonny told me that he was going to kill himself since his tattoo depressed him so much. The tattoo on his arm, "Born to lose" made him feel like a real loser. I told him, that this was no reason to kill himself and if it bothered him so much, he should wear long sleeves until he found the money to have it grafted away; or start to believe himself to be a winner and not to be influenced by a tattoo. He eventually cheered up again and really was happy when he found a girlfriend.

The Jungle Prince

While sitting with Dusty and Sonny, I met 'Jungle.' He was almost two meters tall, skinny and walked barefoot, dressed in a leopard skin-printed cloth, wrapped dramatically around him. He yelled loudly at me, through his missing front teeth, (probably from a fight) in deep, rusty and enormously emotional voice "We don't need no f****** white trash here!" I had such a shock, that I could not hold back the tears and could not find any words to respond. He then added, "Tell me what gives you the right to live." It took me a moment to think and I said, "The fact that I was born and that I have two children." He then said "That's okay," and ordered me a drink. He felt sorry of the way he had screamed at me and it took me a few drinks to get over that one. No one had ever spoken to me that way. He told me all about Nancy who was a white woman, that he had been in love with and who had left him.

I started to feel sorry for him and it started to spark between us. Jungle asked me to live with him so we ended up in his house. I asked him, if he believed in a god. He said, "Of course I do." When I wanted to know what God was to him, he said, "God is a black woman."

He introduced many of his friends to me, amongst them, people who lived in corrugated iron huts, sometimes families of ten or more, living and sleeping in the same room and handing around a chipped enamel cup filled with the local rum. They were poor but lived for the moment, were uncomplicated and glad to be alive and usually owned only a few free running chickens. The richer ones sometimes owned a pig and/or a dog. They were happy with the little they had and TIME belonged to them. *Lack of greed is ideal for our environment.*

Jungle showed me a side of life which I had not known before. Jungle loved art and owned his own private art collection. What I found out, when he locked me up like a prisoner in his house and went out alone, was that he was one of the biggest sexists I had ever come across. I broke the door down and left as quickly as I could. I needed to go to safety.

At least, I had some friends in my favorite pub. A woman, the owner of a clothing boutique, came up to me and asked, if I would guard her shop two afternoons a week so she would have some free time to spend with the man she loved. I told her that I was an artist. She pleaded, "Please do it as a favor to me. I know I can trust you. You can sketch when no customers are in the shop." She offered me a salary and commission. I said, "okay, but I can't promise how long I will be doing that for.(I had tried to work before but got so depressed that I could not prevent my body from shaking or my tears from rolling down my face.)

I agreed to be there the next afternoon. None showed up for at least an hour. Then Dusty and Sonny walked in and said, "We thought you might like this," and handed me an ice cream. They kept me company until a customer showed up. It was a very fat woman who tried on a dress with big flower print and almost broke the zipper since it was too tight for her. It looked so ridiculous on her that I said, "Don't take this one, it makes you look very fat." Let's find you one that flatters you. I found her a dark blue one with fine white stripes, quite wide apart down on it and a big round décolleté. She tried it on and liked it. She had big breasts and it looked good on her and made her look much slimmer. I then grabbed a red cloth rose and pinned it to the side of the décolleté. She went to a posh restaurant with her boyfriend, who said to her, "Finally, you bought a beautiful dress." She came and reported it to me the next afternoon. She would only come into the shop when I was there and bought a dress every time I recommended one to her.

Still, I felt lonely and bored in the shop and got depressions again. I had to quit after working there for four afternoons in two weeks.

I went to see if any of my friends were around. When I took the steps up to the pub and entered the terrace, I spotted three men sitting around a table and one of them looked very sad and lonely. I was mesmerized by the spark in his beautiful big brown eyes. Instant sympathy grabbed hold of me. His golden tanned face was framed by long blond hair and a red beard. He looked like a god.

There was a bottle of whisky on the table and I walked up to them and said, "I bet I can drink you all under the table." They looked at me, kind of cynically and laughed aloud but asked me to join them. I sat next to the man I liked and a glass was ordered for me. One of them filled all four glasses to the rim with whiskey and we all swallowed it down in one go. So we drank round after round. I went to the toilet and stuck my finger down the throat. Then I rinsed my mouth and drank water to dilute the whiskey that still may be left in my system. Then I walked back to my new friends and continued to drink with them. They got more and more drunk and could not understand that I, a woman, was still not falling under the table. I had a crush on the man, whose first name was Taylor. He was so drunk that the others decided to bring him home before they were completely legless.

Taylor lived on 'Joanna', a Tahiti ketch and so we put him into the tender and I rowed him out to his moored boat. It took me all my strength to lift him on board.

Taylor Babb

I laid him on his stomach, on the floor of the cockpit with his face to the side, in case he had to vomit, so that he would not choke and covered him with a blanket I found in the cabin. Then I passed out next to him. After we woke up he said to me, "My home is your home." You can stay as long as you want.

We stayed together. I was totally in love with him. I was grateful to all the previous men in my life, and that the relationships with them did not work out and left me free to be in Taylor's strong arms. We got along so well and real passion overcame us.

Joanna, Taylor's double-ended Tahiti Ketch, was in bad need of repair. She already, as a last resort, was fitted with the 'death shirt', (fiberglass over her wooden hull) and could only sail in Caribbean waters since a change of temperature could expand the wood and split the fiberglass. Joanna was a great little ship to live and day sail, which had the smell of adventure in her timbers and a wonderful feeling. She swung free on a mooring about 100 meters off shore.

Taylor had studied marine biology and had worked in St. Croix as a scientist for Columbia University. He had quit his job on the condition that he could keep on working for two days a week and had the use of their workshop with the use of all the tools that were there. He mostly went on diving missions, since he loved diving. When he went to work, I missed him terribly but used my time to paint and sketch.

I had created enough artwork to accept an invitation, to exhibit my paintings and drawings on the huge wall of the dining room in the Holger Danske Hotel. The owner was very nice and very hard working. His hotel was the best in town and flourished since the food was also excellent. The bar had an international clientele and was open to all. I was very flattered, since the other walls had been covered with Picasso, Dali and other famous named artists.

Taylor Babb

Robbed

We were invited to a party on Buck Island and sailed there. Our friends tied up to us and while the party took place I put my bag on a shelf in the head. A catamaran with three French men aboard, all with the same very short razor-cut hair style that looked like a four o'clock shadow asked for permission to tie up alongside and join the party. We were all in a great mood and invited them on board. After a while, we suddenly noticed that the catamaran with the three French men aboard had disappeared. I went to the head and when I opened the lid of the sea toilet I found my empty wallet and my passport, drivers, pilots and radio license floating in it. I rinsed all my papers and hung them to dry.

Fortunately, I had taken my father's advice to secure the ticket back to Switzerland. I had put aside enough to return a flight back to St. Croix as well. I was robbed of all my spare money, which forced me to either go back to Switzerland or try to stand on my own two feet. Taylor lived on the minimum.

I decided to paint portraits on the street. One day, a reggae band was playing next to me. The man on the steel drum came up to me and asked, "Can you draw a portrait of me?" I said, "Sure." While I worked on his portrait, a few spectators had gathered behind me and started to tell me about who painted in their families. They did not realize how much concentration it takes to paint or sketch. Some came so close into my intimate space, that I could feel them breathing on my neck. It was very hard and nerve-racking, to the point where I lost my equilibrium and screamed at them, "Shut up and let me concentrate!" I did not mean to hurt their feelings.

I found that painting portraits on the street was the hardest thing I had ever done. I sold the first portraits for $3.00. It broke my heart whenever people folded them in four and stuck them in their pockets. I thought I must be doing something wrong. Why would they not respect my work, since I had put all my energy and knowledge into it? I then charged them double but someone still folded the excellent portrait in half. Immediately, I went up with the price again and they did not fold the portraits anymore. I raised the price again and people brought them back to show me how they had been framed. When I went up with the price yet again, they invited me to their houses and let me suggest where best to hang them!

I was invited to exhibit my work at Centre Island. Beside some of my work, I also hung the painting of Taylor which I had created on board 'Joanna' while Taylor was at work. I had turned Taylor into a god. I had priced it at $1000. Someone made me an offer of $999, but I turned him down. I thought that if he liked it enough, he would pay my price. I was not going to let him break my will for $1.00, and was happy to keep it in my private collection.

I got a contract from an architect to draw his 2 1/2 year-old daughter. I went to their house and studied the beautiful little girl intensely. I observed how she would return to the same key ring on the table after moving to other points which interested her. Every time she returned to the keys, I drew some lines. It took me hours but I was happy with the result. So were the parents of this girl. I gladly stopped doing portraits on the street for good.

Life on Joanna

Taylor was so noble. Every time he went to work he left me $1.00 to be able to go and have a beer.

We were invited by the scientists of Fairley Dickinson University to go out on their new powerboat with all the newest and fanciest instruments in it, to measure and sound the sea flora. When Taylor and I stood up to hold the tender alongside to get out, a freckled, red- haired guy (a so-called scientist), shot his new laser gun into our eyes so suddenly that we could not cover them in time. He meant it as a joke but it blinded us for twenty-four hours and we were very afraid. Our eyes were red and hurt. We were not happy and did not find this amusing. The other scientists helped us to get back on board Joanna and were very apologetic for what had happened.

Not A Boring Moment

The owner of the Holger Danske Hotel, where I had my paintings on exhibition and which was located at the sea front, hung a blue towel out of the window where we could see it, whenever anyone wished to see me. I could then just row ashore.

Not many tourists showed up after a war started on St. Croix. It all happened, when three white men who were playing golf on the golf course were shot dead by a black racist. The police were called and those - even worse - fanatics captured and tortured the first 8 eight innocent black men they saw without knowing if they were guilty or not and without a trial. Then they shot all eight innocent black victims. Some of the black folk said that they would kill twenty white people for every black murdered. So almost every week one or two innocent white people were murdered. Then it was a white woman who was on vacation who was stabbed in her hotel room by someone who entered by the window.

The island was so beautiful that one lived in the present and forgot all about the occasional murders. A friend of mine, Frankie, was a mulatto but looked more white than black. He was a family man and the father of small children. We had reserved the first table to attend a jam session that evening and a group of us sat around the round table in the middle, at the front. Frankie said, "I don't understand why some people are leaving the island. If you treat the blacks with respect, they will respect you as well. You won't get hurt if you don't hurt them."

A group of black people walked in and declared, "We want that table!" Frankie told them, "We were here first and have reserved this table and we are not leaving." The blacks then mumbled something to each other and sat at the table behind us. The jam session was great and everybody enjoyed it. We parted and went home. The next day, we heard the shattering news, that Frankie had been found shot dead in front of the place where the jam session had taken place.

Racists of all races are mentally ill and should be treated in mental institutions* before they can cause bloodshed and sorrow* If there is one large enough!

Work On Joanna

Joanna's hull was secure, but the cabin top leaked, the mast tube had to be replaced and the top railing was in bad need of renewal. Almost everywhere we looked there was renovation to be done. To top it all, neither of us had the finances to do it.

Taylor owned two diving tanks and masks from the Second World War. He could fill the tanks at the Columbia University workshop. We found out where there were some shipwrecks and so we dove to unscrew bronze screws and whatever we needed to keep Joanna from being destroyed. We sometimes even dove in murky water.

I helped Taylor with everything I could. He had a piece of plywood left over from doing the cabin top and some polyester resin which he gave to me and I rowed to the shore as quickly as I could to inspect the rubbish bin. In it, I found a rag mop, gloves, a rusty machete, a can with a bit of black paint left in it and some wire. I rowed back to Joanna where I immediately started to create *"The Wild Man."* I laid everything I had collected on the piece of plywood. I took two bits of the old mast tubes, Taylor had given to me and a piece of corral I had collected that would become the ear. I drilled small holes where I planned for the wire to come through, took all the collected materials beside the plywood onto the cockpit bench and painted the plywood with the rest of the black paint in the can. It was a very hot day and the paint dried very quickly in the tropical sun. Then I arranged the materials and fastened them with the wire. I used oil chalks, to enhance the effect and mixed the hardener into the polyester resin before I painted *"The Wild Man"* with it. I was very happy that Taylor liked it very much. He framed it for me and I hung it on the wall with my other paintings in the Holger Danske Hotel.

Taylor and I were asked by 'Jazz' to help sail the "Mongoose" to St. Thomas. Bob, who used to be hired by the owner to sail tourists to Buck Island had been fired since Jazz, the owner's son, had arrived from U.S. A. and taken over. Jazz was known as a flirt and a womanizer. He was good looking but egotistic. We accepted, since we could use what he offered us. Besides, I thought it would be fun to sail in Mongoose since I knew that sailing boat very well.

So Jazz, Taylor and I sailed to St. Thomas. On a clear day, we could see St. Thomas from St. Croix. Jazz brought all the food and drinks. The trip started well until Jazz started to flirt with me, but I let him know that I was in love with Taylor. Taylor got mad. They started to fight. I did everything to talk them into stopping the argument. I almost became physical and got between them, shouting at them, when kind words did not help. I feared that one would begin to lose the argument and start to hit the other. This went on until St. Thomas, where I was relieved to run to the first bar to recover. Taylor followed me and Jazz also showed up after a while. Being on the land had settled their argument but they still did not like each other. At least they accepted each other and finally showed some tolerance. I guess Jazz needed us to sail and we needed to be able to get back to St. Croix. The trip back was just as tense and nerve-racking as before.

Futzli

The scientist friends of Taylor had a problem. Their cat had had kittens and the father was a wildcat. They kept the male since he couldn't get pregnant. they tried to place the female without success. Taylor asked me if I would mind having a female wildcat on board. He believed that she would not get pregnant since 'Joanna' was anchored too far from the shore and cats do not like water.

I loved the idea and Taylor brought the beautiful kitten home. We named her Futzli. She was a beige, tiger-striped wildcat with big ears, short hair, extremely long legs and the marks of the wild cat (three black stripes on the side of her face). She was really wild. Every morning she woke us up by jumping on our heads. We took her in the tender and rowed to a beach with shallow water. Taylor thought it important to teach her how to swim in case she should fall out of the boat while we were sailing. She took to swimming right away and loved the water. Sometimes we took her with us to the land and let her play in the park so she could smell herbs before we took her back to the boat.

Every morning when I got dressed, she climbed up my jeans into my arms. One day, she did not wait until I had my jeans on and climbed up my legs, then slid down them while trying to hold on. I screamed from the pain she caused me from digging her nails into my skin. I grabbed her and threw her over the side of the boat. Immediately, I realized what I had done and wanted to jump into the water to save her, until I saw that she had climbed up the fender and jumped on board in no time. From then on, Futzli would swim ashore and back whenever she liked. She never climbed up my legs again.

We could only pet her if she came up to us for affection, otherwise she would dig her sharp claws into our flesh or even use her teeth. She always came back at feeding time! Every time someone came to the boat, she went straight for their eyes, unless she knew the person. I wrote a big sign, 'WARNING, DANGEROUS WILDCAT ON BOARD' which Taylor hung up. Futzli felt at home on board Joanna and it was her territory. She was a fascinating animal and looked so elegant and had such graceful movements.

Taylor's friends came to visit us. Futzli knew them and did not attack. They handed a joint around and we all got stoned. There was no toilet on board. We used to pull the bucket, tied to a rope, up into the cockpit for this purpose. I was in a hurry but tried holding it back as long as I could, since it was not possible for me to use the bucket because all the men were sitting in the cockpit. I pretended to go for a swim and pulled my bikini bottom down hoping no one was looking. I was so embarrassed, when my shit floated on top of the water.

Everyone thought it was funny and I laughed also (in embarrassment). When I was on board again, we had a conversation about shitting. One of the man said, "I had a shit this morning which was beige and lumpy." The one next to him said, "Mine was black and hard and hurt on the way out." Taylor said "I had such an explosion, that it stuck to the sides of the bucket." Then the conversation shifted onto the subject of which foods could cause which color and texture of bowel movements. We all agreed, that some types of alcohol and smoking could cause diarrhea. I told them how embarrassed I had been just one hour before, when my stool floated. We all had a good laugh and someone said, "Your shit floated because it had grease in it. What did you eat?"

I lost my hang-ups! Everyone has to poop. Living aboard a boat had saved me maybe one year of psychiatric treatment to lose my complexes.

The blue towel hung out of the window of the Holger Danske Hotel, signaling me that someone wanted to see me. I rowed ashore. It was Sonny. He asked me, if I could lend Dusty a pair of my jeans since he had ripped his beyond repair and could not buy a new pair until some money came in for him. I told him, that I only had two pairs and would lend them with the condition, that I get them back as soon a possible. It took much longer then I hoped to get them back. Dusty had sewn a piece of red velvet into the crotch of my jeans, as a thank you.

Taylor and I stayed faithful to each other. We were among the few people on the island, who did not become infected with syphilis. Jazz had carried syphilis with him from the U. S. A. and had caused this epidemic in St. Croix. In my opinion, Jazz behaved like a criminal. Irresponsible people like him should be wearing protection. Some are too lazy, selfish or ignorant to use a prophylactic or to have regular check-ups.

Shark Man

Shark man was 60 years old, when he escaped from Cuba to Puerto Rico in his small wooden rowboat. He was a skinny and tough old man, weather beaten, with an under bite and looked just like Popeye. During his escape, he fended off attacking sharks with the oars from his boat. He then came to St. Croix, where he lived and went out rowing every day.

Ever since the sharks had attacked him, he hated sharks and went out fishing every day in the hope of killing a shark. When they were too large to pull into his boat, he would tie them on a rope and pull them behind the stern to the shore. He would also catch a few other fish which he sold to the hotels. A sailor who felt sorry to see the old man having to row for a living, gave him a 'Seagull' outboard motor. When Shark man tried to pull the string to start up the motor and it wouldn't run after the second try, he slammed it onto a rock, crushed it and went back to rowing again.

    One day, I was sitting in the cockpit of Joanna while Taylor was at work, when Shark man rowed up to me and gave me a fish. I asked him to come aboard and offered him a cup of coffee. He did not stay long since Futzli, our cat did not approve of him and I had to close her into the cabin during Shark man's visit. I was also glad that he did not stay too long, since he smelled like a dead shark. From then on, Shark man often stopped without getting out of his boat just to say hello and speak for a while.

    One day, he asked me to come ashore and told me that he wanted to show me something. I took our tender and rowed to the shore. There, he showed me his wheelbarrow covered with fish. He moved some fish over to one side and lifted up the sacking material from under the fish. It was stuffed full of dollar bills. Many of them where $100 bills. I had been thinking that he was very poor and was amazed at this sight. Then I told him, "Wow, you must have had a good catch, congratulations." He said, "I am not daft, I own a warehouse to store fish that I import from Puerto Rico. I only fish a few fish every day and so my clients believe they are buying fresh fish from St. Croix. They never ask if the fish comes from Puerto Rico." Then he looked at me and asked, "Will you marry me?" I told him that I was in love with Taylor and that he was too old for me. He then said, "By the time I die, you could inherit my whole fortune and be so rich that you could afford to keep as many young man as you liked." I told him that it was nice of him but that I could only be a friend to him.

Tension with Taylor

    Some of Taylor's single friends came to visit. They started to knock women in general. I did not like that since I am a woman as well. They really believed themselves (in their arrogance) to be superior to women, which to me, proves their inferiority. *There are superior and inferior human beings of both sexes and of all races.* Every time those so called friends were with us, Taylor seemed to be influenced by them. Tension had built up between us. I loved Taylor and it hurt when he was down on women. We had some disputes. His friends started to snub me. Taylor turned against me. We made peace again.

I became so homesick for Alexa and Julie. The letters that arrived at the post office from them, kept me going. Every day, I was thinking about my gorgeous daughters. In my mind, I put an invisible glass bubble around them, which could only be entered by people who wished them well and that protected them against bad ones who would drop dead before they could enter their glass bubble.

Things got worse between Taylor and me. I could not help sharing my grief with some of my close friends and told them that I was probably leaving for Switzerland very soon. Taylor was bothered by our age difference of only six years.

The blue towel was hanging out of the hotel window and I was happy to row on shore, hoping that someone needed me. It was the owner of the art shop. She asked me to design a Christmas card with a sugar mill and a Santa Claus on it. Then there was another woman who wanted me to design seahorses to print onto cloth. The design had to be such that one could use the cloth in both directions. This was a great challenge for me and stopped my depressions.

I rowed back to Joanna and started to design right away. I was satisfied with the Christmas card even though I prefer to create my own ideas. Then I finished the cloth print design and was very happy. Taylor liked my design very much as well.

I looked forward to showing them to the women who had ordered them, believing that they would share my feelings about them. First I brought the Christmas card design to the woman with the art shop who wanted to think about accepting my design and wished to keep it until the next day. I was crushed that she had not showed the slightest enthusiasm for my work. I still had hopes for both my designs.

I was very sure of the success of the seahorse cloth print, certain that I had succeeded with my design in creating exactly what she had wished for. When I entered her office, I proudly handed her my design. She looked at it and then said, "I like it but I also have to show it to my partner who will not be back until tomorrow. Leave it here until tomorrow afternoon." I said "okay."

The next afternoon, I went to the art shop and the woman turned down my card design and gave it back to me. She even refused to tell me why she did not like it. I started to get depressed but controlled myself and went to see what was happening with my design for the seahorse cloth print. When I entered the office, the woman handed me my design and said, "My partner did not like it." She also did not say why. I was shattered. I felt as if I had failed as a woman and a artist.

Why, when I gave my heart, body and soul to Taylor, did he not seem to return my love any longer? Why did they not appreciate my work after I had given my best? Was it that I was wrong or were they wrong or had I misunderstood? Why did they refuse to tell me why they would not accept my designs? Why... why....why...?? I felt as if I was trapped in my thoughts and did not know what to do, what to think and where to go.

Taylor was at work and so I went to drown my sorrow with a few rums. I finally gathered my train of thoughts and decided to tell Taylor that I was going to leave him. Also, I started to believe in myself again as a artist. After all I had made several people proud to own an original Maya B. Why should I doubt myself as a woman since so many men wanted me? I guess love can come and go. I accepted the situation without bitterness. I had decided to become the strongest woman on earth.

That evening, I told Taylor that I would leave for Switzerland.

He seemed indifferent and I was not sure what he wanted besides making love to me. We made love most of the night and in the morning. He did not try to hold me back so I picked up the money for the return flight to Switzerland. The return flight was not much more expensive than a single flight so I took the return. I figured if it was too difficult to live at home with my mother's nagging, I could always come back. I loved this beautiful island and the other ones I had seen. The Reggae music, lush vegetation and clear blue water and being able to live in the present made me happy.

What I wanted most of all was to take Alexa and Julie in my arms and spend some time with them and Keys, our poodle. I also missed my father and, oddly enough, also my mother. At the airport, Taylor and I embraced each other with tears in our eyes. I guess he loved me as well but we could not see life together any longer.

When I arrived in Zurich at the airport, I decided to go to the city to shop for a present for my children. I still felt the warmth of the tropical sun on my skin and the smile would not leave my face, until I was made aware of it by the look of frustration on some city dwellers. They looked at me, as if they were thinking, "What is there to smile about in this grey town?"

I took the train to Wil and arrived in the afternoon. My parents had insisted that my siblings and I should all have a key. When I opened the door, Keys had heard me and peed on the floor from her excitement at seeing me again. She would not leave my sight. Then I looked for my parents.

My father's car was not on his parking place so I knew he was on house calls. I went to the third floor and found my mother on the balcony hanging up the laundry. Before I could say hello, she greeted me with, "When are you leaving again?" I felt like turning around immediately but instead I asked her, "Do you mind if I spend a few weeks with Alexa and Julie?" She said, "Of course I don't mind." She then followed me into the kitchen where she offered me fruit, coffee and a cake she had baked, all at the same time.

With Alexa and Julie

My daughters came back from school. Finally, after eight months, I could take them in my arms again! I was amazed to see how much that they had grown. They were 11 1/2 and 9 1/2 years at the time.

When I said goodnight, my mother locked Keys in the kitchen and told me not to let her sleep in the bedroom with me. I obeyed, since I did not want to cause an argument. Keys dug a hole into the wooden door during the night, almost large enough for her to get through. I was touched by the devotion of Keys and the children said, "Look, Keyseli worked so hard to be with Mom!" My father laughed and from then on, Keys was able to have the run of the house again.

She followed me through the thickest crowds, staying with me without ever being put on a leash. I had problems with the power of the small-minded people, when they said, "Put your dog on the leash" and I would reply, "She is on a leash but you cannot see it."

The dog is only as free as his owner.

I was grateful to be able to be with my daughters for a few weeks at least. I wished to be in a financial situation that would allow me to have my girls with me and believed that the success of my artwork was just around the corner. Then, I would be able to realize my dream of having Alexa and Julie and Keys with me all the time.

The divorce from Bob, my second husband, still had not come through. The child support was sent regularly by Howard, my first ex-husband. At the time, all I could do, was to enjoy the present moments with them. Too bad there was no school vacation to give us more time together.

My father was as great as ever. We had a wonderful time. My mother told me, "Your father loves you more than he loves me." I said, "Nonsense, it is a different and platonic love, the same as you felt for Neni" (her father). At last, I knew why she had been so much against me, ever since I had become mature and had a mind and opinion of my own. I was happy that my daughters got along so well with their father and could not understand why my mother did not feel the same.

Jealousy is an illness that causes unnecessary stress and grief.

After everybody went to bed, I went to the pub to see some of my old friends. I hoped it would help me over the loneliness. Ever since the relationship with my second husband Bob, I was unable to stand being alone and needed to fall in love again, to get over the grief. Now I felt the only thing to get me over the strong desire for Taylor, was to find my ideal man who would not be influenced by the outside world and would want to be with me more than anything. He had to love animals and hopefully live on a boat and have the same dream as I, to sail around the world. The men I met in Wil could not compare to Taylor, but the *hope* kept me going.

Never give up hope.

Keys, our poodle, accompanied me everywhere and guarded my handbag. If anyone got near it, she showed her teeth and growled. If they reached for it, she would nip them.

What I had not realized, was that the nagging of my mother about everything I did was her way of throwing me out of the nest. I stayed in the upstairs apartment of my parents' large house and painted while my children were at school.

My mother insisted that I come downstairs and eat all meals with them. I was lovesick and lonely. I dreaded to have to say goodbye again but understood that it was not fair to my parents to stay longer than I needed to. My mother did what she could. She just did not see the world with the same eyes as I. When I told her, that I searched for the truth she said, "That is impossible, no-one has ever found the truth." Now it was I who could not understand her.

Life is truth. If we don't have the courage to live the truth our lives will be lived by the beliefs of others. I wanted to help my mother to understand but it just caused aggression. She probably thought *she knew it all* and definitively believed that children must obey. I believe that one can learn from young generations, but she thought she knew it all.

Children are a generation ahead but parents have more experience. How can anyone who knows it all, avoid standing still or learn anything new?

My parents offered me the apartment at the back of their second residence in Ticino, CH, to use as my art studio. I was thrilled. My father and I drove there to spend a few days. He could not cook and I was happy to do something for him. His brother Freddy joined us and we laughed until our stomachs hurt.

I was glad when the few days had passed, so I could have some time with my daughters. The free time to do and say what you wanted had been needed by my father and I. My mother did everything she could to make Alexa and Julie happy. So did my father, but he was more fun to be around and very understanding and intelligent. He enjoyed life to the fullest and spread his happiness. He could also be serious or very sad. When he was sad, he often stayed in his room with migraines.

Parking meters were fairly new in areas where it had always been possible to park freely. The only reason business people accepted them, was that they were told that their business would increase. It was becoming a real challenge to park the car without being fined. Sometimes I could only find a parking spot by driving around in circles in search of a place. Everybody spoke about saving our environment. It did not make sense to me, to use all that extra fuel just so that the government could make an extra buck on fines, not to speak of the added expense for tax-paying citizens, to install the eye sores in the first place. I felt it to be my duty to act according to my sincere belief, that

Knowledge brings responsibility,

and live the way I was convinced to be the best way. I parked the car in places where I was sure that it was not in anyone's way and did not have to waste extra fuel. When the police stuck a fine notice under the windshield wiper, I would rip it up and throw it away. I was fined very often and ignored it. Every new law made Switzerland less free, in my opinion,

For every new law there should be two old laws taken away.

I did not feel free any longer and started to be very restless and needed to go away again. Just then, a letter from Taylor arrived. He had written that he loved me and that he wanted me to come back to him. My instinct told me that things would become bad again but my feelings said "Go on, don't be afraid, everything will be alright." My feelings won out. I embraced my gorgeous, intelligent daughters, my wonderful parents and Keys, and flew back to be in Taylor's arms again.

Another Round With Taylor

It felt so good to be back with Taylor. People dressed in vivid colors walked stressless through the streets. Their expressions were relaxed. Almost everyone smiled. I was happy to be surrounded by beauty. This sensuous, tropical island almost made me addicted to its great beauty. I can hardly describe how happy and almost delirious I was. Taylor loved me and was happy to see me again. He rowed me to his boat. The familiar reggae sound with the ringing of the steel drums filled my ears with pleasure. The azure blue sky mirrored in the clear almost calm sea. Joanna gently swung on the mooring line. Our wild cat Futzli greeted me by jumping in my arms. Taylor made a coffee. We did not drink it, instead we made wild passionate love. Everything was ok. The next day, I went to deposit the means for a one way ticket to Switzerland, as I had promised again to my wonderful father. I had the best father in the world.

I discovered that the sea horse printed cloth that I had designed was offered for sale all over the island. The woman who had refused to buy the design from me had my work copied, while she pretended to keep it until the next day and show it to her partner. She must have heard about my plan to go back to Switzerland and did not expect me back. I had no idea about the corruption of some business people, or of how to do business. Angry, I went to see the woman in her office and threatened to sue her if she did not pay me $20.00 right away. She paid me the $20 and I signed the paper she handed to me. She must have laughed all the way to the bank.

I met the man who was the printer. He asked me "Maya, do you know that the owner of the art shop had the Christmas cards designed by you reprinted three times already? Each time, there are 200 cards printed!" I was angry that this one had also copied my design. I also threatened to sue her and made her pay the same amount as the one who stole my sea horse design. I found out later, that it is normal to pay the artist 10 % of every meter of fabric sold. This would have given me a constant income while the fabric was on sale. On $20.00, Tailor and I could shop for one week's food supply!

We Live and Learn

The scientists have found out that the crime rate on St. Croix is highest when the temperature is 98.6 degrees Fahrenheit. There were now about two people murdered every week. Here, we lived totally in the present and forgot about the bad incidents. There was a hurricane warning. Taylor was frightened to lose his boat and refused to go on shore. It was his only possession besides the old Volvo he had bought for $100 and was his home. "Joanna" had too much draft to be able to motor for safety up the river. If we stayed on board our lives could be at risk. Taylor said, "If Joanna sinks, I go with her." I said "And so will I." We stayed on board and the hurricane was kind to us. The sea was rough and the waves were slapping on the hull from the high wind but it passed and we were safe. The ropes and the buoy held Joanna tight.

My Job as a Waitress

The owner of my favorite pub had a problem. The waitress had left and he was in desperate need of someone. He asked me if I wanted to work for him. I said, "Yes," since I could really use the money and did not like to depend on Taylor.

The pub was like a haunted one, everybody wanted to drink something different and I was not allowed to write it down. It had to be memorized. Five guests were sitting at a table and all ordered different things. By the time I was at the bar and ordered one beer I had forgotten the rest of the order and had to go ask the guests again. This happened a few times and I got depressed. I tried not to let my feelings get the better of me and carried on. I was determined to stay until closing time. After four hours, I went to the toilet and had a big cry.

When I came out, someone handed me a joint and I took it, thinking it would cheer me up. I found it even harder but pulled myself together with all my strength. The five people who had drunk three rounds of different and the most expensive mixed cocktails had left without paying.

Fortunately, closing time arrived. The 5 1/2 hours work time felt like a week. I was not able to control my tears from rolling down my cheeks. Now I felt not only depressed but also embarrassed. When I went to ask for my salary, the owner said, "Maya, you have not made any money since you let some people get away without paying." Now I was not just depressed and embarrassed, but disappointed.

I ran to the tender and rowed out to Tailor. He held me all night in his arms. In the morning, I was not only feeling depressed but also very angry. Taylor suggested, that I draw a caricature of the event in the pub. I started to let my anger out, by turning the owner of the pub into a crow behind the bar, with eyes popping out on springs and $signs as pupils, while he opened the cash register. I completely let my anger out about everything that had happened, until I found the caricatures so funny, that I had to laugh. My depressions were gone.

Taylor found the caricature excellent and suggested, I show my work to the pub owner. I bought a frame, framed it and took it to the pub to show the man. To my surprise, his feelings were not hurt and he laughed out loud. He said, "I want to buy it, how much do you want?" I gave him a price that I thought very high and he paid me in cash right away. He then said, "Don't waste your time as a waitress, you are an artist."

I'm not sorry that I worked, it taught me respect for people who can do it and I understand how hard it must be for them. The pub owner asked me to hang the caricature up in his living room the next day. It felt so good not to be broke anymore. Tailor and I celebrated it with a steak dinner and a fine bottle of wine. Futzli had a steak as well. I was so happy.

Diligence

Taylor's 'so-called' friends had been visiting again and tried to turn him against me. They did not speak to me, but about me, so I could not defend myself. I thought Taylor should have defended me. I was unhappy because he was not the man he should have been and we had a fight. I demanded to be rowed to shore and then I left him.

I went to the Holger Danske Hotel and sat at the bar where a handsome man started a conversation with me. He said, "You must be the artist who did the paintings on the wall." I answered, "Yes." A little later I told him that I had just left my boyfriend and was not happy about it. He ordered a rum punch, served in a coconut with a piece of fresh pineapple in it, for both of us. He said, "This will cheer you up."

He introduced himself and told me that he had a girlfriend who was working in the U.S.A. He looked very lonely to me. He asked me if I wanted to sleep on the three-masted schooner he owned with two other men. They were planning to sail to St. Thomas to pick up six cars and transport them to St. Croix the next day.

He told me all about the schooner, *'Diligence'*, which used to belong to Metro Goldwin Mayer in Hollywood. They used to shoot pirate films on her. He had fallen in love with the gorgeous ship but Metro Goldwin Mayer had refused to sell it for a price he could afford, so the three friends got together and pooled their money to make a bigger offer. M. G. M. still refused and would rather have Diligence sink than sell her below their asking price.

Diligence became so badly neglected, that she nearly sank. When my friend saw the sorry state she was in, his two friends went with him and M. G. M. finally turned Diligence over to people who recognized the beauty of the old schooner and were willing to take on the responsibility, for a price they only just managed to afford. They became partners, bought two pumps and sailed her to St. Croix. *Diligence* was one of six of her kind left in the world. My friend invited me on board and I was proud and flattered to be asked to help sail Diligence. What a ship!

She was beautiful inside as well and she smelled of wood, salt and adventure. I slept on board and awoke to the scent of fresh coffee. I got up and found the table set with freshly pressed orange juice, pancakes, maple syrup, bacon and eggs. My friend, a crewmember and a twelve-year-old boy asked me to join them for breakfast. My friend told me that the other two 'captains' would shortly be there as well. They had a decision to make.

Diligence's starboard side was damaged. My friend said, "Let's repair those planks properly." The other 'captain' said, "We can't do it in time before the contract today. We need this contract to be able to repair her." The other one said, "Let's seal the leak with tar and use the two pumps if needed and repair her after we come back with the cargo." The first 'captain' said, "Maya, it is going to be a risk", I said, "I know and I don't care."

Soon all three captains were on board and it took three of us to hoist the mainsail. Everything on Diligence was original. Every cleat was carved by hand from wood. No electric anchor winch or sail hoists. All the sails needed to be hoisted by hand. She sailed beautifully in rather strong wind toward St. Thomas. The three captains were eager to get there as fast as possible. Diligence started to leak through the temporary repair on the starboard side. One of the pumps was turned on. A storm blew up and I slept through the whole storm. My friend said to me, "You must have a clear conscience to have been sleeping through that whole storm." I asked him why he did not wake me up and he said, "I did not have the heart to wake you out of the deep sleep." The leak got worse and the second pump was activated. Then the first pump quit working. We were almost half way to St. Thomas when the second pump started to spook. The decision to head back to St. Croix was made, since it was still a bit nearer than St. Thomas.

The weather was great again. The sun was shining and every sign of storm had disappeared. Both pumps had now broken down. Diligence was not sinking but took on water. Just as we where about five sea miles south of St. Croix, one of the 'captains' was at the helm while each of the other two 'captains' were standing on the left and right of him. I sat on the bow and looked out for reefs. The moment I saw a reef, I called out "Reef in front of us!" One of the 'captains' said to the one on the helm, "Go right", the other one said "Go left", so the one in the middle, stayed in the middle and Diligence glided straight onto the reef.

The rescue people were called and arrived within about ten minutes and picked up the two crewmembers and two 'captains' plus the woman who was with one of them. My friend and I stayed on board and took the ropes, which were thrown to us by the rescue people. Then they tried to pull us off the reef, without success. They said that they would leave her and asked if we wanted to go with them. We wanted to stay. They said that they would be back the next day.

Diligence could not sink since she was on the bottom already and the water was calm. My friend and I started to be conscious that every second of not having made the best of life, would not give us those chances again. The moment belonged to us. We started with a cocktail and then ate the delicious food that was on board and he opened a bottle of wine. We sipped an excellent cognac with our cake. Exhausted, we fell asleep in each other's arms.

In the morning we felt the ship moving. We jumped out of bed and hurried onto the deck to inspect *Diligence*. The wind must have blown her off the reef. She hung free on the anchor that had been set the day before as security. We drank some coffee, had a swim and then my friend called the rescue people to come and pull Diligence on shore. We were taken ashore with a small motorboat while Diligence was moved toward the shore. Then we embraced and saw each other for the last time. I found out later that my friend's girlfriend had bought Diligence and paid off the other two 'captains'. I heard also that Diligence was properly repaired. I was glad that this great ship was in good hands and wished them both well.

Reunited

Onshore again, I walked to a spot that I liked especially well and started to immortalize the seascape. When I finished the painting, a tourist came up to me and wanted to buy it. I was very happy that he liked my painting enough to want to own it. He said, "I will buy it with the condition that you carry it to the hotel for me. "Certainly," I replied. I carefully took the painting to his hotel room and placed it on top of a dresser. He immediately paid the price I had asked and then tried to grab me but I managed to throw him off balance and escaped. I was sad, that this undeserving man owned one of my originals. I felt like going back, throwing the money at his head, and taking the painting away but I felt lucky to have been able to escape and was too scared to go back. I needed a drink. Rum is made from sugar cane and could calm my nerves in the past, if I took only one or two. I headed for the pub. When I entered, two eyes were fixed on mine.

Next thing I knew, I was in Taylor's arms again. He said, "It was meant for us to be together again." It was stronger then us. We could not help it and gave in. The spark was still there and turned into a roaring fire again.

Taylor and I sailed to Buck Island to meet some scientist friends. It is one of the most beautiful underwater sanctuaries in the world. We anchored Joanna and rowed ashore. There, we met a hero. The man was the only one from his tribe in the rain forest who dared to explore out of the forest and even go to sea. The superstition of those people claims the sea to be bad and evil. This man was asked, if he would like to sail out with them. He accepted and climbed on board their ship. The rain forest man could not speak our language but could show what he wanted, the way a dog did.

We all felt free to go naked on the beach of Buck Island since there were no tourists there. He was jet black, tall, naked and had untamed hair. When a woman excited him, he made sounds like a dog, " Hu uh uh u, hu uh uh u." He had absolutely no hang-ups about having an erection.

A bunch of us went snorkeling through the reef. I got behind the others because I was feeding the friendly barracuda by hand with some cheese rind, before following the others into the deep. The one in front gave me the signal to look behind me. I could hardly believe what I saw. It was at least a 3 m-long hammerhead shark that swam at the same level as I. I remembered not to show any fear and gently changed direction toward the sailing boat. I tried to swim as calm, steady and fast as I could and swung myself on board. My heart was beating so hard inside my chest and it took me a session of meditation to calm down.

Later, I was told that if the hammerhead had wanted to eat me, I would not have felt a thing. It would have been like a ton of bricks hitting me. I also found out that hammerheads are very docile and rather eat fish than people. I felt so safe in Taylor's arms. I hoped this time it would be forever.

St. Patrick's Day 1973

Taylor and I went to celebrate St. Patrick's Day with some friends at the Holger Danske Hotel. As the festivity progressed, Taylor, a friend and I decided to streak naked through the large crowd and then run along the street through the pedestrians. A policeman stopped me but did not exactly know where to hold me while he tried to put the handcuffs on me. I grabbed the handcuffs in the middle and looked at him with my intense thoughts, "If you try that, I will take those toys away from you." Then I ran away to meet the others.

There was a report about us in the newspaper the next day. Tourists returned to St. Croix, believing the war had ended since people were streaking. Other hotels made offers to us, to streak at their places for money but we refused. We had done it spontaneously and only for fun and freedom.

The problem started again, when someone introduced me as "This is the artist Maya B." and pointed to Tailor, "and this is Maya B.'s boyfriend." Taylor and I had a few more weeks of passion until the flame was so high, that it had to reduce to a spark before it became too dangerous to stay together. We parted again.

Soon I had nothing left but my airline ticket back to Switzerland. I was sitting on the beach in the lotus position and meditating on what to do next, when I felt someone put a glass into my hand. It was a black man, who said, "You look like you need a rum punch." He cheered me up instantly.

He was a sailor and had been hired as the captain of a ship that was due to leave St. Croix shortly. He chased my depressions away and I never forgot him.

As I walked along the pier, another black man with a scar all across his face called me from under a palm-leafed umbrella over the bar he was tending. I had been warned not to trust him. The bar was in the garden of a nice hotel. He said, "Come here." I answered, "You have the same distance, YOU come here if you wish to speak to me." He replied, "But you can see that I am working and can't leave." I thought, *"I have nothing to lose"* and walked up to the bar. He had a plate of food on the bar. He said, "Wait a minute, I'll be right back" and left to go inside the hotel to come back with an empty plate. Then he put half his food on the empty one and handed it to me with the words, "Here, eat. When you are finished you can go."

I am so grateful to him and all the people who helped me to survive. Sometimes, when I was desperate, someone would come up to me and say, "Are you okay?" Just those words helped to give me strength again.

I did not want to go back to Switzerland even though homesickness for my daughters tortured me. Surely the alimony from my divorce would come through soon and help me to be with my children again. I preferred to only visit my parents, without having to live at home and obey my mother. I loved my mother and was grateful to her but I was grown up and decided to go and survive in the rain forest.

Survival in the Rain Forest

I entered the rain forest and started to feel hungry. I was admiring the lush vegetation, when my eye caught the beauty of a very special tree. In admiration, I stretched my arms out to my side with the palms of my hands open toward the top looking up at the tree when a ripe avocado pear dropped into my hand. This was magic to me. It was the best avocado pear I had ever tasted. Now I knew what an avocado tree looks like. I thanked the tree and headed deeper into the forest.

Fighting my fears of uncertainty and not knowing where to turn, I came to the conclusion that if my time was not up for me, I would survive. Suddenly, I spotted some small buildings and went to inspect them. They looked like showers.

Then I saw a person and recognized a friend I had met in town. He said, "Maya, it is great to see you, will you come for dinner?" I responded, "I would like to, with pleasure." He then took me to a wooden house where he was living in a commune with many other members. Healthy children laughed and played while chickens, cats and dogs ran free. The property was surrounded by beautiful trees, bushes and flowers. Here, those people were finally left in peace. They were looked down upon by business snobs (like the ones who cheated me) in town and stamped as hippies.

Since GIs from the U. S. A. had abandoned their station in the rain forest, my friends had taken the place over and adopted all the stray animals left behind by their irresponsible owners. They shared whatever little they had with every living creature. I admire those people. Before dinner was put on the large table, all the pets were sent outside. Everybody sat down and served themselves with delicious fried rice with vegetables and home-baked bread and salad. Tea with honey and lemon quenched the thirst. After the meal, plenty of food was left over. The cats and dogs were called in, jumped on the table and ate every scrap left on the plates and on the tabletop. When they had eaten every corn of rice and crumb of bread they hunted for scraps on the floor and then licked clean the pots and pans. I was very amused. They certainly did not need a vacuum cleaner.

The conversation was interesting. There was no small talk. Those people lived in reality. No TV or newspaper distracted them. They believed in only working long enough to be able to buy what they could not find in the forest or make themselves and drank the occasional beer when they went into town. They all looked so content and satisfied. They did not belong to the consumer society and live consciously and ideally for our environment.

Who lives with the minimum pollutes the least.

I was glad to sleep that night in safety at my friend's house before I continued to venture deeper into the rain forest in the morning.

Maya B.

Impressions and Feelings

The deeper I went into the unknown, the more stressed with fear I became. I had walked a long way and thoughts of, "What am I going to eat or drink and where am I going to sleep?" kept torturing me. If I had only had someone to share the beauty with, I could have enjoyed it much more. Exhausted, I sat down and started to meditate. "I am here because I chose to be here. This is an interesting place. The avocado tree was welcoming me. How many people are lucky enough to be confronted with untamed beauty? Things will be okay." Then my thoughts became dizzy and I fell into a deep sleep.

When I awoke, I saw orchids that had climbed to the top of quite large trees. Birds were singing. How can a creature as tiny as a small bird make such wonderful sounds? I liked the dewdrops on the leaves and chewed on some moss. What a wonderful place our earth is. I whistled and tried to imitate the bird songs. I got up and started walking toward, what I believed to be the west- according to the position of the sun, in the hope of being able to hear the sound of water somewhere soon.

Instead, I heard voices and had a strong feeling of danger unless I changed direction and headed away from those voices, as calmly but as quickly as I could. I discovered more signs of violence by seeing branches that had been brutalized and nature that was disturbed. Birds gave the warning call. Not until I felt the rain forest at peace again, did I slow down.

Then out of nowhere, stepped 'Jungle'. I was almost glad to see him but I also feared him a little. I measure 1m 68 cm and am very agile and quite strong, but he is about 2m tall, has a superiority complex and can be violent. He commanded "You--- come with me." I said, "You know my name is Maya and I don't want to go with you." He answered, "If I want woman, I take her. Before, we eat, you come." He knew the forest inside out. There was no escape that I could see, so I went along with him. Surely, I would find a solution later on.

'Jungle' owned a nice-looking wooden house with a glass front in the middle of the jungle. When we were standing in front of his house, he called a Japanese couple who lived in a shed next to his house and ordered them, "You bring food." The couple's expressions showed fear. They walked into the wilderness and reappeared about 15 minutes later, with something wrapped in a gigantic leaf. Jungle said to the woman, "You show food." When I could see the worms, maggots, caterpillars and beetles on the unfolded leaf, I remembered that it would be the biggest insult to refuse any food given by native jungle people and would be a reason for them to kill you, and thought to myself, "You ate snails, ants and prawns before and it did not taste bad.

Luckily, the man made a fire on the ground while the woman collected some herbs and fetched a tattered frying pan. She put all the insects and herbs in it and fried it well. I was asked to eat it all up. Surprised at how good it tasted, I thanked them and told them that I had really enjoyed the food. I was so glad not to have to eat all the insects alive or raw. It gave me added security to know which insects were good to eat.

Jungle made me go in to his house. I told him that I was still in love with Taylor and that I did not want a relationship with him. He got so drunk that he fell asleep. The door was locked and I could not get out. He was lying in front of the window so there was no way to escape without the risk of waking him up. I fell asleep as well.

In the morning he tried to rape me. I fought him off with all my strength but he said, "If I want a woman, I take her" and so he raped me. He unlocked the door and I ran outside. He followed me and reached into his pocket to take something out. He held me by my arm and stuck the thing in my mouth with the words, "Here, eat this." I believed it to be a candy and swallowed it. After about five minutes, I started to have hallucinations. In a stone, I saw all kinds of live creatures. Jungle said, "You white people can't see without LSD, it's real all the time."

Then he explained to me how to walk in the jungle so that

nothing would attack you. The jungle walk is soft, round, easy-going and slow. It works. I used it later in many situations in the wild. A swarm of mosquitoes flew toward me. Jungle made a movement with his arm toward them and they flew away. I asked him how he did that. He replied, "Easy, just tell them to go." The LSD trip lasted quite a long time and I was relieved when the drug finally wore off.

Jungle high- jacked me back into his house and wanted to rape me again. I noticed the full bottle of vodka and said, "Let's do it properly then. I knew his weakness was alcohol and grabbed the bottle of vodka, saying "Let's celebrate first". A potted plant stood behind me and while he drunk his, I poured mine into the pot. He got intoxicated. Then I heard some voices outside. It was Taylor's friends. There where three of them. Unfortunately, Jungle was not drunk enough and went out to threaten them. They were afraid and ran away. I was content to know that they had found out where I was. Jungle did not realize that he had drunk the whole bottle of vodka by himself and fell asleep. This time, he slept on the sofa. Taylor's friends came back with reinforcements. There were six men now, who returned to help me and I escaped through the window. We all managed to get away.

They brought me back to Taylor, who asked me again to stay and live with him on Joanna. Taylor helped me to get over my shock. I never told him of the rape. We were deliriously happy to be together again.

The next day, I went to check if there was any mail from my daughters at the post office. There was. I missed them so much. There was still no news from my divorce lawyer Bob C. in Baltimore. I asked Bob to replace the alimony I would have had from Howard, had I not gotten remarried to him. I did not hear from my lawyer about this until much later. He wrote that Bob was threatening to reveal the secret that I told him in confidence. (The secret, of my getting married to Charley, in Las Vegas, while both of us were stone-drunk, at a church at 2:00 a.m. Charley had wanted it to be a souvenir that we both would never forget. I was only legally separated from Howard at the time. The next day, when we were sober again, we had the marriage annulled.) I remembered a secret which Bob had told me in confidence, so I threatened him, that I would expose him, if he tried to get out of what he owed me.

Attacked

There were children on the Island of St. Croix who were wild and who roamed without supervision. The youngest was only about five and the eldest of the group of twelve was about fifteen years-old. They were watching me painting on the pier. When I finished the painting they were still there and one of them asked me, "How did you do that?" I asked them if they would like to know how to mix colors, they said "Yes", so I showed them that they could start with yellow, blue and red and how to mix them into orange, green, and brown, that they could lighten with white and darken with black, blue or brown. Then I told them that one has to find one's own style within one's own self but what one could learn was technique and perspective.

No one can teach you how to paint. It comes from within.

They seemed to understand. A few times, when they came up to me, I taught them whatever they wanted to know and hoped that it would help them to survive.

About a week later, Taylor and I were sitting in the cockpit of Joanna, when we saw the same children I had been teaching, onshore. They were violently jumping on Taylor's only other possession, an old Volvo he had bought for $100. I yelled, "Get off the car." They didn't listen.

So we rowed on shore and I told them not to damage the car and said, "You would not like it either, if I smashed your radio." Suddenly, one of the children appeared from behind a wall and threw a heavy stone at me. Another rock was thrown by an older child. They must have had a whole rock collection behind that wall and threw five heavy stones at me and at Taylor. Taylor grabbed the biggest child and threw him into the water, the others ran away since they were afraid to be thrown in as well.

Then, we managed to get into the tender to row to safety. Back on board, the anger gave way to immense pain. Those kids were expert stone throwers. We had open cuts and bruises. We washed them very gently, put iodine on them and powdered them with antibiotic powder. We couldn't sit and had to lie down very calmly. Every movement hurt. I was very disappointed at the falseness of those children. The pain was still pulsating after more than a week.

After that time, we went on shore again to shop for food and fill the water cans. While on shore, we saw the kids going up to one of our friends carrying stones and getting ready to throw them at him. Before we could think of a way to help, our friend jumped up and down, making funny movements with his arms and legs while looking straight at them and loudly saying, "Bug a - Bug a - Bug a!" The boys dropped the stones and ran for their lives. Black children are very much afraid of being jinxed by witchcraft or voodoo.

Taylor took me to the Columbia University Scientific Station. At their workshop, I got a 220 volt shock from the defective cable of an electric sander, while sanding the old paint off Joanna's mast. I went into the house where I met the boss. He was a very nice man. He showed me the whole station and we had an interesting conversation. He said that the biggest problem with Columbia University was that they had too much money and did not know how to spend it all. I thought "How lucky can they get?" Should I suggest to him that they invest in my artwork to hang in their premises? I was too shy to ask him. I also saw that all the females were doing the boring work of checking the aquaria, weighing the fish or other sea creatures, feeding, cleaning and writing down every detail, by the half hour. The men could dive, go out in boats, be outdoors or have big discussions, buy food and drink or even smoke joints. It was strongly segregated. I was accepted since I was with Taylor. It started to dawn on me, that all the men there except for their boss, were suffering from superiority complexes. If the system was like that, no wonder there were so many lonely people in this world! I had read Aldous Huxley's book " The Brave new World." Now I knew what had inspired him.

It is a truth that those who believe themselves to be superior could in fact be inferior due to brainwash. The truly superior do not stand for insensitivity or snobbery.

Streaking the Nuclear Submarine

The almost totally abandoned town opposite Christianstead was called Frederikstead. White people had all left from fear of being killed by blacks. There was only one restaurant left open that belonged to a white man who was known to be an excellent cook. Carlton looked like a ghost town.

Some scientists asked Taylor and I to join them. They knew that a nuclear submarine had arrived there. We found the submarine tied to the pier. All its man were inside. I had heard that wherever a nuclear submarine goes, the fish will turn belly up and die. This was enough reason for me to be proud to be here with them. The sea was already threatened and I was thinking of my children. How will the health of nature on our planet be when their children were born? We had to do something now. We all took our clothes in our hands and streaked on the submarine. The men in uniform opened the lid and swarmed onto the deck. They seemed to be amused but had to chase us off the deck.

We got dressed and Taylor and I were invited to eat at the restaurant. There, we saw the Captain of the nuclear submarine and when he was asked how he could take the responsibility of being the Capitan of such a polluting vessel, he replied, "Easy, I am well paid."

A few days later, Taylor and I started to argue again. We decided to separate for good. He asked me if I would like him to build me a box out of plywood for my artwork to be transported safety back to Switzerland. I was glad he had built me a box. He even fitted a strong lock to it. I was very busy taking my paintings off the wall in the hotel, packing and arranging the box with my paintings to be sent by Swiss air and saying goodbye to my friends.

I had just heard the horrible news of two women in their

early twenties, who were found murdered and cut up into pieces on one of the beaches. I had met them and found them very nice. They were primary school teachers employed in a local school. Everyone I knew was very fond of them. The children in their class liked them very much as well. No one who had met them could understand this disgusting, brutal act of slaughter by such a sick mind, full of hatred and racism.

I am a white anti-racist and I am not guilty of ever having kept a slave or murdered any black person. I don't blame those blacks for their ancestors who slaughtered all the Indians who inhabited the island before they had arrived from Africa. They were not even born then and did not have anything to do with it. It was not the white people faults that their ancestors killed off many Maori or the Maori's fault that their ancestors killed off the aboriginal Maori in New Zealand. It is also not the fault of the white people who had nothing to do with the murder of the many Indians in the U. S. A. so many generations ago.

War is sheer egotism and starts by brainwash from those who enrich themselves on it. Real lowlife at its worst. The excuse of doing away with over-population stands no longer. It is a known fact that population increases after every war. Besides that, there is birth control or sterilization available without having to lose the ability to reach orgasm. I wish all humans, no matter what color or nationality, would be intelligent enough to see the necessity of joining together in peace and would work to save our very threatened environment for generations to come.

Greed kills.

The Manchineel Apple

I tried to become independent from Taylor and went to the Holger Danske Bar. I was suffering from bad depressions and hoped to divert them with some friends. No one I knew was there but I sat down just the same. A black woman put something in my face and told me to eat it. She forced it very hard into my mouth. I ran to the bathroom and spat it out. It was causing me tremendous pain. I

Not A Boring Moment

inspected it and recognized it as a very toxic little green apple from the infamous Manchineel tree. This tree grows in the rain forest of St. Croix. If the natives wanted to torture someone to death, they used to tie the enemy to this tree. It caused an allergy with such unbearable pain that the victim would die a horrific and agonized death. My mouth was burning and itching instantly. Fortunately, I always kept anti-histamine tablets in my handbag in case of allergy caused by wasp stings in the past. I rinsed my mouth really well and took two anti-histamine pills. It saved my life. When I came out of the bathroom, the black woman had gone. I wondered if she was sent by 'Jungle', who probably wanted revenge?

The next day, I said good-bye to our cat Futzli and Taylor drove me to the airport. I didn't have enough money to pay the extra freight charges for my box of artwork, so I arranged to pay for the shipment upon my arrival. Surely my father would help me out. Taylor and I embraced each other for the last time with passion. Tears were in our eyes. I asked him not to write me or try to contact me again. He has respected my wish. I flew to Switzerland.

Keys, our dog heard me turning my key in the lock, at my parent's house. She yelped with joy and was so excited to see me, that she dribbled some drops of urine on the floor. I hugged her. My parents and daughters were totally surprised to see me and I embraced them all. How great to be able to take my gorgeous daughters in my arms again! My depressions were gone. The mood was great and everyone was interested to hear all about my adventures.

The next day the phone rang. Someone informed me that the box with my paintings had arrived. I asked my father if he could help me out to pay for the shipment. He said, "Of course." Both my father and I were shocked to find out, how much Swissair had charged by using their own, very high exchange rate- Dollars to Swiss francs- for the shipping charges. On top of it all, the Swiss government wanted me to pay duty on my own paintings. At this point, my father was upset. He said to me, tell them, that you did them yourself. I did not blame my father but I had to give up my pride and force myself, but did not see another option than to say, "I did them myself." The art expert who was there to value my paintings had lost all respect for me and my serious artwork and considered my paintings, wrongly, as just a hobby. I was let off from paying duty.

I hoped to restore their respect again by throwing myself into life and perfecting my artwork. My parents let me use the small barn behind their house in Ticino as an art studio. My children had their school vacation. We all spent some valuable time in Ticino, Switzerland.

TI 1974, The Artist Jost Blöchliger

I love the canton Tessin. Ticino (TI) is in the southern and Italian speaking part of Switzerland. The climate is sub-tropical and the summer lasts three months instead of three weeks as in the German-speaking parts. When I was a child, it was very romantic. The chickens, ducks and geese ran free in the villages. Donkeys were ridden or carried wood. Vegetation was wild and lush. Today, much has given way to tourism. It is still partly very romantic and nature is still lush but many hotels etc. have been built and an auto route is carving up the landscape of the valleys.

I enjoyed being with my parents, laughing and philosophizing with my father and I loved every second with Alexa and Julie. Relatives came and went and there was no boring moment but I was longing to be in a man's arms again.

My cousin Maya Maurer came to visit and said to me "Let's go to Ascona", so we went and sat in one of the coffee shops on the lakefront of Ascona, (a crazy town) by the Lago Maggiore. It swarmed with tourists. We ordered something to drink and then a man walked up to Maya. She knew him and introduced him to me as, "This is a friend of mine. Maya, this is Jost Blöchliger. Jost, this is my cousin Maya."

He asked, if he could sit at our table and we welcomed him. I liked him right away. He looked like a real character with his long open hair and weather-beaten skin. He wore clothes that did not fit and looked shabby. He made a very relaxed impression and was at ease. His voice was warm. He liked me right away as well. Our conversation flowed like music. We had another thing in common, we were both artists.

Maya returned to her family's second home in the next village above us, while Jost and I drove to my parents' second house in his Renault 4. I said to Jost, "Wait just a minute, while I go and ask my parents if it is okay to invite you to dinner." I ran down the steps to the outside table, where my parents and daughters were sitting. I said to my parents, "I met a friend of Maya Maurer's. He is an artist from Rapperswil, St. Gallen. Don't get frightened by his appearance. He is my new friend and really very nice and fun to be with. Can I invite him for dinner?" While my mother looked at my father, he said to her, " I really like to know who Maya is going out with." My mother agreed and told me, I could bring Jost down for dinner. Everyone liked Jost, including Keys our poodle.

Jost was a guest of Paul and Verena Giger and family but came to pick me up every day. I met the Giger Family and was very impressed with Paul's artwork. In my opinion, he is one of the best. Over a year previously he had visited Jost and asked him if he would join him to go to India. Jost asked, "When are you planning to leave and for how long?" Paul replied, "Right now and for whatever time I like, maybe a year or longer." Jost had told him "I can't do that", so Paul had left alone the same day from Rapperswil heading toward India on his Velo Solex. The day I first met him through Jost, Paul had just returned from India, with his Velo Solex. He was heartbroken that on the way back, all his sketchbooks full of drawings of his India voyage had been stolen from the rack of his Velo Solex.

Jost Blöchliger

Life with Jost

Jost and I liked each other so much, that we fell in love and stayed together. I moved into his apartment in the old part of Rapperswil. It was located on the second floor of a house belonging to Frau Schnelli. She was over 80 years old but still fit and loved to clean all the brass fittings on the wooden front door, to a mirrored shine.

Jost had no shower or bath, just a sink in the kitchen, where we would have a spot-wash with cold water and brush our teeth plus we occasionally did the dishes. Most of the time, we just licked our plates and cutlery and used it again.

We slept on a single bed together. The only heater was in our bedroom. The bedroom was used also as an art studio for both of us, as a living room and office. In a closet, up three steps, was the toilet which could be reached from the hallway which we shared with Frau Schnelli.

In the studio-office-bedroom stood three small tables with Jost's old still-lives on them. The flowers were dried up with their stems liquidized in the vases. Rotten fruit was almost sliding off its position and was covered with mold. Empty bottles stood with a layer of dust next to the rotten subjects. Jost did not want to have them moved or thrown out. I did not care as long as I could work on his easel when he did not need it. The ashtrays on Jost's office table were filled to the top and so was his wastepaper basket under the table. All the ashtrays in the apartment were full. I smoked about two packages of menthol cigarettes and Jost chain-smoked Gauloise blue without filters.

Empty beer, wine and hard liquor bottles cluttered up the studio-bedroom-office-living space. There was an extra room to store the finished paintings in. The wall-space was covered with designs and sketches. Some designs were drawn directly on the plaster. When Alexa and Julie came to visit, Julie said, "What a mess!"

Jost and I visited his parents every Sunday on the way to visit my daughters and parents for the weekend. Keys my poodle, did not leave my sight and chose to stay with me as the children had to go to school. Frau Schnelli was afraid of Keys. Keys took advantage of her fears and barked every time Frau Schnelli came down stairs. Frau Schnelli then threw a biscuit in front of Keys and while Keys ate it, she quickly passed to go downstairs. This was a daily ritual.

One time, Keys really embarrassed me. Frau Schnelli had just finished vacuum cleaning the Oriental rug in the hallway when I came in from a walk with Keys. Keys slid her behind along the full length of the rug. I excused myself and offered to vacuum again for her but she refused and said it was all right and that it did not matter. She was such a nice and tolerant lady.

Jost was drinking too much. He was never vicious but a happy drunk. He never became ill. We got up in the morning, had a coffee and a piece of bread with butter and jam on it and went straight to the pub unless he had contracts or was preparing for an exhibition, and then he stayed sober. I helped him with designs and chose the colors for the stained-glass windows. I helped him with everything I could and created my own artwork. He taught me different technical methods to design glasswork, mosaics, etchings etc.

Jost was not rich but very generous in every way. I believed that if I drank with him he would not be able to afford to drink so much and would stop. I was wrong. He did not stop but I started. Now, we were both drinking too often. I was sometimes unwell but then I became immune to it. We usually went to the infamous rocker bar, the 'Anker', then we had lunch at home or in a restaurant and went straight to the bar again. We had a soup or a sandwich for dinner and went out until closing time again. After that, we usually ended up at Benny's place.

Benny Kohlbrunner was a homosexual lawyer, who liked to sleep all day and live at night. He was always keen on company. All kinds of freedom-loving philosophizing people and other different characters partied at Benny's all night long. Often we partied until four in the morning, while many stayed on until dawn.

What saved us, was that Jost was committed to work on many contracts and that we stayed sober for the family weekends we always looked forward to. Sometimes we went and painted outside in beautiful surroundings. I would choose one subject and Jost another. When I painted in Wil, he liked my paintings so well that he used the same motif. I felt flattered.

Things were easy-going until I sold one of my paintings to one of his customers. Until then, I did not know of his professional jealousy toward other living artists. After all, it is not my fault if the woman preferred to own an original Maya B. rather than another Jost Blöchliger, some of which she already owned. When Jost could sell his work I was happy for him. Why did he not feel the same for me? I could not understand.

Our first arguments started. It did not last long until we made peace again. My parents asked us if we would like to spend some time with Alexa, Julie and they in their second residence in Ticino. It was a very romantic place and was surrounded by vineyards with the beautiful background of mountains and an open view of the Lago Maggiore.

Jost volunteered to paint the façade of the house. My mother wished for a fresco of San Francesco d' Assisi in 'The song to the sun', surrounded by birds. Jost was happy to paint this and I helped by handing him the brushes, mixing mineral colors with distilled water and bringing him rags etc. Both my parents, Alexa and Julie and all who visited us liked the painting very much.

My mother loved to cook and spoiled everyone with her lovingly prepared meals and desserts. The vegetables were freshly picked from the garden. So were the strawberries the grapes and the khaki fruit. My parents told us that we could stay at their house in TI whenever we wanted.

A Herr Peter Stauss from Zurich asked me to paint a wall around a fireplace in one of his holiday homes, a few villages up from us in the Valle Verzasca. Stauss had converted many old rusticos into holiday homes to rent out. I was very happy to get a contract and worked many hours to come up with a design that I was happy with. Then I drove up to his village and showed my design to him with pride. He liked it very much and we decided on a price. I started to paint the next day. After three days of intense work, the painting was completed.

Stauss liked it and so did I. He invited me to dinner and after that, he told me that he would pay me the next day, as he was not able to get to the bank. The next day, Stauss had left. I called him on the phone, but he 'could not speak, since he was too busy' and so on. Stauss, this ugly hunchback, is very wealthy but was not ashamed to cheat others or me. This is what infuriates me about many rich charlatans. They have to look down on honest people to be able to exploit them and often the law cannot touch them. Many people are hurt by them until life eventually catches up with them by causing them to get diseases and to have operations. (Like the dictator Franco of Spain).

Those who exploit or steal have to look down upon their victims but it does not bring honor or respect, just illness misery and loneliness and certainly not love. What good is stolen money then?

A woman came to visit Jost at my parent's holiday house. I felt antipathy at first sight. Jost said that she was a customer. My mother made coffee and brought a cake to the large granite table under the pergola of grapes, where we sat whenever weather permitting.

Of this table, I have wonderful memories of interesting and sometimes serious discussions with much humor, fun and laughter. Birds flew onto the table to eat the crumbs, lizards ate little pieces of meat out of my father's hand and nature was all around us.

I resented that this woman visiting Jost started to knock men. When she said, "A good man is a dead man", I ignored her completely. I was not going to argue with someone so ignorant. The reason I mention her at all, is because she showed up again at Jost's place. But that is for a later chapter in this book.

Jost and I were mostly happy. Life was uncomplicated but interesting and I enjoyed not having to worry about cleaning, washing, ironing or dusting as in my first marriage.

Jost got contracts and I loved to help him. For me, that was the second best thing to having a contract myself. He could do a stained glass window for the new schoolhouse in Eschenbach, do repair work on a saint in a church, portraits, do a family coat of arms in stained glass and etchings, murals and graphics.

He had so much work that he asked me to go to Schmerikon to make a sketch suitable to advertise the new public swimming pool. I was thrilled that he gave me one of his contracts and went straight to the pool for inspiration. With a few quick sketches I produced a very good drawing in his studio. Jost liked it very much. He looked at it intently and laid it on the table in front of him. Then he took a pen and followed all my lines and even signed it with his name. I could not believe what he had just done to my work. When I complained about him having stolen my work, he simply said, "It has to be in my handwriting."

Jost had just hurt my pride and broken my heart. I went to the pub and got drunk. A few hours later, he came and convinced me that he still loved me, so I went home with him, but it left me with a scar. I missed the tropical Islands and tried to talk Jost into joining me in travelling to the Caribbean. He did not want to hear of it and was absolutely happy to stay in Switzerland. Jost did not have the drive to explore the rest of the world like I had.

I was willing to make a compromise and talked him into flying to Grand Canary island. My Aunt Irma and Uncle Freddy had invited us to stay at their seafront apartment, an investment property, in Patalavaca. Gran Canaria was much closer to CH. I was surprised by how beautiful this island was when you got out of the city of Las Palmas and away from the mass tourism which had taken over the west side of Gran Canaria. There were palms, bougainvillea, many other tropical plants and banana plantations with the sweetest, aromatic little bananas I had ever tasted.

Mogan was one of our favorite places and we had some friends there. Mogan had not been taken over by mass tourism and was a quiet little fishing village. We painted and sketched and just simply enjoyed life in the sun, surrounded by beauty, good Spanish food, the sea and nature. A bottle of wine cost less than a bottle of water and the quality was not bad either.

We went to the beach to see the fishermen come in and I planned to buy a fish for dinner, but then I spotted a turtle offered for sale, struggling on his back. I bought it, carried it out a few steps into water deep enough for it to swim. My reward was to watch with great delight, to see how quickly the beautiful turtle escaped. An older native woman was shocked by my action and said "That turtle would have made a very good dinner for many people." I replied," because I let this turtle go, it might lay many hundreds of eggs and your grandchildren may be lucky enough to still see turtles. Turtles have to be saved from being extinct and need to be protected, they are extremely rare." I had the unfortunate feeling that the crowd of people looked at me, as if I was completely crazy for letting the turtle go free. I was happy to have been able to save a precious life.

Animals are our co-inhabitants. We must take responsibility for our planet or the human race will die out as well.

The next day, one of the women I had met came up to me. She asked me for a favor. As the mother of ten children, she had had enough. She asked me to get her birth control pills, but make sure that no one, especially her husband, should find out about it. Her husband believed that the more children he made, the more potent he looked to his male friends. In my opinion, he was not enough of a man to care or understand the woman who gave birth to so many children just because he had a inferiority complex. In fact, he was the inferior one.

I got her the pills and gave a three-month's supply (all I could get) to her as a present, when I saw her alone. That was easy, since he spent more time in the bar with friends than at home with the family. Divorce was impossible because of their religion and lack of financial means. Hopefully their children will have a better future.

Back in the apartment in Patalavaca, I desired Jost more than he did me, which caused problems. At that time, I still believed that if a man did not desire me, he did not love me. I had no idea that alcohol could cause impotence. Alcohol seemed to me more of a stimulant, especially champagne or white wine. Red wine made me sleep like a baby. Jost had been drinking for many years and it had affected his health. The chain smoking did not help him either. What helped him was his active swimming, walking and being outdoors. I exhibited one of my freshly painted landscapes at Gallery Jean Pares, in Mogan. Jost and I drifted apart.

I was heartbroken about it and was forced to go out alone. I tried everything to cheer myself up and went to a nightclub, where I danced with the first man who asked me. He was a very nice Spanish man. A tall blond German with ice cold steel blue eyes stopped me from dancing by pulling me out of the Spanish man's arms and said in German with an arrogant voice, "I don't want you to dance with those damn foreigners." I shouted, "Have you not done enough harm already with your racism during the war toward Jews, Gypsies and Artists?" He yelled, ""We should have killed many more. We should have killed all the Jews." I said, "Get out of my sight, I am a free woman and can dance with whom like. I feel nothing but contempt for the likes of you." He said, "You only speak to me like that, since you feel safe with them in here." and left. I amused myself with the Spanish people and forgot all about the ugly incident. When I got tired, I left.

The German had been waiting for me outside. He surprised me by sneaking up behind me, grabbed me with one arm while pointing an open knife toward me. I managed to wriggle out of the position and get away, running for my life. Fortunately, the apartment building in Patalavaca was not far away. The main entrance was from the road to a bridge over a ditch that was at least three stories high. Over the bridge was a 1.5m gap overlooking the ditch where wooden grill panels were closed against thieves at night.

So I jumped over the ditch and managed to hold on by reaching my fingers into the gaps of the wooden panels, then swinging myself around like a monkey to the balcony and to safety into the elevator, where I pressed the button to the sixth floor and ran down the steps to the fifth floor, just in case the German had managed to follow me and, seeing the elevator light, he would expect to find me on the sixth. On the fifth floor, I knew someone. I knocked at the door and told him what had happened. He gave me a drink and calmed me down. Then, he went to see if the German was in sight. He then accompanied me to the bottom door, where I could walk to the adjoining building, where our apartment was located. Jost was sound asleep so I laid next to him and tried to sleep as well.

The next day, I waited for a man who was coming to the apartment to have his portrait painted. We had made an appointment. I waited an hour but he never showed up. Someone had warned me that one could not make dates with most locals since they would do it 'manana', which sometimes never came, yet I was really disappointed because I was sure he was serious.

Jost and I managed to find each other again. I still desired him but channeled my passion into painting or swimming. Then we even succeeded in having a sex life again.

I met a guy named Scotty Schmelzle from Germany. Jost did not mind if I had an occasional drink with him. Scotty liked to share a joint with me and we took LSD. Then he left and I was alone. I walked among the sand dunes and got very thirsty. Then I got lost. When I came back to Patalavaca, I was still tripping and did not want to go to Jost, until the hallucinations stopped. The thirst was being painful and I was almost afraid of dying from it. It was on a Sunday and all the shops where I could buy some water were closed. The bars were only opened after 6pm in Patalavaca. I looked at the surroundings and all seemed so nice, including the stains of rust on a wall.

I went back to Jost and immediately went to the water pipe and drank and drank until I could drink no more. I could not hide from Jost that I had had LSD. He was not happy about it even though he was an alcoholic. I painted a self-portrait, which I believed to be very interesting but Jost hated it. Finally the reaction of LSD wore off. That was the last time in my life that I took LSD.

Soon our study trip was over and we flew back home. Then

we exhibited in the Kollegium Schwyz. My painting was exhibited in the busy coffee shop while Jost's painting was hung on the wall in the hallway. He was very annoyed about this, which caused tension.

He didn't know jealousy in our relationship but was very bothered with jealousy about the success of other living artists. When a reporter came to the door and asked for an interview with me, Jost said, "She is not interesting", and made him go away. I overheard this from the bedroom. Once again, I felt as if I had been hit in the face.

After a day of being really depressed, Jost bought two tickets to the annual Artist's Masked Ball in Zurich for us so we made up and went there together. I wanted to stay with him but he had disappeared after a few hours, without saying anything to me. I tried to find him without success so I went home to Rapperswil.

I could not believe my eyes, when I entered our bedroom and found him laying in bed with that bitch that had said, "A good man is a dead man." while visiting Jost at my family's second residence. In a state of shock, I was standing there speechless, when Jost said, "Don't you even grant me this little pleasure?" I said, "Of course I do, you can have her!" I packed my bag and hitchhiked home to my parent's. I left Jost for good. I tried not to get bitter and remembered the many good times, of 1 1/2 years of life with Jost. The hope of finding my ideal life's partner was still alive in me but I had to go through a lot more living and to work to bring my own self toward perfection.

Jürg Zollikofer - 1976

Not knowing where to go again, I went home to my parents who so lovingly took care of my daughters. It was great to be able to spend the weekends with them but now I was able to see them every day for as long as things went well with my mother. If I came home with a man, she was fine but if I was alone and hoping to find a man again she had problems with me. I tried everything to make my mother happy but I could not obey like a little girl any more.

Maya B.

During the times my daughters had to be in school I walked through the woods with my dog Keys and often found mushrooms and berries to bring home. I studied nature and made the attic of the house into an art studio with my parents' permission. I lived in the upstairs apartment but my parents insisted that I had my meals with them and my daughters. I was touched. It was so great to see Alexa and Julie grow up. Their intelligence, sensitivity, talents and beauty made me the proudest mother in the world. I never interfered with my parents on the raising of my daughters.

They were both very independent and had strong characters. Alexa was extroverted and Julie had a quieter personality. They both got along well and were close to each other. My mother did not nag them and they spoke to her with humor and intelligence. When my mother began to nag me and started the sentences with "One should" and "One must", it was time for me to go to the pub. If she persisted and continued to tell me and many of our relatives how bad I was, it was time for me to go away again.

I had met the owner of the Gallery Kirchgasse. His name was Jürg Zollikofer. He was as lonely as I was and seemed deeper than most men I had met so we decided to live together. He was divorced and lived in his romantic old farmhouse in a very nice and natural environment with beautiful trees. He painted in one room of his house and I painted in the room next to the one he worked in. His father was an Ober Divisionair which is one of the highest military ranks in Switzerland and the Zollikhofer family owned three castles. Jürg loved his father who, in my opinion, was far too strict with him when he was a child and caused Jürg many problems. Jürg was very passionate and I was turned on constantly but for his crises, which made me see that he was not over his ex-wife yet. I objected to his brutality toward nature but passion kept me from leaving.

It bothered me, that he clipped the gorgeous, natural mature tree next to his house without any feelings. The tree looked beheaded and its limbs were cut so badly that it looked like a cripple. To top it all, Jürg found the tree more beautiful after he had brutalized it. We split up. Home again, Jürg called me on the phone. He told me that he would commit suicide. I drove straight to his place and saw him totally disturbed with a white-green complexion, shaking and trembling. Never have I seen someone in such a state of depression. I said to him,

"It takes more guts to live than to die. Any idiot can kill himself."

He said "That is not true." I insisted that it was the truth, turned my back on him and walked away. I was glad to hear that he had found the strength to survive, I just hope that he got milder with nature and with his own self.

If anger cannot be handled then the following emotion is depression.

Depression can also come from losing someone. I decided to be the strongest woman on earth and not to take any nonsense from anyone. I chose to take responsibility for my life and I insisted on living with and respecting only the ones who respected me, and most of all to find my own true love who is my ideal man and to

Never give up hope.

My Art Opening, February 1976

I was happy to be able to exhibit my paintings in the posh 'Hotel Restaurant Rössli' in Kirchberg, St. Gallen. I had just traded one of my paintings for a car, sold the most expensive of all my paintings to Mr. and Mrs. Wilhelm Heinrich and Elisabeth Epper-Guhl, who already owned a collection of my artwork. I was very happy and it was late. Almost all the people had gone home.

A rich businessman, whom I will call 'Mr. Waegli', invited me to the still-open bar of the hotel and ordered a bottle of white wine. Our glasses were filled and we toasted. Then the conversation started. I found Mr. Waegli arrogant and did not like the cold way he justified war. I was a pacifist and told him so. We started to have an argument. I won the argument and walked away. He shouted, "I will do something you will regret!" It was 2 a.m. and I walked outside to drive home.

Suddenly, I was followed by the police. I was not drunk but had had a few glasses of wine, so I pulled into the next parking place which was just to my side. Three aggressive and brutal policemen hurried to my rolled down car window. I had heard about police brutality from real people who do not lie and who had experienced it on their own bodies and minds. Fear started to panic me and I quickly put the still running engine in reverse gear and headed back into the road driving slalom so the police could not pass me. I believed, that if I stopped in Wil they would not hurt me in a populated area and I could walk home from there so I stopped at the Allée parking place.

By this time, the policemen were furious. I tried everything not to show my tremendous fear of them, by asking them to show me their ID. One of them pointed at his pistol in the white leather holster hanging to the side of his fat, stocky body and said with a harsh voice, "This is our ID." I told him, "You have already done too much harm with those things." They failed to show me any identification, which I heard that they have to show if asked.

My father had told me to never show fear while confronted with sadists. If you show fear, you are more likely to get hurt. The statistics in a medical book showed which professions were most likely be chosen by sadists. They were first, police, second, nursing and third, schoolteachers. In those professions they find victims unable to defend themselves.

The policemen ordered me to get out of the car. Before I could move, they ripped open my car door and pulled me out. Then, they tried to put me into their car and handled me so violently, that the whole left side of my body was bruised. Now, they had made me angry and I made myself so stiff that they could not put me into their car. One of the policemen tried to hit me in my stomach with his square head so I stepped aside, saying "Olé" which caused him to land across the back seats of the police car.

Now I could not help but be amused.

Then, one of the cops grabbed my arm and folded it behind my back. This hurt so much that they could easily shove me into their vehicle. They drove me to the hospital. The doctor wanted my blood. I had low blood pressure and lost a lot of blood when I had my five day- long periods every month. After ovulating, I had to take iron tablets. It scared me that they wanted my precious blood. I screamed, "Take my driving license but don't take my blood!" I asked the doctor, "Don't you have enough work, taking care of sick people, instead of taking my blood?" One of the police folded my right arm behind my back, while I was sitting on a chair and the doctor stuck the big needle's syringe into the back of my left hand and pulled blood out. My hand was swollen and bruised for over a week.

I managed to run out of the hospital and hide in a ditch. Fortunately, they did not find me while searching for me. I was afraid of what they would do to me if they discovered me. I shivered in the ditch, rolled up in a fetal position until I felt safe enough to go home. I knew that Mr. Waegli had called the Autobahn Police from Oberbüren, Thurgau. They don't have a very good reputation.

The next day, I told my parents about it. My driver's license was suspended for six months. I was accused of many wrongdoings against the law which made me write a letter back and state that the list of things they charged me with, was unjust and that in my belief, three men against one woman was against the laws of nature.

A few weeks later, I received an official letter with a date to appear in court. I went to Rapperswil to get advice from my lawyer Bernhard Kohlbrunner. The good news was that he had managed to get my settlement from the divorce with my second ex-husband Bob. I had to hire Benny, who was an internationally licensed lawyer, to get my ex-friend and American lawyer Bob C. to pay out my settlement of $20,000. Bob C. had taken half of that money as his fee, after he had not paid me out for all those years. He probably invested it and kept the profit. I was angry that Bob C. had not been efficient enough to get the alimony from my well-off ex-husband Bob, which I had lost by marrying him in the first place.

Those people in my opinion are the real criminals. That alimony would have permitted me to have my children with me and see them grow up. It would have helped to ensure that we had a roof over our heads and full plates of food. Well, that was the way it was and $10,000 was very welcome to me.

I handed the official letter I had just received to my Swiss lawyer. He read it attentively and said, "Maya, get out of the country as soon as you can. Tell them that you are going on a study trip and don't come back until two years later. By then, your case will be invalid and they won't be able to touch you anymore. They are afraid of people like you and if you get sentenced to jail they can say, "She hanged herself in the cell." I paid Benny for his services and went straight home to discuss the matter with my father.

He suggested that he thought it best to follow Benny's advice. I told him that I had $10,000 and wished to go and live on a South Pacific island with my children. My father said, "I think it will be better, if you leave the children with us. You can give them love, but we can give them love and security. A child needs both. Sleep on it, speak to your daughters and then give us the answer."

I went to see Alexa, who was at a private boarding school not far from Wil. I told her that I loved her but had to go away. I said she could come with me but there were very hard times ahead of us. Alexa said she liked the school and her friends and could see her grandparents often. She was sad I had to leave but she did not mind staying. Then, Alexa cried so hard in my arms that it broke my heart and as I write this down, I still feel a lump in my throat to have had to leave my gorgeous Alexa behind. She was thirteen years old.

Heavy-hearted and again with a lump in my throat, I spoke to Julie and told her that I loved her but was forced to leave, that she could come along but there would be very hard times ahead of us. Julie told me that she would stay since she had just met a boy and was in love. Julie and Alexa loved their grandparents very much. Julie was eleven years old.

I looked up the travel agent and booked a ticket from Cannes to Auckland, NZ on the cruise ship Galileo. I packed a small suitcase with one extra pair of jeans, a pullover, two pairs of underwear, one extra t-shirt, one towel, one bottle of shampoo a toothbrush, toothpaste, tweezers, iodine and a hairbrush. I placed some canvases and sketchbooks on the trolley then strapped the suitcase in front of them. Then I tied a bag with pens, paintbrushes, colors, turpentine and linseed oil on top.

The next day, I embraced my parents and our dog, Keys, and pressed my beautiful daughter Julie tight to my heart. Again, I could not help my eyes watering. I felt her tears on my cheeks. How I would miss them all in those two years. Little did I know that my absence would be almost six years. I felt mixed feelings of sadness and excitement. Heartbroken to leave my girls behind again and contented to be able to see more of the planet and to be free to live and do as I pleased. I waved "au revoir" to my loved ones from the Zurich train.

When I had some time in Zurich, waiting for the train to Milano, I posted the letter to the officials. I had written in it that I was unable to come to court since I was on a study trip and would let them know when I would be back. I rolled my baggage to the train and had a window seat in a compartment. The trip seamed long. In Chiasso, the customs agents searched through the train and checked everyone for passports. I handed my passport to the officer and smiled at him, as if I had no worry in the world. He hardly checked it and I was so relieved when the train was in Italy.

It felt as if I could breathe again. The train stopped in a town about an hour from Milano. A young man came aboard and when he saw me, he said, "Maya, how are you doing, it has been a long time since I have seen you. May I sit down?" I said, "Of course, with pleasure, how have you been?" I hoped he would not notice that I had forgotten his name. I always had problems remembering names but I did not forget the faces of friends.

Knowing I had met him in Zurich, during the time I was in the Ballet Academy, I asked, "What are you doing now?" He said, "I travel to learn more languages to help me in my profession as a opera singer." I asked him how many languages he spoke and when he said 24. I could not help expressing my admiration for him. He said, "I discovered that languages fascinate me; and the more languages you speak, the easier it becomes to learn another. It is only a case of musical ear and memory." I asked, " Where can I hear you sing?", and he replied, "Right here and now", then he stood up, placed his foot on the seat, stretched out his arms toward me and started to enchant me with his beautiful voice. Everyone in the compartment was pleased and I was happy. My friend sang until we arrived in Milano. He had to get out and I stayed on until Genoa.

There, I found the port with the cruise ship "Galileo." I asked someone in the office if I could go on board to the cabin I had booked. I was told that the crew was on strike and the ship was not leaving until three days later.

I didn't want to stay in the city, so I went to Nervi, nearby fishing village, and took a room in a guesthouse, breakfast and dinner included. I had a shower, washed a T-shirt and panties with a bit of shampoo and went out to the seafront. When I saw the cliffs being splashed by roaring wild waters and fishermen who stood on top looking the size of ants, I drew them on the pages of my sketch book which I carried with me wherever I went.

The drawing became one of my mother's favorites. I gave it to her and she hung it in our living room until she died in 1999.

Nervi ,Italy
Feltpen
ca. A 3
1976

Fishermen, Nervi, Italy
Feltpen
1976

While I made the drawing, an artist watched me quietly and when I finished, he started a conversation. He came from Venice and was as lonely as I was in this beautiful place and so we shared some time together. We ate lunch together and spoke about art and life. It felt as if I had known him for years so we went to the guesthouse where he showed me his talent.

There he said, "I will go out of the room and you touch any object, then I will come back in and show you what you touched." While he was outside, I took my sandals off and blocked the keyhole with a towel, and then I stepped into the bathroom and touched a glass. Then quietly again out of the bathroom, and louder in the room, I walked toward the door stopping and turning a few times to sidetrack him and called him inside. He went straight to the glass in the bathroom. I was amazed. We repeated this several times and every time he walked right to the object I had touched. When I asked him how he was able to do this, he said "Easy, everyone can do it, you just have to practice until you are be able to feel the warmth still there from the touch on the object." I tried it as well but it did not work for me.

We had a short but intense time together and he accompanied me to the Galileo, where we embraced each other for the last time. He told me that he would wave to me when the ship was leaving.

Life on the Ship Galileo

I climbed up the stairway and entered the small door to go inside the Galileo, where I was greeted by a crewmember who asked during which of the three shifts I wished to have my meals. He was surprised that I chose the third shift. Most people wanted to eat on the first one. My father had informed me that the first two shifts have to eat in a hurry to make room for the next one. On the last shift, you could have the meals in peace. He and my mother had found this out when they visited me in the U.S.A. and were on board of the 'France'.

Then I was led by a pageboy to the cabin. There were two bunk beds in it and a bathroom to share between the two cabins. The pageboy assured me, that it was not very likely to have to share the room with someone, which I was very glad to hear. The opposite room was vacant too. I parked my trolley with my luggage in the closet and proceeded to go on deck to wave goodbye to my friend.

We waved until we lost sight of each other. I will never forget him. I started to explore Galileo. First I went through first-class to get to the bow of the ship. It fascinated me to look down and see the water being split to an angle toward both sides of the hall, which turned into waves getting gentler as their length increased. This relaxed me. I was thinking about my friend and looked out over the sea in the direction he might be in and threw him a kiss.

I felt so alone and went to the bar. There, I found out that there was room for two thousand passengers on board the ship and two hundred policemen plus over a hundred machine-guns. Galileo belonged to Lloyd Triestino and sailed under the Italian flag. There was a ship's doctor on board and the ship was fitted out with a prison, which later on, I was forced to see from the inside (later in this chapter). There was a long table in front of the bar, where I was sitting. Some people sat down as well. This is how I met Champalou and his girlfriend Carol from Paris, his half sister Helen who had grown up in Russia and her little girl. We all became good friends. There were some musicians and other interesting people.

As Galileo went further out to sea, the ship's laws became stricter and so we all decided to meet there every morning and if one of us was missing we would look for him or her. This continued with new friends who came on board as well. The closer Galileo got to the next port, the more the ships laws were relaxed and the more people forgot how restricted they had been and relaxed. All of a sudden, we were allowed on deck again after 10 p.m. and the doors to the decks were no longer locked. The ship's guards in uniforms were not stopping anyone from walking barefoot on deck again. The next port was Naples. I could see a black cloud of pollution before I spotted Napoli. What a dirty, polluted city- almost as bad as Los Angeles.

I went on shore and looked at the town. I had visited Napoli when I was nineteen years of age, but it had not looked the same. I found the old part of town again and as I walked through an alley where the washing was still dried on lines between the tall narrow houses, I heard a big splash behind me and quickly turned around and saw a bunch of rubbish mixed with vegetable peelings had been splashed on the cobble stones and just missed me. An old woman holding a bucket was looking out of the fifth story window above. She had a big grin on her ancient wrinkled face. I was glad that she had missed me and I could not help laughing.

A little further on, I watched another elderly lady lowering a basket from the top floor with a cat in it. The cat got out of the basket on the ground. There was something very organic about this original part of Naples. The place smelled of coffee, food and urine. I had a drink in one of the old pubs and went back so as not to miss the boat.

I always went on the top deck for the departures and the arrivals. I felt like painting again and looked for a place where I could work. There was nowhere I could be in peace. My plan, which was to create enough drawings and paintings en route to New Zealand to be able to have an art exhibition, dwindled. Trying to sketch in my cabin disturbed me because of the generator noise. There was no way to get peace but by meditation. Then, I noticed the lifeboats on the sides of the ship. I climbed into one of them and found some peace away from the crowd and could not hear much of the noise, only the sound of waves breaking on the hull and the wind whistling. I chose the times when most people were eating or sleeping so as to not be caught lying in my secret retreat.

The regular guests at the large table in front of the bar became like a family. Often, we were speaking several different languages and if someone did not understand, the ones who could would translate. There was Italian, French, German, English and Russian. We all understood each other and were often laughing or discussing together. We also spent much time together at the pool and in the fresh sea air. I loved to be in the bow of the ship but had to go through first-class to get there. The guards started to give me a hard time, so I told them that I was a registered artist and that they could ask at via Brero in Milano to have this verified and if they would not let me go through the first class to get to the bow and sketch, they would be responsible for blocking me as an artist. From then on, I was allowed to go to the very front of Galileo. I met an old woman who told me that she was on her third trip around the world on this ship.

I found it hard to be on this noisy emigration ship. She could not hear so well and the constant noise did not bother her. She told me, that she preferred to be on board the ship, where she could choose what to eat and had her cabin taken care of by the crew. She said that she liked to have her hair done, go to the cinema or the boutique and play bridge or lay in the sun instead of having to go to an old folks' home which would be more costly and boring. She also enjoyed going on land and visiting shops to find presents for her grandchildren. Some shopkeepers recognized her again, which thrilled her.

There were a few characters I had met on board. What I did not like to see, was the armed guards. I had an affair with a man who had to fight to be able to eat at my table since he had signed up for a different shift. The food was very well presented but the waiters constantly wanted to break my head by bringing something other than that what I had ordered and it became a hassle to get what I wanted.

Now, with a man at my table, they would mostly bring what I asked for. This man and I had a great time but our ways parted. My goal was to go to a South Pacific island, where I believed one could live from nature as Paul Gauguin had and find a natural, real man who was not brainwashed into sexism, by sexuality or any other reason, or meet a sailor and sail with him around the world. Soon, we arrived in Port Said. My friend and I said goodbye and went our separate ways. I was alone again.

There were two choices. Either to stay on board through the Suez Canal or take the bus and visit Cairo, then hop on a bus again and go back on board Galileo in Port Suez. I chose to go to Cairo. The bus ride was on a road through the desert.

In the city, I chose to go my own way and first went to see

the pyramids. There was garbage, empty bottles, broken car tires etc. laying in the sand all around the Pyramids. Beggars hustled whomsoever they could. Souvenir sellers followed, trying to talk you into buying their shabby stuff. Half-starved people and worm-bellied children with very thin legs and hungry, neglected, sad looking dogs were the contrast to the fat tourists who swarmed all over the sights. Some were riding on camels and had to be back at the tourist buses after fifteen minutes of exploring the pyramids. This was torture to my mind. It was not what I had expected to find in one of the, supposedly, Seven Wonders of the World. I left, and went to a restaurant to eat lunch.

After cheering up a little, I looked forward to a visit to the Cairo Museum. As I walked along, a thief snuck up behind me and tried to yank my handbag away. It was pretty heavy since it contained all my valuables like passports, traveller's checks, money and sketchbook etc. I pulled it away from him, holding it by the strap and hit him so hard on the head that he fell on his knees. I did not intend to hit him so hard but I had been hustled ever since I arrived in this town and lost my temper. I saw that he recovered and was okay, before I stopped a taxi to take me to the museum.

After I paid for the entry ticket, about six guides were fighting to show me around and I told them to leave me in peace since I wanted to discover the museum by myself I wished to look where, when and at what and for the time I chose, on my own. I told them that if I needed an explanation, I would ask for one of them.

I walked to where ever it pulled me and discovered how they used to make the paintbrushes in the old times. They took green twigs and pounded them at the end with a stone until the fibers showed for the length they needed. The colors were ground out of semi-precious stones.

Then I came to a section where I could see that the old Egyptian drawings had inspired Picasso. It was the most fascinating museum I had ever seen. The gigantic statues were done with such a sense of beauty and perfection that I almost fell in love with the torso of a god in stone.

After looking around for hours, I asked the skinniest of the guards to lead me to the mummies. I felt that he needed a tip. He led me there and I was surprised to see that they had buried some of the mummified bodies in a fetal position, laying on their sides in wicker baskets.

Then he showed me more interesting things and invited me to the cellar where there were many more treasures stored that could not be seen by the general public. There were his co-workers downstairs as well and they were eating. They asked me to sit down with them and handed me some tea.

Then a man came down and said "What, you are still here, the doors are shutting now. If you are lucky you will still make it." I ran upstairs toward the door as fast as I could and just managed to crouch down to safety before the gate shut to the floor behind me.

Then I left to go to the soukh where I found a beautiful Arab dress in heavy silk with cotton. It was decorated with gold borders and had little hand -made buttons all down the front, slits on the side and large pockets on each side. It was not only beautiful but also practical as well as comfortable. The owner of the shop refused to sell it to me, since it was a traditional dress for men. A traveller overheard him and said, "She is buying for me", so the salesman sold it to me. Then the traveller and I went out of the shop. He was a really nice man. I was happy with my favorite dress under my arm.

I entered a restaurant since I urgently needed to go to the toilet. I sat down and ordered a snack and then shot off to the toilet where I could just pull my panties down in time but was unable to find any toilet paper. I stepped out of my bottoms and used them to wipe my rear end. Soon after that, I finished my snack and went outside where a bus arrived to take me to Port Suez.

Inside the bus, a Muslim man started to pester me. I could not speak his language and he could not understand "Fuck off" in plain English so I took out my sketchbook and drew the profile of an Egyptian woman holding her palm against an intruder and showed it to him. He then understood and went to the front of the bus. Muslim men can be very annoying by following women who are on their own, stepping in front of them and even trying to touch them up. Women are looked down at by those brainwashed men who believe that their Allah-God has sent non-Muslim white people to be exploited by them. This makes life so tiresome for people travelling in Muslim countries.

In Port Suez and again on board the ship, I went straight to the cabin and put on my new dress. I wore that dress until its life ended. I was glad to be back and able to relax with my true friends again. Not until later in life, when I was on my own time, came the privilege of meeting remarkable humans in Muslim countries. I will write about that later in this book. I observed that every time the speaker from the towers of the Mosques shouted prayers, many children cried, people shouted and dogs howled. I don't blame them. This caused me, as well, to have to curb my aggressions. Maybe this is why the Muslim men put their bottoms in the air and point their heads toward Mecca. Perhaps they are praying for that ear-busting noise to stop. Christian church bells can also be equally annoying noise pollution to my ears!

On shore in Djibouti, I was surprised at the landscape. I had always imagined Africa to become greener the further south you went. What would tempt people to live here? This town was surrounded by sand. The first thing I did, was to search for a shop where I could buy three postcards, one for my parents and one for each one of my two daughters. This I did at each new place I came to. I also sent off letters to them.

In town, a friend from the ship walked up to me and said, "Maya, let's go and see the parts of Djibouti, which they don't want us to see." This sounded like a great idea. So he and I left the tourist section. The first thing we saw were people celebrating and dancing in the street. When, we got closer, I was shocked to see that some of the people danced on wooden legs, without arms or just with stumps, so many of them were crippled and saddest of all, were the half-starved children with their big eyes staring out of transparent faces. Their thin legs could hardly carry them. Their bellies were swollen with parasites. Some people were blind but they were all happy to be alive and celebrated the end of the war. I wish the warmongers were forced to see this but I doubt that those disgusting mass murderers have enough feelings left to regret any of their brutal and polluting actions toward humans and nature. They should be forced to use their war profits to give free food and shelter to the poor who agree to take birth control measures.

From there, we walked further into that poverty stricken sector. There were no more houses, just piles of rubbish that the poorest made into their homes. The sand was compacted from the many people who lived there. They lived under parts of wrecked cars, pieces of tin, cardboard and whatever they could find. They had barely enough of a roof to squeeze themselves under to sleep. What a sad sight. I spoke French to some of the people, but could only understand the gesture to smoke so I gave them all my cigarettes. They looked like skeletons.

We left and went to the first bar we could find. I ordered six double Cognacs while my friend was in the toilet. The barman lined them all up in front of me. I grabbed the first glass and downed it in one go and then proceeded to the next one. Just then, my friend got back and grabbed my arm before I could drink it. He said, "I know you have had a shock but this is not doing the victims or you any good and will only hurt you." He was a real friend indeed and made me come to my senses. I found out that Air France flew in delicacies like French wine and cheeses etc. three times a week from Paris. I had had enough of Djibouti and we went back on board the Galileo.

One good memory that is imprinted in my brain of the quick visit to Djibouti, is the incredible beautiful and intense sunset behind Djibouti which I had watched from the deck. Not until later, did I have the privilege of spending more time there but all about that in a later chapter. As a passenger of an emigrant ship, the time spent in different ports is too short to study the real situation of any country. Galileo was heading for Durban.

As we crossed the equator around the swimming pool, the worst party I have ever seen took place. Drunken people dressed in weird clothes threw spaghetti and other leftover or rotten food at each other. The sounds consisted of screams, screeches, forced and hysterical laughter, broken glass and unclear, indefinable and intoxicated mumbles. The water in the pool was cluttered with people swimming through putrid fruit and vegetable, coffee grounds, bread, ketchup and spaghetti etc. The color of the water was horrid. The people pushed each other into the pool. Some landed on top of the others. I was turned off. I am all for people having fun but this was sheer frustration.

I walked away from it and went to smoke my pipe on the top deck. I laced the tobacco with some grass. The deck was empty. I needed this rare privacy. A few days later, I went to study the sea chart on the port deck and looked forward to spotting Madagascar. The ship did not stop there. I wished it would, since I had heard of the existence of so many species of animals living there only. I missed my daughters and my dog.

Suddenly, the door I used to pass to go through the first class to get to the bow, was guarded. The guard forbade me to go to the bow again. I found another opening and went anyway. Not many people were there and no one suspected me not being lodged in first class. Having promised not to use the life raft as my retreat any more, going to the bow became indispensable for my freedom. It felt like balsam to my mind to watch the sea being parted into waves. Behind me, I could not see anyone. It gave me a sense of privacy I could not find anywhere else on the noisy ship. Once there, no one seemed to mind. Then I went to the portside deck and was thrilled to see Madagascar coming into focus. The weather was kind of grey and it was cloudy. At the closest, we were too far away to make out the details of the island. Soon we would arrive in Durban. I was looking forward to getting away from the guards who were always trying to break my will and to getting away from the constant noise.

Galileo's crew was on strike again, so all the passengers received enough money for two day's food onshore and we could sleep in our cabins if we did not mind that the sheets were not changed and the bathrooms not cleaned. I welcomed the strike since it would permit me to explore the town for one or two days longer.

I usually preferred to explore on my own since I could choose where to go and did not have to wait for anyone. I first walked along the big paved road along the seashore of Durban. There were hotels, swimming pools and tennis courts along the side. It did not look as I had expected the south of Africa to be. It was like many exploited and newly built tourist towns anywhere in the world. I hoped to find the end of the town and some natural landscape. Suddenly, I noticed that six shady characters were following me. I was afraid of them and started to walk fast. They started to follow me equally fast. It was very isolated and no one seemed to be around except them and me. I spotted a bar and ran inside. The barman said, "Go away, we don't want no woman in here." This made me angry beyond control. I immediately lost all the fear and grabbed a large, heavy crystal ashtray from the bar and threw it with all my strength into the shelves where all the bottles stood. I heard the glass shatter.

In a high adrenaline rush, I ran outside and to safety between the houses and hotels, until I could rest in the market with a cold drink. I paid for the drink and left to see the things being sold from the market tables. I had never seen such a multitude of herbs and spices in so many colors. It smelled very exotic. Also, the incredible brocade and silk fabrics fascinated me. I bought some cards for my loved ones in Switzerland. Then I ate some miniature buns with different fillings which were prepared and baked as a local specialty. They were filled with vegetables, meat, and spicy sauces. They tasted delicious.

I tried to find a piece of hashish. I looked for natives who looked as if they smoked it themselves, but I had no luck. I walked around in the town and then I found someone who promised to get me a piece the next day. We made a date of where and when to meet.

Then I strolled around the town taking in everything that interested me, before I went back on board to sleep. When I awoke, I put on my Arab dress, stepped into my sandals and got off the ship to eat breakfast on land. Then, I walked to the place where I was to meet the man with the hashish. He was there punctually. I paid him for the piece and then he left in a hurry. I was content to have some hashish again, which would sweeten the hectic life on board the Galileo and permit me to deal easily with the annoying crew. Under the influence of soft drugs, I felt it easy to humor nerve racking situations, instead of losing my temper and getting angry.

Today, I don't recommend that to anyone since I have the knowledge that meditation is a much gentler and healthier way to deal with problems.

I spent the day exploring in Durban. When I got to the market again, it was almost 6 p.m. and closing time so I hoped to eat some other specialties. Before I could find any, they started to close the iron gates in the center of the market and shut the vendors in as well before they managed to get out! One desperate man tried to hand me a piece of paper with something written on it through the bars of the gate but a policeman took it away from him and I could not hear what he tried to tell me, before he was shoved into the crowd behind him. This episode scared me and I walked away from there. I was sorry not to have been able to help this man.

Just outside the market, I heard an angelic voice. I followed this beautiful singing voice and was confronted by the saddest sight I had ever seen. The man singing was sitting on a cart with four small wheels. He had no eyes, no nose and his face only had a mouth. His legs were reduced to stumps and I am 99% sure he was a torture victim. I stood there and listened to the sounds of his voice which seemed to be telling a story without words. The man seemed to sense that I was there. With his hands on the ground he shoved the cart he was sitting on toward where I was standing and faced me while his voice reached a incredibly high range in total clarity but sounded so very tragic at times that after about ten minutes it started to depress me. I walked over to him and gave him money. Still hearing his sound in my head, I looked for some privacy. I did not find any so I went on board Galileo and went to my cabin.

I unwrapped the hashish and smelled it. It had no smell. I then cut through it and it did not look like hashish. I tried to light it and it did not burn. It was a piece of compacted earth, covered with dark brown color. I did not care, some people were so poor in this town that I understood a trick like that. In a couple of hours, the ship's bar was open and I went there to have a cold beer. Some of my friends were there and we told each other of the experiences we had had on shore. Someone invited us on deck to smoke some hashish. Time seemed to fly until Galileo, as in every port, took on a new crowd of people and pulled up the lines to start on her voyage to Perth, Australia.

I enjoyed the view from the top deck while Galileo was moving out to sea again. Then I went to my cabin and was surprised to find an old woman in there. Not happy about having to share the cabin but understanding that it was not the woman's fault, I chose to sleep on the top bunk and let her have the bottom one, which was more comfortable for an old person and which she was demanding to have. Then she told me that she wanted the table and for me to clear my things away. I cleared half of it for her but neatly left some of my things there. This did not please her and when she ordered me to give her my key to the cabin it became too much for me and I refused. I told her, I wouldn't do so under any circumstances. I left to find the cabin boy to organize a key for the old girl. I could not warm up to her since I found her very arrogant. After all, she, like I, was in a second-class cabin and had to share with me. Also, every person was entitled to have their own key. After meditating on deck, I walked to the dining room to fight as usual with the waiter, to eat what I wanted, instead of what he wanted me to. I was determined not to let anyone break my will and stayed firm for whatever I felt was my right.

My friends were in the two shifts before mine. There were some people at my table who I had not met previously. They were very nice but were hassled the same way as I was, but gave up after a few days. However, I kept refusing to eat anything, except what I had ordered specifically from the choice of the menu, to stay in good health. Finally, I got Roquefort instead of processed cheese and fresh fruit instead of canned ones etc. but not without a struggle. It became very tiring. The wine was free and as much as you wanted but did not taste very nice. After dinner, I usually went for a walk around the ship then had a few drinks with friends.

There were some new people amongst my friends. Nevel, a pianist, was fleeing from Rhodesia and became my new partner. As the laws were tightened on board Galileo, Nevel and my musician friends started to play revolutionary music. The crew put locks on the pianos. One of my friends forced the locks open with a lever and they all continued playing.

Nevel was in a dilemma. He had left his wife and felt very lonely, not knowing where to go. He believed he was in love with me as much as I was in love with him. He had swept me off my feet. I tried to convince him to join me to live on a south pacific island where we could survive on coconut and fish plus other goodies from nature and build ourselves a hut. If Gauguin could do it, we certainly could as well. This was my belief and Nevel agreed. He was not completely certain what he would choose to do with his future. I tried to convince him to join me. All we could do, was to enjoy the time together in the present.

Having some privacy together was really hard. He was a third class passenger and had to share his cabin with five others. I had to share my cabin with the old woman. That left us with the broom closet. This was not very romantic, so we spent the night in a sleeping bag together between the parked cars, which were transported on board. No one noticed us but when it was too humid or cold we had to find other places or sleep alone. Nevel and

I spent much time together and with my dearest friends Champalou, Carol and Helen whom I had known since Genoa.

The musicians were also amongst my friends and a very special one was the artist John Boyce, who came on board at Durban. He was a very wise man and personality who taught me some relaxing exercises, which have helped me through many stressful situations.

I met my friends at the swimming pool since it was a very hot day. We were somewhere between Durban and Perth. I resented not having the same rights as the men and lay in the sun without a bikini top. No one minded, except a guard who came up to me and commanded me to cover my breasts. I told him that if the men would follow this order, then so would I. He then went into the ship and I was happy that I had won. After a while, he came back and told me that I was permitted not to wear a bra, but only if I would lay on my stomach. My friends, male and female, agreed with me when I refused to let them restrict my movements and to tell me in what position I was allowed to sun bathe. The guard disappeared again and reappeared with reinforcements.

They grabbed me by my arms and forced me to go with them. They took me to the bottom of the ship, where one of them handed me my jeans and t-shirt. I got dressed. Then they shoved me into the ship's prison and locked the door. I laid down on the iron bed in the cell. I felt trapped and panic struck me. I tried to meditate but claustrophobia would not permit me. I got up and walked up and down like a tiger in a cage. Then I laid down again and repeated the whole thing over and over again. I was below the ship's water line.

I felt very thirsty. There was a little square opening with iron bars in the cell door. I could look through it and I saw part of the corridor and a prison guard. I called the guard. He came to the door and I asked him to bring me some water. He did not bring me any. By now, I was feeling not only claustrophobic but was afraid of dying from thirst. I had some felt pens in the pocket of my jeans and started to draw on the walls and ceiling with them. This kept me from going crazy. After a few hours, a guard unlocked the door and let me out.

I went straight to the bar. My friends cheered. They had all been standing on the first class deck, holding up chairs and tables and threatening to smash up all the furniture, if they did not free me from the ship's prison immediately. Thanks to them I was released. Ever since that incident, I suffer to this day from claustrophobia in confined spaces but it is not quite as severe as before.

The ships' laws became stricter again and since some of us refused to wear shoes on deck, the crew scattered glass shards from broken bottles etc., onto the 2nd and 3rd class decks. The doors to the decks were locked at 10 p.m. again.

I only went to my room if Nevel and I were arguing, to sleep, or to have a shower. The old roommate unnerved me. She planned to leave Galileo in Perth and I hoped to have the room to myself and to be able to smuggle Nevel into the cabin.

I went to the pool again but with the bikini bra on. Under no circumstances would I risk going to jail again even though it never made sense to me, that humans were forced to wear clothes to go in the water or to sunbathe.

Wet swimming gear can cause colds, rheumatism etc. and feels clammy and horrible on the skin. Our bodies need the vitamin D from the sun on our entire skin. It should be free for each individual to decide whether to wear clothes or not. Religion and lawyers should not be able to tell us where and what to put on. I don't tell them not to wear their ridiculous outfits, such as the Pope, Bishops etc. like to be seen in, even though it is not carnival time. That is the way I see the naked truth.

I was standing on the starboard side of the top deck, one of my favorite places, watching nature when suddenly, I felt that something terrible was going to happen if I did not leave immediately. I had had this feeling in the rain forest before and know better than to ignore it. I walked away from the spot I was in toward the door to the inside of the ship and heard someone loudly say, "Oh no!" Then one of the guards passed me and walked inside saying, "No, she did not fall overboard." Then I walked through the open door and they were all glad to see me. A friend of mine was there and invited me to the bar to have a drink, where he told me that a guard had falsely informed people that a woman artist had fallen overboard.

From then on, I stuck closely to my friends, especially to Nevel. Nevel had still not made up his mind whether to go to the South Pacific with me or not. We just made the most of the present and I did not mention the South Pacific to him any more. He had a ticket to Melbourne which gave us time. As we got closer to Perth, Australia, the ships laws relaxed, which took the frustration off people's morale and one could hear laughter again. When we arrived there, Nevel and I went with our friends straight to the wild part of the park. We were all overwhelmed to see green again. What incredible trees! I have never heard such a multitude of birds sing. This was paradise and we stayed there until the Galileo was ready to leave.

I had planned to leave but they kept everyone's' passports if they had a ticket to travel further than Perth. Probably an Australian law made to prevent people from getting into their country without a visa. Every country's bureaucrats believe that everyone wants to live in theirs. This seems a paradox to me. When we got back on board, the passports (our personal property), were given back to us. This was the only port where they kept our passports during the time spent on shore.

Galileo's new destination was Melbourne. Without warning, Nevel acted strangely. He cooled off and I couldn't understand why. I was very depressed and my artist friend John Boyce saw the state I was in and asked, "Who is your favorite artist?" I told him, "Picasso", as I never had been so impressed by any painting, as I had been by Guernica. I even dreamed about the screaming people and horses in full color the night after I had seen the original and the pre-sketches of it. John told me, "Picasso had more guts than you, he changed a situation if he did not like it." That made me think. I thought long and hard. Then I went to look for Nevel and insisted that he tell me why he felt the way he did. He then told me, that he had received a phone call from his separated wife and that he was considering going back to her. Anyway, she was coming to meet him in Melbourne. At last I could understand, which made it easier to get over him. Never in my life had I split up anyone's relationship and I did not intend to do so now or ever. Nevel and I stayed friends.

On the high sea again, one of the ships cooks had a fight with his girlfriend, who told one of my friends that the free red wine in the carafes served at dinner, did not have even 1 grape in it but was made out of a chemical powder supplied by Ciba Geigy which was mixed with water. The so-called wine didn't taste good and I drank it rarely. I preferred a cold beer to that terrible stuff. This was too much. In Galileo's advertising brochure, it was written that the WINE came free with the meal of your choice. I complained to the waiter, but could not get a response, so I told everyone around me about it. Most of the reactions were "One can get drunk from it and it's free." They did not care that it was chemical and drank it just the same.

The next evening, "International night" was celebrated on the ship. All classes could mix. Passengers could access the 1st, 2nd and 3rd class. The captain came into all classes to greet the people. When he was in the 2nd class dining room, I went up to him and told him about the fraud of giving us chemicals, instead of wine. He said, if I kept my mouth shut, he would see to it that I would be given a bottle of good wine at every dinner. From then on, the waiter opened a bottle of fine wine in front of me every evening. The captain kept his promise and I kept mine. I let the others fight for their own rights. I keep on fighting for mine and think of my friends.

The weather worsened and the sea was choppy. It looked grey outside. More and more people were missing in the dining room. People's complexions looked from white to green. Some were queued up in front of toilets. Then it got calmer again. Even the bars, library, chapel, cinema and boutiques were almost deserted. Then, the sea calmed and the clouds started to disappear. Everything went back to normal, or as much as that was possible on board that horrible ship. I am glad I never get seasick.

By the time we entered Melbourne the sun was shining. It was Sunday and I looked forward to stepping on land again. I walked alone into town. It looked a bit like a small town in the U.S.A. Everything was closed. Not even a coffee shop was open. There was hardly any traffic or people to be seen. It felt like being all alone in a ghost town. Not even a dog was to be seen. I tried to be happy by sitting on a bench in the shade of a tree and started to stuff my beautiful meerschaum pipe. A gorgeous man's head was carved on the snow white bowl. I lit my pipe very carefully and slowly sucked the whiskey flavored tobacco through the elegant alabaster mouthpiece. I enjoyed every puff of it. That relaxed me. I shook out the finished tobacco and walked around for some time while studying all the details of the buildings in town until it was time to not miss the boat.

There was a waiting room in the port. I went inside and saw Nevel with his wife. I wanted to say goodbye to him as a friend. He acted as if I was a total stranger and pretended not to recognize me. I left it at that and walked away to go on board the Galileo where I asked myself, " What did I see in such a coward?" Now I had cooled off. I was looking for my ideal man again.

I will never give up hope. Men are like dogs, if you lose one you will only get over the grief if you take another.

I had made the decision to travel on Galileo until Auckland NZ. My ticket was valid to there. My close friends Champalou his wife Carol and Helen, an artist who was Champalou's sister, were travelling with Galileo to New Zealand as I was. Too bad, John my artist friend left the ship. I will never forget him. Galileo was on route from Melbourne to Sydney. I was glad not to have to share my cabin with anyone. The cabin across from mine was also unoccupied so I had the shower and toilet to myself. At last, I had some of the much-needed privacy, even though the cabin was noisy. Every day I was thinking of my beautiful daughters Alexa and Julie and hoping they were well and happy.

Maya B.

I went to dinner and enjoyed the fight for my meal with the fine wine. Then I went to sit at the long table in the ships bar. After every port, there were some new friends occupying the chairs of those who had left. We all had very interesting multilingual times there with much laughter. If we did not like the newcomers, we made sure they would stay at the bar and did not desire to be at what we called, 'Our table' any more. We were like a happy family and did not tolerate prudery, prejudice or small talk. We did not mind eccentrics and many of us could identify with them. There was never any fighting even in the hottest discussions between us. Times at our table were very important to us all.

I was invited by a group of my homosexual friends to try opium in a cabin. I was curious since it was my first time. The only thing I knew about opium, was from the opium suppositories that were given to me as the only pain killer that worked during the migraine attacks I had since childhood, until 32 years of age. From then on, I only had migraines when I was partying too much and it was my own fault. I did not remember any negative effects from the drug.

We handed the pipe around. All of a sudden, I felt very sad and lonely. My friends all had each other and I was missing a partner more than anything. I left the cabin and noticed that all the people followed a pattern. They all followed each other up one stairway and down the other. I tried to see what would happen if I would go up where they came down and visa versa. The pattern got confused and some started to adapt to mine by following me. This amused me, until I got tired of it and left the stairway to get some fresh air out in the cockpit. I was more aware of my loneliness than ever. Was this the effect of opium? I did not like this aspect of it but found it interesting. If I ever smoke it again, I hope it would be together with a partner.

I would not recommend trying opium to anyone. As I got older, I stopped smoking and drinking alcohol except for the occasional glass of wine at dinner. I feel so much better and have the strength and energy to do everything I want and like to do.

It went cloudy and grey, the waves got stronger and it turned into stormy weather. Galileo's stabilizers did not seem to work. The dining room where I was eating a big dinner was almost empty. My table was in the middle of the room. The tables on both sides started to slide from side to side. The wind speed must have been about force twelve. It made the last storm seem like nothing. Salt water that the sea threw on deck started to leak through the doors and swamped over the floor into the dining room. People suffered from seasickness, clenching handkerchiefs in front of their mouths. They looked like death warmed over. After the main course, I ate the dessert. Then I wanted to take the stairway and it sucked me right to the top floor. I went down the stairs and was faster than before. Then I went up again and it did the same thing, sucked me right up the stairs. This was very amusing. Galileo was between Tasmania and the Australian east coast. Finally, the storm ceased. The people started to come out of their cabins again. The floors were mopped and the toilets cleaned. Even the dining room started to liven up again. I was really looking forward to being in Sydney.

We soon arrived and the weather was wonderful. It was warm. I stepped on land and this time they did not take the passports off us. I saw the Sydney Opera House in the distance and headed straight for it. What a sight! The marvelous architecture of this building amazed me. I walked around and sat on the steps. Then I lit my pipe and smoked it.

When I went inside a man started to follow me. He caught up with me and introduced himself. He was one of the Directors of the Sydney Opera House. He invited me to his office for a drink. I went with him. He introduced his staff to me and asked me to sit down. One of the secretaries went to the adjoining room and came back, pushing a trolley with different bottles of spirits on it. I liked a whisky so she filled a glass with ice and poured whisky over it. The Director chose the same. We pushed the glasses together and said, "Cheers." He asked me if I would like him to show me the opera house. I said, "Yes, I would like that very much." After the drink we went to see the whole opera house and what the tourists never will get to see. He showed me what the highest roof peaks looked like from underneath. We climbed right under the fascinating, steep roof. Then, he asked if he could invite me to dinner to a very good Italian restaurant. I gladly accepted.

Galileo's crew was striking again so I had plenty of time. Since it was too early to eat, he showed me the infamous Kings Cross. He took me into a sex shop but I was not impressed by the variety of artificial phalluses in different colors and textures etc. Only the real thing will do for me and it has to be part of a real man. The chemistry has also to be right. We looked at the area with all the pimps and whores. Then we went to a bar and had a drink before we went to the Italian restaurant. The director ordered hors d'oeuvres and a white wine with it. Then he ordered the specialty, juicy fillet steaks with herb butter and condiments and an excellent red wine. This was followed by a tiramisu for dessert , a very fine cognac, coffee and delicate biscuits. It was all very delicious and I had a great time. He seemed to enjoy it as well. He asked for the bill and searched in his pocket for his wallet. He could not find it and said, "Uh, I left my wallet at home, could you pay for it? I will give it back to you tomorrow." I said, "No problem" and was glad that they accepted a traveler's check. He took me back to the Galileo, where I went to sleep until it was time to meet him at his office.

He was not there and when I asked his secretary, she said that he had not come in since he had gone on vacation. I had trusted this rich man and was disappointed. It was a hell of a big bill, but I had had a good time. Maybe he did it because I had refused to be a one night stand. The time in Sydney passed rapidly and I hoped to spend more time in Australia to get to know the wildlife and people, especially the Maori which I discuss later on in this book.

It was time to go back to Galileo if I did not want to miss crossing the Tasman Sea. Happy, that I still did not have to share my cabin and bathroom, I showered and changed into my Arab dress. Then I went to our table to see my friends and share the stories of our adventures on land. There was a new guest there. He was a young Maori who loved to laugh. We all loved him. He was very good-natured but full of revolution.

He would go up to prudish looking older ladies and ask them "How do you say, "I want to fuck you" in your language"? We stood there listening to the answers. Some gave him a look of disgust while others just smiled. One lady told him that fuck is a bad word and should not be said, while another explained to him that his way of speaking was no way to woo a woman. Another tried to slap him. This amused me. Sometime later at our table, not completely sober, he claimed to have a tattoo on his penis. Someone said that would hurt too much to have done, so the young Maori opened his fly and showed every one the tattoo on his penis. I saw not just the tattoo but that he had something like a piece of fishing line inserted on his foreskin. I asked him what this was, so he told me that the tattooist had insisted that this would give special pleasure to the woman while having sexual intercourse. Some of those tattooists sell them anything.

A musician friend came up to me and said "Maya, I need your help. I had to smuggle my girlfriend on board, who had to escape from the abuse of her father. We are very much in love and will get off the ship in Auckland. She needs a place to rest. Will you help us, please?" He knew that I had my cabin all to myself. I told him, of course I will help you. She can stay in my cabin and sleep in the bottom bunk. You can visit her there. He was in a third class cabin that he had to share with five other men and it was no place to smuggle a woman in. She settled in and I felt sorry for her to have to be confined in the noisy cabin for the whole trip to Auckland.

It worked well, since the crew knocked on the door before they entered the cabin to make the bed and clean the cabin and the bathroom, which was located in the middle of the two rooms. While my cabin was being cleaned, she moved through the bathroom into the opposite, empty cabin. The crew came like clockwork at the same time every day and never spotted her. My friends and I went to the dining room with a doggy bag and brought her breakfast, lunch and dinner (more than she could eat) and I fed the rest to the fish.

The boyfriend would visit her every day, while I rather preferred to be elsewhere on Galileo. They were really so much in love. When we arrived in Auckland he took her of the ship through first class and fortunately through the customs without a problem. New Zealanders and Australians could visit each other's countries without having to have a visa.

In Auckland NZ

When I finally turned my back on the Galileo for good and entered the building to go through customs, a bureaucrat looked at my passport and gave me only a three week visa, instead of a three month one. I knew that as a Swiss citizen, my right by law was to have a three month visa.

When I pointed that out to the arrogant man, he still refused to give me more then three weeks. I asked the bureauc-rat! why he denied me my rights and he said, "We don't like hippies here." I was wearing my freshly washed T shirt and clean jeans but they had been repaired. My hair was natural and long but had been shampooed that morning. My body and fingernails were clean also. I told him, "I am a serious artist and have respect for people who live positively in our threatened environment." It still did not change this prejudiced fanatic's mind and I gave up for the time being and walked out of the building with my trolley and the three weeks permission to stay in New Zealand.

A handsome man walked toward me. He said, "Are you Maya B. the artist?" and I said, "Yes." He told me, that he was working in a travel agency in town and had heard of my troubles on Galileo. He was there to help me. So I went with him to his mother's house, where she had cooked a wonderful seafood dinner. I was given a room. After a few days, I had rested up very well and did not want to impose any longer. They handed me their phone number to call them if I should need them and told me that I was welcome to come back. I will never forget the kindness and generosity of those people.

I went from one office to another and another and another. I got tired and called a friend who had given me his telephone number while in Switzerland and lived in a commune in Auckland. He said, "No way do you go to a hotel, we have plenty of room for you to stay with us for as long as you want to." I was glad he had invited me and he came to pick me up with his car to bring me to the commune. The beautiful old house was owned by my friend and five other people. They invited me to a delicious dinner with all fresh vegetables right from their garden. The lamb's meat came from their farm and the tea was sweetened with honey. Three people in the commune were part of twenty who owned a farm. Since they worked in Auckland, they only went there on weekends and during vacations. They chose the one who had studied agriculture to live there permanently with his family, while all the others had their own sheds to sleep in, away from the farmhouse but all could use the community dining and sitting rooms if they wanted. This worked out well. The farmer was in charge of the sheep, the ram and the chickens. The musicians had built a big dome out of aluminum triangles covered with plastic. Every month they gave a concert and invested their earnings in the farm, which they part-owned. I was invited there as well and really enjoyed staying at the large, beautiful farm in the spectacular countryside surrounded by sheep, while the ram stood proudly on the top of the hill. His horns framed the side of his head in spiral form. What a lovely place.

Most huts stood individually on the edge of, or just in, the forest. All the villages around had Maori names. The hills looked a light but saturated green with a clear blue sky and cumulus clouds above. The sea was not far. I really admired the twenty peace-loving friends who had come together and realized the dream of a farm. It just showed me what can be achieved, if positive thinking people who wish each other well, get together.

Back in Auckland, I still stayed at the commune but was

searching every day, for some way to get my visa extended to three months. The authorities sent me from office to office, until I was back at the first office again. By then, I was furious. They gave me the run around for nothing. I had sacrificed more than a week of my valuable time visiting the offices and waiting on chairs or benches until an office person would take the time to see me. They often puffed cigarettes while drinking coffee. I was forced to use my valuable time for something that unjustly was not taken care of by an arrogant official who was acting illegally when I entered N. Z. I exploded and told them what I thought. It helped! Now, I was finally given a three month visa.

    I could now take a break and use my time in Auckland the way I liked. While strolling around town, a young man came up to me. He asked me, if I had time to answer a question. I said, "What would you like to know?" and he replied to please come with him into the building behind him where there was a form with a few questions on it. Inside, he handed me the form and I read the first 'question' which said, "You are not perfect." This is why you can learn from us, how to be successful - in perfect mentally and physically health. I handed him back the form and told him that I believed, that there was nothing wrong with me physically or mentally and said that I could not benefit from L. Ron Hubbard's books, since he was trying to convince me that there was something wrong with me and walked out.

    After a few days recuperating and enjoying Auckland and some of the people, I started to try and get a visa for a south pacific island. I applied for Tonga, Fiji and Samoa and planned to travel to the first Island which would issue the visa. I went back to the office for several days in succession but to no avail. I would not be given a visa without a ticket to the island I wanted to go to. Then, I tried to get a ticket to fly to Tonga, Fiji or Samoa, but was not able get one without a visa! What a dilemma!

    I wrote a letter to the King of Tonga, asking him for a permit for Tonga, since it was my life's goal to be there. I waited for a reply but did not get one. Then I called my friend who was working in a travel agency. He sold me a ticket to Tonga, for which I was very grateful but I hope he did not get in trouble for selling it to me. With the ticket, I eventually was able to get a visa and with it the much needed freedom to go where it pulled me. I was very fond of the people from the commune and many other friends, so I felt a bit sad to have to leave them but happy and excited to be able to explore more of the world.

Maybe somehow, somewhere, sometime, we will meet again-

Finally a Flight to Tonga

I took a one way flight from Auckland to Tonga. It was great to be free of bureaucracy. Or was I? When I arrived, they gave me three weeks to stay. This time, I just tried to make the best of my time on this beautiful island and I was enjoying living in the present without letting anything bother or worry me.

I checked into a reasonably priced guest house by the sea. There was my room but also a communal kitchen and bathroom. Tonga reminded me a bit of a Caribbean island, but less touristy and more natural and the sea looked very clean. Where there was water, everything grew.

There was a hospital but unfortunately the missionaries had been there and there were churches. The people were very friendly and liked contact. I told them that religion was evil and a brainwash to keep them from thinking. An official came to the guest house and threatened me, "One more word about religion and you are dead." I kept my mouth shut.

A German guy with a bad limp came to the guest house and introduced himself as Heinz. He seemed very nice and I was very lonely and longed to share the beauty of Tonga with someone. He was living in Tonga and showed me around. Then he invited me to a good restaurant.

The King's son, a nice-looking young man, was sitting at one of the tables next to us. After we finished the delicious dinner, a group of musicians started to play dance music. Heinz, the man with the limp asked me to dance. It surprised me that Heinz could dance even with his handicap. We stopped dancing only to have the occasional drink and then danced closer and closer. I found him so congenial that I did not let his limp bother me. I would have preferred the handsome King's son but hid my feelings so as not to risk being turned down.

Funny, the reaction caused by the lack of confidence! Sometimes my self-confidence was very strong. I guess the struggle for the visas had weakened me.

When Heinz asked me to live with him, I accepted. We were happy together for at least two weeks. Then he decided to give a party for his friends to get to know me. I was impressed with his friends. They liked me as well. The topics of the conversations were very interesting and I found the people very knowledgeable and intelligent. There was a lot of laughter as well. I was having a marvelous time when, suddenly, Heinz hit me straight in the face. Shocked, I demanded to know the reason for this brutal action, which horrified his friends as well. He said, "You are the center of the conversation and I cannot say anything." It was jealousy and I went to pack my bag and left the house and that damned cripple for good. The guests followed.

Amongst them were two businessmen, who lived on Samoa and asked me to go with them. One of them bought me a ticket and said that he could deduct it and gave it to me. The same man, who sold Coca Cola in the South Pacific, offered me his house to live in since he had to go on business trips.

Arriving in Samoa, he took me to his beautiful house, which was fitted with all comforts plus a maid to take care of it and do the cooking. He told me to make myself at home and let me stay in the guest room. The next day, he left on business and I went to paint a seascape, oil on canvas, to give him on his return in gratitude for his friendship and generosity. My friend returned from his business trip. He loved the painting I did for him.

I did not want to stay in a place where the natives were forced to be in their homes by 10 p.m. while the tourists had a 24 hr. free run of the island. This is bound to cause problems or worse, maybe even a civil war.

I decided to fly to American Samoa where I believed I would be permitted to stay with my American Passport. On arrival, I was asked, "How long do you intend to stay?" and I replied, handing my passport to him, "As long as I like." He then stamped five days in it and I said, "Don't I have the right to stay here more then five days as an American Citizen?" He said you would have if you had a job. I said, "Give me any job." He replied you have to have a work permit before you get here. This was another blow.

I started to walk along the beach until I got to a small village. I saw a little girl who was crying. I went up to the child and asked her if she would like an ice cream. She cheered up instantly and asked if I would buy one for her friend as well. I said, "Of course" and she called a little boy over. All three of us liked the ice cream. I missed my children and only got over the pain of not being with them by treating every child as if it was mine, in the hope that everyone would treat Alexa and Julie also with love and kindness.

The little girl insisted that I accompany her to her home. I went with her and she took me to a 'fally', a hut built on stilts made of bamboo and coconut fiber, decorated with woven papyrus leaves on the walls inside. There were four steps, the length of the fally in front of it. The fally could be opened all around to catch the breeze. The girl's family greeted me, invited me to come in and asked me to sit down. There was no furniture, but only the bamboo mats on the floor. Behind a partition made of woven bamboo, were rolled up mats. They used them to roll themselves up in for sleeping (as we do with a blanket).

The main structure of the fally was made with coconut palm trunks and bamboo poles artfully tied together with strings made from coconut fiber or papyrus. They did not use a single nail or screw for the beautiful and very breezy construction, ideal for the climate. I sat down and knew that it was an insult to show the soles of the feet, so I sat in a yoga position. I enjoyed the shade and the breeze, while being sheltered from the enormous heat outside. The girls' mother brought me a glass of freshly- squeezed juice and the girl gave me some food, served in a banana leaf. When I tried to give them some money, they refused to take it. I stayed a bit with them and then went to find a guest house.

After a good rest, I went to a pub where there was a wild sound reaching my ears. The heat had been building up and up until it became almost unbearable, even for most of the natives. Night had fallen and even so the heat did not let off. The fire dance was about to start at the pub. It was celebrated by young, eligible native men who were starting to dance holding lit torches. They only wore short grass skirts and flowers on their good-looking, energetic bodies. The vibrant light of their torches shone and sparkled on the healthy skins of the men, whose perspiration on top of the coconut oil looked like beads, rubbed on to enhance their active muscles. They danced with temperament and tremendous passion on top of the bar and tables. The drums got faster and louder and they moved wildly and ecstatically. I was fascinated by them and the mood in the room and stayed until the end.

When I was leaving, I had to dodge the men who were following me but I managed to get safely back to the guesthouse. My room was on the second floor and I felt safe there. The heat made it impossible to sleep. I finally managed to get some sleep, until I was awakened by a tremendous thunderstorm early in the morning.

I jumped out of bed and hurried to the window to see the rain coming down like a waterfall. The heat reached temperatures I had never known before. I ran downstairs and stood under the strong pressure of the rain drumming a cool massage on my hot skin. I did not care about being naked. I had just experienced the first South Pacific tropical rainstorm. It felt so good. Refreshed, I walked up the stairs to my room and got dressed. Then, I walked to the town.

Puddles of water had formed on the football field. Children

slid through them on their bellies laughing with joy. Everyone I saw had a relaxed face and looked happy. All were in a good mood.

Flowers started to grow everywhere and nature increased its sensuality and lushness. New scents emerged from the mature flowers and herbs. I went to the market to see what kind of fish, fruit and other things were sold. Then, I spent the day swimming and sightseeing.

In the evening, I went to a bar. The barmaid was the famous "Rosy." She was a "mahu", a huge, heavy homosexual who believes himself to be a woman. Rosy was one of those boys who was raised like a girl to make peace between fighting villages. I liked Rosy. If some bloke tried to get fresh with her, she swung her handbag at him and with one blow, he would fall to his knees. She was very strong and her arms looked like those of a prize fighter. However, she was very elegantly dressed and her hair and make-up looked very theatrical.

The next day, I met a sailor who worked on a tanker. He came from Hawaii and was leaving in two days to go back home. He invited me to dinner and asked me to marry him and let him take me to Hawaii, where he would see to it that I could stay. It pulled me to Tahiti and I told him that I could not accept his generous offer since we had to go separate ways but we agreed to spend the short but precious time together. When they threw me out of the guest house for smuggling him into my room, we spent the night on the tanker in his cabin. All his friends knew about it but no one was a tell tale. They all felt happy for us. In the morning, they served us a gigantic breakfast. My friend and I stayed together having a marvelous time until I had to go before the ship was leaving. He gave me three cartons of cigarettes, a bottle of vodka and some 'Buddha stick'.

Since the time of my permission to stay on the island was coming toward the end, I went to buy a ticket to Tahiti. I looked for an island where I could survive from nature and so far, all three islands I had visited were too civilized. They all had churches, schools, boutiques, restaurants and hotels. At the ticket counter they refused to sell me a ticket, unless I also bought a flight from the destination. I chose a flight back to Switzerland. I did not have enough money left to do so and it was not safe to go back before the two years had passed. I was in a dilemma. I was sad that my friend had to leave and felt homesick for my children and depressions knocked me right down.

I went for a swim. After getting some strength from being in the sun, I was still depressed. If I stayed here, the bureaucrats would find me and maybe put me in jail which I could not risk. I asked myself, "What am I going to do?" I had to do something that would make me happy.

I went into town and found a posh restaurant. I told myself that something that would maybe cheer me out of being depressed would be to eat a lobster. When I entered the restaurant, I asked "Do you have a lobster and the waiter replied, "No, but we have other seafood." I said "That won't do," and proceeded to the next good looking place which had a lobster. The waiter led me to a table and handed me the menu.

My father had told me, that trout and champagne or white wine were good against depressions. There was no trout so I looked forward to eating a lobster with white wine. I was very lonely and confused, not knowing what to do and where to go. The waiter filled my glass and placed the beautifully decorated lobster in front of me. While I forced myself to eat, the tears I tried to hold back rolled over my cheeks onto the plate.

A man sitting at a table next to mine said, "Why are you so sad? " I asked him to join me at my table and told him that my time to stay here was almost up and they would not sell me a one-way ticket to any south pacific island without one from there back to Switzerland, which I could not afford. He said, "Go to Tahiti, they like artists there. If they refuse to sell you a one-way ticket, give them my card and tell them to call me." The man was a French Consul who gave me hope and cheered me up immediately.

The next day, I went to buy a one-way ticket to Tahiti. They refused, until I gave them the card from the French Consul. They called him and then the ticket was sold to me. I could hardly believe how lucky I was. I will never forget that wonderful man. Thanks to people like him and my hard head, I could realize my dreams. I found out that

Only those who live let you live.

I sat in the airplane heading for Tahiti and had a really good feeling, thinking of my many friends and those who had helped me along my way. I would do anything I could for them as well. Too bad so many people have been dehumanized by too much bureaucracy. The excuse, "We are only doing our jobs", was what the Nazis said while they pushed 6 million people into the gas chambers and should absolutely not be justified any longer. I was glued to the window and Tahiti was in sight. I was very excited, even though it looked as if civilization had caught up here as well.

After the aircraft landed, I walked through customs. My passport was looked at but not stamped. I got through without a problem. This restored my confidence in the human race again. Papeete was quite a large city. Many shops, businesses, hotels and restaurants were to be seen. I walked around and went to the edge of town near the beach, where I found a guest house. It was a bit costly, but less than one in town. I checked in, placed my luggage and its trolley in the room and went to the beach.

After a good swim, I walked up and down on the madly beautiful beach framed by coconut palms (my favorite trees). I could not help sometimes worrying what I would do when my money ran out. Just then, Champaloo and Carol walked up to me on the nearly empty beach and said "Maya, what are you doing here?" while I was just about to ask my best friends from the Galileo the same question. I had believed them to be in New Caledonia. They said, they did not like it in New Caledonia and that was why they had decided to come to Tahiti. I told them that I had just checked into the guest house and they said, "No way, Maya, are you living there. We have an extra room for you to stay as long as you wish." I told them that I had already paid for the night and would sleep there but gladly accepted their invitation to move in the next day.

I went to enjoy some night life in town and entered a shady looking bar in Papeete. The men outnumbered the women by at least three times. There was bound to be some action in there! I ordered a drink and paid for it right away, enabling me to get out quickly if there was trouble. It felt tense and electric. While I sipped my drink, two men started to insult each other. One of them broke the neck of a beer bottle off, on the edge of the bar. The other one as well. Some others joined them and I made my escape to the beach near the guest house.

I laid on the beach and watched the sky with an enormous number of stars, which looked so clear that I almost felt able to touch them. When I spotted a comet, I made a wish for Alexa, Julie and my parents to be happy and healthy. Then, I went to sleep in the guest house.

After breakfast, Champaloo and Carol picked me up and took me out to a hill side in the wilder part of Tahiti, to their hut. The hut was made of wood. The windows had no glass and the shutters, hinged on top, were held open from the bottom by a stick that could open to three different settings from the frame to the shutters. This is simple and works well. Carol showed me to my room. It was furnished with a mattress and a chair and I had my army sleeping bag, with the waterproof cover, which I had bought so I would be independent. It came in handy now. It was so hot that I slept on top of it. The hut was surrounded with bananas and other plants. There were a few other huts scattered around with Tahitians living in them but no tourists.

Some dogs and chickens were free to roam around the huts and nature was lush and rich but every bit of land was owned by someone. My friends rented it for a very reasonable price but refused to take anything from me. At least they let me share the food with them. I felt so happy being there with them, Helen and the daughter, that I found enough peace to be able to paint again. We had serious discussions and a lot of fun. Champaloo wanted to find work as a plumber and needed to buy tools. He asked me, if I would lend him some money and I gave him what he needed without telling him that I was afraid to run out.

It was three weeks since I had arrived here and felt like moving on again. My next goal, was to visit the Island of Moorea. I asked Champaloo to pay me back when he was able to do so and I would send them my address as soon as I had one, or if there was a post office they could reach me at poste restante. I carefully packed my newest painting, a nude standing firmly on the ground, in the shape of a pyramid looking to the sky, oil on canvas, on my trolley. We said goodbye and I went to the port to take a powerboat to Moorea.

At the Bar Where I met Peter

The crossing from Tahiti to Moorea was wonderful. The boat held no more than about ten people. It was fascinating to see Moorea coming into focus. As we entered the natural harbor toward Pago Pago, the turquoise water was so clear that we could see the bottom and the fish swimming in it. It was so beautiful, that I had to hold back my tears of joy. I had been to the Caribbean and other beautiful islands but never had I seen a place so spectacular and gorgeous as this one. The natural port was surrounded with coconut palms and other trees and plants and mountains. One mountain had a hole and you could see right through it. The scent of frangipani flowers and other delicious perfumes was in the air.

Beautiful people wore only a 'pareo' over their healthy tanned skin and were decorated by flowers in their hair and around their necks. They all had blue- black and shiny hair. The woman's hair was often so long that they could sit on it. The 'pareo' is a piece of rectangular cotton cloth wrapped around the body and fastened in a knot to hold it over the chest for the woman and tied around the waist for men. They come in very cheerful colors, with native prints of flowers on them in yellow, orange, red, blue or turquoise. It was all so sensuous and real.

When I stepped on land, I headed straight along the coconut

plantation to the hotel bar in Pago Pago. This place was entirely built out of local palm, papyrus and bamboo. I booked a room for the night not caring how long my money would last and after a drink I took the local bus to ride around the island. This was my sort of place. I wished to stay here. I realized by now that the world was too civilized to allow me to survive from nature alone, but it would be easier here since I did not have to wear winter clothes or use heating. There were coconuts, fruit and fish here.

When I got back to Pago Pago, I was many impressions richer and I knew where I wanted to stop and explore the next time around. I had met many Tahitians in the bus but had to use pantomime since they spoke only Tahitian, until I realized that most of them speak French.

As I ordered dinner to celebrate my arrival here, a young Tahitian man asked me to sit at his table. I was glad to accept since I hate to eat alone and went to sit at his table. The beautifully decorated fish and salad arrived at the same time as his meal. We ate together, him telling me all about himself and that he worked in his family's pineapple plantation that supplied the French army in Mururoa as well as others, with the fruit. Marcel was his name and I fell in love with his flashing dark eyes and his beautiful body and could hardly wait to take this natural man to my room. The minute we were in the room, he grabbed me and it took just a few seconds before he exploded. Then, he went straight into the shower, then toward the door. He said, "See you tomorrow, I have to get back to my wife." The next day he came while I ate breakfast, so I told him that I would never have made love to him (he never gave me the time to do so anyway), if I had known that he was a married man. However, I would let him do me a favor by finding me a place to live that did not cost too much rent. I was cured of the idea that natural men would not be brainwashed.

He showed me someone who could help me. I went to ask the owner for the place available for rent. He showed me a hut in a coconut plantation, a few meters from the sea front of the natural harbor. Plus, it was only minutes from Pago-Pago, my favorite hotel restaurant-bar, a bus stop and where I could find the Chinese grocery shop. The man charged me $5 a month. I paid him right away and moved in. The door was broken and could not be locked. It was filthy.

I walked to the Chinese shop and bought a broom made of coconut fibers, dish washing liquid, some food, instant coffee, sugar in a jar and some other things. I was so happy to have a paid roof over my head and started to clean the place up. A water pipe came up to a post outside and there was a bucket there as well. There was no bed or closet, no toilet, no fridge, no sink, telephone or electricity. I had a flash light, lighter, Swiss army knife and the army sleeping bag with me. The hut consisted of one room. A roof, the wooden floor, a door, a window without glass and the broken door. Even so, I felt rich to have it. After it was clean, I rolled out my sleeping bag and boiled water on the old gas cooker for a cup of coffee. I stirred the coffee powder and sugar in the cup and went outside to urinate.

When I came back in, the table and the sugar jar where crawling with ants right down to the bottom. I emptied the whole kg of sugar away from the hut. I had forgotten to close the lid on the jar. The sense of smell the ants are equipped with amazed me and those Tahitian ants were faster than the others I had studied. This incident took no more than three minutes.

I walked to the seafront and went for a swim, then lay under a palm tree. Then, I ate some of the food I had stored in an old cabinet with fine, rusty mosquito netting that hung on the ceiling beam. Afterwards, I asked myself why I was so lonely in such a magic place, to the point that not even painting made sense since the outcome would have been as depressing as I felt. I only ate so that I wouldn't starve. The pleasure was gone from my life. I recognized the fact, that nothing made sense to me without a life partner and I lay on top of my sleeping bag and finally fell asleep. At about midnight, I had to chase two native men away by threatening them with a big stick, I had put next to the broken door. They ran and I felt strong enough to survive until I should find love again.

The next day, I managed to find the "Van der Heide" art gallery in Moorea. The owner accepted my paintings for exhibition and I did not have to carry them with me or worry about their safety any longer. When I stayed in Papeete Tahiti, my work was shown at the "Winkler" gallery.

When I got back to the hut, I wanted to throw out the termite-eaten table and reached under the table top to slide it outside from my living space. I was attacked by a swarm of angry hornets that had built a nest under it. Seven of them stung me and I walked fast but as calmly as it was possible under the circumstance, to the road and headed toward Pago Pago.

Luckily, a man in a beach buggy stopped and picked me up. He drove me straight to the medical station. A doctor came from Tahiti once a week and I was lucky again, that I had been stung on the day he was there. When I entered the clinic, I shouted in panic that I had been stung by seven hornets. Two patients were there before me but he told them to wait and took me as an emergency. He gave me an intravenous injection of antihistamine and another of calcium while his Dachshund slept peacefully under his desk. I am a dog lover and found this great. Then, the doctor checked my heart and blood pressure and told me to wait while he treated the other two patients. Later, he checked me over again and gave me some pills to take in case I had problems and reminded me not to drink alcohol.

I left and on the way to my new home, I stopped at the hotel bar and ordered a fruit juice. Then I asked the bartender if he knew of a place I could rent, where the door could be locked. He pointed to a place where a Swiss man was renting out bungalows. I walked over to the main house of the Swiss man and asked him if he had a free bungalow I could rent. He said, "Yes." and showed me a pretty place. He and his Tahitian wife had built the bungalows by themselves and each had a small kitchen, toilet, bathroom, electricity and water and two rooms.

The price sounded a bit high for me, so the Swiss man told me that there was an American vet here who wanted to find someone to share his bungalow and split the rent. "Would you be interested in that?" I replied, "If I like him, then yes." He took me to his bungalow and introduced us and left with the words, "Let me know what you are going to do." The vet asked me to come in. He offered me a drink so I chose a cup of coffee. We got on well and I found him very congenial. I went to the hut for the last time, to retrieve my trolley and returned to him to accept and share the rent with him. This man was as lonely as I was, so the obvious happened, we shared the bedroom.

At first, we were very happy with the arrangement but there was not much passion between us. Intellectually, we understood each other. We were invited to coffee by the Swiss man and his wife. He asked me how long I would stay and I said "I don't know yet but staying here is no problem. As my passport was not stamped, I will be able to live here as long as I like."

After a couple of weeks, the Swiss man and I had a fight. He had chickens and some dogs came into the unfenced land to chase his chickens. None of them were killed. He then took a gun and shot all the dogs dead. I said, "Are you too cheap to build a fence?" I was shocked and called him a brutal bastard which was the mildest of expressions to shout at that criminal who killed man's best friends. He then threw me out of the bungalow, which suited me well since I could not warm up to the vet, who while in a bad mood, destroyed innocent plants and flowers which turned me right off.

I took my trolley and went to the bar. While I sipped a drink and smoked a cigarette, I told myself, that the next man in my life would love animals, flowers, plants and trees.

4 SAILING WITH PETER

Peter Bremer-Kamp

A handsome man came in and also sat at the bar. He waited until I finished my drink and asked me, if he could order a drink for me. I accepted and we started a conversation. Peter was a sailor from Australia and had built his own sailing craft, a twelve meter long double-ended sloop designed by Alan Payne. I had admired his yacht *'Scheherazade',* which was swinging free at anchor in the natural port.

Peter was tall and well built with sun tanned skin. His brown hair was streaked almost white blond from the sun and framed his beautiful face with curls. His eyes were the same as mine, green-brown with just a few very tiny specks of yellow. When he looked me in the eyes, I felt that feeling and spark again. I knew instantly, that he was going to be my next life partner. It felt as if I had known him all my life and we loved being together from the first moment we met. We spent the rest of the day together and when he asked me, if I would like to come with him on board 'Scheherazade', I accepted with pleasure.

We walked from the hotel bar through Pago Pago and then to his dinghy on the beach. He untied the rope from the tree and pushed it into the water. We got in and Peter rowed us out to his boat. He held the dinghy close to the hull and I climbed on deck. He said, "Welcome aboard Scheherazade" and I sat in the cockpit while he opened the cabin door, the hatch and portholes. There was an awning stretched over the cockpit to provide very welcome shade. I enjoyed the gentle sea breeze. The rigging made music on the mast. I liked the free movement of Scheherazade. It reminded me a bit of the times on boats in the Caribbean, just in an even more beautiful and spectacular surrounding. Peter then told me that he had a crewmember from New Zealand who sailed with him, but was with friends on the shore for some time.

Peter Bremer-Kamp, by Maya B.

    He opened a bottle of vodka and made some fresh fruit juice to mix the drinks then he cut some cabbage, onions, carrots, ginger, garlic, raisins and apple pieces into a bowl and mixed it with spices, vinegar and oil. He mixed what he called, 'The ship's salad' and, voila! Dinner was ready. We had a bottle of wine with it. The ship's salad tasted delicious.

    Peter opened a coconut and started to grind it. He squeezed it through a clean tea towel into a bowl and said, "Here is the cream for our coffee." The kettle of water started to sing and Peter went inside the cabin. The tone of the whistle became lower and slower and stopped as he poured the boiling water into the cup, over the coffee powder. As he came up the companion way, I took the two cups from him and placed them on a free surface. He then poured an equal part of the coconut cream into the coffee. It tasted wonderful.

We told each other about our experiences and spoke for a long time. Then we made passionate love and fell asleep in each other's arms.

After we ate breakfast, he said to me, "You can't stay here or Ross, my crewmember, will be upset. His words struck me, as if he had hit me. I did not expect that! I said "Take me to the shore." He did. When I got out of the dinghy, I walked away from Peter without turning back. I was depressed. Maybe I should have taken my father's well-meaning advice, that if I wanted a man really badly, I should let him fight for me. This was not possible to do since to me,

reality cannot hide feelings or play games even if it means getting hurt sometimes unless it is a matter of life or death.

I was in the "What am I going to do, where am I going to go?" situation again. After a long walk, I lay on the beach to meditate. Then I walked to the next village and spotted a very romantic Victorian guest house and restaurant called "Chez Pauline."

It was Christmas evening and I entered the gorgeous tropical garden of the restaurant next to the house. 'Pauline' was in a foul mood and yelled rudely at me, "What do you want?" A lump formed in my throat and tears escaped from my eyes. I asked, "Do you have a room and can I have something to eat?" She showed me to a room on the first floor. It had no door, just an orange curtain with hibiscus printed on it and was tied in a knot. As she stepped down the stairs, she yelled, "Come down and I will let you know if the cook wants to work tonight."

I untied the knot in the piece of cloth hanging in the door for privacy. I put my baggage and the trolley under the bed and had a good cry. Then I washed my face with cold water and went to sit in the dining room. It was the first time in my life that I had spent

Christmas alone.

Morea Tahiti
Feltpen
A 4
1976

    I was sitting lonely in the dining room, when a cat came in and sat on my lap. I was happy to have that sweet animal for company. Then a dog walked up to me and greeted me like a long-lost friend, which cheered me up instantly and made the loneliness and hurt go away. I was petting and talking to both animals when Pauline came in fiercely with something to eat and threw the plate so hard in front of me, that I wondered why it did not spill the food or crack the dish which spiraled around on the bottom of its rim, slowing down until it stopped in silence.

    Then she grabbed a broom and chased the cat and dog out, shutting the door behind them whilst cursing and swearing. Thinking that she might have had a lovers' quarrel, I tried to cheer her up and said, "What a beautiful place you have here" and she yelled sarcastically, "Do you think so?" and stormed off into the kitchen behind the dining room.

    I was so sad and was thinking of Alexa and Julie, my

beautiful daughters of whom I am so proud, and I was so crushed that we could not be together except in thoughts. I was also thinking of my parents and Keys, our dog. I tried not to think about Peter but did not succeed. After I ate some of the food and just sat there drinking the wine, the cook, an older Chinese man, came in and asked me if I liked the food. I said "Yes." He asked, if I would like to celebrate Christmas with them in the kitchen. They were full of emotion, laughing and crying and when I had a few glasses, I enjoyed and even understood them. Then I got very tired and went to my room.

It was hot and I slept with the window open. A noise woke me up which made me jump to the window, where I managed to shut it just as one of the men pulled his fingers away from the sill. Then another tried to get into my room by coming up the steps and I threw him with a judo movement down the steps. It was quiet for a while, before they started to pester me again. I did not get too much sleep and could hardly wait until about 9 a.m. when someone was awake so I could finally checkout.

Then my headache drove me to swim in the sea, which cleared my head. It was Christmas day and I walked to the street, where I decided to stop the next vehicle that came along.

Hungry, I picked up a coconut. After much work I succeeded pulling the husk partly open with the help of my Swiss army knife. Looking at it intently, I found three spots on its shell. I pulled the bottle opener out of the knife and drilled into two spots. This way, I had access to the delicious and sweet coconut milk. Then like magic, another coconut fell from the tree onto the point of a fence and presented itself ready to pull all the way open down to the cracked shell, which I could then pry open. I ate the whole nut.

There was no traffic and just when I almost started to panic again, a man on a Vespa stopped. He was a male nurse who was going in the direction of Pao Pao. I sat on the back of his scooter. About 1 km before Pao Pao, Peter and his friend Ross came toward us and Peter yelled "STOP!" He said, "Maya, where have you been? I looked everywhere for you." It felt as if a big stone had fallen off my heart and I was so glad to see him again. I got off the scooter and thanked the man who had picked me up. Then Peter and I flew into each other's arms. We both had tears of emotion to fight with. Ross left to go and meet some of his friends.

We went to the yacht. When Peter asked me to live with him on Scheherazade, I said, "Are you absolutely certain that you want me to live with you? What about Ross, what is he going to do?" Peter said, "Yes, I am sure and if Ross does not like it, too bad for him." So I stayed with Peter.

On Scheherazade

Life was great with Peter. I was very happy on Scheherazade, but Ross was very hard to live with. I could understand his jealousy. He felt that I had taken his friend away from him, since they had been sailing together since Scheherazade was launched two years previously. Peter had asked him to sail with him since he was not sure if he could do it alone. They had sailed straight from Sydney Australia to the Tuamotos, since Peter had heard that on one island, there were supposed to be many healthy and beautiful young women, fed on coconut and fish which caused them to be obsessed with sex.

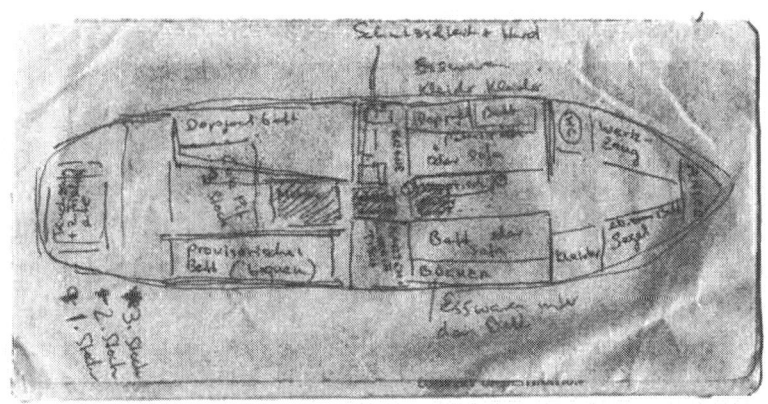

The layout of Scheherazade

There were hardly any men left, since most them were fishermen who were drowned at sea. After having heard this story, they had plotted the way to the Tuamotos. Full of expectations, Peter and Ross arrived there to find out that most young people had left and that the ones living there were mostly old women and millions of flies. They escaped the flies as fast as they could and, disillusioned, set sail for Tahiti. As far as Ross was concerned, I was an intruder. Most of his time was spent ashore since he was working as a bartender and had friends in Moorea.

Peter had just finished some carpentry work in a newly-built hotel and his time was his own. He had originally studied to be a master builder and had worked in Sydney as a building inspector. That had given him the financial means and spare time to build Scheherazade. I started to paint and sketch again. Peter and I did everything together.

When Ross came on board, I was as nice as I could be under the circumstances. Ross ignored me completely. I said to him, "Look here, I won't leave Peter because of you and you want to get back to New Zealand so you will stay on board as well. I don't ask you to like me but the least we can do, is to be nice to each other." He said, "I don't see why I should be nice to you." This was the last thing we said to each other. I was now ignoring him as well.

Peter and I sailed out of the harbor to catch some fish for a few days. If we had too many, I would can them or he would dip the fish (cut in small pieces) into soya sauce and hung them in the rigging to dry.

Reef scene, by Maya B.

This method turned them into a ready snack. I did not have much money left and told Peter about it. He said that it did not matter and that he was sure we could make it together. We tried to save on food by getting fallen coconuts, which were free to be taken by anyone. While Peter repaired the electrics on Scheherazade, I went to the Chinese shop to get some things like rice etc. and made a detour off the road when I spotted a mango tree with fruit on it.

I had picked a fallen fruit off the grass, when a Tahitian man said, "Don't take that one." I said I am sorry, I did not know that this tree belonged to you, I will pay for the fruit." He then said, "The ones on the floor are for the animals. Don't take them. If you only take the ripe ones from the tree there will be plenty of them for everyone." He then picked about ten ripe mangoes off the tree and handed them to me. When I offered to pay for them, he just laughed and walked away without taking the money. What a delicious dessert after a raw fish dinner (a Tahitian specialty). The fresh, raw fish was skinned, de-boned and cut up into small cubes, marinated for an hour in lemon or lime juice. After the fish was marinated and turned white in color, the marinade was poured off and slices of onions, cucumber and tomatoes were added. Then coconut cream, salt and pepper turned the dish into a delicate delight. The bush lemons grew in the mountains, where we also found coffee beans, wild rice and chili peppers. Tahiti was French, which some natives welcomed, but others did not.

I went shopping in Pao Pao. A French policeman came up to me. He said that I was not permitted to stay here and wanted to take me to the police station. I told him I had to be back since the owner of "Scheherazade" expected me back. He said, "Under the condition that you take all your clothes off and swim out to that boat." He was pointing at Scheherazade. He took my passport away from me and told me to be in the police station in the afternoon. The ugly policeman's face was grimaced by his stupid grin. I took of my pareo and bikini bottom. I put the bikini bottom into my handbag and wrapped it into the pareo, which I tied to my head to swim about 600 meters with my head above water back to Peter. He asked me, "What happened?" and when I told him he was outraged.

He swam to the shore (since the dinghy was there) and caught up with the policeman. He told him that I was his official crewmember and that he would complain about the illegal way he had treated me, so that he would lose his job for certain. The policeman excused himself and told Peter, that the Swiss man who had rented out the bungalows, had told him that I was in the country illegally. (The Swiss man had used the confidential information about my passport not being stamped against me, as revenge since his murdering of the dogs had upset me to explosion.) The policeman returned my passport, which was my property and which he had no right to take away under Swiss law in the first place. The next day we both went to the police station where Peter registered me as his official crewmember on the yacht Scheherazade.

It was hot and we were too lazy to row to the shore and fill the canisters with fresh tap water so we used the rest of the tank water on board only for drinking. The clouds grew denser and denser and came closer and closer toward us. I put all the empty pots along both sides of the cabin to be filled with the expected rainwater. Then all three of us stood on the cabin top, stripped naked and rubbed shampoo on our salty hair and bodies and waited until the clouds would burst and rinse the soap off. They did not do that, but instead changed direction and made room for the sun again. We used the remainder in the tank to rinse the soap off ourselves and rowed onshore to fill the jerry cans with tap water to top up Scheherazade's built-in tanks. I used my baggage trolley to carry two twenty-liter jerry cans to the dinghy while Peter and Ross carried them by hand. From then on, we never shampooed again before we were actually standing under water. The bursts of rain can be heavy but also very short and extremely pleasant since they feel like a massage from heaven and cool you down from the sometimes almost unbearable tropical heat. On the boat we could always jump into the salt water every time we felt too hot.

The Russian Dentist in Moorea

Since Peter was working, I was curious to discover more of the island and started walking on the only road that surrounded Moorea. It was another gorgeous day and the crystal clear sea invited me to swim in the inviting blue water to cool off from time to time. My front tooth hurt and a dip felt good. Feeling a bit tired and in pain, I stopped the only car I had seen since I left that morning. It was just my luck, that the man in the car picking me up, was a Russian dentist.

I told him that I am an artist, and asked him if he would fix my hurting tooth in exchange for a painting. He said, "Yes, if I like your paintings." We drove to the natural port and I rowed out to Scheherazade, where I picked up two landscapes and rowed back to show them to him. He liked them so much that he wanted both. I gave them to him and he took me to his home.

There he introduced me to his son, a boy of about 10 years, showed me his romantic place and then to an outside room, with green paint blistering and partly peeling off from its moist thick walls. Inside stood an old drill, which reminded me of one I had seen when I was a little child. A device was attached to it, which had to be started by pumping a foot pedal. I was invited to sit in an old, partly rusty dentists chair and he examined my tooth and proceeded to put a rough-looking needle into the antique looking drill.

Then he left and returned with a bottle of rum and two glasses. He said, "I'm sorry I don't have an anesthetic and it is really going to hurt, so I suggest you drink a glass of rum. I had better have one as well, so my hand will be steady." He poured two generous helpings from the bottle and handed me one with the words, "Cheers." We downed them in one go and he said, "We had better have another." We did, and I was relaxed while he stepped on the pedal. It sounded PF-Pf-pf-puff and stopped so he stepped it on again. This time it worked and he took the drill with a really steady hand. He repaired my front tooth with the same color patch as my tooth.

By that time, the dentist's son had prepared a soup and I was invited to eat with them. We spoke French together. Their place was very wild and romantic. I asked the dentist, if he always told people that it would hurt. He said, "The first Tahitian who came to have a tooth repaired asked him if it would hurt and he told him, "Not much." He fixed his tooth and the great big, strong Tahitian got up and flattened him with his fist. Asking the patient why he did this, he responded, "You said hurt not much, hurt very much." and walked out. "This is why I always tell the truth now." the dentist told me. My tooth was repaired so well, that it is still in my mouth to this day!

On Scheherazade in Morea
Feltpen
A 3
1976

Plan to Sail around the World

Peter's mother, Eileen, had written that she would come and see us and would like us to pick her up in Papeete. We sailed in the beautiful clear, turquoise sea toward Tahiti in a gentle swell and saw a glorious spectacular sunset. I said "Peter, look how gorgeous that sunset is!" He said, "Just like toilet paper." He was not very romantic but had a marvelous sense of humor at times. But I did not appreciate it just at that moment. We celebrated the sunset on deck of the boat with a single mixed drink. This was a ritual we had. Otherwise, we would not drink alcohol while sailing. I took down the mainsail and tied it to the boom, then stepped on shore with the lines while Peter was at the helm. Ross was staying in Moorea with friends. I was glad of that, since his silent treatment made me sad.

Peter's mother arrived from a vacation in the U.S.A. Eileen and I understood each other right away. She was an original who liked to laugh. Peter thought she was the best mother in the world. She was a very generous thinking, tolerant and uncomplicated woman. We took her to Scheherazade where she took over the bunk bed which Ross had previously occupied, while we slept on the sofa bed as usual.

The next day, we took the local bus to go around the island. Peter's mother had tears in her eyes. She told us that she and Peter's father had spent their honeymoon on Tahiti and that it used to be so beautiful and natural then and that the enormous change depressed her. To Peter and I it was still beautiful since we could not compare it as she did. The beach with the black sand was still the same and the native people were not brainwashed by missionaries anymore.

Peter had written to his mother, while she was in the U.S.A. asking her to bring him a tattooing machine and colors, since many of the men in Moorea wished to be tattooed with the less painful machine, instead of the torture caused by shark's teeth, then rubbed with ashes to blacken it. Some had bled to death for their passion for tattoos. Eileen hated to buy it but did it for Peter, who hoped to make an income with the machine. Peter had never tattooed before and practiced on grapefruits until he felt secure enough.

We enjoyed Eileen's visit with us and in a couple of weeks, we met many sailors and spent much time hearing their fascinating stories of adventures. We were invited on board their ships, met in pubs, did a lot of sightseeing, laid on the beach and went swimming. The time for Eileen to fly back home to Sydney soon came.

Peter and I sailed back to Moorea. We became good friends with some of the native people. They were eager to find out if Peter had received the tattoo machine. They invited us to celebrate with them. Every important event was celebrated by starting up the 'umu', a sort of pressure cooker. First they dug a hole in the sand at the beach. Then they laid lava rocks or an iron chain in it. Then straw, sticks and wood were added and lit. When the stones or the iron chain were glowing hot, they choked the fire by putting a wet burlap sack over it. On top they laid the pork, chicken and/or the fish, green papayas, manioc, etc. on it, then it was covered with another piece of burlap and sand. The food in the umu stayed covered in the ground for an hour.

During that time they started roasting a pig. Some played a string instrument made from coconut shell and fishing line. They sang and danced. They did so also at the two hotels for the tourists but not with the same passion as they showed amongst themselves and for the very few lucky ones who were invited to join them. Before we left for Scheherazade, some said that they wanted to be tattooed the next day. Peter told them he had not done it before but they still wanted it.

The next day Marcel showed up by swimming out to the boat. He was the one who had suggested to Peter to get hold of a tattoo machine. Peter told him he would do it at his own risk but was not going to charge him. He disinfected his skin and I designed a tattoo of Marcel's choice on his arms but told him to think about it if he really wanted it. He said that he had been thinking long enough to know.

He really liked my design and Peter hesitated to press the needle into his skin until I told him to pretend that Marcel's skin was a grape fruit. Peter did a really professional job and Marcel was very brave and was very proud of his multi-colored tattoo. The next day a few more native men wished to be tattooed for payment.

Before Peter and I had met, he had invited the village people on board Scheherazade and motored out of the harbor toward a reef where he anchored the ship so they could go fishing, which they loved to do. From then on, they showered us with pineapples, bananas, papayas, mangos and coconuts etc.

One of the men discovered Peter's guitar on board and asked if he could play it. He loved to play so much, that later he would often swim out to Scheherazade where he came on board and made music in the cockpit. We loved to listen to him accompanying the instrument with his full voice.

I received my mail with a letter from Champalou. He was

writing to thank me for the loan which had permitted him to get the tools he needed. He had found work as a plumber, which had made it possible for him to save up enough money and pay me back. Not only was he sending me back what I had given him but added 10 % to it, which I found very noble of him. I was broke and very relieved. It just arrived like magic when I really needed it. We kept in contact by writing to each other.

One day Champalou and Carol wrote that he was homesick for Paris where he had friends and it was easier for him get work. Carol added that she liked to stay in the South Pacific and that she had accepted a job at the Club Mediterrane in Moorea. I was sad that Champalou was leaving and that they would go their separate ways but pleased to see Carol in Moorea. Peter and I went to see her in the Club Med.

She showed us around and told us to go and eat in the dining room where buffets and shelves were covered with delicious food. There were all sorts of fresh breads, lobsters, crabs, oysters, fish, chicken, pork, beef, a variety of salads, vegetables, cheeses, cakes, ice cream and other desserts etc. all at an open buffet. So much food was left over when we and all the guests had finished eating, that all the leftover food was thrown out. Peter and I pretended to be tourists and put on sunglasses. Peter had his camera hung over his chest. We walked into the Club Med. to eat that way about twice a week.

One day we had just chosen all our favorite delicacies and were carrying them on our plates towards the table where jugs of wine had been placed, when someone came and took the full plates away from us. I volunteered to pay but they threw us out. Carol would bring us whole roasts and chickens etc. to Scheherazade. This permitted Peter to keep enough of his hard-earned cash for travelling and allowed Carol to save some of the food from being thrown out.

She was getting very homesick for Champalou and had earned enough to get back to Paris. Champalou was very happy at her decision. Helen, Champalou's sister, later married a young

Tahitian and lived with her daughter and new husband in Papeete.

Peter asked me, "Where should we sail to?" I said, "Let's sail around the world." He said, "Okay, let's make plans." First, we plotted how to stop at many islands before our arrival in Auckland, New Zealand where we would take Ross home to stay. Meanwhile, Peter was expecting a visit from his best friends. They would arrive in Tahiti. Peter gave our Moorean friend, who used to swim out to Scheherazade, his guitar as a going-away present. Then we went to the Van der Heide Gallery to pick up my paintings.

I was thrilled that the owner of the gallery bought my original painting of the nude (oil on canvas) that I had painted at my friend's house in Tahiti. Not just was I glad for it to have a safe place but I could use the financial help with the cost of living. It also inspired me to continue creating in the knowledge that someone loves and appreciates my work.

Our Tahitian friends brought us a whole roasted suckling pig and five whole stalks of bananas and other food for our trip. Ross looked forward to sailing again, even though he still ignored me. I raised the mainsail while Peter turned the tiller in the direction toward Tahiti. Ross manicured his fingernails for hours in resentment at Peter using my help in sailing Scheherazade, which used to be his pleasure, before I lived as Peter's woman and partner.

When we arrived in Tahiti, he was not seen near the yacht until we were leaving Scheherazade to pick up Peter's friends. I had violent headaches and bad cramps in my stomach but wanted to go with Peter. His friends had rented a bungalow, where I was invited to stay while they went to eat at a posh restaurant.

Maya B.

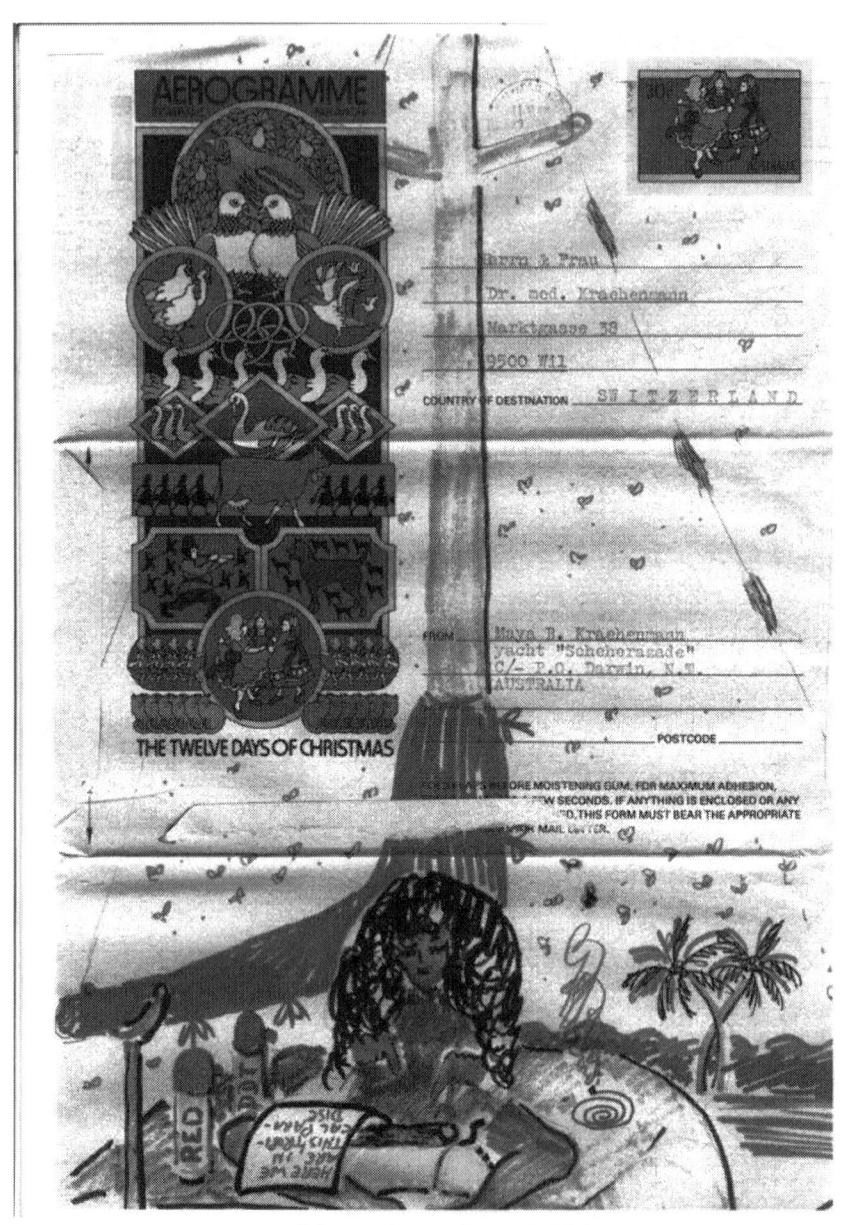

A letter home from Tahiti

Glad to be alone since I could not pull myself together, I dragged my aching body to the toilet to vomit and fell unconscious from raging pain. Now, I wished for Peter to be with me. By the time he and his friends got back, I had a high fever and felt miserably ill and too weak to speak or move from the almost unbearable, pulsating pain. I slept there with Peter in the bed next to me, while his friends rented another room and I almost wished to be dead, just to not have to suffer any longer. The painkillers did not help and only made me sicker.

The next day, I felt a little better and moved back on board. I finally started to get over it and the skin on the palms of my hands and soles of my feet were peeling, a sign that I was one of the lucky 50 % of people who had survived DENGUE FEVER. I had lost about half of my hair as a result of this illness but fortunately, most of it grew back and I recovered well.

Maupiti, Taha'a

Lucky and happy to be alive and well again, I fished for each of the three of us, two fish each of everyone's choice. Fish were so abundant, that I was pulling the line with the cheese on it away from those we did not want for our breakfast. After an hour, I had caught six fish, I had two flounders and Peter and Ross two each of what they wished for. I could not kill them and Ross would do that. Peter cleaned them and I cooked them. Then we went shopping for rice, potatoes, onions, sugar, spices, eggs, canned tuna, toilet paper, etc. for our voyage. We filled the water tank and canisters, checked the sails and all concerning Scheherazade. Then we went to the pharmacy and bought antibiotics for the top and bottom of the body, antihistamine, pain killers, cough medicine, antacids and bandages in case we should need them and checked that all the tools were in their place and everything in order.

It can cost your life and sink the yacht if you don't find the tool you need in an emergency or during a storm. When all things loose were tied down, the voyage plotted on the sea chart and the weather and wind were right we were ready to sail. Maupiti was our next goal.

Approaching Maupiti on Yacht Scheherazade
Feltpen
A 3
1977

The wind was ideal. I was surprised how much Peter dared to angle Scheherazade. What a yacht! I loved this sloop. Peter taught me everything about her except the motor and navigation. Navigation he would not teach me, since with that knowledge I could earn a living on another yacht as a navigator. I loved him and wanted to stay with him and found his attitude ridiculous. For the time being, I was grateful to be able to take a sight with the sextant and take my turn at the tiller.

Ross was on the tiller while Peter and I did the cooking together. I chopped something and he chopped something and he or I asked the other, "Do you think this ingredient, herb or spice tastes good in this dish?" We tried it out and created some really delicious dishes. We hardly ever failed. Once I remember that the tomatoes did not go with the apples and carrots in the salad so the next time we left the tomatoes out for another dish. Just as we had eaten, Maupiti could be made out on the horizon.

Not A Boring Moment

The wind speed increased and clouds formed. The weather made sailing choppy and kind of rough. I reefed the mainsail while Ross pulled down the jib. Peter steered the yacht and suggested to us what he would like to have done. He never said, "Do that." Instead, he would say, "Can you do this?" Usually he discussed what and why he wanted to do things and if one of us came up with a better answer, which was very rare, he would accept it.

By this time, we were almost at the narrow entrance of the reef surrounding Maupiti. We did not want to risk losing Scheherazade by going through there. The large white breakers scared us all.

I sat with my sketchbook on my lap on top of the cabin and drew Maupiti on the page. I wished to remember Maupiti, even if it was too dangerous to get to.

After a while, the weather cleared and the wind and sea calmed. We spotted some birds of paradise. We then decided to go on to Taha'a. Another spectacular sunset turned the sky into a magic spectacle in gold and nuances of orange and red, while we sailed toward the beach in Taha'a still in daylight and dropped the anchor.

Peter dove into the clear water with a mask and snorkel to make sure the anchor had set properly and Scheherazade was secure. We put the sails away, threw the dingy into the water and rowed on shore. We were the only travellers on the tiny island. People came out from the bushes and trees toward us. Their huts were shining through the jungle and they greeted us, happy to have us stop at their island. They said, it was rare that anyone stopped there.

They invited us to their homes and were very nice. Even this tiny island had a church on it. It was lush and green.

I designed a hair grip to be made from the coconut shells that Peter had polished. He sawed them into four pieces and I designed a butterfly to put on them. We made holes in each one that made it possible to fasten them through the hair with a piece of bamboo. Peter melted the design with hot steel over the lit burner on the stove, into the shell. We hoped to sell about thirty of them in Bora Bora. I had painted over ten miniature landscapes during our time in Moorea amongst other creations, which I hoped to be able to sell at the hotel Bora Bora.

From Taha'a, Bora Bora could be seen which made sailing in those islands so easy and pleasurable. It did not require much navigation but reefs had to be watched to avoid running aground. We were at risk in shallow waters and so one of us would look out over the bow for reefs and shout back, "Reef straight ahead," "Port" or " Starboard."

In Tahiti we had run onto a reef. Peter and I dove into the water to inspect the hull. I was amazed that the only damage was a scratch in the paint. Scheherazade' s hull was built with 5 mm thick steel. Had she been a wooden yacht, the damage could have caused a hole. I loved Scheherazade almost as much as Peter. And that was very much! We were the only yacht in Taha'a. After we had explored the island, we said goodbye to our newly made friends and set sail for Bora Bora.

Bora Bora

The sail from Taha'a to Bora Bora was wonderful. I really felt as if I was in paradise. Ross still ignored me but I did not let it hurt me any longer. Peter and I were so happy that he must have felt like the fifth wheel on a car. Peter and I had decided to let him help more with the sailing which he enjoyed. Unfortunately, it did not change his attitude towards me.

After we cooked, I wanted to empty the contents of the bucket with the biodegradable matter overboard. But the potato and carrot peels, banana skins, eggshells and coffee grounds, etc. landed on Ross' head, who was taking his turn at the tiller. I had thrown them accidentally into the wind (on the wrong side of the cockpit). All the food remains looked so funny on his disgusted and angry face, that with the best of intentions, I could not prevent myself from laughing.

Peter took the tiller while Ross and I pulled the sails down. We were motoring through the opening of the reef into the bay of Bora Bora, where we dropped the anchor.

**Bora-Bora
Ink and Feltpen
A 4
1977**

Then we put the sails in their bags and put everything in their place and in order, opened the portholes and hatch to let the breeze through and lowered the dingy over the side. We fastened the awning over the boat for shade before we rowed ashore.

The beauty of Bora Bora was magical. Ross found some friends and Peter and I had time to ourselves all day. We met other sailors and some people on shore who became our friends. There was only one hotel, the Hotel Bora Bora. Peter and I took our hand-crafted hair pins to show the woman at the hotel boutique. She bought them right away. She also exhibited ten of my miniature landscapes in oil. Later, she bought them from me.

Her husband then said to me, "You must not be such a good artist or your prices would be higher." This made me think. From then on, I raised the value of my paintings at once and with each exhibition. The people who bought them from me deserved to have their investment grow.

We met a couple in Bora Bora. The man was from Germany and his wife was a beautiful native woman. They made a living with their black coral culture. I had just learned that coral could be farmed, which cheered me up since I feared that red and black coral was dying out. The man from the coral farm visited us on his sailboard. He loved to sit with us in the cockpit.

While he spent some time on Scheherazade, he lent us the sailboard to sail around in the bay. At first, I would fall into the water just after I managed to stand on the board. Then I was able go straight but fell off every time I turned. Then I finally got the hang of it and thoroughly enjoyed it, until I was warned that those waters were infested with sharks.

Peter was not afraid of them, so I did not see the need to be frightened either. We rowed the dinghy to the reef, put on the lead belt, mask, snorkel and fins and went fishing. Peter had a self-built spear gun. He killed the fish he wanted straight through the brain each time, without making it suffer. Then he gave me the fish and I would swim to the dinghy to throw them in.

I painted a view of Bora Bora on board Scheherazade, which I later sold to the prison director in Port Sudan. We stayed in Bora Bora for several weeks.

I only wished, I could have shared my time in this beautiful part of the earth with my children and not only in the letters that we sent to each other which kept me going. I longed to have them in my arms again. I hoped that soon, I would be discovered as an excellent artist and did everything to improve myself and my paintings. Maybe then, I could send my daughters a ticket to join us. I believed that success was surely just around the corner. At least I never lost hope.

Only a mother who is forced to live apart from her children can know the nagging pain of longing to be with her own flesh and blood. Luckily, I had Peter. I hoped not to get depressed again for his sake and mine and it did not help anyway. It would only hurt me and those around me. I learned self-control and diverted my energy into drawing, painting and wood carving instead. I just hoped Alexa and Julie were happy. My parents loved them and told me that I had given them a new life's goal, by leaving them with them.

I cheered up and we started to explore Bora Bora's mountains, where I found some magic mushrooms growing on top of old sheep's excrement. I had never tasted them before and was very curious. I tried some but did not feel any effect so I picked some more and ate them. About fifteen minutes later, I started to hallucinate. Peter was angry with me, so I went to the beach where I saw a beautiful hand-crafted boat shelter with an outrigger sailing boat carved out of a tree trunk under it. It took me a lot of energy to immortalize this lovely sight in my sketchbook. Proud to have succeeded, in spite of the magic mushrooms, I walked from the shore upwards to where I spotted a pig.

First I felt sorry that the pig should be enclosed. It did not want my pity and showed me how it was able to entertain itself by shoving its food dish all around the pen. It glanced at me as if to say, "Look what I can do." I admired the way it spoke with its eyes and drew the interesting animal with newfound energy. An

American lady who begged me to sell the drawing to her, has it in her possession.

I longed to be sailing a step closer toward my loved ones and so the three of us prepared Scheherazade to continue on our voyage. We then said goodbye to our friends. We would meet some sailors again. We sailed in perfect weather and favorable winds toward Raiatea.

Raiatea

When we arrived at the small island of Raiatea, we tied Scheherazade to the pier and started to put the sails away and clean the yacht up ready to be closed up when we went on shore. This is always work that needs concentration for everything to go into its rightful place. It is very important to find all things aboard even at night.

While we were busy just doing this, the curious natives tried to get on board to greet us. I turned my CD of Pink Floyd, "Dark Side of the Moon" to full blast. The natives became frightened and backed off long enough for us to finish straightening up. Obviously they had never heard such sounds even though one of them was carrying a transistor radio that a sailor had given him. Then in curiosity to hear that sound, they came toward us again.

We then invited them on board and gave them something to drink. They invited us to their huts. Everyone was happy to see us. Their generosity was amazing. They wanted to share their food with us. Not many yachts stop there.

We also met someone who had settled there and who showed us around the Island. Another lush place with very friendly people, tropical plants and coconuts palms, it enriched us. We enjoyed the stay but felt like moving again, this time toward Rarotonga and the Cook Islands.

Peter was a bit worried about Scheherazade not having been out of the water for years. That is why we did not stay longer in most places because Peter's yacht had to be in a civilized country where there were materials and machines to help with the possible work. This would be New Zealand.

Raratonga

We arrived in the bay of Rarotonga and anchored Scheherazade next to an American yacht. Soon a couple of our previous friends anchored next to us in the bay. Some yachts were already there and the people on them also became our friends. Ross preferred to stay on board someone else's boat or on shore. That gave Peter and me some privacy. When Ross was with us, he still totally ignored me. I ignored him as well.

Peter and I took the dinghy and rowed to a place where we hoped to find some fish for dinner. After about a hour of being in the water without success, we rowed on shore and walked through the bushes into an open space. We saw a building with the words "Jehovah's Witnesses" on it. In front of it, we noticed some chickens and looked intently at each other. Peter said to me, "Are you thinking what I am thinking"? I said, "Yes but you have to kill it, then I will clean and cook it. Then he went to get his Gurkha knife out of the dinghy and returned to sneak up behind the chickens. He beheaded the slowest one in one blow. He grabbed it and put it in to his rucksack. We would not ever have taken a chicken or stolen any thing else from the natives, but the missionaries and other religious organizations came here to exploit the people. It rather amused us to get something back from them in return.

When we were back on board Scheherazade, I tried to pluck the headless chicken but it took me hours to do so. I had never done this before and did not know until later, that to immerse it in boiling water would have done the trick more easily. I cleaned the chicken, seasoned it and put it into the pressure cooker, added onions garlic and ginger and cooked it under pressure for an hour. It was getting dark so I fed the chicken giblets to the fish and threw the feathers in as well. Unfortunately they floated all over the bay but luckily for us, no one noticed.

When I opened the pressure cooker and tried to cut the chicken, it was so hard that I pressure-cooked it for another hour. Even then, it had the consistency of rubber but I tore it off the bones with all my strength and chopped it with the Chinese cleaver into minced chicken. Then we were able to eat it. I am sure that it must have been the oldest and toughest one of the bunch. It certainly lost its head for being the slowest.

The next day we were with our friends we had met in Tahiti. Stories of our experiences at sea and on land were exchanged and there was a lot of laughter.

When we got back to Scheherazade, we heard curses and swearing from the American yacht. The owner and his wife were fighting in a drunken state over who had pinched the whisky out of whose liquor cabinet. When the wife shouted, "You broke the lock on my cabinet, you bastard", he shouted even louder, "Here, have this bottle that you stole from mine!" and threw a full bottle of whisky at her. She ducked and the bottle fell overboard into the water. They continued their lovers' quarrel, until at least a half dozen bottles ended up in the bay.

Peter put on his snorkeling gear and went diving for them, handing them to me. He climbed back on board from where we watched the other sailors dive into the water to search for the bottles that we had already stored away.

The next day, the couple were kind of sober again. The husband had been a Navy officer who had his nose tip shot off in Vietnam. Peter and I gave a party on Scheherazade and we invited that couple and the sailors who went diving for the bottles in vain. We all laughed, as we drank the whisky and toasted "Peace!" to the couple who had the two liquor cabinets.

We stayed a few more days, saw new things, met more people and when the wind was ideal, we sailed on to the Cook Islands. Peter mounted a rubber ring in the stern rigging with a fishing line and put a hook on it with a small plastic octopus. When the ring stretched, Peter or Ross pulled the line in. Usually it was a

Tuna, Marlin, small Shark or a Dorado on it. They then cleaned it and I would cook it. Most times Peter and I both cooked it together when we could if Scheherazade did not need our attention. There was a wind vane that Peter had built to steer the boat but it only steered well at high speed. The rest of the time, one of us had to be at the tiller.

We had a wheat grinder on board to grind the wheat for our bread by hand. We then mixed it with eggs and a bit of beer and fried it since we did not have an oven. For the times we did not feel like cooking we had cabin bread, (dry bread and crackers) stored in a large tin can.

Sometimes when I was sailing, I longed to be on land and when I was on land I longed to be at sea. What I did not like, were the night shifts. To be woken up out of a deep sleep was not my thing but I found it only fair that I share the responsibility with Peter and Ross. I did not dislike Ross, even though his jealousy made him behave like a sulking child instead of an adult.

Cook Islands

We arrived well and happy at the Cook Islands. These islands are British territory. It looks pretty civilized with shops, hotels, restaurants etc. but still has beautiful tropical plants. Peter and I went diving. There was less sea life than in Tahiti or in some places along our voyage but we saw some fish, sea cucumber, coral and sea shells. Peter loved to dive or snorkel. I got to know so much about sea life with Peter who is an expert.

When I first saw a three-meter-diameter sting ray with a skin pattern like a leopard (in Tahiti), I was afraid and gave Peter the signal to go up. As soon as our heads were above water, I asked, "What was that?" He said, "That is a leopard sting ray. They are very curious and if we are lucky, he will come back and we can have a good look at him. Don't be scared, he will not attack us." We went down once more and had the chance to see this beautiful, rare animal again. Peter took the fear right out of me. He enriched my world by sharing his knowledge. He also taught me not to be afraid of reef sharks since they are very docile.

We met a sailor who had just come from Palmerston Island which we planned on visiting next. He said, "The people there need spark plugs for their outboard motors, aspirin and batteries." We went to buy those things and started on our trip to Palmerston Atoll.

On the way there, Ross slipped and almost fell overboard into the deep water but I grabbed him and pulled him into the cockpit. He was not glad enough to discontinue the silent treatment.

Palmerston Island

We dropped anchor before the reef in front of the island and while we got Scheherazade ready, we saw that men in two boats were rowing out to us. The first to arrive with their boat, were allowed by the Palmerston peoples' agreement to be our hosts. To make this understandable, I will fill you in on some of the history of those 64 inhabitants who have lived on the island for three generations.

In 1977, I was told by Papa John, (at 82 years-old, the oldest descendant living in Palmerston on the atoll and who was in charge of making all the important decisions), that about 450 members of the family had moved away because of the space problems and overcrowding. They had settled in New Zealand on the Cook archipelagos and in other places. Papa John was a cousin of the Queen of England. His great grandfather William, took over this island by pulling up the anchor of the one who had tried to claim the island before him.

He set his own anchor in place of it and claimed the then uninhabited island. William's goal in life, was to produce as many children as he was capable of. To do this, he married the two daughters of a chief. The two wives were jealous of each other, which split the family in two. They almost made peace again, until one man from the wife's family left the island to study religion. He returned as a priest and tried to convert both wives' families, to become obedient Catholics. He managed to convince most of his tribe to build him a church out of the wood from shipwrecks around Palmerston. The descendants of the other chief's daughter then commanded the influenced ones, to stay only on their half of the tiny atoll.

We were invited by the family of Papa John. They wanted us to sleep at their house but we insisted on sleeping every night on board Scheherazade. It was not safe enough to leave her unattended. If the wind should suddenly change, we would have to immediately head out to sea and make sure the yacht would not risk getting stranded on the dangerous reef, as quite a few ships had done already. We rowed in every day.

Papa John told us all about their history. All the people were so generous to us. We went fishing on the reef of a nearby atoll with all the young men of both families.

When it came to survival, they would all work together. The young men's chore was to catch fish for all the people on Palmerston for three days. They managed this by spearing the fish with prongs and with such accuracy, that it took them only 1 1/2 hours to catch enough fish. A prong is a piece of straight wood from a bush or tree, growing into three branches that are carved into very sharp points.

They cleaned the fish and then took them to their boat. Then, they returned to Palmerston where the fresh catch was strung up between two poles to dry. The ones to be cooked that day, were brought to each family's oldest daughter who was in charge of cooking and the household duties until she was married. Then the second daughter had to take over the tiresome task.

Papa John's family insisted that we eat lunch and dinner with them. The food was delicious, sometimes cooked in coconut juice and seasoned with bush lemon or chili.

They had some papaya and mangoes on the island. They also

had some chickens they had to cook, since for no reason, they knew, some would drop dead before they became one year old. They also had a pig. At that time no one knew, including some vets, that the reason for this, was because chickens and pigs should not be kept together.

A ship arrived once a year to exchange sugar, rice, coffee and other things they needed for copra and coconuts plus handicrafts. The people wove hats out of papyrus leaves and made a variety of beautiful things with seashells and coconut shells.

While the oldest daughter was cooking, I went to talk to her. She had no self-confidence and believed herself to be too ugly to be married. I told her that she would see her own beauty, if only she would believe in herself. I told her also, that those who told her she was ugly, only spoke about themselves and that many a man would be glad to be with her.

" No one speaks smarter than they are."

I promised to write the girl a letter and kept my promise. I also sent her an article I spotted on how to turn dried grass and leaves into earth, which should give her some attention when she shared it with her family.

To try and unite the two sides, I asked the young men from both families if they would like to learn self defense. They loved the idea and so I gave them Karate lessons.

When Sunday arrived, Papa John asked us, if we would like to go to church. We told him that we were not religious. He said that he wasn't either but it would be an interesting experience for us to see, even though he could not join us, and added, "The church is worth seeing." So we went to church.

What a unique and wonderful place! It was all built from boats' timbers, decorated with carvings and other beauty rescued from sunken wrecks and lovingly restored. We sat on the bench at the back so we could leave unnoticed if we had enough. Suddenly, the older women in the church started to sing so intensely and loudly that we almost had a shock. It was fascinating. They sang all the sorrows and joys out of their systems with such great passion. None of the three of us had ever experienced this before. The beautiful mahogany staircase and gorgeous railing up to the pulpit used to be part of a large and luxurious shipwreck. Everything had been rebuilt with love and dedication and artfully put together with the means that were available. Papa John was right. We would not have liked to miss this unique experience.

The day before we planned to continue our voyage, both tribes decided to celebrate a football (soccer) game party for us. First, football was played by all the youngsters and adults, female and male, of both sides who wished to. Peter and Ross joined them in the game as well.

Afterwards, we all walked to a field situated between the coconut palms and bushes. Our eyes feasted on the beautiful and mouth-watering sight of different foods- all displayed on banana leaves laid on the grass and decorated with tropical, intensely-perfumed flowers like frangipani, hibiscus and others. Different kinds of fish dishes, chicken, turtle, manioc, green papaya, vegetables and much more graced the banana leaves.

Everybody sat on the soft grass around the food. We were handed their highly treasured silver cutlery stamped with the name "Britannia" to eat from. Papa John told us, that the yacht visited them every year and everybody from the island was invited to board the Britannia while the people of the Britannia would spend the day on Palmerston. The cutlery had been given to the family as a gift.

We were also told that every baby born on Palmerston Island had his afterbirth buried with a coconut palm planted on top of it. This tree then belonged to that baby and to no one else. I found this such a good tradition and felt that every child born should have a tree planted and dedicated to him or her. We said goodbye to all our friends. Papa John had made a beautiful ashtray out of coconut shell for Peter and me, as a souvenir from him. We treasured it. I was given two artfully handcrafted bags, made of coconut and papyrus for my daughters and a hat for me, which was decorated with flowers. I will never forget those wonderful people. We all waved to each other until they got smaller and smaller and the island disappeared from view while Scheherazade was heading toward Niue Island.

Niue Island

Peter and I were very happy, even though Ross was still sulking and ignoring me. I did not care any longer since Peter made me so happy. I respected him for keeping his word to bring Ross back to New Zealand but we looked forward to sailing with just the two of us. Two is ideal but three is a crowd. Four is better then three but not ideal either and we had no desire to take someone else just to keep Ross company. He had our company as soon as he would accept us being together. On land he would go his own way for which we were very grateful.

Niue Island also had a dangerous reef and we had to anchor in front of it and row the dinghy through the opening to arrive at the beach. There was a small village consisting of a few houses and a road. I bought some postcards to send to my loved ones and then Peter and I went to explore some of the many caves on the other side of the village. The large pieces of lava rock had been smoothed down by wind and water over years, which made going barefoot on them enjoyable.

The caves were free to enter at your own risk and were spectacular and interesting. We were delighted to find some small but beautiful sandy beaches in romantic coves surrounded by bushes with not a person in sight. The water was clear all the way down to the sea flora and alive with sea creatures. It was enriching to watch the fish, crabs, shells, anemones etc. and delightful to swim and be there. The weather was hot and clear. Too bad, that we were forced to leave after only three days because the wind had changed. We sailed toward Vava'u, Tonga.

American Samoa

On the high sea in a strong wind, Scheherazade made an average of 10 knots. While we were heading toward Tonga, Peter and I celebrated our birthdays together as we crossed the datum line. My birthday was on July 12th before the date line and Peter's was on the 14th, just after the date line.

The next day, it was cloudy weather and while Peter was taking a sighting of the sun at the precise moment when it could be seen for just seconds and long enough to take a sight with the sextant, the precious instrument broke into two pieces which ended up in Peter's hands. It was the only sextant on board. This forced us to change the destination.

Instead of Tonga, we changed course for Samoa. Peter took the radio and moved the antenna toward the strongest signal which was American Samoa. During the night, we all took our turn in the cockpit. It was a dark, rough and not very pleasant night watch and a bit scary. Fortunately, we had no encounters with other ships. There was no radar reflector on Scheherazade but it would not have helped us anyway, since most vessels only have the radar turned on to enter a port. At dawn we could see the silhouette of Samoa. The weather was calmer and a few hours later we sailed into the harbor of Samoa and anchored.

Peter wrote a letter to his mother in Australia and asked her to send him a new plastic sextant as soon as possible and have the beautiful old brass sextant repaired for him. He put the broken one in a box, added the letter and sent it off together with three of my letters, one to each of my daughters and one to my parents. I sent all of them a postcard from all the places that had a post office. Our address for the next three months, was: Post restante, Yacht Scheherazade, Pago Pago, American Samoa, South Pacific.

The population consisted of Samoan people who looked more like Africans than (or) Maoris and Indians who had immigrated to the island afterwards. The Indians had shops and businesses while the others fished or had jobs. When I asked the original Samoan people, who invited us to join them at a 'Kava ceremony', what they thought of the Indians taking over government positions etc. , they replied, "If they give us a hard time, we will just eat them."

The Samoans used to be very feared cannibals. We met two brothers, (grown-ups) whose grandfather was still a cannibal. A 'Kava ceremony' is held, when a girl becomes eligible for marriage. The root of the Kava bush is pounded to a pulp in a large ceremonial wooden bowl with a big piece of wood. Then it is prepared by the eligible girl who squeezes the pulp through a cloth and mixes it with water. She serves it to all the men who are interested in her by handing them each a half shell of coconut with the white-beige liquid in it. If they want to drink the Kava, they clap their hands, receive the bowl, and drink it empty in one go.

There used to be no other women attending. The first time we were invited to a Kava ceremony was in Raiatea, where I was the first woman who was ever asked to attend. In Samoa, people of both sexes drink Kava, but then it is not a celebration any more. They produce an instant powder to mix with water whenever they want to. I don't like to drink it because it tastes like dirty dish water and doesn't have any effect except to make your lips numb.

In Samoa there were schools, churches, hotels etc. Some Samoans wore beautiful, hand printed tappa cloth around their waists. Many were tattooed with sharks' teeth even on the most tender parts of their bodies. Some of the natives wore western clothing. I exhibited my paintings at E & M. Maugaside Restaurant, Pago, Samoa in 1977.

African – Maori looking Samoans lived on the island. Peter and I were inseparable and went up to see the magnificent waterfall. On the way down, we walked through a coconut palm plantation. I was hungry. Peter carried his bag with important personal belongings, a Gurkha knife and a piece of cloth in it. He took out the cloth and wrapped it around his feet to climb the tall tree and to cut a coconut down for me. The Gurkha Knife was tucked in his belt. There were nuts lying on the ground but the young, unripe ones on the tree were filled with a jelly, which is very nutritious and is a mouth-watering, sweet-tasting delicacy.

Peter was just about to cut a coconut off, when a big muscular man with shiny black hair and fiery eyes walked up to me. He said, "What is this Palongy doing up the tree?" (Palongy is a slang word used for a white person by the natives.) Peter shouted down from the tree, "Sorry, my woman was hungry so I wanted to get a nut for her. He made a move to climb down when the big man said, "Go cut all those nuts down for her." Peter said, "We only want one," but the man insisted that he cut them all. So Peter reluctantly cut all four or five nuts and threw them on to the soft, sandy ground. He climbed down. The man said, "I have never seen a Palongy climb a coconut tree and did not know they where able to do this." He added, "Call me John, I am the oldest son of the highest chief of all the chiefs of all Samoan islands."

We became good friends and he showed us much of their culture. When we asked him, where he had learned to speak the English language so well, he told us that he and his brother had studied at a University in California. When Peter said to him, "You must have got those muscles by climbing the coconut trees," he replied, " I don't know how to climb the trees but I got those muscles by working out at a health club."

We met his very nice and handsome brother, who had studied medicine and we were invited by their parents to join them for dinner. They lived in a modern house that the American government had built for them. The U.S.A. needed their large natural harbor for their ships. The first man in space came down in his capsule into the Samoan natural harbor. We were told by John that the American government wanted the island as well and had offered the high chief a million dollars for it. They also said, that if they would not accept this offer, that they would take Samoa by force. So they had to move to one part of the island, while the U.S.A. took the other part.

I thought --- Is this the way, so-called 'civilized countries' operate --- while they condemn the hungry people for stealing a loaf of bread? Well, I do know some intelligent and civilized human beings in America as well and know it's not their fault. Unfortunately, the intelligent and positive thinking people who take responsibility for their own actions, are still in the minority all over our planet. It would be great if America and all the other countries had one of them as their leader. Maybe then, the utopia of world peace could come true.

    We got to know John and his brother really well. John had a crush on me but for me, there was only one man in the world and that was Peter. We were invited out again and one day, Peter told them of his tattooing machine. John, his brother and many of their friends wanted to be tattooed with the machine and not by sharks' teeth, which caused too many people to bleed to death. We were short of money so we agreed to do it. I drew the patterns they chose from the samples we had onto their skin with felt tip pen. Then I told them to sleep on it and come back the next day, if they still wanted it.

    They all came back and I poured them a glass of whisky, before Peter tattooed them. I almost got sick seeing their freshly tattooed skin swell up with beads of serum on the wound, but they were all very brave. They not only paid a modest price but showered us with gifts as well and invited us to their homes.

    A man showed up with an old tattoo with the name of his former friend (who had betrayed him) on his shoulder. He begged me to do something to help him. I designed an eagle on top of the name, holding a snake in his claws which pattern would hide the name. He loved it and when Peter had finished tattooing it, he had to hold back the tears of joy.

    From then on, I was called the tattoo artist. John wanted to set us up in a tattoo business on shore and have us live on their island but we wanted to continue our voyage instead.

    They asked Peter if he wanted to come and watch them playing football. He told them that he did not like football but that I loved it. I did not have the heart to tell them that football bored me, so they invited me to watch the 1 1/2 hour long game instead.

Peter received the new plastic sextant and was happy that its accuracy was very good. It took three months for his brass sextant to arrive with new silvering on the mirrors and very well repaired. Now we could make Scheherazade ready for the voyage. We filled the food cabinets and water tanks, inspected and repaired the sails etc.

The day before we started on the voyage to Vava'u, Tonga, John, his brother and friends threw a big going-away party for us. We all went to a beautiful bay to swim and then to their home where an incredible buffet of different delicious foods all beautifully decorated was awaiting us in the garden.

We said the sailors goodbye* to our friends on shore and to the ones on their yachts in the port. Before leaving, we visited the weather station to study the weather forecast sent from the balloons and from the barograph.

*Someday, sometime, somehow we hope to meet again.

Toward Tonga

We prepared Scheherazade for our sailing voyage toward Tonga. The awning was stored away, the dinghy was tied upside down over the front hatch and Peter had started to motor out of the harbor, while Ross tied up the anchor and I was hoisting the main sail, a job I really liked to do. To feel how the wind fills the sail and pulls the boat forward is such a pleasure. Peter turned off the motor and set the wind vane. What bliss to only hear the wind, the water and the seagulls! We all just relaxed.

Saved

I fell asleep on top of the cabin and woke up very thirsty. When I moved to the side of the cockpit, I nearly slipped into the water (still sleep drunk). Luckily, Ross reached up to catch me and prevented me from falling over board. I knew then, that he did not wish me to die, even though he still kept up his silent treatment toward me. Nevertheless, it cheered me up that he had stopped me from falling into the sea. Scheherazade was quite fast and even though I was able to swim like a fish, I might not have been able to catch up with her at the speed she was going. It also showed me, that Ross remembered me saving him previously from falling in. None of us were ever attached or wore a life vest. We had a rescue ring fastened to the stern.

About every two days we had a large fish on the line. We cooked fish in all sorts of different ways. Sometimes I longed for a steak.

Vava'u

I looked forward to getting to know a new Tongan island which I had heard was very beautiful and had not many tourists. I could also hardly wait to get my mail. The sail had been smooth and pleasant and we dropped anchor in the bay of Vava'u in front of the hotel. The water was not quite as transparent as in Tahiti but it was clean with plenty of sea life. The sunrises were beautiful and the sky looked spectacular at sundown.

The people were very friendly. They invited us to their huts and informed us about their way of life. The King of Tonga gave every eligible young man some acres of land. The men could choose their land. If there was no water, it would be delivered there according to their needs. They then had to pay a small amount in taxes to the king annually. This they were easily able to do, if they sold a bag of coconuts or whatever they decided to grow on their very fertile soil. Usually they would get married and have children. The eligible girls had no land given to them. The hospitals were free of charge for all Tongans.

I find this system very good. However, in my personal opinion, it would improve conditions if they were to give the females half of the land and the males the other half. (Birth control would be inevitable to keep that freedom for the people in the future as well. The catholic missionaries had already been there as well and this is, apart from Islam, the worst religion where freedom (not only for the woman) is concerned. Personal freedom for the people gets kissed goodbye by religious brainwash.

Still, the system seems to be the best I have seen so far and the people are content and even happy. I guess all the citizens of the world are in different stages of development. I met a wood carver, who sold a beautiful and intricately well done carving to a tourist for only 1 $. When I asked him why he sold this masterpiece so cheaply, he answered, "Tomorrow is Sunday and I need $1 to put into the poor box at church." The people had built the church and the school with their own hands in hard labor for no pay. Then they celebrated by bringing and preparing their own food for the party.

It seems to me unfortunate that slavery is by no means a thing of the past. Will it ever be? Not until all the 'isms' caused by religions, superstitions and other brainwash are done away with (for good), can the people of the earth live in peace and grow to be intelligent human beings capable of taking responsibility for their own actions that could make this life a pleasure.

There was a market on the island. Some sailors had told the people, "This is what we wear to church", and handed them pyjamas. The people actually went to church in them. There was a strange mix of two civilizations. You could see women wearing grass skirts and cross-the-heart, stepped bras. Some wore coconut half shells to hide their breasts. The men wore sarongs or western shorts. When the King visited from Tongatapu (the main island), they all had to wear shirts to cover their chests in respect for the King.

The King was so heavy, that his Rolls Royce had been fitted with special springs. The people loved their King and told me that he was a real expert and excellent on water skis. I admired the King for being against nuclear tests.

I am not sure whether the loss of my hair was from the dengue fever or from the nuclear tests in Mururoa while I lived in Tahiti in 1976-1977. I was glad when most of my hair grew back. I also suffer from glaucoma even though we don't have this eye illness in our family. I have heard that many Tahitians are blind as a result of the nuclear tests in Mururora.

I got a contract at the Hotel Vava'u to paint a mural on the dining room wall. I also painted a portrait of a beautiful young lady for her parents. Then I painted a nude for a man who was going to give it to his girlfriend. I rowed him out to Scheherazade, where he lay on the sofa while I painted him and Peter was watching. He was very happy with the result and bought it right away. Then, we rowed him to the shore with the still wet painting and indulged in a drink at the hotel with some sailor friends.

In every port, we exchanged the books we had already read for ones that interested us with other sailors. I have never done so much reading, as during the time on Scheherazade.

A native man in a dugout canoe came to the boat and I ordered some fresh vegetables from him. I gave him some money so he could buy the vegetables from a friend of his. An hour or two later, he showed up with a basket of beautiful, fresh vegetables and papayas. It did not cost very much.

Ross had his friends on shore. Peter and I went to the market. There was a whole slaughtered cow there. Most natives just bought 1 kg of beef from any place on the cow. The butcher then just hacked off a piece of meat from the cow's carcass with an ordinary axe. I saw that the fillet was still there and asked him how much he wanted for it. He replied, "Same as all meat, $2 a kilo." We bought the whole fillet. It was delicious after I used the ground seeds of the papaya as a meat tenderizer, before I fried the thick juicy slices of the fillet in margarine with garlic, soya sauce and honey. It made two large meals for the three of us. What a welcome change from fish!

We sailed around the island and went swimming and diving at different bays. I nearly panicked when I saw the poisonous sea snakes so close to me, until Peter told me not to be frightened since they are not able to dislocate their jaws like other snakes. He also mentioned that they would come close out of sheer curiosity but would not hurt anyone, unless they felt fear if someone tried to hold them. He said that the temperament of sea snakes is not aggressive at all; however if they felt threatened and succeeded in biting part of a finger or anywhere else where it was possible with the small opening of the their jaws, then they could be deadly since their venom is extremely toxic.

I lost my fear and was able to enjoy and watch them as they came up for air and rested coiled up on the surface of the water for some time. There were grey ones and pretty black and white ones. We also saw them around many other island reefs. I learned so much from Peter and admired his knowledge.

Anchored back in the bay in front of the hotel with Scheherazade, some new yachts had arrived and the social life started up again. We had interesting times with a lot of laughter together.

While exploring Vava'u we came to a small original native village. The people were very happy to see us and invited us to their huts. We became friends and were very honored to be invited by them to a Kava party. They owned some piglets, chickens and dogs. The village was built along the shore and had its own sandy beach where children and dogs were playing.

One mother had five children at her side. She pulled a stick with fishing line out of the water, unhooked the fish and handed it to the smallest of her flock who ate it with the scales and intestines in very short time. Then the mother proceeded to bait the hook again and lowered it into the sea. She gave the second fish to the second smallest child and repeated the action with the third, the fourth and the fifth child. She continued fishing, until all five children were full. It took her no more then twenty minutes. The last three fish the mother ate with guts, head and scales as well and in record time. Then they went home.

We promised our new friends in that village, that we would visit them the next day. The conversation started with them asking us if we had children, parents, uncles, aunts and names and ages of children etc. We would ask them the same. When we felt like moving again, we told them that we planned to sail in a couple of days. They insisted that we come back the next day for a goodbye party. We promised.

Back on board, I ordered fresh vegetables from the guy in the canoe for our coming voyage to Fiji. He asked me for a written recommendation for future business with other yachts which I gladly gave him. I then handed him the money as usual. We never saw him, the ordered vegetables or the money again. I hope he was not ill, but did not know how to find out, since I could not remember his name.

While we were in Samoa, Peter had some popcorn sent to him by his mother from Australia. He thought it would be an interesting contribution to the goodbye party. The day before we left, we walked to our friends' village with the popcorn and a large pot with enough oil in it to pop it in.

When we arrived they were just drowning a piglet. This is the way they kill pigs and I had to pull myself together, not to stop them or to show any concern. After all, they were preparing this feast for us, which was very generous of them. I guess they don't feel the same sentimentality as we do.

The umu was already prepared to put the pig and other foods in, before they covered it with wet sacks and sand as on other South Pacific Islands.

Peter told our friends, that he could do magic. He asked for a gas burner, which they sometimes used for cooking on as well. Then he put the pot on it and showed the bag of popcorn to them. He then poured it into the pot and stirred before he put the lid on. It started popping while all around had their eyes fixed in fascination on the pot. When it finished popping, the lid was slightly raised and when Peter opened it they were amazed to see the amount of popcorn. They did not dare to eat it, until we tried it first. Then they all ate it with fascination and found it very good.

I had to use the toilet and so the children accompanied me to a wooden shed poised over a ditch and equipped with a board and hole cut through it, as a seat. There was some sort of a door which the children kept open to be polite and to keep me company while I had a bowel movement. I asked the children if they had some paper and they just looked at me while pointing to the sand. I got up and grabbed some leaves. This was a new experience and I did not blame Peter when later, he was holding it back, until we were on board again.

The food was decorated with a great sense of beauty and served with so much kindness. It was all so delicious, especially the suckling pig. I ate it since it was already dead and it would live on in everybody who ate of it. When we had all eaten enough, we all sat on the beach in the shade of the coconut palms.

Our friends showed us how they caught fish by chewing coconut, spitting it into their hands and throwing it out over the water. When the fish jumped to eat the coconut pulp, they shot them with stones from their home-made slings and grabbed the stunned fish with a net tied to a branch of wood. They were very proud of their technique.

Then they slung a stone at a beautiful bird. He was not dead so they tied the bird's leg to a stick in the ground and when the bird's partner tried to free him by pecking at the tie. I managed to stop the men from killing it with the stone sling by waving a dollar bill and offering to buy the bird. They sold him to me and I untied him gently and let him fly loose. It almost brought a tear of joy to my eyes when the two birds were flying happily away together. One of our friends said "That would have made a good meal." I then told them of the time in my childhood when I found "Jacqueli", my pet magpie that was my friend and so tame, that he accompanied me everywhere by sitting on my head or shoulder.

Then the people said goodbye, blessing our children, parents, aunts, uncles, friends and us and we blessed them and their loved ones to stay healthy and happy and wished that they would all live to a very high age and be lucky in life and always have enough to eat and, and.........

We walked back and had a last drink with some of our friends from the yachts in port and on the island and got a nights' rest on Scheherazade before we sailed on the next day toward Fiji.

Tonga, at Sea
Feltpen
A 3
1977

Toward Fiji

We all longed to sail again. I felt at home in Peter's arms and on Scheherazade. Peter was at the tiller motoring out, while I hoisted the sail when a lizard fell from the mainsail to the cabin top. He must have come on board with the vegetables. We were too far from shore to turn back to let him go on shore so he became our beloved pet. I placed a dish of water for him behind the compass where he often liked to be and we gave him corned beef and egg and tried various foods on him. The lizard did not want to come into the cabin. Even at night he wished to stay outside. This was all very well until a few days later when the wind and the waves increased and we could not find him any more. We were all sad since he must have fallen, unnoticed, overboard. We had gotten quite attached to the little fellow.

Pets are not ideal on a boat. I knew many sailors who owned a cat or dog. All the pets I meet were happier on land, except one Cocker Spaniel called "Lobo", the pet of our German friends, who preferred to be on their boat and liked sailing. When they took him to the shore they had to force him to get out of the dinghy.

Scheherazade's seacock started to leak. Water poured in and overfilled the sea toilet and floated the floorboards in the head. It was night and I mopped the floor while Peter pumped the water out of the porcelain. Peter, Ross and I took turns pumping out the toilet in intervals of every ten minutes all through the night.

In the morning at daylight the weather was gentle and we reduced all the sails except a small triangle to keep Scheherazade on course. Then Peter tied a rope that was attached on board around his waist for safety, put on his snorkel and fins and went overboard to knock a plug through the opening. It still leaked but we had to pump only every hour. No one used the head and we all did our excrements overboard. The leak through the broken seacock got worse again but fortunately we soon anchored in Wakaya.

There, we spotted poles sticking in the ground of the beach. He inspected them and as the tide came in Peter motored Scheherazade to the poles and tied her up. When the tide went out some people wanted to came on board. Peter told them that it was too dangerous and that the boat could fall on its side. It took all three of us to keep them away, so that Peter could seal the hole properly in the short and valuable time before the tide came in to float Scheherazade again. The repair was done in time and then we anchored her out in deeper water, where we put everything away and rowed on shore to look at some of the beautiful Island of Wakaya.

I managed to draw a landscape in color. We met a man who

lived there and who told us that many super rich people had already bought property and intended to have their luxury houses built there. I hoped that paradise would not become threatened. We snorkeled and caught some fish for dinner. I also found some seashells without the animal inside.

The next day we started to sail early to Fiji. There was a sudden hurricane warning and the winds heralded a storm. We decided to find shelter in a bay off the main island. Other yachts stormed into the larger bay and we headed for the smaller one since we would be the only boat in it.

Peter and Ross set three anchors out, while I tied everything down or away. The wind blew about a force eight. We could hardly believe it, when another yacht came in and threw his pick not far from ours yelling, "Hope you don't mind if we anchor in your backyard." Before we could say, "It is too dangerously close and too much of a collision risk," he had already lowered his anchor. Luckily the hurricane did not come closer and the winds dropped.

We slept all night and when we got up, we ate breakfast and rowed to shore. We walked to the entrance of the river we intended to motor up, all the way inland to Suva, Fiji. The sky was blue again. Back on board we pulled the anchor up and motor-sailed to the river. Peter had found out that it was no problem and deep enough for Scheherazade to go through.

There was a bit of tension between Peter and me because he chose Ross to help him through the river, instead of me. It was the first time he had ignored me. I went down to the cabin and let them get on with it. I felt sad to be ignored by Peter as well. I made myself a coffee and laid on the bed with a book. Suddenly, the boat trembled and had run aground. The cup fell off the table. I ran up the companionway to the stern of the boat. Ross had untied and lowered the dinghy and Peter took the main sheet (rope) with a dinghy anchor to the side of the river, where he dropped the anchor. Ross then winched the boat, until the angle permitted them to slide Scheherazade sidewards and free her up in deeper water. Then Peter tied the dinghy to the stern and took the tiller.

Ross sat in the cockpit as well.

I asked, "Would you like me to keep a lookout?" Peter replied, "No, Ross can do that." My feelings were hurt. I asked myself if Peter still loved me. Unhappy, I stretched out on top of the cabin away from Peter and Ross. Oops! It happened again. This time, I headed straight down into the cabin and said, "Call me if you need me." It was a hot and humid day and I did not envy them for having to pull the ten-ton heavy steel sloop to deeper water. They did it and the voyage through the romantic river with mangroves on each side, kept forking off in different directions. Now they were lost.

A native woman in a canoe was rowing in the river. Peter and Ross wanted to ask her for directions to Suva. She got scared and rowed into the mangroves as fast as she could to get away. I thought, serves them right for ignoring me. But immediately told myself, "These are not positive thoughts."

I asked them if they wanted a cup of coffee and they did not, so I went to stand on top of the hand railing at the bow and tried to enjoy the view over the mangroves and trees. Sometimes I could see small villages with huts and a few people across the sides. I felt lonely and almost sorry for myself. Another woman in a canoe was spotted and I went straight downstairs.

As they tried to ask her, she started rowing in the opposite direction and they begged me to come and ask her, as a woman. So I came up and called her with a smile and asked if she could tell us which side of the river to take. When she saw me, she turned toward us and said, "Go to mango tree, then to left and straight to papaya, then right when river is big again, all straight to coconut, left to Suva ask again. Bye bye." Standing in the bow, I could see where the deep water was by the darker color. I yelled, "Turn to port" (left) but Peter was still ignoring me for no reason and instead of turning, he ran aground again. This time, I felt no guilt for having my thoughts.

They got lost again and found a man in a canoe, who gave

them directions with trees as signs to turn. To make a long story short, they had ran aground seventeen times and arrived totally exhausted in Suva.

After anchoring, Peter fell asleep in my arms and I felt happy again. Life was wonderful and we enjoyed every day, swimming diving, socializing, exploring and I painted, sketched and carved wood. We also sailed to Ovalau, a green and mountainous island surrounded by a reef (a real fish paradise) with beautiful coves. Then we sailed, not through the river again (!) but by sea back to Suva.

Fiji, Suva

To be able to go on shore again, Ross went his way and only came back to sleep. We did whatever we wanted or needed to do. Peter had to have some chlorinated rubber paint to repaint the cockpit. We found it at the ships' chandler. He bought several pots of it to have it later as well for the cabin top.

Our friends Alan and Atao were also in the port. It was good to see them again. He was a young Frenchman and the son of a fisherman. Alan had bought an aluminum life raft for $200, fitted it with a telephone pole mast to turn it into a sailing boat, raised the sides of the hull enough to be able to sit down in the cabin, used electrical cable for rigging, built a small cockpit, added two lee boards and sewn his own sails. He had a seagull outboard motor with an extended propeller shaft which he fastened to the side of his boat.

When he was ready to sail, he showed it to his father who knows the sea and approved 'Nayla' as seaworthy. Alan had also made arrangements with a publisher to buy every article written by him with the title, 'To sail around the world at 20 years old'.

Fiji Sunset
Ballpoint and Feltpen
27 x 36 cm
1977

The interior of Nayla was not completed when he started his voyage. He had a small cooker, used jerry cans to store water and as a sink he had a plastic basin. When he single-handedly arrived at a Marquise island he fell in love with Atao, who was the daughter of a fisherman. Her father approved of Alan and Nayla and so the couple stayed and sailed together. We had known them since Tahiti.

Alan needed to step his mast a bit forward to improve Nayla's performance so all the sailors got together and helped him to pull Nayla on shore by rolling her on tree trunks up to where his boat stayed dry even during high tide. We all envied him since our boats were too heavy and depended on expensive slipways.

Every once in a while we met up with previously known sailors again in different ports. This was always cause for celebration. Some of them had been forced to sail back to the last port and pay the newly invented harbor fees for yachts which had they tried to avoid by sailing away. When they arrived here, they were denied permission to stay unless their harbor fees had been paid in the last port. This new law was only a phone call away.

I had been disappointed with Peter for having paid but now I was glad that he did avoid having to sail back and obey this (in my opinion), stupid law. We admired one of the sailors for his idea of going to the airport and asking a pilot who flew there to pay the fee for him. This saved him a trip back.

Most sailors are adventurers and are not financially well off. They had to find work in different ports to keep their boats and themselves going or work for the wealthy ones by guarding their yachts as Peter had done in Tahiti.

An American owned a stainless steel luxury yacht and was anchored next to us. In his absence Peter charged his batteries. We heard a noise and rowed over immediately to find that the heavy cutting board on top of the dishwasher had turned on the switch on the wall behind it and had started the motor of the machine. A wave must have made the board jump up. Peter tied it down.

Back to Fiji again, this new law of paying harbor fees for yachts must probably have come from the ever-increasing charter-boat tourism which threatened to crowd out the beautiful sailing ships from harbors and bays. They threatened to create mass-tourism and a nuisance for the still beautiful nature of those islands. It is okay to charge commercial ships. Most ports I had been in so far, did not have any facilities like showers etc. and at least those should be provided when non-commercial sailing boats are charged harbor fees.

Peter and I explored Fiji where I found the art gallery "Suva Fiji" which was very interested in exhibiting my work. I was very, very happy about the positive critique and an interview that the reporter of the newspaper wrote about me.

Fiji was very beautiful and the anchorage was just in front of the hotel. One sailor who had a job there as bartender, lived on his yacht and owned a surf glider which he used every morning. He sailed on it to the shore, wearing his shoes, suit and tie and then walked to work. It beats me how he managed to never fall off or even get wet. Everybody was amused to watch him and we all occasionally visited the bar there.

We were also delighted at the first opportunity in every port, to head straight to the post office and pick up our mail. I was so happy that Alexa, Julie and my parents always kept in regular contact. Those letters were treasures to me and I safeguarded them all.

My old typewriter's ribbon was really used and hardly had any ink left on it. I laid black carbon paper under the writing paper and sent the copies which were more readable than the original to my daughters or wrote by hand.

Peter, Ross and I went shopping to stock up on food for our long voyage to New Zealand and also filled all water containers with water from the pipes on shore in order to fill Scheherazade's tanks for the long trip ahead and made her safe and ready for sailing. When the wind and weather were ideal, we made our next move and I hoisted the sails.

Toward New Zealand

Now all three of us were together for 24 hours a day. There was absolutely no privacy whatsoever. When I reached an orgasm Peter held his hand on top of my mouth and whispered "sch-sch-sch." I could not control it and screamed "O-O-O" instead. We just had to learn to live the way we were and accept each other. Ross got used to it.

The hole in the hull for the ship's toilet was sealed up and the head could not be used so were forced to have our bowel movements over the side, which we would do at open sea anyway. We were all able to speak about the texture and color of our excrement by then and had discussions about which foods could cause which kind of stools. This means Peter told me or I told Peter or Ross told Peter or Peter told Ross. Ross still ignored me, so I still ignored him. When Peter asked, "Could you make us a coffee?", I always brought three cups out and each one grabbed one of them.

There was not a single atoll in sight. Just sea and sky around us. There were wonderful and unforgettable sunrises and sunsets. We never had disputes.

When the wind and the waves were calm we swam in the sea holding onto a rope tied to the ship. I will never forget the feeling of delight, swimming in the deep, blue sparkling water. What an immense pleasure!

We pulled in fish that were caught on the plastic octopus from the line tied to the stern. Ross always sat in the cockpit, grooming his nails when he was bored. I felt sorry for him not having a life partner. Peter and I were so happy.

Dolphins swam with us. There was a whole family. The mother, father had two babies who swam with them. They passed us and then swam at full speed toward the bow before turning away to the sides at the last second. Dolphins followed us on many other occasions since Tahiti. They cheered us up to no end. I admired their acrobatic skills. While their heads were out of the water, they looked at you and said "pfff."

Once I sat on the side of the hull and dangled my feet toward the water to try to gently touch one dolphin with my foot, while he swam by. He liked it and came back for more. I wanted to jump into the water with them but Peter said, "Don't do that, they will think that you need rescuing and will try to push you to shore, which would be too far to swim."

Peter was not military minded and so each of us was keeping night watch as long as we could and letting the others sleep. Nights during the dark of the moon could be very spooky. I was always relieved when daylight made the black nights disappear. We usually planned our voyage to arrive at the next destination during full moon and hopefully, during daylight.

We lived with no more then two liters of water each per day to be assured that the supply in the tanks would last until we arrived in Auckland, New Zealand. Even the spaghetti was cooked in half sea water. We still had enough potatoes, onions, wheat, fresh fish, crackers, spices, dried foods and rice on board to last for several weeks. It took us 24 days to sail from Fiji to New Zealand.

Fishing-Trawler, Auckland NZ
Feltpen
A 3
1980

According to law, we hoisted the yellow flag on Scheherazade. She had to be tied to a special place for the health inspector, police and customs to come on board and check our health, passports and ship's papers. This has to be done upon arrival, before entering each new country.

The doctor and police gave us the okay and left. Then the guy from the customs arrived with a beautiful black Labrador search dog. He sent us out of the boat and we stood next to it on the pier. Peter allowed me to take marijuana on board, but only as much as I could smoke in a single day. I only smoked it on special occasions and otherwise, I had stopped smoking my pipe and cigarettes in 1977. The guy just finished his search and seemed extremely irritated, not to have found anything illegal. We climbed on board and noticed that he had even turned the mattresses upside down. He then frantically pulled the drawer out of cabinet and inspected it. He spotted a single hemp seed at the bottom of the drawer. He showed his open palm containing the seed to the dog, which was supposed to bark but ate the evidence instead. The guy could not do anything and left annoyed. We were free to go.

Anyway, if I smoked a bit of grass on the high seas, I certainly did not commit a criminal act as each person is allowed to live by his own law twelve miles out from land. It used to be only three miles in the past.

We cleaned up the mess that the man from the customs had left behind, and it was afternoon by the time we arrived in the port of Auckland. A big crowd of people applauded us as we sailed in. They believed that were part of the 'Whitbread Round The World Race', which had more racing yachts still to arrive.

The fastest ones had already tied their mooring lines to the bollards on the pier. I jumped on the pier with the rope to tie up Scheherazade (a privilege that was mine since I could move very securely thanks to ballet and karate) and we all cleaned the boat and put every thing in its place ready to lock up and go on shore. We were immediately invited to celebrate by some of the racing yachts' captains.

We had a marvelous time hearing their stories and telling ours, while we sipped champagne and fine wines and ate many different kinds of delicate specialties. We observed that some yachts had military regimes, with an exact timetable of duties and were showered with orders by the obnoxiously snobby captain who clearly suffered from an inferiority complex. The crew looked exhausted and miserable in their uniforms. Their small food portions were not allowed to weigh more than so many grams; and their little baggage was not permitted to include any of their personal things because of the extra weight, which could slow the speed of the yacht. How ludicrous! The entire crew had the same short hair cut and looked enviously over to the yachts with the individually dressed sailors, whose captains and crews where laughing and celebrating happily while singing and playing their musical instruments.

Guess who did better in the race? You are right, it was the individual and contented ones, who sailed into Auckland before the strict ones arrived. This proves to me the importance of keeping the morale of the crew or people in general as high as possible, to get the best performance out of them. Well-fed and happy people will be stronger, to cope with the enormously hard tasks and human stresses of such a very demanding race.

I could hardly believe it. Something very unexpected surprised me. Ross spoke to me! He was very nice and we even had a conversation in the present, without either of us mentioning the past. Before he left Scheherazade for good, he even bought one of my paintings - a landscape in oil on canvas. It felt so good being at peace with everyone close to me. I am sure Ross felt better also for getting rid of his jealousy. This takes strength and I congratulate him for it. He will be rewarded with more freedom. I wished Ross well.

Peter was forced to move Scheherazade out of the port and make room for the incoming racing yachts. We sailed through the drawbridge that had been opened for us. Then we tied Scheherazade to a pier in the industrial section of Auckland where Peter hoped to find work.

He also had to do some repair work on his yacht so I went to the post office to pick up our mail. There was mail for both of us. I opened my three letters in the park in Auckland sitting under a tree. I read the happy news from Alexa, Julie and my parents.

Then I went shopping for fresh food. Peter and I arrived in Auckland with only $5 between us. First I bought a huge cabbage and a large zucchini and went to the butcher. I asked him, "Do you have an ox tail? He said, "No." Then I continued, "Do you have pig's feet?" He replied, "No." So I dared, "Do you have calves brains?" He said, "No". When I asked him, "Do you have bulls testicles?", all the people in the butchery roared with laughter and so did the butcher himself. I then bought four mutton steaks.

The next stop was a bakery, where I chose the biggest loaf of bread. Then I still had some money left for two liters of fresh milk (to make our own yoghurt). and a double liter of sherry.

By the time I got back to Peter, the repairs were done and we felt rich to have so much fresh food on board. We were especially glad to have meat for dinner again.

The next thing we had to do, was to inspect the hull, anti-foul it and repair the seacock. For the time being, we used a bucket on a cord that we pulled out of the water into the cockpit when needed. It was not long before we could use the slipway next to the pier to continue and make Scheherazade shipshape. I painted the anti-fouling we had on board onto the hull while Peter did the repair on the seacock. While we were on the hard, a family of rats came to beg for food. I threw them some vegetable peelings. I heard that if you feed them regularly outside they will not come on board. This was true. We rather enjoyed watching those clever animals.

Merry Xmas from New Zealand, on the back of a letter home.

We were happy to be able to lower Scheherazade back into the water and tie her to the peer again. A floating ship feels much better then a land-locked one.

We got to know the people who worked for the business next to the pier, who do repairs on tankers and cargo ships. They were all very nice and we became good friends.

The boss of the place was a very generous man from Scotland who had emigrated years before to New Zealand. He invited us every day to his house for dinner. He loved our company and we loved his. Finally, Peter confronted him with the fact that he needed a job. He was hired as a ship's welder for confined spaces.

As soon as he was working for the boss, we were not invited at his house again but Peter earned very good money. Even though the work was hard, he never complained and everybody liked him.

I started to paint on an old sail that I had found washed up on shore. I washed it three times at the laundromat and left what did not come off as background. I stretched it out on the pier and started to paint. Later that day, a young woman came up to me and said, "I was sent by Dr. Tizart, the Director of the Auckland Society of Art, who wishes to see you. Will you please come along with me?" So I went happily along with Margaret who was Dr. Tizart's secretary. He had seen me painting on the pier.

The Universal Flag

Margaret took me to the Auckland Society of Art building and showed me an art studio with an easel and running water which was available for me use, A space, where I could complete my painting, entitled "The Universal Flag." I had only three colors left and one tube of white, plus some white emulsion.

Then I met Dr. Director Tizart, a really intelligent, kind and gentle man. He told me, that if I could finish my painting in three days, he would have a opening of two weeks in his gallery to exhibit my work free of cost. He would personally unveil the "Universal Flag" and Margaret would call the press. I was thrilled by this offer. What a pleasure to have a proper studio!

With this work, I wanted to stay free of mental or physical prostitution. I was lucky enough, to not ever have to do this now, before or after. My head and body belongs to me and I will never sell it. What I have to offer, is my serious work and sometimes, I also do graphics or other contracts that have to do with my chosen profession. I am an artist.

I was painting without a break and mixed my brushes up, instead of dipping them in turpentine, I dipped them in water and visa versa. This brought me out of the feverish state and I started to correct my mistake by homogenizing the two media of water and oil based color, into one precise line on the linen. This is how I discovered a mixed media that proved to be very strong, even when later swamped with salt water from the red sea which left "The Universal Flag" or other artwork painted with the same technique, unharmed.

I had hung my other paintings on the wall the day before. Two shady looking characters entered before my latest work was completed and threatened to kill me, if I should exhibit this work. They had watched me paint through the window and could read 'Life is legal' on it and were unable to cope with the truth. I told them to go to hell. An hour before the art opening and the unveiling took place, my latest painting was completed. It was hung on a wall by itself and a large piece of white cloth was carefully draped over the still wet painting. I invited everybody I knew and asked them to bring their friends. Several hundred people showed up and witnessed how Dr. Director Tizart unveiled " *The Universal Flag.*"

This took me from being an artist to becoming one of '*The World's Leading Artists'* at the Auckland Museum of Art. Later on, this creation was exhibited and published in many newspapers in different parts of the world. It was also registered in Switzerland at the Bundeshaus in Bern by Herbert Mäder, the famous artist-photographer and politician.

I created the universal flag for world peace and freedom and against brutality and oppression toward the human individual.

About a week after the unveiling, I was walking with a friend along the cay when two men passed us in a silver grey convertible sports car and one of them aimed a pistol at me and pulled the trigger. Fortunately, the bullet went through my hair on the side of my head and did not harm me. I figured that since my time was not up, no one would succeed in killing me. I also hope to beat the English Queen Mother in age before I give up living.

Peter was working very hard and I had gotten so used to spending time with him, that I missed him terribly. I was glad to have my paintings and drawings exhibited at The Grayson Gallery, the Parnell Art Centre and the ANZ Bank in Auckland, N.Z. I also sold five paintings to artists at my art opening at the Pandora Gallery, which flattered me especially since they could recognize the energy and quality I put into all of my work.

On September 1978, I entered The Universal Flag into a competition at the Pakuranga Community Cultural Centre in Auckland. They did not let me hang up my work but promised to hang it in a good spot. I went back to see where they had placed my Universal Flag but could not find it hanging on any of their walls. When I found it behind a wall, carelessly thrown on the floor, I lost my temper and screamed and yelled at those 'so called' responsible. The judging had taken place without my creation being exhibited, but at least they hung it in front of me in a good spot for the rest of the time of the exhibition. The best art critic of N.Z., "O' Brian", had written an article in the paper and gave me the title, *One of the best artists,* which cheered me up and gave me courage to go on.

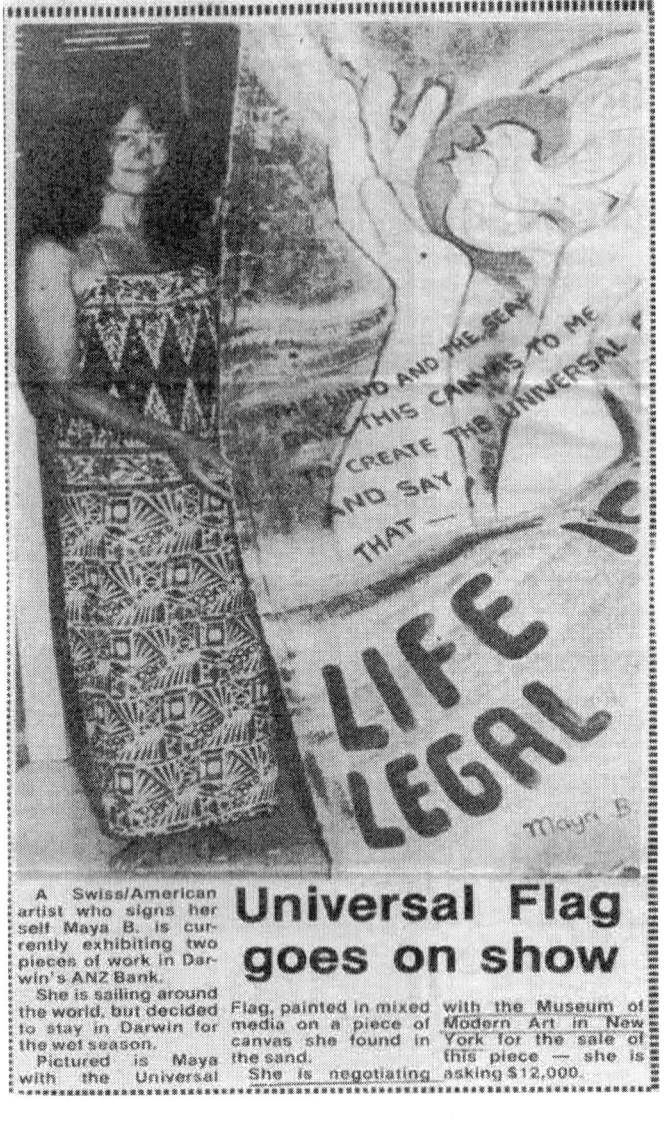

Maya B.

The N.T. News, Oct. 26, 1979

Universal Flag goes on show

A Swiss/American artist who signs herself Maya B. is currently exhibiting two pieces of work in Darwin's ANZ Bank.

She is sailing around the world, but decided to stay in Darwin for the wet season.

Pictured is Maya with the Universal Flag, painted in mixed media on a piece of canvas she found in the sand.

She is negotiating with the Museum of Modern Art in New York for the sale of this piece — she is asking $12,000.

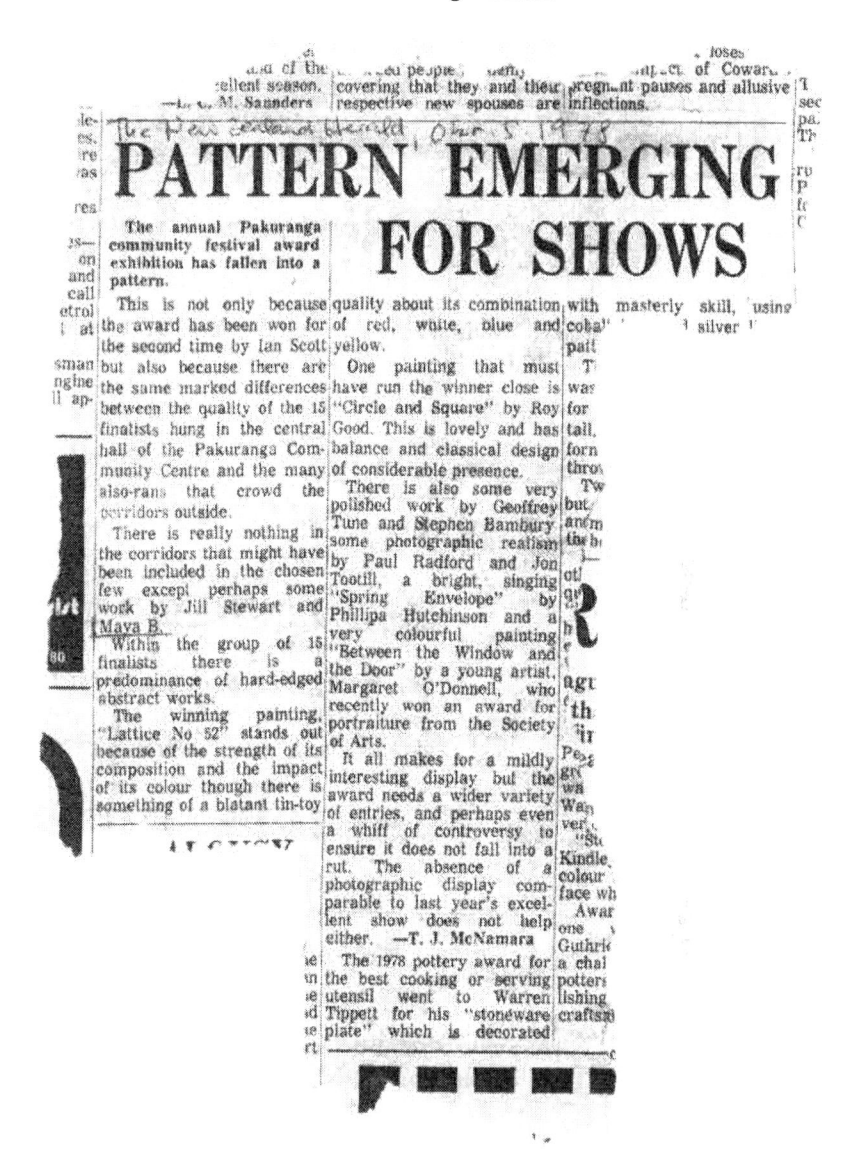

> **PATTERN EMERGING FOR SHOWS**
>
> The annual Pakuranga community festival award exhibition has fallen into a pattern.
>
> This is not only because the award has been won for the second time by Ian Scott but also because there are the same marked differences between the quality of the 15 finalists hung in the central hall of the Pakuranga Community Centre and the many also-rans that crowd the corridors outside.
>
> There is really nothing in the corridors that might have been included in the chosen few except perhaps some work by Jill Stewart and Maya B.
>
> Within the group of 15 finalists there is a predominance of hard-edged abstract works.
>
> The winning painting, "Lattice No 52" stands out because of the strength of its composition and the impact of its colour though there is something of a blatant tin-toy quality about its combination of red, white, blue and yellow.
>
> One painting that must have run the winner close is "Circle and Square" by Roy Good. This is lovely and has balance and classical design of considerable presence.
>
> There is also some very polished work by Geoffrey Tune and Stephen Bambury, some photographic realism by Paul Radford and Jon Tootill, a bright, singing "Spring Envelope" by Phillipa Hutchinson and a very colourful painting "Between the Window and the Door" by a young artist, Margaret O'Donnell, who recently won an award for portraiture from the Society of Arts.
>
> It all makes for a mildly interesting display but the award needs a wider variety of entries, and perhaps even a whiff of controversy to ensure it does not fall into a rut. The absence of a photographic display comparable to last year's excellent show does not help either. —T. J. McNamara
>
> The 1978 pottery award for the best cooking or serving utensil went to Warren Tippett for his "stoneware plate" which is decorated

The Banjo Mandolin

I spent some time in the city of Auckland. A free bus drove around and around all day so that people could park outside the city. When I got out of the bus, I spotted a beautiful old instrument in a pawnshop window, which I believed to be a banjo. Peter had mentioned to me that he would like a banjo. It pulled me straight to the instrument. Fortunately, I had just sold a painting and worked on some contracts, so I could afford to buy it.

The strings were in a mess so I went into the park and sat under my favorite tree, where I tried to string the instrument. I did not succeed since the strings jumped off the bridge the minute I tried to play it. I gave up and took it to the small music shop. A sympathetic old man looked at the instrument and told me that it is a banjo mandolin but was too old to repair. He also told me that it was made in England but had been discontinued for many years since it was not lucrative enough. I insisted on buying new strings for it anyway.

Back on board Scheherazade, I managed to string it but they still jumped out of the bridge. I looked around the yacht and found a piece of plastic of the same thickness as the bridge and cut it to the right size. Then I filed the grooves deeper than on the old bridge and found a piece of rubber that fit on the bottom of the new bridge as a cushion between the skin and the bridge. I proceeded to fit the new strings. Now I could play it, without the strings jumping out and was enchanted by the beautiful sound it made.

When Peter got home, I offered that already-loved Banjo Mandolin to him. However, he was not interested in it and so it became my friend.

After a while of intensive playing, the thinnest two strings broke. I went back to the old man in the music shop and asked him to put a set of new strings on my beloved banjo mandolin. He looked at it intently and spotted the bridge I had made and then said, "If you tried it, I will have a go at it as well. Leave this Instrument with me and I will completely restore it. First I will take it apart and clean it. Then I will replace the old skin with a new one." (The old skin had a cigarette burn in it, when I bought it.) Then he said, "I will build a new bridge for it and my son will help me with the restoration."

I told the wonderful old man that I did not have the money

for the restoration but if he was willing to make exchange business for one of my paintings of his choice, currently on exhibition at the ANZ Bank, I would be very happy. He said, "So would I." He picked my favorite painting, a self-portrait in oil. This showed me that he understood a lot about art. I also found out that he was a violin builder and restorer. The violinist Sir Yehudi Menuhin, would only have his violins repaired or restored by this great old man. I felt very fortunate indeed. When it was restored, it sounded even more beautiful then it had before. I became addicted to my banjo mandolin. Unfortunately, I forgot the man's name but I will not forget him. He lived on Ponsonby Road in Auckland.

Leonie Bremer – Kamp, Voyage North N.Z.

Peter's sister, Leonie came to visit us. She had her flute with her and we played together. A friend from a yacht joined us with his violin. We all enjoyed it. Leoni was not just young and beautiful, but an intelligent and very talented artist with great fantasy. We both missed her when she left. Later on, I received a letter from her saying that she was living and sailing with her boyfriend and missed her art studio. I am sure she made the right decision about whether to live on land or on the boat.

So often, I longed for an art studio but I never managed to have my own place to work in, until the year 2000. Peter was working every day and I got a bit lonely. I had many friends and often went to the pub to have a drink. My friends sometimes insisted on inviting me for another drink and so I started to drink again. Time went fast when I was in the pub but I usually managed to get to Scheherazade in time to have a cooked dinner on the table by the time Peter came home.

One day, I had left the boat when the tide was high. I always went to the post office before I went shopping. Then I ate a sandwich and would paint or sketch, or walk to the laundromat, or straightened up the boat etc. I would only visit the pub, if everything was done. I had such a good time with my friends that when I looked at the clock, I was late. I got up and ran home in such a hurry, that I forgot that the tide had gone down by five meters.

Auckland, NZ
Feltpen
A4
1978

Not A Boring Moment

Normally, I would jump from the pier onto the boat. I fell five meters down and landed with my rear end right on the tip of the anchor that laid on deck. Peter just said, "Serves you right for getting so drunk." I agreed with him. I had broken my coccyx (tailbone). The pain was almost unbearable. It healed well and I did not go near the pub for a long time.

It was so great, when we went sailing to small islands, not terribly far from Auckland for a few days. There were many oysters to pick and fish to catch. Peter soon made enough money to continue our voyage but first I, heavy hearted, took eight of my paintings to be auctioned off because of lack of space on the boat.

I had a toothache and finally managed to find a dentist, who filled my teeth, doing exchange business for my drawings. I also had a contract with a fisherman to paint a symbol on the hull of his boat. This was not easy, since his ship was swinging free on a buoy and rocked with every wave. I stood in the dinghy with the paintbrush in my hand and was very pleased with myself for having succeeded. The man was so happy that he wanted me to paint his portrait as well and paid more than I asked for, which helped to stock the boat up for the coming voyage.

Scheherazade's tender disappeared and Peter and I searched for hours, to finally find it abandoned on a shore.

A Swiss guy came to Scheherazade and asked us to come for dinner at his mother's house where he lived. He was a boring person and we did not especially want to accept but he insisted, saying that otherwise his mother would be very disappointed. The mother was rather nice and a good cook.

Afterwards, this Swiss man pestered us every week, until we agreed to take him with us across the Tasman Sea to Australia. We were so looking forward to just being the two of us, and now this guy had managed to talk us into taking him along. Peter set the date and said, "If you are not here on time, we will sail without you."

He was not there and we left without him, being happy at last to be sailing with just the two of us. New Zealand is so lovely and beautiful. Scheherazade moved swiftly through the water in perfect wind and we watched the sheep grazing on the velvet green hills, while the deep blue water turned into white foam that caused ever-changing patterns absorbed by sizzling light beige sand on the beaches. Cumulus bassus played the shade on the sunny surface of the island.

We were sailing to Whangarei, where we visited Ross after securing Scheherazade on a pier. Ross had just opened a restaurant in partnership with his friend who was also a pianist. We were invited by them to a gala dinner in their elegant and posh restaurant. They had hired a cook, Ross served behind the bar and his friend played the piano while a waiter opened an excellent New Zealand bottle of wine and served the several-course gourmet dinner.

I was glad that I had bought a floor length, burgundy dress with matching hat and mink stole in an Auckland second-hand shop. It came in very handy, was hand crocheted and lined with soft silk. I felt very comfortable and beautiful in it. Ross and his friend treated us like royalty.

We slept well and sailed on the next day and visited Tutukana, Russell Island and then Hauhora. We caught fish and ate oysters from the rocks. The Bay of Islands is quite large and very spectacular. It consists of many small Islands and has a rich sea life but can get very rough.

Not A Boring Moment

Swiss-American artist, Maya B.
(nee Krahenmann — 12.7.40)

is sailing around the world on yacht Scheherazade.

For the past 18 months she has been painting in the South Pacific.

Maya B., a former ballet dancer, has been educated in classical ballet, flying and karate, as well as art.

Come see her sketches and paintings at the

Pandora Art Gallery
96 Karangahape Rd (Grafton side opposite top of Queen St. — upstairs)

from July 24 to August 11

Hours 10 a.m. to 5.30 p.m. Monday to Friday (late night Thursday)

Evening viewings — for appointment ring 370-323

Peter collecting oysters

N.Z., Tasman Sea, Lord Howe Island

We arrived after a spectacular sail and anchored Scheherazade in Houhora. Then , we rowed to shore. The village was small but had a wonderful view of the sea. The vegetation was rich in bushes and trees. It was warm and sunny. Our spirits were high. The few people who lived there were very friendly and interested to hear about our voyage.

One woman told us about her son being at sea in his yacht. The next day, she was standing on shore with a big box and called us over. We rowed in and she handed us the large box with fresh vegetables from her garden for our trip. We were really touched at her kindness and we said the sailor's goodbye, rowed back to Scheherazade and got ready to sail further north to Paua.

There we anchored in the bay. During our time on shore, we met a man who invited us to his house. He was nice and very handsome. He looked very passionate and awakened thoughts of desire in me. If I had not been with Peter, I could not have resisted him. He felt the same about me but I turned him down when he asked me to stay with him. He took us into his garden and we all ate fresh beans from his plants.

He also invited us to stay for dinner. He cooked while we had a drink and watched him. Suddenly, I was violently ill. I had stomach cramps, developed a high fever and passed out. I woke up feeling miserable in bed, in the man's guest bedroom. Peter was at my side. I had just come down with botulism poisoning. I never ate raw beans again. When I felt better, we went to the boat and when I had fully recovered, in a short time thanks to my strong constitution, we decided to sail on.

Before we had time to lift the anchor, a motor boat passed by and dropped off the Swiss guy who had wanted to sail with us. He had hitch-hiked up here to join us. Peter and I could barely hide our disappointment. We took him with us. He was very clumsy and often in the way. The weather was magnificent and the sea was calm with just enough wind to sail gently to the North Cape.

At the most northern tip of New Zealand, we tied Scheherazade onto the rails of a shipwreck. A whole tanker was wrapped around the cliff like tissue paper. The power of wind and water amazed and impressed us. We got out and inspected it. The steel ship was totally crushed. As we looked out to sea, it looked ever so gentle.

We got back on board Scheherazade after having felt the last of New Zealand ground under our feet, before we set the sails ready to cross the Tasman Sea, which has quite a bad reputation.

The wind speed increased and we made at least ten knots. The Swiss guy started to order me around but I told him off. "Get the sandwich yourself, I am not your maid or your mother!" He started to put all women down as inferior. Then he got seasick. Secretly, I felt that nature had revenged herself for his stupid and arrogant attitude. I gave him some crackers to eat which temporarily settled his stomach. I hated him and he hated me. He irritated both Peter and me.

He proved totally useless on the boat and was incapable of learning how to operate anything to help with the sailing. His fears and clumsiness were annoying. We were glad, when he laid in his bunk so we did not have to keep an eye on him and so that he would not fall overboard. Peter made him wear a life vest.

Peter and I took turns at the helm. When the wind was light, the wind vane did not work but Peter managed to repair the auto pilot. We repaired everything right away if the weather permitted.

I chipped rust on the railing and painted it, then I repaired the sail using a 120 year old Singer hand sewing machine that I had bought at a auction in Auckland for $8, while sitting on the top of the spray dodger.

Peter spotted three mating whale couples. He called me in big excitement to come and look. We were thrilled. This was indeed a very rare and beautiful sight. We felt so lucky. The six grey whales were about twelve meters long and did not come closer then ten meters. Those magestic monsters played so gracefully and released a fine spray from their backs. They glided elegantly in and out of the sea with their wide tails dripping and splashing, as they rose up out of the water.

Their huge mouths were full of tassels. They only fed on plankton. Their backs were battle scarred and many barnacles were attached to them. A strong and fishy smell filled the air. Not for one second did we feel threatened that they would turn over or attack Scheherazade. If they had felt threatened, I am sure they would have been able to do so but they were so docile.

The whales stayed with us for three days until Peter started the motor to charge the batteries while sailing. This unfortunately drove them away. The Swiss guy could not enjoy it very much since he was still seasick.

He was still not a very nice person but I tried to help him by making tea and very light things to eat. He was fat and would not die of starvation. I believe in his case, he was sick because of his fear of the sea, since I have never met someone who was seasick and was free from fear of sailing. The weather was cloudy and the Tasman Sea looked grey. Then the weather calmed and the sun was shining on the clear blue horizon.

We arrived at Norfolk Island. There we met Shaun, a sailor who had left Canada with only $100 in his pocket. He had fixed two dugout canoes together to turn them into a catamaran with a wooden deck in between and tied his canisters of water to the mast in the middle. When we met him, he had already been dismasted three times and his hull was very worm-eaten. He was working in the shipyard to make enough money to sail to Australia.

Shaun was a very likeable man and a character. He never arrived in Australia and no one had seen him in other ports, until someone arrived from Tasmania, who had met him there and said that he had fallen in love with a Tasmanian girl and decided to stay there. All who had met Shaun were relieved to hear the good news.

The Swiss guy finally felt better. We only stayed a day and night and then left Norfolk Island and set the course toward Lord Howe Island. As we sailed along for some time, we spotted a very steep island that was shaped like a huge sugar cone but out of rock. We knew then, that we were on the right course.

Later on we found out that two sailors had decided to climb

the steep mountain and believed themselves to be the first ones who had mastered the truly difficult task of climbing to the top, only to find an empty champagne bottle lying up there!

Soon Lord Howe Island came into focus. What a great feeling to spot land after some time at sea. The timing was such, that we would be arriving at Lord Howe Island in the afternoon. Peter was always spot-on in navigating and I usually took the sights. I tried to learn about navigation but Peter still did not want me to learn. I took the sails down while Peter was at the tiller motoring to the anchorage. Then I dropped the anchor. The yacht dragged it along the bottom of the sea that consisted of such foul holding ground, that we had to lower the anchor in three different places until it dug in.

We raised the yellow flag, as was required, signifying our arrival and waited for the coastguard police to show up. The guy arrived so fast with his motorboat, that I just managed to stretch my legs out over Scheherazade's hull and toward his boat to fend him off and prevent him from ramming us. This caused him to immediately release the accelerator. He then yelled at me, "What are you doing?" and I replied, "I don't know if you care about your boat but I protect this one." He then tied his boat on the railing and clumsily flung his awkward and fat body onto Scheherazade, without asking permission to come aboard, as was the polite thing to do. He had a folder with papers and permits with him. First, he wanted to come into the cabin. He sat down and bombarded us with bureaucratic questions and started to mark them on the forms he had brought with him. Suddenly, he became violently seasick. He held his hand in front of his mouth and ran up the gangway to the cockpit, where he just managed to vomit over the side in time.

Peter suggested that it would be easier to go to shore with him and sign all the papers but he stubbornly refused, until he was so sick that he agreed to do the bureaucracy on shore. It took so long, that Peter just wanted to sail away but I insisted on seeing the Island. We then went exploring but the mood was broken. Peter was worrying that the anchorage was not safe enough so all three of us returned to Scheherazade and sailed away.

Australia

Dolphins accompanied us for a while and we saw many sea birds. When we spotted Frazer Island it was afternoon. By the time we passed toward the Australian mainland, where we hoped to anchor, it was too deep and we continued in the dark. It was cloudy and rough.

A storm brewed up and surprised us. We were in a place we did not know, somewhere toward the Mary River (where we had planned to go), behind Frazer Island and the mainland. A storm is less dangerous at sea since the vessel cannot hit up on anything except (very unlikely) another ship. Here it was pitch dark and we could not see if there were cliffs or shallow reefs which we could be thrown up against or get pounded on, or grounded. We were all worried but there was no time for fear.

We pulled down all sails just in time to not get them ripped by the storm, put all movable things away and stuffed up the ventilators etc. The Swiss guy laid in his bunk which made the job easier to do and was one less worry with him out of the way. Peter fetched the sea anchor and attached it to the stern and threw it out to slow down Scheherazade. The sea was so choppy, that the rudder could not grab or help. Peter tied the tiller down with a rope to both sides of the cockpit. Then he attached a car tire and threw it overboard to slow the speed of the boat. I tied the jibs to the railings and the mainsail to the boom. Then I brought the storm triangle (our smallest sail) up and attached it to the mast and boom to help with holding the course. I was grateful for everything I had learned from Peter.

Lightning was all around us. It was quite spectacular. The storm was very intense and lasted 1 1/2 hours but felt much longer. We were relieved beyond description when it was finally over and celebrated with a much needed glass of rum. We shoned the spotlight from time to time to see if anything was around us until dawn arrived and the sunrise took all worries away.

Then I took a sight and Peter plotted the exact spot where we were. We pulled the sea anchor and the tire on board and I replaced the storm sail with the mainsail, reefed it and repaired the jib, while Peter replaced the bronze sail hanks on it that had ripped off, before I was able to pull it down in the storm. Then we cleared the boat and I mopped up the salt water that had managed to enter the cabin from the cockpit.

We all shared a hearty breakfast. Having survived this violent storm gave me such a great feeling of power, that I felt as if nothing could hurt me. I spoke to Peter about it and he said that he felt the same. We all loved and admired Scheherazade for getting us through that storm.

We soon saw the entrance of the Mary river and tied the boat to the pier, waiting for the bureaucrats to arrive. The bureaucracy was very fast and the ships' doctor and coastguard were nice.

Then we all slept very deeply and woke up refreshed and started to motor up the river toward the town of Maryborough, where Peter had sailor friends who had settled there.

About ten miles before we reached this town, the prop shaft broke. We anchored immediately and lowered the dinghy into the river for Peter to push the propeller shaft further into the stern tube and tie it in place in order to keep the water out. Then he put the outboard motor on the dinghy and headed to his friend in Maryborough to have him come down and pull Scheherazade up.

The Swiss guy and I stayed on board and watched the boat. It took a few hours until Peter and his friend came back with a yacht to tow Scheherazade gently up the river. Good that the tide came in and was with us. Peter's friend took us to a private slipway where Scheherazade was pulled up on land. She was full of mud and the firemen (friends of Peter's friend) came and hosed her down with fresh water.

We lived on the yacht and anti-fouled her hull. Peter had the

Maya B.

old propeller shaft on board but had replaced it in N.Z. with a bronze one he had thought was stronger. In fact, the steel one was better.

Peter also found a job for the Swiss guy and finally we had the boat to ourselves again. It is not nice to live on a ship on land. Mud gets tracked in and makes life very hard. We hurried to finish all the necessary work and were glad to be back in the water again. We tied Scheherazade to the pier and walked to Peter's friends.

T. and L. T. had built the second of the three ships constructed from the same plans as Scheherazade. The three friends had found the plans in an empty building and Peter was the third one to build his boat. He learned from the mistakes the other two friends had made and this caused Scheherazade to be the best.

We planned to go to Sydney and visit Peter's family and also Alan Payne, the marine architect who had designed the plans for "Gretel" at the age of twelve, and which were used again, to build the three yachts. Peter wanted to pay him for the plans that were used illegally and also desired to meet this great man.

T. had been with his yacht in Tahiti when he fell in love with L., a very beautiful Tahitian girl with shining black hair so long that she could sit on it. They had a baby and that is why they bought a gorgeous Victorian house on the waterfront of Maryborough in Queensland so they could anchor their boat in the river in front of their house. The house had a terrace under the roof all around it and a beautiful garden.

Peter's other friend and B, his Malaysian wife, also had a son and had moved into the next house, also a large Victorian one. Their yacht was also anchored in front. Their house needed restoring, so Peter was hired to do the work and moved Scheherazade just up from them.

Those people were so real and frequently invited us. There was never any small talk but very interesting conversations accompanied by laughter mostly in the evening. All four of them cooked well. During the time Peter was working, I painted, sketched, did the shopping and of course checked the post office for news from Alexa and Julie and my parents and friends.

Maryborough was a small-large town and I exhibited "The Universal Flag" at David Johnson's Department Store, in the window next to the entrance and some of my work on the second floor.

One day, B. and I went shopping and she had her four-year-old son with her. When we entered a vegetable shop, she taught her son how to steal. I could not believe it, since here husband was well off and very generous. When we were outside, I said, "Why did you do that? It is very dangerous and if you are caught they will maybe take the child away or you will end up with a criminal record." Anyway, you don't need to have your son to steal. She then said, "It is important for him to learn to survive."

Then she told me about her life. She had been born in Malaysia and when she was a small girl her brother tried to boss her around. She refused to obey him so he stabbed one of her eyes out. Then she was given to another family, since there was not enough to eat at home. When she was eight years old, they told her to go into town and wait for her mother to come and pick her up. No one showed up and she was frightened and depressed. An old woman felt sorry for her and took her home with her. The woman just barely had enough for herself, so she taught B., who was then only eight years old, how to steal. B. is an artist and one of the most intelligent women I had ever met. I told her that life is different in Australia and convinced her, that it was not necessary to steal.

B. and I became very good friends and I trusted her 100%. I learned so much about nature from her. She started a banana culture in their garden with only two banana trees. She told me to cut them down after the fruit is picked, so that the banana tree would multiply and many other things. I learned how to understand those poor people who steal for survival.

Some rich men, even politicians, steal from people even

though they do not have to, getting large salaries which are more than they really should be earning.

On rainy days, I often visited the library and spent hours there. Until one day, they decided to throw me out since I did not own any shoes. I always washed my feet and kept them clean. I had gone barefoot for so long, that it hurt when I tried on a pair of sandals. The soles of my feet were as thick as natural leather hide. I stayed barefoot.

Peter took time off from work to be with his mother and sister Leony who were visiting. They had driven the car there and then took us back 1200 km. to Sydney. On the trip, we saw the Glass House Mountains National Park, kangaroos, bush babies and all sorts of interesting wildlife and landscapes. Queensland is beautiful and my favorite state in Australia. The climate is very pleasant, especially along the sea. When we have summer in Switzerland it is winter in Australia and New Zealand. The Moon is waxing there when it is waning in Europe.

Sydney, Peter's Family

We arrived in Sydney in May, 1979. Peter's mother Eileen was an excellent cook. She felt so sorry for us not having an oven or refrigerator on board Scheherazade, that she pampered us with so many kinds of roasts, cakes and desserts, that we could hardly move after dinner. Leony lived with her mother and had her art studio there.

It was colder in Sydney than in Maryborough but mostly sunny. There was a beautiful park, almost like a tropical forest, near Eileen's house. There was much wildlife in it. White cockatoos with yellow beaks and crests on their heads flew to Eileen's window to eat out of her hand. They were a protected species and one of their favorite pastimes, was to do gymnastics on the TV antennae. Almost all of them were bent. To watch the spectacle we had to get out of bed at five in the morning but it was worth getting up.

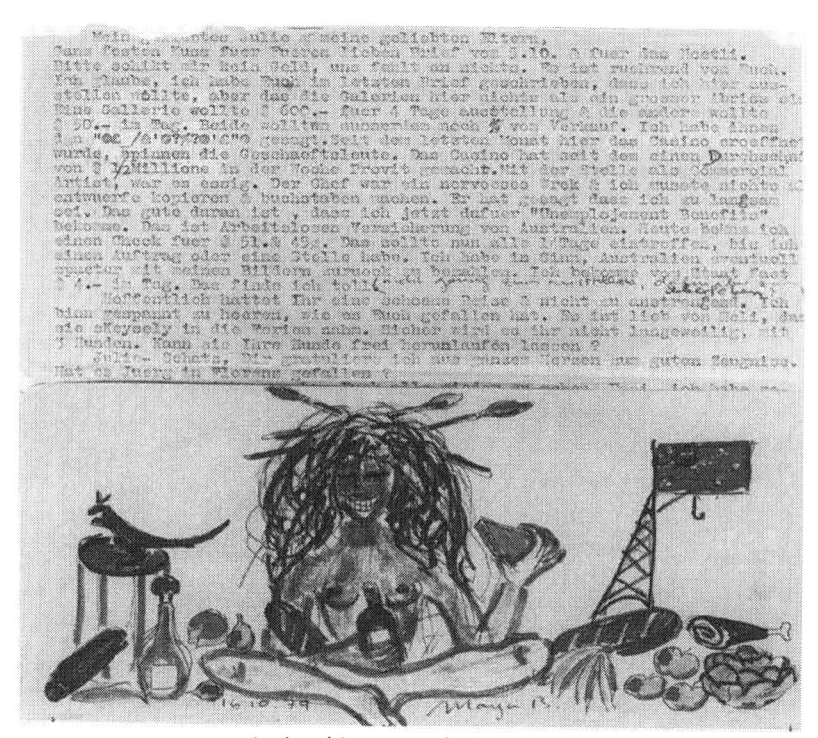

Arrived in Australia! A letter home

There was a party almost every day and Peter showed me around Sydney. I loved the beaches, especially the wild ones with high waves ideal for surfing.

We went to the shipyard where Peter had built Scheherazade. Everyone who knew him loved him. Peter has a golden sense of humor. He finds almost everything funny. The guy from the second hand boat parts shop was glad to have a few good laughs with him. What a fascinating place. Peter had bought many things from him while he was building his boat. The bronze anchor winch on board came from this place as well. The man had five dogs who guarded the multitude of interesting ships paraphernalia.

We also went to see Alan Payne, the ship's architect. Peter offered to pay for the plans. Alan Payne wanted to know everything about Scheherazade. When he heard that she had survived turning over in a storm with a 60 mile-an-hour hurricane wind, with all three men on her safe and the mast still standing, (just the rigging had to be tightened), he said, "No, Peter I don't want you to pay. Instead, I would like you to tell us about this incident on the tape recorder here." Peter recounted the experience in detail and then Alan said, "Thanks, this is the best advertisement for me."

Time went quickly and Peter wanted to earn a bit more for our future voyage. We had a marvelous time in Sydney and said "Goodbye" to Eileen and Leony. Peter had another sister Cherry, who was married in Holland. We planned to visit her later. She was the first woman to climb K1 alone and without oxygen.

Then we took a train back to Maryborough and to Scheherazade, which was guarded by Peter's friends. We both found travelling by train to be very hard. When we sailed in our home, Scheherazade, we were really at home, private and free wherever we were. Also, travelling by wind force on water is a very special feeling and almost addictive.

Tired out from hours in the train, we were happy to be back on board and anchored in the middle of the Mary River, with the boat freely swinging in the tide.

After a day of rest, Peter went to work on the restoration of his friend's beautiful Victorian house. My favorite place was on Scheherazade, watching the wildlife while relaxing in the cockpit under the shade of the awning.

Many pelicans lived there and with the tide out, the mud on the banks was exposed. One of the pelicans arrived for a landing and came in a bit low. He tripped over his feet and slid on his belly which was covered with mud. He looked so embarrassed, that I had to laugh, so he gave me a dirty look as if to say, "What are you laughing about, that could happen to anybody." It amused me greatly. Another time I watched a pelican with a fish stuck in his mouth. He could not get it up or down. Before I could go and help him, his mate stuck his beak in the other's open mouth and turned the fish around so he was able to swallow it. The intelligence and sensitivity of those animals never failed to amaze me. Sometimes, I peed over the side and every time the catfish jumped to drink my urine. I am wondering if they needed the minerals in it.

Peter brought his friend to the boat for a drink after work. It was the first time that he knocked all women. I felt insulted, since I am a woman. It t shocked me because he had never done that before. When his friend detected the expression of disappointment on my face, he said, "I did not say that." I cooled off toward Peter until he apologized. I am writing this down so that men can learn from it.

If you show no respect for a woman the strongest relationship will die a little.

Peter took some time off from work and we motored down the Mary River to Frazer Island, in the hope of seeing the dingos. We rowed on shore and were lucky to see a whole family of dingos, the bitch, the dog and the pups. We were very amused to watch them playing. We spent many hours on Frazer Island before taking the rising tide to head back to Maryborough.

We had now been there eight months and Peter's work was done and so we partied with our friends. An older couple, who I was very fond of, was anchored behind us. They lived on their 'Water Witch'. I was impressed how practical and roomy it was on that small sailing boat, without any walkway along the cabin top. The cabin top went right across the hull and one walked on the entire width of it. The couple was Jewish. I had not met any Jewish people who were sailing before. They were not orthodox but free spirited. They had sailed for many years and had just bought one of the houses there to retire in. They bought four of my drawings for their new home.

Peter and I prepared to move on. Someone wanted to give me a gorgeous six month-old dingo. I really liked the wild dog and he liked me. The owner told me that he had ripped a sheep and on board a yacht, he could not do that. Peter refused to have the dingo on board, which made me very sad but I could understand that a yacht was too small for such a freedom-loving animal. I hope his owner found him a more ideal place.

We planned to sail to Darwin in the Northern Territory. The final goodbye party took place on the pier and all the sailors and other friends came with their families and dogs. Everybody brought their own drinks and something to eat and it was wonderful, until the police came and stopped us for no reason at all. We were not disturbing the peace since we were not in a residential area. They said it was illegal for so many people to party together. What party poopers! All of us, but especially the children, were disappointed.

I walked to the abandoned industrial center for the last time and climbed my favorite- the highest, of all cranes left there to rust. It felt almost like being in an airplane and I observed the marvelous view for the last time. The next day we were under way on our journey toward Darwin, N. T. and looked forward to swimming and diving off the Great Barrier Reef.

The Great Barrier Reef

What freedom, to be just the two of us again! Peter and I were happy. The weather and sea were ideal and Scheherazade glided gently and swiftly through those feared waters with her new coats of anti-fouling. We always anchored in front of uninhabited islands if the ground was holding the anchor and explored the reefs around us by snorkeling or diving. The sea life was spectacular. I saw creatures that I had never seen before. We also got to know many of the islands.

Wild goats lived on one of them and on another the animals and birds were so unafraid of humans that we could see them very close up. Fortunately, they had not been confronted with the violence of some so-called human beings. I hope they never will.

On some of the islands, we found ripe bush lemons. On shore we rarely collected fallen or washed up coconuts. Coconut palms are sparse on the beaches of Queensland because greedy, stupid people have cut down the trees to collect the nuts. This lack of consideration deprived other humans and future generations of the abundance of these magnificent and useful trees with their (sometimes life saving) nuts filled with delicious, high energy fluid. The leaves can be braided to use on huts.

On one island, I had climbed to the highest spot to get the best view, when I was confronted with a two-meter long, grass-green lizard. It was the biggest one I had ever seen. He was very shy and immediately sped away from me. I hoped to see him again but searched without success. I counted myself to be very lucky to have seen this gorgeous creature. I will not name the islands where I saw such rare species of animals, fish, birds, plants or trees in order to *Protect nature from mass tourism.*

At the time we were sailing, the charter business was starting to take over in some of the most beautiful places but the navigation computers for public use were very costly and still in their first stages. Navigation was time consuming and difficult to learn. Today, every idiot can navigate, thanks to today's advanced techniques in electronics. Where there are reefs you cannot depend on the sea charts since the growth can cause differences in depth.

We caught different kinds of fish for every dinner. We fried, boiled or marinated them in bush lemon juice or soya sauce with onions and/or garlic, accompanied by rice, noodles or potatoes and often with raw cabbage salad. We also ate stone crabs. We took lobsters only occasionally and only the large males in order to not threaten the species.

I found empty seashells to send to my children. Around one of the islands we had visited, the fish were in such multitudes, that we caught twelve fish in record time. I canned them for harder times.

Every once in a while, we caught up with friends we had met in other ports since Moorea, Tahiti. This was always a reason to celebrate on their yacht, on Scheherazade or on shore.

One time, Peter and I were both tired and hoped to get into a difficult port for a good night's rest. The port was in a dangerous location on the mainland and we had to pass through a narrow entrance between high cliffs in strong currents. Without a motor, this would not have been possible without the risk of losing the boat. Inside the small port the holding ground was so poor, that we set two anchors and hoped that they would secure Scheherazade.

As soon as we were anchored and had put everything in its place, our friends Bill and Jenny arrived in their beautiful 'Tahiti Ketch'. We had first met them in Bora Bora. They were both 72 years old and had started to sail from the U.S.A. They were both unable to swim and so afraid of the water that they wore rubber shoes to drag the dinghy to the shore. Bill was a retired and ingenious electronics engineer who had been working for Howard Hughes.

While we were in Bora Bora, one of Peter's two radios had been broken and so he and Bill had made a deal. Peter cleaned off the barnacles from the hull of the Tahiti ketch in return for Bill repairing his radio. Not only did they have many things in double, but in triple. Three radios, three TVs, three sextants, etc. Everything on their yacht was reinforced by Bill in stainless steel.

They were a lovable couple but very complicated. One day while in the South Pacific, they had invited us for coffee. Bill turned the engine on to turn on the generator in order to generate the power needed to power the electric water heater to heat the water for the coffee. It took poor Jenny over an hour to hand the full cups to us. We sat on one of the two sofa beds with our heads tilted painfully forward because the TVs took the head room and were mounted so low that it was impossible to sit comfortably.

Jenny had such a nice smile. She missed her grown up children and her grandchildren and sometimes longed to be back in the States. Bill loved his beautiful boat and sailing. They were a very close-knit couple. After the long stretch of sailing in the Great Barrier Reef, we were tired out and so were they. We all decided to go to sleep and meet the next day.

When we woke up, Bill and Jenny had gone. We could not believe that they had not said goodbye to us. The next day we hoisted the anchor and motored through the tight passage into the safer deep sea and sailed 1 1/2 hours to the next island. To our surprise, Bill and Jenny were there and so we anchored next to them. They told us what had happened. In the middle of the night, Bill went into the cockpit to have a pee over the side. He called to Jenny, "I think we are moving", Jenny came out with the spotlight and they discovered that they had drifted through the dangerous passage to the sea so they kept going until dawn when they anchored on the island and we met again.

This time, we invited them to have coffee brewed on our kerosene stove in a fraction of the time and we sipped it in comfort. We met them later again in Bali, where they told us of another incredible happening but I will write about that in a later chapter of this book. Soon we said

the Sailor's Goodbye: "Sometime, somewhere, somehow, we will meet again",

and sailed on to increase our knowledge of this beautiful planet and to be closer in distance to my daughters, my parents and our dog Keys.

Townsville, Queensland Australia

After having visited many ports and islands of the Great Barrier Reef, we arrived in Townsville. It was a quiet place and felt very good. It was easy to get to know people who told us what would be interesting to see here. We went to the museum. I especially remember the drawings from the eighteenth century. They showed how the Aboriginals stored their food then. There were humans, white and oriental, females and males hanging by their hair in trees with their hands tied behind their backs. They were kept alive until ready to be cut down and slaughtered as needed for the next meal. Their favorite meat was from Chinese people since they had been nourished by more healthy food than the whites and therefore tasted better. The breasts and thighs of oriental woman were considered a special delicacy.

I found the Aboriginals of today to be loving and kind people, even though they are still discriminated against by some of the brainwashed ignorant whites.

During the writing of this book in November 2008, I just heard about a young Arab girl who had been raped by three brutal Muslim men. What happened to them? NOTHING. What happened to the innocent violated girl? She was stoned to death for not being a virgin before marriage. You can imagine why that religion is considered the most inhumane. That it is still being followed in this day and age is incomprehensible, but they are unfortunately now still where Christianity was in the year 1500. It took many wars to chase the Christian dictators out of Europe but some of the more primitive immigrants seem to bring a no less evil religion back in. For survival's sake, make room in your brain for knowledge.

I was raped by a commandant and two soldiers of the French foreign legion but I will describe this horrendous incident, which is still haunting me with nightmares to this day, in a later chapter of this book.

Before Peter and I continued on our voyage, we swapped sea-charts with sailors heading in the opposite direction. Peter found it impossible to part with the very marked charts. I understood him very well. There are many important markings and memories on them. I copied a borrowed chart we badly needed in those tricky waters by hand and spent all day drawing all the depths on it, where we intended to sail.

We really admired Captain Cook for measuring all the depths of those waters in the Great Barrier Reef and charting them and the various areas. He did this by sending part of the crew in a rowing boat ahead of his ship '*Endeavour*' with a lead on a string. The string was knotted at one-foot intervals. That way they could count if it was deep enough to get "Endeavour" through. What a painstaking and slow job to create the first sea charts in about 1770. Today, electronic navigators make sailing much easier and safer. The negative thing about this, is that sailing has almost become mass tourism.

I believe that sailing should only be done by those who take responsibility for their own actions and respect life. Those who don't will endanger their own life and that of future generations of all species, including the human one. It is even public knowledge and a fact known since the 1960s, that the sea and life in general have been threatened. Even so, the pollution and abuse by some fishing and other industries continues (not to speak of the bloody, brutal and desperately polluting war industry) by those who made their (in my opinion criminal) fortunes, not only by raping the earth but by continued slaughtering and torturing animals and humans alike. The problem was taken seriously by too few of them.

I admire Prince Charles for his concern and frankness and wish other leaders would take notice of him and change their irresponsible behavior. If only they were less greedy, more earnest and understood the urgency to make this world a better place.

When I painted 'The Sea Flag' in order to save the whale in 1978 and asked Jacques Cousteau for his support, he never answered me. I met someone who had worked with him in the South Pole, who told me of Cousteau's real character and then I was not surprised that Cousteau hadn't responded to me. In fact, we looked at the film from the South Polar expedition and my friend who had been there commented "This is true." and "This is not true." during the whole film.

The wind and weather was ideal to continue to sail to Cairns. We stopped and anchored Scheherazade in different bays and islands and were fascinated by the different fish and other sea life. We also saw rich bird life. There was a marine biology station on one of the atolls. We met some interesting people there, who let us explore the reefs.

Arriving in the canal of Cairns, we were happy to tie the yacht to a safe pier. Hardly anyone was there, until we got off the boat and walked to the nearby town center. How nice it was to sit outside at a pub and sip an ice-cold beer in the shade from the big afternoon heat. We met some people and had interesting conversations. We were also told where we could find things in Cairns and were invited by the locals, who were eager to hear our stories.

I was terribly homesick for Alexa and Julie, my beautiful daughters and was so happy when I could pick up a letter from them. I will not reveal what they wrote in order to protect their privacy, but I was proud of their intelligence, positive thinking and sense of humor. They had good contact with their father and grew well, in the loving care of my parents who made it possible for them to have a good education. Both were speaking English, German and learning French and Italian. I was so proud of them. If I just could take them in my arms again. I forced myself to think of something else in the present, to prevent my hot tears wetting my cheeks again. After all, I was safe living with Peter, a wonderful, kind man, on his beautiful yacht Scheherazade and was surrounded by beauty, having my dream fulfilled to sail around the world, which was every reason to be grateful and happy. However, the bond between a mother and her children is so strong, that it can torture you by the physical distance. In my mind, I would cover my girls with a glass dome that would come up around them if anyone tried to hurt them.

Again, it was time for the sailor's goodbye and we motored out of Cairns toward Cooktown and toward new impressions. I really enjoyed hoisting the sails and we stopped at Palm Cove, Port Douglas, and some other islands. We found out more about Captain Cook on his third voyage in Cooktown, where they did repairs to make the 'Endeavour' seaworthy again after the famous ship had been pretty badly damaged on the reef.

We always studied the weather before sailing and were hardly ever surprised by unexpected storms, but I can imagine how dangerous it can be there in high winds or suddenly changing weather patterns. Maybe there is hope that sailing mass tourism will not threaten the nature of the richest sea life areas after all.

Hopefully! We enjoyed resting at Cooktown before the long voyage toward the feared Torres Straits, which lay between New Guinea and Australia.

We stopped at Lizard Island National Park, the Howick Group, Stanley Island and other places and then anchored just before the Torres Straits near a pearl culture. We did not get off the boat until the next day, in case someone was watching to see if we would steal pearls. No one was watching and so the next day, we rowed on shore to fill our water containers before we prepared to pass through the Torres Straits and across the bay of Carpentaria.

We found water and were delighted to meet an Aboriginal family still surviving in the desert. Some men fished with a long wooden spear that was sharpened to a point. They aimed and threw them with such accuracy, that a fish was speared every time. We plotted where we planned to go on the chart and our next stop was Entrance Island.

We found out, that our Polish friend "Spissec" (I am not sure if I spelled that correctly!) was stranded on a reef in the straits but had received help from people to rescue him off the reef. Also, if needed they would repair his boat free of cost.

Spishec was a handsome and deep-thinking man. He managed to escape from the then-oppressed Poland by getting the press to publish that he had repaired a small and old wooden boat to circumnavigate the world single-handedly and 'Do something for Poland'. Everybody who knew him loved and respected this courageous man. He showed me his boat. It was pretty but he could not stand up in it. The mattress on the floor took up almost the whole length. It was very crowded but delighted my sense of smell with the scent of sea, salt and aged wood. It was good to know, that he was being helped and okay. Anyway, if we could not see him there, we would meet him again in Darwin.

The currents in the Torres Straits were incredibly strong. They made steering difficult but seemed to have sucked us straight through in less time than we had estimated. It was a bit frightening to watch the closeness of the reefs on both sides of Scheherazade but it was exhilarating and I loved the rush of adrenaline. Peter, who was fully aware of what we had just gone through, was getting very tired. In the safety of the open sea, we had the wind from behind and poled both jibs out to catch the maximum of the wind. We both went to sleep and then I cooked a big meal in the wok on the primus stove on the gimbals. We ate it with the hunger of wolves.

Gulf of Carpentaria, Near Collison, Wessel Island

As we were crossing the north of the Gulf of Carpentaria toward Wessel Island, it was getting dark. We spotted a big tanker and this made us believe that we were too far north and in the shipping lanes so we headed to the south, out of what we thought to be the official course for tankers. Peter was very exhausted and I was still in good shape, so he said to me, "I am going to sleep. You can handle it. Take over Scheherazade and don't wake me up for any reason before you see the lighthouse."

The wind was still blowing from behind and the jibs on the double fore stay were poled out. I was at the helm. It was pitch black and there was no moon. I figured that in about 1 1/2 hours, I would be able to see the lighthouse but when this time had passed and I still could not see the lighthouse, I looked to see if Peter was awake. He was sound asleep. I believed that the speed of the boat must be less than I had anticipated, when suddenly I heard huge waves breaking on the cliffs in front of me. I tried to pull the poles out without success. I woke up Peter and screamed, "Come quickly, it is urgent!" He jumped out of the bunk and we both managed to pull the poles out and get the jibs down. I reefed the mainsail and he took the tiller and changed direction.

Then, he went back to sleep and I took the tiller again, taking each wave at an angle and not letting any wave get over our bow until the weather calmed. Then I headed in the direction where we believed the lighthouse to be. This was the first time I was frightened. I had the responsibility of Peter, Scheherazade and my life. I felt so alone and realized how hard it must be for single-handers. I also learned, that one should not be influenced by what one sees (like the tanker). One should be guided by one's own self and knowledge.

Had we not altered course, we would not have been so close to a life-threatening situation. We had been lucky not to have lost Scheherazade or our lives by being smashed up on the cliffs. Had we waited to sail until we would have had the aid of the full moon shining, it would have been a safer and more pleasurable sail. The good thing about mistakes is that you will learn from them.

Finally, after four and a half hours, I was very relieved to see the light from the lighthouse. I gently woke Peter up and was too excited to go to sleep. We both had coffee and something to eat in the cockpit and time went fast until we rounded the lighthouse and changed direction for the Wessel Islands. I was totally exhausted and slept like a baby.

The following day, we arrived at the Wessel Islands. What a magical place, not a soul around except birds, millions of seashells and crabs. The anchorage was good and Scheherazade was safe there. I collected some empty seashells to send to my daughters and we watched the crabs. When they saw us, they dug themselves like corkscrews under the sand and did not come out until we stepped further away from them. What a wonderful and restful place. I loved being there! After we rested up, we continued to sail to Darwin.

Peter and I did not have to speak. We could understand each other just by looking in each others' eyes. We spoke just to hear each others' voices. We read a lot and I played the banjo mandolin. The weather was with us and the wind vane or autopilot steered the boat. I took the sights with the sextant and Peter did the navigation. We took turns steering as needed and Peter mostly set the sails while I did the reefing or hoisting and pulling in of the sails. Dolphins accompanied us part of the way and entertained us with their acrobatic skills and delighted us with their sounds. Occasionally, Peter pulled in a fish and we would cook and eat it.

It was morning when we saw the entrance to the sea basin of the Island of Melville before Darwin and we were thrilled. The thrill changed into total surprise, when the swell was something we had never experienced before. It moved Scheherazade up and down like a nutshell in a whirling big sea and we lost all sense of direction. The compass changed heading constantly and it felt as if we were in one of those crazy rides on a fairground. There were some fishing boats around us, which made the situation even trickier. One of them came so close that we could fortunately ask him for the course to Darwin. We were so glad to have this information.

Upon arrival in Darwin, we tied Scheherazade to the pier. It was Sunday and people came up to us and wanted to know where we had sailed from. Some of them invited us and we accepted all invitations. We also received an honorary membership card to the yacht club where we could get drinks and food for half price. We were also invited to watch Scotsmen in kilts dance for us. We were allowed to stay on the pier for twenty four hours and then had to make room for other boats so we anchored in the River basin where quite a few yachts and fishing boats were staying.

Crocodiles and many jellyfish swam in the salt water basin. It was so hot, that we jumped in and swam regardless. Crocodiles are reptiles who watch the habits of their prey. It is important that you do not repeatedly get out of the boat on the same side or in the same place. When you jump into the water, the jellyfish automatically float away from you. Once, an artist was painting a landscape even though people had warned him not to return every day to the same spot with his easel and canvas. An almost five meter long crocodile had a fatal go at him. The crocodile was caught and killed. They found the artist swallowed, clenching pieces of grass in each fist, where he had tried to hang onto the shore. Crocodiles were also infamous for swallowing dogs, who approach them out of curiosity, to sniff this often completely still reptile, which is capable of snapping them up at a surprisingly high speed.

The climate was hot and sticky in Darwin. It felt like the most agonizing climate I had ever experienced. The hair stuck to the sweating scalp and clothes were a nuisance. I cursed having to wear clothes in this climate but on board I only wore the bikini bottom. At least I could jump into the bay and cool off.

Shopping was torture. The asphalt was so painfully hot, that I ran from shady spot to shady spot. To make things worse, the existence of mosquitoes and sand flies (midges) even at night, was sheer hell. To sleep with a sheet pulled up over your head was too hot but kept the sand flies from biting. The tiny pests lay eggs under their victims skin which hatch and cause agonizing itching and sores from scratching. I finally figured out when I treated fresh stings, that alcohol (which we had on board to preheat the burners for our stove), would kill the eggs and stop the itching. I shared this newly acquired knowledge with everyone I met there.

Most people in Darwin were real and unforgettable characters who more than made up for the unpleasant, hot and sticky climate with the annoying sand flies. After a while, they would not sting so often any more. I believe that they prefer new blood and prefer to sting the ones who freshly arrive in the northern territory.

Darwin

We intended to stay in Darwin for three months until the hurricane season was over before we sailed on. Peter was searching for a job. He was taking any work that came along and said, "By the time they find out that it is not my profession, I am already doing it." I always admired his flexibility. No matter what he did, he did it well. The bosses and colleagues were always sad to see him leave. He would work until he had $3000 and that had to be enough to live on, until he needed to find work again.

When we took the dinghy to row on shore, we had to pass a few boats. The people living on them were very nice and some became close friends. The yacht 'Taharoa' with the Swiss couple Peter and Arlette and their cat "Son", who was nine years old and slept almost the whole day, were here and so was the yacht 'Nayla' with the couple Alan and Atao, described on an earlier page of this book.

They had just come together again after having been separated for a whole year after having a fight. A year previously, she had been thrilled to announce her pregnancy to Alan. They were both in their early twenties. Alan was more realistic and said that they could not afford to have a child just yet and that their boat was too small to raise a family. He suggested, she have an abortion. She terminated the pregnancy but did not forgive him.

Atao left him without taking any money and with just a few belongings, to hitch-hike around Australia. She was faced with enormous language difficulties during that trip because she spoke only her native language from Tuamotu Island, where she had grown up. She had only known animals like fish, birds, chickens, pigs and natural people with a simple, uncomplicated lifestyle. We all admired Atao's beauty, intelligence and courage. She learned fast. Atao had even tried working in a massage parlor until she found out that she was supposed to masturbate men. She managed to escape. I am sure she could write a book about her experiences during that year around Australia. When she got back to Darwin, she was so happy and relieved to find Alan still there. He felt the same way as Atao. They became inseparable.

Spissec, our Polish friend who had been stranded on a reef in the Torres Straits, had arrived well and happy in his small, pretty yacht which was still in good shape. It was a good thing we did not know before, that every reef, rock and island in the Torres Straits were named after the ships that had been wrecked on them.

I went to town to check out the art galleries, to return very disappointed. One gallery wanted to charge me $600 for four days of exhibition. The other one asked for $50 a day. Both galleries wanted to take a percentage from the sales as well! This was too much for me and I told them "& * é à!*%?*è'!?ù*!"

Then I went to the ANZ Bank and asked to speak with the director. I followed the secretary, who took me to Mr. Hammer. He asked me to sit down. Then I asked him if I could exhibit my creation, 'The Universal Flag' and showed him my curriculum vitae, exhibition record and press cuttings plus a photo of my creation. He then proceeded to show me a very privileged place on the wall between an original Picasso painting and a Miró, where I could hang my original the next day. An original from Hundertwasser also hung on the same wall. I was so happy.

Mr. Hammer called the press. I got an excellent article in the newspaper. Mr. Hammer wished me to come and see him once every week. I was so happy that things went so well for me.

When I got back to the boat, the bucket there was full with giant shrimps. A fisherman friend of ours had filled it to the rim and we shared it with our other friends. We cooked them onshore and they brought the wine, potato salad etc. We had a real feast. The fishermen were invited as well but could not come since they had to sell their catches etc.

Peter's "Volvo Penta" motor failed and he could not figure out what the problem was. He realized that the motor had to come out and was upset about that.

Just a short time later, he was offered a job as a mechanic and felt that he could only learn from this new occupation. One of his co-workers was looking for someone trustworthy to look after his friends' house in their absence for six weeks and to also take care of their two dogs. I am a dog lover and was all for it when Peter told me about the house and dog sitting job. Peter accepted on the condition, that we could use the washing machine and dryer, have friends come to visit us and use their garage to take the motor apart.

I asked a friend who was a fisherman, if he could help us pull the motor out of Scheherazade. He said, that was easy to do with his boat's yardarm. We had already struggled to get the motor to the cockpit where it was a cinch to pick it up. It was lowered it into the back of our friend's pick-up truck parked on the pier, where it was transported right to the house that we had agreed to watch.

There was a beautiful boxer dog chained up in the garden and a brain-damaged miniature poodle that constantly hid under the sofa, barking frantically. I hoped to be able to straighten out the tiny, over-bred dog and to gain his confidence with a lot of patience and love. I unchained the Boxer.

When Peter came home from work, we dismembered the motor. We took apart every piece, nut, bolt and screw. All pieces were then carefully scrubbed with a soft toothbrush in a plastic basin containing diesel oil, before we marked them and placed them onto a sheet of cardboard to dry. After about three weeks, the motor was still in pieces and we hadn't found the problem. Peter asked a friend at work to come and have a look at it. The friend arrived and inspected the cylinders. He looked and at one glance he said, "Here is the problem, it is obvious. There is a scratch right here." We looked but could hardly see the scratch which was much tinier than the thinnest hair. Then Peter's friend said "You have to send the block to Sydney to have it fitted with a new cylinder. This is what we did and the time for the truck to get the part to Sydney, repaired and back was estimated at about three weeks.

The weather became so bad that the truck with Scheherazade's motor part could not be driven because of the floods. We went to Scheherazade to check if everything was okay.

Peter and I had one of our very rare arguments. I threatened to jump off Scheherazade and swim to the pier which was about 1 1/2 km away from the anchorage. Peter said "You will never do that." I jumped in and fortunately had the tide with me to arrive safely.

Some fishermen noticed me climbing up to the pier in my wet dress. They asked me on board their ship and I accepted. They gave me a cabin and I could take a shower while my dress and slip were hanging in the breeze. While a big meal was prepared, the men handed me a whisky since they knew how upset I was and shared the feast with me. After eating, I was so exhausted, that I fell fast asleep in a bunk of the cabin, when somebody knocked on the door. Peter entered. I put my dress on and stood there. He came toward me and took me in his arms. I was so glad to see him.

He had searched all over for me without success. Then he had hurried to the police station, where he told them of my disappearance after I jumped into the bay. They said, "Must be an aboriginal woman - we will not search for her." (You can imagine of what I think of that!) Peter replied, "She is my girlfriend and comes from Switzerland." The police answered, "In that case, we will find her." As Peter returned to the pier, one of the fishermen had been looking for him to tell him that I was safe on board their trawler. We made up and were happy to be together again.

When the weather cleared up a little, I took the dinghy and motored down to the pier, where I tied it up and walked into town to do some shopping. By the time I was back in the dinghy and headed up the river, it was getting dark and the stormy weather surprised me. The outboard motor quit and waves came over the side. It was so rough, that I nearly panicked since the more I rowed up, the more it pulled me down the angry river. I managed to grab the raft of the digging station and shouted for help. The guard came out of the shed and helped me to tie up the tender. Then he took me inside and poured me a cup of coffee before fetching his strong powerboat and pulling me up to Scheherazade. Peter had been worried about me and we were both grateful to this really nice man, whose help I desperately depended on.

We cooked something to eat. A friend of ours offered to take over our house and dog-sitting responsibilities on the weekends while we were on board Scheherazade. Back at the house, the dogs were happy to see us again. We invited all our sailor friends to do the laundry at the house and to have a bath if they committed themsleves to clean the house up before the owners returned.

The little poodle would only eat when I put his food under the sofa. He refused to come out, except to follow when I took the boxer for a walk. Both dogs walked without being on a lead. I also gave the Boxer the run of the house. The poodle seemed slightly improved but could not bear to be touched. I respected this but felt sorry for the poor little beast, whose brain damage was entirely a direct result of man's perverted urge to alter nature.

This is the result of greed- to force nature into something it shouldn't be, with a careless disregard for suffering of innocent victims of all species. It is urgent call for all mankind to start to respect the animals' and other living beings' birthright, to choose their own partners without man's interference.

Man should help each other and share the planet with all other species. Leaders must take their responsibility to protect nature very seriously if we are to survive. No one has the right to abuse nature. If they do, it will not only hit back on them but also affect many innocent unfortunates, before the abuser gets a full dose of nature's revenge.

The house was cleaned up so spotlessly by our friends, that the owners of the house gave us more money than they had said they would. The part was back from Sydney and the motor rebuilt and reinstalled. However, it was too late to sail and we had to wait another three months until the rainy season was over to continue our voyage.

The rainy season in Darwin was so stormy, that we left the anchorage and motored Scheherazade up the river where she would be safe. Then we set two anchors. We were so happy to be back on board our home Scheherazade. It had been great to have running water and electricity but to watch nature in real life- instead of on TV, was to live in reality with our own mobile roof over our heads. We could feel the waters movement while hearing the lines on the rigging ringing like bells according to the wind speed.

I am so grateful to Peter and Scheherazade for making my dream of sailing around the world come true. Thanks to them, I was confronted with so much beauty already.

We were invited by friends living in Darwin to visit Margaret, a friend of theirs, who rescued kangaroos. She and Charley, a 1 1/2 year-old kangaroo, greeted us at her front door. Charley was rescued out of his mother's pouch, who had been killed by a car. Margaret intended to keep him as their personal pet and he had the run of the house and large garden. She and her boyfriend showed us the other kangaroos, whose lives they had saved. Over a dozen were kept in a sock, each under heat lamps and needed to be fed every 1 1/2 hours. They took care of twenty-four kangaroos and wallabies.

Margaret worked as a part time nurse and did this admirable work with her boyfriend and using their own money. When the animals came into puberty, she would let them go free in a nature reserve where they would not be shot or run over. People like them restore my belief in humanity.

The visas for Indonesia we had applied for still had not arrived. I visited Mr. Hammer at the ANZ Bank. He desired me and hoped I would go to a hotel with him. I told him I was in love with Peter.

He invited us to his home for a dinner party. I met his wife who is a very sensitive woman and their many guests. The food was delicious, the wines as well, and the mood was great but I could not understand why Hr. Hammer did not wish to stay faithful to such a pleasant woman. When he still urged me to sleep with him, I just said, "I have a date" or used some other excuse.

After three months of stringing him along, he told me to take my painting off the wall and said, "I will see that you will never be able to exhibit your artwork in any English bank." I was so fed up by men who offered to buy my work if I would have sex with them. Had I accepted their offers, I would be a very wealthy prostitute by now but my aim is to be a serious artist, with a non-prostituted head or body. I do not look down on prostitutes - each person has the right to choose their own life.

I carefully rolled 'The Universal Flag' together with 'The Sea Flag' and my latest creation, 'The Holy Flag', between sheets on a roll and covered them with plastic and stored them safely in the boat alongside the rest of my work. I managed to sell a few drawings but not enough to survive.

I wanted to help Peter and applied for a job to do graphics at the Government Printing Office. They asked me to choose a script with impact and space out the spelling of a slogan. When they saw me working on the poster, they said, "Use the computer. We don't do things like that by hand here." I admitted that I had no idea how to use a computer but that I was willing to learn if someone would show me how. The boss said, "We don't have time to teach you, you have to leave." I said, "What am I to do? I am completely broke." He said, "Get unemployment benefits." Humbly, I went to the office and was accepted to have a check sent every month to an account that I had to open. This meant that Peter could save his hard-earned salary for the voyage and Scheherazade's standing, sand blasting and repainting before leaving while I took care of the food and the stocking up of Scheherazade's cover and shelves for the coming trip we planned to Indonesia.

Peter's mother visited us in Darwin. We went out together while Peter was still working. I took her to one of my favorite pubs where I had many aboriginal and other friends. It was the wildest pub, except one of the truckers' cafes we also visited later. I accepted a dance. Eileen, Peter's mother also danced and we had a great time. Then, I directly caught the intense eyes of a man and had to ignore my true feelings for him. I fell immediately in love with him but denied the truth to myself since I wanted to be true to Peter. After a week staying with us, Eileen had to fly back to Sydney. My thoughts were constantly with that man called 'Bill' and every time I stepped on land I hoped to get a glimpse of him.

The Power of the Erotic

I felt guilty for desiring that man since I also loved Peter. My whole body ached and longed for him. It was a power that was stronger than me. No matter how I tried, I could not stop thinking about that gorgeous man called Bill.

He was a healthy blond and blue-eyed man who looked like a

God with irresistible sex appeal. He wore a sleeveless T shirt that revealed his muscular arms. I longed so much to be in them. His Poseidon-like face was framed with a blond beard that had a red shine to it. At the same time, I wished to stay with Peter. I went shopping for food when Peter was at work and did not look for Bill. Then I went shopping again and Bill looked for me.

    We spoke to each other. He felt the same desire for me. I told him about Peter and he told me about the woman he lived with. We agreed to have a drink together. We were sipping on a second drink, when we both realized that it was no use at all to fight this thing called love. We drove to a motel and ended in an embrace. Something occurred that never before had happened to either one of us. We both had multiple orgasms which would not stop, until someone knocked on the door to interrupt us, at the time we had arranged, to let us know when it was 5 p.m. Just as well. Otherwise, we would have continued until we died of exhaustion! What a way to go, but not yet, please.

    We both had the need to go back to our partners. We jumped into our clothes and made a date for the next day. Then Bill drove me to the dinghy and I motored up the river to Scheherazade where I prepared dinner and motored back to shore to pick up Peter who was coming home from work. I still floated, feeling Bill's warmth.

    Peter sensed something. I told him that I could not resist Bill but would take the full responsibility and consequences of my own actions, which were so powerful that I could not control them. Peter said, "Whatever you do, please don't leave me." I was so touched by Peter's words that we made love that evening.

    The next day, I kept my date and Bill and I ended up in his fishing boat. He had also made love to his girlfriend. Bill and I tried to get together again but it did not work out. We tried again the following day, but neither of us could reach orgasm. Maybe, because we had been back with our partners. We parted as friends, richer for an unforgettable memory and returned to our partners.

The motor had been sent back from repair in Sydney and was installed in its old place on board. It was time to have Scheherazade pulled out of the water and get on with all the work we planned to do before leaving. A price was agreed for the use of the slipway and the cradle plus the special overalls and sand. Peter looked like a sponge diver as he removed all the paint from Scheherazade's hull by sandblasting. We were amazed at the good state we found the steel to be in after having it stripped. It had been at least five years since that had been done. I helped with painting and anti-fouling. Scheherazade looked like new and I loved that beautiful ship which got us safely through the most dangerous situations.

Peter and I never mentioned the love affair with Bill again. When Scheherazade was anchored safely in the bay, we went to the out backs of Darwin. It was a real wildlife paradise. Sometimes we would motor the dinghy up the river into the gorge and to the bush.

Often, we walked for hours watching the wildlife. We even spotted an albino water buffalo taking a bath in one of the natural pools together with some brown ones. There were many species of birds and reptiles. I remember the crowned herons, penguins, crocodiles, kangaroos, wallabies, bush babies, insects and other life.

Aboriginals had warned me not to go barefoot any more since it was too dangerous for people who had not grown up in the bush. I ignored their well-meant advice. There was a narrow stretch of track, which was totally overgrown on each side. Peter went ahead of me, since I preferred to go slowly and inspect the overgrowth for beasties.

When I decided to follow Peter, a fully-grown brown snake blocked my way and took the attacking position. She was coiled up with a raised upper body and with her head moving toward me with the mouth open. I shouted "Sch- sch- sch and clapped my hands but she would not move away. Then I took a stick out of the bushes and hit it on the ground in front of her but she still remained there. I wanted to catch up with Peter, so I jumped over her and did not look back. Had she bitten me, I would have been dead in less then a minute. The Brown Snake is the most toxic of all Australian snakes.

Peter and I caught up before dark. The sunset was intense, spreading a red-golden sheen on the sand and bushes which looked magical. Darwin in the distance started to come alive with electric light.

Welcome Visitor on Board

I was sitting under the awning's shade in the cockpit, when a grass-green lizard about 60 cm long climbed up Scheherazade's fender and sat on the stern of the boat. Slowly, I tiptoed to the gangway and looked at Peter with the index finger in front of my lips, waving to him and pointing to the stern. He moved slowly up to the cockpit and we both watched this beautiful reptile in amazement. It was panting and had probably been chased by a predator and looked for shelter. It seemed to know that we were not going to hurt it. After a while it relaxed and stayed with us for almost an hour. We were privileged to have him as our guest since those lizards are extremely rare and normally very shy.

A few days later, I sketched a praying mantis, which sat on Scheherazade's stern railing. Peter and I had lived almost two years in Australia and were ready to expand our horizons by sailing to new places. Our friends Alan and Atao from the yacht 'Nayla' and our friends Peter and Arlette from the yacht 'Taharoa' planned to leave the same time as we did and meet us at the King George River Waterfalls twenty four miles above Bonaparte Bay. Before sailing, we all stocked up our ships with food from the bulk food store at reduced prices because of the need for big quantities. Then we filled our tanks. Bonaparte Bay was going to be our last Australian destination. We tried to obtain permission to go there but to no avail, so we decided to sail there anyhow. The freedom of sailing a boat is that you can go anywhere you like.

Toward Bonaparte Bay, Freak Wave

I went to my favorite pub to say goodbye to all my aboriginal and other friends. The police came in and went toward an aboriginal woman and accused her of being drunk and disorderly. She had only had a couple of glasses of weak beer and laughed. All the aboriginal men and women in the room got up from their seats and protected her from being taken to the station. I admire their courage to stand up and defend each other from discriminating policemen or anything else. The police went away. I had a last drink with all that had become so dear to me and then went back to Peter.

The next day, Scheherazade was ready to sail and so were we. Alan and Atao, Peter and Arlette were almost ready to go as well. We all planned to meet again at our next destination. Peter and I were the first to start the voyage.

The Australian Air Force followed us every day with their planes. Sometimes they even followed us twice. We were not happy about their invasion of our privacy and I was tempted to moon them but Peter thought this would not be a good idea. We could not think of a reason for the pilots to follow us. We were happy with the weather and would not let this spoil our good time. We had been followed before and got kind of used to it, that big brother was watching us. They did it to all the yachts sometimes. I guess they have nothing better to do.

We approached the Bonaparte Bay on a late afternoon. We turned toward the river on our left and got into such shallow waters that we were forced to make a quick 180° turn and then aimed for the other river on the opposite side of the bay. We just managed to pass the sandbank on the bottom of the river on the incoming tide. After crossing the bank, we were in safe deep water and could sail 24 miles to the waterfalls on top. The river was wide enough to sail all the way and the tide helped us to get there faster. We only had a few hours left before the tide would change but made it to the top in enough daylight to tie Scheherazade under a cliff where she could not be seen by the air force.

What a gorgeous and magic place! There were three waterfalls there. The cliffs on both sides of the river consisted of some of the oldest stones in the world and were horizontally striped in colors from pastel pinks to red, beige, ochre and purple. We lowered the dinghy and rowed with our laundry and empty water canisters to the smallest of the three large waterfalls that fell from the platform, at least thirty meters above.

We checked out all three waterfalls and found the biggest one large enough to take Scheherazade under it the next day to wash her and her sails clear of all the salt water. Refreshed from enjoying the shower under the waterfall in this absolutely paradise-like environment, we returned to Scheherazade where Peter immediately caught a fresh fish for dinner. As the tide went out, a multitude of oysters could be discovered on the cliffs where Scheherazade was tied.

For breakfast, I took some wild bush lemons and the hammer and screwdriver into the dinghy and ate about thirty oysters fresh off the cliff. Peter preferred his usual porridge. I ate oysters every day we were there and never felt better. I was free from guilt since they were in such abundance. In the afternoon, we untied Scheherazade and motored her under the waterfall. Peter was at the helm while I stayed on the bow. When we were under the waterfall, the water pressure knocked me straight down onto the deck and I was unable to get up but enjoyed the powerful, invigorating massage tremendously.

The red rocks were full of wild life and so was the clear blue water. There were lizards, snakes, butterflies, turtles, crocodiles, and a multitude of fish etc. Soon, Alan and Atao in 'Nala' found us and so did Peter and Arlette in 'Taharoa'. They arrived last, since they had constructed their yacht out of concrete.

A full-moon party was in order to celebrate us being together again. The men went fishing and Peter caught a 1 1/2 meter-long grouper fish, while we made a fire on shore. Atao wanted to cook the grouper. She knew many different ways to cook fish. I canned some of the fish and all six of us ate the rest in the next two days for lunch and dinner. Peter and Arlette's cat "Son" ate from it as well.

The men had decided to go hunting for a change of diet. They took their guns and left us women behind. I felt so lonely without Peter. To top it off, we had had an argument, which made me utterly miserable. I never liked to be apart before the argument was settled. I started to feel depressed and homesick for my daughters again. Trying to make it go away with yoga and meditation, I walked to the nearest sandy beach and started to sing. In this beautiful place, I composed a song for Alexa and Julie called, *Nature is all*.

It was the first time I started to regret not being able to write music but I managed to play it on my mandolin banjo and to jot it down later. Since I had no money left, I sent them this song, (a waltz) for their birthdays.

Nature is gentle and Nature is tough
Nature is smooth and Nature is rough
Nature is lovely and who are we
Nature is you and Nature is me
You are your senses - see what you are
Hear what you sound like - touch what you are
Smell what you taste and that you will be
Nature is you and Nature is me
Nature is all and so are we
Nature is all and so are we

After having composed the song, I was happy and felt strong again. I had learned to get myself out of depression quite fast by diverting my thoughts and creating something.

The men came back from hunting without having seen an animal to be killed and I was glad about that. So again, we had fish for dinner as usual. After a few days, a pilot spotted us while flying acrobatics down the plateau towards the cliffs under which all three of our yachts were tied.

Our friends also planned to sail to Kupang and Timor, as we did and so we all took advantage of the tide going out and sailed down the large river into the bay and out to the Timor sea where we lost sight of each other. The weather was grey and the wind was quite fast and we made good time toward Timor.

We did not worry too much about night watch and each of us just had a look around from time to time. There was no heavy traffic. It felt a bit chilly, so we mostly stayed below. The sea looked smooth. After we had a good night's rest, the porridge was simmering in the pot on top of the gimballed stove.

A freak wave hit us and lifted Scheherazade up and threw her onto her side. Water poured through the vents like fire hoses and down the companion way, which flooded the whole floor and swamped the mattresses. The worst thing was that the pot of porridge was thrown off the cooker and the porridge, mixed with salt water, made such a mess, getting stuck even in the smallest cracks and spaces. We still found porridge three months later. The best thing was that we were inside when the enormous wave surprised us. Otherwise, we could have been washed overboard. What was a mystery, was how exactly this gigantic freak wave could arrive in the middle of a gentle swell. We were both a bit shaken up but did not let it bother us and started automatically to clean up the mess. We tied the wet mattress on top of the spray dodger to dry, pumped the water out of the floor, cleaned the porridge and salt water mix the best way we could and watched the waves from the cockpit, while we drank a strong cup of coffee with rum in it. I noticed that every eighth wave was slightly bigger than the rest of them. Probably, there was shelving bottom below us which resulted in the freak wave and crossing waves that caused each eighth wave to be the largest.

Kupang, Timor

The grey sky turned bluer and bluer the closer we got to Indonesia. We were so happy to spot land again. Faintly in the distance, we just could make out the islands of Timor and Roti which came slowly more into focus and we sailed between those two islands in weird currents and toward eastern Timor, where we dropped the anchor in front of Kupang on May 14, 1980.

We had heard that the war there was over but it still went on in eastern Timor where it was forbidden to go. We were forced to waste two days for bureaucracy to get a permit to stay, even though we showed them our visas. We had to fill out form after form of a whole stack of papers. The men who were working there, seemed not to have anything to do and wanted to practice their English on us. They all asked, "You have present for me?" They wanted money, clothes and especially (there, illegal) Playboy magazines.

A lieutenant in uniform carrying a machine gun, was motored out to Scheherazade to watch our boat while we were taken to the commanding officer who wished to see us. There was nothing we could do, except go along with them and leave Scheherazade to be watched by the stranger. We were driven by a chauffeur in a Land Rover to an official building. Then we were accompanied up the stairway to a room where we were introduced to the top commanding officer.

He stood in front of us in his decorated uniform and greeted us in a very welcoming manner. He invited us to a very posh restaurant on the western side of Timor Island for dinner. The food was beautifully decorated and delicious, the dessert was mouth-watering and the wine was excellent and so was the after dinner brandy. Peter and I mostly let him speak. He told us that the average income in Timor was $150 a year, school was not obligatory and the life expectancy was 50 years. There are Muslims and Christians. Before religion arrived, the boys had to steal something of value before they were allowed to marry. Then the Muslims cut of their right arms to stop them from stealing. For 100 rupiahs (5 cents) one can eat a meal at the Warung (little restaurant). There was no toilet paper and the rear end is cleaned with water and the left hand. They eat with the right hand.

The commanding officer told us of the lush beauty of Timor and that the next day we were expected to be ready for him to show us a very beautiful place 55 km from Kupang. He also said, that neither he nor any of his men were from Timor but came from other Indonesian islands and that they often felt lonely and homesick away from their families. We enjoyed the dinner with this man and we were driven back and motored out to Scheherazade by his chauffeur who took the guard with the machine gun back with him.

We slept without waking up until morning as a welcome change from the night watches at sea. Meanwhile, 'Nayla' and 'Taharoa' had anchored next to us. The owners of Nayla were not allowed on shore and were forced to sail back to Darwin to get a visa that they refused to issue them in Timor. They hoped to meet us in Bali again. We shouted over to Taharoa, that we would see them later since we had a date on shore.

The guard was dropped off again on Scheherazade and we were taken to the shore where we slid into the rear of the Land Rover driven by the chauffeur. The chief commander in his uniform sat in the front seat next to the chauffeur. First they took us to a place in town and we got out of the car. The commander stayed inside.

Immediately, we were surrounded by people who stared at us in amazement. Most of them had never seen a white person before. The braver ones touched us gently to see if we were real. They all looked half-starved and poor. One of their babies started to cry when it saw us and turned in fear toward its mother. We gave the people smiles and touched their hands. We felt like the animals in a zoo with the difference that we could escape back into the car.

The chauffeur drove very fast out of the section to a road outside town. Huts could be sometimes seen on both sides of the road. The chauffeur drove so fast, that he drove over a pig and sometime later, over a chicken. He did not stop to find out whose treasure he had killed. I asked the chauffeur to slow down. Then we noticed that the natives who saw the director, almost turned into stone and their expressions showed shock and fear. Some people had covered their faces with white clay so you could see only the eyes, nostrils and lips. Neither one of the men could tell me the reason they did this. The chauffeur pressed the gas pedal right to the floor again and once more, he killed some chickens that belonged to the very poor, before we arrived at a gorgeous place in the jungle.

We got out of the car for a swim in a natural pool under a waterfall surrounded by very large and impressive, ancient trees. We were amazed by the beauty that surrounded us and filled our hearts with delight, until we noticed that the whole area was guarded by military personnel who saluted the chief.

The magic of the jungle was gone. I had to pull myself together to not show resentment. We felt it dangerous not to keep them on our side. After this place, they drove us to see the large land turtles and Komodo dragons which had been given to them as a gift from Komodo. The land turtles were from Timor and were kept in a large field.

The Komodo dragons, a male and a female, were fenced in by chicken wire. I called the two wonderful reptiles over to me and they responded. I spoke to them in Swiss German (my mother tongue) and they seemed to understand every word I said. The guard threw a live chicken to each and they put one foot on it and pulled the head right off. Before the chicken could realize what had happened, it was decapitated and eaten.

The dragons looked like the oldest animals I had ever seen. Their heads were almost square and their grey blue, thick and textured skin was ancient. It looked older than the elephant or crocodile. From the back of the head down to the tail they were graced with a zigzag. They react like gigantic lizards with muscles like crocodiles but are much taller. They looked directly into my eyes and moved their large necks under their almost square heads which rather resemble snakes. They are able to move their blue, slim, forked tongues very quickly. Their lips are pink and their almost-scales grey-black. Their finger nails are nearly ten inches long, pointy and black. Their eyes are very expressive and they close them with the lid from the bottom up like a chicken. I feel lucky indeed, to have seen this rare and magnificent species of animal and will never forget them.

I was told that a man who attacked a Komodo dragon was killed. This happened only once because those gorgeous animals are protected. They are known to be very docile and on Komodo Island they go free and are not afraid of men who leave them in peace. It is considered to be bad luck if you hurt or kill one. The land turtles were also very interesting and the largest ones I had ever seen.

We also found out that the hospitals were not free of charge but that the poor could buy remedies for everything, even to make vaginas smaller or penises larger for only one cent a piece from the jungle doctor.

We were invited by the commander again the next day but told him that we had promised to see our friends and wished to go to the market and buy things we needed for our soon-continuing voyage. We thanked the chief for his generosity and said goodbye.

When we were dropped off at the yacht, Peter and Arlette on 'Taharoa' had prepared dinner for us and our friends on 'Nayla'. Arlette was an artist and professional cook. We all had dinner together and told each other about the Timor Sea, the time on shore and the damned bureaucracy, etc. and laughed together.

The next day Arlette and I decided to go to the market in Kupang while the men worked on the yachts. Peter asked, "Can you bring back some chicken?" Arlette and I rowed on shore. We came to a watch post. They made us show our passports and visas and fill out papers again. We told them that we only wanted to buy food at the market but they sent us, followed by a soldier, to the next post where we were left waiting to fill out more papers. When we did, they wanted us to go to yet another watch post.

Arlette had enough and said, "We are going back home." I replied "Look, we fought to get through two posts already, let's not have them break our will, lets find out what they are trying to hide from us." So we were accompanied to the third post. Again, we had to wait and were then forced to fill out more forms and had to promise to take the bus straight to the market and not go anywhere else. After the long struggle, we were finally free (?) to go.

I noticed that we were followed. For some reason, they did not want us to go on our own. We took the bus and got out at the market. We also looked for chicken meat but there were only live roosters. Arlette bought a beautiful rooster and asked me if it was okay for her to return to the boat. I said, "It's ok if you don't mind if I stay."

We parted and I managed to lose the man following me. I went to explore the section I had heard was so dangerous. I found it to be too depressing to be described by words and returned to the market to fill my bag with fresh vegetables and fruit. Then I bought a gorgeous live rooster and wanted him as a pet. With shopping bag over my shoulder and the rooster in my arms, I took the bus back. The people who spoke broken English asked, "Is good fighting cock." I replied, "Fighting no good, cock is my friend." They thought I was crazy but smiled at me, some of them with red juice from the betel nut they chewed running down from the corners of the mouths to their chins. When I was back, I shouted my high-pitched "Uh-Uh!" sound out to Peter who came and picked me up with the dinghy. He was not too happy about my new pet.

We and our friends on 'Taharoa and 'Nayla, were angry at the bureaucracy and planned to leave. For the FIRST TIME we were forced to go on shore and do more paperwork to get A PERMIT TO LEAVE. There, one of the bureaucrats said to Peter, "You go to Bali, girls have big eyes and small pussy."

Arlette had killed her rooster and prepared him to be eaten cold. We all decided to leave this place the next day. No way could I kill my rooster. He had the run of the boat and loved to sit on the railing. He did not want to come inside. I fed him wheat that we had to make our own bread and the left over salad. We ate fish and went to sleep.

At midnight "Elvis" as I had named the rooster, started to crow. Peter said, "For God's sake, shut him up." I jumped out of bed and patted him while talking to him. He seemed calm so I went back to bed. Fifteen minutes later he started to crow again. Peter said, "If you don't shut him up, I will kill him." I got up again and noticed that he had to lift his neck and head up to be able to crow. So I put the bucket over him and went to bed. It took less than a minute for him to throw off the bucket and before he went on the cabin top. I returned to bed and when he crowed again, I hurried to hold him in my arms for an hour, before I went inside again. I fell so deeply asleep, that I did not hear anything. Peter was sound asleep as well.

When we got up in the morning, Peter went to the cockpit and noticed that Elvis had eaten most of our fresh vegetables and wherever he had defecated, on board, the chlorinated rubber paint had melted. I promised Peter that I would repair it but he was still annoyed. Elvis sat on the railing enjoying the sunrise, which showed off his beautiful multicolored plumage. What a proud rooster he was.

Peter and I ate a hearty breakfast and then he said "Let's get ready to sail, can you hoist the anchor?" While I was turning the anchor winch handle, I heard a faint "Cro-w.......!" and looked back to see Peter with the machete in his hand, having beheaded Elvis on the chopping board. At sea again and with tears in my eyes, I prepared and cooked him. We ate him for dinner and then I blew my nose and dried my cheeks with the comforting thought that Elvis would live on in me. I could understand Peter's reaction and he could understand my disappointment but we both found it better to live in the present and enjoy life.

I loved Timor's mountains, tropical nature and fertility, which reminded me of Tahiti but just hundreds of years behind and more primitive. The air and water was clean. Timor has beautiful ponies, they export fish and cattle and have found uranium and oil. No wonder the Portuguese did not want to lose their colony.

I hate war! It is a dirty way to acquire financial gain by

milking, suppressing, brainwashing, mutilating or killing people and robbing their land. I could understand a poor devil who steals something to eat. But he will be punished by man-made laws. It would be good to make a law against the mental cannibalism of the greedy, unscrupulous warmongers who threaten the health of our beautiful planet more than the so-called "ordinary people" can ever do.

On the other hand, I found some of the primitive and poor people very cruel as well. The nicest people I found were the sailors, artists, fishermen and small farmers.

Sumba Island

We were sailing in the Suva Sea of the Indian Ocean toward Sumba Island. The wind and waves came from all directions and the waves were 11 feet high. We were forced to tack often and our voyage felt quite rough for a while.

Peter pulled a large fish up on the line attached to the bow. Dolphins accompanied us a small distance away, which always filled our hearts with joy. The clouds had left and the sunset was celebrated with the first and last drink of the day, while sailing. A 1 1/2 meter stingray jumped out of the water. We had never seen that before. He was probably chased by a predator.

At sunrise, I went on deck and took a sight of the sun with the sextant. Every once in a while Peter and I looked out for land with the aid of binoculars. Every time we spotted land we got excited. It proved that our navigation was spot on. When the bay of Waingapu came into focus we were happy that our estimated timing was right as well. To measure the water speed, Peter threw a log over the stern. To check the wind speed, he used an anemometer attached to the rigging.

We approached the port and dropped the anchor on May 14, 1980, in rather shallow and murky water. Scheherazade's keel lightly touched the sandy bay bottom. Before we could put everything away, nearly twenty native men followed the harbor master and climbed on board without permission. They all stood on one side of the yacht. We yelled at them in panic, that Scheherazade could fall on her side and it was not easy to convince them to spread their load out evenly but they finally understood with the help of quick sketches I had drawn. I blocked the companion way so they were unable to go below, while Peter spoke to the harbor master. They had only come to greet us and were like children. We managed to make them understand, that they could come back the next day, since we were tired and had to put the sails away plus go on shore to do the bureaucracy which was nearly as bad as it had been in Timor.

After a lot of wasted time filling out forms, we got permission to go on land to explore Sumba Island. Sumba means sandalwood but there was not one single sandalwood tree left. We went back to the yacht and some of the natives came to visit.

In Darwin we had been told by other sailors to bring jeans, jackets, sunglasses and tennis shoes for trading with the natives in Indonesia. We had checked out some second hand shops and had brought all those things with us. We showed them to the men and they brought us beautiful hand-woven and natural colored blankets that took four months to weave, antique silver and other artifices they traded with us for old clothes. They almost fought each other over the six pairs of sunglasses. It was very hot but that did not restrain one guy from wearing the multicolored ski jacket he had acquired by trading his stuff for ours.

We looked at Sumba but did not feel free. It was taboo to point to anything with the index finger, to stroke your hand over the head of a child and to put your hands on your hips. When you walk freely, they sometimes try to throw stones at you. Those little islands are hardly ever visited and the people are afraid of visitors. The Indonesian food is delicious but the bureaucracy annoyed us so much, that we decided to leave and not to visit Flores, Komodo, Simbawa and Lombok as planned but instead headed straight for Bali, the "Tourist Island", where we hoped to find less bureaucracy.

Peter motored Scheherazade out of the Waingapu Bay and

out to sea. There was not enough wind and the old Volvo had to do hard labor all night long. We still had to make about 200 miles to Bali and were grateful for enough wind to be able to give the motor a well-deserved rest. We discussed which sail to set and pulled them up. The winds increased and we made good time on our long run toward Bali.

I put new strings on my banjo-mandolin, while a beautiful tropical bird rested on Scheherazade's railing. He was already with us for 1 1/2 hours. Flying fish flew on deck and Peter threw the living ones back into the sea but fed the dead ones to the bird who stayed with us for thirty minutes more.

We could see Flores and Komodo as we passed them and just before Simbawa, we believed we were being followed by a pirate ship. I made some Molotov cocktails out of empty bottles by stuffing them with rags drenched in petrol ready to light, should we be threatened. Peter had the Gurkha knife hidden behind the compass box. The old sailing ship seemed to follow us and got closer and closer. Then Scheherazade was overtaken by the rough looking Indonesian sailing vessel while the men waved friendlily to us. We were SO relieved!

We passed Lombock and the swell en route to Bali was so strong and against us, that it took hours to try and get there in daylight. We saw that we could not make it and headed away into deep water to be safe for the night and would head for Bali again just before dawn. We had not realized how far we had drifted off course and it took us all day just to arrive at dusk and anchor Scheherazade in front of the Benoa yacht club in Bali.

Bali

On the morning of May 25, 1980 we went to the office as was demanded of us, to show our passports and visas and obtain a permit to stay. The office was full of people and the heat was almost unbearable. After we had been waiting for 1 1/2 hours, I became dizzy and because there were no chairs, I sat on the window sill. The uniformed bureaucrat behind the counter yelled at me and commanded me to stand up immediately. He would not serve me in my turn but said, "You come last." After Peter's papers were checked, I told him not to wait for me and I was served three hours later.

I noticed that all the bureaucrats who were male had grown their little finger nails up to about 5cm in length and stuck them out like an old lady drinking her tea, in order to not damage them. They grew their nails so long to show the world that they were better than the rest and did not need to do manual work, which proved their stupidity to me. Unfortunately, their pay was higher than that of the rice field families who do something constructive.

I was not in a great mood when I got back to Scheherazade but Peter cheered me up. The water tanks on Scheherazade were low and there was only half a canister of water left in the cockpit. We poured it into the tank and loaded the cans into the dinghy. Then we rowed on shore to fill all our empty jerry cans.

When we got back, Peter did not want to pour them into the tanks since he was not sure how good the quality was. We used the water to make coffee, tea, soups and for boiling but I drank it unboiled. I drank water from the pipes everywhere and never became ill. This time I was so sick and had such stomach cramps and fever and diarrhea, that I nearly gave up. I almost feared it may be typhoid fever. Peter brought me the mail from Alexa who was by then living with her father in the U. S. A. and was studying drama and Julie who was in gymnasium in Switzerland and news from my parents. Their letter with so much love, helped me to recover very fast. We boiled the water before drinking it for a minimum of twenty minutes while in Bali.

'Taharoa' had already arrived there since they had sailed without stopping straight to Bali. We also met new sailors and made friends on shore. We took the bus to explore the island and as soon we got away from the tourist mecca, we were astonished at Bali's beauty.

To eat on land was more reasonable than to cook for

ourselves, so we did not prepare our meals on board any more. There were many native people cooking with woks on top of burners attached to bottles of gas at the side of the streets. If they looked healthy, we would try their food since they ate the same. They usually cooked chicken, fish or rice with vegetables and desserts for next to nothing and they tasted wonderful. One of my favorite dishes was "sate", beef pieces marinated with a special flavor chili and peanut sauce and fried on a stick. Often the delicate food was seasoned with ginger, garlic, chili, coconut, peanuts, cinnamon and other exotic spices.

I met some tourists who were afraid to eat the delicious native food and preferred to eat American hamburgers or Swiss sausages in Kuta where you could find such things as restaurants, bars gift shops and kiosks but not what I needed- an art gallery.

I found out from a sailor, that you could get an omelet with magic mushrooms in Kuta. Peter had to do some maintenance on the motor, and was edgy and refused my help. Instead, he went to call his friend from another yacht to come over. My feelings were hurt and I took a bus to the market on my own. When I got back, I asked Peter for the small amount of cash needed to go and taste the magic mushroom omelet since I was completely broke. He refused, so I made it my goal to get that omelet any way.

I took my camera and went to Kuta. There, I saw two young men who offered to play a game of chess for money. I asked one of them if he wanted to play a game with me and if I should lose, I would give him my camera but if I should win, then he would help me sell the camera and find me the place I could get the omelet. They agreed. Since I don't like to play games, it took all my concentration to win. The man sold my camera and took me to a woman who showed me the mushrooms before she put them into the omelet and I ate it with pleasure.

I was amazed how much money I had left and invited the man and his friend for a drink. I did not miss the camera, which was not of the best quality but had been all that I could afford to buy second hand. After the drink the mushrooms started to work. I walked to the beach. A group of musicians were playing for their own pleasure. They came from Lombok, Bali's neighboring island which was visible from there. They told me about Lombok. Everything looked very intense. I tried to analyze my impressions the best way I could and not be afraid of the reactions and to use my body and mind to do my own research.

When I stroked my hand through the air I made the discovery that:

Many red green and blue dots showed a pattern in strict order, which filled the space behind my movement for an instant before melting to invisibility with the atmosphere. Energy became visible.

I also noticed that all smokers had a sick yellow-green complexion and the bottom of their eyelids were dark red underlined. Quite a horrible sight but I never regret any of my experiences, since this would not do any good and it is better to learn from them.

However, I DO NOT recommend the use of drugs since they can be very hard to deal with or become addictive, dangerous or even deadly.

Later on, I found that life is best with a brain free of drugs, alcohol or tobacco. (I am not speaking of life saving medicines). Back at a Kuta side road, I watched two old women fight for a leek. They each tried to snatch the vegetable, using one fist to fend the other off for dear life. I found this very sad and had to restrain myself from taking it away from them, breaking it in two and giving each of the women half. Then I thought, a lawyer would probably give them each only one third and keep one third for himself. This way he could make a leek soup as well. I would not like to be a lawyer.

I got the bus back and suddenly, I started to feel sorry for all the people who looked unhappy. I had to hold my tears back. My brain tried to cope with every impression and I got a hold of myself by looking at nature. Trees and bushes calmed me. When I got out of the bus half an hour later, I was still feeling the effects of the omelet and found Peter having a drink with friends at the yacht club of Benoa.

I went to join him and a sudden panic struck me. Peter said that anyone who would eat poisoned mushrooms deserved to die. His words cut like a razor. Peter had never smoked or tried drugs and could not understand why anyone did. I imagined his remark to be the result of my unfaithfulness to him with Bob in Darwin but I had been faithful to my own feelings.

I felt grateful to be finally free from the effects of the drug. The Benoa Yacht Club consisted of a primitive hut with a corrugated tin roof, only three walls, a long bench and table plus very small bar. It had an earth floor. In front of the hut, I could see a native couple. She was sitting on a chair while he stood behind her checking her hair for lice. Then they changed positions and she looked for lice on him. This was a sign of affection which brought a smile to my face.

We were a whole group of sailors who came to know each other and shared adventures. We gave each other information about ports and bureaucracy and we exchanged sea charts etc. We also helped one another out when needed and lent each other tools. We all had the love of freedom and nature in common and felt happiest on our boats but also enjoyed a good party with lots of laughter.

Sometimes in ports, there was the odd pompous owner of a motor yacht, whose uniformed crew was forced to polish the brass every day in military manner while the owner stood importantly over them like a peacock. He shouted commands standing there with a fat belly, his captain's hat on and with a drink in his hand. This we could observe in some ports and even though we should have felt pity for those men with their inferiority complexes, we could not help laughing at the comedic situation.

We met Holger who was a doctor of medicine from Germany.

He was one of three owners of a concrete sailing boat. They had argued, 'As three women would in the same kitchen' so he bought the others out. Even two real men are a problem in a small space. It will only work if one of them is the leader and the others are followers.

Holger had invited us to his yacht. 'Likedealer' and introduced us to his friends Dieter and Yuyun. Dieter was a tall and handsome young biologist from Germany and Yuyun was a beautiful young woman from Bali. She was one of four female poets in Indonesia, which is a very honorable position with more rights because it is a vocation. Dieter and Yuyun were so much in love but had to hide their feelings onshore, since it is forbidden for Hindus to fall in love with Christians or any other religion. The leaders of religions may preach love but keep on brainwashing and selecting people which will only result in more inbreeding, illness and grief in the human race.

Hindus have four castes. The highest, the Brahmins, are the richest, who are allowed to have a TV. They are not allowed to marry, unless they come from within the same caste.

The Bali newspaper sent a reporter who asked me for an interview. He also photographed me holding up the Universal Flag on board Scheherazade. The reporter asked us, if we knew somebody who lived aboard a yacht and was willing to let him write an article for the newspaper. I asked Holger on 'Likedealer', who was all for it. We were photographed again on 'Likedealer' with Yuyun, Dieter and Doris, who was another medical doctor from Germany who planned to settle on Bali with her boyfriend.

They were building their own house with their own hands out of bamboo from the country side. The next day Dieter and Yuyun invited us to join them on a inland trip. Yuyun knew Bali like her own navel.

First we went to see the Indonesian temple dance school. She showed us how the girls were dressed by being wrapped in sixteen meters of the finest silk cloth for the dance ceremony. They also wore beautiful headdresses and jewelry. It was very interesting, colorful and charming to see the positive side of the Hindu culture and I almost failed to see the underside of the religion.

We were also invited to a Hindu mass. A Hindu band played traditional music on their instruments while professional dancers enchanted us with their graceful movements. Bowls with lighted candles were passed from one to the other amongst the worshippers sitting on benches in the large Hindu tent during mass. After the mass ended, food was served. The next three days we spent in Piliatan, Ubud and surroundings. We had a really good time.

At the Loswum (guest house) they charged us the sum of $1 a night for a room with 2 double beds, accommodating 4 persons. It was in a romantic setting and was part of a dance school. Most of the Indonesians artists live in Piliatan and Ubud.

I met a 70 year-old artist who had grown up in Bali with his Dutch parents. He had lived in the Australian bush and spent eight years living in a cave where he survived on rats etc. He was a fascinating man who had many stories to tell.

Our friends spoke Indonesian which made this trip especially interesting. We swam in a glass-clear river and stood under a wonderful waterfall. It was so private, that no clothes were needed. We ate different delicacies. A tropical fruit salad with coconut was between 25 and 100 Rupees.

About a week later, Dieter and Yuyun escaped from Bali. When Yuyun went missing, the airport and harbors were put under guard without success. I am still curious about how the lovers did it and how they got on. I wish them good luck, freedom and happiness.

Religion f*** off-----------------I refuse to see a crime in love

I was wondering why the newspaper had not printed my

Universal Flag and asked why. I was told it was because of technical difficulties but it should be printed soon. When it was finally printed, they had cut the bottom off where I had written **Life is Legal.** I resented their censorship, since my work had been unveiled with the message on it:

The wind and the sea gave this canvas to me to create the universal flag and say that life is legal.

I try to get the human race to live on a higher level of intelligence for the sake of the survival of life on our beautiful planet.

We were able to have our visas extended another six weeks because Peter told the customs chief, that it would be too dangerous to sail and that he needed to do work on the motor first.

Exploring Bali

There were many hustlers trying to sell carvings, pictures, batik, sandalwood fans, carved bones, toys, etc. and themselves in the tourist area. This section was nervous and unpleasant. We were followed constantly. There are so many people who tried to survive but even though some of the things they sold were beautiful, I could not afford to buy something and was glad to go to the countryside where the people are nice, helpful and not pushy at all.

The higher we walked into the hills, the poorer the people were, even though nature was very rich. They were so brainwashed, that they could not see the fruits on the trees. People could not think how to make their lives easier.

We saw small children no more than two to four years old, who carried two 20 liter canisters full of water up to 4 km, down to their families. They balanced a bamboo stick across their backs from shoulder to shoulder with a container hanging on each side. There was enough bamboo to construct some sort of a pipeline but they could not think and I did not speak enough Indonesian to make it clear to them. The older children had to carry up to 80 liters of water. I was so sad not to be able to help them.

On the way down from the mountain, we passed the rice fields. There were many families working together. They were poor but were the most contented people we saw in Bali. Their faces looked happy, they smiled and some were singing. The old women did not wear bras and just had a piece of cloth wrapped around the waist. It looked like back-breaking work, standing in water and planting rice in the tropical heat. They all wore straw hats. Every once in a while someone got bitten by accidentally stepping on a snake.

Back on board, we enjoyed the sea breeze while Scheherazade swung peacefully and free on her anchor. Here we could relax and enjoy the view, the gorgeous cloud formations, the spectacular sunsets and the multitude of stars in the clear sky. The world was wonderful on Scheherazade when, like most times, we enjoyed each other's company.

Helmut had friends from the little village of ""Nusa Dua" who invited him and us to attend a Hindu Festival that had never been seen by tourists. In Nusa Dua there is a temple, which is surrounded by the most beautiful trees of the forest, adjoined by a sandy, white beach and the sea.

The celebration started at 3 p.m. with cockfights while the musicians stimulated the brutal happening, the men placed bets for a hell of a lot of money. They played bingo and other games. People were everywhere. Hustlers and people with clothes stands, tables with food or other things tried to sell their wares. It was like a fairground. Starving dogs, mostly skinny and with diseased skin, tried to get a bite to eat.

The tables were covered with tropical fruit and bananas, pork, chicken, rice, noodles and turtle eggs. Everything was presented beautifully, like in a picture book. At 6 p.m. everybody was allowed to eat. There was no electricity but oil lamps spread a golden light and it smelled of flowers, food, dust, Indonesian Kretec cigarettes that are laced with cloves, petrol and sweat.

Woman carried up to 1 1/2m high towers of food to the place of sacrifice in the decorated temple. There the food was blessed by the priests and symbolically given to the gods before they were allowed to be eaten.

Women who were menstruating were not allowed inside the temples. Music was being played non-stop by musicians with xylophones, bamboo flutes, bongo drums, bells etc. Most people wearing sarongs (colorful fabrics) wrapped around their heads and hips, were there in honor of the Hindu God who lives in the trees and were responsible for the beautiful wooden masks which are kept in four different villages.

Men, women and children of every age from all four villages were present. In the evening at darkness, the dance with the wooden masks took place, which can only be done twice a year and in this place. It was a clear and 3/4 moon lit night.

The Barong (male God) in the form of a big dragon decorated with gold, hair, mirrors etc. showed up, carried by two men. The bad ghost Rangda, an ugly creature with hanging breasts (female Devil), arrived. The Barong was trying to fight her. The music got louder and wilder. So did the dances. People were hypnotized. Some went into a trance, while others screamed and cried. It looked as if Rangda was winning and Barong was loosing and the crowd went mad.

In the center, some men who felt guilty for having done wrong tried to stab themselves with a Kris (Indonesian knife). Dancers in wooden masks became so intense, that the dust and sand rose up and up from the ground. Before the men could break their skin with the dangerous knives, the priest took them out of their trances and other sinners started to get into the center and into trance.

While Barong and Rangda fought each other it was magical but almost frightening, with all the noise and screaming of the mass hypnotized until the Barong won and Rangda lost. Everyone was relieved to be forgiven for their sins.

Once more, we could see that all religions we had been confronted with discriminated against women. Whoever discriminates against women, also is doing so against man and humanity, just to allow them to be milked by tyrants.

Leaders would benefit in my opinion, if they would loosen the screw. Show me happy people and I am convinced the leader is good, as in Tonga.

I admire the Chinese for their strict birth control which should be copied the world over.

Even though, as a thinking person I am not a believer, I was fascinated and impressed by all the colors, the odors and the ambiance, the spectacle. The Hindu ritual ended horrifically, with a man biting off the head of a live chicken and swinging the cadaver in a circle to make the blood squirt onto the people around the center, which disgusted us and our friends.

Bali has 3 million inhabitants and in the rest of Indonesia the population was 135 million, which makes a total of 138 million. Many of them eat in warongs (small restaurants) and paid about 200 Rupees for a meal in 1980. Only 20 Rupees was charged for a coffee. I could imagine that after a while, I would enjoy being back at sea but at that moment I wished to be nowhere else. I was happy to discover Bali, where everything is decorated and wanted to collect as many new impressions as possible.

We went to collect the mail. Peter's package from his mother had been opened up and half the goodies stolen out of it. I received letters from my loved ones. Those letters were indispensable to me.

We were told of an awful incident a few years ago, when racist fanatics had organized amongst themselves to kill all the Chinese people. In one night they surprised and slaughtered all of them. There were over 10,000 men, women and children of Chinese origin. The Indonesian murderers were no better than the Nazis in Germany, with the difference, that no one speaks of it except very few. I was tortured with nightmares after we heard of this and I feel disgust for those who are responsible for race- and other ism's. Fortunately, not all of humanity are perverts. Many families embraced up to five different religions and lived in harmony under the same roof. Even so, I prefer animals to most people.

The animal life is very interesting. There, amongst many species, were ant bears and beautiful monkeys. Some looked like meerkats. I fell in love with a black, long- haired monkey that smooched with me. I would have liked to take him with me but that would not have been fair to him. Three monkeys sat on Peter and did gymnastics on him. One of them reached in his pocket and found his sunglasses very interesting while another wanted to play with his ball point pen. The babies should not be held since the parents would bite or urinate on you. What makes me sad, is that so many turtles were caught.

The animal world appears to still be intact in Sumatra. I hope to be able to study it later in life. I have heard that there are orangutans, birds, reptiles, wild oxen, tigers, even bears amongst the wildlife in the mahogany and teak woods.

I find truth in nature which is the basis for my paintings. Truth brings harmony. It is like a tree that has to wind itself around obstacles to grow in height.

Peter wrote an article about the Kimberleys. He hoped to sell it and I wish him success.

An American man who lived alone with his white poodle for company, took the dog everywhere he went. He owned a motorbike and had put a piece of foam rubber across the tank where his pet could sit and loved to ride with him. I befriended him because I love all dogs and can't resist talking to them or other animals. This man was called Goldfinger since every thing he touched, turned to gold, someone told me.

We were invited to come to a party on his motor yacht.

Goldfinger told me, "You have dedicated all your life to art. I would like to do something for you. I would like to lend you $1,000,000 for one year, without charging interest rates. When you get back to Switzerland, open an account and mail me the number, I will then send you the money." Peter and I spoke about this and he said this could be true, since this could cause him to save taxes on his income. I will write more about the outcome of this offer in a later chapter.

We hardly ever ate meat anymore since we saw it in the market covered with flies. We had fun discussions with other sailors. One of them cursed about Bali and I said that people of all countries were like nature and consisted of contrasts like positives and negatives. He then said that 50% of the world's population suffered from hemorrhoids while the other half were perfect assholes.

Agung Dalem

A handsome and sympathetic young man rowed in a dug out canoe (carved out of a tree trunk) out to Scheherazade and introduced himself as Agung Dalem, the wood carver. We asked him on board. He showed us some impressive pieces of work. Peter pointed to the bulkhead inside and asked how much he wanted to carve a small fish being chased by a bigger one which is chased by an even larger one until five fish would grace the bulkhead. Agung wanted a piece of paper and started to sketch. Peter liked the drawing and was surprised at the affordable price. Agung left and came back the next day to show Peter a beautiful peace of teak wood and wanted to know if we liked it enough to have it carved. We agreed and told him we were happy and looked forward to seeing the carving. After a week, Agung came back with the finished work. What a beautiful, well done sculpture! All our friends came over to look at it and many of them ordered sculptures from him.

He became our friend. Agung was so nice and real. We spoke about art and he took us to meet his master at the carving school, where he was in the fourth year of the eight years of apprenticeship needed to become a master carver. His master was a memorable, sensible and kind older man of inner and outer beauty. I fell in love with one of his works and was so sad that I could not afford to buy it even though the price was very reasonable. He had carved a snake in ebony rolled up to form a bowl. One could almost feel the snake breathe. I will never forget that incredible piece of the finest art.

We sailed with our Swiss friends Peter and Arlette from 'Taharoa', to Nusa Basar in a Bali outrigger canoe. We stayed there for a day and a night. It was a real pleasure. For the first time in a long time, a New York newspaper came into my hands and I had a real shock. It is amazing how sensitive one becomes without TV or radio. Our entertainment was conversation with real people and real things. Time is too precious for small talk. That newspaper stole my time and caused me to become depressed and nauseated at the many lies it told. I was glad that we did not own a TV. The depressions soon left when I watched the waves gently foaming from the water splitting on Scheherazade's keel and felt her familiar movement while she was swinging sweetly on her anchor in the welcoming breeze.

I longed to be free, sailing out at sea alone with Peter again. We had been in Bali for three months and planned to sail the 500 miles to Christmas Island on June 25,1980, like our friends on 'Taharoa' and 'Nayla'. Then we planned to sail 600 miles to Cocos Keeling. Next, about 16 days to Chagos where we hoped to stay 14 days and then continue for about 11 days , arriving in the Seychelles around August 21st. After staying a while, it would take us about 15 days to Djibouti, then about 8 days to Port Sudan, after about 12 days to Port Said, where we planned to sail in the winter wind. Approximately mid October or the beginning of November, we hoped to arrive in Cyprus or Kreta, Greece. The dates could vary and depended on wind and weather, our moods and the bureaucracy.

As a going-away present Agung Dalem presented me with a beautiful teak wood name plate on which he had carved *Maya B.*

Artist and which he had decorated by carving beautiful Bali symbols around my name. I was touched and I am very proud of the gorgeous present. I consider Agong as one of my best friends.

Our American friends Bill, the electronic engineer, and his wife Jeanne, (both over 70 years old from the U.S.A. on their 'Tahiti Ketch'), had just returned to Bali from Jakarta, Java. Everyone who had been there, had advised them not to go there because everything gets stolen but they went there anyway. They slept in the cockpit to make sure no one tried to get on board without them hearing it. In the morning, they woke up and saw that the boat was empty and all the things were gone. Fortunately, everything was insured but it was a real nuisance to have to wait for the check to replace everything and so they ordered a compass and a sail and returned to Bali to order the rest of the things they could not get in Bali either. We all felt sorry for them. If anyone could, they would help them.

'Canard Lucky' arrived with a Swiss man and his German wife aboard. They showed us magnificent photos they had taken while sailing as far north as they could until they were blocked by icebergs and could not go any further. Their stories were incredible. We met so many fascinating people who were sailing.

Christmas Island

Not A Boring Moment

Typing a letter home

In transit to Christmas Island

On July 5, 1980 Peter pulled the anchor up from Bali and I was at the helm. The captain of "Canard Lucky" was swimming. I aimed toward him, ready to change direction before it became dangerous. When he saw me coming at him, he panicked. I turned the tiller in more than plenty of time but felt very bad to have scared him. It was only meant to be a bit of fun. I hope he has forgiven me.

At the same time as we sailed away toward Christmas Island, so did 'Taharoa' and 'Clair de Lune'. A few hours after it was dark, we lost sight of each other until July 10th. All three yachts arrived within two hours of each other at Flying Fish Cove off Christmas Island. The weather and the sea were ideal. The wind was gentle and the climate tropical and mild.

We had been accompanied by dolphins again. The closer we got toward the island, the more species of sea birds we saw. We spotted frigate birds, tropic or bosom birds, seagulls, doves, boobies, little blackbirds, and others. The sunrises and sunsets were breathtaking. On the whole route we did not see any ships and mostly slept without a care through the whole night.

During the day, Peter and I read, ate and drank, slept, played and sang while the automatic pilot did all the steering. On

Christmas Island we caught a big tuna fish and cooked it with black bean sauce. It was delicious. We were welcomed like royalty. The boat club was free and at our disposal so we could take as many warm showers as we liked. This was a real luxury for us. There were also infra-red ovens and a large freezer free for our use, plus two refrigerators stocked full of cold drinks that we could purchase for the same price as in the shop. There were four barbecues including wood there for our use. The people almost fought each other, to see who could invite us to their homes for dinner. It was not necessary to hitch-hike since every vehicle stopped and wanted to take us along. We felt very privileged, indeed.

The inhabitants where Chinese, Indians, Indonesians, Malaysians and Europeans. The only industry on Christmas Island was Phosphate (mountains of guano {bird droppings}) that were worked into fertilizer or explosives. We had arrived there at a very interesting time. Everything was in flux.

The phosphate industry had held the people, predominantly freedom fighters, like slaves. People were forced to work seven days a week and were paid very poorly. The island had belonged to Singapore.

Australia had just bought the island and made the people Australian citizens if they so wished. Now they worked five days for good salaries ever since the unions had mixed in. There were no taxes there and the minimum income was A$20,000 a year.

Bananas, papayas and lemons could be taken for free in the beautiful jungle. Coconut trees were also in abundance. The population consisted of about 3500 people. There was also a hospital and there was a shortage of women.

The inhabitants of all races drove Lamborghini's, Mercedes, Alfa Romeos, Jaguars and Japanese small cars. There were also Jeeps and Holdens. They all drove on the left. All routes were tarmacked.

The vegetation was lush and fertile. Fish that had all died out in other places, swam happily amongst other rare species through the coral reefs surrounded by crystal clear water.

On the evening of July 15, 1980, we were invited by our Chinese friends. Choy was born on the island and Poo had emigrated from China. The two were in love. Choy was 21 years old and the sixth generation of his family, who was an expert in Kung Fu Karate and had a black belt. Both were remarkable and generous human beings and drove us all over the island and accompanied us to the jungle to pick bananas, lemons and coconuts. They seemed to know every tree and bush and told us to take what we liked. Loaded with '1000 year old' eggs, mangoes, and new sandals for Peter (since his had broken on the way), plus many other things, we got back to Scheherazade.

Choy's father had been banished with many other old people. The previous regime had sent them back to China, Malaysia, India or Indonesia to make room for the young "profitable people." Choy and his family were sad about his father being sent back to China, but could understand that on this small island, they were forced to make room. I can't help finding it inhuman to send people who had raised their families and lived 50 or more years there, back to their old countries.

Since Australia had taken over, the only old to be deported, were those who had relatives with land in their old country. Under the new system, the young have the possibility to save for their retirement and will receive a pension.

My friend Janet Cheng wrote to me later, that all the people from Christmas Island were given the right to go and live in Australia, take jobs, get an education and work there or receive a pension.

During the rainy season, thousands of vivid red crabs go from the land to the sea to lay their eggs and fertilize them. Then they walk across roads and gardens towards the forest, where they are much appreciated for keeping the jungle clean. They eat all dead things, even colorful leaves. One can see them all year round. There are also the larger blue crabs which are becoming rare and are protected like all the birds.

It was estimated, that in eight years the phosphate industry would not be able to continue to operate and that is why the leaders tried to find a way to replace it by 1988 with another profitable industry. Agriculture would have been difficult since the many grasshoppers and crabs also love it. Unfortunately, they were discussing the tourist industry but it was understandable. People can't live without an income. I just hoped it would not become mass tourism for nature's sake.

A large airport had already been built. Telephones and buses were free on the island. The apartment blocks were a real eyesore. What they need there, is a nature-loving architect and artists. The profit hunger of the industries is too visible and ugly. For the working people, it was a big step forward and they are happy to live in the horrible housing cubes that look like beehives for a reasonable rent. Everything was clean like in Switzerland, which was a pleasure after Indonesia. There was no poverty and birth control was established. The language was English and the currency was Australian Dollars. Most groceries were imported from Australia for the same price as in Sydney. The two cinemas were free of cost and mostly totally crowded. Culture was practically non-existent, except the one carried on from their ancestors.

Besides lizards and slow worms, there were no reptiles. The only dangerous animal was the centipede but one could see them easily and so stepping on them could be avoided. Anyway, most of them were not deadly.

We hoped to be able to return the generosity of our friends by inviting them for dinner on Scheherazade. I had cooked chicken, fish, vegetables and salad. They arrived with a large box under their arms containing chicken, chips, drinks, curry and other goodies. We were surprised that they had brought anything at all.

After they had been on board Scheherazade for five minutes, both felt seasick. It was a bit wavy and they tried to hide their feelings but when I asked them after ten minutes if they would prefer to go on shore, they were relieved. I suggested we should eat at the boat club but they could not think about food and went home to sleep it off. They left the food with us and Peter and I ate until it nearly came out of our ears. The rest was heated up at the boat club and shared with our sailor friends, who were delighted.

The next evening we were invited again by our friends ashore. Choy was also a herbalist and massage therapist. He massaged Peter's aching back and also offered him acupuncture for free but Peter did not want to have anything to do with needles. He found the massage very helpful. Choy also taught me new Kung Fu exercises while I showed him con Korean ones. Loaded up again with all sorts of massage oils, Chinese booze and lucky symbols they had given us and rich in new impressions, we rowed back out to Scheherazade.

We spent the rest of our time with Choy and Poo, our sailing friends and other acquaintances. Peter and I often went diving and he caught many fish, which permitted us to thank Choy and Poo for their enormous generosity and hospitality.

On Saturday, July 19th, we lifted the anchor and set the sails for Cocos Keeling. Peter was seasick for the first time in his life and could not eat. The sea was wild and the waves chased over the whole boat into the cockpit. The fore hatch started to leak and I put two buckets inside under it to catch at least some of the entering water.

Fortunately, I never found out what seasickness felt like. At night, Peter started to sleepwalk. I woke up and followed him, taking his hand in mine gently and asking him where he was going. He did not respond and walked with my hand holding his through the companion way the full length of the boat to the bow. I whispered, "Let's go below", while I tightened my grip on his hand. He followed me and we went to bed. The next day, Peter did not remember the incident. He felt a little better but was not completely well. When I ate half of a big, juicy beef steak with great pleasure, Peter could not watch. I threatened him, that if he did not get well soon, I would eat all of it plus the stew as well. He got better and managed to keep the rest of the stew, an apple and tea in his stomach. I was glad for his recovery, felt well, even excited and needed Peter to share it with.

As we neared Cocos Keeling, it was cloudy and dark outside. We trailed the sea anchor to slow down Scheherazade's speed because we were unfamiliar with the reefs in those waters. We were almost rocked to death in the high sea, with an about five miles off- course drift of strange currents. Daylight arrived and we could correct the drift upon spotting the island. What an experience. We slept like babies in a mother's womb after our arrival. When we woke up, the sky was clear blue and the sun was shining.

Cocos Keeling

I was glad to have learned everything I could steal with my eyes, about navigation. Peter was glad as well. He taught me the rest, since he saw the importance for both of us to be able to navigate. I wrote it down so that I would not forget. By July 21st, we had sailed about halfway towards Cocos Keeling. We arrived at Cocos Island on July 23rd. What a beautiful place! The water was turquoise blue and clear.

Coconuts galore and it reminded me of the South Pacific. We had anchored in front of one of the coral atolls. There were a few yachts there. One of them had problems with navigating and was afraid to sail. He had been there eight months already and was surviving from nature. He had no bureaucratic problems, but it was impossible for him to get a job there.

There was nothing besides the coconut industry. If the natives wanted to leave they could. However, they could not come back because another person would have filled their place. It was all still very primitive.

The island belonged to a private millionaire and landowner,

Clunies-Ross from Scotland. His grandmother, Queen Victoria, had given him the Cocos Islands as a gift, to do as he pleased. He planted coconut trees and imported people from Malaysia to work for him like slaves. His grandson and great-grandson, also Clunies-Ross, were pressured to sell the islands to Australia, which owns them now.

The people worked for a co-op and the profit was shared twice a year. They were made Australian citizens. The "Home Island" is only open to visitors by invitation.

A few days after us, 'Taharoa' had finally arrived and anchored there as well. Peter and Arlette had left Christmas Island a day after us and picked up the mail I was waiting for and brought it to us. I received a long, beautiful birthday letter with news from my daughters and parents plus a card. I can hardly describe the feelings of happiness from this mail delivery.

It was good to have our friends with us. On August 1st, we celebrated the Swiss National Day with a big bonfire on the snow white, sandy beach framed with my favorite trees - the coconut palms. The turquoise blue of the water glowed. We celebrated with our friends Pierre and Ute from 'Canard Lucky' and Peter and Arlette from 'Taharoa' until late that night. Together, we were three Swiss, one Swiss-American, one German and one Australian citizen. The next day, 'Nayla' arrived with Alan and Atao, which was reason to celebrate again.

Peter and I spent three hours in the water fishing while the others cooked, baked and prepared for the fiesta. It was so beautiful to snorkel. The reef was like a gorgeous garden. A shark nearly had a heart attack when confronted with me. I did too but the shark zigzagged at incredible speed away from me, while I hurried out of the water. I felt ashamed of myself for being scared of a docile reef shark. The more I learn about fish, the less I am afraid of them. None are as unpredictable or false as humans can be. Anyway, fish prefer to eat other fish rather than people. If places are over-fished by the greedy fishermen, I understand that they might eat a human if they are hungry and there is nothing else.

Meanwhile we had met 23 year old John Clunies-Ross, Junior, a healthy and nice but shy young man, with intense dark brown eyes and frizzy sun-bleached hair. He was a picture of health and we became good friends. Scheherazade was the first sail boat John had ever been on. He came on board carrying an ice chest full of food, beer and a bottle of Southern Comfort. We spoke freely about anything and everything.

We all objected to the blue toilet cubicle that the United Nations had erected as a gift. The ugly toilet was locked up and very visible and stood just a few meters from the waterfront of the white sandy beach, where it created a real eyesore on the magnificent, uninhabited coral atoll. I used the cube as background for my then, latest painting and graced it with two mating dogs with big grins on their faces, which amused the people and cheered them up.

When the Australian Air Force showed up, they photographed me in front of my mural on the plastic cube. They sent the photos to my parents in Switzerland, together with copies of the ones they had taken of Scheherazade while following us.

The Air Force men invited us to eat steaks and drink ice cold beer with them on the beach. Peter did not want anything to do with them, since he was still angry about them "spying" on us and photographing us while we were sailing in Australian territories. I accepted a welcome ice cold beer. The more we spoke, the more I liked the men. They told me that they loved to fly so much, that they only did their job of seeing where we were so as to be able to be flying. I could understand this very well. I would take an ideal job like that if I could.

On second thought, I found sailing with Peter was great and better than having been in any air force for me. One of the men swam out to Scheherazade with me and we talked Peter into coming ashore to join us. He accepted and did not regret it. The pleasure of eating a succulent, thick steak and ripe tomatoes accompanied by cold beer is a welcome change from fish. The conversation was very interesting as well.

It is important to do something in life that you enjoy. Peter from 'Taharoa' shot two hares. He gave me their pelts and I treated them by washing them in salt water and covering them with salt on the inside while stretching them out to dry in the shade and wind. Then I washed them with clean water and dried them in the breeze. They turned out nicely and I thought that maybe I would make gloves out of them. It had gotten a bit colder but was still 28 degrees in the shade. Only a bikini bottom was needed.

I just thought about the port-o-potty the United Nation gave as a gift. Maybe this was the beginning of a horror. The next thing, could be that policemen stood on both sides of it. One of them could give fines for not using the ugly cube while they deprived nature of the natural fertilizer we would bury and cover with sand while on shore. Then they could hire someone to sell toilet paper and use chemical cleaners on the bowl. Then they would need housing for the employed and jobs like cashiers for fines. Then some coconut trees could be sacrificed to build a church and school and so on and voilà, before you knew it the water and land would be as polluted as the rest of civilization. Ha- ha- ha- uh -hu- oh. ; but enough of the bad and dirty jokes.

I repaired the mainsail using the over a hundred year-old hand sewing machine that I had bought in New Zealand at an auction for $8. It was so tough, that I could sew through leather with it. Peter did all the hand work on the sail. Then he fixed the burners on the stove, repaired the sea anchor and pumped out the bilge while I washed the laundry. Then he charged the batteries and we collected coconuts for the coming trip.

It was cloudy and rainy on our last night in the lagoon of Direction Island. Peter and John joked and promised to make the sun come out for our departure in the morning. I handed a letter for each of my daughters to John and ask him to mail them for me. Then we said goodbye. On August 7, 1980, we left Cocos Island in the direction of Paros Banos and we would not receive mail because there would be no post offices until we arrived in the Seychelles.

Paros Benos

Out in the Indian Ocean again, dreams started to occupy my brain of what to do with the $1 million 'Goldfinger' had offered to lend me without interest for a year. I was planning to invest it at a bank for 15% interest and would try to borrow a "Freedom Forty", a sailing boat that really impressed me since it had no rigging, was very fast, easy to sail and looked good. I wanted to become the first Swiss woman to sail across the Atlantic single handed. I could then write a diary, which I hoped to sell with photos taken with my would-be-excellent-camera, sell my adventure story and could then buy the Freedom 40.

I hoped, if my plan should succeed at the end of the year, I would not only have the boat of my dreams but also the interest from $1,000,000 = $ 150,000 which I could then partly invest again and live on the rest. Before being able to realize all this, the return to Switzerland, the opening of an account in a Swiss Bank, the writing to Goldfinger and him sending the cheque would be essential. All that could be done was to wait and see.

Meanwhile, I enjoyed life to the fullest, travelling with Peter on Scheherazade. I sketched, painted and played my banjo mandolin. Flying fish landed on deck and then in the frying pan. We ate them like chips by the dozen for breakfast. They were among my favorite fish. It was wonderful to watch the waves spread out from the keel and hear the spray of the water. I felt so lucky being there.

The weather turned cloudy and rainy and Peter was threatened with seasickness again. He overcame it by lying down, relaxing and not eating for two days.

When we changed sails, I almost froze. The wet suit was drenched even on the inside by the waves slashing at me. After that, I was trying to design a wet suit that was warm, dry, waterproof and easy to put on and take off. There is nothing worse, than getting cold and wet while sailing. A good outfit, spray dodger, wind vane and self-steering can really help.

Bad weather, rough sea and hard wind with large white capped waves all happened to us at latitude 7 and longitude 80 degrees. I was worried as to how it was going to be in cold climates. On Monday, August 18, 1980 at 4.24 Greenwich Time we were at 6 degrees latitude and between 74 and 75 degrees longitude. We had been motoring at about 3 knots for the last 23 hours and were about 150 miles away from our next anchorage. The swell was quite high and inside the cabin it was 33 1/2 degrees.

The last fish we caught was a beautiful Mackerel. In the morning we spotted the first frigate bird since our departure from Cocos Keeling. This was a sign, that we were no further from land than 150 miles. Peter used the stars to navigate. He picked a star with the sextant and determined the distance by lining it up with the horizon. When this happened, he called immediately down to me "now" and I wrote the time down. An error of 4 minutes would mean we were 1 mile off course. There is great satisfaction in knowing where you are. I mostly took the sights at sunrise, at midday and at sunset.

Sometimes it was not possible to navigate because the sky was overcast and we could not see the sun, stars, planets or the moon. If that was the case, we used the transistor radio as a crude radio direction finder and followed the bearing thus discovered. There was a lot of guesswork, until we had spotted land that was not easy to see on the low coral atolls since the highest points there were the coconut palm trees.

Besides the canned goods, the powdered, freeze-dried and grain food we had some coconuts, three limes, some pumpkins and 2 kg. of shallots left. We had figured out pretty accurately, how much fresh food we had needed. We were looking forward to being able to collect fresh food soon again. I had dreamed of a juicy steak the night before. We also had two small salamis, dried beef and a block of cheese left and were sprouting some munge beans in the galley.

The motor coughed and died completely. We were wondering why this happened and worried about approaching dangerous reefs. We could no longer depend on the motor which could normally get us out of tricky situations and away from lee shores. We nearly panicked. Peter took the filter out and replaced it with a new one and checked the oil. Nothing happened, so he bled the engine which contained a lot of air. With the air out, the motor ran like a charm again. What a relief! That was a lot of panic for a bit of air.

Salomon Islands

On the August 20, 1980, we arrived in the beautiful lagoons of the Salomon Islands, Diego Garcia, Chagos, where we anchored in front of an atoll. Since about 1973, this Salomon Island had been deserted and only the settlement on one of the atolls left. Where we anchored there were no inhabitants except one hermit, an ex hockey star Karl Heinz Gutersohn from Germany who had lived there for five months already, before our arrival.

He was a highly intelligent and philosophical individual who had the deepest respect for nature and only killed what he needed to eat. He had no money and did not need any except for flour, rice, tea, sugar and matches, all of which he still had plenty of. The American army had leased Diego Garcia from the British to use as a military base in case of emergency. They had threatened Karl Heinz with jail if he did not leave, but he told them, "If you throw me in jail you will have to feed me." Finally they left him in peace.

The almost ruined houses on the island were still standing and so was a church, jail, copra sheds and a small hospital. All the buildings were overgrown with plants. Huge water containers stood near the damaged roofs with pipes attached to collect the rain. One or two still supplied water.

Turtle shells and shark fins, some furniture and all sorts of junk were lying around. When Peter and I arrived, we were alone on the island and explored everything with the curiosity of two children. Bottles of medicines still stood on shelves of the long abandoned hospital with most of the liquid dried out.

The cells of the jail were without windows and too small for any human to be comfortable. We felt sorry for anyone who was thrown into such inhuman conditions. I guess there was a dictatorship over the imported and exploited Malaysian people who were taken off the island and transported to the Seychelles since the coconut industry no longer made enough profit.

The island was turning back into a tropical paradise with all sorts of trees we had not seen before. One large tree had longish fruit growing out of its stem which when cooked, almost tasted like tomatoes and could be made into a sauce for spaghetti. A cat came up to us and wanted to be petted.

We were having a ball exploring every building and looking for fruit trees etc. when we came to a house with the door wide open and entered it. The walls were constructed of half-meter thick limestone. It was furnished with church benches, a large table, a kerosene cooker, books and a tape recorder and looked as if someone lived there. On the table laid a note, which read *"Yachts", please make yourself at home and take whatever you need. We went to Paros Benos but will be back on August 20th.* It was signed Karl Heinz Gutersohn.

A few hours after we arrived, the yacht 'Papalagi' pulled in and anchored next to Scheherazade. They were Elisabeth and Brend from Germany with their 10-year-old son Michael. With them was Karl Heinz. After a big welcome, the men went out fishing and Michael started a fire. Elisabeth made a heart of palm or "millionaires' salad" while I squeezed oranges, limes and lemons

The menu for dinner was:

Fresh fillet of coral trout, (from a 12 kg heavy fish) grilled with garlic, Millionaires' salad with freshly squeezed lemon and lime dressing, bread fruit baked in its own skin with coconut cream

sauce, raw marinated mussels with soya sauce and coconut cream, freshly squeezed orange juice and tea.

We ate like this every day. For breakfast, we fried "Roti" a bread made from coconut or whatever turned us on. Everything grew on the island. We never wore clothes and forgot that we were naked. I felt as wild, real and beautiful as one can only be without the constant brainwash and pollution of our civilization. I composed a song while walking along on the gorgeous, white, sandy beach and sang it as loud, high or low as it felt good and made my chest and head vibrate. It was so intense and free, almost delirious to be surrounded by so much beauty.

When I walked into the wind, a new species of crabs presented themselves by crossing in front of me. They had long antennae, which they could turn, with eyes on the end of them. They were able to be completely covered by sand or water and just stick their eyes out. I was thrilled to find that dream places like this still existed.

On August 23rd, I was unhappy to leave but also happy to have experienced this beautiful paradise and to get closer to my loved ones. On the same day, we arrived in Coin Island, Paros Benos. The lagoon was not as picturesque as the Salomons and the anchorage was deeper and rougher but nature was even lusher than in the previous atoll. We almost went berserk at the variety of fruits, nuts and fish there. The settlement was slightly bigger but was mostly overgrown by ivy. There was diesel and gasoline on Coin Island and we filled Scheherazade's tank. We watched many animals and the almost tame varieties of birds. By walking into the wind they could not hear or smell us and permitted us to watch them close up. We collected shells (no live ones except the ones we wanted to eat) and had a great time cooking on shore with a wood fire, swimming and playing.

Before we left, we took a large bag of oranges, a sack of lemons and limes, plus a huge bag of de-husked coconuts etc. with us. From August 28, 1980 we were sailing toward the Seychelles (Mahe Island). It was an interesting sail and we were surrounded by millions of small green crabs for several hours. The whole time we were going down wind and Scheherazade was hardly leaning at all. It was a real pleasure and we had a wonderful time at sea.

Seychelles

On September 3, 1980 we sighted land and I looked forward to eating a steak on shore that evening. A flag stood on a tiny island and was marked "Quarantine Island." We anchored Scheherazade. The ships' doctor arrived to see if we were healthy. Then we moved to Mahe Island, where a customs official checked our papers and searched every corner of Scheherazade. I tried to put the man in a good mood by playing Gaby Lou's tape, 'Sweet bacalolo'. Peter told me to stop the music but the man stopped Peter. He liked the sound.

He found Peter's homemade spear gun and took it and us on shore. We were forced to follow him to the police station where the spear gun was taken away and locked up. After that, they took us to the courtroom where the judge asked why Peter had carried this arm on board. Peter said that this was not a weapon and he used it exclusively for what it was intended to do. That he had constructed it for the sole purpose of catching our dinner. Peter found it more humane to kill the fish by spearing it through the brain which caused instant death without suffering. The judge sat up so high that everybody was forced to look up to him. There stood a table next to me and I laid on top of it so the judge had to look at such an angle that his eyes were not able to look down at me. Peter and I had to swear and sign, that what we said about the spear gun (which was broken) was the truth. It was true and we did sign. A receipt was given to us and we were told that we could get the spear gun back as soon as we were ready to leave. Relieved, we walked in to the village.

There were three letters at the post office which had arrived from Alexa, Julie and my parents. This cheered me up totally. While we looked around for a place to eat a steak, our attention was drawn to a shop with mouth-watering French pastries. We ended up eating so many pastries, we had no room left for steak.

The people were Creole and spoke half African mixed with French. They were fine-boned, agile in their movements, friendly but distant and looked frightened. We had the impression that the people's spirit had been broken.

The island was spotlessly clean and we saw people in blue uniforms sweeping alleys, streets and in front of their colorful wooden houses. We found out from other sailors, that the Island Mahe had been taken over by two Englishmen in June 1977. When one of them left to visit England, he received a letter from the other. It told him told in writing of the new Dictator's decision to keep the Island for himself and not to attempt to come back. Cannons were lined up outside the large house of the new ruler (who was never elected by the people). This looked to me like fear. The laws were tightened and we found out from people who told us that they had been much freer under the French government and that life had been easier and better.

Mahe was spectacularly beautiful with its beaches and coves, high mountains, and rich vegetation. The colors were those of the South Pacific. What had been missing on this magic island, was individualists, music, song and laughter. The prices were incredibly high except for tea, coffee, fish and bananas (grown on the island). We were charged for showers and fresh water from the yacht club.

On September 11th, we were invited to dinner on the yacht 'Anastasia' by our friends. Peter and Alf had worked together for Universal Diesel in Darwin, Australia. Alf's girlfriend Carol was from England. They had sailed non-stop from Christmas Island to the Seychelles in 42 days. They owned a Honda 125 cc motor bike and when they were not using it, they lent it to us. This helped us explore the island.

Mahe had four different highways, one went all around the island and another went right over the top of the 3000 ft. high mountain and we enjoyed an absolutely heavenly view from there.

A sailor friend was forced to leave because he was caught singing in the street. The police and the army could be seen everywhere. The captain of another yacht was thrown off the island for crossing the road next to the zebra stripes. There was no traffic at the time. The two women who had employed him, were afraid to sail without him and angry that they had to buy him an airline ticket to the U. S. A. Nothing that the women said or did could change this narrow- minded and ridiculous verdict.

In the Seychelles, there existed the only species of double coconuts in the world. The male double coconut tree is equipped with a flower shaped like a giant penis while the female palm has the fruit, which looks like a big vagina. The nuts tasted delicious but were illegal to export except for the shells which could be bought as souvenirs.

We went to the impressive park and studied the collection of many different carnivorous plants plus other interesting tropical vegetation. Scheherazade was anchored quite a way out from shore so I only wore the bikini bottom while on board. A native man rowed out and started to masturbate while staring at me. Peter swung his Gurkha knife in the air and the man took off like lightening. We met our friends from the yacht 'Sapho Smith' that we had met on Christmas Island and then again on Cocos Keeling.

The boat was an old classical wooden sloop owned by two remarkable women, Jeanne and Kate. Both were nurses from England and were doing a circumnavigation.

We received a note at the post office for us to pick up Peter's and Arlette's mail for them and bring it to them in Djibouti since they had changed their route to the Maldives instead of the Seychelles. We were looking forward to seeing them again since they had become like our brother and sister.

We had a pain in the gut from eating meat as a change from fish. We had both been attacking it like hungry wolves. This made us so ill, that we had to nurse ourselves with the rest of the bottle of brandy and then we slept for several hours. I was completely broke and could not go and enjoy a cold beer with other sailors in the yacht club. This was good for my health but miserable for my spirit. I didn't let not owning one cent bother me too much, since I knew that a door would open again as it always had done in the past in my life.

On September 20th, we left the beautiful island of Mahe. First to go was 'Anastasia' and second 'Sapho Smith' and lastly, we also sailed again into the open sea. The trip started with excellent wind and weather conditions. We passed both of our friends' yachts in a short time with full sails. I was so proud of Scheherazade.

We played chess or did something to entertain ourselves or each other and laughed a lot, etc. There was not a boring moment. Time went quickly.

On September 23, 1980 we neared the Equator and were in the doldrums. There was hardly any wind and then it stopped blowing completely. It was so hot that we could not walk on deck without throwing water over it with the bucket.

We ate the last of our French bread (toasted) with fresh tomatoes, cucumbers, capsicums and salami (still plenty), or sweet with peanut butter and jelly. For lunch it was fried rice with dehydrated meat and fresh vegetables and for dinner the rest topped with fried eggs. Fish did not seem to bite when Scheherazade sailed slowly. The next day, we ate huge amounts of pancakes for breakfast topped with bananas and honey and a pot of tea hand picked by us in the Seychelles, flavored with fresh lemon and caramel sugar. Often, we prepared a big salad with cabbage, garlic, chili peppers, onions and whatever turned us on. Eating was one of the main pleasures for us at sea.

We had only done 300 miles in 3 days with 20 hours of use of the motor. The sky was clear and the stars were bright. A beautiful full moon illuminated the night. The last signs of the Southern Cross were the two pointers still visible. Orion was very clear and so was Scorpio. The stars were our friends and so were the occasional dolphins and sea birds.

What fascinated me was the often big swell in the absence of wind. One lives completely in the moment while sailing. Everything is conscious and there are no outside influences, except the books one is reading. The head becomes clear and the brain opens new channels. It is peaceful when calm and active while rough. One becomes part of it, part of all. This may only be my observation.

At the equator it was so hot, with a slow swell but completely wind still, that we both jumped into the inviting deep blue, clear sea and swam around Scheherazade. When we dove under the water we could see millions of small air bubbles and it looked magic. The tiny sail triangle we had set, was the smallest on board, with just enough area for the automatic steering to keep the boat on course. As we frolicked in the sea a sudden small breeze blew up and we looked at each other, headed immediately toward the boat and just managed to pull ourselves back on board while the wind speed so drastically increased, that Scheherazade glided through the water at great speed. This experience explained the mystery of the Bermuda Triangle to me. From then on, one of us stayed on board when the other went into the water, with a rope attached to the yacht to hold on to.

On September 26, 1980 we were about 2 degrees north of the equator. The temperature was nearly 40 degrees. We were still in the doldrums and becalmed.

The day before, Peter had given the engine an oil change and nearly freaked when he detected water in the oil. He feared a damaged head gasket, so we were not using the engine except for emergencies. We were doing about 30 miles a day.

Fishes jumped everywhere and Peter got tense and excited trying to catch them without success. Dolphins showed up and swam with incredible speed toward the bow turning off just millimeters from getting hit. What acrobats! Hundreds of sea birds tried to get the left over bits of food that the big fish missed. To our surprise, we also noticed the frigate birds who normally don't go further then 100 miles away from land. We were 1000 miles away from the coast of Africa. It must have been individualists of the species.

We kept night watch since we had spotted two large tankers. We sailed in one of the shipping lanes known as the busiest but after the two ships, we did not see any others. For entertainment, Peter threw little bits of paper into the water to see how fast we were going while I sketched.

Breakfast was cooking when Peter came into the galley from deck and said, "Guess what, I had a beautiful brownie, six pieces are my average. Are you not happy for me?" "Oh yes but you must have had a goat in your family – did they ever tell you about your Uncle Ma-a-a-ax? Did you know that carnivores have darker stools then the vegetarians, that whole wheat bread really cleans you right out and that constipated people get up-tight quicker than others? Did you know that fish eat shit and catfish jump to get at it, before it has a chance to hit the water?"

This was my experience while anchored in Mary River. My spirits would lift if I urinated standing up instead of crouching down. It is good not to feel guilt or be ashamed of a natural body function. Speaking about shit, the next day we planned to make a ship's omelet with cabbage and tomatoes. We were having evolution for dinner! So much for the lesson on Scatology.

It comes and it goes – this is evolution. It takes and it gives – this is the solution. It is not mine, it is not thine - but it is ours.

Days can feel like months or months can feel like hours.

Our conversations could be very organic at times. Possibly stemming from prudery during the years spent in a catholic nun's school.

Sailing between Africa and the "Socotra Islands" which were infamous for pirates, we had to pull ourselves together and concentrate with all our strength on getting through those very strange and tricky currents. A few days later, we had slowly but surely arrived in the Gulf of Aden. It was still hot. We cooled each other by throwing buckets of water at each other.

A large shark was swimming near the boat. The temporary, shady roof I made became indispensable. Again, we collected over twenty flying fish who threw themselves on deck. We fried them, flavored them with lemon juice and ate them with pleasure. I repaired the ripped main sail and gratefully kissed the old Singer hand sewing machine, which was worth its weight in gold.

A special delight, was to have some kind of a booby bird, an owl and a sparrow who hitch-hiked and kept us company while sitting on Scheherazade's railing. The sparrow flew under the spray dodger near the compass. The birds stayed for several hours. The owl is nocturnal, who's visit flabbergasted us in the middle of the afternoon. All birds refused food but enjoyed the ride. We later found out that they had done this on other yachts as well.

We sailed without using the motor successfully through the treacherous coral reefs before Djibouti. On October 10, 1980, after 20 days at sea, we arrived save and healthy in the port of Djibouti.

Djibouti

We both suffered from a culture shock in the port from all the generator noises, other sounds and from the bright lights. Peter did not have any desire to go on shore and I was getting impatient to go on shore but tried not to show it since it only upset Peter.

Then a very handsome Italian man with intense blue eyes from Milan, rowed out to us and introduced himself as "Jean Paul" from the two masted schooner 'Nautilus'. He was like a godsend and invited us to have a drink on board his boat, one of the most beautiful old timers I had ever seen. He had fallen in love with this gorgeous ship in Malta and sailed her from Malta even with her deck leaking badly and the bowsprit almost falling off. On board 'Nautilus', we admired all the beautiful original carpentry below and all the original cleats, hatches etc. Jean Paul had done some repairs to make the boat more seaworthy but it needed much more work done on it.

He was in love with a beautiful woman from Yemen. She had more rights than other women since she was considered to be a heroine for being the first woman in Yemen to ride a horse. She and her sister owned and operated a travel agency in Djibouti. Jean Paul tried to talk her into sailing with him. He also took on several Ethiopian refugees as crewmembers who would help him to sail 'Nautilus' to Sri Lanka and then to Malaysia where he hoped to have her restored for a fraction of the cost in other parts of the world. The wood was still available for reasonable prices there.

Jean Paul's girlfriend could not make up her mind whether to go with him and lose her independence or whether to stay in business with her sister. While she was at work and Peter preferred to be alone to repair the motor, Jean Paul and I went to the yacht club (best restaurant in town). There he got me a contract to paint a 5 x 8 meter mural on the wall of the dining terrace with the condition of completion over the weekend, since they did not want to close the terrace to their customers any longer than that.

I finished it in time with the help of Jean Paul and Peter. I was in top form to work standing on the ladder, then descending every time to observe every stage of my work at a distance. I asked Peter to fill this out with blue, etc. and Jean Paul to fill that out with green etc.

Unfortunately, I did not own a camera to immortalize the mural so I will describe it. I tried to unite France and Djibouti by painting an Arabian Dhow flying a French flag and a large portrait of a Djibouti girl with her face showing. I completed it by drawing the sign of the Universal Flag on it. All three of us signed the mural, my signature on top and the two men's' underneath. I was so happy that people not only accepted my work but really liked it as well. I was given the lifelong right to anchor the boat in front of the yacht club and eat there for free during my stay.

I went to pick up the mail from my daughters and was so happy to have received news from them and to be a step closer to being able to take them in my arms again. I can't describe the longing for my sweet, charming, wonderful, intelligent and talented young ladies who were 19 and 17 years old. More than four years had passed since I had last embraced them.

In the Seychelles, I had picked two mangos from the most magnificent tree which was between 25 and 30 meters in height. We ate the mouth-watering fruit with delight on our voyage and I put the kernels into a dish with water on gimbals and they grew into two trees on board Scheherazade. One had six leaves and the other had eight.

I handed them to the Mayor of Djibouti whom I met in the bar of the yacht club, with the condition that when they were mature enough they should plant them in town where the poor could eat of the fruit for free. He promised me officially in front of Jean Paul, Peter, the owners and customers of the yacht club, to give them into the care of his best gardener and would see that my wish was respected.

I remembered from my visit to Djibouti in 1976 (page 303), that it was filthy, dirty, poverty stricken and depressing place with awful reminders of the horrid war and many crippled and blind people, sick children and starving dogs and enormous heat.

This time I found Djibouti beautiful. Everything grew when watered. Trees and bushes had been planted and the climate was not so dusty and dry since the plants had attracted moisture. Houses were repaired, the streets swept and many businesses flourished. Even the poorest seemed healthier and dogs looked better. French delicacies were still flown in from Paris. Most of the people were nice and friendly. The sunrises and sunsets were intense and spectacular like the ones I had remembered. I was pleasantly surprised by the change. The park was spectacular. We looked at as much as we felt like and bought fresh fruit and vegetables and drank an ice cold beer while sitting outside a pub.

Back on board, we took the containers and the laundry on shore, we filled the jerry cans, washed the laundry (mostly towels) and ourselves and went back to fill Scheherazade's water tanks and hang our things to dry.

Peter started to work on the motor again. A sailor is best off knowing as many trades as possible. He is a mechanic, shipbuilder, cook, welder, sail repairer, painter, plumber, diver, fisherman, builder, navigator, captain, and lover. He was not only all of that but much more. I was fascinated by beautiful Arabian dhows which were decorated with carvings on their bowsprits and hulls and graced the harbor. It rained for three short times during our stay.

I was sad to say goodbye to Jean Paul and watched him with tears in my eyes while we sailed away. We waved to each other, until we were cut off by the distance. On October 28, 1980, we left Djibouti and sailed with the off shore evening breeze about 10 miles from Djibouti. Then the wind decreased drastically.

The next day there was again only a little wind but enough to get us to Perim Island, which was controlled by the U. S. S. R. and was located near the tightest, most southern point of the Red Sea. After Perim, the wind blew very strongly and the weather was beautiful. In the east, were South and North Yemen who were shooting at each other and attacked yachts; and in the west was West Ethiopia who was at war against yachts as well. Fortunately, we had the wind with us and managed to sail between the two countries at excellent wind speed, while we heard the bullets shoot past our heads without getting hurt. Before we realized what had happened, we were in a safe zone again.

We caught a barracuda and a tuna on the line baited with a plastic octopus and tied to the stern, railing. We changed our sails for smaller ones. Several big ships were around us. Sometimes we could count half a dozen of them. One of us slept while the other sailed. Sometimes we were both awake but never both asleep. The wind speed registered about 50 knots.

We anchored at Hamish Island to sleep and for diving. While I was deeply asleep, Peter had already scrubbed the hull free from barnacles for two hours under water, caught two groupers and prepared them.

Hamish is a volcanic island with shining ochre sandy beaches and dark brown cliffs. Behind, are the silhouettes of the deep blue mountains that fade into delicate blue grey toward the firmament. The color of the water changed, depending on its depth, from emerald green to dark with white foam. The morning and evening sun caused everything to glow with a red – golden, magic shine. One could see long and clear. On Hamish grew a few meager bushes and a fly or two. There were supposed to be gazelles but we could not find any. Seven days after we had left Djibouti, we sailed at 2 knots into the harbor of Port Sudan.

Port Sudan

I had fastened a small version of the Universal Flag (as a ship's flag) on the rigging, as I had done before in Djibouti and we did not have to go through the very annoying bureaucracy. When the police came, one of them pointed at the flag and asked, "What is the idea of that?" I replied, "This is the Universal Flag and includes Sudan as well. If I can't do what I believe in as an artist, I will be finished in my profession, would you want to be responsible of this?" I was told, "You are free to do what you like." We did not have to go through the bureaucracy.

We had heard that about six yachts a year were wrecked or damaged on the reefs there. For three days, Peter had worked feverishly on the motor again and finally found the problem. The shaft of the water pump had to be replaced. Peter had a piece of stainless steel on board and made a new shaft out of it in an olive oil factory repair shop, where there was a lathe for him to use, on the condition from the owner that his workers could watch and learn how to use the lathe as well. Peter spent an extra afternoon teaching them, while I was watching also.

During the time that the motor was out of use and could not turn the generator, Scheherazade became very romantic, lit only by oil lamps. However, we were glad to have the motor and everything else in working order again. I was also happy to be able to play music tapes again.

The mail system was lousy. Packages were known to not arrive. All post went through Kartoum and took about a week, depending on the possibility of a flight. No one knew how long the post lay in Kartoum. Telegrams and telexes were only possible three days a month or when there was electricity.

In Port Sudan, there were many flies, Arabs, dust and heat. Even so, it was a fascinating place. What made me sad were the many people, and especially children, who had been scarred by deep cuts across both cheeks. They had been marked according to the area in Sudan they came from by 1, 2, or 3 large cuts. I found that as perverted as branding.

Peter did not feel adventurous so I went exploring by myself. The Muslims were not emancipated and prayed five times a day. One could hardly see any women. I walked barefoot through a piece of dessert to study camels and other animals.

Then I came into a little village entirely built from rusty car parts and trash. Cows walked through broken glass to eat from the rubbish. Camels ate paper, then came the cats. After the cats, the goats arrived and then the birds ate the ticks from the camels. Somehow even with all the dirt, there was harmony. Skinny children made toys out of empty cans or played with stone pebbles. I spotted some palm trees in the distance and headed in their direction, hoping to find an oasis.

The Arabs were very tiring. First, two of them came and commanded me to follow them into a tent. I said "No," since I intended to go somewhere else. When they followed me, I got angry. We had disputes. Women crept from behind the car wrecks and parts. The curiosity was big. Probably they had never seen a woman stand up against men and were amazed. Suddenly, there were six Arabs who ordered me to go with them. I ran and was faster than them. They then signaled by blowing and whistling through their fingers and another half a dozen skinny, small shouldered, and not at all tall men appeared who signaled to a third group. I sidetracked them by pointing my finger in the opposite direction from where I intended to go and while they looked in the direction I had pointed to, I ran. I repeated the same thing with the next group. Fortunately they were plump, weak and slow while I was in best form, agile, and fast. I outsmarted 18 Muslims with the help of a brave nomad woman who stood in front of their tent just on the outside of the car part village. Next to her was a table covered by a floor length tablecloth. She wore a long skirt and gestured to me to hide under it.

One of the many men came toward her and looked under the table. He found nothing. Then the woman hinted to me to move from under her skirt to below the table. I then moved under the table when she raised her long skirt from behind. The Arab then looked under her skirt and inside the tent without finding me and angrily, he stormed back like a ragged Napoleon, to where he had come from. He probably continued to search in the pile of rubbish. The nomad woman then prepared me a cup of delicious spiced tea for me. I was grateful that she had maybe even saved my life. She was a beautiful middle-aged woman with dark fiery eyes and the wrinkles of a hard life marking her interesting face. A man and children were in the tent. Two goats were tied up in front. After a while, she told me that it was safe to leave and pointed me in the right direction of Port Sudan.

It was so hard for a woman to be alone in non-emancipated places and sometimes I wished I had three bodyguards or a superman. There were so many things I wanted to discover. My best weapon, was that I lost all fears most of the time and loved to throw myself into life and then write about it. It also intensified my paintings because I learned something every time.

Back on Scheherazade it felt like a safe oasis again. This allowed me to relax and permitted me to visit, live and explore the most beautiful and interesting places on earth, which otherwise I would not have had a chance to see. Peter was a real sweetheart, who mostly accepted me the way I was. Most of the time, we had a wonderful and happy time together, even though we were two individualists. However, at this time, we had some friction in our relationship which made me very depressed.

Peter needed more time alone, while I was unhappy to be without my partner. A large Lloyd's Bank building stood in town and I went there to try and insure my paintings for the rest of our voyage up the Red Sea. Those waters are dangerous since there are many reefs and the traffic was very heavy. The Red Sea can be very rough.

I was sent to the Bank Director, who showed himself to be extremely nice and asked me in a very welcoming fashion, to sit down in the easy chair. His secretary brought a drink trolley with several different bottles of spirits to choose from and asked me what kind of drink she should pour for me. I sipped on an excellent, smooth and very aromatic cognac. Then the Director wanted to know, how high I intended to insure my work. I told him for as much as possible and that I was broke but would like to do exchange business with him, by paying with my work, which he could see on the yacht Scheherazade. I had asked him very nicely but he got annoyed and told the secretary to take the drink trolley away and accompanied me to the door and closed it behind me. There was no answer and no goodbye. They had treated me very impolitely and rudely.

I had hoped that my work would be recognized and so famous, that it would not be affordable for people like this guy, who look down on the 'Active living' with their greedy eyes, while they sit with their fat bellies in air conditioned offices and order those who work for them around. This low class director had not just insulted me with his bad behavior but did not even want to see my work. He had (like most of his kind) no feelings or understanding of art and artists.

Back on the boat, I put on a see-through, powder pink shirt with matching long pants over my naked body and went out in a rage to make opposition to the system which would not give me a chance to survive. It was six months that I had not had one red cent in my pocket. European men on ships smiled and whistled at me.

They told me that all women should wear my kind of clothes. Even some white dressed Muslims liked the way I looked and I told them that I was against female circumcision and compulsory black dresses for widows to wear in that heat. I continued by saying, that women and men should be able to wear anything of their own choice.

As I started to walk hesitantly back to Peter and was not sure what his reception would be, a young, tall, fine boned man came up to me and said, "Are you the artist and would you like to know the Sudanese way of life?" I replied, "Yes." because I had nothing to lose. He asked me to accompany him since his brother the chief of police wished to meet me. I went with him and he walked to a part of town I did not know. Then he approached a white stone wall with green painted wooden doors and pulled a large key out of the pocket of his striped Muslim dress to open the first door. We stepped inside and I realized I had been taking a big risk when he locked the door behind me.

In front of me, I saw a manicured lawn, a tree and a pretty wooden hut with running water. He said that he would let me use it as an art studio. We walked around the hut and behind it was another building which was the kitchen with a modern gas oven. He introduced the cook and other employees to me. I was asked to sit down in the next house and was given tobacco and snuff.

I waited five minutes and was brought tea. The, about 30 year-old man, "Esedin" asked me to marry him. I said, "No," since I was with Peter. He then said that he wanted to introduce me to his brother just the same. So "Esedin" and I walked between different houses behind the long wall with the green doors. There were ducks and a pond as well. The floor between the small houses was packed with hard trodden sand. Then we came out of one cement enclosure into another with a lawn and a high official building. Then I asked Esedin, "Where are we?" and he replied, "This is the prison."

He took me to a large office, furnished with a highly polished and stately looking desk, TV and upholstered chairs and asked me to sit down on a comfortable looking arm chair and ordered more brands of cigarettes and Turkish coffee. Thoughts rushed through my brain, that I might be thrown into jail for walking around naked whilst on Scheherazade. But then, the hospitality would not have been so generous. The coffee arrived and so did Esedin's brother Masher.

He was the director of the prison and a well groomed, tall, skinny and fine boned man, I had never seen without sunglasses. He wore a uniform decorated with three stars on each shoulder and many medals. He took my hand with a firm grip and asked me if I had any paintings for sale. I said, "Yes." and that I would let him see some of my work. He asked me to bring them to him and that he wished Peter and I to have dinner with him and some of his friends. He wanted me to be back in an hour with some paintings and I promised to do so. Then he shook my hand and someone unlocked all the doors and showed me out.

I walked with fresh courage back to Peter, who was glad to see me and I told him of what happened. I took our friend Amin, Peter's tennis partner and navigation student with me since Peter preferred to do something to the motor. Amin carried two framed landscapes, while I carried the map with some of my unframed work. After Masher had inspected my work, he chose the two framed landscapes (oil on canvas) I had painted while living on Moorea Tahiti in 1977, and Bora Bora and bought them both. He also invited us to hang them up in the formal dining room before we all ate dinner. Masher, Esedin and all their friends loved my work.

The large table was covered with a tablecloth and genuine silver cutlery. It looked formal and very high class. We sat down and dinner was served to everybody. It consisted of different salads, fresh corned beef, lamb, filled vegetable leaves and all sorts of delicacies. My mouth started to water. I know that people here preferred to eat with their hands instead of cutlery and all sighed with relief immediately when I started to eat with my fingers while supporting my elbows on the table and attacking the food like a cannibal. Conversation was almost absent and one could hear the intensive gobbling noises with the sound of ooh, aaah and mmmmm. Almost nothing was left over.

For dessert came bananas, ice cooled pineapples and coffee. Fresh lavender soap was unwrapped and everybody washed their hands in the sink just a few steps from the table. Then we all sat into comfortable chairs and smoked. We had interesting and amusing conversations. All of the men wore thin, snow white and still immaculate Muslim dresses with deep pockets that were practical and ideal for the climate there and I complimented them so Masher presented me with a brand new, white Muslim dress.

I found it hard to separate from two of my favorite paintings but was glad to see them in a safe place, without the risk of them maybe being destroyed on the voyage in the Red Sea, Plus, it felt good to have money again.

Back on Scheherazade, Peter and I slept soundly in each others arms. The next morning, I put my new white Arab dress on. It was too long and I cut it off and made a matching turban out of the rest. Then we went as usual into town and ordered yoghurt for breakfast. We sat at a table under the arches and it was served to us in a large soup plate full to the brim and with two large, round, flat, Arab breads, for next to nothing. The breads were still warm from the wood oven and were so large that we took the second one back with us. We filled it with cheese, salad or whatever we wanted later on board for lunch.

Every time I was by myself, native men would come up to me and start to annoy me. Sometimes, they even tried to touch me up and I had to get physical by using judo to throw them out of balance. Others proposed marriage to me and promised to buy up to four pairs of shoes for me if I would say yes. Those I waved off much more gently. Not until later did I find out that if they wanted a divorce, they had only to say three times to their woman, "We are divorced" and then they were declared not to be married any longer.

The new white Muslim dress was the most comfortable I owned and the large pockets replaced having to carry a handbag. I embroidered a small version of "The Universal Flag" on the back of it and was wearing the white dress when a group of Muslims approached and angrily demanded, "What is the idea of a woman wearing our national costume?" I replied, "I feel very honored to have been presented with it and thank Allah for this great gift. They took a few steps backwards and gazed at me with admiration and said "A-a-a" holding their hand's on their chins. From then on I was not pestered any longer and felt free again. THANK YOU, ALLAH!

Toward Christmas, it was more ideal to sail up the Red Sea to Suez. So we had to wait until the wind changed. In the north it blows south and in the south it blows north at this time of the year. Port Sudan is the wind-changing point.

We were not bored with having to wait. There were nine yachts in the port. Three of them we knew from Djibouti. Two others were on the way and should arrive at any time.

Port Sudan had been built in 1920 but gave the impression of being 2000 years old. Cars had not been imported until lately. Sometimes there was no petrol and then the traffic moved by donkey. Some of them had masterful patterns lovingly clipped into their fur. Their owners were proud of them.

Most of the few woman that were visible, were veiled with colorful cloths and the men wore night-shirts, mostly in white and almost all of them had a turban wrapped around their heads. Some of them had intense dark eyes and beautiful faces and were fine boned.

Too bad that their girls still get misshaped and crippled by female circumcision. Together with nurses and doctors, I fought against it. A family came up to me and told me that they refused to do it to their daughters and were classified by their relatives and others, as outcasts.

In contrast to Djibouti, there were no cripples who had been distorted for begging. People ate a lot of meat here and at the market, we could hardly see the meat, which was covered with swarms of flies. The fruit and vegetables came from around the Nile and the grapefruits were sweet and juicy. The bread was freshly baked and tasted wonderful. We could even get cheese. Everything was inexpensive. We ate at the best hotel restaurant and ordered a mixed grilled skewer with potato salad, fish, sausages, beef and ham and paid only $2 for both of us.

Even in this hot climate after 8 p.m., there was hardly anybody around. One could see an old aircraft from time to time. Regular flights were non-existent. Lufthansa had an office in town, which had not been opened yet.

Shoes were a status symbol and many people could not understand why I preferred to walk barefoot. I washed my feet every time I went on board and treated every cut or puncture with iodine after searching for splinters, which I took out with tweezers. The soles of my feet had become like thick leather. Peter also treated all his cuts and wounds with iodine and that is why everything healed for us the same way as in Europe. Many sailors used penicillin, creams and powders and had chronic open wounds and infections. There were no mosquitoes but flies instead.

I was invited by three sailors (mechanics) from Australia, who had just serviced the only Porsche in Sudan, which belonged to the owner of the cooking oil factory, to go along on a trial-drive to Suakin. One drove on the desert highway constructed by the U. S. A., while the other sat next to him. Fritz and I sat tight on the small back seats with our heads gently touching the roof. The air conditioning was a welcome relief in the tremendous desert heat.

We arrived in Suakin in less then an hour without any problems. There, we were welcomed and served hot spiced tea and I had the big pleasure of meeting nomads. The men had the most deep, fiery, wild eyes that I had ever seen. Their hair was covered in clay against the heat. They had camels, goats and horses and wore swords that were long and heavy and were beautifully decorated with genuine gemstones and silver. They strapped them on their backs while riding. I will never forget those magnificent intense faces.

Suakin used to be one of the biggest slave markets in Sudan. A few houses were still standing amongst the ruins. It was very interesting and beautiful. Some hand carved mahogany doors and shutters were still there. Camels, goats and donkeys searched for something to eat amongst the piled up stones of the ruins.

A few people also lived amongst the debris. Between the debris, one could see pieces of boards covered with ripped cloth or with the remains of old paint on them. A few sensual penis shaped towers on Mosques threatened as in Port Sudan and other places, their brainwash songs, sounding many times during the day and night.

In the background, one could make out the white-beige-ochre colors of the desert under the clear blue sky and together with the white calcified debris, plus the ruins, a magic landscape was formed. I could imagine what it used to look like and was glad as a woman, to have seen it then and not while it flourished as the slave market.

Two of the friends separated for an hour while Fritz and I went to explore. We spotted a large baroque-style portal which attracted us like a magnet. A few dogs lay lazily around. To the right of the portal, we could see a few buildings and then a sandy beach with a clear blue lagoon.

We stepped through the portal and heard people calling us. The voices came from the building. They were Muslims dressed in traditional long night shirts and turbans. One of them was gorgeous, without his turban and with thick curly hair. His eyes were full of fire and nearly black and the light played lively in them. Such a man would be a woman's dream if he were civilized. I felt secure and glad to have Fritz with me. We were invited by the man for dinner.

Everything was cooked with care and the best ingredients.

The fish was seasoned with wonderful spices and was our favorite. We all ate with our fingers and after the meal, the table looked as it may after a Roman orgy. The building had been constructed with thick white walls and the floor was pressed earth and sand. It smelled like earth, sand and moist walls, fish, vegetables, spices and others, and felt pleasant and cool. My nose almost had an orgasm. The tea was sweetened with sugar and spiced with cloves. After the meal, there was Turkish coffee and all kinds of tobacco to smoke. Hashish exhilarated the senses even more and is not illegal. Smoking means a lot to the people.

Fritz and I were sad to say goodbye but needed to get back in time to meet up with our two other friends who had the Porsche with them. As if bewitched, we floated out to meet the others. During the drive back, the four of us witnessed something incredible. We stopped and got out of the car. The blue-grey sky was splitting above the horizon. From the top, the wind drilled with fearsome speed into the red sea. Seen from the front, the clouds formed a white cube. On top of the cube another smaller cube formed. Then a brilliant white stripe formed upwards and into the clouds. Thunderbolts struck into the clouds from above. We could hear the sch-sch-sch sound of the wind getting louder and closer. We were fascinated and impressed and could not help being amazed. The wind speed was increasing and moving in a circle while rapidly getting closer and closer. The sand started to be lifted and we got back into the Porsche.

We had just witnessed a hurricane forming and were caught in the resulting sandstorm. We could just see through the rising sand outside, that a group of nomads had wrapped their faces up in turbans and covered themselves with blankets while riding on camels for dear life toward mountains in the northwest of the desert. My friends and I stayed put in the Porsche since we could not see anything through the dense and fast moving desert sand. We waited for about twenty minutes until the storm had calmed. Not a grain of sand had entered the air-cooled Porsche.

The highway could barely be made out under the sand, which

blew so strongly across the surface that we had to stop again and wait until the sand dropped below our eye line, to be able to continue our drive back safely. We were all exhilarated by that unforgettable experience but we felt sorry for the nomads (those brave individualists) who were forced to go through it.

The price of freedom can be very high

We really stood out and the Sudanese stared at us because cars were very rare. Life here resembled biblical times like a few thousand years ago. Cows and donkeys pulled wooden-wheeled carts. Veiled women, Muslims and nomads with wind- blown, wild-looking hair, children, goats, camels, cats, dogs, chickens, crows and other birds lived there amongst the dust, heat and mud- built houses.

They sold everything at the market- even bits of paper and rubbish, bananas and other fruit, vegetables plus meat with flies, intestines, spices and many other items. Men with floor length shirts threaded ancient sewing machines while others offered their wares for sale. My friends dropped me off at the port.

I prefer two-seaters, even though the little Porsche was very fast and exhilarating, had four seats and air conditioning. It was well sealed, a pleasure to drive and proved to be a very good friend in the desert.

Peter was glad I had returned safely and greeted me happily. He had managed to put the motor back together and it worked like a charm. The next day we all went back to Suakin. We were all friends from various yachts- 'Anastasia', Vanessa from 'Swan view', 'Roulette' and 'Scheherazade', sharing the rental of a Land Rover.

We drove in a pastel morning mood to Suakin and then into the mountains to Aqua Vit. The blue-grey silhouettes of the mountains with the harsh rustic desert, the very few bushes and cacti constantly fed my emotions. Everything looked so new and yet so ancient. Peter constantly said that he liked it in Australia and the South Pacific much better than in this poor, bare, uninteresting part of the world. Later he told me, that he was more impressed than he acknowledged at the time.

We could find stones and pebbles in green, red, blue, brown, black, white, beige, ochre and grey. If I had been there for longer, I could not have resisted creating a mosaic. At the hotel Aqua Vit, we ate quite well. The things I liked best were the little goat cutlets and the appetizers baked in leaves. I missed the wine, since the Muslims were not allowed to have alcohol.

Back on Scheherazade after a hard day, I was glad to feel my banjo mandolin, to relax and block out the city and harbor noise by playing cassettes. It was good to be able to have the batteries charged again and to forget the noisy mosques and the very busy harbor for a while. I bought light bulbs and a new cooker for Scheherazade, cheese, olives, pipe tobacco and other goodies. I invested in ivory, mother of pearl, black coral and a bottle of gin for emergencies. I changed some Sudanese money for Egyptian currency with a crewmember of a big ship. It was so good to have money again. We were ready to continue our voyage again.

Sanganeb Lighthouse, Jeddah, Port Safaga

On December 5, 1980, we left Port Sudan. Our friends on 'Anastasia' sailed at the same time. We met again in Sanganeb, where a huge lighthouse stood. The reef was incredibly beautiful, if you didn't try to approach it at night. We were lucky to get away with some scratches on the hull. The lighthouse keeper, his helper and the people from the diving school came with flash lights to show us the way and a place to tie Scheherazade.

We were soon served tea again. Our private life had vanished and the lighthouse keeper was a freedom-loving, young, thinking man who had been put on Sanganeb, so he would not be a threat to the system of the mainland. He took us up to the top of the lighthouse, where we could see the mechanism and the spectacular view.

Our friends on 'Anastasia' arrived a day after us. It was party time again and on of December 28th, we continued our sail closer to my loved ones. How much I longed for my daughters and parents. I was wondering if my dog Keys was still alive, since I had had no news about her for so long. Keys would then have been 10 years old. Among our favorite themes, belong the stories of our dogs. Peter and I could speak for hours about our dogs.

We anchored by St. John's Island but it was not safe, full of reefs and Peter dove four times. Once to get a fish and twice to untangle the anchor. We wanted to leave before the wind changed so as to not risk ending up on the reef, so we set the sails for Jeddah.

When we motored into the port and tied to the pier, the harbor police arrived and told us that there was no way we could stay there or get a visa for Saudi Arabia. We told them that we needed fresh food from the market and that we were very tired and desperately in need of rest. They then let us sleep through the night and told us, that they would get our needed supplies the next day.

During the whole time, a uniformed guard watched us, while sitting on a board in a three-sided/ one-man shed as a shelter. It was open at the front and the officer held a machine gun on his lap. He was sound asleep as soon as the other policemen were gone. The next day, some men came with all the food we had listed. We paid and left. We resented not being able to go on land. This was the first and last time we were restricted in this way.

The next anchoring place for Scheherazade was located in front of a beautiful beach without any people and we swam on shore. We walked on Saudi Arabian soil enjoying the clean beach and had a great time, before we swam back and moved on.

On December 5th, it was very hot and we were already one day away from the tropics at Latitude 24 and Longitude 36 in the direction of Daedalus Reef, where we hoped to see the lighthouse the same night. We did not know if we could anchor there. We hoped to receive mail in Port Said, even though we had heard that the postal system was lousy in Egypt. We hoped it would be better by the time we arrived there and that the mail would have arrived for both of us. Poor Peter had not received any of his mail from Australia. From December 11-18, 1980, we stayed in Port Safaga.

As we motored through the pass of the reef, I insisted that Peter attach the anchor to the chain. The motor stalled and we had just enough time to hoist the sail and sailed a few kilometers before we anchored. The oil filter was blocked and Peter cleaned it enough to get us to the pier. He did not know which pier to aim for and handed the tiller to me. Two men waved and signaled us to the left. I was steering in the direction the man had pointed.

Peter became so angry, that I nearly had a shock. Even though I was doing my best, he ripped the tiller out of my hand and steered in the opposite direction to the industrial pier between two large tied up ships, where I jumped on land with the rope to tie Scheherazade onto a large cleat. We and our yacht were powdered by bauxite, cement and corn dust within seconds.

In front of us, the British ship 'Ataman' was berthed. The captain and crew called us to have a drink with them. I was eager to join them but Peter called like mad, "Where is the harbor master?" I was so angry because I hate bureaucracy. In Djibouti and Port Sudan we had had no problems since we had not run after the bureaucracy or raised the yellow flag and instead, I had raised "The Universal Flag." We were respected, did not have to pay anything or waste our valuable time by filling out unnecessary papers, produced by killing trees which deprives living things of their oxygen. Instead, we were left in peace.

Peter suddenly suffered from a crisis. This happened rarely but when he suffered so did I, while the idiots ripped us off. First, the doctor came and took $20 of my last $30 away from me for a cholera vaccination I had not asked for. This was forced on me, even though it would be at most, 40% effective and there was no cholera in the area. I made such opposition when they wanted to give me a shot against yellow fever, which the doc signed without giving me the injection. Where we planned to go, there was no danger of yellow fever or cholera. Then, we had to pay to get a shore pass to go on land. This was not enough, since we had planned to go to Luxor and we needed a taxi for 120 km to Hergada and back to pick up a visa. The bank receipts for money changing had to be shown in order to prevent people from being able to change it on the black market for a better exchange rate.

Meanwhile, we befriended the crew and the captain of the 'Ataman'. We were invited to eat with them and take as many showers as we wanted. That was no luxury in the dirt and dust. We were also welcome to use their washing machine.

As we were having a really good time at the bar, up-tight policemen appeared shouting arrogantly, "Get that woman out of here!" I was shocked, disappointed and annoyed at the nerve and disrespect of those sexist, ill mannered and uneducated, ignorant cops and tried not to let it get under my skin. I quietly kept sipping on my drink and smoked a cigarette as the cops shouted like maniacs at full moon. They were so unsure, wearing their too large and rough shoes, of getting safely down the ladder and I had to help them to not slip off. (My good nature amazes me at times.) Even though I told them that I was not a prostitute (and don't look down on them) but an international artist, they forbade me as a woman to ever visit another ship again while in Port Safaga.

At night, two cops were placed, without our permission, to sit in the cockpit of Scheherazade and spy on us. I felt sorry for them having to shiver with cold and even made them tea. I guess I did that in the knowledge, that one cannot change parasites either. It is not their fault to have been born to be brainwashed.

During the day there were from one to three cops who watched our every move. Every time we went on land, we had to show our papers. They searched through our pockets and we were forced to inform them of all our actions. We were asked where we had been, what we did and why and how much money we changed, what we bought and for how much.

In the evening I needed to have a walk on shore and was stopped even though I had a shore pass with me because I was an unaccompanied woman. When I protested, they threatened me with prison and torture. Instead of Peter supporting me, as I expected from my life partner, he lost his head and hit me with the bread board and locked me inside the boat. While I was a prisoner in the cabin, I decided to leave him at the next best opportunity. It is awful what fear can do to people. I needed a man who was as free as I am and did not let fear turn him into cripple. I saw that it would be lunacy for a woman to travel alone with only $10 in her pocket in a non emancipated police state. I hoped to leave Peter in Crete.

Compromises only lead to hate and cut you off from any real chance in my opinion. The next day, I went along to Kena and Luxor just the same because I wanted to see as much as possible of the world (which belongs to me as well). Peter was sorry and did everything to make peace with me. I liked him very much but was no longer in love.

I can only love a free man. I cannot change my nature or anyone else. I will not tolerate having my freedom and rights taken away and will fight for them if needed. Only in a matter of life or death, will I give in temporarily until I find a way out.

Peter had already warned me, that he would ask for the whole bureaucratic menace again in the next port. I expected that we would get punished, robbed and dehumanized over and over again by officials.

I will fight, if I see a chance of winning. Peter could not do anything else since he was slightly brainwashed in my opinion. He was a good friend but he was holding me back. I outgrew him. I needed a man with whom I could make our damaged world well again.

The temples and graves in Luxor were very interesting but most of them were locked to tourism. There were a lot of hustlers and many tried to rip you off. The Valley of the Kings was wonderful and it was fascinating to ride on a bicycle through the welcoming green into small villages. From Kena to Luxor everything was planted and watered. Camels, goats, cows, chickens, dogs, water buffaloes, horses and birds fill the landscape.

Black veiled women with expressions of fear in their eyes, children in pyjamas and men with striped night shirts stood everywhere. "Baksheesh" (a tip) was their favorite word. One even wanted to exchange his bicycle for a woman.

My mother had read the book "Tutankhamun" to us when we were children. It was so fascinating. When I finally had the opportunity to visit his grave, all the chambers except for one room were locked. With great anticipation, I entered the room where the golden coffin of the young deceased king stood. What a big let-down! My disappointment showed and an archaeologist noticed me and asked if we would like to see a grave that he was excavating and had to key to. We accepted gratefully and were among the first to witness some of Egypt's latest historical finds, without fighting for viewing space among the masses. Alf and Carol were with us. It is good to have real friends.

Stefan and Hans from the yacht 'Roulette' had also arrived in Port Safaga. We went to the center of the village where I learned, that a huge shipload full of wheat sent for the poor people, by the U.S.A., had been dumped at sea since the people were too poor to pay the tax on it to Sadat. What a crime!

There was a legal opium den in town and we could see through the windows, how old men were enjoying sucking the smoke out of the hoses attached to the large water pipes. Their faces looked dried from the sun and marked by hardships.

The bread was put on planks along the side of the street to rise in the sun, in front of the bakeries, which were equipped with handmade clay ovens over a man-high and heated by wood, dried animal dung, paper or other combustibles.

I have learned to make the best possible out of every

situation. My survival instinct is very strong. I saw it as my goal in life to find my ideal mental and physical partner.

We were at sea again. Our next stop was Hurghada. I don't remember if it was before or after Hurghada and just know that it was somewhere in the Red Sea, that a snowstorm forced us to tie up to an oil rig. I was very angry since I was made to wait in their office while Peter was given a tour. They told me women were not allowed to see the inside of the rig. Peter explained to me later, that I would have been shocked at the pollution etc. and would have made a big fuss and opposition to it.

Scheherazade was covered with ice and snow. We were bitterly cold, drank a hot tea with rum and went to sleep in each others arms, with all the blankets around us. The next day, the weather eased off and we could continue our way up the Red Sea. We were glad to have a Swiss Army sleeping bag with a watertight cover, which was great to sit in while steering Scheherazade during the cold night watch.

I have heard that American Army sleeping bags (for two people) are even more ideal because the warmth of bodies against each other is the best form of heating. I recommend it to all sailors or people who are forced to live outside. The watertight, hooded cover replaces a tent even in sub-zero temperatures.

Hurghada

On the December 31, 1980 Peter and I were one heart and sole and thrilled to have found the way to each other again. We only stayed overnight in Hurghada but met interesting new friends from a small wooden sailing boat, who cooked spaghetti and invited us to eat with them. Peter does not smoke so I smoked the water pipe with them. The captain was an artist and his wife was an author. There were two crewmembers on their boat. Those people had a lot of aggravation and problems from the port authorities because they had obtained five gallons of drinking water from a German ship, instead of buying it for a rip-off price from the ships' chandler. We were lucky that they did not notice the hose pipe with water leading from the German ship into our tank.

We then followed the ship and anchored next to them. They invited us to dinner and Peter was given a big can of grease he needed for his motor. The propeller shaft had rusted and grease could prevent the water from leaking in. It leaked a little but we had to get used to the thought of having Scheherazade pulled out of the water in the near future. Peter already had a piece of bronze on board to replace the rusted shaft.

At the beginning of the Gulf of Suez, the weather had turned so bad that we anchored. We secured Scheherazade with three anchors for two days and it was ice cold, windy, wet and it even hailed. 'Anastasia' anchored as well. After 2 to 3 days of sailing and tacking up the Gulf of Suez, while being made utterly uncomfortable by strong winds and high waves, we were exhausted from the hard work of constantly having to change sails. We were soaked to the skin, even though we wore wet weather gear until I decided to do the sail changes naked and towel dried myself immediately afterwards and then jumped into the last dry clothes.

After that, we did not exactly feel warm but the weather got better and then the sun warmed us a little. Scheherazade did not take water on board and the sea calmed. I even baked bread. We enjoyed life again. Peter was a remarkable, nice and handsome man and I was in love with him again. Sometimes we played chess or drank a bottle of wine or I played my banjo mandolin, which let me forget the grim reality for a while.

I created "The Universal Flag" as a demonstration to the world that with good will, it is possible to recognize that national boundaries and the divisions and wars of greed (which they engender), are totally destructive to both the planet and to all life thereon. In my view, those organizations and authorities which continue to profit from the present political scenario, are little more than criminals of the worst kind.

Suez, The Prince of the Red Sea (?)

We were wondering how long the bureaucracy would take in Suez before we could go through the canal. It was hard for us to be cut off from contact with our loved ones. Poor Peter had not received mail since Bali, except for one letter from his brother-in-law, who had arrived in Djibouti. Peter and I were heading toward Suez, when a tug boat came alongside Scheherazade. I did not know if it was owned or leased by Mr. Shaker's outfit. They offered to tow us but we refused.

Then, near Suez on January 1, 1981, another vessel pulled alongside us with a stocky corpulent employee named Said and a Buddha-bellied guy called Ibrahim, who showed us good hospitality. Said started to be very pushy to do the paperwork and managed to put me ill at ease. We had previously done an incredible amount of filling out and showing papers while in Port Safaga and Hurghada (both in Egypt) and I did not want to have any more to do with bureaucracy so I let Peter fill out whatever forms he was forced to do. Our friend Stefan was pressured to fill out papers before he could read them. I hoped our trust would not be abused. Then, on the second tug-type boat, we were shown photographs of other yachts and people. On one photo was our friend Jeanne on the yacht 'Sapho Smith', whom we had met on the beautiful island of Mahe in the Seychelles with a recommendation to see the 'Prince of the Red Sea' for this business.

We berthed Scheherazade in the port of Suez since it would be safer from thieves than anchored in the open water. The port was all fenced in. Then we were put under pressure again, to get into their tug immediately with them, if we still wanted to get on shore that day.

After we stepped on land, we were told to sit in a small, military, port authority shed and we were brought a cup of tea. Then we tried to hop onto the back of Ismail's motorbike but decided to take a taxi instead, to visit the office. By the time we got into the taxi, we were in possession of a shore pass. They took our passports and ship's papers and we did not see them again until we visited Cairo on January 6, 1981, just to have them taken off of us again on the return from Cairo by the Travel Agency of Mr. Shaker.

This was Peter's first trip to Cairo, so I could show him what had impressed me and find new places. When we went into the Cairo tower and were ready to enter the lift to the top, an old friend, colleague and ex-lover stepped out of the lift and we had a big reunion after many years. It was the artist Maurice Frido from Ascona, TI, Switzerland. We did not have much time together since Peter understandably wanted to get back to Scheherazade.

In Mr. Shaker (also called the Prince of the Red Sea's) office, we were handed a photo of Antoine's ketch and dinghy with details of where he was heading for and that he planned to anchor up the creek from Salvador Dali's property and hoped to maybe meet us there. After seeing several more photos, we agreed to let 'The Prince of the Red Sea' organize the trip for us to go through the Suez Canal.

We were offered the chance to suck on a hose attached to a water pipe which had been heated by charcoal and was stuffed, by a shy, skinny 12 year old boy, with honey cured tobacco, topped with hashish. As a non-smoker, Peter refused with a friendly smile but I accepted.

The Prince liked me so much that he added, as a compliment, some opium to the water pipe. When I noticed an exquisitely bound red book decorated with gold and took it in my hands and said, "Nice", they all turned pale and heavy silence filled the room while the prince snatched the book out of my hands before I could open it. He said, "This is a holy book, the Koran and it is forbidden for any woman to touch it except at her marriage." I smelled danger and said," I am sorry but no one has ever told me of this law and I promise never to touch this book again." They forgave me.

We were served tea by the boy. I asked if he was his son and the 'prince' said "Oh, no." Then he explained that he was a child who came from a large family and worked for him for something to eat and a place to sleep. The boy scrubbed the floor of part of the office and was yelled at and ordered around. I felt so sorry for that shy little fellow.

Then the prince wanted to order me to paint something to his specifications. When I suggested to him that we should discuss the price, he chickened out. Before I wanted to discuss business, he had offered to let us have a shower at his place but then he was engaged in an important matter in Ismailia.

We were invited to Ibrahim's apartment, where we meet his wife and 18 month- old daughter. Their hospitality was very generous but the shower was lukewarm and the system was very primitive. It was better than standing in a cold breeze while taking a quick shower with cold water in the cockpit. It was the first time we had been in an Egyptian home and it was very interesting. Ibrahim paid 10 pounds rent a month for the dingy little place located several flights up a cold and dusty stairway. We could look out of the windowless opening and see a neighboring house with a roof garden where he kept ducks, before reaching the floor where Ibrahim and his family lived. The apartment was crowded with furniture. A color TV was turned on. They did everything to make us welcome.

The baby was a little roly-poly and looked like his father. The family looked as if they enjoyed fattening food. We were asked to enter the dining room and were amazed. There was delicious highly spiced fish soup, salad, bread, rice, filled cabbage leaves, ice cold water and orange juice. They had uncovered the godly, gold color painted furniture especially for us. A western style wedding picture graced the wall. Ibrahim's hair looked fluffy and I could hardly recognize him without his usual white cap. Alf and Carol from 'Anastasia' were with us. What struck me as unusual was that neither Ibrahim nor his wife ate with us but after the meal Ibrahim smoked the water pipe with us in the adjoining living room. It was nice to have met his family.

We were on the waiting list and yachts had to give way to the many tankers and ships, who had the right to go through the canal first. Before I left, I picked the most beautiful shell I had collected in Australia and intended to give it to the 12 year old, exploited boy at the bureau, when the baron of the red sea or also called Mr. Shaker snatched the sea shell out of my hand with the words, "This is too good for the boy, I will keep it for myself." Peter noticed my anger firing up toward an explosion and whispered in my ear, "Pull yourself together and say nothing, otherwise he will take it out on the boy."

It should be illegal for any child or grown up to have to work in the condition of a slave. Children all over the world should be protected from any exploitation. I wish I could make a better world, where all children have enough to eat. With birth control this should be possible. A roof over the head and a full plate of food, as long as they are in need of it, with the condition of having their tubes tied or a vasectomy. This should be made possible within a generation, with the financial help of the exploiters and would be a chance for those people to ease their guilty consciences. Or have they become so monstrously inhuman, crippled by their lack of feelings and compassion that they have become incapable of taking the responsibility of their own actions? Therefore, should they be forced to pay back for their greed or be prosecuted and jailed (in my opinion)? The world would be a much better place to live in and for our future generations.

We moved Scheherazade to get ready to go through the canal. Jean was anchored next to us on his luxury motor boat. He had a machine on board, that converted sea water into drinking water. Peter asked me to row to Jean and get our jerry cans filled. When I arrived at Jean's boat, he asked me onboard and told one of his crewmembers to fill the containers and lift them into my dinghy. The other crewmember brought some ice cold Heineken beer and coffee. We enjoyed philosophizing and the conversation flowed easily. While we were drinking together, the jerry cans were filled and loaded up. Jean then invited Peter and me to come for coffee after lunch.

Just after lunch, the 'Prince of the Red Sea' had arrived to pick up Peter and take him on shore to do the rest of bureaucracy to get through the canal on the following day. When Peter did not return, I went to John for coffee by myself and we got stuck into wine and whisky. I found Jean very sensuous and when he wanted me to stay with him, I could not have thought of anything I would have rather done but was reluctant to because I did not want to hurt Peter. When he told me that he would pick me up at 7:30 p.m. for dinner and that he would kill me if I did not show up, I felt flattered and happy that he desired me as much as I did him.

I rowed back to Peter and told him of my plans, laid in bed and slept. I must have had more alcohol than I thought and did not wake up until the middle of the night, when I walked up to the cockpit to empty my bladder over the side. In half-sleep I thought it funny that all the yachts around us had gone. I went back to bed until I realized that Peter had moved the boat. He told me that he had rowed over to Jean and threatened to shoot him between his eyes if he tried to get near his boat. It tickled me to know that I was so desired.

On January 8, 1981, they brought a pilot to us because the law prohibited us from guiding our own boat through the canal and it was obligatory to hand over the helm to a hired pilot. The same day, this was done to our friends on 'Anastasia'. We motored to Ismailia.

The pilot was a very quiet man who just sat there steering without saying a word. Before we let him off in Ismailia, he demanded "Baksheesh" and Peter gave him $1, since he was on a salary from the 'Prince of the Red Sea'. He complained that this was not enough.

In the morning, they sent us a different pilot. We were anchored in the harbor all night. The new pilot was a real turn on. He was very cheerful and entertained us the whole time and pulled out a piece of hashish. We smoked together and he steered the boat for long stretches at a time. It was Sunday and there was hardly any traffic in the canal. Big tankers were not allowed in while yachts were passing.

I was amazed at the organization of the Suez canal but the scenery was not very special. Flat and sandy. Sometimes sand dunes in the background. Trees were being planted and some shrubs had grown but there were hardly any birds since the bastards eat them. The markets were full of pigeons, sea and land birds. On January 9, 1981, we arrived in Port Said where we tied up at the yacht club.

Port Said. Crete

First thing, I went to the office where I inquired about the mail we were expecting. I was very disappointed when they informed me that it was lost. Peter received one letter but all the stamps had been stolen off it. If it had been up to me, I would have left the yacht club immediately without paying. Peter thought differently. We were held at the yacht club like prisoners and were locked up after 7 p.m. until 10 a.m. while guards constantly watched us. For me, Egypt's bureaucracy and corruption put a damper on an otherwise interesting country.

We decided not to buy the diesel from the ships' chandler, who demanded 17 Piastas instead of the 3 Piastas a liter charged by the service station. At the police station, they acted like gods and denied a white person permission to stay for a week. We had the option of prolonging our shore passes after three days.

I managed to get even with the bastards by climbing the largest of the pyramids (illegal) and enjoyed the cheering crowd and the musicians playing while I climbed down. The police bawled me out when I was back down and wanted to take me to jail but I talked them out of it by saying that I had not noticed the sign and giving them a lecture to not try and climb up, since it was too dangerous. I was photographed and interviewed and a camel and a horse were offered to me to ride for free.

Back in Port Said, £9 was charged for a permit to leave, which we were forced to pay if we wanted to have our passports back, which the cops had not been entitled to take away in the first place. Passports are private property but that was not acknowledged in Egypt. They tried to charge us an extra £2.50 but did not get away with it.

After not having worn shoes for nearly five years I bought a pair of sandals made from water buffalo leather since my feet felt too cold to walk barefoot. My feet were so sensitive that I had to get used to wearing them, even though I had to treat the blisters with iodine.

After stocking up Scheherazade with diesel that we had collected by rowing the dinghy to the service station and filling the jerry cans, we went shopping for fresh food and bought a sea chart for £10 (we had decided against the 1981 Nautical Almanac for £50). The mosques disturbed our peace with the noise pollution of their loudspeakers attached to the towers. The shrill, threatening, loud, whining sound attacked my nerves and sensitive ears.

On January 12, 1981, we were relieved to leave Port Said and Egypt. Happily we set Scheherazade's sails (even though the weather was doubtful) for Crete. The wind was blowing like stink and it was wet and cold. My only rubber boots were leaking and the wet weather gear was as good as one could expect, second hand for $8. We could not hold the course, since the next day headwinds started to blow. A few days later, we saw Cyprus but made our minds up to head for Crete no matter what.

Scheherazade was picked up and knocked down by a freak wave, just like she had been in much warmer waters between Australia and Indonesia and was pounded onto her side. That wonderful, strong boat came up again. Water poured in from the cockpit and through the ventilators. Finally, after six days that felt like a month, Crete popped up over the horizon. Even though night was approaching, we anchored with the help of a beautiful full moon in a rough little anchorage, with the hope that the anchor chain would not break. Scheherazade hobby-horsed in such a way, that with each blow the decks got wet.

The next day, on January 19, we left for Palekastron. The skies were overcast with the sun desperately trying to shine through. It was a gorgeous and intense sight. The anchorage was beautiful. I had a big urge to step on shore but Peter did not want to leave the boat in those rough conditions. I did not blame him.

We stayed there for two days, then we took a risk and started sailing in a force nine to get around the point and head for Sitia. At one stage, we were even debating if we should turn back. I could hardly believe our luck. We arrived safely but exhausted.

Sitia was a picturesque fishing town but had a lousy exposed anchorage. Again, we hobby-horsed and worried about the boot breaking loose. It was impossible to row to shore. Later, we shopped for fresh food and a bottle of wine. We could not believe how inexpensive the wine was. We slept well that night. The next day, we went to the pub and were surprised that we were given 'hors d'oeuvres' with each order of drinks.

They consisted of different plates with Greek cheese, olives, peanuts, chips, salad and chickpeas, on which I cracked a filling. Unfortunately, I did not find basouki players and Greek dancing, which I had developed a taste for while living in the U. S. A., but enjoyed it just the same. Greek men sat quietly with stern faces and weather beaten expressions. Some played cards. One of them came up and challenged me to arm wrestle. He won and I judged it was due to by my broken or sprained little finger, which happened previously during an unexpected moment, as a wave hit the boat and I had fallen on my finger with my whole weight. By the loud noise that escaped my mouth, my play mate probably thought I had cursed because I had lost. It set up a storm in the pub and to my great embarrassment, the rest of the men gave this poor fellow hell.

We stocked up Scheherazade and sailed to Nikolaos with one tack in beautiful, but still rough and cold weather. The place looked very romantic. Then we lowered the dinghy into the water and it broke loose during a hailstorm and smashed up on the wharf. It was bitterly cold and Peter hurried into the diving suit and swam after it. I was really worried about him. The waves were breaking with such force that it sprayed across the road. The seats had been ripped out of our aluminum dinghy and the oars were floating separately. Peter managed to get the lot to safety within half an hour. He was freezing and his skin looked blue from the cold, even though he was wearing a wet suit.

The fishermen volunteered to fix the dinghy which had previously belonged to Peter's friend Ken Furley, who sold it to us in New Zealand for $50 since we had lost the old one. It had been around the world 1 1/2 times and was 28 years old and had great sentimental value. When we got it back from the fishermen it looked like new and we wanted to pay for it but they refused. Peter insisted on giving them some ship's paint which they gladly accepted. We became good friends.

On March 15, 1981, we were anchored in Nikolaos in front of the harbor when two fishermen pulled up and told us that they knew of a better place to anchor, so we followed them and they gave us their mooring. I invited them for tea but we all just sat there and pantomimed.

In the morning we motored into the harbor and tied up alongside the wharf. The formalities were next to nothing. A small fee was charged to tie up. The harbor was small and picturesque. There were no tourists. There was no supermarket. Just small shops and it was a really magical little place.

At the post office, there was mail from my parents which also included my daughters' letters and Peter received a telegram from his mother with the date of her arrival on it. We were both happy to hear from our loved ones.

It was really nice and warm there. What a difference from the previous two months. The almond trees were in full bloom and flowers grew everywhere. The wind still persisted which is characteristic for Crete.

We met George at the fish shop. He spoke good English and helped us with everything. He even gave us special prices when we bought fish, meat or cheese at his parents' shop. George admired

Peter and helped him sell older paint and ship's putty for a good price since we were getting low on money.

Peter's 63 year-old mother and her 70 year- old lover had been visiting us for weeks since February 3rd. First I thought, "Rats, this is going to be tight on a small boat like Scheherazade with the galley, bunks and toilet all in the same cabin", but it had gone surprisingly well. It had been almost all laughter and happy times and no one got on anybody's nerves. The two of them were madly in love with each other and he wooed her all the time, which she loved.

He was a big man and she was a fragile-looking woman who was really quite tough and when they were asleep she was snuggled in his strong arms with her head on his shoulder. Then they snored in duet. That was very humorous and did not bother us since we slept extremely deeply with Scheherazade in a secured place.

We were invited to the discotheque opening of 'Nick the Greek'. Nick himself looked like a guru with fire in his blood. He had a long grey, natural beard and long grey natural hair and his dark brown eyes sparkled. He moved with the grace of a cat while he played the records. Peter's mother danced almost the whole night while her lover, riddled with arthritis in his legs, suffered with jealousy but was proud to watch her move like a 40 year old.

Someone had sent a bottle of champagne over to her and the waiter explained to her, "Someone likes the way you dance." We all got very stimulated and it was not easy but a lot of fun to try and make it down the steep hill that took us back to the boat. I held the lover and Peter held his mother, while we guided them in safety. Peter's mother was laughing so hard that her bladder let go which brought tears of laughter to our eyes. The hardest part was to get the lover, who weighed about 16 stones, from the wharf over the about 1 1/2 meter gap and over the railing, into the boat. We did it. Dry and safe, we all fell asleep with all our clothes on.

We waited for better weather and when it became clear and

sunny we rented a car for sightseeing. First we drove to Kritsa, a mountain village and then beyond and to the top of mount Korifi. Peter's mother was frightened as we drove through snow and slush so we turned around instead of risking getting stuck.

I found a rock which I carved. Then we went to look at all the old stones left from an ancient village with a palace and picnicked. We crossed the island to Irapetra. The crossing was interesting after the breathtaking view from the mountain, with its many windmills and innumerable hot houses. Then we took the road to Lithined and to Sitia. We all agreed that we liked the views better from the north side of the island.

The drive back from Sitia to Nikolaos was simply magnificent. We drove through unspoiled towns and could see the medieval sight of men riding donkeys with black dressed women urging the poor animals on with sticks, to keep them walking. There was hardly any traffic. Olive trees were every where. Some had thin stems while others were all knobby with age. They can reach 2000 years of age. We took other rides to Heraklion and Knossos by bus.

Overland to Switzerland

I had sent all my paintings and sketches to Switzerland where my parents had stored them in the attic of their house.

On March 24, 1981 we accompanied Peter's Mother and her friend to Athens. We took a cruise with a stop in Santorini. When we went on shore, I watched a waiter rubbing his hands together, while he walked toward us. Before he could speak, I told him, "We don't want any." This remark took him by surprise and he invited us to his restaurant for free drinks with appetizers.

We then ordered some fish dish which was delicious but we did not have enough time to explore Santorini, but what we could see was beautiful and very romantic and it was not overrun by tourists except those from the cruise boat.

When we arrived in Athens, we stayed with Peter's mother

and her friend in a hotel until the 31st, when they planned to depart for Australia. While Peter and I ate breakfast, Peter's mother's friend joined us at the table and said, "I think she has flipped a coin. She is jumping like mad on the bed." When she appeared with a big smile, Peter asked her, "Why did you jump on the bed?" She replied, "I want to do everything I was not allowed to do when I was a child." We all laughed.

After breakfast we went to see the famous Greek Temple which disappointed me after having seen much better temples in Sicily. I found the old part of Athens interesting but preferred the countryside or quiet beaches and coves to any city. Too many people make me nervous.

After saying goodbye to Peter's mother and friend at the airport, we got a ticket for on a bus trip to Germany with a stop in Milan. It was a long and tiring voyage and the bus was completely filled to the last seat. Peter and I were sitting on the bench along the back. It was hot and unpleasant. Every once in a while the bus stopped to let everybody out for only 10 minutes to stretch their limbs or run to the toilet. It was funny to see them hurrying into the WC, with pinched faces and come out sighing with relief and wearing relaxed expressions.

I tried to talk the chauffeur into letting us out in Switzerland, since he was passing through on the way to Germany but he said, "No" since it was forbidden for him to do so. Sore and sticky from sitting for so many hours, we got out in Milan and I asked a woman travelling alone, if she was interested in sharing a room with us to reduce the cost. She was all for it and so we tried to book a hotel room. The guy at the desk wanted to inspect our passports and saw that we all had different names. He said, "Maiale" (pigs) to us and threw us out. I felt like defecating in front of that hotel but Peter wanted to avoid troubles and so I refrained from expressing what I thought of that man with the dirty mind. The travelling woman went her way and we were dead tired but found a room with a shower in a guest house.

In the morning, we hopped onto a train to Switzerland.

What a reunion! With tears in my eyes, I hugged my gorgeous daughters and pressed them to my heart. Both Alexa and Julie had grown so much. Then I hugged my parents and Keys, my dog, who recognized me immediately. Then I hugged my girls again. I had waited so long for that moment.

Everybody liked Peter right away. My parents had already lined up a job for him, as suggested by my Uncle Paul's wife Beatrice, whose family owned a shopping trolley factory and needed a welder.

After a few days of rest and getting acquainted, my father lent his car to us so we could go sightseeing. Sometimes we went all six of us and Keys. Keys would not leave my side and accompanied me everywhere.

Peter was happy about the job but had to go by train from Wil to Gossau which took 20 minutes. My aunt Maria lent him a bicycle so he did not have to walk from the train station to the factory, which belonged to the family Mitcheta. Peter cheered everybody up with his humor and the interesting sailing stories. He liked the job and was happy to be able to save his salary for sailing while we stayed 4 months for free at my parent's house.

Alexa and Julie were 18 and 20 years- old and very independent. I was so proud of them and grateful to my parents for everything they had done for my flesh and blood.

All my relatives thought very highly of Peter. We were all sad to have to say goodbye. Separating from my daughters was heartbreaking but they could understand that I had to leave again and were glad that Peter and I got along so well, again. I spoke to Keys who understood that she was to stay with Alexa and Julie.

We took the train to Venice and then changed for one with a sleeping car which was leaving for Athens. We had booked a bunk each and laid in it. The train filled up with a dense crowd of stressed people, which made Peter think of the ride suffered by the poor Jewish people on their way to Dachau. It felt as crowded as in a chicken battery. A woman with children wanted my bunk but there were so many mothers with children that I said, "No." My back was fragile from a previous injury and I did not want to be standing for hours to come. They could have reserved as well. The toilets were overflowing and it stank. They leaked in to the hallway mixed with used wet toilet paper and human excrements. Children where crying and mothers were shouting.

We tried to quench our thirst and ate all the oranges my mother had given us. They helped to prevent our throats from drying out. The smell of rancid food, body odor and axle grease drenched the air. The windows were open and people stood body to body like tinned sardines. The temperature was nearly unbearable. I felt sorry for them, gave up my bunk and ended up standing with one foot on my suitcase and one arm out of the window. I had to hold on because of the shaking and squeaking old wagons. Whatever I touched was sticky. I was unable to move without winding myself through sweaty bodies.

In Belgrade, an old Yugoslav sold home brewed coffee from the outside of the train and I handed him the 1000 Lira he asked for through the window. Peter and I shared the only half-filled cup. It felt like a godsend all the same. Hallelujah!

We waited until some of the crowd got out and wiggled through the rest of the bodies to go out of the train and find a WC and a water fountain and could just jump and escape to the side, at nearly being run down to the ground by the thirsty masses. We drank after they had gone and washed ourselves as well as we could and filled the empty orange juice bottle.

We managed to get back to the train before it started to move. Peter and I had the top bunks again in the cabin for 6 people. Later, 2 men from Ireland, 1 man from Greece and 1 man from England with a 14 year old son and 2 guitars joined the cabin and we had our enormous long and almost unbearable hot time shortened by conversation and entertainment.

When we arrived in Athens and got out of the train, it almost felt like an orgasm. We were very tired and in bad need of a bath and swore not to travel by train ever again if we did not desperately need to.

We took a taxi to Pyreus and were pleasantly surprised to still be able to book 2 bunks in a 4- person cabin on the ship 'Ariadne', one for women and one for men. There were 3 other women and a baby in the cabin. I searched the whole ship for a shower, carrying a towel, fresh clothes and a bottle of shampoo under my arm and finally found one. I stood under it for a 1/2 hour and felt like new human. Wonderful! Then I met Peter and showed him where the shower was.

I enjoyed a cold beer in the shade of the upper deck and watched how the backpackers, reserved a place to sleep by placing their sleeping bags and other baggage on the deck. The ship held 1400 people. Peter returned from the shower, glowing with a big smile. We were amused to watch the masses preparing for the night on deck.

After 7 pm the dinner in the self service restaurant was available. Again, the masses nearly ran each other down worse than wild animals to get in. We wanted to go to the better restaurant but were turned away for not having a 1st class ticket. So we got a piece of goat meat, thrown on top of the over-cooked noodles and Greek salad from the hectic tourist self-service restaurant and fought for a place to sit down. We gobbled down the meal (prepared without love) with a wolf's hunger.

Before going to sleep, we drank another beer and a Metaxa which smelled like spirit but helped to digest the food. Then we each went to our cabins. The women were asleep and so was the baby. I slept in the air conditioned cabin very deeply for a few hours until I woke up feeling ice cold. I put on my warmest pullover and went into the warm night air to warm up. It was a clear night with many stars.

A lonely Greek man spotted me and followed me across all the sleeping bodies. I did not desire any company but ended up smoking a cigarette with him. He got sticky and I disappeared into the cabin, where I found the switch for the air conditioning and turned it to low. Then I fell deeply asleep again until I was awakened by the screaming, of the, probably wet, baby. That was not too bad until the grandmother talked non-stop in Greek to try and calm the baby until 6 a.m. in the morning and until the steward came and woke us up in Heraklion.

We let the masses fight their way down the stairs while we drank a cup of coffee. Then we stepped on land and walked to the bus station to deposit our bags there. We went to see the yacht port where every place was taken up. People were chased out of parks by the police. They were all back-packer tourists. It looked weird, how they all put on their clothes, grabbed their sleeping bags and baggage and took off. It was forbidden to sleep in public parks since many of them left excrement and rubbish behind. Peter mentioned that the first "backpacker" could have been the hunchback of Notre Dame.

Back in Nicolaos, we went to see our friend Janos and family from the restaurant Kri Kri, who welcomed and kissed us. They could watch Scheherazade from their place and had volunteered to guard Scheherazade in our absence.

They then wrapped up a beautiful dinner with vegetables, potatoes and fish for us to take to the boat and gave us back the dinghy and the keys. We rowed back to the boat and were relieved and happy to find everything the way we had left it. Even the batteries still had some charge in them after 4 months of absence. Scheherazade was a bit dusty and we scrubbed her.

There was an empty birds nest in the boom. We were anchored in the Minos Bay. Since we got back, the wind had increased which was very pleasant in the 32 degrees of heat in the shade. For sailing it was a bit too wild. Scheherazade was clean and everything was in order. The motor worked well and we were almost ready to sail. The trim tab for the wind vane had to be repaired, the shopping was done and we had to say good bye to all our friends.

I danced the basouki on top of the table for the last time with my Greek friend and dancing partner, who came every day to the Kri Kri while we were there and had asked me to dance with him. Peter did not mind, since he did not like to dance and watched us. I sold one of my sculptures I had carved out of tropical wood at sea, to George, who was a friend of ours.

To New Adventures

We had been asked if we would do some chartering, but Peter said we only would take no more than 4 people for an afternoon's sailing in the cockpit. The cabin was for us only and was our bedroom and private space.

We went out sailing with tourists only 2 times but met some really nice people who brought all the food and drinks with them and invited us to dinner after the sail. They left all the unconsumed food and full bottles plus they were extremely generous. We laughed together. Later we received a letter from Germany, where they stated how much they had enjoyed the first sail of their lives. I have forgotten their names but not their faces, like so many other wonderful people who left a mark in my memory as well.

On August 28, 1981, we left Nikolaos and sailed to different places on the west from Nikolaos. We anchored the same day in Spinalonga. On the 29th, we arrived at Standia. On the 30th in Kalives and on September 1st, we arrived in Stavros.

We really enjoyed ourselves being surrounded by beauty and sailing short distances in perfectly beautiful weather conditions. We swam, walked inland and met locals and explorers. In Crete, there were over 10,000 species of flowers and plants that grew nowhere else in the world. This attracted many botanists. The island was interesting to archaeologists as well. Crete and its people had been great to us.

On September 2nd, we left Stavros and arrived on the Island of Antikythera. It was a tiny island without tourists, hotels, bars or coffee shops and scarcely inhabited by a few fishermen and families.

We anchored in a deep natural port and rowed on shore. Then we climbed up the steep stairway to the only village on the island. People came out of their simple houses and greeted us. They looked very poor, dressed in shabby looking clothes, had weather beaten faces which expressed their hard way of survival.

We asked if there was a pub in their village where we could get a drink but they said, "No." Then a commotion took place amongst the people and the men took their rifles with them and headed out of the port in their rowing boats. Excitement was in the air. Peter and I wanted to know what was going on. We could not understand much Greek and heard many shots. We saw over the cliffs that the men had shot at a dugong.

We shouted "NO, STOP!" but they kept on shooting and took the gorgeous animal back on shore with them. We ran down the steps to him. He was so badly wounded that we were unable to do anything to help him. I stayed with him and gently caressed his beautiful head. His big round eyes seemed to tear, so did mine, then he died. I asked the men, "Are you going to eat him?" They said "No." Then I wanted to know why the fuck they had murdered this magnificent, docile animal. They claimed, "Because they eat all the fish." Peter and I knew that this was a lie, since dugongs where extremely rare in those waters.

We were so disgusted at their brutality and greed that we went back to Scheherazade, immediately pulled the anchor up and headed for Kythira.

On September 3rd, we arrived in Kythira. This island was larger than the dugong slaughter island. Kythira had a much better feel to it and a picturesque sandy beach invited us to walk. We did not desire to meet people but could not avoid it and were pleasantly surprised how nice and welcoming they were. The sunset was beautiful. The inhabitant's curiosity was great since not many sailors stopped there.

On September 4, 1981, we stopped at Porto Kagio in Peleponnesus. On the 5th in Methoni and on the 6th, we arrived in Pylos, Greece where we stayed until the 8th.

I wanted to see the oldest olive tree in the world, aged more than 2000 years. I hugged the tree trunk, which was so big that my arms were by far, too short to embrace the whole trunk. This tree made a spectacular impression on both Peter and I.

An older man told us that we could pick as many olives as we wanted. When I told him that I had no idea how to prepare them, he explained that we had to put them into salt water for " 21 days " but had to change the water every day. Then we should season them with garlic, rosemary bay leaves etc. and fry them in olive oil, then let them cool off and can them. The next day, we took a bucket to the tree and picked enough to last us for a while. I started to put them in clear sea water which was changed every day. After 22 days, we ate and canned our own delicious olives from the oldest tree in the world. I am wondering if that tree is still alive. In my memory I still feel and smell this special and unforgettable tree.

We had also met a young couple on a motor bike who had driven all the way from Germany to Pylos. They had many stories to tell and were interesting to listen to, even though their rear ends were in pain from the long voyage. We left Pylos on September 9, 1981.

Collision with an Oil Tanker, Reggio Calabria

The 300-mile sail from Pilos to Reggio, Calabria in Italy, which we had estimated to take two days, took six days with the motor. We had hardly any wind. There was a full moon. The self steering broke down and we had to hand steer for hours. At the first rainfalls, I got a bit worried about storms brewing up but fortunately my worries were in vain. The full moon was bright and Scheherazade's white hulls could be seen and we had lit the mast head light and all others. We did not spot any ships and were out of the ships road and to the north of it. Peter and I were so tired, that in the calm of the wind, we both fell asleep.

At about in the middle, between Greece and Italy, it banged so loud that everything flew around in the cabin. I thought that we had hit a reef, even though there were no reefs in the middle of the Mediterranean Sea.

When I grabbed the spotlight and ran up to the cockpit, I could see that we had been hit by a 6000 ton heavy Oil Tanker. My imagination ran wild - at a hundred miles an hour and I believed that we were sinking. I shone the SOS sign with the powerful spotlight at the big ship. They turned back and stayed with us for an hour, until we had inspected Scheherazade and saw that she was not sinking and there was no water seeping in.

Luckily, we learned that the 6000 ton ship had only touched the bow of the 10 ton Scheherazade with her rear end. Besides the steel railing and the anchor roller, nothing was damaged. We really had luck on our side and celebrated with a glass of Ouzo and toasted to the fact, that we were alive and well. Probably the captain of the ship was also asleep.

When we arrived in Reggio Calabria, on September 13, 1981, we were asked, "O Madonna – what the hell had happened to you?" Peter told them that we had a collision but would not name the ship, since the people on it would have all lost their jobs. I can tell, now, that it was a Russian ship.

The people at sea stick together and don't tattle-tale on each other. The people in port know this. They arrived with welding equipment and, free of cost, repaired Scheherazade's railing and anchor roller like new.

The mainsail was so ripped, that we had it repaired by a sail maker. The people were so eager and very dependable to help us. We were deeply touched by their aid, generosity and friendship. As we walked to the market to buy fresh food, the cars stopped and offered us a lift with our goods and drove us to the harbor.

About 20 sailing yachts were stationed in the port. There was not a boring moment. We were invited by an Italian industrialist who drove us around and showed us the beautiful Piemont and invited us for dinner and lunch. Then he gave us a huge crate of mouth- watering grapes, special amaretto cookies, flowers and perfume for me and picked us up the next day again as his guests for lunch at his home. Then he showed us his factory and took us to a restaurant in the evening. He loved to hear our stories and had a bit of a crush on me but respected both Peter and I. I had never been on an aero foil cruise so Peter surprised me with two tickets to Sicily and back which we enjoyed greatly.

The following day we visited the Museum to look at the magnificent gigantic antique Greek bronze statues that had been found on the seabed and repaired. I believe they represented two Greek, male gods and looked very realistic with their enamelled eyes. One could see every vein on them and every detail of the whole process of restoring was documented and photographed. I had to smile when an Italian man stood in between one of the sculptures and I and stared at me with the expression, "Look at me, I am alive." I got a bit annoyed when he would not move but then I pretended to walk away and he moved as well and this gave me the opportunity to study the Greek gods. A sight I will never forget.

Soon we were on the move again. There was an incident concerning the police and which I will describe LATER by copying a letter Peter sent from Sardinia to my parents in Switzerland.

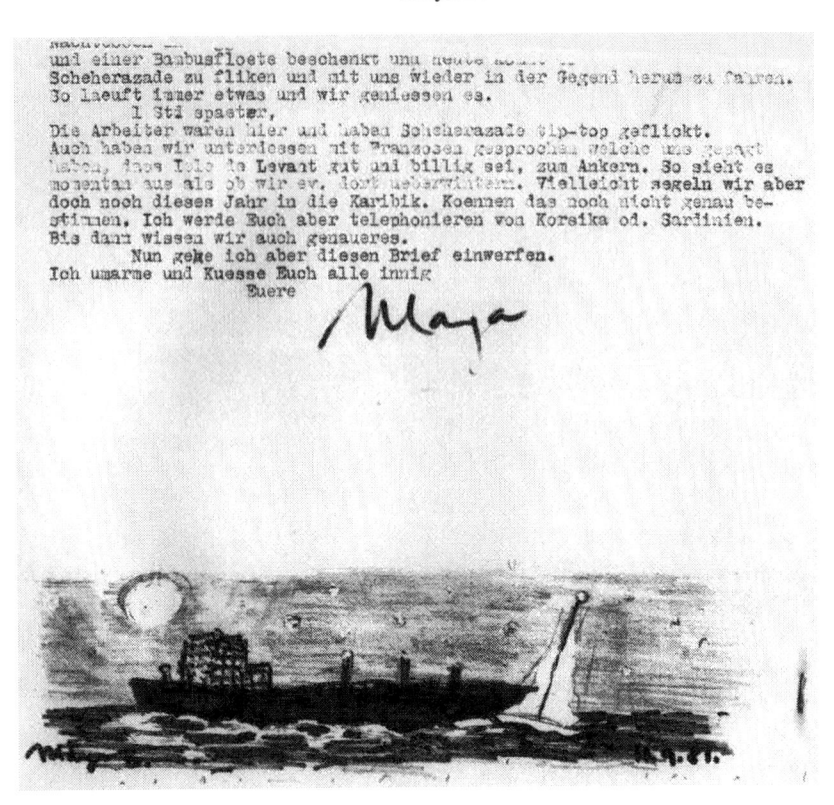

Letter home about the collision

Lipari Islands, Sardinia

I picked up pumice stone floating near Volcano Island at sea toward the Lipari (Aeolian) Islands.

It was impressive to see the fire and smoke rising up into the sky. The water was deep blue. We did not stop since the anchorage was not ideal. We went to Lipari Island instead. What a romantic place but nothing compared to the South Pacific for me.

I loved Peter but was thinking about leaving him. He was such a good friend, that I felt guilty about my thoughts. I wanted and needed passion again or I was going to go crazy. I sensed that I could find it, given the courage to live alone for a while and find a studio to paint in again. I tried to tell Peter but he would not hear of it and changed the subject.

We went to see Salina Island and Alicudi Island and then sailed toward Sardinia. Just before Sardinia, we were surprised by one of the worst storms I had ever experienced. The wind increased so suddenly, that we hardly had time to pull down the reefed main sail and replace it with the storm triangle before we were completely surrounded by violent waves and wrapped in thick dark clouds.

We could not see the shore or our direction. The compass swung around. Peter started the motor but the propeller spun often above the waterline and so he turned the motor off again. We threw out the sea anchor. This slowed Scheherazade slightly but we were worried that she could run aground, not knowing how close to the shore we were. It was spooky and we both just hoped to ride this storm out. There was nothing to do but wait and hope that Scheherazade and we would be okay.

Thoughts of, "Do we have such bad karma since I did not have the courage to tell Peter about leaving him?" sprung into my brain. Then I told myself not to be silly. The storm calmed after about 3/4 of an hour that felt like a week. We were very close to the shore but headed back out and toward Cagliari and managed to get to the port just before dark.

I do not remember the exact date of arrival but it was in October, 1981. It escapes my mind, if we were anchored or tied up but what I do recall, is that we needed to go on land. So we ate dinner together in a cute little restaurant and indulged in a bottle of wine to celebrate having survived that horrible storm. We didn't want to stay in the big city any longer than necessary, just long enough to have Scheherazade pulled out of the water and repaired. They gave us a price but when Scheherazade was lifted half way out by the crane, they raised the cost to twice the amount and threatened that if we did not agree, they would leave Scheherazade hanging in mid air. On top of all that, we were not allowed to do our own work but had to unload a package to pay the workers. We were relieved when Scheherazade was repaired and back in the water again.

After a good night's rest we sailed around the cliff of Stella del Diavolo and dropped the anchor in the Gulf of Salinas, where we enjoyed the beach before sailing to Olbia the next day. Other yachts were in the port and we met two single-handed sailors whom we invited for dinner on Scheherazade. I thought that this would be the ideal time to leave Peter, since he would not be alone. I took a few of my things and hitch-hiked to Palau, since that name attracted me.

I felt guilty about leaving my best friend Peter but I had to do it, even though I knew that it would be very hard to be on my own again.

After Leaving Peter. Involved with the Mafia.

A bit worried and nearly broke, I walked in a northerly direction until a car stopped. The driver was a Swiss woman in a Mini Cooper. She invited me to a pub for a coffee. We got into a conversation and she suggested that I should go with her to Arzachena where her friend from Norway owned a mill. She had rented an apartment there. I gladly accepted and looked forward to meeting her friend and seeing the mill. When we arrived there, two donkeys, two parrots and four cats greeted us. It was a very romantic and wild looking place with beautiful plants and trees in the garden. The sound from the untamed stream and the singing of the birds transformed my soul like magic. A big tree stood on the riverbank and spread its shade across the very large table under it.

The Swiss woman asked me to sit down while she went to speak with her Norwegian friend who lived in a stately looking house and who had travelled all over the world, before she married an Italian man who had a boyfriend but gave her the mill to live in. He was rarely there and she was faithful to him but very lonely. My Swiss friend lived in a smaller building. Since the large mill room with the fireplace and the large bed was not inhabited, I asked if I could have it as my art studio and do exchange business for one of my paintings in return. She agreed, if I would have one that she liked. She let me sleep in that wonderful place for the night and in the morning the Swiss woman drove me to Olbia.

Peter and Scheherazade were in the port. Peter had done his first single-handed sail from the Gulf of Selinas to Olbia and I was proud of him. I picked up the rest of my things, the banjo mandolin and my paintings that were rolled up. I felt a bit guilty for having left him but needed to be free and paint again. I hoped that the two single handed sailors in the port would console Peter and that he would find a wonderful person to sail with him or find the courage and confidence to sail on his own.

It had been a great and valuable time sailing with Peter and I am eternally grateful to him and his wonderful strong yacht Scheherazade, which got us safely through dangerous situations. Peter told me that if I left him, never to try and contact him again. I kept this promise even though it was hard to not try and find out if he was safe and where he was. I hope he is well and happy. He deserves it.

Funnily enough, I had said the same thing to Taylor when we separated in St. Croix, U. S. V. I. in 1974. Back at the mill in Arzachena, I unrolled my paintings and showed them to the woman from Norway. She loved one that reminded her of a Botticelli and hung it on her living room wall. I took over the large room of the mill but liked to paint outside. I was very productive but had the urge to go out toward the evening.

While hitchhiking to Porto Cervo, which was not far away, I had found out that Porto Cervo was a town built by the Aga Khan. I walked through the town, which had many boutiques, shops, hotels and a few very nice restaurants, pubs and coffee shops. The port was full with some beautiful yachts. I sat in a pub and watched the people go by.

Then I hitch-hiked back to Arzachena and went to sleep. The next few days I did not go out, since the owner of the mill told me that she would be glad if I would eat up all the food stored in my room before it went bad. There were canned, dried and pickled foods available to me. This was paradise and I could hardly believe my luck. I felt that nature was on my side. What a pleasure to paint in such a wonderful place!

I worked very intensively toward my next exhibition. I did not know where or when it would take place. Feverishly, I continued to create, until I ran out of canvas. Then I hitchhiked again to explore Sardinia and met Marcello who wooed me, until I could not resist him any longer. I went back to the two friends in Arzachena and said goodbye, packed my things and the still slightly damp paintings and went to live with Marcello.

He took me to see his two houses and asked me which one I would like to live in. One was located on top of a mountain and the other was overlooking the port of Cervo. I preferred the one with the spectacular view near the sea and he showed it to me. It was a very nice house. He made a coffee for us and we sealed our new life together. Marcello wanted to introduce me to his friends, so I washed up the two empty cups. He yelled at me, "Don't do that, you are not my maid, you are my woman." This I found weird but other countries have other customs.

We had a great time driving around and meeting his friends. In the evening we went to dinner. We walked into the private dining room of a restaurant, where about a dozen men were sitting around a very large table. He introduced them all to me and then said to them pointing at me, "If you try any thing with her, *rompa di balle*." Which I believe translates as *'Or you will be castrated'*. Convincing myself that he had only joked, I accompanied him to his work, with the condition that I be quiet and wait for him in the back of the same room at a table with another woman who was waiting as well, while the men played poker for money. Then we went to sleep in the house I had chosen. The next day he had to go somewhere while I started another painting. I put it in the hot sun to dry.

At dinner we went out again but to a different restaurant. The whole gang was there again. After dinner we all went to a nightclub. Marcello forbade me to dance with anyone. He would not dance so I thought, "Why should I let him dictate what I can and can not do?" and accepted a dance with the first man who asked me. Marcello walked up to me and hit me in the face.

I escaped and went to the police who accompanied me to the house, which was locked so they could not get my bags, paintings or my passport. I did not trust the Police and walked to Porto Cervo where I hid on a bench sheltered by bushes and slept in the park. I was awoken up by a torch shining in my face. A policeman told me that it was forbidden to sleep in the park so I told him of my troubles.

It was one of the Aga Khan's private policemen who told me not to worry, that everything would be okay in the morning and took me with him, to slpend the night in a room at his house. In the morning, I showed the policemen the house and fortunately Marcello was not there. They managed to open the house so I could get my things.

I binned most of them, leaving my favorite, red hand-crocheted dress, red hat and antique mink stole visible next to the container and kept only what could be strapped on my trolley. The paintings were rolled up and tied to the top and I headed for Olbia to catch the ferry boat to the mainland of Italy.

I met some crewmembers who were leaving that day and wanted to do exchange with a drawing or a portrait for a ticket since I needed to keep my last cash to buy a railway ticket back to my parents. They smuggled me as a stowaway onto the ship and spoiled me with food, drink and conversation.

While walking to the train station, I noticed that I was being followed by a man but thought I would be able to shake him off. In the train I felt safe. It was a long train ride. In Zurich and in the process of changing trains, I was followed by the same guy again. This time I knew every corner of the surroundings and managed to lose him for good.

I arrived at my parent's home and was greeted first by my dog Keys, who heard me come through the ground floor door. She wet the floor, she was so happy to see me again. I went up the stairway and found no-one in the kitchen or living room.

Then I heard the beautiful sound of the flute coming out of Julie's bedroom on the third floor. I sat on the stairway with Keys on my lap and listened to my daughter's playing. I was so touched by her intense feelings that tears of enchantment rolled down my cheeks. When Julie stopped playing, I entered her room and we were in each others arms again and I was happy to be back.

My daughter Alexa was living with her father in Baltimore U.S.A. where she was in college studying drama. My parents returned from shopping and gave me a warm welcome. My father decanted a special bottle of Robert Mondavi, Californian Cabernet Sauvignon, while my mother prepared a delicious meal. All tiredness had vanished and we were all glad to be together again and filled each other in on many new stories. We called Alexa on the phone. She informed me with joy of the news that her father had bought her a car.

Peter's Letter to my Parents and Julie *

Scheherazade Olbia, Sardinia Oct 27, 1981

Dear Heli, Ruedi & Julie,

Greetings from the cold & windy south. The flamingos have flown south, the tourists have gone back to work & the yachtsmen are not going anywhere. It seems that winter has stuck with a vengeance! Well, of course the reason that I am writing this letter is to tell you that I am no longer looking after Maya.

She has been struggling within herself for the last year & I'm sure would have stayed in Kreta but for our visit to you in Wil. However, on returning she completely forgot those 4 months and immediately returned to her rebellious ways. I could not compromise any longer, as I found that I was accepting more & more and realized that if that was the life she was determined to lead it, would not be right that I prevent her, and in fact necessary that she fulfill the desire that she is searching. However, now that she is on her own, she is a lot quieter and is in fact almost a different person.

     She seemed to reach a crisis in order that I demand that she go. I could not begin to tell you about those various crises. However one in particular was very amusing & happened in Reggio. About 6 pm, Maya & I were returning from shopping when she decided to climb a 40m security light tower in the Port. She got to the top while I watched from the cockpit of Scheherazade. After 10 minutes the Fire Brigade & 20 men arrived, then the Port Police with 30 men, then the Customs & Immigration with more, then 100 spectators! When they climbed the tower to bring her down she locked them out. Soon they came to me, but I told them I could do nothing. They wanted to know if she was drunk or under the influence of drugs or did she want to kill her self? I told them she was perfectly sober & was enjoying the "bella vista." They could not understand this & said they would make big trouble, I asked "Why me?" Well after smoking a cigarette she came down & was immediately descended upon by the Chief of Police, the Chief of Immigration, the Fire Chief all asking questions at once. It was like a Gilbert & Sullivan opera. Fortunately, she could speak Italian. So they took her off to the station, searched Scheherazade for drugs & took me along to the station for interrogation. However, when we arrived Maya was making portraits of them all! The poor fellow trying to make the report never got further than putting the paper into the typewriter. The Chief arrived & announced that she must go to the hospital for an alcohol blood test. So together with 5 policemen she went off to the hospital, stopping for coffee on the way & on return! At the hospital, she also entertained them with ballet & Kung Foo exercises & of course never took the test but just signed the paper. It was all typically Italian & had a happy ending.

     Even the next day when I went to pay the harbor fees the Harbor Master congratulated her & said that the place had been very dull & only charged us for 3 days instead of 7! However the unfortunate thing was that now she felt that she was immune to the law & could get away with anything. Although there were many embarrassing & hair raising adventures afterwards, no one suffered. And as I said, now that she is on her own the crises appear to be over.

She has been to collect the rest of her belongings & says that she has stopped smoking & drinking (perhaps she can't afford it). Anyway, that is encouraging.

She is living about 30 km north of here on a property with a Mill & I understand she is living in the Mill. I'm sure she will write to you soon if not already. It is unfortunate that I could not make her happy, but as the French say...c'est la vie! If you have any post for me please send it to C/-Poste Restante, Olbia as I imagine I will be staying here for the rest of the year.

All the best,

signed Peter

(I found this letter in the year of 2008 inside a box with letters written by me to my parents and daughters.)

Maya B.

Loneliness

After gratefully accepting my parents' offer to use the upstairs flat in their house, I started to prepare for my next art exhibition. My parents were so kind and insisted that I take my meals with them and Julie. My father, Julie and I had wonderful discussions and saw the world in a realistic way, while my mother worried about what people thought. She became edgy and irritable and started her sentences to me with "One should" or "One must." My answer was "You can do this or that if you want to" or I went upstairs to paint.

I preferred to work in the attic above the apartment. The view was great and it reminded me of my adventures as a child. Still tempted to climb the roofs, I only refrained because I realized that my weight would probably damage the roof tiles.

Key's kept me company. What a wonderful dog. Poodles are so smart. It is a shame that they often suffer from infected ears because of over breeding. The mixed breeds are more resistant to illnesses.

After dinner, I usually went to one of my favorite pubs. Julie was in college and had her friends. She was very independent and planned to study biology at the University of Bern. I am so proud of both my daughters.

I met Hannes Meier, an actor had who opened a private kindergarten. My mother admired him. I found him very nice and agreed to watch him in his private kindergarten the next day. He showed me how he could tell the character or mood of a child by the colors they picked to paint with. Hannes was anti-authoritarian and let the children do what they liked. When they started to fight, he would take his guitar and play. This stopped the fighting and the children began to listen. They all enjoyed being there and loved Hannes.

At midday they were all picked up by their mothers. Hannes said to me, "Watch this, the mothers in their unconsciousness will unfortunately undo everything I do try to free them up and to make them think for themselves. The mothers showered the children with commands like, "Give Mr. Meier your hand, say thank you, etc."

Hannes was as lonely as I was since his girlfriend was angry at him for trying to get her off heroin which she seemed to prefer to him. So we decided to live together. I asked my parents if I could invite him home for dinner. They said "Yes." My mother cooked with special care. She was an excellent cook. She delicately seasoned the food with herbs and spices and was an expert on pies, cakes and cookies as well. My father loved to eat, laugh and have discussions and was a specialist in fine wines. Julie and my parents liked Hannes and were not surprised that we had decided to stay together but my mother sighed, "If it would only last this time!" I answered, "Only time will tell."

It lasted exactly two weeks until it became obvious to me that Hannes was still in love with the woman that he could not have and we separated as friends. Alone, without a man, I went to drown my thirst for a real man by drinking with some friends. They consisted of all sorts of people like artists, musicians, rockers, poets, gentlemen of the road, intellectuals and professionals who came from many different walks of life. They all had one thing in common. They were individualists who loved freedom, were real and nothing was phony about them and we would cry or laugh together. We had discussions, shared adventures and lived in the present.

The pub was also visited by those who would still sit in the same places and the same chairs and were still complaining about their same jobs, the same things, the same bosses and the same girl - or boyfriends as they had done six years ago, before I had left for my voyage. They were not capable of changing their situations and we felt sorry for the helpless ones whose lives were controlled by their superiors (?)!

5 LATER YEARS

Emil Gegenschatz

At the "Marktplatz" pub we couldn't avoid making eye contact and it filled both Emil and I with wild desire and the urge to become lovers. His intense blue eyes sent shudders of hot and cold and down my spine. I knew right away why I had had to leave Peter (whom I always will love, feel grateful for and respect).

The force of the erotic is the strongest of all emotions,

and was impossible for a healthy woman in the productive years like me, to control.

Emil was tall, well built, muscular, in the best of health and with blond hair that stood up from static electricity on the top of his head. His hands were beautifully formed. His voice was like music to my ears. We were both lonely even though we had many friends.

After we had a drink together, we both went to his room in the basement of his mother's house. We stayed there for three days and made love over and over again and got to know each other by sharing stories of our past. It was the first time in my life that I had the desire to open up every part of my body and soul. We could not get enough of each other.

Emil's history was sad. He, his brother and his sister had been regularly beaten up by their father. When his mother stepped in between or tried to protect her children, she was brutally treated with her husband's fists as well. As the one who was most rebellious, Emil was beaten more and worse than his siblings. His beautiful hair was brutally shaved off when he did something wrong and he was locked in his room to wait for the beating for an hour. Often, he wet himself out of fear of the coming torture. After the insane punishment with the belt buckle, he could remember sometimes waking up out of unconsciousness. Often he laid on the floor covered in bruises and bleeding.

His mother told me that this mistreatment had gone on from the time that her children were very small and that she did not get any help from anyone because they did not believe her. As a postman, her husband gave such an ever-so-friendly smile to everyone, that no one ever suspected him of being a sick sadist.

I had to go to Julie and my parents and explain that I had found real love and to tell them not to worry. Emil did not want me to go without him but I found it better, since I knew my mother and needed to prepare them to meet Emil. When I told my loved ones about Emil and some of his past, my father said to my mother, "It would be better to know who Maya goes out with." My mother agreed and invited him for dinner.

Julie and my parents approved of Emil, who was so real that one had to like him. My father, having suffered from an authoritarian upbringing as well, could understand Emil's revolutionary nature. Emil was invited to stay in the upstairs apartment with me. We were grateful to be invited to join them for the meals downstairs.

Before I met Emil, I had arranged a date for my art opening in the beginning of 1982. He helped me carry and hang my paintings at the 'Hof' of Wil, St. Gallen. The Hof was the most important historical building in my home town comprising a museum, restaurant, gallery, many function rooms and a brewery. I exhibited my work on the two top floors.

When I hung up the "HOLY FLAG", the owner of the Hof made me take the painting down and threatened to throw tar on it, if I refused to do so. I had created this important work for the freedom of women.

My creation was later lost or stolen, together with many others which were rolled up in my studio in Brezilhac, France while

I was absent. It was a portrait of an about 80 cm large vagina with the writing

"You came out of your mother's vagina."

on it. Any woman who chose to live instead of being lived, would understand the necessity of this important work of art. *If real women were treated equally to men, real men would benefit as well. The only ones who let you live, are those whose heads are truly alive.*

Zombies cannot understand this. I invited my parents and many people to my art opening. Hannes volunteered to give a speech for me and played the guitar afterwards. There were many paintings from different stages of my life in the exhibition, including the erotic series. My mother started to apologize to people about my work and was very ashamed of me. She managed to turn many people against me with her bigoted and prudish attitude. Only two of my paintings were sold.

I never invited her to any of my art shows again. Herbert Mäder, the famous photographer and politician, wrote an excellent critique of my work in the papers and registered *'The Universal Flag'* at the Bundeshaus in Bern, Switzerland.

Emil worried about being forced to join the military again. There were only a couple of days left, before he had to go and it was too late for my father (a retired doctor) to help him. Emil, heavy-hearted, had to go if he did not want to end up in military prison again.

A few days later, he ran away and came to the pub where he told our friends and me of the horrendous conditions at the army barracks. We all organized ourselves and took him straight back, hoping to smuggle him in, without being caught, so he would not be punished. We drove to the barracks and stormed right by the guards with him in the middle and penetrated into the sleeping quarters.

I could not believe my eyes when I saw three rows of boards with thin mattresses on them on top of each other, with not enough space to sit up in. The room was dark, dingy and the poor men were sleeping like apples on shelves. The space was full of those people-shelves, the ventilation was very bad and there was no privacy. There was only one window, which was closed since it was winter. The smell was putrid and the men looked miserable and exhausted after having been pushed into running with 80 kg bags on their backs through long stretches of difficult, muddy grounds, in pouring, cold rain.

Switzerland has its army only for defense, which I respect but I am sure that if the men had comfortable, light and warm uniforms with better shoes like the U.S. Army, they would not be so miserable. In my view, some comfort would help the men to fight an eventual enemy much better. Good rest in a better place would add to better sleep and well being. I could see that this was sheer sadism and did not encourage anyone but a masochist to join up. No wonder military service is still compulsory in Switzerland.

I went up to the officer and told him that I had shared my man long enough with the army and wanted him back. He said he wished his wife would tell the ones above him that she wanted him back as well but unfortunately, he did not have the power to let Emil go. My friends and I were questioned and then went back to the pub.

I missed Emil like crazy. The three weeks of separation felt like an eternity and Emil and I were deliriously in love. What a pleasure, when I could pick him up! My father had written a letter to his colleague who examined Emil and to the army doctor, wherein he stated, that it would be better for the Army and for Emil if he did not have to go back to military service again. Emil was discharged from military duty by a military court. We went to celebrate.

Emil Gegenschatz

Revolution with Emil. Teeth Smashed Out

Emil worked as a street worker during the week and so we decided to spend the weekend in Zurich. When we arrived there Emil could feel friction in the air and followed it until we came to a house for the young.

Heinrich Gretler, the late Swiss actor, had left his entire property with the park to the young people in his will. Those responsible for carrying out his wishes as he intended, found it to be too good for the young and so they kept this property for the City of Zurich substituting instead, a sad, busy parking space without a single tree. Just concrete, busy streets and terraced houses all around a beautiful house that stood once surrounded by trees, bushes and flowers in a peaceful setting. The young people rightfully felt betrayed and were angry. A revolution was planned.

Signs were put up by the youths that any cars left in the parking area after 2 p.m. would be damaged. I was surprised to see the parking lot still quite full. At one side of the parking area stood the police waiting with clubs and guns containing hard rubber bullets. The bullets were approximately 3 cm long and hexagonal. I had heard that some demonstrators had lost their eyes from those kind of bullets. On the other side of the parking place stood the young, brave rebels lined up in front of their house. Emil stood in front of it and was the first to move toward the police. They all carried sticks and stones. They started to bash in windshields, smash headlights and stab tires. The police looked frightened behind their shields but then got excited at the opportunity to start to beat up the people with their batons and to shoot rubber bullets at them.

Emil and I managed to escape without getting hurt but some others were not so lucky. We then went to the Niederdorf area to have a cold beer. Then we walked around and saw all the smashed up shop windows in the old part of Zurich.

We came to Maxim's nightclub and bar. There was a hole in the middle of the showcase window, which was spidering out in all directions. Behind, were photographs advertising the strippers who worked in this club. Emil walked up to the glass, grabbing the hole with his index finger, while gently shaking it and said, "This is against human relationships and love." It looked funny but did not break.

Just then, the bouncer stormed out and brutally hit Emil to

the ground. (Emil's right to defend himself had been taken away from him when he refused to join the military and he had been thrown into prison, with a police record still hanging over him.) While he laid on the pavement, the bouncer wanted to hit him again, so I stepped up and grabbed his right arm and pulled it away before he could hit Emil again.

The bouncer, Angelo Thomaso, then took illegal 'hitting rings' (brass knuckle dusters) out of his pocket and slid them over three fingers on each of his hands. They looked like three steel rings attached to each other with a knife sharp edges that pointed upwards. He hit me so hard in the face with his armed fist that with one blow, he split my upper lip on the side all the way down to my molars, while the force of this professional blow knocked me down to the ground. When I tried to get to my feet, he hit me down again. A big crowd gathered but no one helped me. A third time, I tried to get up but was beaten to the concrete again.

A real man stepped up with an open pocketknife and threatened the bouncer. Meanwhile, I had walked to a nearby water fountain and washed the pouring blood from my face. The man who has defending me so bravely, came up to me and said, "If you want to sue him I will be your witness." I stopped the first taxi I could see but he tried to refuse to take me to the hospital because of the blood, so I sat inside so fast and refused to come out. I held my T-shirt over the wound, so as not to mess up the taxi. Emil and the man came with me.

I was dropped off at the emergency section, where they immediately treated me. I spat out two healthy teeth which had been knocked out of my mouth. A 5 1/2 cm cut on the upper left part of my lip and two large cuts on the back of my head were stitched up. I suffered from bad headaches and nightmares and could not chew on the left side. This was the first time in my life, hat I had ever been beaten up.

Unfortunately, it was not the last time in my life, as you can read in a later chapter of my autobiography. I sued Angelo Thomaso. His boss at Maxim's nightclub called me on the telephone and suggested that we settle the matter out of court but I did not trust him and chose the legal way instead.

Since I had no fixed income, I had a right to a public lawyer who was there to defend people like me. Unfortunately, he did not once speak for me in my defense, so I shouted the truth to the judge who questioned me like the criminal instead of the one who had been my brutal abuser. My lawyer just sat there in silence. I was wondering if he had been paid off by Maxims. The whole case was thrown out of court. I appealed and when I tried to get a different lawyer, I was refused, so I was stuck with him again.

Three years later, I received an invitation for a court hearing in Winterthur. Again, I endured the same questioning. I had brought the doctor's report and the bills from the hospital plus those from my cousin Paul Schefer, who in my view and many others was considered to be the best dentist in the world. He had made a bridge for my teeth and said that I could pay for it, only if I received the money. I was so happy that I could chew again.

Now I tried to get the money for those bills, and some more for the pain and future expenses resulting from those armed blows. I also figured, that the abuser would think twice before he hit a woman again, if I could make him pay. After over an hour of fighting for my rights, the judge just hit the hammer down and only made my opponent pay the two bills. My pain, scar on the face, phone calls, train rides, fears, nightmares, registered letters and time was not taken into consideration. I felt bitterly let down.

The only thing left for me to do, was to take the case to the high court in Bern but I could not find a lawyer and the one I had, was turning me down. In no way would I wait another three years, so I gave up, utterly disappointed by the injustice of the so-called justice. Well I know now that they need criminals to keep them in a job. In my opinion, I would have won, if I had been as wealthy as the boss of Maxims but I would not have been happy in my skin.

Money blinds weak characters to the truth.

Ticino, CH

My parents felt it a bit strained to have Emil and I in their house all the time and suggested that we move into the apartment above their second home in canton Tessin, where I could paint while Emil could look for a job until we could find our own place to live, there in the south of Switzerland.

Emil was 11 years younger than me and I found it necessary to free him up. The only time he had lived away from his mother and my parents, was when he had worked as foreman on a building site in Arabia. It would be good for him to learn Italian and to travel. I tried to talk him into cashing in his life insurance and buying a small bus to live in with the money. This way, we could avoid having to pay rent and save enough money to spend the winter in a southern country. He said, "We can't live without electricity, water, toilet or bath." Emil did not want to hear of it and we continued to live in my parent's second residence.

The 'rustico' with its hand-cut granite slab roof was in such a romantic setting in a small village in, Valle Vercasca. We sat at the granite table under the pergola of grapes and enjoyed the semi-panoramic view and lush nature. The garden was at the front of the house, with vineyards below, right to the edge of a cliff that dropped off down to the river Verzasca. The guest apartment was situated above the house, under the car park next to the street, which curved all the way up to Valle Verzasca and to the mountains.

All along it, one could find original villages surrounded by chestnuts and other trees in wooded areas, which often led to waterfalls. When we followed the waterfalls, we were rewarded with total privacy and the sights of lizards, salamanders and other creatures that had probably never encountered people and were so tame that they came so close to us that we could have touched them. The lakes were set between two waterfalls with crystal-clear water and we could choose to lay on a big rock, on grass or in water to make love. It was truly magical. I had finally found a man who desired me as much as I did him. The many species of birds gave us a concert. Emil grabbed me at least five times a day and three times a night. We were both delirious.

Emil soon picked up enough Italian from the people in the Italian part of Switzerland to get by.

My parents called me on the phone and said that they planned to come to Ticino and had hoped that we would have found an apartment and work for Emil since they needed privacy. They gave us three weeks. Emil tried to ignore it but I would have been glad if we could have been more independent.

When he did not make a move, I took off, heavyhearted, on my Puch Maxi mobilette in search of an apartment and did not go back, until I had found one in Bigorio. Then I called Emil and told him, I would not be back until he found a job. He had been drinking in the kitchen during a thunderstorm and said to himself, "If Maya does not come back, I want to die." At that moment lightning hit so close that the light bulb in the lamp above the kitchen table exploded. He took it as a sign to get work and went to the pub to inquire. He found 'black' work in construction and I went back to him. What a "reunion" for both of us!

When my parents arrived, we borrowed my father's car and went to buy an old Renault station wagon. Then we had dinner together with my daughters and parents.

Before Emil and I moved into our own apartment, we visited Emil's boss- a shady Swiss German, who had refused to pay Emil and his colleagues for their back-breaking work on the 'black'. We had called him several times before but got the same negative answer any time of the day and were very annoyed and because we really needed the money. We decided to pay him a visit but his wife said that he was not there. I said, "Okay, we will wait for him", then I brushed her aside and took a seat on the sofa in their living room. Emil sat next to me.

A home-baked tart was displayed on top of the coffee table decorated with a pink rose in the middle. I said to the woman, "We can't afford dinner because of you and your husband." I also loved marzipan and so in defiance, I grabbed the rose from the center of the tart. To the tight woman's horror, I bit into it. It broke into two pieces and nearly broke my teeth because it was made out of plastic. She said, "I could have used that rose over and over again." which confirmed how cheap they were. Plastic decoration on a tart, ha – ha! How very low class and ordinary.

The woman was short and fat with her eyes close together and the corners of her mouth were drooping downward in deep creases, revealing her unpleasant character. She called her husband on the phone, who said to tell us that he would not be home that day. We got tired of waiting and left their big square house, eager to find our nest in Bigorio.

Bigorio

Bigorio was a small, quiet mountain village. Our apartment was on the second and third floors of an old house. I liked the place, as it was ideal to use the third story, open but under a roof, as an art studio. The view was magnificent and one could see the mountain 'Denti della Vecchia'.

Emil liked the place as well. It had a new bathroom, a new fitted kitchen with sitting place, a bedroom and a living room with a balcony.

Once we had settled in, I suggested that Emil invite all his friends and colleagues for dinner at full moon. When they had all arrived, we planned to visit the boss who did not pay his workers.

After dinner we all prepared sticks to take with us and at midnight we were all standing in two rows each equipped with a large stick in front of the boss's house. Someone stuck a matchstick in to the doorbell. The window opened on the top floor and the boss-couple looked out. Someone yelled, "Hey, if you don't throw down the money that you owe us right now, we will smash all the windows and doors and beat the hell out of you!" The boss went to fetch a bag with the money and lowered it down to us. Someone counted it and it was all there. The primitive seem to only understand one language and this was *fear*. Everyone in the group below was relieved to collect their hard-earned cash.

Emil had a new job. He worked for Stuag as a road worker. It was very hard labor and he had to mix tar and do other unpleasant work in the hot summer heat, while breathing exhaust fumes as well. He was paid SFr. 3.50 an hour and counted himself lucky, not to have to work for 2.50 only, like a man from Italy who crossed the border to come to work in Switzerland.

When Emil got home he was so stressed, that he could not eat dinner without first drinking at least two beers to unwind and to then wash the dirt off in the bath. Our sex life declined to 1 or 2 times during the night.

While Emil was at work, I painted, sketched, went sight-seeing or climbed a mountain. When I wanted to climb the 'Denti Della Vecchia' for the second time (I could easily reach the summit), I would tie my moped to a tree at the foot of the mountain. I always climbed barefoot to the top. When I reached the highest peak, I felt like descending to Italy but needed to go back the same way to reach home in time to prepare dinner.

I climbed down so fast, that I tripped and sprained my ankle. It hurt like mad but I kept on going with the pain. The fog was creeping in and I had to hurry to be able to still see where I was going. By the time I reached the moped, the fog was so thick, that I had to ride really slowly. At home I threw something easy into the pot and put my foot up high. Luckily, it was not broken and healed well.

Our landlord lived below us and visited us too frequently. She asked me each time, if she was allowed to clean our windows and I let her. She was not too nice a person and had the nose of an eagle, just not as pretty but a heck of a lot bigger. I usually made her a cup of coffee but the small talk irritated me. Sometimes, I just told her to come back some other time since I would rather paint or do something constructive.

I bought freshly-laid eggs from another neighbor. He was a very nice old man with a sunny disposition, who insisted that I drink a 'Nutino' or two with him. The Nutino was liquor that had been made out of nuts, was very strong but delicious and had been made by the only priest left in the presbytery located at the top of the village. The old man and I laughed together. He worried about his, even older, brother who was ill and would be coming to live with him but was looking forward to the nurse that would come to attend to his brother.

Sometimes I invited him for a coffee or a glass of wine at the romantic restaurant with huge terrace overlooking a breath- taking landscape. The property was run by an ancient man and his two old spinster sisters. The youngest must have been at least 80. A large wood-burning oven stood inside with the pipe running right across the whole dining room and which let the smoke out through a window pane lined by a metal ring. Mandolins hung on the wall and the tables were very large and made out of dark old oak. So were the chairs. A cat slept on one of the tables. One of the old sisters sat in the corner, sewing on an antique Singer sewing machine.

The entrance and garden were filled with plants and flowers of all colors. What a welcome change from most other restaurants that were furnished with plastic and stainless-steel and with flowers made out of paper, even if the service was faster. The good thing, is that one can still find places of character in Ticino and some other cantons of Switzerland.

When I had not been in my studio for a few days, swallows started to construct their nest. I kept on painting while I spoke to them and they were not afraid of me. Then an idea came to me. I drew a television set on a piece of cardboard and wrote on it, 'What swallows think of television', and laid it under the nest when the eggs had hatched. It was great to watch the birds and I watched the parents feeding the young. I also witnessed the babies' first flights. At the same time the whole family of swallows created my idea for me. When they flew south, I sprayed thick varnish on it and wrapped it up.

While unwrapping it years later in the south of France, I found that it had suffered so much that it was not worth restoring. Polyester resin instead of varnish would have done the trick and plywood would have been better suited than cardboard. We live and learn.

The 6 marihuana seeds in my garden grew well and I watched their progress every day for nearly 3 weeks. Then at night it rained and in the morning all 6 plants had been eaten by snails. They had left me not one single one of them. I loved the plants for their elegant feathered leaves and beauty. How can one declare anything that nature creates as illegal, even though such laws do make the Mafia rich and make it more interesting for abuse by young people since it is more attractive in its illegality? The state also gains money from fines, etc.

The plant was once farmed to make ropes for ships, cloth, oil and more. An excellent remedy against cold or flu is a brew of 1/3 hemp, 1/3 thyme and 1/3 sage seasoned with honey and lemon. It worked for me, even though it did not make me high.

Emil desperately needed to have a vacation. We decided to visit his Friend Köbi and family in the south of France.

France and Andorra

Once Emil stopped working, our sex life had increased again. Before we drove to Köbi's trout farm in the south of France, we laid a mattress and sleeping bags in the back of the Peugeot station wagon and then packed some dried and fresh fruit, nuts and cookies into a plastic container and filled jugs with water to take.

Then, we started our voyage. I could not understand why Emil was frightened to sleep in the car. Only when he was too tired to go on, did he stop in the pitch dark and mostly we were surprised to wake up in the morning and find ourselves in interesting places. Then, we would start to drive until we found a coffee shop and order coffee and pain au chocolate.

We stopped in medieval towns and in Carcassonne, which impressed us, and tried special French food like bouillabaisse and others. Emil tasted snails for the first time, was surprised how good they tasted and picked up a few French words every day. He had already learned to speak Italian since we met.

We arrived at Saint Hilaire and went into a pub to find out where the small road was, to drive up to Greffeil. We had a drink and found out that they knew Köbi well and gave us a drink on the house. Then we took the piece of paper the pub owner had drawn on and looked at the very interesting old convent before enjoying the drive through vineyards and wilderness. When we arrived at the old mill that Köbi and his wife Joelle had built up from a ruin stone by stone, it looked like paradise and was very romantic, right on the river Aude. They owned a lot of land.

Köbi had built a water wheel and a reservoir from which water was led to the mill. Next to it there were three pools with small, medium and large sized trout breeding in them. The property was in a wooded setting with lots of wildlife. We drove over the bridge and parked next to the Aude under a tree.

Köbi and Joelle greeted us with open arms and insisted that we should sleep in their bedroom for the entire time of our stay and they moved into the guest bedroom.

Köbi made a fire. He placed some individual pieces of aluminum foil on a large table and put some on large cleaned trout with onions and spices on them before wrapping them up and then took more pieces of foil on each of which he laid cabbage leaves and two halves of potatoes filled with a thick slice of cheese and then closed the foil. Then he placed the filled packages onto the embers while we sipped an ice-cold beer. Joelle prepared a wonderful mixed salad from their garden.

Köbi and Joelle had two children. They helped setting the table. The boy was about six and the girl maybe five. They were adorable. Köbi opened a good bottle of wine with dinner. When the children were asleep the drinking continued. Joelle got angry with

Köbi and went to bed. We got to sleep late and did not wake up until the coffee being brewed reached our noses.

Joelle was still uptight and every little thing made her annoyed. She was very frustrated. I tried to help her but to no avail. Köbi said, "Don't worry, it is her character." I felt sorry for them. The next day, the situation improved. Andy and Heiner, two friends of Köbi's, arrived from Switzerland in an old car. Emil, Andy and Heiner helped Köbi to clear some land to grow fresh food. This gave me some time to get to know Joelle and find out why she was so unhappy.

She had grown up in Paris and was a total city person who was homesick and hated the country. She worked as hard as her husband to build everything up and felt that he preferred the company of the boys to hers. She also told me that their daughter loved nature but their son was not showing the least interest in the fish farm like his sister and preferred to be indoors with her. Joelle said that Köbi was upset about that and did not let the daughter help him but insisted that his son did. This showed me the stubbornness of patriarchal men. I tried to smooth things over between them but had not much success and gave up. Köbi was okay with me and we got along well.

Emil and I continued our trip to Andorra. We drove to Limoux and approached Andorra from France. Then, we drove up a mountain road with hairpin curves, which took us to 'En Champ'. We looked around for tax free goods but could not look in peace since hustlers pestered us like in Arab countries.

We looked at the interesting menu outside, advertising a big variety of foods for reasonable prices and discussed what we would like to eat. Then we entered a restaurant, where the waiter let us choose the table we liked to sit at. When we tried to order some dishes, they had run out of everything on the menu but could make us an omelet.

When we wanted to get up and leave, the owner of the restaurant told us the truth. He showed us the marks on the wall, still moist from the last flood. Some people had lost their lives and others were injured. They had all suffered in one way or another. Business was so bad that many people were hungry. We ordered the omelet and some wine. The people owning the place sat with us and insisted on treating us to another bottle of wine. We talked until late in the night and then went to sleep in the station wagon which was parked in a guarded parking place.

We woke up completely dressed and tightly embraced in each others arms under all the blankets and sleeping bags with frozen condensation on the windows. It was two degrees below zero outside and clammy-moist on the inside. Emil started the motor and put the heater on maximum, while I scraped the ice from the windows. Then we drove for a while until we found a coffee shop to have some breakfast. We drove through a high mountain valley, which was very spectacular with some ski lifts leading to the top of the peaks. Then we got stuck in the snow.

This angered Emil to the point of explosion. It took me all my skill to calm him enough, so that we could find a solution and dig ourselves out. After about half an hour, we were ready to move on.

The mountains of Andorra are very impressive. We headed for Sant Julia where we shopped at Maya Super market for tax free cognac, whisky, other alcoholic beverages, truffles and other things and went through the toll without any problems even though Emil worried himself half sick. Then we drove to the Spanish coast and explored some of the beautiful bays but got annoyed at all the ugly high-rise hotels and apartment complexes which blighted the gorgeous landscape.

We crossed over to France and I especially loved Banyuls-sur-Mer and Collioure but not the crap that materialistic egotists without taste had started to build for mass tourism. I bought a few bottles of Banyuls sweet red wine for my father and one for us. It tastes delicious but is quite a strong dessert wine.

Emil sold the bottles of spirit to a barman, making a profit. Ports have a special attraction for me and I loved to look at sailing boats while Emil preferred to drink something while waiting for me. Then we continued our voyage over the high hills to Greffeil and back to Köbi.

Andy and his brother Heiner were not there any longer. They had gone out for a few drinks and, completely intoxicated, ran off the road, down a cliff toward the river Aude and landed on top of a tree. Someone saw it and called the fire brigade, who made a rescue exercise out of saving them. It took them a while but they managed to get the car with Andy and Heiner to safety. The two young men were lucky to get away with only a bruise or two. The old car was scrapped and they went back to Switzerland by train.

Köbi was glad to have Emil's help for two weeks, before we drove back to say, "Hello" to my parents and daughters plus Emil's mother and before we drove on to our apartment in Bigorio. Emil had to find a new job since we both felt that to do unhealthy hard street labor for such small pay was exploitation. I still tried to convince him to buy a small camping van.

Just then, we passed a garage where they had a Renault Estafette camping car for sale out front. I convinced Emil to stop and just look at it. When he saw the inside with two upholstered benches and a table in the middle, plus cabinets on three sides for clothes, a cooker and sink etc., he realized that this was going to be fun and wanted to buy it but didn't know how he could afford it.

He had a life insurance that he would not benefit from either before or after his death and decided to have them pay it out. He not only got enough to pay for the camper but also enough to not have to worry for a while about getting a job. He sold the old Peugeot station wagon for a profit and felt really proud driving his newly acquired van. We had our own roof over the head wherever we went.

New Job. Tension in Apartment

A friend of Timothy Leary, whose name I forget, had a business in Tessin and did special restoration of old, original Ticino rusticos. His astrological sign was Aquarius like Emil and he had already a crew of seven aquarians working for him. Every time he saw me, he asked me to have Emil get in touch with him. He offered excellent pay for the work. When I told Emil about him, he said, "I can't do that work." I tried to restore his self-confidence and told him that he could do everything if he really wanted to and that he was intelligent enough to learn whatever he wanted to as well.

There was a thunderstorm brewing up as Emil and I made love. Like magic we both reached orgasm together precisely at the same moment as the thunder was ro o o O O lling!

When Emil had a crisis he would drink too much. The only thing I could do, was to drink with him. This caused him to be aggressive and we could end up in a fight, separating for a short while which felt very long. One time, I locked the door behind him. He smashed it in with his fist and I managed to get away. The owners of the house made him pay for the door and threatened him with the police if he did not. Then they threw us out of the apartment. We made peace and love again and moved our things out. Emil threw a bar of butter into the heating room before we slammed the door for the last time.

The live-in van was a godsend. We met the rustico-restoring specialist again and this time, he convinced Emil to work for him. The rustico they were working on, was in a beautiful, romantic, quiet and private setting and we parked the Renault Estafette in front of a field of sheep.

While Emil was working, I sketched and watched the sheep lambing. I did all the cooking in the van and the water tank held 50 liters. I could also get drinking water from a fountain and fill the solar shower bags which held 5 liters each. We would hang them under a tree to shower. Life was great but Emil came home and said,"I should never have taken this job."

He told me that he was expected to figure out how many steps and at what height they had to be to make a stairway. I told him that it was better than doing a crossword puzzle. I told him, that if I wanted to, I could do it and volunteered to help him if he would give me the measurements of height and tread. This gave him enough courage to figure it out for himself. All he needed, was to regain his self-confidence, which had been beaten out of him when he was a child. He started to be proud of his achievements and was almost sorry when the job was done.

Our emotions were like an uncontrollable roaring fire. We had a tango relationship and decided to part only when it would get life-threatening or too violent. We loved and fought over and over again and when we were apart, we felt sad and miserable without each other. Too proud to give in, we both had one-night stands and then we found out (sober in the morning) that it was each other that we wanted and no one else could take that place.

When, after a fight, I was back in my parent's house, I knew what I needed was a camper van to myself. I just had sold a portrait and did not touch the money. I saved up for a second-hand van. When my father and I went to visit my uncle the garage owner, I spotted just what I wanted and pointed to a used Renault Estafette. When I said to my father, "That is what I am saving up for." He replied, "If you want it, I will pay for half of it." We went to look closer at the van and I was so happy to be able to pay easily for it since my father helped me out again. I bought it with the condition that a roof window would be installed and never forgot the thrill of picking up my own, mobile roof over the head. I felt free.

My mother gave me sheets, pillows, blankets, cooking pots, towels and whatever I needed and my father gave me a radio. I took them for a ride in it and got so busy installing a Singer hand sewing machine and loading it up with painting materials, a portable easel, food and whatever else I needed, that I forgot Emil for a short while. I was excited to be independent.

My father said, "But this is too small to live in." I said, "Come with me, Papi, and you will see how possible it is. Where would you like to go?" He said, "To Murten on the lake." My mother preferred to stay at home so we drove over the Furka Pass, where I prepared sandwiches and we ate in the van before we continued our voyage to Murten.

    There we went to see an old friend of mine, who owned a restaurant and invited us to dinner. Then we drove to a natural and wild looking place, where we parked the van next to the lake of Murten and spent the night. After breakfast, we drove over the hill with vineyards and looked at some picturesque villages, before we continued along lake Neuchatel to Yverdon. My father had good memories from there, so we stopped in the big green park which was ideal for sleeping in the Estafette. I cooked a simple dinner and we slept very well after a bottle of Neuchatel wine.

    My father got up in need of relieving himself. As he slid the door back to go outside, he saw that we were surrounded by wagons from the Circus Knie. He woke me up and said, "Quick Maya, we have to try to get out of here, or we will be stuck until they move on." Since the Renault Estafette was painted white like their wagons, they thought that we belonged to the circus as well. We just managed to get out between two wagons and were guided by the people of the circus through many more circus vehicles to the exit of the park. It took us half an hour to get out. Finally out of the park, the Estafette ran out of fuel.

    I stopped a man in a car and asked him, where we could get some gasoline. He said, "It is Sunday and all the garages are closed." He noticed how disappointed I looked and said, "Come with me and bring your canister." My father and I sat in his car and he drove us to the garage he owned, filled our canister and brought us back and told us to put the gasoline in and follow him. We did and he filled the tank at his garage. It was so nice of him to help us out.

    Then we drove to a beautiful old town on the lake of Neuchatel. There, we bought some fresh croissants and parked in a small port. I brewed fresh coffee on my stove and we ate breakfast on a bench outside. The weather was beautiful and the climate was mild. Birds sang everywhere and swans and ducks liked the old bread we had with us.

My father showed me some interesting old towns. One of them still had an old ditch in the middle of the cobblestone street where people used to throw the rubbish and excrement during medieval times. Rainwater would clear it from time to time. No wonder many of them died of cholera, etc.

My father needed his comfort so we drove back to his house in Ticino where my mother and daughters were happy to see us again. My father explained to all of them that it was really possible to live in the Estafette. When we told them about the circus, they all had a good laugh.

I drove to Wil, where I hoped to find Emil in the pub again. I knew this area well and parked in a nice spot. Emil really was in the pub and we got together again, he in his van and I in mine. We went almost everywhere in convoy. Emil visited his mother alone, since I did not like her boyfriend. It got colder and I had found a parking place for my van just outside of Wil. Then I went to visit my family and ended up sleeping in the van. In the morning, the water in the tank was frozen solid. I decided to go south. Emil agreed, since he had saved up as well. After we had prepared for the voyage and said "Goodbye" to our loved ones we drove in convoy toward Italy to overwinter.

Rammed by Fire Truck

Emil and I were happy to drive each in our own living space to Italy. We aimed for Venice. Somewhere after Vincenza, I was driving gently on the right side of the road, when a large fire truck approached me. He came at high speed and had a ladder attached to the side nearer to me. There was no way I could avoid him, when he drove his monstrous vehicle into the side of my van. The whole length of the Estafette was ripped open. I nearly cried. The fire chief got out of the car, excused himself and told me where to go and have it repaired at their expense. I wanted him to sign this but he refused and said he expected me to trust him since he was the chief of the fire brigade. There was nothing to do then to trust him since I could not force him to sign.

I then drove to the place he had told me of. Emil followed me. When we found the repair shop, I told them what had happened and they said that they would fix the damage right away and get in touch with the fire department, but could not do it unless I could leave the van for two days.

Emil and I then drove to the coast which was brutally marked by greed and overbuilt with concrete complexes for mass tourism. The season had ended so everything was closed and we parked Emil's van to sleep in. The day after that, we went sightseeing but the next town looked the same as the last one. At least we found one pub open, where we could have a drink and something to eat.

The day after, we went to pick up my van. It was repaired but I had to pay for it because the people of the fire department had refused. I was angry to have to part with some of the 'over-wintering money' because of the fault of others. Emil was angry as well.

We decided to alter our plans and not spend one lira in Italy and instead of going to Venice and further south, we headed straight for Yugoslavia. We had to buy gasoline coupons since gasoline was rationed for Yugoslavian people. I bought more than I expected to use and so did Emil.

We drove all along the coast and were surprised how low the prices were. A good meal with wine was a 10th of the price in Switzerland. So was the food. Sometimes the shops did not have coffee, meat or other things and we were limited to taking what they had to offer. The next day, they might have had coffee or meat but no noodles.

We went to explore some of the islands we could see from the shore and found a beautiful deserted camping place with water and a toilet but no person around. We spent about a week there, before we followed the coast as far as possible, stopping at small restaurants to have a drink or some food.

Maya B.

I loved Cavtat, Dubrovnik and Molunat where we installed ourselves for a while. We parked our vans with the sliding doors facing each other, with a gap in between that formed an extra space with a tarpaulin over the top of both vans. One van was used to sleep in and the other to cook and eat in. We enjoyed a spectacular sea view from our spot.

If we walked a few steps down the hill, there was a clean, sandy beach without people. This was paradise. Not like Switzerland, where we were chased out of every nice spot by the police, where there was rarely any free parking and the payable parking places were for a limited time only.

When we awoke, there was a man welcoming us with a bag of oranges from his trees. He was a fisherman and took us straight to his home, where he cooked a fish dinner for us.

He also suggested that we could use his address to have our post sent to. His name was Thonko. We became good friends. I asked him where I could find a studio to rent, since I felt like painting again. He pointed to an empty pavilion that stood in solitude just before the beach which we overlooked from our van's parking place and said, "If you clean it up you can use it for free." Emil cleaned it up and I used it. It made a great and peaceful art studio for me and was very spacious.

To thank the people of Molunat for allowing me the use of this space, I created a mural for the outside wall, which they held in high esteem. An old woman with a hunchback, called Nikitsa wanted to get to know us. She invited us to her house for coffee. Nikitsa loved animals and took in all the stray cats, even though she could hardly afford to feed them. All cats had the run of the house. We brought her food for the cats every time we visited her. She even fed them our left over spaghetti which they gobbled down.

What I did not like, was that Thonko and Nikica constantly asked questions like "Where have you been, where are you going, when will you be back, why are you going there?" etc. We felt that this was not their business but did not want to hurt their feelings.

Questioning seemed to be part of their culture. Also, they wanted to be driven around.

Nikitsa asked us to drive her to a funeral so we took her there. While we waited outside, I saw a beautiful lost puppy dog. I inquired about it but they all said that they did not know where it came from and that I could have it if I wanted it. We took the puppy to the vet and had it checked out, vaccinated and de-wormed. Emil did not want to own a dog, but ever since "Keys" my poodle had died, I had longed for a dog again. I took the puppy with me as my dog. She was female and was an English wire-haired terrier. I called her "Zora." She became my constant companion. Wherever I went, she came with me.

Her bed was under my bed in the van and she was house-broken within a very short time since she preferred to do it outside and away from her food dish, that stood next to the water dish on the side of the floor in the van. I wanted her to grow up free and taught her to follow me without a leash and come whenever I called her. She was a very intelligent dog, who knew how to survive without people. I had to teach her lovingly, not to eat used paper tissues or human and other excrements. She understood the word "No," if I held a treat in my hand to reward her and made a big fuss of her when she obeyed me. She learned incredibly fast.

Wherever my van stood, I left the door open for her to go in and out as she pleased. She was still so tiny that I made a step for her to get in or out. Emil liked her as well. Zora grew well and gained some weight. I fed her only fresh cooked meat or fish with raw grated carrots and an egg, plus a spoon of olive oil every week. Sometimes she ate almost everything we ate except salads.

When she was about six months-old, she could jump into the water and come out with a fish in her mouth. She was the only one of my dogs who could do that. Her best friend in Molunat was a 1 1/2 m-long slow worm, the longest one we had ever seen. She also showed me Salamanders and other animals but did not hurt them.

I sketched Emil and her over and over again. Emil and I had a good time. Because of the questioning, we calmed our relationship with Thonko and Nikitsa a bit. We still saw them but not as often.

We met Rosa and Bozo who lived in a luxurious house that their daughters had built. She was working as a top model in Paris, France. A fireplace needed to be built into the living room and Bozo asked Emil if he could do it for a high price. He accepted and built them a beautiful fireplace. He had learned how to do that while working for the rusticos-restoring-expert in Tessin. They were very happy and called their daughter who sent the money right away.

We became good friends and Rosa was a wonderful person with a big heart who loved to laugh. Bozo loved to drink and had all sorts of liquor stocked in part of the cellar behind a door. He used to go to the barrel with a jug and fill it. Rosa did not drink much and would sometimes get upset in fear that he would drink too much for his health. They insisted that we ate with them. The house was very posh and beautifully decorated. It had a gorgeous kitchen with modern appliances, a large dining and living room, plus several spacious bedrooms and luxurious bathrooms.

Rosa and Bozo preferred to live in the cellar of the house where they made fresh coffee for us by roasting green coffee beans in a small container over a wood fire in a converted steel drum. The coffee was then ground on a hand-turned coffee grinder by Rosa and put into a Turkish coffee pot with lots of sugar and brewed for just the right amount of time. The delightful aroma filled the large cellar. The coffee tasted wonderful. Bozo insisted the coffee had to be accompanied with a home made 'racky', straight from the barrel into a jug. The racky was very strong.

The cellar had two big doors that opened up and revealed the magnificent garden with a multitude of flowers of all colors. Unfortunately, Bozo insisted that his gorgeous German shepherd watchdog was chained up all the time. No matter what I said, he would not listen. At least the female dog had her kennel to go in and was fed very well but she looked lonely and pregnant since she could not escape from the many dogs that had got into the garden while she had been in heat and mated with her.

Their son, a musician, his wife and their son came to see them. We were invited to dinner and to meet them. He had his guitar with him and taught his son dirty songs. The small boy loved to sing those songs while his father accompanied him on the guitar. This was a great idea to get his son to appreciate music.

The mother of the boy had studied psychology. She had grown up in a Mostar Muslim family and her clitoris and lips of the vagina had been cut off in a religious ritual. So many women were still disfigured in that brutal and perverted way. If the small girls bled to death or died of an infection, they believed that it was Allah's wish.

In my view, Allah must be as brutal as all the other man made gods, or even more so. The poor woman could not have an orgasm and wondered what she had missed. I liked her very much and told her that I had met many other women who could also not reach orgasms either. I think this is because some men do not understand women or they do not understand men or their own selves.

If you live a lie you will not understand the truth. Deliberate manipulation and brainwash are lies that cause fears, brain damage, misery and suffering.

If there were a perfect and real God or Goddess, he or she would certainly have made mankind in a perfect way and would not want humans to disfigure, hurt or kill what he or she had created.

Power should be used only with responsibility, if life on our beautiful planet is to survive.

Rosa and Bozos daughter came to visit them. She was shocked to see her parents living in the cellar and gave them hell. She said, "I built a comfortable house for you and what do you do? You live like primitives in the cellar."

So while the daughter was there, they moved upstairs and when she was gone, they moved back down. Rosa said to me, that they preferred the simple life downstairs since they did not have to worry about keeping everything spotless. She did not like kitchen machines anyway. The world of their daughter was different from theirs.

When Bozo killed all the puppies in front of their mother, I refused to go there again. I was sad not to see Rosa again but I am sure she understood.

Emil Thrown Out of Yugoslavia

A man begged me to sell him some of my gasoline coupons, so I figured out how much gasoline I would need to drive around and get me back to the border. He offered me double what I had paid for them. Emil sold him some of his as well.

I met some Jewish people, a man, his wife and her sister who was a scientist. They were very nice and invited us to a formal, classical concert in Dubrovnik.

Emil was not interested but I was. He was going to watch Zora, my dog. I needed a long dress for the occasion. Previously, I had bought a three meter piece of cloth that had caught my eyes and used it as a sun shield when it was very hot in the van. It was just the thing needed for the occasion so I turned it, with a few stitches and a belt into a gown, without cutting into it. They all liked it and the woman's sister lent me a pair of shoes. She was a scientist and a beautiful, young Russian woman, who reminded me of my daughters.

She played the violin with so much feeling that I had a hard time holding back my tears. After dinner they invited me to a delicious gourmet dinner at the best restaurant.

The scientist said that women did not need men any longer to have babies. I said that it still needed sperm from a man and that a child needs a father and a mother. We discussed the matter seriously but it is no secret that I prefer the natural way and would find it depressing to have an in-vitro child, when so many children need to be adopted. If homosexuals, lesbians or single woman want children, then there are plenty of them who need a loving home. This would help to slow down the population explosion as well.

    I liked my new friends. I was wondering why the first thing that all Jewish people told me after we met, was "I am Jewish." I never heard a catholic or protestant tell me their religion. Is it that Jewish people consider themselves as a race? Black people don't tell you "I am black." Neither do other people emphasize their race.

    Zora was not used to me going anywhere without her and greeted me like a long lost friend. So did Emil. About 20 children came to visit me while I was in my studio. They brought me flowers. I was touched.

    After a week, Thonko came with some letters for us and a package from Germany under his arm. The package was from my new Jewish friends and had been opened. I ask Thonko why? He said, "I found some lighters in it and took them out." When I objected to it, he said, "You would have given them to me anyway." I said "Even if I did, you had no right to open my mail."

    Then he proudly spoke of Dolphins that he slaughtered because they ate all the fish. I got angry and, pointing my finger in his face, and said, "That will bring you very bad luck." Our friendship had ended. I called my parents and daughters not to send the mail to him again.

    My paintings were on exhibition at the "English Pub" in Cavtat, Yugoslavia in 1984. They could send the mail there. Emil and I felt like moving and parked our vans on a different place in Molunat right next to the sea.

    An old Mercedes van was parked there as well. It was owned by a very likeable couple who met each other and fell in love when they escaped from East Germany. They had to go through so much hardship and the woman had been forced to drink her own urine so as not to die of thirst in jail. They had a black dog which loved to eat so much, that it was way too fat to play with Zora. Those people were wonderful and not bitter at all and we enjoyed their company and laughed a lot together. They had a golden humor.

Emil loved to make fires and even though there was a sign that forbade making fires, he said, "I am a free man and I can make a fire if I want." He collected driftwood and branches and drank a bottle of wine. Some people warned him, that it would mean trouble but he sent them away. The fire was roaring when the police arrived. They accused him of acting against the law and being drunk and told him that he had been heard speaking against Tito. I told them that this was not possible, since Emil had nothing but admiration for the great man who had brought all five departments together and created peace amongst the people. But he was handcuffed. I told them not to punish him, that it was my fault that he had had too much to drink because we had had a fight. Nothing I said could made them change their minds about taking him to the station. The police told me that they would question him and that he would be back with me in a half an hour.

This time passed and he was not back. I waited a bit longer and then went to inquire. I was then told that he would come out in an hour. When he still did not come, I went again and told them that I was in contact with the Swiss consulate and if they laid a finger on him, they would be in trouble. Two men waiting in the office turned pale at my words. The police told me to wait again. After waiting 20 more minutes, someone told me that Emil had been taken to the court in Dubrovnik. I did not know what to do.

Finally, the next day, he was dropped off where we were parked and told me that he had to be out of the country within 24 hours. This was not possible since it took 3 days minimum to reach the border. Emil and I had difficult emotional times behind us. I was glad that he wanted to leave without me but when he really was gone, I missed him again and so I went to the pub.

I heard that Nikitza wanted me to take her and all the (over 20) cats to another town and let them out and that some guys found it funny to make a donkey drunk by feeding him a bottle of booze. This all disgusted me and I went outside with Zora. While I looked at the view, I heard Zora yowl. Then I noticed that someone had thrown a canister of fuel on her. Another guy struck a match and I grabbed his hand, threw him on the pavement and took Zora under my arm running to the van.

I washed her gently with shampoo in the water and rinsed her then I creamed her skin with an anti-burn cream. I had had enough of cruelty and said goodbye to our refugee friends, who were also leaving, but in the other direction. Zora and I then drove to Cavtat without stopping.

At the 'English pub', I listened to 'The Gipsy Kings' and the 'Screaming Joe Hawkins' records that I had received in the mail from my daughters.

While I was painting a seascape in Cavtat, I met a Yugoslavian woman who wished to invite me to the pub. When I finished the painting, I went with her and entered the pub of her choice. Conversation came easily since she had studied Karate as well and was the most emancipated Yugoslavian woman I had met. Men were watching a football game on the pub's television. They commanded us to be quiet. She said, "This is a public place and we have as much right to speak as you have to watch the TV." We were asked to leave by the owner. A man followed us and tried to grab her but she grabbed him instead and threw him with one movement down the steps.

I love to be on boats and there was an old-timer tied to the pier that had been converted into a restaurant and bar. The owner was very nice and his mother cooked, cleaned and helped him with everything. I often went there with Zora to eat or have a drink at the bar and we became friends.

The mother was a hard-working woman with a sunny and vivacious personality who loved to laugh and was proud of her son. The ship was leaking and they needed some business. I pointed everybody who wanted to know where to go in their direction.

My van was parked near them and I felt safe to sleep there. One day, I could not get up because I suffered from time to time with back problems because of sitting in the draught or lifting too much and this could take as long as two days to cure, laying down and keeping warm. At the same time, I caught the flu. I was unable to move without sharp pain and when my friends on the ship did not see me, the owner's mother came to see what had happened to me.

She brought me soups and other things and the man sweeping the streets brought me a whole big bag full of oranges. I was really touched by their kindness. I left the van door open for Zora to be able to get in and out. After a couple of days I was well again, thanks to them.

The Mom, as I called her, asked me what color I liked best and I said, "All colors are beautiful." Then she asked, "What color would you pick for a vest if I wanted to crochet one for you?." I said, "Orange." She hand-crocheted a beautiful vest for me.

Suddenly, I had the urge to move on again so I had a last drink with my friends and went to pick up my paintings at the English Pub, wrapped them up and sent them to Switzerland because of lack of space in the Estafette. I then continued to drive along the coast and took a ferry to the island of Korcula.

Marco Polo was born here. What a fascinating, stone-old, place. I looked at all the architectural details and then entered a lively pub where I met a very handsome man. We immediately fell in love and he told me that his two friends were in big trouble and had to escape from the island since the police had found two marijuana plants in their garden. They could expect two years in jail if they did not escape. He said someone already had organized for them to work on a ship but they had to be there the next day. The police were very feared for their brutality. He asked me, if I could smuggle his friends off the island and take them to Dubrovnik.

I do not believe that any plant should be declared illegal and agreed to help them. Early the next day, we took the two young men into the back of the van and covered them up, to go on the ferry then we drove to Dubrovnik. There, we went to see friends of my friends and left them there.

We returned to Korcula, where he introduced me to his mother. She was really happy to meet me and told me that her husband had died when her son was very small. She had brought him up by cooking, cleaning and sewing to make ends meet. When my new friend went outside, she told me that she was afraid of her only son since he would beat her up when she denied him money for drinking and that he refused to work. She told me to be careful. When I heard her say this while looking directly into my eyes, I knew she was not lying and immediately fell out of love with him, blaming my feelings for this guy on being horny.

When he came back in, he looked ugly to me. Since he followed me, I suggested that we go to his favorite pub. He ordered two beers and his friends joined us. I excused myself to go and get some fresh air with Zora (white lie). He said, "Don't go without me, wait 10 minutes." I said Zora has to go and walked out. I went straight to the van without looking back and headed for the ferryboat that was, like magic, ready to load. I drove straight on it and crossed over.

Then I took the direction to Switzerland. Just before the Yugoslavian customs, two men asked me to smuggle them across the toll to Italy. I told them I was at the wrong place and did not intend to leave Yugoslavia, since I was afraid of them. They looked strong and primitive. I used my acting skills when needed.

Then I drove on to another toll crossing and traversed Italy to Switzerland. I lived in the van and visited my parents and daughters regularly. In desperate need of an art studio and broke, I asked the people of the town hall in Wil, SG if they had an empty place somewhere I could use but they turned me down. One man who worked there, called me to his office and said, "Ask the architect, Mr. Ruedi Elsener."

When I visited Mr. Elsener he was working on a project to

restore the 'Korn House', a beautiful ancient building, used to store wheat. Since then, the building had been split down the center for two purposes- As a retirement home on the left side of its impressive original stairway and the right side, it was turned into an orphanage. This had not worked out with success since the old people were annoyed by the children's' noise. The orphans were not happy either, since they had to be quiet. After that, the 'Korn house' was turned into a 'Poor House' and then the situation really went downhill.

Ruedi Elsener wanted to rescue the historic 600 year old building. He gave me a large room with a magnificent view and the use of the kitchen and bathroom. When I asked him what he would charge for it, he just waved and said, "I don't need this space until I am ready to work on it and then you have to leave, but not for 6 or 8 months."

I could hardly believe my luck to have a roof over my head, with running water and electricity for free. I was on the orphan side and my friends, a couple, were on the old folks side of the staircase on the same floor. They loved to give parties and invited me as well. The food was cooked in a huge, tiled wood-burning oven which heated their place as well in the winter.

In St. Gallen an exhibition for artists from Canton St. Gallen was being organized. Professional artists were asked to bring three paintings each to be selected for exhibition. I had just been turned down, when I saw the magnificent work of a gorgeous old artist with long, snow white hair and beard, who had come on an ancient bicycle, also being turned down. I could not believe it and felt so bad for the old wise-faced man, that I almost got a lump in the throat and could have cried. Some of the so-called artists really took the "Mickey" out of the so-called experts. Then I got angry with the so-called art experts who don't estimate fine and honest work unless the real artist has died.

I returned to my studio and thought about it. Then I inquired at the town hall, if I could put a poster for my next exhibition in the window next to another artists advert. When they turned me down and I asked, "WHY?" The bureaucrat explained that the artist with the poster in the window was famous and I was not. I asked him, "How can I be, unless you give me a chance?" The bureaucrat turned me down.

I hung my posters all over the town and the next day, I was forced to take them all down or pay a big fine. I invited everyone I knew to my "Art Opening" on the huge staircase of the 'Korn House'.

About 800 people came to my art exhibition and my best friends Wilhelm Heinrich and Elisabeth Epper –Guhl showed up and even went to get more cases of wine when we had run out, before buying the most expensive of my paintings with the title 'Befruchtung' for several thousands of Swiss Francs.

This permitted me and Zora my dog to live, instead of just existing. I bought art materials to last me for at least a year.

A musician friend of mine introduced a refugee, whose name was Francesco, to me. All refugees were doing lowly paid jobs. Some could not go back to their own countries. They were forced to get out of Switzerland within three days. Francesco was one of them. His life goal was to go to Sweden and meet a blond and blue-eyed woman. He was a black-haired young man from South America with fiery dark brown eyes who needed more time to make his dream come true. While he stayed hidden in my studio, I moved into my van with Zora.

His friends had organized a party before leaving and we drove in my van to join them that night. Those South American people really understand how to have the best time, living in the moment. There was food, drink and live guitar music to dance to and many couples took turns to make love in the adjoining rooms of the apartment. It was their last night in Switzerland. I found it personally very cruel to throw them out of the country in such a limited time. In my view, we are all citizens of the world and it would be great if we could choose where to live, as in the old times when you could sail without a visa or passport. Materialistic thinking only causes life to be threatened. Yesterday on February 23, 2009, I found out from IUCN on Wikipedia that:

1 in 4 species of Mammals, 1 in 8 species of Birds, 1 in 3 species of Fish, and more than half of all flowering plants and insects worldwide are endangered. The problems of racism, war and pollution all stem from the same thing......... G r e e d.......! No other animal but the human messes up his own oxygen.

Escape To Live In Caves. Jumped to Safety from Moving Van

My daughter, Alexa, was studying Mandarin in China. My younger daughter Julie had successfully completed her masters and was looking for a job working for the benefit of the ecology. Originally, she wanted to specialize in reptiles but had to settle for termites. I am so proud of Julie for being true to her beliefs and I admire her strength. She had chosen to study and pass the diploma and teach biology in Bern. She discovered that she did not like to teach kids of the most difficult ages. While Julie was still studying, about three months before the final tests, she wrote to me that she did not believe in it any longer and wanted to quit. I should have agreed with her instead of saying, "It is a shame to give up after all these years just for three more months." She listened to me. I am so proud of both of my daughters and am very glad that they have not chosen to live like me or I would have been constantly worried about them.

They both had good contact with my parents, their father and I and planned to spend every vacation with their father in the U.S.A. They both have very positive outlooks on life and hardly ever speak negatively. They accept life the way it is and make the best of it. I envy them for it. They are beautiful, intelligent and talented. Wherever they go they are loved.

Emil and I got our hot relationship back together after what felt like a long rest. The flame of passion started to consume us again. We decided to spend the winter on Gran Canaria Island. I stored my van at an uncle's garage.

My parents suggested that I leave my dog Zora with them for the four months we were gone. Heavy hearted, I left Zora behind. My mother loved to take her for a long walk every day. Emil and I left in his van and headed south. We took the autoroute to Genoa and followed the coast, stopping here and there, all the way to the south of Spain.

It was getting colder but Emil was an expert at making a fire on the beach wherever we stopped. This would, almost every time, attract the police. When they arrived, I made them a cup of hot tea or coffee and they enjoyed drinking it near the fire and left us in peace.

The south coast of Spain was still pure and beautiful without hotels - or apartment complexes. The sandy beaches were free from mass tourism. Sea- and other- birds were singing in the bushes. This beautiful landscape was a mixture of wild and lovely. The ever-changing cloud formation was spectacular or could reveal a fresh blue sky. We did not like to go into towns, except for the necessary shopping or to fill the tank.

We did look forward to seeing the rock with the monkeys on Gibraltar. What a disappointment when we got there. There was a high fence with barbed wire on the top all around the whole area. Armed army guards stood ready for defense inside. We could see the rock in the distance but could not make out if there were monkeys living on it. The foreground was cluttered up with ugly army barracks.

Depressed, we moved on to Cadiz. There, we got ferry tickets to Las Palmas, in the Gran Canaria islands. I was very upset when I saw the dog quarters right next to the noisy funnel on the ship. The cages were very small and the dogs looked miserable.

According to Pink Floyd or Emerson, Lake and Palmer, the hearing of dogs is 150 times better than the hearing of humans. I watched the tests. With such sensitive ears, I can imagine how much they suffered because of the ignorance of mankind. One of the dogs laid in his own vomit. I went up to talk to them and the dogs were glad to see me. I complained about it but to no avail. They just forbade me to visit the poor dogs again. I was glad that "Zora" was staying with my parents.

Emil felt seasick and laid in his cabin not wanting to be disturbed. By the time we arrived in Las Palmas, Emil felt well again. We drove along the north coast and then over the Roque Nublo to Maspalomas. It was an interesting ride through mountain villages with bougainvillea and other tropical plants gracing the snowy whitewashed houses. People were very friendly to us. The long sandy beach of Maspalomas would have been beautiful if not for the mass tourism and ugly buildings which had turned us off.

We drove on to Mogan. There we headed up the mountain and found an ideal place to park right near a fresh spring, with clear drinking water on one side and a small grass field next to a stream on the other to park the van on. Emil built a fireplace out of the stone which laid around and we cooked on it. Everybody assumed we had bought the plot and left us in peace.

The only people who passed on the small rough road, were tourists equipped with cameras in their rented safari vehicles. They came in handy, since they would pay Emil well for fixing their punctured tires.

We did our shopping in Mogan. Everything was as inexpensive, just as I had remembered. The wine was still more reasonable than a bottle of water. Food was less than one third of the price in Switzerland. We could buy fish directly from the fishermen. We did not pay rent, water or electricity since we lived in Emil's Estafette. We used an oil lamp and flashlights. The van also had lights that were connected to the battery. We had water straight from the source. Life was good and we had a ball.

We went to Mogan to get our mail and went to eat out or to just have a drink and meet some people. We met one fascinating man, who had lost his legs in a motorbike accident and was living in his van with his pretty wife. He had a really sunny disposition and would play football in his wheelchair. He mostly won. His wife was so jealous of every woman who spoke to him. There were lots of characters around.

One day, Emil received some bad news in the mail. His beloved grandmother had died. I could understand that he wished to drown his sorrow. The problem, was that he could not control his aggressions. When he started to insult the Guardia Civil, which is a dangerous thing to do, I went back to the van. When he got back, he took his aggression out on me and I ran for my life, leaving my handbag with my wallet behind. I just had enough cash in my pocket to get some bananas, a chocolate, some bread and a salami.

I searched for a cave and found one. Someone had even put a door on it. It had a splendid, panoramic view over Mogan and the sea. I slept well in it, until the police climbed up to the cave. They said, "We don't want hippies sleeping in caves here and I said, "I am an artist who wants to be inspired". However, nothing I could say, prevented me from having to leave. I grabbed the food under my arm and went in search for a more hidden cave.

Spotting a police helicopter, I hid and then found a cave they would not find me in. It was very difficult to reach but my ballet training helped me to get to it. I did not feel hungry because I was upset and tired. It was just getting dark and I fell asleep. In the morning, I was woken up by the noise of the helicopter but they had not seen me. I saw that the mice had visited me during the night and eaten all the chocolate, bread and most of the salami. They did not eat the bananas. Mice pellets were everywhere.

There was a beautiful bouquet of chamomile growing in front of my habitat. The cave consisted of ochre red stone, and the floor was the same cultured sand. I was really getting hungry and climbed down to the seashore in search of something to eat. I could not find seaweed, sea urchins or seashells but spotted a man who was about to bite into an appetizing sandwich.

I went up to him asked, "Does this taste good?, took it out of his hands and bit into it. He was totally surprised and speechless. After a pause, he said, "I will buy you all the sandwiches you want if you teach me to swim." Relieved, I replied, "It will be a pleasure to teach you how to swim." He bought me some sandwiches with a drink and after I had eaten, I gave him the lesson. He seemed big, plump, heavy and scared and I started to believe that he was too clumsy to learn. Almost giving up, he then swam skillfully into deep water like a pro, grinning from ear to ear. I laughed as well.

When we went to the pub together, a friend of mine came up to me and told me that Emil had been badly beaten up by the Guardia Civil. They had been armed with bats. Emil was laying in the van unable to move.

So, I went back to him. He looked pale, almost green and moaned. He could not sit up and I gave him a bowl to urinate in. There was a drop of blood in his urine. Then I made a soup and fed it to him. I looked at his next urine and was glad that it was free from blood. He was in a sorry state and suffered from pain but refused to let me take him to a hospital or a doctor. He had been beaten up by four policemen. Four armed men, against one sad, unarmed drunk - how low can they get.

Or did Emil asked for it and missed the beatings his sadist father had given him when he was a child? I read in my father's medical book entitled, 'Sexual perversions in medicine', that sadism and masochism went hand in hand and that sadists could turn into masochists and vice versa. Had I fallen in love with a sado-masochist? It did not make sense to me, because Emil could be so affectionate and felt so deeply for nature.

He recovered well and we were happy again. Of all the places I had visited more than once, this was the only one that had improved. Instead of four days of rain a year, when I was visiting here for the first time, it was now 154 days annually. The trees and bushes planted around the properties had attracted moisture. New golf courses and plants had been watered by salt water converted to sweet water. The island looked greener and healthier.

Time passed so quickly in Gran Canaria and it was February 1984 already. We took the ferryboat to Cadiz and drove to

Portugal. We looked at romantic villages in spectacular settings along the south shore.

I was recently shocked to see on "Google Earth" that most of them have been built over for mass tourism and lost their charm. How sad. Why can't they keep the mass tourism in the same places that has been messed up already, like the Costa del Sol in Spain? Fortunately, the top of Europe's "Cape St. Vincent" looks as pure as we experienced.

We drove along the west side of Portugal and found an ideal place for us on Praia da Amoreira in the Algarve. What a beautiful place! I painted a watercolor seascape with a cliff, which reminded me of a pregnant woman lying on her back. When the owner of the coffee shop saw me, he came up to me and gave me work creating a new menu card and paid me very well.

To the left of the beach was a huge cave, which could only be entered at low tide. Thousands of bats lived in it. It absolutely fascinated us. We often went back to it. The water was just warm enough to swim in. Delicate sisters bloomed on their bushes in almost transparent, pearl white and soft pink. The long stretch of sandy, light beige beach was free from tourists and rubbish and it was very peaceful.

The low tide exposed large rocks with plenty of oysters and clams on them. We only picked the largest ones, opened them and slurped them down as an instant meal.

We did the shopping in the village of Aljezur. We had our mail sent there as well. Emil needed his shoes repaired and found a shoemaker who glued and stitched up the side and front of his favorite combat boots for only 35 cents. Emil then wanted to give him more business and had a belt repaired. When he wanted to pay, the man said, "No," and he did it for free because he had done his boots before. Emil then insisted that he take the money for his children, since he was happy with the work he had done on his boots.

We went to the restaurant bar, which was the meeting place of travelers and had a good time eating and drinking for a reasonable price, before driving back to park in our ideal place again.

The next time we went shopping and to the post office in Aljezur, we had mail waiting for us. I had good, but Emil had bad news. It was a death announcement of his beloved grandfather who could not cope with his wife's death and committed suicide at 95 years of age, by hanging himself in the bathroom, where his granddaughter found him. Emil was in shock him and I feared, that he needed to get stone drunk again. He wanted me to join him so we went to get drunk together.

Suddenly, he wanted to leave. I was glad there was hardly any traffic to be seen while we headed for the beach. There, Emil turned to the left and drove up a hill cliff where he planned to kill himself and me, by running down the cliff of a lee shore. The ground was sandy. I managed to pull open the door and jump onto the sand, rolling my body up and landing safely on my feet, while Emil's van got stuck in deep sand just before the edge of the high and steep cliff. In anger, he tried to dig his wheels out and in doing so, he sobered up enough to lose his depression.

His aggressions were still at the point, where I found it unsafe to stick around. This time, I grabbed my bag and ran. I walked toward Aljezur and slept in an unlocked car for a few hours but got out before daylight, in order to not get caught. Then, I walked again, until it was dark and started to rain. I could not find shelter until I got to Aljezur and spotted an empty telephone booth. Totally exhausted, wet and shivering I entered and rolled myself into a fetal position on the floor, falling deeply asleep.

Then an older man woke me up. I shouted, "Go away, I was here first!" The man then insisted I go with him. I was embarrassed at having tried to send him away, when I saw that he must have been close to 80 years old and was no threat to me. I accompanied him, being curious about where he was going to take me. He went up to an old restaurant with a bar that belonged to him, opened the door, led me to the bar and asked me to sit down. He poured me a brandy and told me to wait for him.

He went upstairs and came back with a plate of food, which he placed in front of me. I gladly ate it. Then he pointed to the large, red sofa and said that I could sleep there for the night. He went upstairs to sleep. In the morning, he came in with fresh buns and made me a coffee. When I wanted to pay, he refused to take anything but I had to promise him that I would come and see him again, if ever I should come back to Aljezur. I will never forget that wonderful old man.

After I left, I went to the pub. Some friends I met earlier, planned to drive to Lagos and asked me if I would like to go along with them. Since I believed it to be too early to go back to Emil, it was a welcome change for me. The older of my friends was driving the pickup truck along the highway, when a car came directly toward us at very high speed. My friend could only avoid a frontal collision by steering onto the gravel next to the highway. The truck got away with being hit slightly on the backside. The guy that hit us escaped. We all had a shock and went to the next pub to order a double brandy.

The men stayed there and I left to walk to the next town and sleep in a nice guest house. I returned to Emil the next day, who was glad to see me again. We celebrated by passionately falling into each other's arms and a few days later we continued our voyage along the west coast of the Iberian peninsula.

When we were passing the prison grounds of Lisbon, we saw five policemen standing around a shirtless prisoner who was bleeding. All of them were brutally hitting him with their police batons. I told Emil to stop and wanted to help the victim but he stepped on the gas and said, "You are crazy, they would beat both of us up and maybe we would never be seen again."

In Lisbon, we looked at the port with its monument and explored the old part of the town hoping to forget the ugly jail incident. The same day, we drove out of the city and stopped at different villages or beaches along the way. On the Praia de Afife, I found not only sea shells but two hand blown glass balls that had been attached to fishing nets in their past. We saw many things and met some interesting people on our stops before we crossed the borders of Portugal and Spain.

Then we drove to Biaritz and went on to the south of France to visit Köbi and his family on the way to Switzerland.

Invited to Sing With Gypsies, Gang Raped

Köbi and Joelle welcomed us, but we insisted on living in the van near their mill on the side of the River Aude, instead of occupying their space. Köbi was always very happy to have Emil help him with his land. This made Joelle and I a bit lonely. When, even in the evening, they preferred each other's company to ours, it made me disappointed, then angry and depressed.

The next day it was still early, when I invited Joelle for dinner in the old section of Carcassonne. When we entered one of the so-called best restaurants and were shown to a table, I was thrilled to be so near a real gypsy band playing and singing. The flamenco was just what I needed. We ordered an aperitif and dinner and then the band took a pause and sat at the table next to ours. We were invited by them, to join them. Joëlle said to me, "On ne parle pas avec les gitanes." (One does not speak to gypsies). I could hardly believe what she said and after swallowing, I said to her, " If that is how you feel, I don't want anything to do with you." I took my glass and joined the gypsies at their table. Joelle got up and left.

The band leader offered me the chance to sing with them. When they returned to the stage, they took me with them and handed me the microphone. I felt so flattered and privileged for that great honor. I sang with all my feelings to the point that all the heartache and depressions disappeared. The band and the public loved it and gave big applause but the owner of the restaurant was mad that we had not asked him first and forbade me to sing again at his place and threw me out.

I walked to the town and wanted to visit a musician, whom I had accompanied with my voice while he played the sousaphone, at a fête on a previous occasion. Before I could get there, three French foreign legionnaires walked up to me and asked, "What do you think of the army?" Instead of saying, "I have no idea, since I never was there", I said, "If no one went, there would not be war." They looked at each other and one said, "She is against us."

They grabbed me at dawn, right in the pedestrian precinct in the center of town and dragged me up the street. When I screamed for help as loud as I could, the house shutters on both sides of the street closed and the people around were too scared to come and help. Then they forced me to cross the highway and into the public park. There, they took me behind bushes and when I screamed, the commanding officer made a movement with his index finger across his throat and threatened to cut my throat if I did not stop shouting. The officer said, "We only want to make love to you." When I shouted, "How would you like your mother or sister to be raped?" and tried to defend myself, each of the two soldiers grabbed one of my arms and the officer hit me in my face with his fists over and over again. I tried to protect my teeth by blocking the blows with the elbow but could not move it much since they held me in such a tight grip.

After having been truly beaten up, they pushed me to the ground and one of them ripped my underwear off. The first that raped me, was the officer. Then he commanded one of the soldiers to rape me as well and he masturbated while he watched. He told the second soldier to rape me also. Since I feared that they would maybe kill me, I whispered into the ear of the second soldier, " Please help me. I have two children who need me." He then said, "You are illegal in this country." I caught on quickly and said so that his mates could hear it, "Please don't tell the police that I am illegal in France." The officer then raped me a second time. When he was finished, he got up and threatened me, "If you go to the police, we will kill the next woman."

Then, all three of them looked to the right and then to the

left in a cowardly way, to be sure no one was coming and took off. I did not go to the police since they had not helped me when I needed them in the U. S. A., Switzerland or France. I ran to the duck pond and washed my body frantically, since I felt so soiled by the three brutal and disgusting legionnaires.

I ran to a bar and wanted to use the telephone to call Emil. The owner saw the state I was in (all swollen, bruised and bleeding), so he chased me out saying, "We don't want trouble here." I stopped a car to take me back and when the driver asked me what happened, I told him. He was not planning to go in my direction but felt sorry for me and took me all the way back to Köbi's fish farm.

It was hot but I felt chilled to the bones. The men asked me what had happened and when I told them that I was raped, Joelle said, "On ne parle pas de ca." (One does not speak of this.) I said, "But it is necessary for women to speak of this."

I did not feel like being with anyone or even with Emil and went into the forest for a week where no one could find me. I drank the water from the Aude and ate moss and plants even though I did not feel hungry but I didn't want to starve. Thoughts about everything that had happened would not leave my mind. I wanted to know if it was my fault or theirs.

When I came out of the forest, I started to write everything down and then came to the conclusion that the rapists must have been treated awfully by their superiors. It must have been a vicious circle. Being taught to kill and rape by the system is a disgusting thing. Understanding this and knowing that boys having problems at home or with the police and that they are most vulnerable to blandishments, they enter the foreign legion without realizing what is going to happen to them. I managed to get a bit of distance from that horrible crime. But the shock had a tendency to come back and haunt me for a long time.

To this day, I get a cold shiver down my spine when I see a man in a military uniform or even any other man with a shaved head. Nightmares and fears that this could happen to my daughters tortured me for years. I would rather be raped again, than have this happen to them and would give my life gladly for them if needed.

One of my front teeth was wobbling but grew back on while the other front tooth turned black from the nerve being damaged by the blows. I also got bad attacks of headaches and dizziness.

There was an art gallery owner in Carcassonne who liked to exhibit my paintings but I was unable to go to that city again until years later. I also found out, that even the whores had left Carcassonne and moved to Toulouse in fear and because their pimps were beaten up and they were raped by the French foreign legionnaires. I was informed that this happened all the time and that some women were even killed, so often that the press was not interested in it. My thoughts tell me it could be out of fear.

Emil and I drove back to Switzerland . I had promised my daughters to pick them up at the airport in Zurich when they came back from their vacation at their father's house. Emil drove the van into a post and we had to have the bump straightened out. I called my parents to tell them that we may not be able to get back in time because of the accident but that we were trying to be there. My father told me not to worry, since they planned to meet them as well, whether we were there or not. We managed to get there just in time and I was happy to be able to take them in my arms again.

My parents assumed that I looked so bruised up from the accident but when my daughters wanted to know what had happened, I told them the truth. This was hard for them and my parents. I don't believe in telling lies except in a matter of life or death.

I admire the courage of Mister Mandela tremendously. It helped me to speak to other women about being raped and was horrified how many of them had similar stories to tell, but all agreed that they had received no help from the police and were worse off after having been questioned. There was a woman who told me that after having been raped near the lake of Konstanz by eight rockers, she went to the police, and they asked her if she had enjoyed it! She told me they even had become excited by her report. She suffered from bad depressions, fear and shock.

Red Factory, Zurich, Thrown Into Prison.

Emil and I had a crisis again. He told me, that I was "Too old and past it" for him and that he was looking for a younger woman who would obey him. Not only was I shattered, but I was naïve enough to believe that I really was too old and past it, even though I had not quite reached my 45th birthday.

Fortunately, I had my own van but it was difficult to find a place to park. So I drove to the Red Factory, which had been declared 'independent-autonomic' space , where I parked the van. The Red Factory was built next to the lake and had been constructed many years before out of red brick. The young people took it over and artists turned rooms into their studios.

A restaurant with good food and a self-service cafe was organized by some people. I saw a naked guy, dressed only with an apron, bringing food out the table. Those who ran the place were all individualists. Others people organized concerts or plays on the premises. A small circus erected their tent and gave performances. A kindergarten was located in one building. Music lessons were offered, even a bicycle repair shop was opened and many other things. It was a very interesting place to be and those who visited, returned again and again.

I met the owner of 'Circus Mouse' there, with all his animals who consisted of a pig, goats, dogs, birds a cat and a mouse etc. They all got along very well. I also met old friends there from time to time. It was never boring. The only thing that was annoying, was all the garbage that had been thrown everywhere, along with broken bottles and spat out chewing gum.

It was also impossible to find privacy, except when I lay in the bushes behind the open lawn, which had not been discovered. I looked everywhere I could to find the best place for me to paint and found a row of sheds hidden from the most-visited areas. They were all locked up so Zora and I parked our van to the side of them and made this place our home. Zora knew all the free dogs that were around and loved the place. She never went out of earshot so that she could hear me when I called her.

The next day, I started to clean up the entire area where I was staying and intended to paint. It was summer and when it became almost unbearably hot, I just jumped into the lake to cool off. There was also a float further out, that invited me to lay on it when no one else was there. Some linen sheets I had bought at the second-hand store were rolled up in my van. I unrolled them and hung one of them on a shed wall. Then I grounded it with water-based white paint and it dried very quickly leaving it tightly stretched with the grain of the wood imprinted on the canvas. Then I started to turn it into a modern piece of art with oil colors. Completed to my satisfaction, a new problem was created for me. I knew that Zora and I could sleep, cook and live in the van but where was I going to put my wet paintings which were larger then my bed?

The City of Zurich then took over the Red Factory since it had become fashionable for the rich to visit the restaurant, concerts etc. and it was no longer available to artists who really needed a place, but was rented out to the ones who drove expensive sports cars and were selected by the so-called art experts. Unfortunately, I was not one of them since they make it very hard for any artist who has been away to come back. I had to help myself again.

There was a long wall behind the last sheds extending about 10 meters into open space. The wall of the shed plus the wall behind formed a perfect triangle so if I could succeed in building two walls and a roof, I would have a room to work in when it was raining plus a storage room for my paintings. Happy with this idea, I started to look around in rubbish skips for discarded building materials I could recycle, so that I could start my project.

When I asked the people in the restaurant if I could hang the wet painting on the wall, they helped me to put it on exhibition. I was glad to have found a temporary place for my piece, where it was safe.

It was amazing, what I had found in the trash container. A big picture window in a frame, probably thrown out by a shop keeper, a beautiful arched door, Posts, wood, ply wood and all sorts of useful things. I took the screws and nails out of old wood and straightened them with a hammer.

My father had given me good tools which I treasured. I loaded the things I needed on top of the bed and drove them back to the Red Factory. In the trash bin at the Red Factory, I also found a lot of stuff that helped me build my new storage and working place. It was very hard work and I felt strained.

Zora and I walked into town to find food for her. The co-op restaurant was an ideal place for that. Most people have the tendency to take more food than they can eat. On the trolley for used plates, I found halves of steaks, sausages, chickens and other leftovers, which I put into a plastic bag to give to Zora. The chicken place also had a bin with half eaten drumsticks in it. It amazed me, what could be found among the waste.

Necessity made it possible for me to get over my shyness and hang-ups and help myself. When I own a pet, it is important that I can take care of it. Zora was not just a pet, she was my best friend, my guardian angel, my companion and she needed me. I needed the responsibility of her to not lose the will to live. She cheered me up and made me laugh. I was so lonely.

Without a man as my life partner, nothing made sense. Whenever I saw a man that I found handsome, I heard Emil's voice saying, "You are old and past it" and, believing it, I cut myself off from any chance of finding a partner again. When I meditated, I realized that we create our life up to a point by ourselves. Theoretically, I understood this but practically, it took many years to get over those thoughtless words.

Concentrating on building my house, I hurried too much and tried to continue working, even after I had made a mistake. Then I was forced to undo all the work and correct the fault before going on. I pulled myself together and managed to finish the walls. Someone was kind enough to help me with the roof. I found all the furniture in the bin. Two chairs, a table, cups and saucers, curtains etc. I learned a lot by building this, even though it had been very hard to work in the extreme heat while the sweat was pouring off me.

So glad to have this place, I started to paint intensely. My daughters, sister and mother came to visit me. Then Emil came with a larger van, a Peugeot J7 he had exchanged for the Estafette and parked next to me. I was not ready to forgive him and I behaved quite coolly. He invited me to the restaurant and after a few drinks, I could not resist him any longer so we made hot passionate love and then he left me again.

Even sadder than before, I sat on a bench with my arm around Zora next to me and stared out over the lake, devastated beyond tears. I had to wait until my latest paintings were dry enough to roll, before I could go away and change the scenery.

My 45th birthday was coming up and I went to buy a piece of smoked salmon for breakfast, to celebrate the event the next day. When I opened the vacuum sealed plastic around it, it was rotten and stank to high heaven. I took it back to the shop it had come from. They refused to take it back so I walked around the shop and stole a roast of about the same value as the rotten fish from the freezer and carried it out in my handbag. I felt proud of myself, even though my heart pounded against my chest with unusual force. Since they had cheated me, I did not believe this action to be theft. Zora and I enjoyed the roast that I cooked in the pressure cooker inside the van.

Some days later, I went to see the 'Theatre Spektakel' (Theater Spectacle/Festival) in the park of Zurich, beside the lake. A group of artists from the theatre, comedy, magic, acrobatics, dance, music, circus and pantomime were on show. There was also food and drink being sold.

I looked around and crossed the bridge to Saffa Island. I could not believe my eyes. There were NO signs to forbid anything. There was not even a 'forbidden to park' sign, so I parked the van and went with Zora into the tent, where food and drink were sold from the counter. I met some people who cheered me up and began to enjoy life again.

After a while, I felt sleepy and went to lie down in the van. I fell asleep with the sliding door open so Zora was free to come and go as she pleased. There were many dogs around and she loved to play with them. When I woke up, a man from Africa was knocking on the van. He held two necklaces out of real ivory up to me and said, "Will you buy them from me?" I answered, " I can't afford those and need the money to buy food and gasoline." He replied, "I will sell them cheap." Desperate, he urged me to give him 20 Francs. I took the note from my handbag and he left the necklaces with me and hurried off.

Then a man with a Zurich accent showed up and said, "You can't park here, go away or I call the police." I said, "No, it is not forbidden to park here and who are you to speak to me this way? You go away!" He left and I dozed off again in the heat of the afternoon. Suddenly, police were violently beating on my van and I just managed to slide the door shut but there was not enough time to roll up the windows and one of them stuck his arm through and opened the door from the inside.

They shouted at me to come out immediately but did not give me a chance to get out by myself and yanked me outside where one of them crossed my arm behind my back and pulled it upwards which felt like agony, while the other shoved me into the paddy wagon. I pleaded that my dog was outside and I wanted to have her with me, but they did not listen and threw me into the hot iron wagon with just a slit covered by wire netting for air.

A woman had witnessed this event and asked me, "Can I make a phone call for you?" I shouted the telephone number of my parents through the slit and she promised to call and let them know what was going on. I had no idea what was going to happen to me or where they would take me. I was left to sweat and worry about Zora for 1 1/2 hours and nearly passed out. Then I felt the vehicle moving and after about 10 minutes it stopped. The iron trap door was raised and a policeman yelled, "Get out quick or we will hit you over the head with the door." I was terrorized even more by the threat of being raped by one of the policemen if I did not move fast enough. Inside, they questioned me without letting me answer for about a quarter of an hour and then one of them asked, "Do you take drugs?" I answered "Sometimes." He said, "What drugs do you take?" I replied, "Painkillers or antibiotics or others depending on what medical problems I have."

They pushed me into a jail cell with a shatter-proof window, a table and a chair after having denied me the right to make a phone call. They also took my handbag away. I felt like taking the chair and throwing it through the window, but realized that it would probably not break and that maybe I was being observed and that this action would not bring anything but more problems. I saw someone walking outside and screamed as loud as I could to get his attention but the thick glass was too solid for me to be heard by anyone. They left me in there for over an hour and then the door opened and Zora was given to me to my great relief and the door shut again. She greeted me like a long lost friend and I inspected her to see if she was ok. She was. We were left in the cell for another hour before a police member came to release us.

Then I was told, that I could leave but had to be back there in exactly two hours. They kept my bag, Zora's leash and my shoes. I was in state of shock and very thirsty. I saw a restaurant and entered. I asked the owner if I could eat and drink something and could pay later but was insulted when he saw my bare feet. With a string of aggressive words he threw me out. I went to the park and sat on a bench. Zora sat next to me.

A man sat under a tree next to his bicycle with trailer, which was loaded with a box the size of a coffin. On the box was written,

'The smallest home in the world.' He took a look at me and asked, "What happened to you?" I told him and said, "I don't even have the money to call my family since the police have taken my handbag away from me." The man gave me the phone money and invited me to the stand where he bought me a bratwurst with bread and something to drink. When I asked where I could find him to pay back the money, he refused to take anything back. I left to find a telephone and made a phone call.

My daughter Alexa answered. I informed her of what had happened and that I had to be back at the "Stadelhofen Police Station." She said that she would leave right away and would meet me there. I started to relax a little but had to force myself to go back to such an awful place. Alexa had to drive 60 km to get there but showed up shortly after I got there.

I was told that my van was parked in their private parking place behind the police station. Alexa kept her cool and when they told her that I was not in any state to drive, she told them, "Yes, she is perfectly capable of driving." They handed me the van keys and then let me go, without giving a reason why they had put me into jail in the first place, or why they had denied me the lawful right to make a phone call . Alexa, Zora and I were relieved to get out of that horrible police station and away from those awful policemen.

Upon entering my beloved van, I noticed with disgust, that they had not just driven my van from the Saffa island to the Stadelhofen police station without my permission but had also opened all the cupboard doors and snooped into every corner of my mobile home. They had walked through the van with their heavy, dirty boots and left imprints with mud and grass up to 2 cm. thick on my bed. They had not even cleaned their own mess up behind themselves. Disgusted, I cleaned it up as well as I could in the depression and sadness that tortured me.

I respect everybody's property and asked myself, "Why do we have to pay taxes for those who work for the law and don't respect it and never have the slightest consideration for you or your property?" That does not mean that I don't respect all laws.

But there are too many of them in my view. For each new rule and regulation, there should be three old ones taken away. To top it all off, afterwards, a 'forbidden to park' sign, was placed on Saffa Island and the police had the arrogance to send me a parking fine.

Isola d' Elba. Klaus.

I left Zurich and the shed I had built in the red factory to say au revoir to my daughters and parents. My parents had given me SFr.1000.- for my 45th birthday which made it possible for me to drive to Italy and explore the Island of Elba.

I tried to make this money last as long as I could. At Piombino, my van was loaded onto the ferry boat and I stayed on deck looking out to see if I could spot a good place to park on Elba. To the left of the ferry port 'Porto Azzurro' I could see a beautiful, empty and sandy beach in a small bay with a street leading to it. That is where I planned to spend the night but first I enjoyed a pizza and some wine.

Then I looked to find out 'what was where' in town before heading to the Naregno Beach for the night. Zora and I had the whole beach to ourselves. We went to sleep deeply, until we were brutally woken up at 4 a.m. by the police hammering with their fists on the van. Zora barked in fury. One of the policemen yelled for me to, " Come out right now!" I slid the door open and held Zora who stopped barking as I told her to. When I stood outside, one of them shouted, "What the hell are you doing here parked with a van?" "Why did I not go to a camping place?" Before I could answer a policeman inspected the van and looked under the bed.

Then I pointed to the articles of my last art exhibition in the window and told them, that I hated camping places and as an artist, I wished to immortalize the beauty of this place. I added, "Would you like a cup of coffee?" They read the advertisement and excused themselves, saying that they had thought that I might have a prisoner who had escaped hidden in my van and that from now on, they would leave me in peace and I could go and do anything I desired, since the Italians liked artists.

The next day, I drove to Porto Azzurro and shopped for food. Then I went to have a drink. Zora accompanied me everywhere. If I had to leave her outside when I went into places such as into supermarkets, I left the van door open and her water dish filled. The van was her home and she knew I would be back. She never went far from me or the van. The minute I called her, she came running to me. What a wonderful dog!

We drove along the coast and stopped to look at many interesting sights and then went to Porto Ferraio. Sailing boats were a special attraction to me, so I looked at them and quickly found one that I almost fell in love with. It was a Hershof designed old-timer called 'Rose of Sharon'. Then I felt thirsty and sat at a table outside a coffee shop. The owner served a drink to me and said that I must be new here because he had not seen me before. I answered, "Yes." He asked me if I was on holiday and I told him, "No, I am an artist who lives in her van and wants to paint here."

He was so nice and told me to come to the bar for a free sandwich since he was making one for himself as well. His wife was nice to me as well, even though she was not nice to most other people. Then, a weather-beaten man arrived in the bar. He ordered something and we got into conversation. When he spoke of sailing it turned into a real conversation about the subject. I liked him. He then invited me onto his yacht, 'THE ROSE OF SHARON'!

His name was Klaus and he became my next lover. Klaus had escaped through the Berlin wall, after having thrown a stick in the air which pointed toward the flag when it landed on the floor. This put him under suspicion and he had to escape with only his swimsuit and a towel strapped to his bicycle, so that if asked where he was going, he could answer, "Swimming." We told each other a lot about our lives and had a good time for several weeks until suddenly, Emil showed up.

Somehow, he had found out where I was. I could not resist him, even though I tried to and we made hot passionate love again. Klaus was disappointed. He could not understand that I would fall for, 'This gorilla in leather', as he called Emil. I hoped that Emil would stay with me but after a while, he left me lonely and hurt again.

I drove around Elba and sketched a lot to keep my mind off of him. I found a wonderful place called Marciana dell Enfola and parked there. In front of me, I could see the peninsula Enfola and the sea was on both sides of my van. It was magic. I climbed to the top of the mountain on Enfola , where I enjoyed a breathtaking view. This area was uninhabited and so Zora and I felt free to pick fruit that tasted like strawberries off the bushes. We found many other interesting plants. I was sad that I could not share it with a man I loved.

Klaus could not walk without pain since his hips hurt him too much. We stayed friends but had become more distant by then. I still loved him but was not in love. Emil was in my head. I asked myself, why I was in love with a man who did not feel the same about me? I started to doubt myself .

When I saw a man who turned me on, I would look the other way, so that he had no chance to turn me down. I could not handle the thought of accepting another man, who would leave me again. Loneliness drove me nearly mad. I could only be alone if I chose to be by myself. Otherwise, I had to go out in the hope of finding a partner again and had a tendency to get drunk, if I continued to drink after the third glass.

Men liked me and often my body insisted that I had another and another drink with them. I met some friends. Francesco was the one who suggested that we all ate together, one bringing the fish, or chicken or meat, the other bringing the bread, the next the wine or cheese and so on. We all ate very well for minimum cost this way . Francesco let us use his kitchen and dining terrace overlooking Porto Ferraio and his romantic garden. After a while, I got homesick for my daughters and drove back to Switzerland. Elba was so beautiful that I returned there a few more times later.

Moosburg

I did not want to be a burden on my parents so I chose to go and look for a place where I could park my van in peace. My father had just bought a painting from me and insisted on paying for it, even though I would have been happy to give it to him as a present. It had to be a place near enough so I could visit them and my daughters. Usually, I went to see them every Sunday and my mother looked forward to cooking everything I liked best.

Lakes had a magic attraction to me, so I drove to Güttingen where there was a shower in the port and parked nearby. I walked to a beautiful old garden restaurant where I ate fish with condiments from the Lake of Konstanz. Then I went to sleep in the van. In the morning I made a coffee and went to drink it on a bench outside.

Three men walked up to me and asked if I had slept in the car. I said, "Yes", and they wanted to know why. I answered "Because it is my home." "Why don't you want a flat?" one of them asked. "Because I am an artist and don't have any work", I stumbled. He suggested that I should go to Moosburg and ask the owner Mr. Greff, if he had a place for me and that he would not charge much.

I thought, "Not much," could be too much for me but curiosity got the better of me and so I followed the man's directions and drove there, about 1 km. I was overwhelmed by the beauty, charm and romance of this ancient château and farm estate, located right on the lake with its own sandy beach and surrounded by gorgeous trees. Two peacocks greeted me. The male had a high screechy voice and the female a deep squawky one. Several old houses and barns stood as part of the landscape in the wooded area and birdsong enchanted my ears.

Zora immediately liked the place as well. She loved to smell all the different herbs dogs need to eat for vitamins. She ate a bit of sage, mint and other herbs. When she wanted to empty her stomach, she swallowed grass.

Dogs who live in the city, miss out on herbs and should be taken to the country or woods to catch up on what they need. Remember that if you keep your dog healthy and happy, you will feel better and in form as well.

My van was parked in front of the château and I was standing at the door ringing the bell. Mrs. Greff answered the door and when I introduced myself and told her that I was an artist who looked for a place to live and paint, she led me up the staircase into a large living room where her husband was sitting. Mr. Greff was happy to see me and got to his feet reaching out his hand to me. I was asked to sit down and if I would like a cup of tea. Mrs. Greff went to make the tea and I told Mr. Greff why I had come to see him.

He said, "What I have to offer to you is really too primitive. I told him I needed no luxury- just a roof over my head to paint under. He then took me across the gardens to an old house and showed me the upstairs of a barn. It had water, electricity, a toilet and three empty rooms, one of them overlooking the gardens, the château, fields and woods. The other rooms had a view to the fields with a small house that a couple was renting. The third room would make my bedroom. The second my studio and the first the kitchen.

Mr. Greff let me rent it from him for a song. I was over the moon and paid him two months in advance without a contract so we were both free. He could throw me out and I could leave any time I liked. I parked the car next to the barn and took the broom, dustpan, sponges, soap and a basin up to my new place and cleaned it spotlessly. I just left the spiders and their webs since they fascinate me. Spiders also catch flies, which suits me well.

Then Zora and I went to town and bought a bottle of gas and a table top cooker with two burners. There was a sink but nothing else in my new place so we made a visit to the second hand shop and bought a table, a chair and a mattress. The painting materials, sewing machine, pots, pans, cutlery and what else I needed came out of the van.

Then Zora and I inspected our new environment, went swimming and walked to the next town all along the front of the lake. Across the lake one could see Germany and toward Austria. Often, there were bright cumulus clouds gracing the magic blue sky.

When it was Sunday and time to go and see my daughters and parents, they were happy to hear the news of my place. They all came to visit and found my flat a bit primitive but loved the surroundings. My best friends Willy and Beth came to see me as well and bought a painting from me.

Things were going well for me but I was lonely for Emil and missed him very much. I was sure he would like this place and would be happy there since he loved nature. My pride would not let me ask him back since he had left me in Elba.

I met the six young people who had rented a house. Their commune was just to the left of the house that I lived in. They invited me to a delicious health food dinner. Then, they wanted me to drive them to where they wanted to go but I told them that I was not a taxi. They respected that and we became friends.

Five of them owned a sailing boat, which was tied to a buoy out on the lake and asked me to become the 6th part owner. They managed to talk me into it, so I paid a 6th share of the boat. It was not an especially pretty one but it looked like fun anyway. The trouble was, that everybody wanted to sail on an ideal, sunny day but no one was tidying up behind themselves. I cleaned it up on the condition that everyone would take their rubbish back to shore and would leave the boat the way it was, before they came on board. They agreed but no one cared enough.

When I wanted to go sailing, I found sticky lunch wrappers, used paper napkins, empty bottles and beer cans, full ashtrays and other muck scattered around the boat and on top of the bunk. The cockpit was full of wet clothing and the sail was not fastened correctly. I was disgusted and fed up, left the boat with the mess and went back and told them I wanted to get out of being a part owner.

They said, "We can't let you do that since we don't have the money to give back to you." I answered, "I don't care about the money, I just want to be relieved of the responsibility, since your lot doesn't seem to give a hoot about the boat or the responsibility it requires.

Sailing in a neglected boat can be life-threatening. Sailing in lakes can be more dangerous than at sea when a storm comes by surprise. At least the sea gives you the possibility of getting away from land and avoiding running aground.

I decided to build my own dinghy. I went to hunt in the trash bins of the industrial center for materials and found two very thick, and long pieces of polystyrene. I cut it with a bread knife into the shape I wanted and cut a rectangle 3/4 deep into the 50 cm thick material to make the cockpit. Then I wrapped the whole thing in sticky plastic foil before covering it all with plywood and painting it. I made the frame from the wood taken from an old closet. The sides were reinforced with metal to support the rowlocks that held the oars. On the stern, I attached a metal ring for the rope. On the bottom, I screwed on three strips of wood as keels, then I went to try it out. It behaved well and was easy to row. I could sit on the, about 30 cm wide, rim with my feet either in the cockpit or stretched out in the bow space. Two people could sit on it. I was very happy to row with Zora along the shore to the restaurant in Güttingen. There, I celebrated by drinking a glass of champagne, instead of wasting it by throwing it over my new dinghy when it was launched. The weather was a perfect and beautiful with a light wind and we rowed back to Moosburg. I don't believe it would row well in hard weather but preferred to go out when it was mild anyway.

My neighbors from the commune stared at my new dinghy and one of the men said, "I bet it will not hold two people." I answered, "Yes it will." He said, "If it will, I will invite you to dinner." He and his best friend went out to the lake in it and tried to capsize my small boat without success and invited me for dinner at my favorite restaurant on the lake. Unfortunately, someone sabotaged it and it took me many hours to repair it. Then it was smashed by force by some sick person in such violence, that it was unrepairable. I was heartbroken and I don't understand why anyone gets a kick out of destroying someone else's property.

A Great Gift. Back with Emil

The farmer from down the road came to see me and asked me to follow him him to the beach where he wanted to show me something. I went with him and he pointed to a 6 1/2 meter long, beautiful fin-keeler, open yacht and said, "She is all yours." I couldn't believe that I had heard him right and asked, "Why would you want to give me this beautiful sailing boat?" He replied, "Because I need the room and if you don't want it, I will burn it." Gratefully, I accepted this wonderful present and was delighted.

The boat was an elegant, streamlined, Italian design out of fiberglass with air chambers all around and a water tight compartment at the stern. It had one mast with stainless steel rigging and a sail. Even ropes came with it. Everything was in excellent condition. Only the box around the keel had a small leak on one side. This did not worry me, since the fiberglass factory was not far away. I bought some fiberglass, resin and hardener then went back to repair the small damage by putting on four layers. I let it dry in the hot sun and the next day, I pushed it into the water and enjoyed sailing.

She sailed like a dream. I felt so lucky. The farmer and I became good friends. He was a very handsome man but had a family. I can say with pride, that never in my life have I ever split up a couple or destroyed a marriage.

Moosburg made me bloom up again. I was living in my dream environment. Painting came easy. In the evenings, I got very lonely and longed to be in a man's arms. Going out, I would meet someone from time to time but he was usually not enough of a man for me to fall in love with. Sometimes my hormones made me believe I was in love again, until the next day and then I came home more lonely than when I went out.

People liked me and I made some new friends. Emil was still in my head and under my skin. I longed to be in his arms again but also wished to forget him, but no matter how I tried, this feeling for him was stronger than I.

On my 46th birthday, my best friends Willy and Beth came to see me in their old-timer Peugeot convertible. This car was a thing of real beauty, built on a strong steel chassis with swinging curves over the very large, round headlights to the sides of the chromed cooler, running boards under the doors and original buttoned leather upholstery. It had wooden spokes (if I remember correctly) and white rimmed wheels. The top was folded down on the back. My friends gave me a ride in it. They brought me a huge bouquet of red roses in a handmade Murano vase.

Then they invited my other six friends from the commune and I, to a posh dinner in the best restaurant of the area. We ate the best gourmet delicacies and tasted the finest wines for four hours and had a great time. Then Willy and Beth Epper drove me home and bought one of my erotic paintings for their collection of original Maya B. s.

On the following Sunday, my birthday was celebrated again in Wil with the family. It was always good to see my daughters and parents. My daughters planned to go and travel in China together, where Alexa intended to continue her Mandarin studies. Both my daughters had developed into beautiful, fine boned, intelligent and charming young ladies who filled me with pride.

After the next Sunday dinner at my parent's home, I broke down and went to the pub, in the hope of seeing Emil again. He was there with his friends and came right up to me. Then he ordered some drinks for us. It was obvious that he had missed me as much as I had missed him, and his friends were pleased for us. When I asked him if the bit about, "Being old and past it", had been his mother's and her boyfriend's idea (because I was older then him and had my tubes tied, which made me unable to produce a grandchild for her), he said, "Yes."

Now I was able to forgive him and we could move on together. He followed me with his van and loved Moosburg so much, that he offered to pay the rent. I accepted him back. We were deliriously happy to be together again.

Emil's many male friends came to visit us and they all loved Moosburg so much that they returned too often and I resented not having Emil to myself. They brought booze with them, and that caused Emil to have crises again. I tried not to keep wine in the house and kept drinking as a strictly social thing. For my self-protection, I never kept any alcohol in the place I called my home, unless there was invited company.

Relationship With Emil. Kuddi with Aids. Joe Cocker.

The relationship with Emil was very happy for a short time and otherwise miserable and lonely. We could not live with each other or apart. Both of us suffered to the point, where we had to replace each other with love affairs that did not last because what we really needed, was each other. We were anchored in each others' heads and were both very hard-headed, to the point that made it impossible to make compromises. This stubbornness drove us apart. The longing to melt into each other's arms again, drove us back together.

Alone again, nothing made sense to me. However, the responsibility to my daughters, parents and my dog Zora kept me from committing suicide, even during the worst of my depressions.

Mr. Greff, the owner of Moosburg, came to visit. He said that he had thrown the people from the beautiful, large apartment next to mine out, when he found out that they were addicted to heroin. He asked me if I would like to move into the much better place. When I asked him how much the rent was there and he told me a higher price, I said that I could not afford it. However, Emil stated, "But I can," and so we moved into the better place.

The people who had lived there before had taken off all the layers of paint from all the beautiful old wooden doors and window frames. It had been turned into a real bijou just a few steps from the lake. Emil and I lovingly furnished the apartment with antiques from the second hand shop. The lake was just wonderful and we had a really good time. This time, our relationship lasted longer, maybe because we were doing everything together without interference from anyone. Then it went downhill again, into the big, sad, repetitive loneliness. I lived in the hope that Emil would come back to me.

The people from the commune invited me for a beautiful dinner prepared fresh from their garden. They told me that they would soon be seven people since they planned to take in a young man called "Kuddi", who was suffering from AIDS. They asked if I would help take care of him. I said "No, I am not a nurse and I need to paint, which I can't do unless I feel free." Also, I hoped to find a partner again which was essential to my life.

The commune people then asked, "Could you just drive him to the doctor in an emergency if we should all be at work?" I said, "Okay." Kuddi arrived in a really sorry state. He looked terrible. His skin was all broken out with rashes. His lips were swollen and dripping. He could only take little unsure steps and his shaking hands could barely lift the constant supply of beer and cigarettes in front of him up to his puffed lips. His long thin blond hair was hanging limply without shine. Kuddi's eyes were red and sad. He told me with a clouded voice, that he had been infected by aids while using a dirty needle during his addiction to heroin.

One day, Kuddi limped over to my place and paid me a visit. He was cursing with the pain. I opened a beer for him and one for me. He used my toilet, washed his hands and dried them. I put on rubber gloves and cleaned the toilet and hung up a fresh towel. Kuddi felt insulted and cursed. I said, "Sorry about your feelings being hurt but I certainly don't ever want to suffer the way you do or risk my other guests catching this terrible AIDS disease." Kuddi understood but was bitter about having to die so young.

He came to see me several times. Often, he was left alone and called me if he needed help. Sometimes I asked him to join me for a drink in a pub, which he always loved to do. I could only take him to rough places, since he insulted all the waitresses by telling them, "I want to fuck you up the ass." When the waitress was shocked, I told her not to take any notice, since Kuddi was mortally ill and only said that out of bitterness at having to die young. The waitresses came to know him and did not worry anymore about his crude remarks.

Half the people from the commune did not have a vehicle at their disposal, since the other half with the cars were not there. They had tickets to the Nina Hagen concert in Konstanz. They invited me to go to the concert with them, if I took them there in my Renault Estafette. I drove them there and Nina Hagen had her speakers turned up so high, that my ears hurt.

To my great surprise, Joe Cocker appeared in the second concert. He is one of my very favorite singers and I felt very privileged to be at his concert which was like balsam to my ears. At no one else's concerts did I go up to the front of the stage as I did at his. It really pulled me closer to the man with that sensual and passionate voice. Joe Cocker could not see me because of the spotlights but he took steps toward me as if he felt my presence.

One of the men living in the commune, and I, had ear damage from Nina Hagen's concert. 'Rolli' was treated with vitamin injections at the hospital of St. Gallen for eight days, while I did nothing about it. We both suffered with high pitched whistling in the ears for a whole year after the concert.

Signatures against Cruelty. Fight To Keep Moosburg. Zora's Puppies.

It was the year of the Olympics in Korea and when I heard that the Koreans torture dogs so they will taste better to eat and saw the photos, I was so horrified that I collected, single handedly, over 1000 signatures to stop the Olympics unless the cruelty and eating of dogs was stopped immediately. Many other animal friends also collected signatures.

I promised Zora that she could have puppies once. She got pregnant by the beautiful Bless from Güttingen who had been her best friend since we arrived there.

The real estate investors got wind of Moosburg and made such a high offer to buy Moosburg, that Mr. Greff agreed to sell it to them. They were going to destroy this beautiful place and build a housing estate with over 200 houses, dig canals from the lake of Konstanz to the houses for the stationing of private boats, build restaurants and a shopping center. This would be a terrible shame and another beautiful old historical place lost to speculation and greed, not to speak of the gorgeous park with rare mature trees, the woods and fields plus the rich life of nature being destroyed by that brutal action.

I felt like fighting for my dream territory and visited the mayor. He asked, "Do you have money?" When I said "No," he replied that there was nothing he could do and claimed that I had not paid the 35SFR dog tax. I informed him that my mother had paid it in Wil, so that he would not charge me again. Then I visited every restaurant and bar and spoke to all the people about how awful it would be to lose Moosburg and its rich natural life, to those greedy men with their ugly plans. When I made it clear to them that they would lose out on business and have nothing to benefit from, they all agreed with me and wanted to keep Moosburg as their recreation area.

One day, I walked outside and saw with horror, that they had cut some healthy mature nut trees down. They used to be essential for the squirrels, birds, insects and humans alike. The Greff's were on vacation and some gypsies showed up. They were badly in need of a place to stay. I told them that they could stay if they would leave before two weeks when the Greffs were expected to be back. They gratefully agreed. No one ever found out that they had been there and they left the place immaculately clean.

Emil came back. For a while we were deliriously happy and

enjoyed every minute of it. Some refugees came to our door and begged us to hide them. They were totally exhausted and in desperate need of resting up before moving on. I showed them a caravan standing in a barn and told them that they would be safe there. I brought them food. After two days, they went on their way again.

By doing away with borders, so much suffering and fear could be eliminated. It would be great if all creatures could share the planet in freedom. Egotistical regulations created by greedy, mentally-ill men of law, politicians and phony religious leaders threaten the survival of all species and the human race on this planet. It is high time that every sane human alive is allowed to take their own responsibility seriously.

Zora gave birth to five healthy puppies. Emil gave me a hard time and complained about each puppy being born after the first one. I shouted at him to leave but he refused. I told him that Zora needed peace. I fed her some lukewarm milk during her labor. Emil was jealous of the puppies and I pushed him away from the scene with all my force and threw him out of the apartment. I was amazed of my sudden strength against the 11 year-younger and very tall, muscular Emil. My responsibility was to keep Zora and the puppies safe.

Emil could come back when he had calmed down. He did come back and calmed down. His friends came to visit us. Emil and his male friends went to the beach at night and did not want me to go along. I had suspected that he was bisexual but did not want to admit it. This time, I went to spy on them, which is against my nature but verified my suspicions. He could have saved me so much grief by telling me the truth. This would have permitted me to make up my mind whether to accept the situation or not.

Since I am 100 % heterosexual I knew that it would not have worked out, since I don't like to share my panties or the man I am with. This time, I well and truly had my nose full. His friends had gone and so I asked him to leave for good. He attacked me and said, "I am going to kill you." I just managed to put the puppies into a basket, grab it and run to my van with Zora following. I got all dogs into the car and drove straight to the police who refused to help me.

I slept in the van and went again to the police, to ask them if they would accompany me to the Moosburg where I wanted to remove my paintings, my colors and some clothes. They refused again and so I asked for a court order to have Emil thrown out.

In the meantime, I lived in the van and visited my parents and daughters until Emil was out. Then I returned.

All the people who had wanted to take a puppy while Zora was pregnant had chickened out, except the musician who took over my former apartment. The Greff's grandchildren played with the puppies who were enjoying the outdoors. Mr. Greff came out of his manor steam-raving-mad and yelled, "You have betrayed me, by not asking me if your dog could have puppies." I told him, "It is my responsibility not yours."

The puppies were two months old and I soon found places for all of them. Zora was glad, since it had been hard work for her. She often played with her puppy who was with the musician.

After my art exhibition in Wil, when I picked up the unsold paintings, I noticed that two of them had been cut with a razor blade right across the canvas and found out that Emil had done it. That was the absolute end of our relationship.

It was my birthday and I heard the musician's puppy scream. The people from the commune, the musician and I all ran out of our places toward the puppy. It looked as if someone drove over it. We took it to the vet who saw that its back was broken at two places and suggested we have it put to sleep. We all had tears in our eyes. 'Carlos' was such an adorable puppy dog. Just when the puppy died, a huge storm built up and blew mature trees to the ground. They all pointed with their tops toward Greff's manor house.

After thinking about everything, I decided it would be best to take Zora to the vet to have her tubes tied. I did not want her to be neutered. At least this way, she could still have safe fun.

A woman called me and made a date to come and see me for advice on how to improve her newly painted still life. We made a date for the afternoon. I was menstruating and, since I did not want to block up the drains, I wrapped the used sanitary napkin up in newspaper and threw it into the waste paper basket in the bathroom. The woman showed up with the painting. She looked very sophisticated. I asked her to sit down, while I brewed a coffee for us. Then I sat down with her and we started to discuss what she could do to improve her work.

Zora unwrapped the sanitary napkin and brought it onto the living room carpet. She started to eat the bloody part out of it. When I saw this I went, embarrassed, up to her and tried to take it away. She growled at me. She defended it and the woman did not know what to do or where to look until I broke down in laughter. We laughed together while Zora devoured her find. The woman said she could not remember when she had such a good time. She paid me for my advice and left.

I needed to go away from Moosburg, so I went to Wil and said goodbye to my loved ones before heading for Italy with Zora to protect me.

Cinque Terre, Italy. Fire at Moosburg.

I lived and enjoyed the moments again, driving toward Italy with Zora. Italy had always attracted me. There was so much I wanted to see. For the first time, I headed along the coast and over the mountain toward the Cinque Terre which my father liked so much when he visited. At that time, they could only be accessed by boat. Since then, a road had been built that led from Monte Rosso to Corniglia and Vernazza.

Between the wild, high cliffs that reached out to the sea were five bays with sandy beaches framed by fishermen's houses with mountains behind them. It was so pure and there were no tourists. The road was steep but the ancient colorful houses on the cliff presented a romantic sight and the view was absolutely breathtaking. I watched the spectacular sunset and then went to a small fish restaurant, where I ate mouth-watering food with excellent wine for a reasonable price.

The Italians are easy to have contact with and so a lot of laughter followed with dessert. Zora and I slept well in the van and we watched the pastel cultured sunrise with fascination. The huge cacti, aloes and other subtropical plants formed an impressive foreground to the sunrise. Birds were singing, cicadas chirped and insects hummed. Everything came alive. The clear blue of the sea and the sky formed a magic contrast to the black cliffs. I felt so lucky to be here and it made me realize how much I had missed the sea.

I was thinking of Peter and Scheherazade and was wondering how he was doing. I was also thinking of "Carlos" (I believe I met him in Porto Venere or a town more north). Carlos was over 80 years old and lived in a romantic old house which overlooked a smallish town. He had spotted me when I got up from sleeping in the van and invited me to his house for breakfast, lunch and dinner. What an intelligent and delightful man!

He was very tall and his handsome face was framed with silver hair. At his house stood several gorgeous models of ships made lovingly by Carlos himself and worked in every detail to a perfect quality. He used to lead a "contra band" when he was a young revolutionary and ended up in prison because of it. This also made him an honored hero in town. Everybody loved and respected him. It was in prison, that he taught himself the craft of miniature boat replica building. His ships were so beautiful that the museum bought all of them that he was willing to sell.

I was deep in thoughts while looking over the sea, until Zora wanted my attention so we both walked down to the beach. I loved the Cinque Terre. I stayed a few days until I called my parents and daughters.

Maya B.

My father told me of the terrible news, that the house in Moosburg with my apartment-studio had burned down. I drove straight back to Moosburg worried sick about all my paintings perhaps being destroyed. When I arrived, I found all my paintings and art materials saved in the barn next door. The firemen had rescued all my work. I was so relieved and happy. All my worries had been in vain.

The house looked a mess. I cleaned it up as well as I could and stretched a plastic sheet over the roof. At least, I still had some kind of roof over my head and a place to paint. The odor was awful and it smelled like coal, tar, ashes and moisture. There was no more electricity, just some cold water, no showers and no telephone. How quickly one can get used to all those luxuries!

Even so, it was better than sleeping in unlocked cars, climbing under the covers of boats, entering building sites and tying the hammock between poles plus having to be out early, before getting caught by construction workers, sleeping on the beach, in caves, in phone booths or under the bench of a bar.

I was determined to save Moosburg, especially after Martin, a reporter who lived in the commune, showed me photos he had taken of three explosions blowing out of the roof which had started the fire. (When I later asked him for a copy of those photos, he denied ever having taken them.)

I started to finish my latest painting on the ground floor, since it was dryer than my apartment. Greff walked over and said, "Leave this place, they want to break down the building." I said, "You sold it, it does not belong to you any longer, I am not leaving." Greff walked away. I continued to work on my painting. Suddenly, the wall cracked and a bulldozer was coming through. I grabbed my wet painting and my favorite sable brush and ran outside just in time, before the house collapsed behind me.

Those monsters would not have cared if I had been killed. Life does not mean anything to them. I hoped they would have to eat their dirty money.

You can do good things with money as well. I thought that if I had the chance in the future to help nature survive, I would do it with pleasure. I now have the chance to describe in a later chapter, how I will continue to do so.

I left my dream place, Moosburg, and went home to my daughters and parents, stored all my paintings in their attic and rested a few days before planning the next voyage of my life.

My father said, "Maya, ask for an invalidity pension, which is designed to help people like you. I cannot die in peace unless I know that you have enough to live on." I replied, "Papi, I don't want you to die and I know that you mean well, but I am not disabled." He said, "But you often have bad depression which is a handicap, please do it for me." I could not deny my father anything and gave up my pride to ask for a disability pension.

They sent me from bureau to bureau, until I got angry and demanded a date with the director. I got a date but the chief never showed. I insisted to get another date and got one. This time, he showed up but did not excuse himself for not missing the first meeting. I was treated like an outcast, which caused me more depressions. Then the bureaucrat wrote something down and said, "We will see what we can do." He wanted all sorts of information and I told him that I lived in my van and it was very hard to find a place to park that was not forbidden to stay for more than a few hours and planned to go out of Switzerland on a study trip, but would keep in touch with my parents who would give me all messages and forward all mail to me. The man promised to let me know of news but said it would take a while.

When I told my father, he was relieved to hear that I had applied. I decided to go to the island of Elba, since it was only a 1 1/2 day drive away from my parents, who by then had become frail. My daughters were independent. I had friends on Elba, where my parents could reach me and I would call them every Saturday at 6 pm. Before I got into the van, my father shook my hand, leaving some large Swiss Franc notes in my palm. My mother also handed me some money.

Adventures at Elba

It was great being surrounded by Elba's beauty again. I drove straight to Porto Ferraio, where I parked my van in the harbor. Then I walked with Zora to Julio's bar, where my sailor friends were hanging out. Julio's Bar was called 'The little sailing club' by the sailors. Julio greeted me like a long lost friend and so did Klaus with whom I lived on his yacht- the beautiful 'Rose of Sharon', a few years ago. Many other friends were there as well. They all cheered me up but what I wanted, was to fall in love again. I needed to get over Emil.

This time, I would go into a relationship with my head, not with my emotions. I met a lonely artist in Julio's who started a conversation with me. He was in worse state financially than I and did not own a van to sleep in. I felt pity for him and when I got to know him better, I invited him to live with me in my van. Surely one artist would understand another. Zora liked him as well.

We sketched together and were invited quite often since the Italians love individualists and artists. My friends accepted him but he felt as if he was in my shade. Everywhere my friends treated me like the dominant one. Once we were invited to join some people at a night club. My new boyfriend hated to dance. Having studied ballet, I loved and needed to dance. When a man asked me to join him on the dance floor, I accepted even though my companion forbade me to dance. No one is going to forbid me anything. I had fought for too long to be free to start obeying the one I took in because he had nowhere to go or anyone else to go to.

My dance partner and I danced so wildly with pleasure, that the audience cheered us on for more. When I got back to my artist friend, he hit me right in the face. I told him, loud and clear, to get his bag and piss off and leave me alone for good. Then I pulled my leather belt with the big buckle out of the pants loops to defend myself against him if he tried to step toward me again.

He did come near me and I held the belt ready to hit him. However, a German tourist saw it and unexpectedly ripped the belt out of my hand. In doing so, the hook of the buckle ripped the inside of my index finger and palm of my hand so deeply, that the artery pulsated the blood out of the wound. My hand had to be put in a tourniquet. It was 2 a.m., when I was driven in a hurry to the hospital.

One of the doctors was on duty but three surgeons were called out of bed. All four doctors operated on my hand, while the nurses handed them the instruments. They used micro surgery to stitch the artery, veins and nerves back together for 4 1/2 hours. When they finished the operation with success, the one in charge of billing asked, "What do you do for a living?" I said, "I am an artist." He replied, "In that case you don't pay anything." He gave me some painkillers, bandages and cream, all for free.

Fortunately, I never saw the aggressor ever again. I found out that pity is not a base for a relationship.

Alone again, I had my friends. Francesco came from Switzerland and owned an, about 20 meter-long, oldtimer, wooden, motor sailing, fishing boat called 'Nikito.' Francesco was a positive-thinking hedonist with beautiful sparkling eyes and his gorgeous face was framed with dark, shiny, curly hair. He loved to drink, smoke, laugh and eat. Everybody loved him. I admired him as well, but he was married and had a family so we stayed simply friends. His wife did not share his love for boats and lived in Switzerland. He asked me if I would park my van next to his boat and live on board to watch it, since he had to go back to be operated on.

I jumped at the chance to be on board a ship again and was flattered by the confidence and trust Francesco gave me with this big responsibility. I said, "I would love to watch 'Nikito' but if my parents should need me, I have to go back." He said, "You watch it as long as you can and if I should not be back, I will arrange that a friend of mine will take over if you cannot watch it any longer. You can invite whoever you trust, as long as the boat stays clean." We had a drink on his boat and he showed me where everything was. Then he introduced me to his friend who would take the boat watch over if I had to go.

Zora liked 'Nikito'. I asked Francesco what kind of operation he needed and he told me with a cigarette in his hand, that years of smoking had damaged his veins and they had to be replaced in the front side of his throat. I felt so sorry for him and hoped that this operation would be a success. I knew that it would be a big risk but hoped he would be lucky.

Life on 'Nikito' was great. My old friend Alberto and other friends came on board with food every day. We cooked fish, steaks etc. on the grill which was on board and drank wine. They all helped to clean the boat and kept it immaculate. For about three weeks I enjoyed watching 'Nikito', then my mother called Julio at the little yacht club and left the message to call her back. I did and found out that my father was in the hospital and being operated on. I told Francesco's friend about it and he immediately took over the watch.

I caught the next ferry boat to Piombino and drove back to my home town and to the hospital in one go. When I arrived, I found both parents in the same room. My father with a prostate operation behind him and my mother bandaged up with a broken skull. Somehow, while out walking the dog, she had fallen and hit her head, which landed her in the hospital with a concussion. I visited for a while but both were tired, so I went home and rested from the long drive and went to visit them the next day. I found my mother alone in the room. She said, that they had taken "Papi" to the hospital in St. Gallen since he had complications and had to be operated on again. I stayed with my mother a while and then raced 30km to my father's bedside. My father, as a typical doctor, had waited too long for the small operation to be successful and had to go through the big operation.

I visited both parents each day. My mother got fed up with staying in the hospital and begged me to take her home. I spoke with the doctor who said, "You can take her home if you take the responsibility of seeing that she lies quiet and lets you help her. Otherwise, she will have headaches for a long time." I made my mother promise to lay still and took her home.

My mother was very headstrong and took the clothes pins out of my hand when I hung up the wash. She wanted to do it. I told her she should lie down but she had the harder head than I. I picked up my father from St. Gallen and stayed in Switzerland until both parents felt fit again.

When they felt better, I went out to my favorite pub to spend a little time with my friends in the evenings. I met a young man called Pius who was in a dilemma. He just had been released from the psychiatric hospital without money and nowhere to go to. It was bitterly cold outside and everybody was afraid of him, since he had been in the psychiatric hospital for two years. No one was willing to help him. I asked him why he was in that institution and he replied that he did not know why, except that his parents had insisted on it.

Then I wanted to know how he felt about his parents. He informed me that his mother had been in a German concentration camp and still had many problems because of it and that his parents had never loved or wanted him. He was very upset, sad and frightened. I ordered a round of beer and calmed him down by assuring him that he could sleep in my van overnight since I could stay at my parents house.

I spoke to my parents about Pius and we all were disgusted that Switzerland and other countries did not look after prisoners fresh out of jail or patients out of the psychiatric clinics. On top of it all, most people are afraid of them and it is hard for them to find jobs or rooms. I went out with Pius every evening and since we were both lonely we found comfort in each other's embrace.

Pius had told me of his voyages to India and that he had a big urge to go there again. He told me that in Aadorf TG, the bureaucrats were holding back his invalidity pension which was supposed to be paid to him each month. This I believed right away, especially since I had not heard from them in my case either. I took him to Aadorf and demanded to speak with the director. When I asked him why Pius had not been paid out, he whined, "He would only spend it outside Switzerland."

I said, "It is not your business to tell him where he can spend it. It is your job to see that everyone the court has awarded it to, will be paid out on time. These people depend on it for their hard survival and where Pius is concerned, in India he would be accepted more easily than here. Anyway, I will go with him." "Are you taking the responsibility for him?" he asked. "They would not have released him if he could not take the responsibility for himself, but I will be there to help him if he needs it," I replied.

Pius was paid out and gave his bank number in India to him so he could send the monthly payments there. I told my parents of the plans to go to India and parked my van in my uncle's garage parking lot. I sold the pharmaceutical bottle collection my father had given to me, to Zora's vet for SFr.3000. This allowed me to pay for a return air ticket to Bombay - Goa and have some spending money. By the time we had the visa and the ticket, four weeks had passed. Pius and I got along just well.

My parents insisted that I leave Zora with them. They loved her very much and my mother liked to walk with her three times a day. She explained that this would keep her fit. I missed Zora but knew she was in good hands. Pius had some problems but I believed that with love, I could cure him. In late Fall, 1990, Pius and I took a flight to Bombay. (Mumbai)

Bombay "Mumbai", India. Goa.

Glad to be able to stretch our limbs again, we got out of the crowded plane and were surprised by the incredible sunrise. It was gorgeous and Bombay was starting to wake up. We took a taxi and noticed a whole string of people defecating on the sides of the street while chatting to each other. This was the first time I had been confronted with such a scene. It did not shock me but brought a smile to my face. The closer we got toward the town center the denser the population became. It was a very hot day and smelled of urine, dust, food, exhaust fumes and incense.

When we got out of the taxi, beggars started to hustle us. If I had given each beggar something, I would have been broke in next to no time. Amongst the dense crowd of people were meditating Yogis, Hindu and Buddhist priests, women dressed in glittering saris, travelers and people from all parts of the world, business people, hustlers and other folks. It looked really colorful. The shopkeepers would try to get you to come into their shops. The shop windows were crowded with unusual and usual things. People with stands on the sidewalks offered many different wares for sale.

Pius suggested that we check into the hotel, where he lodged during his previous journey to India. It was right in the center of Bombay on a street with so many unique shops. Pius was tired so we entered a tall house with the 'so called' hotel on top. Homeless people were sleeping on the steps. Betel nut juice was spat on the walls of the staircase and ran down them. A junkie injected himself with heroin. I felt as if I had landed right in the bowels of Bombay.

The heat was almost unbearable. All I wanted, was to take a shower and explore the city. When we entered the shady looking hotel, I asked, "Does the room come with a shower?" The man gave me an insulted look and said harshly, "Of course there is a shower right opposite your room." He showed us to a tiny room with a bed on each side of the tight walking space between them. It looked more like a closet than a room. One bed looked used, so I immediately laid on the other one and put my suitcase on the bottom part of the mattress so Pius would take the other bed. There was a big fan running just between and over our heads. It was supposed to be fastened to the ceiling with screws but two of them were missing, which made the fan turn oblong instead of round and threatened to decapitate us if it should drop off. Even so, we kept it running since the sweat was pouring off us.

Pius fell asleep and I went outside to find the shower. When I could not find it, I asked the man to lead me to it. He took me to a green painted, claustrophobic room where a water filled oil drum was standing and handed me an empty tin can. He filled it with the water from the oil drum and handed it to me, saying, " With this you can wash yourself." The floor was tiled and had a hole for the water to drain. The man went outside and I tried to cool off by pouring water over myself. Then I returned to the room.

Pius woke up and I asked him if he would like to go and eat some breakfast and explore Bombay. This room gave me claustrophobia. To my surprise, Pius started to psycho-torture me. In Switzerland, he had been so nice and a real gentleman. Now, he tried to imprison me in that horrible place. He certainly did not want me to go out on my own. He refused to get out of that awful room and threatened me with violence if I did not obey him. I could only outsmart him by pretending to like staying in and not caring to see Bombay either. This defused him enough to suggest a move into the outside world. My confidence in Pius was instantly gone but I felt it to be my responsibility to stay with him. I slept with my bag which contained my papers, money and other belongings under the pillow and never let it out of my sight. Outside the broken window of our room, there was bamboo scaffolding tied together with string and fastened to the façade of the ancient and neglected house. It would have been a cinch for a thief to climb to the top and enter.

When we finally left the room to go and eat, I could hardly believe how low the prices were. Everything was at least 10 times less costly than in Switzerland. I found a bank and opened an account to deposit the money I wanted to keep safe. I kept some travelers checks with me for the rest of the stay. We entered a pub-restaurant where many travelers met and ate. We drank and enjoyed the conversation with people who had experienced travelling in interesting places around the globe. Soon, I made new friends and Pius pulled himself together again.

I bought some pieces of beautiful silk material and wore it like a pareo. It felt good, was light and was washed and dried in next to no time. I also invested in two beautiful Australian opals as a nest egg.

Pius became more tyrannical than I liked and I felt confined with him. He wanted to go to Goa and I went with him, since he claimed to not be able to live without me. Goa interested me as well, since it was the least populated part of India. We took a flight there and headed in a three wheeled taxi for Calangute, since Pius had a friend from Yugoslavia who owned a beach pub there with his wife from Switzerland.

When we arrived at the beach, I waited at the shed of a beach bar with our bags, while Pius went to Candolim beach to see if his friend was there. I was so overwhelmed by the beauty that surrounded me, that I could not hold back the tears of joy that heated my eyes. I had never seen so many intense colors. There was an acrobat in front of me, who was bent backwards with a trained cow standing with all four feet close together on his stomach, while he played a tune on his flute. Cows ate seaweed on the beach and Pakistani women offered their jewelry for sale. They wore colorful decorated clothes and carried their wares wrapped in a large towel on their heads. Children and relatives followed them and their husbands were never far away. The older women and children were carrying their belongings.

The sea was wonderful and I could hardly wait to swim in it but it would have been an invitation for thieves to take our bags. I did not have to wait long until Pius got back with his friends and we were invited to eat with them. Then we left the bags there, while we searched for a guest house and found one a few steps from the beach.

It was primitive but clean. The water was brought in a bucket filled from the well outside. We mostly ate breakfast, lunch and dinner out since it was so reasonable and smoked hashish or grass every day. Pius needed it and it calmed his nerves. An Indian man came up to us and begged us to have him give us a massage since he needed the money to feed his family. We accepted and from then on we often had a massage. The man was an expert and had strong hands.

A nasty looking guy came up to me and before I realized what happened he had stuck tweezers holding a tiny pebble of stone in my ear and said, "You have dirty ears. I will take it out if you pay me Rupees. I was so afraid he would drop it into my ear, that I did not dare to move my head and said okay. He took the tweezers with the pebble out and claimed to have found it inside of my ear but I paid him anyway and told him not to ever come near me again.

There were a whole swarm of ear cleaners on the beach that ripped off newcomers every day. I recognized them from afar and gave them such a look while waving them off that they did not dare to come any closer. Magicians, acrobats and snake men all tried to make a buck from the travelers. The tourists hardly came out of the posh hotel where they paid European prices and swam in the chlorinated pool. They felt safe there and ate from European menus. I was invited to a buffet dinner and was amazed at all the appetizing food laid out on many tables, but nothing looked typically Indian.

Pius could not swim and it was impossible for me to teach him since he could not get over his fear of the sea. After a lot of patience on my part, he dared to walk in less than knee deep water. I asked myself why I still desired this man who was so possessive and jealous.

When Pius did not desire me for too long and refused to go out with me but demanded that I to stay in the room with him, I escaped and went to a concert. I feel that I have the right to live the way I want to and that every moment of life that I don't do what I desire without hurting anyone is lost and never comes back again. At the concert, I met a man who I needed as much as he did me and so we got together and made wild passionate love. Then I had an attack of stupid guilt and went back to Pius who was happy to see me again.

But then, he had a crisis again and got worse and worse. We moved to another place near another beach more north and rented a small house. We went every morning to eat at the terraced restaurant and ordered coffee, orange juice, eggs, pancakes, fruit salad and yoghurt for a small price. One morning, when we went out for breakfast he had such a terrible crisis that the owners were afraid of him and put a tranquillizer into his orange juice. He heard voices and complained that people cursed and threatened him and got so furious when I could not hear the same voices. Nothing I did or said calmed him down. When we got back to the house he collapsed on the bed. Then he slept for two days.

I hung my hammock on the Banyan tree just in case I had to run for my life when he woke up. But that sleep did him the world of good and he woke up peaceful. There was no toilet in the house and we had to pick a tree to squat under and had to fend off the pigs who fight each other to eat the stools before they have a chance to drop on the lawn. There was no toilet paper, so we had to take a jug of well water with us to wash the anus. I never ate pork again in India.

I only took the money with me that I could spend in one day and put the rest that was not in travelers checks, into an empty jar and hid it in a hole in a stone wall, which I closed with a stone, closing the gaps with sand.

The police had a tendency to take handbags and search them for dope. If they found a piece of hashish, they would then take all the money and dope in your bag or threaten you with torture and jail if you refused to let them have it.

I learned a lot from Indian people about bush medicine and the Banyan tree, which eats everything with its roots in the ground and in the air. Nothing grows under the Banyan tree. Touching the tree gives strength and solves many problems. That is why it is called the holy tree. Since people from civilized countries are not used to the dirt, they often become ill with infections.

I could hardly sit because of two ulcers on the bottom of my rear end. When I visited a bush medicine man, he told me not to eat fish, meat, eggs, milk products or fat. And not to drink coffee, tea or alcohol. When I asked him what I could eat, he answered, "All the vegetables, fruit, rice and water that you want." I listened to him and got rid of the ulcers in less than two weeks and felt great.

Pius had another relapse and demanded that I stay with him. I did for a long time but then I had the urge to go to the beach for a swim. He threatened me and I escaped. Believing myself not to be followed, I looked back and saw him approach. I ran but he caught me in the narrow path behind the beach, while I was climbing over the sharp stones. He pushed me so hard, that I fell with the small of my back onto the sharp end of a rock, which caused a deep and painful wound. He felt kind of bad and led me back to the house, where I demanded that he washed the wound and poured iodine on it. Then I treated it with penicillin powder. It was hard not to go swimming before it healed. To this day, the small of my back still gives me problems sometimes.

We went to the interesting Mapusa Market together, visited different temples and walked along many beaches, where I swam while Pius relaxed on the beach. We ate in different restaurants and met people and new friends. I loved to play with the wild dogs and took food to them. They really needed feeding.

We met Indian friends outside a hut restaurant under a tall coconut tree. We sat with them. One of them was a father with a 12 year-old son. He wanted the son, who was afraid of heights, to climb the tree. I told him that it would be too dangerous but he insisted that the boy go up. I disagreed and we walked away. The next day, we found out that he had given the 12 year-old a drink of beer for courage and forced him to climb up. The boy fell down and died of a broken skull. His father was heartbroken to have lost his son because of his own damned stupidity.

India was a weird but sometimes wonderful place. It consisted of huge contrasts and we lived, mostly, entirely in the moment. The confrontation of life and death was an everyday thing. But some discoveries caused me to be in a state of shock. When I got over them, I had learned something. Some of the shocks still give me nightmares.

One time, as Pius and I walked from the Calangute beach to Anjuna. There was a horrible stench in the air and we saw a dead woman with the hair cut off from her head. Her cadaver was laying with its belly on a rock and the clothes were ripped. The back side was exposed in a pornographic looking position. Her body was covered with bruises and her ankles had been eaten by crabs. Never in my life had I seen a more violent, sad and disgusting sight. I found out that the dead woman was 22 years of age and had been murdered by her Indian husband and a gang of his mates because he found out that she had fallen in love with another man. This discovery not only sickened and shocked us but made us want to leave the area.

Pius wished to go to Arambol since he had never been there. This interested me as well. For the moment, we were getting on quite well. A fisherman asked if we would like to hire him and his Goa-built beautiful wooden boat to picnic on one of two tiny, uninhabited river islands toward Siolim. Pius was frightened since he could not swim and did not enjoy being stuck on the boat, even though he was wearing a life vest, but I felt privileged to be on this boat.

On many beaches stood traditional Indian, wooden boats that have not one nail or screw in the planks but were tied together through holes drilled into them for the coconut ropes to go through, which were then made watertight by being brushed with tar. The bows were often decorated. Many sailors wished to own a boat like that but it was forbidden to export them. They are used for fishing and pulled out of the sea, by rolling them up the beaches on tree trunks. As many as 20 men are needed, to haul a large boat up. Usually the people of the whole village came and helped. Then the fishermen or their wives sold the catch on the beach. Many of them were Catholics since their ancestors had come from Portugal.

I was heartbroken when my camera did not work anymore and went to Panjim to try and have it repaired. Electronic cameras were unknown in Goa and it was not possible to have it repaired. The only cameras which were not broken down, were the hand operated ones, since Goa's climate is moist. I wished to have an old Kodak or Leica but could not find one. Many people who had left their cameras unattended for just a moment, had them stolen.

There were so many motifs and interesting things I meant to capture through photography. My life with Pius was much too hectic for painting.

Arambol

Before we left for Arambol, I said goodbye to the two girls who carried the water from the well, washed our laundry, made our bed and cleaned the house. I paid them and gave them an extra tip since they really needed the money for their studies. They were really happy when I handed them all the clothes that I was tired of carrying with me, except for those that I needed and the ones my daughters had made for me while travelling in China.

Then we headed for Arambol. It was an interesting trip, through lush and tropical vegetation, coconut trees, beautiful beaches, interesting small villages, market towns, temples and rivers. We met all sorts of interesting and unique people. Sometimes it seemed as if the world had been transformed into antiquity. Roughly hand-built wagons with heavy loads were pulled by buffaloes with long and pointy horns. People worked the land with primitive tools.

When we arrived in Arambol, we sat at a table and relaxed in the outdoor restaurant and asked where we could rent a place to live in. A man told us to follow him. He took us to an old house that had a covered terrace with steps down to a private and fenced in garden. We liked the place and rented it for a song, with the condition that we would move out if the owner, (an artist from England) should came back. The house was large but had no water or electricity. We could take a shower at the well outside and get the water to drink and to use from the well. The cooker in the house consisted of a built-in table made out of stone. On top of it, was place for a wood fire with three large stones on which to sit the pot or pan. We used an oil lamp and candles to light up the place. It was very romantic.

We used the garden as a toilet and buried it under the compost or in the ground. It was so dry that the plants liked the urine. Since Pius and I loved nature, we took our showers in the garden with buckets of water and no soap. We rotated the showers amongst the trees and flowers in the garden and the colors started to turn from beige to green. Then we could watch how it all started to bloom in many shades of different colors. There were lizards and more birds arrived when I started to feed them. Butterflies and other insects displayed their beauty. The place started to liven up with the water.

We moved the bed onto the terrace so that we could watch life waking up. A large spider had built his web on the corner of the terrace. We could watch him over the foot of the bed. In the evening, we ate on the terrace and threw the leftovers under the bushes where birds and other living things could get what they wanted and leave some as fertilizer for the plants. Then Pius suddenly, and for no reason at all, had another attack of outrage and tried to wake me up by hitting me over the head with a wine bottle. I was half awake and managed to roll out of the way and the large spider attacked and stung Pius right into his back. He screamed and grabbed my bag.

I ran away and asked for help to retrieve my bag with all my important papers in it. The man who rented out the house got some of his friends and we all went back to the house. Pius had gone, and locked the door with a pad lock. He had also taken the key. The men went to get a crowbar and broke the lock. I entered but did not find my hand bag with my papers and realized that Pius had taken it. I went to the stone wall in the garden, where I had some money hidden in a jar and took it all out.

I was forced to wait for Pius to return because I needed the passport, return ticket and other things inside. I practiced karate in the garden and felt less fear of him. He returned at night but I had had an afternoon snooze on the beach and was alert to every move he made. He still did not hand me my hand bag and I opened some beers for us and drank mine very slowly while I waited until he went to bed drunk. Then I reached gently and slid my bag out from the side of the bed he was snoring on. It was nearly morning and I hurried to throw the things I needed into a cloth bag and escaped toward the jungle.

In the Jungle

A short walk out of Arambol there was a simple restaurant located almost like a swallow's nest on top of the cliff above the beach. My friends frequented there and I enjoyed a good breakfast before resting on the beautiful beach in company of friends. Behind the beach, stood several huts built from coconut wood and leaves where one could choose a variety of dishes cooked in a wok or cold for next to nothing.

A little further north, there was a gorgeous and sensuous place. A sand dune between a sweet water lake and the sea made it a very special and magic paradise. I could swim in the sea and have the salt water washed off my skin and hair while diving into the fresh water lake. On the north side of the lake, were the first home built shelters in the jungle surrounded by tropical plants. I followed the stream up from the lake to the jungle and found a place between two trees to string up the hammock.

The contents of my light cloth bag consisted of a hammock, a flash light, spare batteries, two silk pareos, iodine, tweezers, penicillin powder, a muslin blanket, a plastic bottle freshly filled with water from the stream and a pair of jeans. In my handbag I carried all my important papers, my wallet and private things.

I knew that I was safe from Pius since he feared water and the jungle. I met one of the men who lived in the shelter north of the lake. He asked if I would like to live in his hut since he was leaving. He showed me his half hut which was closed on three sides but open to the great view of the lake, sea and the cliff where sea eagles had their nests with young and monkeys lived.

The monkeys were chased by a dog every morning and did their elegant acrobatic exercises from tree to tree to escape but the next day they came back to enjoy this game again. Their size was a bit smaller then a human, they had grey bodies, white faces and black fur on their heads that made them look as if they were wearing caps. Their long and slender limbs and tails made them move with great agility. I loved to watch that spectacle every day while I was there. The eagles impressed me no end with their flying skills and when the young were flying I watched with amazement. Every night I could hear the frogs and watched the moon upside down with a bright star directly under it over the sea, accompanied by the sound of the waves on the shore.

I was glad to have the muslin blanket for the rather cool nights. In front of the hut was a paraffin cooker and a wok. Behind the hut, stood a jerry can with oil to fill the lamp hanging in a branch, as well as the cooker. There was also a bucket and the mattress was woven from coconut leaves like the hut, with a piece of plastic under it.

I was warned about the police coming, even into the entrance of the jungle, to annoy people and steal their money. When I was still living with Pius, I found out, that they have to pay a lot to become a member of the police and try to get that money back when in office. They steal money, hashish, marijuana, cocaine, and heroin for resale and throw the ones who do not possess money into jail and threaten to torture them, if friends or relatives do not pay a fortune to get them back out.

I met an Indian family at an illegal party (so called because the police did not know and could not cream off money) who were crouching around a fire. The party took place at night in a secluded place one had to walk up to. People from villages all around offered all sorts of food for sale while the music played. For added warmth, the dogs surrounded the family by laying next to the people when they were not looking for food amongst the stalls.

An older woman embraced her husband, who laid next to the fire. I heard her cry. Her husband was on the floor and did not move. I sat by the fire behind them and when I wanted to go up to her and find out if I could help her, the arm of the woman next to me stopped me. She got up and pulled me gently to the side and whispered in my ear, that the police had tortured the old man by hanging him from the ceiling by his hands, hitting him repeatedly with canes on the sole of his feet and had castrated him in front of the people who could no longer pay to get their relatives out of jail. A policeman told them, "If you don't pay, we will do that to your son."

I heard that they often take and force poor and innocent people from the street to do this disgusting thing, which is far worse and sick than someone maltreating their own body in desperation for drugs. I was even more afraid of cop brutality than I was of Pius, who in my opinion should not have been released from the psychiatric clinic. What I learned from living with him, was that no amount of love could cure that poor mentally-ill man who suffered from brain damage but was even so more intelligent than some people I have met, which also made him more dangerous. It is funny that so often psychopathic men can have power over women but can become life-threatening to themselves. The best thing is to show them no fear, defend yourself or run.

To avoid being confronted by the police, I penetrated deeper into the jungle. I followed the river upwards and had started to climb a cliff, when I saw a cobra sunning herself in the way of where I wanted to go. This forced me to go more to the right, where bushes made it harder to get through. While I was hustling out of a bush, giant ants attacked me. I pulled one of them off my back. While I did this, three others bit me as well. I climbed out of the bush as fast as I could and ripped them out of my flesh. Each one had taken a piece of my skin with them leaving four deep wounds in me. It hurt like mad.

A plant seemed to be calling me. I went over and picked it and rubbed it on my wounds. Instantly, the burning sensation was gone. I heard later, that some people let ants bite them on top of wounds and then separate the ants' heads from their bodies, to stitch the cut or wound. They leave the head in, until the wound is healed.

I continued to pull my body from stone to stone, up to the top and came to a clearing where there was a temple. I was totally alone. The view from there was wonderful and helped me to regain my orientation. I hoped to see the monkeys, since I had noticed that every morning they would head in this direction. They really appeared in the bushes surrounding the area and I managed to get close up to them, by pretending to be a monkey speaking monkey language with them and they were as curious of me as I was of them. Unfortunately, I had nothing to eat for myself or them and they left.

Suddenly, I became depressed because I could not share this beautiful place with anyone. I felt alone. I wished to be someone who could be alone without suffering. No matter how much I tried, I always lived in the hope of meeting a life partner again. I did some yoga relaxation exercises and then kept walking into the unknown until I was so tired, that after rolling myself into a fetal position under a tree, I fell into a deep sleep, without worrying about cobras, ants or anything else until the sun came up.

I headed north and downwards in the hope of finding something to eat from the sea. Just when I was starting to worry, two boys from the first village outside the jungle showed up and sold me some oranges and cake their mother had baked. It tasted wonderful. With new force, I entered the wilderness again and found a magnificent Banyan tree. Climbing up it gave me new energy and took the depressions away. I did not feel the urge to smoke in the forest. Heading north, I came out of the jungle onto agricultural land and into a village consisting of a few houses and some people and chickens.

The people were friendly and gentle but there were no pubs or shops so I went through the jungle with more confidence than before. I enjoyed watching birds, insects, butterflies, snakes, lizards and many species of plants I had not seen before. I ate moss and other plants but was looking forward to eating a meal back in civilization again.

After some time in the wilderness, I returned to my favorite place and went swimming in the sweet water lake and walked to the beach of Arambol to delight in a wok-cooked meal. Then I laid in the sun for a while and when I found out that Pius was not around any longer, I relaxed with friends.

I found a hut for rent near the last few houses before the jungle. There was no electricity in the village and people living there refused to accept free cookers as bribes for having electricity. They preferred to cook on a wood fire outside their homes. They had no desire to pay electricity bills. Surrounded by wilderness, the trees supplied them with plenty of dead wood for cooking.

The family had built their huts to earn an extra income and rented one out to me. It was empty so I headed to the next village with a shop and bought a mattress which was rolled up, while I carried it with the sweat pouring off me to my hut. The bucket, paraffin cooker, oil lamp, pot and broom followed on the next day. The daughters of the family accompanied me to help me carry all the stuff plus some food from the village, back to my hut. Below the houses was a river, which had to be crossed by walking about 1 km along the waterfront to a bridge, that we crossed before going the same distance to the small road which continued to the village.

When I came back from shopping and was inside my hut, a shy female wild dog came to the open door to beg for food. I gave her something and she just looked at it but did not eat. Then the male came out from under the bush and she let him eat it. I spoke gently to both of them and went to bring out more food. Then they both ate and became my friends. Every time I went somewhere, they would accompany me up to 1 1/2 km and when I got back they greeted me like a long lost friend. I did not want them to get too tame since that would only make them vulnerable and so I did not encourage them to come into my hut. Normally, wild dogs lived in a pack put those two were definitely a couple.

I liked living there, since I could enter the jungle just above the house and could come back and feel safe sleeping in my hut at night. It made me frustrated and lonely not to have a partner to share it all with. I went to pay the very reasonable rent in advance, in order not to lose the hut to someone else while I was away from it. I locked up my hut and hired a motor bike taxi to take me to the big river, where I took the ferry across to the bus which drove south to Calangute where I planned to call my parents and daughters.

While there, I looked up my friends who informed me that Pius had fallen in love with a young Swiss woman and was living with her. When I met her and warned her that she should be careful since he could get very violent from one second to the next, she replied that she did not care and wanted to make her own experiences. I felt sorry for her but there was nothing more I could do. I just hoped she would be fine.

When I was still living with Pius soon after we had come to Goa, I had never found out how he had found me when I escaped during his crises. Whenever he found me, he tried to beat me up. Once I managed to escape from him by swimming out to a small island and waiting there until he was gone. Another time, I picked up a heavy stone and threatened to smash his head in if he did not leave me alone. Another day, he found the guest house I stayed in and stole my money and the silk blouse I treasured, since it had been given to me by my daughters who had had it specially tailored for me while they were travelling together in China.

Now, I did not have to worry about Pius any longer, since he had fallen in love. Even so, I kept away from him and was very relieved that he was no longer my responsibility. I felt so light and happy again.

In Love with Punitan

I followed my instinct and it drew me to a restaurant which I remembered from the past. It had one enormous big table with all the guests sitting around it. The food was exceptional and the ambiance was great. There was an empty seat, so I sat down and ordered a plate with different seafood, lovingly garnished and a drink. The conversations that took place amongst all the guests was interesting, without any small talk and became more humorous and louder as time went on.

Amongst the guests, was a gorgeous tall man with beautiful

green eyes and curly dark hair. When his eyes met mine, I felt that magic feeling again that told me, that he would become my next deep love. I hoped that this time, it would last for life. We were the last guests to leave and he took me on his restored red Royal Enfield motorbike. I held onto him from behind and my skin tingled all over. He parked the bike and we sat in the moonlight on the beach where we got to know each other. He told me, that he had escaped from eastern Germany and had a sister there and no other family. He had moved on from there and landed in an Australian jail for surviving outside the law. After he was released, he had come to India where he was working for Bagwan.

They lived like one big happy family there, until everybody left after the great Guru died of mercury poisoning and Punitan came to Goa. He took me in his arms and told me that it was love at first sight, when he looked into my eyes. I went to live with him in his hotel. I did not worry about the hut I had rented, since I had paid for a month's rent in advance and we could go there later if it was not too primitive for him.

Punitan wanted to do some business with people he knew and he asked me to marry him. I was flattered by the offer but did not believe in needing the permission of the law to tell me it was okay to live together or make love or paying for the bureaucracy and so we did not mention marriage anymore but enjoyed every moment together in so called "sin." Anyway, I know from experience, that marriage does not guarantee happiness; but getting out of it requires a lot of patience, nerves and time.

Punitan didn't just help me to forget all my past lovers in my life but even Emil. He was so affectionate and passionate with a totally free spirit. I was walking on air. After having been together so happily for a while, we went to see friends of his who had invited us to their place. We all had some cocaine after dinner and the host invited us to sleep there overnight. Punitan did not want to spend the night there and when he stood up, he nearly lost his balance since we had all had more than enough to drink.

I was still in much better condition but he claimed to be able to ride the Enfield. When he just managed to start the motor and asked me to trust him and sit behind him, I had nothing to lose and sat on the back of his bike. He drove a few meters and we ended up in a sand heap. He picked up the bike and convinced me, that he was okay to drive and to sit back on it again. I did and we drove along the road, until I screamed at him in fear and made him stop to let me off.

I heard music coming from a restaurant and told him, I would fetch some food and Coca Cola to dilute the alcohol before driving again. He agreed and I thought that he would wait for me. I got what I wanted at the restaurant and hurried back to him. He was gone and my feelings were hurt. I went to a guest house and searched for him in the morning. When I came to his hotel, the room was locked and I asked for the key. It was still where the receptionist had put it. He stated, that Punitan had not been there since we last left together. I took the key and found the room untouched and empty.

Worry started to torture me. I asked where the nearest hospital was and went to see if he was there. He was not. I asked all his friends I met, if they had seen him, but without success. Three days passed without a sign of Punitan. I went almost crazy with worry. While I was passed a restaurant, I heard someone call, "Maya!" A friend of Punitan came up to me and told me, that he was in the Panjim hospital and if I wanted to see him alive, I should go there soon.

I went there immediately and before I got into the hospital, something pulled me straight to the room he was in, amongst at least twenty patients who were dying, giving birth or recovering. Then it drew me directly to the bed Punitan was laying in. His hair had been shaved off and his beautiful body was naked from the waist up. Even deadly ill, he still had sex appeal. A crowd of people he knew, stood around him and looked like a flock of vultures. I gave them one intense look and they all disappeared.

Punitan was laying on his back and it took him all the strength to lift his arm and hand up from his elbow to reach for my hand. Then he whispered, "I love you Maya." He wanted to tell me something, so I put my ear to his mouth but even so, I could not understand what he had said. Then he added, "Now go." I was heart-broken when he sent me away, because I wanted to stay with him. I respected his wish and walked outside, sat under a tree and sobbed.

Then I took the bus back to Calangute and stayed in the guest house until the next day. I went to the beach and was doing some yoga exercises to get me out of my depressions, when I suddenly felt a freezing cold shiver run down my spine. I knew that Punitan had died.

I went into the beach bar and ordered a whisky which I downed in one go. Then I ordered another. Vincent, a friend sat next to me and asked, "Did he just die?" "Yes," I replied. Vincent put his head on my shoulder and his arm around my waist. He just sat quietly next to me and gave me comfort. We drank to Punitan in silence and I admired Vincent's sensitivity so much, that he became my next big love.

After a few days, Punitan's best friend came up to me and told me that he had died on the very day and at the exact time, that I had felt the chill. He also informed me, that he had to fight to get Punitan's body back, since it was his wish to be buried under the ash tree. They nearly sold all his organs to Bombay. Punitan had died because the police had poked a stick into the spokes of his Royal Enfield as he was driving by, which made him fall off and hurt himself so badly internally, that he died at only 48 years of age. He was buried under his favorite ash tree.

Vincent

Vincent was a very tall, well built and an extremely handsome man with black wavy hair and striking grey blue eyes who was born in Ireland. He was younger than I but we really got on well and stayed together. The trouble was that he was addicted to heroin.

It hurt me to see him go away for a fix and sleep for up to an hour afterwards. I really liked Vincent and wanted to help him get off the stuff. Vincent had a tropical ulcer on his back which would not heal until I took him to the Banyan tree and held a root, which reached almost to the ground in my hand and held it over the pus-filled wound. The root sucked the wound dry and from then on it healed. I was as amazed as Vincent.

Once, while Vincent shot himself with heroin, I saw a man who was badly hurt. His leg had been deeply cut by a piece of metal that he had tripped over. He did not know what to do. Fortunately, he lived just a few steps from there and had some clean water so I could wash the wound. Then I asked him if he had some alcohol. He pointed to a bottle of whisky so I fetched it and handed it to him and said, "Drink some against the coming pain," and then took the remaining whisky and poured it over the wound. I saw on his face, how much it hurt but he was very brave. Then I took a clean T-shirt, ripped it into strips, and wrapped up the wound to keep it clean since there was nothing else.

His name was Freddy and he was Swiss. We had a long conversation and I found out that he sniffed out vintage Rolls Royces, bought them, had them done up in Goa and shipped them to his clients in Europe. That is how he made his living.

Out of curiosity, I attended an acid party, although I did not take a pill but wanted to observe what was happening. The people were all dancing to acid house music, each one by themselves and their loneliness was extinguished by believing themselves to be watched and admired by everyone else. Their faces were smiling in self-satisfaction and trance. There was no way I was ever going to swallow one of those pills.

Vincent and I had been living together in my hut and in guest houses for some time, when I told him that I had just lost one man and could not bear to lose him as well and that he had to choose between heroin or me. He chose heroin and left me. I was deadly unhappy and lonely without him. I missed him like crazy. I did not see the sense in staying there any longer with him gone and I did not know where he was. Totally shattered, I planned to go back to Switzerland and booked a flight to Bombay where I hoped to rest up before flying home.

In an antique shop, I bought a cane for my father with a sword in it that could be pulled out. At least this way, I could go out alone in safety even at night and then bring it to him as a gift. There was so much I wanted to see that the new expectations drove away my depressions.

Before I intended to look for a hotel, I needed a drink and went into my favorite restaurant in Bombay. Two intensely beautiful eyes met mine. The first man I had met in Bombay was here and it was Vincent. We immediately jumped into each other's arms and stayed together once more. I never again tried to cure him of heroin. It was his decision and I could accept it.

We went for a meal and I met his two best friends who were also addicted to heroin. They were both handsome and one of them, especially, had a highly sensitive personality and was kind and considerate. The other one was rather quiet. They were well-educated and came from upper middle class families. Both accepted Vincent as their superior since he was the most dominating. All four of us stuck together and always went out to eat in each other's company.

The hotel we were staying in looked grim. Our quarters were accessed by going through a shabby corridor into a cellar. There were no windows, just a hole in the wall for air. A square water tank out of galvanized steel stood in one room. There was an old bed in each of the two other small rooms. That was all. The walls were full with messages, monograms and sketches that were partially lifting off with the paint because of the moisture. It was horrible but I did not care as long as I was with Vincent. They had rented this dump since, there, they were left in peace with their addiction.

Vincent and his friends needed to heat the powder on a silver spoon and shoot it into their veins. At least they could get syringes from the pharmacy without any problems. The quiet friend shook so much, that one of the others gave him the injections. Vincent had to sting himself into the vein of his leg since the one in his arms was too wrecked from all the shots. It depressed me to have to watch those three young men.

I told Vincent, that if he was going to die from heroin he should get me some as well, since I did not want to live without him. He yelled, "If you take heroin, I will not have anything to do with you again. I tried to give it up many times for twelve years without success and went straight onto it again. Don't you ever think about taking heroine again!" he emphasized. Thanks to Vincent I never tried heroin except for once, when I smoked it before I met him and it made me so nauseated and ill with diarrhea that I never tried it again. I also have a horror for injections.

Every evening we sat in the same bar to drink a cold beer. Then we ate at the restaurant across the street. Often one of the three men's heads dropped toward his chest, as if he was falling asleep so one of us gave him a gentle prod to wake him up. It was not easy for them to go travelling or exploring since they had to have their regular fix or would become uncontrollably frustrated and shaky. They used to be freedom-loving men but could not cope with a society whose product they had become. Their freedom was victim to addiction just as mine was to smoking tobacco. I was never addicted to marijuana or hashish since I was able to take it or leave it but usually did not turn it down when it came my way.

The heroin addicts were also always living with one foot in jail because of the illegality of it. I felt sorry for them. If it were legal, the Mafia types could not make profit from it and the whole legal system would not profit from their illegal addiction. I liked the young men so much and was totally in love with Vincent.

Every time we went eating, we handed a plate of food out to the children. Vincent took them in his arms and laughed with them. We all hugged the skinny children. They seemed to need affection almost as much as food. We refused to give anything to mothers who crippled or burned their children for begging purposes. If we had given, the children would have eaten but the cruel misery would have gone on. If no one gave, it would stop and save future generations from continuing to abuse their children.

I spotted an advertisement for the boat that crossed from Bombay to Elephant Island. We decided to go there. When we arrived there, four men came toward us carrying a Sedan chair. They begged us to have them carry us since they had families to feed. Vincent and his friends refused but I accepted. Sitting on that throne, they lifted me up onto their shoulders and carried me up the stairs and along the path right to the other end of the island, while my friends followed on foot behind me. Everybody was looking at me and I loved it as much as I had loved being on stage during the time I was dancing ballet. We walked to the carved caves and were amazed by the huge elephants cut right out of the cliffs inside. In the middle stood an, about 70 cm- tall, phallus carved out of stone that Hindu women would rub their vaginas on once every year as part of a religious ceremony.

The vegetation on the island was interesting but we had to take the next ferry back since heroin called to the three men who were already showing signs of frustration. Back in the claustrophobic cellar rooms, I went out alone while the three men slept after their injections. Since I intended to see the nightlife in Bombay, I took my sword-stick with me for safety. When a whole group of shady looking characters followed and tried to surround me, I pulled the sword out its scabbard and swung it around me. They took off like lightning.

It was time to call my parents again, so I went to make the call. My father told me, that my mother had been found unconscious while she was walking with my dog Zora and was in the hospital and that he would be glad if I could come home. I went directly to book a flight back. The next plane was leaving in two days. I called my father and told him. He had good news from my daughters in China and U.S.A.

Vincent understood that I had to leave and gave me an address where I could reach him in England since he planned to go there. He was never short of money because, when he needed it, he bought silk carpets and had them sent to a friend who sold them for a high profit in England and immediately sent him the money. When the time came to leave, we held each other tight and I had to hold the tears back. I took my bags and sword-stick and joined the line for the flight.

At the customs post stood a policeman, who yanked the sword stick out of my hand while yelling, "I know what this is!" He pulled the sword out of the scabbard and said, "It is not legal to take this on an airplane" and forbade me to get through, saying, "You are not flying anywhere." I told him that the sword was a gift for my father and urged him to let me go, since my mother was in the hospital. However, no matter what I said, he refused to change his mind, even when I told him he could keep the sword stick. He said that he would give it to the people at the Air Kuwait office, who would put me on a flight in a week's time. So I called my father and went back with Vincent.

The same day, I visited the Swiss Consulate, who did not help me to get back sooner. Vincent and I made the best of our time together and he hoped to get enough methadone for the trip back to England, that he planned to make two weeks after I had left. After week, it was time for us to say goodbye again.

I was looking forward to seeing my parents and Zora again. Sitting next to me in the horrible jumbo jet, was a young man from Kuwait who was in an airplane for the first time in his life. He was frightened and asked me every few minutes, how long it would be before we would arrive. I finally figured out that he could not read the time and explained the clock to him by showing him that when the small hand was here and the big hand was there, the plane should be at its destination. Then, a steward came with some forms to fill out. I noticed that the man from Kuwait could not read nor write, so I filled the papers out for him. He still asked me all the time, when we would arrive, so I pretended to fall asleep.

When I felt a nudge on my shoulder, I opened my eyes and the steward handed me the sword stick. The airplane flew into air pockets. The weather was bad. We flew so low that I asked why the pilot did not fly over the clouds instead of under them, where it would not be dangerous but was told that he knew what he was doing better than I. I told them that I was a pilot. They asked me to be quiet. I was glad when the shaky machine had landed. Instead of letting us out, a film was put on the screen until we were allowed to leave.

The hostesses and the steward made sure that all the shades on the windows were pulled down. When I pulled mine up to see what went on outside, someone from the crew immediately ordered me to pull it back down again. I did but left a small space open that I blocked with my head when looking outside. All the baggage and big crates were rolled out and loaded onto wagons which were driven off. Then stuff was loaded on again. I could not make this out. It did not make any sense to me. Then the film ended and we were allowed to get out of the plane. Not until later, did I figure out, that they may have been taking out arms for the war.

I had about six hours to spare while waiting for a plane to Zurich. Hoping to see something of Kuwait, I walked to the door where I was stopped and told that I was not allowed out of the airport hall. People who worked there seemed frightened and stressed. Some stalls had some food for sale. I sat on a chair in the hall and tried to relax. I studied people and then took out the sword to see if it was not harmed. A man behind me jumped up towards me and said, "What are you doing?" I said, "It's a present for my father and I was just looking at it," and put it back in. I promised not to take it out again. It was a long, lonely, hot and boring wait for the plane to take me away from there.

I arrived at my parent's home okay. My father was relieved to see me. Zora yowled and ran in circles when she saw me again. My father opened the best bottle of wine for us and since it was late, we went to see my mother the next day in the hospital. She could not remember what had happened to her but had a concussion and was forced to lie still and have tests done. We figured out, that she might had been hit over the head from behind. Fortunately, she had been found by someone who recognized her and who had called my father and an ambulance.

My mother was happy to see me and soon we could take her home. She recovered well and did not need me any longer. The tension between us built up.

I tried to reach Vincent in England but my letter was returned to me with "Unknown address" stamped on it. Vincent did not contact me in Switzerland either. I hope he did not give himself the 'golden shot'. But since he had been on heroin for over twelve years, it would not surprise me if he had. I felt very sad.

I felt it was time for me to go away again. Since I had some money left from India, I planned to drive to Elba again in my Renault Estafette. My generous father insisted on pressing more money into my hand, even though I told him that I did not need it. He asked me to let Zora stay with them since my mother was so attached to her and said that I would be more free without her and could get another dog. I tried to hide my disappointment but how could I say, "No," to them, who had done so much for me. I spoke to Zora and told her, she had to guard my parents and I would be back again. She seemed to understand. No way could I get another dog. She could not be replaced. I embraced my parents and Zora and went on my way to Elba.

Raymond

I slowly drove along the coast and stopped in many ports to look at boats and have a few drinks in a pub in the hope of meeting a life partner again. I felt so lonely and started to drink quite a lot but never alone. I became a social drinker and didn't realize that this was not the way to meet a partner.

Often, I couldn't drive in the morning because my head hurt as a result. Luckily, I did not have to escape as so often before, when some men found out that I was living in the van alone and tried to get sticky. There were plenty of men who wanted me but none of those turned me on. I am sure that we can all learn something from everyone but I compared them to past loves and they could not match up to them. Loneliness drove me nearly insane unless I painted, sketched, swam or was with friends.

All my life, I could not be alone. I missed my daughters and Zora. No way could I spend the evenings alone and had my meals in pubs. I did not care how much I spent but saved the money that my father had given to me to be able to return if I had to. By the time I got to Elba the rest of the money had decreased a lot and I started to worry, but even so, I made sandwiches in the van or cooked something. I went out every evening anyway. Elba had beautiful beaches and spectacular scenery.

My friends cheered me up. I parked in the same places I knew so well. One day, I walked along to the port to find my friend Francis's fishing cutter and got a shock when I found the beautiful old motor sailing ship on the ground with only the bow with the galley out of the water. I asked Julio in the bar what had happened to Francis, whose boat I was watching when last on Elba and he told me to ask his friends who were sitting outside. One of them explained, that Francis had fallen in love with a woman who owned a sailing boat and the two were very happy and sailed to South America together. This did not make sense to me since I knew that Francis would never abandon his beloved ship.

Later on, I was told the truth, that Francis had not survived the operation to renew his veins, damaged as a result of smoking too much. I was shattered and when I confronted the one who had lied to me, he replied, " I did not want to make you sad." I told him that if he was a real man, he would not lie to me again and I forgave him.

I drove around the island and discovered new places where I found settings to draw. However, loneliness made me return to Porto Ferraio where most of my friends lived on boats or on land. I parked my van in the port parking place only a few steps away from the telephones, a pipe with drinking water, post office, shops and pubs. The wall behind me sheltered the van and in front of me was a spectacular view of the harbor and over the sea into the hills.

It did not rain often and when it did it did not last long. One day when it was raining, I did not go out but stayed in my van. I wished so much that a man would come into my life. Someone knocked gently on the van. I slid open the door and was pleasantly surprised to see a very handsome man standing outside. He introduced himself as 'Raymond Blithe' from 'Yacht Seraki' . He asked me to join him for dinner. I accepted with pleasure.

Raymond had long, wavy, silver hair and a full white beard. His eyes were sparkling blue and his words were interesting, sounded like music and were often humorous. He was a wildlife photographer and showed me some of his impressive pictures. He was able to capture a glow worm with the light showing. He was also a brilliant and sensuous cook. He wanted to know everything about me and I was just as interested in him. Our conversation flowed like music in the soft light of the oil lamp and we enjoyed a bottle of wine together. He then asked me to stay with him and so we started to live together on his beautiful, wooden sailing boat.

Raymond had been born in Little Hampton, England. He had sailed single-handedly from England across the English channel, then motored through all the locks in the French canal system and took the Rhone to the south of France and sailed from there across to Elba, all alone. His aim was to sail to Corsica, then to the Gulf de Foss and motor up the Rhone into the little Rhone and to the Etang de Thau, then continue to the Canal du Midi.

He asked me, if I would like to help him sail the boat, since he had not been in the best of health ever since he had been in the hospital with a broken back when he fell off his boat in a lock on his way here. I replied, "Of course I will help you, this gives me a new life goal as well and I am looking forward to it."

First, we had to pull 'Seraki' out of the water and get her ready for the voyage but before we could do this, he had to make some extra money since he was nearly as broke as I was. Raymond took any job that came along. He de-brambled gardens, worked for the sailing club, etc. and kept up his photography. He sent his photos to England where they bought the ones they wanted and sent back the rest of his slides with a check for those they had kept.

We tried not to spend more than absolutely necessary and saved up for the trip. After the market had ended, we collected the fruit and vegetables left behind and I cooked and canned them. First I was shy about doing that but got over it quite fast. We opened every trash can and found all sorts of food and clothes in them. Behind the bakery factory was a big bin with bread and pastry that had not been sold the day before. A woman who worked there, saw me take it out and said, "Don't take that, I will put a plastic bag full with goods in this corner of the bin for you to lift out every day." I found the big bag for me that was so full of goodies, bread and rolls that we ate from it and gave some to sailors who could find no work and needed it. We also shared our bounty with my artist friend, 'Cony', an 82 year old man who survived with the bare minimum and fed the rest to the seagulls and other hungry animals.

Life with Raymond was not boring. He took me with him when he did photography and I learned a lot from him. He had butterfly larvae on the boat and waited for them to hatch so as to capture the event with his camera. He also kept a praying mantis, who I watched and he photographed while she laid the froth with eggs in it on the stem of a plant. Then we let her go free where he had found her. When the eggs hatched, about 1000 praying mantis babies swarmed over the whole boat. It was impossible to save them all but we caught as many as possible and let them go in a place where they had a chance of survival. We kept some of them.

Every day, Raymond inspected dog shit while on shore, to see if there were any flies on it that he could catch for his praying mantis who only ate live insects. People looked at him in a funny way but it did not bother him or me.

We had our first argument, when Raymond put a swallowtail caterpillar into the refrigerator so it would be too cold to move when being photographed. I believed this to be a cruel thing to do.

He got so angry at me, that I left. After about two hours of staying heartbroken in my van in depressive state, he came, apologized and took me into his arms. We went back to 'Seraki' together.

The same day, he saved a swift from being run over on the street and tossed him up into the sky where he happily spread his wings and flew toward us as if to say, thank you and then we watched him getting further away until he disappeared. Swifts cannot take off from the ground.

Raymond and I had a 'tango' relationship. Either we were extremely happy or deadly sad. Raymond's moods could change from one moment to the next, then we separated until his crisis had passed and, back together again, we would celebrate as if on honeymoon again.

When he drove me out with his foul moods and I could not understand why, since he refused to speak to me. I went to the pub, heartbroken, and got drunk with friends. Then I slept in my van and he would come to get me again.

During one crisis, I occupied an abandoned boat in the port, which was large enough to use as my art studio. I cleaned it up, slept on it and started to paint the next day. A man saw me painting and asked me, if I would paint his portrait the next day. We made a date but he did not show up. This depressed me and I went on shore to the next bar.

There, I met my friend who I asked, "Do you know a psychiatrist who can help me get over my depressions? He said, "Let me be your shrink" and called the bartender for a bottle of whisky. Then he filled a fresh glass full to the rim and said, " Drink this and it will make you feel better." I drunk it in one go right to the bottom and it helped. After drinking two full glasses of whisky, I started to live in the moment again and forgot all my sorrows and we started to laugh together, finding everything funny.

We became such good friends that his mother wanted to meet me. He knew that I was in love with Raymond and did not want another man but his mother wanted to invite me for lunch just the same, so I accepted. My friend was a street cleaner and I was amazed that his mother lived in a very rich looking house and wore beautiful jewelry. The place had an impressive staircase and was furnished with good taste and real antiques. The food was exquisite and so was the wine. My friend had to go back to work and his mother asked me to stay for a while and keep her company. She told me that her son had finished his studies at the University but did not like it and found out, that what he really wanted, was to be outdoors with his mates. That is why he preferred to sweep streets. His mother was upset when she told me this but I told her that she should be proud of her son having the intelligence and the courage to do what he really wanted and that we all have only one life.

If we do, just for one moment, what we don't want to do, that moment of our life will be lost forever. It is not important what other people are thinking, only what we think of ourselves matters. We all have a right to life if we don't hurt someone else. My friend's mother agreed with me.

It can be hard to live in a so-called civilized country with too many man-made laws, regulations and bureaucracy, especially for those who live with the bare minimum.

The second day on the abandoned ship, I felt sad and lonely again. There was no sign of Raymond and I had to find a way to cheer myself up again. I tried it with a few drinks then climbed to the top of the mast and enjoyed the night view over the boats and the harbor when, of a sudden, I heard the sirens of police cars and ambulance. I looked all around to figure out where they were heading to and they stopped on the pier next to the boat I was on. Police men stormed out and spotlights shone their cold intruding light on me. A cop yelled up at me, "Come down right away." The people resembled little ants down there and I said, "I will come down when I want to, but in my own time. I am not ready yet."

One of the men from the ambulance pleaded, "Please don't jump!" I said, will I come down on the promise, that I can take over this abandoned ship and use it as my art studio. I need a place to paint. A policeman started to climb up and threatened me, so I thought it better to give in and come down. Then they grabbed me but gave me the option to choose whether to go with the ambulance or the police. I chose the ambulance and was driven to the hospital, where I was shown to a room.

By that time, Raymond had been alarmed and joined me. He was not happy. There was a small window in the room and the nurse pointed to it and said to him, " She will not be able to climb out of this, will she?" and Raymond answered, "Yes, she will." I felt betrayed by him. I was locked into a windowless room, while he returned to his boat. After an hour's wait, suffering terribly from claustrophobia, the nurse unlocked the door and took me to the psychiatrist. He told me to sit down and we spoke for a while and he asked, "How do you feel about life, do you like to live or die?" I answered, "I like to live," and he signed a release from the hospital and told me not to climb up masts again since people were not free enough to understand the fun of it. He smiled at me and showed me out.

I went straight to Julio's bar, where I was celebrated by my friends before going to crash out on my bed in the van. The next morning, I nursed the hangover on the empty beach and swam. Then I visited the market and drank a liter of milk, swearing to myself, never to touch alcohol again. However, it was too hard to keep that promise for more than a week.

The usual thing happened and Raymond came to take me back again, convincing me that we had something special and it would be a shame to give it all up. Since I believed I was unable to live without him, I ended up going back to him. He cooked dinner and erotically decorated my plate with the food looking like a big penis with balls on it and used parsley to add the pubic hair. We had fun and it tasted good and I hoped that our relationship would last forever. We were deliriously happy again.

Raymond had to take beta-blockers every day. It was an awfully hot day and he felt ill, so he swallowed some medicine from a bottle and collapsed on the floor. It took all my strength to drag him from the cabin across the center cockpit onto the bed in the after cabin. I hung a blanket over the boom across the boat so that he would be cooler below and when he was still unconscious after I had sponged him with cold water, I fetched the ambulance. When they arrived, he was checked over and they wanted to take him to the hospital. He was half awake and refused to go with them, crouching in the cupboard to the side, so tight that it was impossible to get him out without using force.

I begged the men not to take him against his will and signed a paper to take full responsibility for his life. I tried to drip some water in to his mouth but he just dribbled it out again. When I feared that he could die of thirst, I went to get my friend Linda, a nurse, who lived on a boat in the port. She and her man Toni came right away and while he held Raymond up, she made him drink. She also checked his pulse and listened to his heart and told me to continue to sponge him with cold water and they would return the next day. Raymond was ill and slept for 4 1/2 days.

This was a tremendous strain on me and I was happy to see him wake up. He told me I was a liar when I informed him that he had been out for 4 1/2 days. When Linda confirmed this, he fell instantly into a rotten mood and was so nasty, that I would have left, if I had not been so committed to him and intent on staying on until he was on his feet again. I cooked , kept the boat in order and did everything to cheer him up but he kept on psycho-torturing me until I left.

This all was so stressful to me, that I could not control my depressions and walked to the top of the cliff behind Padulella beach, thinking how easy and painless it would be to jump to my death, while listening to the music on my headphones, and I could be free from the suffering of loneliness and depressions forever. While these thoughts were in my mind, I suddenly slipped and automatically grabbed the cliff and it took all my strength and energy to pull myself up to safety. From then on, I knew that I could never commit suicide and was grateful to be alive.

I returned to Raymond and demanded that he tell me straight in the eyes, if he wanted me to stay or go. He wanted us to stay together and finally his bad mood had gone away.

We saved up enough money to have 'Seraki' pulled out of the water at the wharf, where we scraped the old paint off, Raymond repaired the planks and I painted the hull. Raymond found a bicycle in the trash, lent me his tools and showed me how to repair it. This meant, that I did not have to fill the van's tank so often.

Checking the post office for mail, I discovered that there was a package from my parents with letters from my daughters. There also was an official letter, which stated that I was eligible for the Swiss disability pension that I had asked for three years previously. This was great news. No more worry about starving. It was as if a big weight had been lifted off of me.

I found out later, that the problem was, that I was labeled as by being on welfare and many people looked down on me and did not take me seriously. This wounded me deeply and I hoped to be able to sell my paintings at a price that would regain their respect for me.

I had my easel in the ship's wharf and worked hard on my erotic series and seascapes. The artist Cony liked my work very much and I considered him to be a real art expert. I had different stages of painting. Realistic, abstract, cubism and erotic. Then I started to combine them and to get back into realism again.

Since I had a pension, I did not need to do any menu cards, decoration and the sort of work that I had done solely to be able to put gasoline into the tank or buy food. With the first check, I stocked 'Seraki' up with food.

While Raymond and I were cooking hamburgers, a beautiful but skinny shipyard's grey tiger cat was attracted by the scent of meat and jumped up on the ladder to the boat. We were sitting in the cockpit and shared our food with her and she stayed with us. After a few days, she had enough confidence to let us take her to the vet for a check-up, de-worming and vaccinations. I also had to get her a health certificate and buy a travelling cage.

My parents wanted to meet Raymond and so did my daughters, who were with them during their vacation. I also planned to go to the bank in my hometown where my first check had arrived. My van was in a garage waiting to have a new set of cylinders, so we took the ferry to the mainland and travelled by train to Switzerland carrying the cage with the cat. She was so good, that I could take her out of the cage onto my lap . However, when we moved, she felt safer in her cage and refused to eat or drink until we were at my parents' home. We had a great time with my parents and my daughters. Zora was happy to see me, liked the cat and the cat liked her. They played together after they had lost their fear of each other.

Kitty cat had diarrhea so we took her to the vet in Switzerland, who gave us some pills to cure her and informed us that she was pregnant. Raymond looked forward to photographing the birth of the kittens on 'Seraki'. The whole time while in Switzerland, he never had a bad mood.

Back in Elba, we were still happy and watched the five kittens being born on the sofa of Seraki. They grew fast and were about 2½ months old when we were ready to put Seraki back into the water and start on our trip. Four kittens had already found places with friends but one of them was still with us and so was Kitty cat. We had her spayed just a week before. To my horror, Raymond wanted to abandon them at the last moment. I could not believe it, since he loved them, was photographing them over and over again and had given them so much affection. He exclaimed that, we had helped Kitty cat to survive with the kittens but the sea would not be a good place for them and that they would surely find a new place to stay. In my grief, I talked to a sailor in the wharf, who told me that he needed a ship's cat and took in the kitten, then I ran to the office and spoke to the secretary who promised me, that would feed Kitty cat.

My van was repaired and locked up at the wharf's parking

Not A Boring Moment

lot and I made arrangements to pick up my vehicle once we arrived in the Midi Canal. I jumped on board Seraki and we sailed with an ideal wind out of the port. When we arrived on the open sea, the waves got so rough, that the ties of the huge batteries under the cockpit ripped and the batteries jumped out of their support across the hull. Raymond had to chain them down which was not easy at all. If Kitty cat and the Kitten had been aboard, I would have been really worried about them falling overboard. I had to admit that Raymond was right to see that the sea was no place for a cat.

I was so used to sailing, that I automatically wanted to help him with everything that needed to be done on a boat, as I had done on Scheherazade. This made him so mad, since he was used to being a single-hander. He insisted on shouting commands at me and ordering me around. This I couldn't do and so much friction built up, making me wonder, if it would not have been better to have listened to my old friend Cony's advice, "Whatever you do, don't sail with Raymond. It would be too dangerous for you." Fortunately, Raymond calmed down and when I cooked a meal, he was grateful for it and admired me for being able to do it, even though the sea was rough.

I could tell that Raymond did not like to sail in the open sea and understood why he wanted to be back in the canal. He nearly panicked when we were approaching the port of Bastia but everything went well. We found a good spot to tie Seraki to on the pier in the harbor and the fees were affordable.

The last swallowtail larvae in his jar on the boat was about to hatch in the next days, so we took a train ride to the top of the mountain and watched, in a coffee shop, how the larva hatched into a beautiful butterfly. We watched him dry his wings and he became the star in Raymond's photos. Then we took him to where there was fennel growing. It was one of his favorite plants to eat and we released him the moment we spotted a female swallowtail. May they live happily ever after together and go forth and multiply in this paradise-like beautiful scenery!

Back from the mountain, we explored Bastia and were

amazed at the low prices for the magnitude of food and specialties offered in the supermarkets compared to Italian prices.

After a while, we decided to sail around the north of Corsica and go to Marine d'Albo. There was a beautiful bay, where I could tell it was safe to anchor for free but when I suggested it to Raymond, it put him instantly into a bad mood and he claimed it would be dangerous. He decided to go into the port instead. We had to pay a lot of money, and extra for a shower as well, but obviously it was worth it for him to have his own way and to feel safe amongst hundreds of yachts. I loved him just the same.

After resting for two days, we continued to sail across the Ligurian sea to Nice. We were dead-tired and sailed into the port. Then we motored to a pier and tied Seraki up. We had to cross over six yachts, to get to shore to find out about the fees. When we had that information, we filled the jerry cans with drinking water, stepped over the yachts once more to Seraki and sailed straight out again. We could not afford to pay those prices which were higher than the cost of a room in a luxury hotel.

Some sailor friends told us about a river we could anchor in and so we aimed to get there before the predicted storm the next day. We just made it and Raymond threw three anchors out to hold Seraki. He was so uptight, that he did not congratulate me on my birthday and when I told him that I wanted to go on shore for a while, he refused to let me go and made my day a disaster.

The next day, it was blowing like stink and we went onshore together and walked to the next village. He was still in a bad mood but was much better than the day before. When we got back, some boats had ripped loose and some had drifted but Seraki was still on her three anchors and in the same place. This made Raymond so proud, that he instantly got into a good mood. The storm calmed and the clouds cleared.

In the morning, we continued our voyage to St. Tropez where we tied Seraki up on the bank of a small river between two marinas. We stayed there for three days and sailed on to Ile d'

Hyeres and Ile de Porquerolles, where we anchored and enjoyed the peace and quiet- ideal for resting up. The sky was clear blue and the surroundings beautiful. The wind was great for moving on.

The Golfe de Fos was easy to find. The entrance to Port- St.- Louis- du-Rhone was in the mist, but we found it when we got closer and went through it and along to the anchorage of Port St. Louis and secured Seraki. Then we rowed to the shore, where I ate two dozen oysters with freshly squeezed lemon juice and drank white wine. Raymond ate something else. We were so happy again and I realized that once his bad moods blew over, there was peace and pleasure again. I just had to learn to be more patient.

He told me about his childhood and I was surprised, that he was not more messed up. He had been adopted by a nurse and the rich and much-older owner of a pharmaceutical and chemical factory, who had married her after being nursed by her while in the hospital. She wanted a child but had no idea about children and was a sadist. Her husband did not want any more children since he had two nearly grown-up ones from a previous wife.

The father did not give a hoot for Raymond. He was driven by the chauffeur to school every day but lacked nest warmth and understanding. When he fell off his bicycle and broke his arm, his adoptive mother beat him up. She was often fighting with the female cook and the two of them beat each other and let their frustrations out on this innocent child. His adoptive father did not want anything to do with them or little Raymond.

He did have a good education in schools but decided to study photography and went to South Africa to specialize in wild life and orchids. Raymond's former wife committed suicide and he had lost contact with his daughter Sera. Raymond named the boat after her. 'Seraki' means "Little Sera" in Greek. He missed her very much but could not afford to visit her in England, where she was married. He told me, that she blamed him for the suicide of her mother who had been a pilot, licensed to fly supersonic jets and was the chief of an airport.

I started to save some money from each monthly check so I could surprise him with a ticket to England in the future. Raymond believed that he would be able to square things between his daughter and himself , if only he could see her.

One day, Raymond and I were sitting in the cockpit watching the dolphin, who visited Port St. Louis and jumped to get the fish children had thrown to him. This graceful mammal had been there for a few weeks already and people loved him. We went shopping for some food and then motored to the entrance of the Rhone, to step the masts so that we could get through the locks of the river.

As we came to about one third of the way toward Arles, the tide was so strong that even with the motor at full speed, we just inched forward. Just afterwards, we ran out of diesel and tied Seraki to a tree, while rowing to the nearest farm, where we asked for some fuel. The farmer filled the can to the top and when we wanted to pay, he just shook his head and waved goodbye. We were so grateful to him for helping us out.

Then, we had the good luck to discover a beaver family. A great photo opportunity for Raymond. This was not easy because we had to wait until they lost their fear of him. I sat still and watched this rare view with fascination.

Then we continued to motor to Arles. We went into the small port and tied Seraki up alongside the pier. Since I always had contact with my family and they knew where to reach me, my daughter Alexa and her husband P. came to surprise us. They invited us to dinner and we had a wonderful time together. All four of us slept on the boat. I was sad when they left but I was grateful for the valuable time we had spent together.

A Russian Jewish single-handed sailor arrived in a small wooden sloop. Instantly, we became friends and we invited him to dinner on Seraki. He was an older man, weather-beaten and skinny with a beard. He stretched a rope from tree to tree and taught me to walk the tightrope. Before he left, he gave me a beautiful book with etchings of different Russian hussars in their uniforms on horseback, which I will always treasure.

We had to pass by a gypsy camp and other fascinating sights on our way to the old town of Arles, which is very interesting and full of character. Sometimes, I went shopping all by myself while Raymond was busy with something else. There were small shops which I preferred to the supermarkets and so I walked through the old back streets that smelled of freshly baked bread.

There were also small pubs and I met an old gypsy man. His name was 'Papa Jean' and he was the family elder. We became good friends and I wanted to paint him. He took me to his favorite pub and the next day I returned there with art materials and a canvas. He was there and the painting of him was finished the same day. He liked it so much, that I gave it to him and he handed it to the pub owner, who hung it on the wall of the pub. I have a photograph and the memory of Papa Jean. He drank quite a bit and did not eat. His family was worried about him.

Raymond and I went to the square several times, where the real gypsies were playing and singing flamenco. Plane trees shaded the different coffee shops which surrounded the stage. They tempted us to sit down, to sip a cold drink while listening to the passionate sounds of the music. We did some sightseeing and exploring. Before we left, I visited Papa Jean. He preferred to sleep in a beach chair outside, rather than in his caravan. He did not touch the goodies that I brought to him . He looked very weak. I knew that this was the last time I would see him and felt privileged to have met this extraordinary man who had been married five times during his life and was respected by all who knew this colorful and unique character.

The First Roof of my own, over my Head

Our voyage took us through the Petit Rhone, whose banks were full of wildlife. We saw many flamingos, birds, butterflies, lizards, grasshoppers, fireflies and other beasties before entering the Etang de Thau. The Etang is quite shallow at times and it can be rough and dangerous around the oyster beds and we were very careful not to run aground.

Then we entered the Canal du Midi, which was a real paradise, until it was declared a World Heritage site and was groomed to look like a cemetery garden for tourism. There were herons, kingfishers and many species of birds who lived in the trees and bushes. Bulrushes and irises and many wild plants graced the banks and the odd snake could be seen fishing in the water.

We met people on barges, sailing boats, yachts and even British canal boats. There were even water lilies growing in different parts of the canal. It was great to be able to go through locks, aqueducts, tunnels and villages and to be able to tie up whenever we wanted and to go exploring or eating in a restaurant near the canal.

I sketched and we met some interesting people and saw some charming places. Raymond and I were attached to each other but even so, we had some depressing rows along the way.

Our goal for the time being, was to get to La Porte de la Robine and leave Seraki safe with Ted and Marianne who would look after her while we went to Elba to pick up my Renault Estafette van.

When we arrived at the wharf in Elba, we found the van just as we had left it and Kitty cat came to greet us. She had been adopted by the secretary who loved her. We slept in the van overnight and when the time came to leave, Kitty cat looked so sad that we could not take her with us. Raymond still felt that she would have a better life there and it nearly broke my heart.

We loaded the van onto the ferry and then drove back to La Porte de la Robine. When Raymond had one of his moods and got nasty, I went to the woods to search for mushrooms. There were many species and I studied them with the help of my books. Then I picked some thyme and other herbs, which are good for eating and to use for my cooking.

I met new friends. There were two homosexuals who both had the name Malcolm and owned an idyllic restaurant next to the canal. One of them was fat and the other skinny. So we all called them the Big and the Little Malcolm. Big Malcolm was a bully and the masculine part of their passionate relationship. Little Malcolm was sensitive and nice but suffered for being so much in love with the big one.

They gave me a contract for two pen and ink drawings of their place. They were really pleased with all the intricate details that I had put into my work and paid me right away. I had saved up enough money to give Raymond a ticket to go and see his daughter in England while I stayed on Seraki. Little Malcolm came to see me often, while he was walking their German Shepherd, Helen.

One day, he was very nervous and depressed. He told me that Big Malcolm had threatened to kill Helen because he was jealous of the dog. We had a drink together and I let him stay on the boat while I tried to make peace between them. Walking across the bridge and over the aqueduct, I found big Malcolm just as miserable but he showed it with anger. I told him that if he should hurt the beautiful and innocent animal, he would not only eliminate his chances to ever see his lover again, but had to be prepared that I would have him turned over to the SPCA. He then assured me, that he loved Helen as much as little Malcolm did and he would never harm Helen. All of a sudden, his expression looked sad and he told me that he did not want to live without his partner and asked me to ask Little Malcolm to come back to him.

The two made up and I had a free dinner at their restaurant called 'Cascade' that evening. I met many people there, since the ambiance was good and the food delicious, in that romantic place with a waterfall to enhance it even more.

Raymond came back from visiting his daughter in the same white shirt and pants he had left in. It was just as spotless as when he had first put it on. I don't know how he could manage that. I was thrilled to see him and had missed him very much. He had been gone only a week because his daughter told him, "I survived without you for so long and I don't need you now either. Go away." I felt so sorry for him but could not comment since I didn't know their situation but did everything to try and cheer him up.

We moved Seraki out of La Porte de la Robine and motored to the free mooring the Malcolms had offered to us. We lived in peace for a while, until I was forced to leave Raymond temporarily because of his bad temper. Sometimes Raymond was happy to see me back and at other times he was in such a mood that I thought about leaving him for good.

I was grateful to have my van and to be financially independent. I searched for an apartment to rent, a place where I could live and paint, in vain, until I visited the town hall and asked the mayor if there was a place to rent in his town. His secretary told me of a house that was for sale for only F Francs 50'000, which was about S Fr. 10'000 at the time. I went to look at it and it was the smallest house in the village and 200 meters away from the Canal Du Midi.

It had a kitchen with a fireplace and a sink on the ground floor, which was only 2 1/2 meters wide. There was a bathroom installed under the stairway, containing a French squat toilet with a shower hose mounted on the wall. The steps led to the bedroom on the first floor and the attic above. There was no garden or view but beautiful walks into the countryside with gorgeous woods and rich wildlife. The village had no post office but one grocery shop and a bar.

I called my parents on the phone and told them about the house and asked them if they could lend the money to me, suggesting that I could pay some of my pension money back to them every month. My mother handed the phone to my father who said, "Buy it. We will deduct the money from your inheritance so it will be fair to your brother and sister."

I bought the small stone house and moved in and kissed the ground of my first, own roof over my head, which was located in Argens-Minervois. Raymond moved Seraki there and our relationship continued. We turned the attic into another bedroom and studio. A neighbor gave us a beautiful antique, carved, oak double-bed that Raymond made longer and fitted next to the small window across the attic. I fitted a board to the wall, which I used to paint on. Raymond replaced the broken old tiles of the kitchen floor with new ones. As soon as I could afford it, I bought a cooker and then a washing machine. It was so great, not to have to do the laundry by hand anymore. A neighbor let us hang the washing on their line. It was also nice not to have to carry water any longer and to turn on the lights using a switch instead of getting oil to light the lamps, but I refused to have a TV in my house.

The first roof of my own over my head

Marseillette

Since my little house had no garden, I needed a piece of

recreational land to give my plants a good place to continue to grow. Their pots had become too small. I looked through the newspaper ads and found:

For sale in Marseillette, 4750 square meters of recreational land, with well, fruit and other trees next to the Canal du Midi.

I had just saved up enough to buy it and we immediately made a date to see it. The man had single-handedly planted all the trees in this magnificent garden for his daughter, who was not interested in it since she had married and moved to Perpignan. Her father was happy to sell it to me because I could not hide my feelings of delight. It was just what I needed, a very romantic place- so private that I could walk around naked.

It was fenced in by 24 year- old, dense cypresses. The trees consisted of: nut trees, meddler, plums, three sorts of cherries, four sorts of apples, peaches, apricots, three sorts of pears, pines, quinces and garnet apples. One part was wild and untouched with berries, different trees plus two sorts of wild orchids. There grew also three varieties of grapes, asparagus, rosemary, thyme, laurel and more. Raymond liked the garden as well. It was a real paradise.

The hotel restaurant next door was convenient but could not be seen through the two rows of dense cypresses. There was land on the other side, left wild by a neighbor who had built on it without asking for permission, but lived somewhere else. He gave me the right to collect the water from his roof and I used it to fill the pond I had dug out for the benefit of wild life.

I bought a caravan from the owners of the hotel next door and had it pulled by a farmer with a tractor to my garden and placed under the pine trees. Then, I attached a big sign with '*Refuge Natural*' written on it.

A shed stood on my land and it shocked me to see all the different bags with poison in it. The apples, pears and grapes were full of the stuff. I threw the toxins away and never used those evil powders again. The man who had sold me the land, had also raked all the leaves and weeds away. The ground was suffering and when it was raining, I would sink in almost up to my knees.

Because of my jungle experiences, I knew that if you leave nature in peace, it will recover automatically and the insects are essential for fertilization of trees, plants and flowers. Weeds don't exist. I want all plants, except the ones that were deliberately manipulated and used during the war, like false wheat that spread like a cancer but bares no fruit. The seeds of those had been thrown out of airplanes over Vietnam according to Freddy, a former war veteran, who pointed them out to me. The pear trees were struggling so much, that the former owner believed that they could not be saved. I just left them to it and they rewarded me after two years with the most beautiful, sweet and juicy fruit. An apricot tree's branch was dead and when I wanted to clear it off, a gorgeous woodpecker was pecking the insects out so I did not clear the deadwood from the trees unless I wanted some to cook on. I left all leaves, branches and fallen fruit to rot and enrich the soil. Every year the earth got richer.

I planted vegetables on the bottom of my land, nearest to the canal. I planted salads, tomatoes, beans, artichokes, zucchini and eggplants. Wild strawberries surprised me. I was given a water pump, which I used to pump the water out of the canal to give to the plants. I only cleared enough herbage to make a hole to plant the vegetables in. The rest protected the ground and plants from drying out during the big heat.

The compost heap was used by many beasties. I walked around naked and free. Every time Raymond had a crisis, I drove to my garden and stayed there until I thought he would feel well again. Every time I ate, birds came around to beg for food. Even a pair of partridges and some wild pheasants and a squirrel showed up.

I was very happy but sometimes sad and lonely. Raymond was often ill and did not tolerate any pity or help from me. I insisted on paying for the doctor and the dentist if he would go and he finally accepted. The doctor sent him for tests and a gastroscopy to the hospital and the dentist said it was high time to treat the infection in his tooth with strong antibiotics and have the rest repaired. Soon he was well again and came to the garden to photograph the fireflies and other wildlife while I painted.

My paintings were exhibited at the restaurant Troubadour, in the Cave de Malice in Argens, Minervois and at the Gallery Jean Baptiste Viquereux in Lezignan- Corbieres. I had some contracts as well.

Cats

There were many stray cats in Argens, that came to my house begging for food. In the winter even the shy, wild tiger cats showed up. Normally, they lived in the forest and only came when they were really hungry. We never turned a hungry animal away. I had to go to Switzerland and Raymond stayed in the house. When I was at my parent's house, Raymond rang up and told me that all of the cats had gone away because it had snowed very much. However, one black cat remained in front of the door with snow on his head, begging to come in. He asked, "What should I do?" I replied, "Let's adopt him." When I got back, we were three to share my tiny house.

'Kitty Cats' was a big black male. He had no hunting instincts since he had been castrated by the his former owner who had died in a car accident. Kitty Cats had been on his own for 1½ years, according to people in the village who knew him and sometimes fed him. I bought him a very nice bed but he preferred to sleep with us on ours and was very attached to Raymond, who he considered to be his savior.

No one could touch him, unless he came up to them first. If you tried to gently glide your hand over his fur in any way, he would bite and scratch you bloody. He was also very tyrannical and when I did not feed him before I made the coffee in the morning, he scratched and bit me. I threw him outside a few times for 10 minutes until he learned not to hurt me again.

When I was back from Switzerland, I discovered that Raymond had crashed my beloved old home, the Renault Estafette, into a tree on the banks of the canal, on the way to the Malcolms' restaurant. I was heartbroken but told him, "That could happen to anyone," and tried to not let him know how sad I was. I was glad he was not hurt and knew that material things are not so important for survival.

When I told my parents, they sent me the money and deducted it from my inheritance so I could be mobile again. I bought a used Citroen AX Tonic. I had taken the train to Switzerland and back since I could only drive the old Estafette outside of Switzerland. I feared that I would be unable to pass Swiss inspection, since any vehicle with the slightest rust would not pass the test, tarnishing the Swiss image. Not to mention the dangers to the environment that the throwaway society was causing.

Later on, the police were menacing my parents and threatened to put me in jail the minute I should cross the border, if I did not send back my license plate. My father pleaded with me to send it back. I did, but not before I had copied it onto a piece of aluminum to replace it with.

I insured my van in Narbonne and kept it in good shape by taking off the slightest rust and painting it with anti-rust solution. I also had it checked at the garage regularly and drove it in Italy and France legally, without any problems for many more years, until it was totaled in Raymond's accident. I did this because I don't believe Switzerland should be a police state which can terrorize or blackmail old people like my parents or abuse the natural environment just because of vanity, image or materialism.

When our friends and animal lovers, Jacky and Lucy, came to visit, Lucy wanted to pick Kitty Cats up and I warned her not to, since he could get vicious. She just ignored me, saying, "No cat has ever hurt me," and lifted him up to kiss him. He scratched her bloody, straight across the face. Jacky uttered, "You should have that tomcat put down." I replied, "Your wife should have taken my advice. Every animal wants to be respected and probably something has happened to him that caused him to be afraid of people. This is no reason to have him killed." We stayed friends but they never came to my house again. Instead, we went to visit them. They owned five dogs and seven cats and Jacky was a great cook. Lucy was an artist and part- time nurse.

Separation from Raymond after 4 1⁄2 Years

Raymond accused me of having said something that I knew I did not say just to pick a fight. He tried to push my head into the toilet so I told him to go to hell and leave me. I insisted that he give me back the key and he threw it so hard at my forehead, that it bled. He left Kitty Cats behind and went away. I really hated him but it would have been better if I had not felt any thing for him at all any more, since love and hate are both similar and very strong emotions. This time he had gone too far and I would not give up my pride and invite him back again.

About a week later, I started to miss him but was still wounded by his mental and physical abuse. Why were the men that I wanted to share everything and my life with, always hurting me? I asked myself many questions and tried to analyze the lonely and miserable state that I was in. I chain-smoked and went out in the hope of meeting my ideal man.

A registered letter arrived for Raymond and I knew it contained the check for his photographs. I knew he depended on it and so I took it to his boat and saw that he was not there anymore. Someone told me that he had gone to the Malcolms to tie Seraki to their mooring. This left me no alternative then, but to drive there and deliver the important mail in person. When I arrived, Big Malcolm was standing outside. Before I could speak, he said, "You can't see Raymond, he is with us and I am sure he does not want to see you." I held the large envelope with Raymond's check in it up to him and said, "This is important registered mail for him and I wanted to give it to him personally." Big Malcolm snatched it out of my hand with his fat fingers and with the words, "You can trust me". He turned away and left. I started to ask myself, how can

Raymond prefer his company to mine and was I right during a past fight, when I had called him a sadist homosexual?

I worked on myself to get rid of such negative thoughts and to do everything to be happy again. Every evening I did yoga and meditation. I tried to give up smoking but when I went out and saw my friends light up a cigarette, it was easier to say, "I'll stop tomorrow."

My hormones started to torture me but I was determined not to masturbate and rather share it with a lonely man. Often when waking up sober in the morning, I started to compare the new lover to someone I had loved intensely in my past and this blew the chances for me and for the man in bed with me.

My paintings became dark. They lightened up with some contracts. It always animated and cheered me up, if someone liked my work enough to order a portrait or landscape depicting their house, etc. Often, my good friend the art gallery owner, Jean Baptiste Viquereux, poured me a whisky and cheered me up.

Lezignan was only a few kms away from the town I lived in. I had another good friend there, whose name was Clemence. He was an American writer who was living in the Hotel Luxembourg. Clemence wanted to write my autobiography. He listened to my life stories for hours and noted everything down. Then he fell in love with a charming woman from the U.S.A. and told me that they were moving there and would get married. He then emphasized, "Maya, you have to write your autobiography, you owe it to the world." I replied, "I want to do some living first, but when I get old, I will write the book with my memories."

Diana

I had six beautiful old windows saved from the dump but had nowhere to put them. Joras, a Swiss friend who lived in the village, offered to store them in his attic for me. I did not know where to use them but just wanted them for their beauty and found it a shame for them to be destroyed. When Joras needed the space, I told a man in town about my dilemma and he offered to store the windows behind his old house under a roof for me. When I moved the windows there, I saw that two beautiful but skinny hunting dogs were chained to the wall.

One of the dogs, I knew since she had come up to me twice after a hunt and I had fed the shy animal. This was the third time I had seen her. I felt sorry for the dogs but could not help them all. When I mentioned that they were a bit on the skinny side, the man did not respond and I eventually forgot about them. When I went back, I only found one of the lonely and skinny dogs still there looking sadly at me. I took the windows and moved them to Marseillette, where I covered them up with a waterproof sheet behind the caravan. A few days later, I returned to my house in Argens.

I was unable to sleep that night and kept thinking about that sad-looking bitch. The next day, I went to see her. What a horrific sight. She was chained so tightly in an iron cage, that she could hardly move. I broke open the cage with an iron bar and released her from the chain. She followed me home and I called the man and threatened him, that if he did not let me have this dog, I would go to the SPCA and complain.

Her back was cut almost down to the bone and she had the mange. He gave 'Diana' to me and said, "I paid F Francs 7000" for her." I replied, "And even so, you did not take better care of her." Diana was a beautiful 9 year-old Griffon Nivernais with a very nice character, extremely sensitive and very intelligent. She had refused to hunt any longer and had been abused because of it.

Those horrible hunters don't deserve to have dogs. I am against hunting, since they have decimated or killed off many species of our precious wildlife. Why don't they shoot clay pigeons or each other?

I took Diana to the vet. He took care of the wound and treated her for four types of parasites, the mange, infected ears and diarrhea. To top all that, her front teeth had been knocked out by the so-called 'men' kicking them out with their boots. With the help of the vet, it took us six months to get the poor animal back into shape. I never regretted having adopted her for even a second and she became my best friend and companion. I needed a responsibility to make life more valuable and she needed me as well.

Kitty Cats was jealous and attacked Diana, who was so good-natured toward all other animals. Every time he clawed Diana, I threw him outside for 10 minutes. If he did it again, it became 20 minutes and so on. When I was upstairs or to the toilet, Kitty Cats thought I could not see him, so when I saw that Diana's nose was scratched, I threw him out again and he could not understand how I had found out. Finally, he learned not to hurt Diana any more.

When we were not in Marseillette, Diana and I walked three times a day through forests, fields or along the canal. Kitty Cats would accompany us for up to a kilometer. He was frightened of being in the car and when I had to go somewhere, I had to find someone to feed him and take him in until I would be back again. Diana came with me wherever I went and even followed me in the house. Diana preferred to sleep on one side and Kitty Cat on the other side of me on my bed even though they both had their own beds. Diana's hobby was to bark out of the window every morning and to get an echo from all the village dogs.

I did the shopping at the market so Diana could stay at my side. She did not need a lead and followed me through the thickest crowds. Where she was not allowed, I did not go either. In coffee shops, she sat next to me on the blanket that I took along everywhere for her.

Once, I gave a party in my house. We celebrated until I was so tired, that I went to bed and let the guests carry on without me. Diana lay next to me. I was woken up by a total stranger and Diana jumped for his throat growling loudly and it took all my force to hold her from attacking him. He asked, "Does your dog bite?" I said, "Yes she does and if you don't get out of my house immediately, I will set her on you." He ran for his life, never to be seen again.

A guy on a moped passed through the small road in front of my house every day. Diana hated this man and attacked him every time but I could hold her back while she fearsomely growled at him. When I found out from a respected older village woman, that she had witnessed him beating Diana with a stick before she was with me, I understood and gave Diana the chance to chase him and growl at him to let her anger out, while I held her tight.

The man filed a complaint with the Mayor of Argens, whose secretary called me to come to the town hall. I took Diana with me and had to listen to the guy's complaint about Diana threatening him every day. His friend objected to Diana's barking. I told the mayor, that the vet had said that barking is healthy for a dog's lungs and that the woman had told me about the man with the moped beating Diana with a big stick while she was tied down and that it was natural, that no dog would forget such an ordeal. I mentioned also, that he did not have to pass my house every day but could choose the equally convenient other way to the village center and if someone should to be punished, it should not be Diana, or me, but that animal abuser.

The mayor then said, "But they told me she is a dangerous animal who bites. I opened Diana's mouth and said, "How can she bite, who had her teeth kicked out by the boots of this kind of man?" The mayor sent the man away and Diana and I left as well. I took the cat and Diana and we lived in my caravan for a while.

The people from the hotel next door, gave me leftover meat for my pets almost every day. 'Kitty Cats' made friends with them and went there in person to eat the scraps that the tourists would feed to him as well. He became almost wider than long and slept most of the day in the caravan. When I went somewhere, the people of the hotel would see to it that he would not starve and gave him plenty of love.

The caravan had a roof hatch that I left partly open with a cat ladder, that I made for him so he could access it going up and decending the roof, which allowed me to lock up when Diana and I went somewhere. There was always a full bowl with water and dry food, in case I should stay away overnight. Too bad cats can't travel like dogs. It would have made my life so much easier.

Diana

Friends and Lovers

My first friend in the village was Robert. He looked like a hippy and was very gentle but liked to drink. His father was a big shot in the military and had treated him and his siblings to a very strict and brutal upbringing. The mother was too frightened to take her children and run since they were then living in Algiers where her husband was stationed. To this day, the whole family hates him.

Robert told me that his father demonstratively put a bar of chocolate on the table and left the room. The children each took a row of it and their punishment was that all of them were beaten in turn for an hour. I asked Robert, "Did your father not get the cramps in his arm?" Robert replied, " I hoped he would but the bastard was too stubborn to stop."

Today, the father is only a shadow of a man who looks ill and is a total alcoholic. Robert and his mother take tranquillizers every day. The rest of the family had moved out. Robert lived in a room in the basement in his parent's home.

He came to my house often and smoked a joint with me. The trouble was that he would not leave until all the wine was gone. We had a love affair for a while, until he cheated on me with a man. He admitted it and since I respect the truth, we were at least able to have a platonic friendship. I had a blood test and was happy to be find myself to be in the best of health.

Someone told me about a young woman from Portugal who lived in a small tent outside the village. I went to see her. Her name was Paula. She had been pestered by an old married man, which annoyed her. I knew how that felt from experience, so I offered Paula the chance to stay in my guest room to rest up. She was a cheerful and beautiful young woman with a free spirit who had the courage to do what she wanted. I enjoyed her company.

Soon she found a little old house to stay in for free on the condition that she renovate it. It had no shower and no electricity. The guy who owned the house was a financially very well-off grape farmer who used her for work without payment. However, she could not see that because she was so happy living on top of a hill with a great view (but with absolutely no comfort, except a roof over her head and running cold water). She could also lock the door and feel safe.

An older man showed up at my door with a bag full of freshly laid eggs. I asked him to come in and sit down and poured him a coffee from the thermos flask. He then told me of that whore who lived in the house on top of the hill. I said, "How dare you speak of my friend that way? I bet you are just angry because she did not let you in. Take your eggs and get out of my house before I lose my temper." Paula told me that he had pestered her and become so sticky, that she had to get nasty to make him go away.

I exchanged my Citroen AX for a Peugeot Station Wagon so I could sleep in it whenever I was tired and Diana had more room to stretch out since she was a large dog. One market day in Lezignan, I met a pianist in the coffee shop. I loved to browse through second-hand shops and when he told me that he liked them as well, we made a date the next day to look for some treasures. We drove to Narbonne and when he saw a beautiful old piano, he sat down and played so well, that all the people working there applauded and egged him on to play some more. I was very impressed.

We went to dinner together and when he asked me to live with him, I said "Yes." I took him home with me since I had to arrange for Kitty Cats to be fed. Paula liked my cat and was happy to take care of him in her house. I took Diana with me.

When we arrived in Ribot where my new partner lived, I was amazed at the romantic old village next to a river at the foot of tall hills. We were happy together until about two weeks later, when I went to get bread without him and before getting back into his house, a man greeted me outside. He only said, "Bonjour." My partner yelled angrily, "Who is talking to my woman?" and came out pointing a shotgun at the friendly neighbor who ran for his life. After that, I gave my partner a lecture, to never behave that way again because I did not consider myself anyone's property and would only stay with him as long as I wanted to.

We made up and on the weekend we went to his favorite bar, where he knew many people. He invited all his friends to the house and opened many bottles of wine. Toward the morning, almost all the folks went home and only a few stayed on. My partner danced with another woman which I thought odd but when he kissed her on the mouth, I grabbed my things and hurried with Diana to my car where I locked the doors and started the motor. He came like a fury toward the car and threatened me, that if I didn't open the door, he would hit me. As I drove away, he kicked the door so hard, that it left a big dent in it.

Sometime later, he called me on the telephone. He pleaded with me to forgive him and to come to his birthday party. I told him that I wanted nothing to do with him anymore and that he had killed my love for him. He kept calling again and again and invited all my friends as well and assured me that he only wanted to stay friends with me. He pleaded until I gave in.

Not A Boring Moment

On his birthday, I took Diana and three of my friends with me. The pianist had cooked a huge paella in a beautiful wild garden near the river. He asked everybody to help themselves to wine and food and urged me to try the paella. I took some on a plate and gave Diana the fat from a piece of meat that was on it.

My ex-partner snuck up behind me and hammered me on my head with the back of his fist, so hard, that I suffered from headaches for years afterwards. I told my friends what had happened and asked them to leave with me since this guy was dangerous but they preferred to stay. I then drove away with Diana.

When I got to Lezignan, at about 4:30 a.m., a man in a car sped out of an alley to my left and rammed my Peugeot Station Wagon so hard, that it was a total wreck. Diana was okay and I got away with a couple of bruises. I got out of my car and the driver got out of his. He claimed it was my fault and I told him it was his. I was on the main road and he had rammed me from the left which made him the one at fault.

He then yelled at me and since I was only 5 km from my home, I left the car in the middle of the road, took the key and walked with Diana to my house. In the morning, the police arrived and asked me why I had left the car there. I told them, that I was afraid of the man who had rammed me. They understood and his insurance covered the value of the Peugeot, which was just enough to buy a Volkswagen Transporter from the gypsy family a few houses away from mine.

Robert spoke of people who lived in teepees and asked me if I would like to go with him to see how the Teepees were constructed. This sounded like a good idea and so we drove to the woods in South Corbières. Friendly people greeted us and invited us into some teepees. It was autumn, and cold, so we sat around the fire inside a teepee. The inhabitants of the interesting Indian tents told me that the hunters had bought the ground and they were forced to go away.

One of them said his dog had just given birth to a litter of puppies and he did not know where to go. I felt sorry for 'Jens', his dogs and his two friends and invited them to stay in my garden in Marseillette until the puppies were old enough to find a home. They accepted gladly. Jens drove a very old Ford Transit van from the mid 60's. The others owned no vehicles, so they all followed me in the Transit to Marseillette. I did not offer them my caravan but Jens parked the Transit there and the other two slept in tents.

Roland Stauffacher was a really nice guy from Switzerland who had been rescued by his aunt when, on a visit, she found him as a toddler chained to a bed all bruised up in an orphanage. She was a comedian who raised him all on her own. Roland earned his money by doing a pantomime impression of Charley Chaplin and tricks with his, very loved, small dog.

Rolly was very sensitive and too proud to beg like the other two. After four months, all three of them were still living in my garden even though Jens' puppies had all been sold or given away. Jens and his other friend exploited Rolly. Whenever he went to Carcassonne to perform his act with permission and came back with money, he was forced to give it to them or be beaten up. When I found this out, I told the other two to get out of my garden. As a result, I was threatened with a beating by Jens.

I could not go to the police since they had not helped me or Paula when we had been robbed and attacked by the crazy owner of a second-hand store for trying to bargain over the price. He had ripped the F Fr. 100 bill out of my hand and pushed me to the ground outside, where his mates watched him trying to hit me with a iron bar. I rolled away to avoid getting hit and when he tried again, Paula pushed him and he turned on her. Then I attacked him until Paula got off the floor and we both ran for our lives. None of the men watching helped us but seemed amused by the whole incident.

Arriving at the police station, they let us wait for an hour before taking our statements. When it was time to sign the report, I wanted to read the statement first. The gendarme said, "You don't have to read it, you can trust us." I read it just the same and told him I would not sign anything without reading it first. Fortunately, I did read the lies in it that made us look as if we were at fault. I complained that the statement was not written truthfully and demanded that it be rewritten the way we had told it to them. We had to wait again and saw, through a partly open, door the second-hand shop owner handing some money to a cop. Then we were handed the same form as before and I refused to sign and walked out. So did Paula.

I took Rolly to the house with me. He repaired the shelves in my kitchen and insulated all around the inside of my roof to keep the draft out. He helped me with everything and was good company. Diana and his dog liked each other. When I wanted to pay Rolly for all the work he had done, he refused to take anything.

Rolly was much younger than I but declared his love for me and loneliness made me accept. He was a man alone and I, a lonely woman. I admired his nobility. It did not work out between us and he left. I heard that he had fallen deeply in love with a young woman who felt the same about him. I was so glad for him. He deserved it.

My parents were getting older and needed me from time to time. My sister could not go since she worked full time as a manager for Swiss Television. My brother wasn't able to help out either because he was ill. He lived alone with his cat in the mountains and did not drive. I liked to go and see my parents.

My mother had become more understanding of me and a lot less tyrannical. My father and I enjoyed a good bottle of wine and my mother loved cooking and baking. Mostly, we all sat at the round, pear-wood table in the kitchen. Family members and their friends visited often.

One day, Uncle Paul, my father's brother, dropped in and we started to discuss relationships. Paul told me that I was like him, always choosing the same type of man while he chose the same kind of woman. He added, "If we were able to change this pattern, we might have the chance to find happiness." This made me think, even though I realized that if a man looked me in the eyes and made me feel a certain way, my emotions would be stronger than my reason. I always believed I would find my ideal partner in life.

Rosa

Rosa was my neighbor. She was a cheerful old woman who trusted everyone and was very good natured, but too naïve for her own sake. She came to my door waving a typical letter from Readers Digest in front of my face and said, "Maya, I have just won F Francs 1,000 000!" I took the letter and read the small print on it, that stated she had won the right to enter a competition to win up to 1 million. I explained it to her and told her, that they only wanted to sell their stuff by making her believe that she could win. Poor Rosa was not able to read the small print, even with her glasses. She came back almost every week with award letters, believing she had won a million.

One day, she asked me where I was born. I told her, "In Switzerland." Rosa said that her son was in Marseilles and wanted to know if Switzerland was near Marseilles. I got the atlas out and showed her where we were in France, where Marseilles was and where Switzerland could be found on the map. She said Switzerland is not far, and Marseilles not either. I tried to explain how many kilometers in distance it was. However, Rosa had never been out of the village further than the next town in all her life and could not relate to distances. Rosa had an old boyfriend in the village and the two of them met up and went walking in secrecy together in order to not upset their families.

One day, Rosa came and told me that her son wanted to buy her house but would let her live for free in it for the rest of her life. This sounded great to her since her old age pension was so low, that it was not enough to live on and too much to die. I told Rosa, that as long as the house was in her name, she would be free instead of dependent on her family, who could throw her out of the house. However, she believed they would never do that. She sold the house to her son, (I believe, he was a policeman) and soon after that, she was put into an old folks' home. Poor, good-natured old Rosa's boyfriend died and she lives on, in the hope of winning a million Euros. Last time I saw her, she was so frail, visiting her own house on a Sunday, with all the family around talking down to her. She looked sad and lonely. I remember what a cheerful woman she once was.

Hitch Hiker from the Azores

I will give him the pseudonym 'Azor.' I met him standing sad and lost near the pay booth of the autobahn on my way back from Switzerland. He was dressed in a T-shirt and pants, was barefoot and had no luggage. When I asked him where he would like to go, he said somewhere he could find a job picking grapes. I told him that I knew two men who might have a job for him in the village where I lived and he was relieved to have some hope of work. It was a cool late summer's day and he looked chilled.

I took him to a second-hand store and bought him some shoes, a sweater and a leather jacket, socks etc. Some people had helped me when I needed help in the past and now it was my turn to help this poor man. I cooked us a big meal and he was very hungry. Then he did the dishes and told me that he had escaped from prison in the Azores. He was imprisoned because they had caught him with marijuana. I offered him a joint and invited him to use the shower and the guest bedroom and assured him we would look for work the next day. It was not easy to find work because machines had replaced most men, but he was lucky and found a job as grape carrier for a rich Arab grape farmer. Dead tired, 'Azor' used to come back in the evening with blue marks on his shoulders from carrying the huge and heavy drums full with grapes to the tractor. Then he insisted on cooking dinner and washing the dishes every evening.

That was very nice of him. After dinner we relaxed at the table with Diana sleeping in her bed under it. Kitty Cats liked him as well.

Azor was small but muscular. He was many years younger

than I and I desired nothing more than his company. He wanted mine. We were two lonesomes sharing some time. He slept in the guest bedroom and I in my bedroom-studio in the attic. This went on for several weeks, with my friends joining us around the table most evenings.

Azor's job at the winemaker was over but he only received a small part of his promised salary and when he complained, the Arab told him that he would make problems for him for working 'on the black' if he said one more word. Azor was upset and disappointed. I told him to go back and threaten him with problems for hiring him illegally, if he did not pay up right away. The Arab paid. It makes me so angry that some rich people avoid paying the poor workers what they owe them.

One night while I was asleep, Azor sneaked upstairs and half woke me up with a kiss. Before I was totally awake, we made love. After I told Azor that this was not supposed to happen because I wanted a man at least my age and wanted him to find a girlfriend his own age. He excused himself and told me he was really in love with me. I let him know that I liked him very much but did not wish more than a platonic friendship.

I took him to a concert in the Minerva's and met a man I spoke to. Azor was not drinking anything so he could drive my Volkswagen Transporter home. He drove all the way home at full speed in first gear. I yelled at him but he was determined to break the engine as revenge for me speaking to another man. When we got home, I asked him to take his things and get out of my house.

He refused and got so mad that I picked up the phone and pretended to speak to a policeman and said loudly, "Okay, you will be here right away," before I hung up. Azor locked the door and put my keys in his pocket. I was afraid and escaped through the small window. Diana was outside and we got away with my handbag and the car keys.

By the time I had driven around the village, Azor had gone. He stole my treasured 18 Kt. gold bracelet Certina watch given to me by my father for the birth of my second daughter, my entire collection of first world war and other antique money- a gift from my father as well, two ivory necklaces, a pearl and amethyst necklace and some of my favorite CDs. I was heartbroken and never stopped for hitch hikers again, except once for an old woman.

I was glad that 'Azor' was out of my life. Diana and I drove to my garden. Jens and his friend were not happy to see me again and greeted me with, "How long are you staying?" "As long as I like," I replied and moved into my caravan. When I had a walk around my land, I was so upset about the mess the two beggars had left, that I yelled at them to clean it up. They made a fire and burned some of the rubbish.

Then they told me that the best day to beg was in front of the Catholic church after mass on Sunday. They said they could make at least FFrancs 500 each in a hour's work sitting there with a hat in front of them and a sign with "Take any work" written on it. Jens said that no one ever threatened to give them work, which was fine with him. He also showed me his German passport with the name Jens von Sachsen printed on it and claimed to have been thrown out by his blue-blood father for appearing at a formal dinner in torn jeans, instead of a traditional black suit with tie. I did not believe that one, and even if that was true, I did not warm up to him since he had taken over my garden against my will. I wanted to know if they had taken my gas bottle from the back of the caravan and they said "No."

I did not stay there any longer since I did not feel at home with the beggars in my garden. They assured me, that they would be out, as soon as they could find a place to park Jen's van. When I got back to Argens, my friends Patrick and Linda said that they had bought an almost full bottle of gas from Jens. I recognized it as the bottle that had been missing from my caravan.

A few weeks later, I went back to my garden and those thieves-liars-beggars were not there but a totally wrecked car had been left on my land. I stayed there until they showed up the next day and lied to them that the police were looking for them. Jens said, "My girlfriend had an accident and we had to hide the car here." I said that they should tow the car to a scrap yard and disappear before the police came back and fined them, or even threw them into jail. I warned the two bums, that the police had only left because I had promised to call the police station from the hotel next door the minute they came back to my garden. This frightened the intruders and they pulled the wrecked car to the scrap yard and disappeared from my garden after having stayed there for two years.

Normally, I don't believe in lying but under the circumstances I had to use a lie to protect my garden from being further destroyed and to get them out for good. It took me a month to clean their mess up and I never invited anyone else to stay there without me again.

Baba. Emil's Death. A Shot in my Window

'Baba' was a photographer who wanted to explore the south of France. I had met him at a party and we started to live together. The natural caves, dolmens, castles, romantic, historic towns and beautiful landscapes were his subjects. It was interesting being with him, however he was completely broke and I paid for the food, hotel rooms, films and gasoline for my van. I figured this was costing me less than a school to learn more about photography and I thought I was in love with him.

When he left me to go back to his mother in Nantes, I took him to the airport. On the way there, I felt freezing cold running down my spine and stopped the car to get out. Baba asked me, "What is the matter with you?" I stumbled, "Someone I love has died."

It was Emil, the man I had lived with for 7 1/2 years, who had been killed (or murdered?) in Cuba. He was on his way to city hall to get married to the daughter of Fidel Castro's best friend, when his car broke down. He was laying under it to fix it.

Strange, I knew for a fact that Emil could not fix anything mechanical and used to panic every time there was something wrong with the van. Then, he was run over by a German who crashed into their car. He died instantly and so did his girlfriend and one of the witnesses. The other witness was taken to the hospital in critical condition and I heard nothing more about the case. Having known Emil very well, I could easily imagine that he could have tried to take over Cuba. Like so many men who became political leaders, he would have been a tyrant. His death made me very sad for a while but I finally had to cope with the fact that he was gone for good. I really became free in my head to move on again.

The men since our relationship had only been compromises, even though some were deep friendships. I did not hear anything from Baba until a year later, when he asked me to model naked for him and I hung up the phone. That was the end of Baba for me. I am not a prude but had no urge to return to the past or be exploited again. I did just one more compromise out of loneliness. His name was "Jean" and I will write in a later chapter about life with him.

The needed wood for my fireplace and so I drove to the dump and picked up wood to throw into my van for heating. Some hunters were shooting birds there. I told them that it was disgusting and a terrible shame to murder birds and there was not enough meat on them to make a meal. I was sad and angry and told them it was a shame that so many species of animals were extinct or dying out and there would not be any wild animals left for their grandchildren, if they continued to keep killing the way they did. I drove back home with Diana and made a fire to heat my house.

Then I heard a shot and ran upstairs to the guest bedroom to see a bullet hole in the window. I knew that one of the hunters had shot it and was glad not to have been in that room when it happened.

My Father's Death

My mother and my sister called me on the phone and told me they could not take care of my father any longer and he had to go to the hospital for observation since he suffered from irritable bowel syndrome and then to the clinical care department for old people since he was nearly blind. They begged me not to tell my father anything about this, since he believed that he would be coming back home after the tests. I said to them that this would hit back like everything that we do, that it wasn't right.

I told my mother that I would come home right away. I took a few things and Diana, locked up the house and drove straight toward Switzerland. I spent the night in a hotel in Orange, where Diana was allowed to stay in the room. I shared a steak with Diana and then we got some much-needed sleep. When I arrived in my parent's house, my father was already in the hospital.

I went to see him the next day during the visiting hour and he had been pumped full of Valium and other drugs. He recognized me immediately but was so tired, that I just said, "Hello", embraced him and left to come back the next day. It broke my heart to see my beloved father so weak and helpless in that damned institution.

My daughter Alexa was in Wil visiting me and my mother. My daughter Julie, who lived in Bern, came to see me as well, which brought some sunshine into my life. We all realized, that my mother could not take care of my father since she was old and frail as well. She was 81 and he was 84 years old. My mother had good friends coming over and was still very independent. If she needed my daughter or my sister or me, the one who was free would go and help her right away.

When I got back to my home, I discovered that I had been robbed. They had taken my hi-fi, a clock and other things. I had more important matters to worry about and called my friend Lucy the artist and part time nurse. I asked her if she would like to take care of my father in his home. She said, "Yes," and would have liked to live in Switzerland in my parent's house, which had an apartment on the top floor for her to live in. I was so happy about Lucy helping my parents and called my mother to share the exiting news with her.

    I told her that my father could come back home since my friend Lucy was prepared to take care of him and she replied sternly, that she did not want another woman in the house and that she wished for my father to stay where he was well taken care of , and that she went to see him every day up to three times a day and took him home cooked meals. She also mentioned, that they were better equipped where he was. My father always asked, "Why can't I come home?" and so I asked his doctor, if I could take him with me to the south of France if he could lie on the bed in my van.

    He said, "Can you help him take a bath? Do you have stairs in the house?" I had not thought about that and could not offer him the comfort he needed. Then the doctor said, "Don't you realize that he would not be strong enough to survive a long journey like that?"

    I was the one in the family who had no commitments and so I visited every two or three months and stayed for a few weeks. After my father had been turned passive and weak from all the tranquillizers they had drugged him with, he was moved to the old folks' ward. It was so hard for me to watch my father fade away for two long years. The last thing he ate and drank was the caviar and the champagne I took to him before leaving again.

    A week later, Julie called me and told me that if I wanted to see my father still alive, I should come as soon as I could. Diana and I drove straight to Wil without stopping, but he had died in Julie's arms at the age of 86 years. His last wish, was to be buried without the presence of any priest. Also, he wished that no one should wear black and that there should be a party with food, drink and music for friends and family to be happy instead of sad.

    The morgue was next to the chapel and several bodies were laid out in different rooms, as was my father. My mother, sister and I went to pay our last respects. When they were ready to leave, I told them I wanted to be alone with my father for a bit longer. His body looked so young, the way I remembered him from my childhood. I stood there and spoke with my thoughts to him, that what they had done to him was not fair. Then I felt him standing behind me, with the warmth of his hand on my shoulder, saying his last words to me, "Joggeli (his nickname for me) forgive them, they don't know what they did, you can go now."

I walked out of the room and headed for the large main door. When I wanted to open it, it was locked. I panicked and believed they wanted to keep me there. Then I forced myself to think what to do. I pulled the lever on top down and the lever on the bottom up, and pulled the door open.

I wanted to get Diana out of the van to attend the funeral with me but my mother told me that this was no place for a dog, so I obeyed against my will in order to avoid an argument. The party took place in the Hof (the most important historic building with conference rooms and a restaurant in Wil). Julie had arranged for a trio, who gave a beautiful classical concert and everyone who wanted to say something about my father could do so. There were many anecdotes recounted with tender love and great respect for this wonderful man, whom I was privileged and proud to have as my father.

Bundesrat Ogi, who was a friend and one of his classmates, attended the funeral and came to the party with his wife. Uncle Paul was also there, even though he was very weak with cancer and died just two weeks after my father. My old friend Willy and his wife Beth were also present and many people paid their last respects. An artist friend of mine, "Toni Calcaferi" made the tombstone for my parents. My mother wished to be cremated after her death and the ashes buried in the same grave as my father. The tombstone is a work of art and her name could be carved next to my father's when her time came to die. I hoped she would last a few more years.

Jean. Choked by a Drunk

I met him at the Black Mountain, while I was out looking at some houses with a friend. The properties were less expensive there and I hoped to replace my small house with a barn that I could turn into an art studio. I could not find anything for the equivalent price of my existing house, so we went to the coffee shop in Labastide-Rouairoux for a drink. I gave Jean my address and he gave me his, then I drove my friend home.

When I got to my house, I parked the car and approached the door while Diana was playing with another dog down the road. Suddenly, a drunken man attacked me and wanted to force me to open the door and take him inside. When I refused, he grabbed me around the throat and started to choke me. I thought that if he was trying to kill me, I was not afraid to hurt him and aggressively scratched him with my long fingernails down his entire face, leaving him with marks full of blood. He then turned away and I quickly opened the door, went inside and locked it again.

A few weeks later, I received a marriage proposal from Jean and went to see him. I still did not believe in marriage but was prepared to live with him, rather than stay lonely. Jean was a vegetable farmer from Belgium. He shared his big house with me and I paid for the groceries, except for what he grew in the many gardens which people had lent or rented to him.

He invited me to meet his mother in Belgium and that was the first time I was there. The mother was a really good cook and she and all the other Belgian people were gourmets and very generous. I loved the Belgian cuisine and Jean showed me many interesting places including the second-hand market in the center of Bruxelles.

He had inherited an apartment from his grandfather with his brother who had restored it and we stayed there. Jean went out with the boys and my feelings were hurt when he left me behind. I went to the next bar and had a few drinks before looking at the town and then returned to the apartment to sleep. Jean came back toward the morning. He told me that men would go out here without their woman. I told him, "Suits me well. I will also go out with whomever I feel like."

Back in Labastide, Jean and I worked together. I helped him pick the vegetables and let him use three strips of land between the rows of apple trees in my garden in Marseillette to grow some of the organic vegetables he sold in Carcassonne.

We had been living together for a year, when his friends from Belgium came to visit and I invited everybody to my garden where I roasted a leg of lamb on the open fire. I also wrapped filled potatoes in cooking foil to put them on the embers. I bought a dozen of bottles of wine as well. Jean's friends ignored me and so did he, without giving me a reason why. It was depressing when they talked only to each other.

I went into the caravan with Diana at my side while the boys were continuing to party around the fire. I heard a lot of laughter and fell asleep. Jean woke me up and said, "Time to go", so we drove back to his house where we made passionate love. One of his friends was still there. We were happy together. The day after that, Jean told me, "I don't love you anymore and I don't desire you anymore. You have to go away." I thought he was joking but he added, "I am serious." When I asked why, he did not answer and Diana and I left him and drove to my garden.

I looked for the fault in myself but could not find one. I had done everything in my power to make him happy and had believed that he was happy as well, since he often told me that he loved me. Depressions kept me from thinking straight and I walked around the garden and along the canal, not understanding the world.

The ducks and the birds in the trees seemed to say to each other, "Will she live or die?" Then I said to myself, "I will live." When I went to the Restaurant in La Redorte for dinner, Kathy, the owner, told me that a friend wanted to find someone who would do exchange business for a house with his sailing boat. I told her that I was very interested in that proposition since I could tie up the boat to a tree on the bottom of my garden and live in it. Surely I would not be as lonely on the canal, where I hoped to meet a sailor again. This gave me new hope.

I was fed up with Argens since I had been robbed there twice already, and most people in town were weird and inbred. The mayor suggested making a competition for the most beautiful garden but the daft buggers sabotaged each other's gardens since all wanted theirs to be the best and win the prize. The gardens looked as if they had been struck by war. A Swiss man who lived two houses away from me, tried to convince me over and over again that I had to believe in God and accept the Bible.

That's a book that constantly contradicts itself and doesn't make any sense to me. I prefer the reality of science any day.

I gave Kathy my address in Marseillette where the man could find me.

THE MAN OF MY DREAMS

It was a hot day and I had watered some of my plants while walking around naked in the privacy of my garden. Everything lived and it had become a beautiful jungle like wilderness with a multitude of trees bushes and flowers. I had just cultivated a small part to plant vegetables between the wild herbs whose shade protected them from the hot summer sun.

When I walked up to the caravan, a very handsome man walked toward me. I forgot that I was naked until I saw the embarrassed expression on his face and hurried into the caravan to put something on and then came straight out again. As he introduced himself and our eyes met, I felt that feeling again but much stronger than ever before. Not just did it feel hot and cold down my spine but from the top of my head to my little toes and my vagina started to pulsate. I more than desired him, I was instantly and deeply in love with him at first sight. This happened on July 5, 1998.

He is an Englishman who has since told me, that he felt the same desire as I. However, out of respect for me, he found it incorrect to sleep with me on the first day we met . So we had shared a bottle of white wine together and made a date for July 7th (my father's birthday), at the Café de la Poste in Olonzac and sealed our love on his boat.

He likes to stay anonymous and I respect that. I was 58 years old when we met and we've been together 13 years, (as I write this) and we are even happier now. First we had a few disagreements because he wanted me to stop drinking and I thought that he wanted to restrict my freedom.

When I made the decision to stop drinking alcohol, I realized that I had gained more freedom. So I even stopped smoking of my own free will and feel really liberated to do what I really like. I had no idea that a relationship could be so good. We each have our own homes and for a while I had my own houseboat. We are each financially independent of the other and are together out of our own free will. I do anything to keep him happy and he does the same for me. I introduced him to my mother before she died. She was glad for me and relieved that I had finally found my *******Soulmate and Partner. *******

My mother was getting weaker and weaker with cancer. I asked her who she would like to have with her when she had to die and she told me that she wished to die alone and in the hospital. She also told me that like my father, she also wanted a celebration of life without a priest, for all the guests who attended her funeral, instead of a sad last supper. All the family members and friends who could attend were there and so was Diana. My mother died of cancer three years after my father had gone and her ashes are in the same grave. Tony Calcaferi chiseled their joint tomb stone with my mother's name next to my father's.

Unfortunately, Tony, a brilliant sculptor killed himself in his studio soon after Anita, his woman, had committed suicide. He was one of my best friends and I will never forget this sensitive artist.

Not A Boring Moment

I had created a miniature sculpture for an art competition for a fountain, which was designed so that dogs, birds and other animals could drink as well as people. Before I entered the competition, I asked Toni if he would build the fountain from my model if I should win. He told me that he would be very happy to do it. I entered my model and had to go somewhere during the exhibition and evaluation. I got back in time to pick up my work. They could not find it, until I insisted that they immediately search for it. It was found in a back room, hidden behind a door and had never been on exhibition. When I told Toni about that injustice by the community heads of Wil, who benefitted from the artists who joined and had hidden my work, he said, "Maya, they always choose and know in advance who their winner will be. The struggling artists are just milked."

When I die all the friends and dogs will be welcome to attend my funeral and bring their own bottle and sandwiches to the burial place. As music, I would choose Emerson, Lake and Palmer, Mark Knopfler, Steve Winwood, Iris De Ment, Johnny Cash, Sydney Bechet, Louis Armstrong, Joe Cocker or any other music except martial music. On the other hand, I probably won't care anymore what happens after my death, since it will be no longer my responsibility. As far as I am concerned, they can feed my body to the hungry dogs.

I hope to outdo the Queen Mother in age. At funerals and weddings we usually meet again or when there is a family reunion at which nearly 200 people would be present if they could all attend. My father was a gourmet who liked a good cognac, fine wines and smoked cigarettes. My mother was a non-smoker didn't drink alcohol and was a vegetarian. Both my parents died at the age of 86 years.

I am in love with the most gorgeous and real man in the world. My dream of meeting him came true but since he wants to stay anonymous, I will continue my life story with (I) instead of (we) even though I am no longer alone.

Pepieux

I bought a historic barn in Pepieux, with its small steep garden descending to the river Aude. It had a gorgeous, arched front portal. After a hard time getting the neighbors permissions, I had it supplied with water, electricity and main drainage and could finally go ahead with the work. Before I could use it as my art studio, the owner of the bar told me, " You foreigners don't have to believe you can crawl into any old space and get away with it." This turned me off so much, that I sold that beautiful historic barn to a man from Germany who loves it as much as I did but had the courage to stay in that racist village.

Artis

I bought a 12 meter long Catamaran hull and had it built up to a house boat with Mollycroft windows, a toilet and shower room, a rear deck with an outboard Yamaha 50 horse-power motor and a covered front deck with the steering. One could walk along the narrow walkways outside from front to back for easy handling through the locks. The galley had a hot water heater and was part of the large cabin with a double bed to the rear with a spectacular curtain across, two sofa beds along each side with a coffee table in between and a round table with six chairs in front of it. Opposite the galley was a large buffet and a wood burner to heat Artis with.

I loved living on the boat and had many friends come and visit me. Diana liked to be able to go out and be in nature. She had her dog friends to play with and loved cats.

What disturbed me, was that the VNF (Voies Navigable de France, a government agency controlling all the navigable French waterways) started to destroy the wildlife and cut the wild flowers and grasses before they had a chance to seed. Butterfly eggs and all living things had no chance to survive. Plane and other trees had their beautiful natural branches brutally cut with chainsaws and looked like people with their arms cut off. They did not hear if I complained.

Not A Boring Moment

Hire cruiser companies sprung up in all the ports and tried to push the beautiful barges, sailing and other boats out. They hired out specially designed very plump plastic parlor boats that looked like monstrous bathtubs and were driven by noisy drunken tourists who had no idea about a boat. They sped without a license so fast, that the soil on the banks was washed away from the roots of the trees and threatened the people who lived aboard by running into them.

Artis got hit twice but was lucky not to suffer much damage. We all had to scream at them to slow down. They destroyed the water lilies and other plants which had graced the canal banks and that the VNF could not reach with their damned machines. Herons, kingfishers and other animals panicked and flew away. Fireflies and dragonflies as well as other insects started to disappear.

Suddenly, we were charged a high price to be on the canal, not to speak of the fees in the ports even though we all spent money with the shopkeepers, pubs etc. When the VNF sent people who wanted to cut nature down at the side of Artis, I got angry and stood in front of the flail mower, whose driver did not stop until a few centimeters from my feet. I told him that I had paid to be in this spot and did not want my wild garden to be murdered. I explained and named many plants and flowers to him and took him to the VNF bureau, where I tried to explain to them the importance of safeguarding wild life.

When I was away shopping they came and destroyed it all.

Maya B.

Artis

Inside Artis

The foredeck of Artis showing the control post

Maya B.

Artis at La Redorte, France

Happy on the catamaran Artis

In the Flood

In November 1999 Diana and I were on my boat. It rained like mad outside and in no time, the rain quickly raised the water levels of the canal. It was so uninviting to go outside and so I postponed moving my VW Transporter until when the wind and rain decreased in ferocity. It increased even more and one of the two lines that was holding Artis to the mooring post broke. There was no way I could go on shore. My love's sailing boat next to mine broke a line as well and when it bumped into my boat, I tied the two together in the hope, if one got loose the other would hold it.

I tried to sleep but was too nervous to get much rest. Artis was swinging across the canal and then a plane tree fell on her roof and held her in place. The next day, the water was over the banks and the houses stood in water. The current dragged two boats in the strong current alongside Artis and out over the banks into a vineyard. Boats were scattered everywhere and floating out over the land.

I tried to chase my fright away by taking photos and filling Diana's dish to the top with food and water in case I had to swim for it. I watched my van slide into the middle of the roaring canal waters and finish up with only one wheel sticking out, upside down. If Artis were to be washed out of the canal, it had two possible routes. One was into the vineyard, the other was to be banged around the trees of the forest.

When the water had lowered a bit, a friend came to tell me that they had called the fire brigade who would come and rescue me. I was so glad but could not imagine that they could fly a helicopter in this violent storm and rain, until I saw a man being lowered onto the boat tied next to me. Immediately, I took Diana and went across to wait for the man. He urged, "Quick, get into this loop" and I uttered, "Not without my dog."

Diana was frightened and refused to get into my arms and the man said, "You come up with me and I will go down again to get her." I got into the helicopter and the man went down but came up without Diana, saying that he could not make her come with him but would get her later that day. I had left the door open on my boat and hoped she would stay inside.

During the whole rescue mission, the pilot kept the helicopter in the same spot despite the storm and weather. I admired that hero's clear head, skill, concentration, strong nerves and steady hands. I was fascinated by my first flight in a helicopter. The pilot hovered over a drenched field in La Redorte, Aude and I jumped out from about a meter above ground so he did not have to land and could continue to fly to the next rescue mission.

My second-hand fur coat was soaked and I headed to the 'Gigy' bar. There were several of my friends who had been rescued from the top of their roofs who greeted me like a long lost friend. We were so glad to be alive, that we celebrated with strong stuff. Kathy was sad to have her restaurant swamped and damaged since she had put all her money into it to have it restored.

The third floor was still okay and she invited us all to share whatever she could find and save from the kitchen. When we got to her place, we grabbed a full bottle of wine and whatever we could floating in the kitchen and went up the steps into the safety of her third floor apartment. She took all sorts of delicacies from the fridge and a cupboard and put it all out onto the table.

My friend Lola from Spain cried and refused to eat. She had lost her father a month before and her car in the flood and everything except what she was wearing. We all tried to console her but she was heartbroken and was sitting on the floor. I took half of my piece of bread to her and said, "If you don't want it, you can give it to someone who is hungry. This cheered her up enough to realize that being alive is more important than worrying about what cannot be changed. We all ate and drank with a lot of pleasure, not worrying about lost material things, just being happy to enjoy the moment and being alive.

Kathy got tired and so the rest of us left to go to the pub. Next to it was a big place, where we were given dry clothes, bottles of milk and food for free.

My Love was in England. His cousin and her husband came to look for me and took me to their house which was on top of a hill. I phoned the fire brigade and asked if they had rescued Diana. I was told that they had to get people first and could not get my dog until later. I kept calling but always got the same answer. Homesick for my Love and for Diana, I fell asleep exhausted.

The next day, my Love showed up with his son from England and Diana. I was the happiest woman on earth. My Love had only heard of the flood, when he was trying to get out of the auto route in Carcassonne and they told him he could not get out because of the flood. He said he had to, since his woman was in danger so they made an exception. He found Artis open, my van in the water and Diana shivering on top of the wheel. My Love and his son borrowed a dinghy and rowed out to rescue her.

They had had to walk back a kilometer to his van and carry my exhausted and weakened dog, Diana while walking through up to half a meter of thick mud and were very tired. I knew that my Love was the best man in the world and I was the lucky one who had his love.

Artis aground but upright and mostly undamaged, the author's van becomes a write-off, and my Love's boat is still seaworthy.

No other vessel survived quite as well as Artis!

The Inheritance

I inherited enough money from my parents to buy a gorgeous 16th century house with two barns, two studio apartments and a garden on top of a hill in Allée du Château, at the end of a small village called Brezilhac, in Aude. The view from the living room was incredibly beautiful and one could see over hills and valleys into the Black Mountains. On a clear day, I could see the Pyrenees mountains to my right from the kitchen window and also see across the park with magnificent trees, where the mayor lived with his family and horses. This made me feel as if I lived in a tree house.

The barn had been built later than the house to which it was attached, after the revolution from the stones of the old fortress. In 2000, this became, 'My own, First Art Studio'. What a Millennium!

The façade of the house was built in the year 1500 and rendered over, so my friends Alan and Leslie removed all the render and pointed the beautiful blue-grey stones like jewels. I had known Alan, a sensitive, kind and gentle man since 1992, when he did a wonderful job fixing the roof of my house in Argens, while

Leslie (who met him through me) mixed the cement. Leslie came from the U.S.A. across the Atlantic on the raft, 'Floating Neutrino', which she had built with four or five others. They survived by playing jazz. Leslie played the sousaphone. Alan was indeed a very special man who was loved by everyone.

    I had a shock, when I found out later, that he had choked to death in Leslie's arms because he did not have his asthma inhaler with him and had believed he did not need it any longer since for many months, he had been free from asthma. I felt so sorry for Leslie, as they were so much in love and about ready to go sailing on a raft that Alan had built for them. He will live on in the memory of all who met him.

    The people of Brezilhac were all very nice. There was no shop or anything to buy. The baker would honk the horn of his van when he arrived three times a week. The supermarket van honked every Friday and the butcher twice a week.

    People ran into the village center even if they did not need anything just to have a social gathering. In the middle of the center stood a war memorial with a huge iron cross, with an almost life size suffering Jesus nailed to it and painted pink. This disturbed me and I suggested they change it for something less depressing. It was just the sort of thing that reminded you of the middle age brutality and the times when the church had tortured and murdered the Cathars and could cause nightmares. Unfortunately, no one had the guts to remove him and he is probably still there now.

    Once every year, I exhibited my newest artworks and sold prints made into post cards. My Love moved to Normandy to be closer to his children and grandchildren. I sold my house and was living temporarily with him, until we found a place near an airport in Bretagne so I would feel closer to my children and grandchildren.

    Diana was not feeling well and had cancer. I was thinking about taking her to the vet to end the suffering. She had rheumatism and could hardly hear and I gave her hand signals and clapped my hands together, which she could hear. Soon afterwards, she ran straight into a car and howled short and loud and died in my arms. I hoped she would only be in a coma but the vet verified her death and took me into his arms. We both cried. Diana was 17 years old. I still miss her. She was an intelligent and exceptional dog and is immortalized in many of my paintings.

Dans le journal ' Ouest France ', jeudi 17 Juillet 2008

Le Chatellier

L'amour et la paix sur la toile de l'artiste Maya B

Maya B, artiste peintre, expose ses peintures à l'agence BNP-Paribas de Flers, jusqu'au 14 août. Paysages et vaches en Normandie, lys, langoustine sont parmi les thèmes exposés : « J'ai choisi ces tableaux, parce que je voulais quelque chose que tout le monde comprenne. Des peintures comme la langoustine ou l'ail sont le reflet de ma passion pour la cuisine. »

Dans sa maison plantée dans la campagne normande, le visage encadré d'une épaisse chevelure, la voix teintée d'accents venus d'ailleurs, Maya B se raconte : « J'ai peint toute ma vie, c'était mon désir profond, ma passion. Dès l'année 1972, j'ai pris la décision de ne rien faire d'autre que la peinture. » Née en Suisse en 1940, Maya a sillonné les mers du monde en voilier, elle a vécu aux quatre coins de la terre (Etats-Unis, Nouvelle-Zélande, Australie,...) De ces voyages, elle a rapporté des images, des couleurs, des souvenirs de rencontres mémorables : « Je voulais trouver la vérité, je voulais être moi-même sans obéir à personne. » Puis elle est arrivée en France ; Maya a vécu quelque temps dans l'Aude, puis elle a découvert la Normandie et le Châtellier où elle est installée depuis deux ans : « J'adore la Normandie, ses arbres, ses forêts, sa verdure et ses habitants, accueillants et chaleureux. » Cette nouvelle terre d'accueil est devenue source d'inspiration pour la peinture de Maya.

Aujourd'hui, elle a, à son actif entre 400 et 500 tableaux : « Je travaille de manière très intensive. Je donne tout ce qui est à l'intérieur de moi. Quand l'énergie est épuisée, je me repose quelques jours, je me ressource dans la nature, puis je reprends la peinture. Pour chaque tableau, je ne m'arrête pas jusqu'à ce que ce soit parfait. »

Le désir de Maya est de transmettre, par sa peinture, un message d'amour, de beauté et de paix. D'ailleurs, ses tableaux sont autant de fenêtres sur la beauté simple et pure de notre monde.

Maya et l'un de ses tableaux fétiches : la bannière universelle. Elle expose à l'agence BNP-Paribas jusqu'au 14 août.

A new Universal Flag on display in Normandy

While packing my work prior to moving to Normandy, I discovered that a large number of my most important works had been stolen from my studio in Brezilhac. Imagine my despair. All I have left of the original is this photograph.

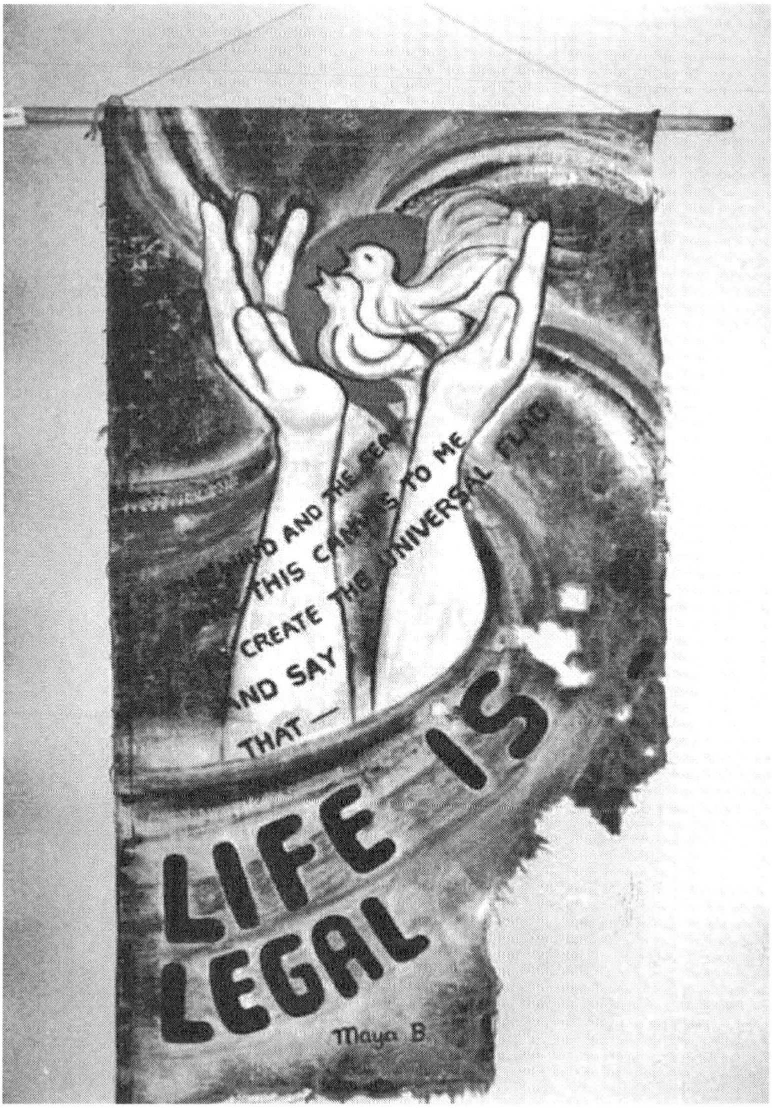
CREATE THE UNIVERSAL FLAG
AND SAY
THAT —
LIFE IS
LEGAL
Maya B.

6 RETROSPECTIVELY

Looking back at my life and having studied human nature in every walk of life, I have come to the conclusion, that the human is but another animal, which is led by its instincts. When homo sapiens gets into breeding stage, he or she thinks of little other than sex. If he or she gets hungry and there is not enough food around, this person will get greedy. If a person feels threatened, he or she will defend themselves and their young. When frightened, they will run or hide.

Most leaders in governments are short of the understanding necessary to handle the power, which they wield and they too often act with their emotions. Their greed leads to them attacking other countries and stealing from them.

Soldiers are here to defend their country and it is wrong to send them to invade other countries. This causes many soldiers to be cheated out of their lives because of the stupidity and greed of the politicians.

Apropos food: Life on earth is threatened because of lack of understanding and, again, greed. Greed is an emotion and has absolutely nothing to do with intelligence or knowledge. If fishermen dredge up the sea's flora, they destroy the food of the fish. If you want species of life to survive and to multiply, you will not succeed if you don't respect *their food*. Plankton thrives on carbon dioxide and feeds many species of small or large fish, even whales, and helps to protect humanity from the pollution they create.

Monoculture has taken too much living space away from many species of animals and deprived human and beast alike of valuable oxygen by destroying too many trees.

When I was a child, we all had rosy cheeks. Today's children are pale. The lower we eat into the food chain, the more species will die out and life on earth will be threatened for the human as well.

Wars are greed and greed is polluting. I am sad to see that most leaders lack the intelligence and understanding to be able to replace emotion with intelligent thinking.

For the humans who think positively, I created the Universal Flag in 1978- to try and unite the world for peace and progress in a positive way. All those who are for it, deserve to fly this flag all over their planet.

My aim in life IS, to find a good and safe place for my substantial life's work.

I found a place in Brittany, ideal to create a wildlife reserve and where I planted hundreds of trees.

My goal *was* to find my ideal partner. We found each other in 1999, in my wildlife sanctuary in Marseillette. We have been living a quiet life in happiness together and hope to reach a very old age in good health.

I wish you all intelligence, knowledge, peace and love!

HAPPY END!

Many thanks to those people who helped me to create this book by sharing parts of my life with me and to Alexa, Jack and Julie for the preparation of this work by proofreading and text correction.

To learn more about *Maya B.* please visit www.maya-b.net. You can also find the photgraphs in color there.

ABOUT THE AUTHOR

Maya B. (Maya B. Krähenmann)
I am an artist currently living with my dear partner in Brittany, France.

I lived my life from adventure to adventure on different parts of the globe in search of *truth* and freedom and to find my ideal partner. Often my friends advised me to write my memoirs. Lawrence Dahl, a writer whom I met in the south of France, and I, became good friends. We met frequently in the Hotel Luxembourg in Lezignan and he took notes of my experiences and wanted to write a book about my life. He then met a woman from the U.S.A. and the happy pair moved to the United States. Before he left, he told me that I owed it to the world to share my memories, and that I should write my autobiography. I replied that I would do so when I was older since I still had some more intensive living in front of me, before I would be ready.

Thanks to Lawrence's encouragement I started to write my autobiography in 2007 and it took me three years to complete it. The book is a true account of the events of my life as I remember them. Others may have a differing viewpoint. I hope that you will enjoy reading my life story as much as I did both living it and writing about it.

Made in the USA
Charleston, SC
06 September 2013